RANDOM HOUSE
ESSENTIAL
SPANISH
DICTIONARY

RANDOM HOUSE ESSENTIAL SPANISH DICTIONARY

Originally published as *The Random House Spanish Dictionary, Second Vest Pocket Edition.*

Edited by
Donald F. Solá
Cornell University

Revised by
David L. Gold
Doctor in Romance Philology
University of Barcelona

BALLANTINE BOOKS • NEW YORK

A Ballantine Book
Published by The Random House Publishing Group
Copyright © 1995, 1983 by Random House, Inc.

Library of Congress Cataloging-in-Production Data
Random House Spanish Dictionary
Random House essential Spanish dictionary/edited by Donald F. Solá.
     p. cm.
   Previously published: The Random House Spanish dictionary.
   New York: Random House, c1983.
     ISBN 0-345-41078-5 (pbk.)
     1. Spanish language—Dictionaries—English. 2. English language—Dictionaries—Spanish. I. Solá, Donald F. II. Title.
   PC4640.R26 1997   96-35117
   463.21–dc20   CIP

This edition published by arrangement with Random House, Inc.

Printed in the United States of America

www.ballantinebooks.com

First Ballantine Books Edition: February 1997

12

Foreword

This bilingual dictionary has been designed as a practical tool for the general use of the English-speaking learner of Spanish and the Spanish-speaking learner of English. Travelers and students will find that this up-to-date and accurate reference work has been carefully prepared to meet their everyday needs.

The editors have taken great care to make this dictionary as useful and informative as possible for its size and scope—we hope you will enjoy making the most of it.

Prefacio

Este diccionario bilingüe se presenta como instrumento práctico destinado al uso del hispano-hablante que aprende inglés y del anglo-hablante que aprende español. Los viajeros así como los estudiantes encontrarán aquí una obra de consulta puesta al día para llenar correctamente sus requisitos cotidianos.

Los editores se han esforzado en hacer este librito todo lo más útil e informativo posible, en vista de su tamaño y su alcance. Esperamos, pues, que le sea del máximo provecho.

Concise Pronunciation Guide

Spanish Letter	Pronunciation

Spanish
Letter   Pronunciation

a   Like English *a* in *father.*

b, v   At beginning of word group and after *m* or *n,* like English *b.* Elsewhere, like English *v,* but pronounced with both lips instead of upper teeth and lower lip.

c   Before *e* or *i,* like English *th* in *thin* (in Northern Spain); like Spanish *s* (in Southern Spain and the Americas); elsewhere, like English *k* in *key.*

ch   Like English *ch* in *child.*

d   At beginning of word group and after *n* or *l,* like English *d.* Elsewhere, like English *th* in *either.*

e   Like English *e* in *bet.*

f   As in English.

g   Before *e* or *i,* the same as Spanish *j.* Elsewhere, like English *g* in *get.*

gu   Before *e* or *i,* like English *g* in *get.* Elsewhere, like English *gw* in *Gwynn.*

gü   Like English *gw* in *Gwynn.*

h   Silent.

i   Like English *i* in *machine,* but more clipped. Before or after another vowel, like English *y* (except when accented).

j   Like English *h,* but more rasping.

k   Like English *k.*

l   Like English *l* in *like,* but with the tongue behind the upper front teeth.

ll   Like English *lli* in *million* (in Northern Spain); like Spanish *y* (in Southern Spain and the Americas).

m   As in English.

n   As in English.

ñ   Like English *ny* in *canyon.*

o   Approximately like English *o* in *vote,* but more clipped.

p   As in English.

qu   Like English *k.*

r   Not at all like American English *r;* a quick flap of the tongue-tip on the roof of the mouth.

rr   A strongly "rolled" or trilled version of Spanish *r.*

s   Like English *s* in *lease.*

t   As in English.

u   Like English *oo* in *boot,* but more clipped. Before or after another vowel, like English *w* (except when accented).

v   See *b* above.

x   Like English *x;* although before consonants many speakers pronounce it like Spanish *s;* like Spanish *j* (in Mexican Indian words).

y   Approximately like English *y* in *yes.*

z   Like English *th* in *thin* (in Northern Spain); like English *s* in *lease* (in Southern Spain and the Americas).

Spanish Stress

In a number of words spoken stress is marked by an accent (´): *nación, país, médico, día.*

Words which are not so marked are, generally speaking, stressed on the next-to-the-last syllable if they end in a vowel, *n*, or *s;* and on the last syllable if they end in a consonant other than *n* or *s.*

Note: An accent is placed over some words to distinguish them from others having the same spelling and pronunciation but differing in meaning.

Spanish Irregular Verbs

Infinitive	Present	Future	Preterit	Past Part.
andar	ando	andaré	anduve	andado
caber	quepo	cabré	cupe	cabido
caer	caigo	caeré	caí	caído
conducir	conduzco	conduciré	conduje	conducido
dar	doy	daré	di	dado
decir	digo	diré	dije	dicho
estar	estoy	estaré	estuve	estado
haber	he	habré	hube	habido
hacer	hago	haré	hice	hecho
ir	voy	iré	fui	ido
jugar	juego	jugaré	jugué	jugado
morir	muero	moriré	morí	muerto
oir	oigo	oiré	oí	oído
poder	puedo	podré	pude	podido
poner	pongo	pondré	puse	puesto
querer	quiero	querré	quise	querido
saber	sé	sabré	supe	sabido
salir	salgo	saldré	salí	salido
ser	soy	seré	fui	sido
tener	tengo	tendré	tuve	tenido
traer	traigo	traeré	traje	traído
valer	valgo	valdré	valí	valido
venir	vengo	vendré	vine	venido
ver	veo	veré	vi	visto

Las Formas del Verbo Inglés

1. Se forma la 3ª persona singular del tiempo presente exactamente al igual que el plural de los sustantivos, añadiendo **-es** o **-s** a la forma sencilla según las mismas reglas, así:

(1)	teach	pass	wish	fix	buzz		
	teaches	passes	wishes	fixes	buzzes		
(2)	place	change	judge	please	freeze		
	places	changes	judges	pleases	freezes		
(3a)	find	sell	clean	hear	love	buy	know
	finds	sells	cleans	hears	loves	buys	knows
(3b)	think	like	laugh	stop	hope	meet	want
	thinks	likes	laughs	stops	hopes	meets	wants
(4)	cry	try	dry	carry	deny		
	cries	tries	dries	carries	denies		

Cinco verbos muy comunes tienen 3ª persona singular irregular:

(5)	go	do	say	have	be
	goes	does	says	has	is

2. Se forman el tiempo pasado y el participio de modo igual, añadiendo a la forma sencilla la terminación **-ed** o **-d** según las reglas que siguen.

(1) Si la forma sencilla termina en **-d** o **-t**, se le pone **-ed** como sílaba aparte:

end	fold	need	load
ended	folded	needed	loaded

want	feast	wait	light
wanted	feasted	waited	lighted

(2) Si la forma sencilla termina en cualquier otra consonante, se añade también **-ed** pero sin hacer sílaba aparte:

(2a)	bang	sail	seem	harm	earn	weigh
	banged	sailed	seemed	harmed	earned	weighed
(2b)	lunch	work	look	laugh	help	pass
	lunched	worked	looked	laughed	helped	passed

(3) Si la forma sencilla termina en **-e**, se le pone sólo **-d**:

(3a)	hate	taste	waste	guide	fade	trade
	hated	tasted	wasted	guided	faded	traded
(3b)	free	judge	rule	name	dine	scare
	freed	judged	ruled	named	dined	scared
(3c)	place	force	knife	like	hope	base
	placed	forced	knifed	liked	hoped	based

(4) Una **-y** final que sigue a cualquier consonante se cambia en **-ie** al añadir la **-d** del pasado/participio:

cry	try	dry	carry	deny
cried	tried	dried	carried	denied

3. Varios verbos muy comunes forman el tiempo pasado y el participio de manera irregular. Pertenecen a tres grupos.

(1) Los que tienen una sola forma irregular para tiempo pasado y participio, como los siguientes:

bend	bleed	bring	build	buy
bent	bled	brought	built	bought
catch	creep	deal	dig	feed
caught	crept	dealt	dug	fed
feel	fight	find	flee	get
felt	fought	found	fled	got
hang	have	hear	hold	keep
hung	had	heard	held	kept
lead	leave	lend	lose	make
led	left	lent	lost	made
mean	meet	say	seek	sell
meant	met	said	sought	sold
send	shine	shoot	sit	sleep
sent	shone	shot	sat	slept
spend	stand	strike	sweep	teach
spent	stood	struck	swept	taught

(2) Los que tienen una forma irregular para el tiempo pasado y otra forma irregular para el participio, como los siguientes:

be	beat	become	begin	bite
was	beat	became	began	bit
been	beaten	become	begun	bitten
blow	break	choose	come	do
blew	broke	chose	came	did
blown	broken	chosen	come	done
draw	drink	drive	eat	fall
drew	drank	drove	ate	fell
drawn	drunk	driven	eaten	fallen
fly	forget	freeze	give	go
flew	forgot	froze	gave	went
flown	forgotten	frozen	given	gone
grow	hide	know	ride	ring
grew	hid	knew	rode	rang
grown	hidden	known	ridden	rung
rise	run	see	shake	shrink
rose	ran	saw	shook	shrank
risen	run	seen	shaken	shrunk
sing	sink	speak	steal	swear
sang	sank	spoke	stole	swore
sung	sunk	spoken	stolen	sworn
swim	tear	throw	wear	write
swam	tore	threw	wore	wrote
swum	torn	thrown	worn	written

(3) Los que no varían del todo, la forma sencilla funcionando también como pasado/participio; entre éstos son de mayor frecuencia:

bet	burst	cast	cost	cut
hit	hurt	let	put	quit
read	set	shed	shut	slit
spit	split	spread	thrust	wet

El Plural del Sustantivo Inglés

A la forma singular se añade la terminación -es o -s de acuerdo con las reglas siguientes.

(1) Si el singular termina en **-ch, -s, -sh, -x** o **-z**, se le pone **-es** como sílaba aparte:

match	glass	dish	box	buzz
matches	glasses	dishes	boxes	buzzes

(2) Si el singular termina en **-ce, -ge, -se** o **-ze**, se le pone una **-s** que con la vocal precedente forma sílaba aparte:

face	page	house	size
faces	pages	houses	sizes

(3) Una **-y** final que sigue a cualquier consonante se cambia en **-ie** al ponérsele la **-s** del plural:

sky	city	lady	ferry	penny
skies	cities	ladies	ferries	pennies

(4) Los siguientes sustantivos comunes tienen plural irregular:

man	woman	child	foot	mouse	goose
men	women	children	feet	mice	geese
wife	knife	life	half	leaf	deer
wives	knives	lives	halves	leaves	deer

Spanish Equivalents of 'you'

Whereas contemporary English has just one second-person pronoun, **you,** today's Spanish has several equivalents of that word. These guidelines give basic information on how to use them.

A. Addressing the Deity
The Deity is addressed by **tú.**

B. Addressing Human Beings
1. Addressing One Person
Choosing the correct translation of **you** is hardest when addressing one person. Since conventions differ from one country, social class, time, speaker, and occasion to the next, hard-and-fast rules cannot be given, just as it would be impossible to formulate exceptionless rules for English about addressing others **(Smith? Dr. Smith? Ms. Smith? Barbara? Babs?).** If you are just beginning to study Spanish, you often have to play it by ear, but as you learn more of the language, you will come to have an intuition for which pronoun is appropriate in which circumstances.

The younger the addressee or the better you know each other, the likelier you are to use **tú.** Thus, an infant is invariably addressed by that pronoun, as is a small child (except of extremely high rank, like a member of the Spanish royal family). Likewise, two good friends or close blood relatives would normally use **tú.**

The older a stranger is, or the greater the distance between you, the likelier you are to use **usted.** Thus, for a stranger at the end of adolescence and the beginning of adulthood (around the age of seventeen or eighteen), **usted** becomes more and more appropriate.

Someone performing a service for you, like a barber, flight attendant, or waiter, will address you by **usted,** since that pronoun may also connote deference. By way of reciprocation, you should use **usted** in addressing such a person, with these two exceptions: if the person is a child (say an eight-year-old bootblack), you would use **tú** and be addressed as **usted;** or, if you and the person performing the service are on friendly terms, **tú** would be appropriate in both directions.

If you are addressing an adult whom you have never seen (as in a letter) or an adult you are seeing for the first time, **usted** is appropriate, at least initially.

As people get to know each other, they may switch from **usted,** which connotes deference, respect, distance, formality, etc., to **tú,** which connotes informality, friendship, solidarity, and the like. That change often goes through three stages:

[1] When people are on formal terms, **usted,** but not the addressee's given name, is used. Thus, you would be addressed as **usted** and as **señor López, señora López,** or **señorita López** and you would address the other person in the same way.

[2] At stage two, you would continue to use **usted** to each other but switch to the given name. In certain relationships it is normal to remain at this stage. For example, two colleagues may address each other by their given names because they are on cordial terms, but since they want to show deference or maintain a degree of formality, they continue to use **usted.**

Since it is possible to go right from stage one to stage three, stage two is optional.

[3] If proceeding to stage three, people call one another by their given names and **tú** is used in both directions.

Thus, **señor López, señora López,** and **señorita López** are incompatible with **tú,** whereas **usted** is compatible with either a title + family name (= stage one) or the given name (= stage two).

Besides age, rank, and the nature of the relationship, gender may play a role in determining which pronoun is used: people of the same gender might more readily use **tú** (or switch from **usted** to **tú** earlier in their relationship) than people of different genders. Therefore, a woman who wanted to fend off a would-be suitor would insist on **usted** in both directions, whereas a woman who invited a man to switch from **usted** to **tú** would be intimating her interest in him.

Except in addressing infants and small children (when **tú** is the only appropriate pronoun except, as we have said, if the child is of extremely high rank), you would be well advised to follow this rough-and-ready rule: if the other person speaks first, notice how you are addressed and use the same pronoun in return. In that way, you will be neither more nor less deferential than the other person. In following that rule, you accomplish several things:

[1] Since your addressee is likely to be a native speaker of Spanish and thus adept at choosing the appropriate pronoun, you are relying on someone who probably knows better than you which one is suitable.

[2] By not choosing the pronoun yourself, you are absolved of responsibility if the wrong one is chosen.

[3] By seeing which pronoun the other person spontaneously selects, you can infer something about how that person feels: is the tone one of formality? cordiality marked by a degree of distance? out-and-out friendliness?

[4] You can then put yourself on an equal footing with your addressee by using the same pronoun yourself.

If, however, you are the first to speak and you feel that you are in that gray area where the choice of pronoun is not clear-cut, the proper choice is **usted.** In that way, if you are too formal, your addressee will good-naturedly invite you to use **tú,** whereas if you began with **tú,** it would be embarrassing to be told that you had overstepped the bounds of propriety.

The foregoing suggestions rest on the belief that society should be egalitarian and that people in a subordinate position should be treated deferentially, but you may find that in the Spanish-speaking world, certain people have a different view of things. Thus, someone may address you as **tú** (when you think that **usted** is appropriate) yet expect that you show deference by using **usted.** When two people do not use the same pronouns, the implication is that the person using **usted** is in a subordinate position and the one using **tú** in a superior position, just as in English we signal that lack of equality by a difference in address forms:

"Johnny, take these trunks up to my room."

"Yes, Mrs. Smith, right away."

In such cases, you have an alternative: you can swallow your pride and allow yourself to be treated less respectfully than you would wish; or you can switch to **tú** to show that you want the same respect you are expected to show. In the latter case, your addressee will either get the message and switch to **usted** or protest that you're not showing enough respect, upon which you can politely say that you expect the same measure of deference you are expected to give.

If a Spanish-speaker switches from **usted** to **tú,** you are being sent one of two messages: either "I now consider us to be on closer terms than before" or "I now consider myself to be your superior." In the first instance, you are being invited to switch to **tú,** whereupon you can accept the invitation or, if you want to maintain a certain distance or deference, you can continue to use **usted** and suggest that your addressee do the same. In the second instance, you can accept your now inferior status or you can explain that you want to be treated with the same deference you yourself are expected to show (that can be accomplished by continuing to use **usted** in the hope that the subtle message will get across or by explicitly stating that you prefer **usted**).

Several criteria may thus be applied for deciding whether to use **tú** or **usted.** If the criteria conflict, the result will be either uncertainty on the speaker's part or disagreement about which pronoun is appropriate for which addressee. One incident will illustrate the point: in the late 1970s an adult male guest in his thirties arriving at a hotel in Barcelona was surprised to hear the desk clerk, a male of about the same age, address him by **tú** when, because of their different status (guest vs. employee), he was expecting **usted** and would have given **usted** in return. In choosing **tú,** the employee had followed only the criteria of gender and age, disregarding the difference in status and the fact that the two were strangers.

In many parts of the Western Hemisphere today, the pronoun **vos** is used. In at least one country (Argentina), it is used in everyday speech and in most writing to the total exclusion of **tú** (certain Argentinians do, however, use **tú** in writing, especially when addressing other Spanish-speakers). In some countries, **vos** is used in certain areas but not in others (for example, **tú** is used in most parts of Cuba and Mexico and **vos** in a few parts). And in some countries, certain social classes use **tú** and others **vos** (Costa Rica for instance).

The guidelines offered above for **tú** apply to **vos** as well only in areas where just one of those two pronouns is used, as in Argentina. If, however, both are used, as in Costa Rica, the rules for selecting **tú, vos,** or **usted** are much more complicated and you will have to play it by ear even more than when the choice is only between **tú** and **usted.**

Still another equivalent of **you** is found, though less and less as time passes, in the Cundinamarca Savanna (Colombia): **su merced,** literally 'your grace', which is more formal than **usted.**

In certain kinds of impersonal address, **tú** may be used to establish rapport. For example, before elections, billboards might read **Tú, que sabes leer, puedes votar** 'You, who can read, can vote' (at least in Mexico) or **Es importante que votes** 'It is important that you vote' (at least in Puerto Rico). The implication here is that a seemingly impersonal message—addressed to anyone reading the billboard—is actually intended for YOU and no other, as if a close friend or relative were speaking to you in private. Likewise, in certain kinds of publications (like a book of poetry or memoirs), authors may use **tú** in addressing the reader in the introduction to establish an intimate bond or create a cozy feeling. The implication here is that the book was written just for YOU.

2. Addressing More Than One Person

In most of the Western Hemisphere today, you need not be concerned about which pronoun to use in addressing more than one person because only one is used: **ustedes.** Thus, **ustedes** is the plural of **tú,** of **usted,** and of **vos.** Only in the Cundinamarca Savanna is there a choice: **ustedes** or the more formal **sus mercedes** (literally 'your graces'), though the latter form, like the singular form (see above on **su merced),** is obsolescing.

In Spain you must make a choice: **vosotros, vosotras,** or **ustedes.** If you are addressing a group of two or more people and to each of them you would say **tú,** address the group as **vosotros** if at least one of them is a male or their gender is indeterminate; if all of them are females, use **vosotras.** If, however, you would say **usted** to at least one member of the group, use **ustedes** in addressing all of them.

In sum, while English-speakers have somewhat subtle choices when it comes to addressing others, Spanish-speakers, depending on the kind of Spanish they use, have overt choices in form: between **tú** and **usted,** between **vos** and **usted,** between **tú, vos,** and **usted,** between **tú, usted,** and **su merced,** between **ustedes** and **sus mercedes,** and between **ustedes, vosotros,** and **vosotras.** After a while, you will acquire a feeling for which one is appropriate in which situation. Also, since native speakers will probably realize that Spanish is not your first language, they will usually be understanding if you make a mistake. To be on the safe side, if in doubt use the deferential pronouns **usted** or **ustedes.**

C. Omission of Subject Pronouns

Since the endings on Spanish verbs almost always indicate the person and number of the subject (**quiero** can only be first-person singular, **quieres** second-person singular, **quiere** third-person singular, **queremos** first-person plural, **queréis** second-person plural, **quieren** third-person plural, etc.), the subject pronouns are usually superfluous. Thus, to express 'I want', **quiero** suffices, unless the subject is stressed or contrasted with another subject (for example, **¡Yo quiero!** '*I* want to!' or **Yo quiero ir pero ella dice que es muy tarde** '*I* want to go but *she* says it's too late').

However, since **usted, ustedes, su merced,** and **sus mercedes** are used with verbs in the third person, third-person verbs are semantically overburdened, as a result of which a subjectless third-person verb might be ambiguous even in context. **Está nadando,** for example, could mean 'he's swimming', 'she's swimming', 'it's swimming', or 'you're swimming' ('you' = **usted** or **su merced**); and **están nadando** could mean 'they're swimming' or 'you're swimming' ('you' = **ustedes** or **sus mercedes**).

Therefore, with third-person verbs, subject pronouns tend to be used somewhat more than with other verbs, since ambiguity might otherwise be the result. For example, if you're asked 'Where are John and Mary?' and want to say 'He's in the kitchen and she's in the living room,' you must either repeat their names (**Juan está en la cocina y María está en la sala**) or use pronouns (**él está en la cocina y ella está en la sala**). If, however, no ambiguity might arise (and the pronouns are not being emphasized), the verb alone is sufficient. For example, if someone asks, **¿Dónde está Ana?** 'Where's Ann?', you would say **Está en la biblioteca** 'She's at the library'. Although out of context that reply could also mean 'He's at the library', 'It's at the library', or 'You're in the library', the context here is enough to show the underlying subject of the sentence.

Since **usted, su merced, ustedes,** and **sus mercedes** are used with third-person verbs, the foregoing remarks apply to them too. They tend to be used more than the other Spanish equivalents of 'you', which tend to be omitted more often, since they are used with unambiguous verbs (thus, **tú quieres** 'you want' can be reduced to **quieres** without any ambiguity).

There is a second reason why **usted, su merced, ustedes,** and **sus mercedes** tend to be omitted less often than other equivalents of 'you': since they are deferential pronouns, it is felt that repeating them every once in a while in a conversation or letter reminds the addressee of your respectful attitude. Thus, in making a request or asking a polite question, you would be well advised to use the pronoun. For example, if you address someone by **usted,** you have, in principle, two ways of asking 'Would you like to eat?': **¿Quiere comer?** and **¿Quiere usted comer?** The second variant is more deferential than the first one.

The foregoing paragraph not withstanding, in one instance it is obligatory to omit **usted, su merced, ustedes,** or **sus mercedes:** if any of those pronouns is the subject of both the main and subordinate clauses of a sentence, it may be used in the main clause but never in the subordinate one. Thus, to say 'You're right, but you shouldn't punish them', you have a choice between **Usted tiene razón, pero no debe castigarlos** and **Tiene razón, pero no debe castigarlos** (the former is more deferential than the latter), but no one says **Usted tiene razón, pero usted no debe castigarlos.**

Thus, on one hand, Spanish-speakers use the equivalents of **you** less than English-speakers do, but on the other hand, Spanish-speakers use **usted, ustedes, su merced,** and **sus mercedes** more than they use **tú, vos, vosotros,** and **vosotras.**

Having seen in **Omission of Subject Pronouns** that in certain circumstances those pronouns are omitted or omissible, we may now return to the **Spanish equivalents of 'you'** to make this addition: even if you omit the pronoun, you still have to choose the correct form of the verb. For example, the most explicit translations of 'You are very kind' are **Tú eres muy amable, Vos sos muy amable, Usted es muy amable, Su merced es muy amable, Ustedes son muy amables, Vosotros sois muy amables, Vosotras sois muy amables,** and **Sus mercedes son muy amables.** If you omit the subject pronoun, you must still choose the correct form of the verb: **Eres muy amable, Sos muy amable, Es muy amable, Son muy amables,** or **Sois muy amables** (of which only two are ambiguous: **Es muy amable** can also mean 'He's very nice' or 'She's very nice' and **Son muy amables** can also mean 'They're very nice').

In conclusion, whenever you come into contact with someone for the first time (whether that person turns out to be your life partner or just someone who sells you something in a minute's time before you part ways forever), you must make a decision. If a relationship continues, you may have to make decisions too ("Should I switch from **usted** to **tú?**") and in the course of a conversation not everything is automatic either ("When should I use **usted?**"). However, after a while, proper use of the Spanish equivalents of 'you' becomes second nature.

D. Addressing Animals

One animal is addressed by **tú**; more than one is addressed by **ustedes** in the Western Hemisphere, by **vosotros** in Spain if at least one of them is male, and by **vosotras** in Spain if all of them are female.

As noted in section C, the subject pronouns are much less frequent in Spanish than in English, being used mostly for emphasis, to disambiguate third-person verbs, and, in the case of **usted, su merced, ustedes,** and **sus mercedes,** to connote deference. Therefore, there is no need to disambiguate third-person verbs for animals; and since it would be highly unusual to speak to an animal with marked deference, **ustedes** would be out of place in such situations. In most cases, none of the four pronouns mentioned in the preceding paragraph is applied to animals. Consequently, for all practical purposes that paragraph may be reformulated in this way: imperative verbs take these forms when directed to animals:

[1] if one animal is addressed, the verb form is that corresponding to **tú,** for example, **¡Ven!** 'Come!'.

[2] if more than one animal is addressed,

[A] the verb form in the Western Hemisphere is that corresponding to **ustedes,** for example, **¡Vengan!** 'Come!' and

[B] the verb form in Spain is that corresponding to **vosotros/vosotras,** for example, **¡Venid!** 'Come!'.

D.L.G.

English Abbreviations/Abreviaturas Inglesas

a.	adjective	govt.	government
abbr.	abbreviation	gram.	grammar
adv.	adverb	interj.	interjection
aero.	aeronautical	interrog.	interrogative
agr.	agriculture	leg.	legal
anat.	anatomy	m.	masculine
art.	article	mech.	mechanics
auto.	automotive	med.	medicine
biol.	biology	Mex.	Mexico
bot.	botany	mil.	military
Carib.	Caribbean	mus.	musical
chem.	chemistry	n.	noun
coll.	colloquial	naut.	nautical
com.	commercial	phot.	photography
conj.	conjunction	pl.	plural
dem.	demonstrative	pol.	politics
econ.	economics	prep.	preposition
elec.	electrical	pron.	pronoun
esp.	especially	punct.	punctuation
f.	feminine	rel.	relative, religion
fig.	figurative	S.A.	Spanish America
fin.	finance	theat.	theater
geog.	geography	v.	verb

SPANISH-ENGLISH

A

a, *prep.* to; at.
abacería, *f.* grocery store.
abacero, *m.* grocer.
ábaco, *m.* abacus.
abad, *m.* abbot.
abadía, *f.* abbey.
abajar, *v.* lower; go down.
abajo, *adv.* down; downstairs.
abandonar, *v.* abandon.
abandono, *m.* abandonment.
abanico, *m.* fan. — **abanicar,** *v.*
abaratar, *v.* cheapen.
abarcar, *v.* comprise; clasp.
abastecer, *v.* supply, provide.
abatido, *a.* dejected, despondent.
abatir, *v.* knock down; dismantle; depress, dishearten.
abdicación, *f.* abdication.
abdicar, *v.* abdicate.
abdomen, *m.* abdomen.
abdominal, *a.* abdominal; *m.* sit-up.
abecé, *m.* ABCs, rudiments.
abecedario, *m.* alphabet; reading book.
abeja, *f.* bee.
abejarrón, *m.* bumblebee.
aberración, *f.* aberration.
abertura, *f.* opening, aperture, slit.
abeto, *m.* fir.
abierto, *a.* open; overt.
abismal, *a.* abysmal.
abismo, *m.* abyss, chasm.
ablandar, *v.* soften.
abnegación, *f.* abnegation.
abochornar, *v.* overheat; embarrass.
abogado -da, *n.* lawyer, attorney.
abolengo, *m.* ancestry.
abolición, *f.* abolition.
abolladura, *f.* dent. —**abollar,** *v.*
abominable, *a.* abominable.
abominar, *v.* abhor.
abonado -da, *m. & f.* subscriber.
abonar, *v.* pay; fertilize.
abonarse, *v.* subscribe.

abono, *m.* fertilizer; subscription; season ticket.
aborigen, *a. & n.* aboriginal.
aborrecer, *v.* hate, loathe, abhor.
abortar, *v.* abort, miscarry.
aborto, *m.* abortion.
abovedar, *v.* vault.
abrasar, *v.* burn.
abrazar, *v.* embrace; clasp.
abrazo, *m.* embrace.
abrelatas, *m.* can opener.
abreviar, *v.* abbreviate, abridge, shorten.
abreviatura, *f.* abbreviation.
abrigar, *v.* harbor, shelter.
abrigarse, *v.* bundle up.
abrigo, *m.* overcoat; shelter; *(pl.)* wraps.
abril, *m.* April.
abrir, *v.* open; (med.) lance.
abrochar, *v.* clasp.
abrogación, *f.* abrogation, repeal.
abrogar, *v.* abrogate.
abrojo, *m.* thorn.
abrumar, *v.* overwhelm, crush, swamp.
absceso, *m.* abscess.
absolución, *f.* absolution; acquittal.
absoluto, *a.* absolute; downright.
absolver, *v.* absolve, pardon.
absorbente, *a.* absorbent.
absorber, *v.* absorb.
absorción, *f.* absorption.
abstemio, *a.* abstemious.
abstenerse, *v.* abstain; refrain.
abstinencia, *f.* abstinence.
abstracción, *f.* abstraction.
abstracto, *a.* abstract.
abstraer, *v.* abstract.
absurdo, 1. *a.* absurd. **2.** *m.* absurdity.
abuchear, *v.* boo.
abuela, *f.* grandmother.
abuelo, *m.* grandfather; *(pl.)* grandparents.
abultado, *a.* bulky.
abultamiento, *m.* bulge. — **abultar,** *v.*

abundancia, *f.* abundance, plenty.
abundante, *a.* abundant, plentiful.
abundar, *v.* abound.
aburrido, *a.* boring, tedious.
aburrimiento, *m.* boredom.
aburrir, *v.* bore.
abusar, *v.* abuse, misuse.
abusivo, *a.* abusive.
abuso, *m.* abuse.
abyecto, *a.* abject, low.
a.C., *abbr.* (**antes de Cristo**) BC.
acá, *adv.* here.
acabar, *v.* finish. **a. de . . . ,** to have just . . . .
acacia, *f.* acacia.
academia, *f.* academy.
académico, *a.* academic.
acaecer, *v.* happen.
acanalar, *v.* groove.
acaparar, *v.* hoard; monopolize.
acariciar, *v.* caress, stroke.
acarrear, *v.* cart, transport; occasion, entail.
acaso, *m.* chance. **por si a.,** just in case.
acceder, *v.* accede.
accesible, *a.* accessible.
acceso, *m.* access, approach.
accesorio, *a.* accessory.
accidentado, *a.* hilly.
accidental, *a.* accidental.
accidente, *m.* accident, wreck.
acción, *f.* action, act; (com.) share of stock.
accionista, *m. & f.* shareholder.
acechar, *v.* ambush, spy on.
acedia, *f.* heartburn.
aceite, *m.* oil.
aceite de hígado de bacalao, cod-liver oil.
aceitoso, *a.* oily.
aceituna, *f.* olive.
aceleración, *f.* acceleration.
acelerar, *v.* accelerate, speed up.
acento, *m.* accent.
acentuar, *v.* accent, accentuate, stress.

acepillar, v. brush; plane (wood).
aceptable, a. acceptable.
aceptación, f. acceptance.
aceptar, v. accept.
acequía, f. ditch.
acera, f. sidewalk.
acerca de, prep. about, concerning.
acercar, v. bring near.
acercarse, v. approach, come near, go near.
acero, m. steel.
acero inoxidable, stainless steel.
acertar, v. guess right. **a. en,** hit (a mark).
acertijo, m. puzzle, riddle.
achicar, v. diminish, dwarf; humble.
acidez, f. acidity.
ácido, 1. a. sour. **2.** m. acid.
aclamación, f. acclamation.
aclamar, v. acclaim.
aclarar, v. brighten; clarify, clear up.
acoger, v. welcome, receive.
acogida, f. welcome, reception.
acometer, v. attack.
acomodador, m. usher.
acomodar, v. accommodate, fix up.
acompañamiento, m. accompaniment; following.
acompañar, v. accompany.
acondicionar, v. condition.
aconsejable, a. advisable.
aconsejar, v. advise.
acontecer, v. happen.
acontecimiento, m. event, happening.
acorazado, 1. m. battleship. **2.** a. armor-plated, ironclad.
acordarse, v. remember, rec-ollect.
acordeón, m. accordion.
acordonar, v. cordon off.
acortar, v. shorten.
acosar, v. beset, harry.
acostar, v. lay down; put to bed.
acostarse, v. lie down; go to bed.
acostumbrado, a. accustomed; customary.
acostumbrar, v. accustom.

acrecentar, v. increase.
acreditar, v. accredit.
acreedor -ra, n. creditor.
acróbata, m. & f. acrobat.
acróbatico, a. acrobatic.
actitud, f. attitude.
actividad, f. activity.
activista, a. & n. activist.
activo, a. active.
acto, m. act.
actor, m. actor.
actriz, f. actress.
actual, a. present; present day.
actualidades, f.pl. current events.
actualmente, adv. at present; nowadays.
actuar, v. act.
acuarela, f. watercolor.
acuario, m. aquarium.
acuático, a. aquatic.
acuchillar, v. slash, knife.
acudir, v. rally; hasten; be present.
acuerdo, m. accord, agreement; settlement. **de a.,** in agreement, agreed.
acumulación, f. accumulation.
acumular, v. accumulate.
acuñar, v. coin, mint.
acupuntura, f. acupuncture.
acusación, f. accusation, charge.
acusado -da, a. & n. accused; defendant.
acusador -ra, n. accuser.
acusar, v. accuse; acknowledge.
acústica, f. acoustics.
adaptación, f. adaptation.
adaptador, m. adapter.
adaptar, v. adapt.
adecuado, a. adequate.
adelantado, a. advanced; fast (clock).
adelantamiento, m. advancement, promotion.
adelantar, v. advance.
adelante, adv. ahead, forward, onward, on.
adelanto, m. advancement, progress, improvement.
adelgazar, v. make thin.
ademán, m. attitude; gesture.
además, adv. in addition, besides, also.

adentro, adv. in, inside.
adepto, a. adept.
aderezar, v. prepare; trim.
adherirse, v. adhere, stick.
adhesivo, a. adhesive.
adicción, f. adiction.
adición, f. addition.
adicional, a. additional, extra.
adicto -ta, a. & n. addicted; addict.
adinerado, -a, a. wealthy.
adiós, m. & interj. goodbye, farewell.
adivinar, v. guess.
adjetivo, m. adjective.
adjunto, a. enclosed.
administración, f. administration.
administrador -ra, n. administrator.
administrar, v. administer; manage.
administrativo, a. administrative.
admirable, a. admirable.
admiración. f. admiration; wonder.
admirar, v. admire.
admisión, f. admission.
admitir, v. admit, acknowledge.
ADN, abbr. (**ácido deoxirribonucleico**) DNA (deoxyribonucleic acid).
adolescencia, f. adolescence, youth.
adolescente, a. & n. adolescent.
adónde, adv. where.
adondequiera, conj. wherever.
adopción, f. adoption.
adoptar, v. adopt.
adoración, f. worship, love, adoration. **—adorar,** v.
adormecer, v. drowse.
adornar, v. adorn; decorate.
adorno, m. adornment, trimming.
adquirir, v. acquire, obtain.
adquisición, f. acquisition, attainment.
aduana, f. custom house, customs.
adujada, f. (naut.) coil of rope.
adulación, f. flattery.

adular, v. flatter.
adulterar, v. adulterate.
adulterio, m. adultery.
adulto -ta, a. & n. adult.
adusto, a. gloomy; austere.
adverbio, m. adverb.
adversario, m. adversary.
adversidad, f. adversity.
adverso, a. adverse.
advertencia, f. warning.
advertir, v. warn; notice.
adyacente, a. adjacent.
aéreo, a. aerial; air.
aerodeslizador, m. hovercraft.
aeromoza, f. stewardess, flight attendant.
aeroplano, m. light plane.
aeropuerto, m. airport.
aerosol, m. aerosol, spray.
afable, a. affable, pleasant.
afanarse, v. toil.
afear, v. deface, mar, deform.
afectación, f. affectation.
afectar, v. affect.
afecto, m. affection, attachment.
afeitada, f. shave. — **afeitarse,** v.
afeminado, a. effeminate.
afición, f. fondness, liking; hobby.
aficionado, a. fond.
aficionado -da, n. fan, devotee; amateur.
aficionarse a, v. become fond of.
afilado, a. sharp.
afilar, v. sharpen.
afiliación, f. affiliation.
afiliado -da, n. affiliate. — **afiliar,** v.
afinar, v. polish; tune up.
afinidad, f. relationship, affinity.
afirmación, f. affirmation, statement.
afirmar, v. affirm, assert.
afirmativa, f. affirmative. —**afirmativo,** a.
aflicción, f. affliction; sorrow, grief.
afligido, a. sorrowful, grieved.
afligir, v. grieve, distress.
aflojar, v. loosen.
afluencia, f. influx.

afortunado, a. fortunate, successful, lucky.
afrenta, f. insult, outrage, affront. —**afrentar,** v.
afrentoso, a. shameful.
africano -na, a. & n. African.
afuera, adv. out, outside.
afueras, f.pl. suburbs.
agacharse, v. squat, crouch; cower.
agarrar, v. seize, grasp, clutch.
agarro, m. clutch, grasp.
agencia, f. agency.
agencia de colocaciones, employment agency.
agencia de viajes, travel agency.
agente, m. & f. agent, representative.
agente de aduana, mf. customs officer.
agente inmobiliario -ria, n. real-estate agent.
ágil, a. agile, spry.
agitación, f. agitation, ferment.
agitado, a. agitated; excited.
agitador, m. agitator.
agitar, v. shake, agitate, excite.
agobiar, v. oppress, burden.
agosto, m. August.
agotamiento, m. exhaustion.
agotar, v. exhaust, use up, sap.
agradable, a. agreeable, pleasant.
agradar, v. please.
agradecer, v. thank; appreciate, be grateful for.
agradecido, a. grateful, thankful.
agradecimiento, m. gratitude, thanks.
agravar, v. aggravate, make worse.
agravio, m. wrong. — **agraviar,** v.
agregado, a. & n. aggregate; (pol.) attaché.
agregar, v. add; gather.
agresión, f. aggression; (leg.) battery.
agresivo, a. aggressive.
agresor -ra, n. aggressor.
agrícola, a. agricultural.
agricultor, m. farmer.

agricultura, f. agriculture, farming.
agrio, a. sour.
agrupar, v. group.
agua, f. water. —**aguar,** v.
aguacate, m. avocado, alligator pear.
aguafuerte, f. etching.
agua mineral, mineral water.
aguantar, v. endure, stand, put up with.
aguardar, v. await; expect.
aguardiente, m. brandy.
aguas abajo, adv. downriver, downstream.
aguas arriba, adv. upriver, upstream.
agudo, a. sharp, keen, shrill, acute.
agüero, m. omen.
águila, f. eagle.
aguja, f. needle.
agujero, m. hole.
aguzar, v. sharpen.
ahí, adv. there.
ahogar, v. drown; choke; suffocate.
ahondar, v. deepen.
ahora, adv. now.
ahorcar, v. hang (execute).
ahorrar, v. save, save up; spare.
ahorros, m.pl. savings.
ahumar, v. smoke.
airado, a. angry, indignant.
aire, m. air. —**airear,** v.
aire acondicionado, air conditioning.
aislamiento, m. isolation.
aislar, v. isolate.
ajedrez, m. chess.
ajeno, a. alien; someone else's.
ajetreo, m. hustle and bustle.
ají, m. chili.
ajo, m. garlic.
ajustado, a. adjusted; trim; exact.
ajustar, v. adjust.
ajuste, m. adjustment, settlement.
al, contr. of **a** + **el.**
ala, f. wing; brim (of hat).
alabanza, f. praise. —**alabar,** v.
alabear, v. warp.
ala delta, hang glider.
alambique, m. still.

alambre, *m.* wire. **a. de púas,** barbed wire.

alarde, *m.* boasting, ostentation.

alargar, *v.* lengthen; stretch out.

alarma, *f.* alarm. **—alarmar,** *v.*

alba, *f.* daybreak, dawn.

albanega, *f.* hair net.

albañil, *m.* bricklayer; mason.

albaricoque, *m.* apricot.

alberca, *f.* swimming pool.

albergue, *m.* shelter. **—albergar,** *v.*

alborotar, *v.* disturb, make noise, brawl, riot.

alboroto, *m.* brawl, disturbance, din, tumult.

álbum, *m.* album.

álbum de recortes, scrapbook.

alcachofa, *f.* artichoke.

alcalde, *m.* mayor.

alcance, *m.* reach; range, scope.

alcanfor, *m.* camphor.

alcanzar, *v.* reach, overtake, catch.

alcayata, *f.* spike.

alce, *m.* elk.

alcoba, *f.* bedroom; alcove.

alcoba de respeto, guest room.

alcoba de huéspedes, guest room.

alcohol, *m.* alcohol.

alcohólico -ca, *a.* & *n.* alcoholic.

aldaba, *f.* latch.

aldea, *f.* village.

alegación, *f.* allegation.

alegar, *v.* allege.

alegrar, *v.* make happy, brighten.

alegrarse, *v.* be glad.

alegre, *a.* glad, cheerful, merry.

alegría, *f.* gaiety, cheer.

alejarse, *v.* move away, off.

alemán -ana, *a.* & *n.* German.

Alemania, *f.* Germany.

alentar, *v.* cheer up, encourage.

alergia, *f.* allergy.

alerta, *adv.* on the alert.

aleve, alevoso, *a.* treacherous.

alfabeto, *m.* alphabet.

alfalfa, *f.* alfalfa.

alfarería, *f.* pottery.

alférez, *m.* (naval) ensign.

alfil, *m.* (chess) bishop.

alfiler, *m.* pin.

alfombra, *f.* carpet, rug.

alforja, *f.* knapsack; saddlebag.

alga, *f.* seaweed.

alga marina, seaweed.

algarabía, *f.* jargon; din.

álgebra, *f.* algebra.

algo, *pron.* & *adv.* something, somewhat; anything.

algodón, *m.* cotton.

algodón hidrófilo, absorbent cotton.

alguien, *pron.* somebody, someone; anybody, anyone.

algún -no -na, *a.* & *pron.* some; any.

alhaja, *f.* jewel.

aliado -da, *a.* & *n.* allied; ally. **—aliar,** *v.*

alianza, *f.* alliance.

alicates, *m.pl.* pliers.

aliento, *m.* breath. **dar a.,** encourage.

aligerar, *v.* lighten.

alimentar, *v.* feed, nourish.

alimento, *m.* nourishment, food.

alinear, *v.* line up; (pol.) align.

aliño, *m.* salad dressing.

alisar, *v.* smooth.

alistamiento, *m.* enlistment.

alistar, *v.* make ready, prime.

alistarse, *v.* get ready; (mil.) enlist.

aliviar, *v.* alleviate, relieve, ease.

alivio, *m.* relief.

allá, *adv.* there. **más a.,** beyond, farther on.

allanar, *v.* flatten, smooth, plane.

allí, *adv.* there. **por a.,** that way.

alma, *f.* soul.

almacén, *m.* department store; storehouse, warehouse.

almacenaje, *m.* storage.

almacenar, *v.* store.

almanaque, *m.* almanac.

almeja, *f.* clam.

almendra, *f.* almond.

almíbar, *m.* syrup.

almidón, *m.* starch. **—almidonar,** *v.*

almirante, *m.* admiral.

almohada, *f.* pillow.

almuerzo, *m.* lunch. **—almorzar,** *v.*

alojamiento, *m.* lodging, accommodations.

alojar, *v.* lodge, house.

alojarse, *v.* stay, room.

alquiler, *m.* rent. **—alquilar,** *v.*

alrededor, *adv.* around.

alrededores, *m.pl.* environs.

altanero, *a.* haughty.

altar, *m.* altar.

altavoz, *m.* loudspeaker.

alteración, *f.* alteration.

alterar, *v.* alter.

alternativa, *f.* alternative. **—alternativo,** *a.*

alterno, *a.* alternate. **—alternar,** *v.*

alteza, *f.* highness.

altivo, *a.* proud, haughty; lofty.

alto, 1. *a.* high, tall; loud. **2.** *m.* height, story (house).

altura, *f.* height, altitude.

alud, *m.* avalanche.

aludir, *v.* allude.

alumbrado, *m.* lighting.

alumbrar, *v.* light.

aluminio, *m.* aluminum.

alumno -na, *n.* student, pupil.

alusión, *f.* allusion.

alza, *f.* rise; boost.

alzar, *v.* raise, lift.

ama, *f.* housewife, mistress (of house). **a. de llaves,** housekeeper.

amable, *a.* kind; pleasant, sweet.

amalgamar, *v.* amalgamate.

amamantar, *v.* suckle, nurse.

amanecer, 1. *m.* dawn, daybreak. **2.** *v.* dawn; awaken.

amante, *m.* & *f.* lover.

amapola, *f.* poppy.

amar, *v.* love.

amargo, *a.* bitter.

amargón, *m.* dandelion.

amargura, *f.* bitterness.

amarillo, *a.* yellow.

amarradero, *m.* mooring.

amarrar, *v.* hitch, moor, tie up.

amartillar, *v.* hammer; cock (a gun).

amasar, *v.* knead, mold.

ámbar, *m.* amber.

ambarino, *a.* amber.

ambición, *f.* ambition.

ambicionar, *v.* aspire to.

ambicioso, *a.* ambitious.

ambientalista, *m. & f.* environmentalist.

ambiente, *m.* environment, atmosphere.

ambigüedad, *f.* ambiguity.

ambiguo, *a.* ambiguous.

ambos, *a. & pron.* both.

ambulancia, *f.* ambulance.

amenaza, *f.* threat, menace.

amenazar, *v.* threaten, menace.

ameno, *a.* pleasant.

americana, *f.* suit coat.

americano -na, *a. & n.* American.

ametralladora, *f.* machine gun.

amigable, *a.* amicable, friendly.

amígdala, *f.* tonsil.

amigo -ga, *n.* friend.

amistad, *f.* friendship.

amistoso, *a.* friendly.

amniocéntesis, *m.* amniocentesis.

amo, *m.* master.

amonestaciones, *f.pl.* banns.

amonestar, *v.* admonish.

amoníaco, *m.* ammonia.

amontonar, *v.* amass, pile up.

amor, *m.* love. **a. propio,** self-esteem.

amorío, *m.* romance, love affair.

amoroso, *a.* amorous; loving.

amortecer, *v.* deaden.

amparar, *v.* aid, befriend; protect, shield.

amparo, *m.* protection.

ampliar, *v.* enlarge; elaborate.

amplificar, *v.* amplify.

amplio, *a.* ample, roomy.

ampolla, *f.* bubble; bulb; blister.

amputar, *v.* amputate.

amueblar, *v.* furnish.

analfabeto -ta, *a. & n.* illiterate.

analgésico, *m.* pain killer.

análisis, *m.* analysis.

analizar, *v.* analyze.

analogía, *f.* analogy.

análogo, *a.* similar, analogous.

anarquía, *f.* anarchy.

anatomía, *f.* anatomy.

ancho, *a.* wide, broad.

anchoa, *f.* anchovy.

anchura, *f.* width, breadth.

anciano -na, *a. & n.* old, aged (person).

ancla, *f.* anchor. **—anclar,** *v.*

anclaje, *m.* anchorage.

andamio, *m.* scaffold.

andar, *v.* walk; move, go.

andén, *m.* (railroad) platform.

andrajoso, *a.* ragged, uneven.

anécdota, *f.* anecdote.

anegar, *v.* flood, drown.

anestesia, *f.* anesthetic.

anexar, *v.* annex.

anexión, *f.* annexation.

anfitrión -na, *n.* host.

ángel, *m.* angel.

angosto, *a.* narrow.

anguila, *f.* eel.

angular, *a.* angular.

ángulo, *m.* angle.

angustia, *f.* anguish, agony.

angustiar, *v.* distress.

anhelar, *v.* long for.

anidar, *v.* nest, nestle.

anillo, *m.* ring; circle.

animación, *f.* animation; bustle.

animado, *a.* animated, lively; animate.

animal, *a. & n.* animal.

ánimo, *m.* state of mind, spirits; courage.

aniquilar, *v.* annihilate, destroy.

aniversario, *m.* anniversary.

anoche, *adv.* last night.

anochecer, 1. *m.* twilight, nightfall. **2.** *v.* get dark.

anónimo, *a.* anonymous.

anormal, *a.* abnormal.

anotación, *f.* annotation.

anotar, *v.* annotate.

ansia, ansiedad, *f.* anxiety.

ansioso, *a.* anxious.

antagonismo, *m.* antagonism.

antagonista, *m. & f.* antagonist, opponent.

anteayer, *adv.* day before yesterday.

antebrazo, *m.* forearm.

antecedente, *a. & m.* antecedent.

anteceder, *v.* precede.

antecesor, *m.* ancestor.

antemano, *de a.,* in advance.

antena, *f.* antenna.

antena parabólica, satellite dish.

anteojos, *m.pl.* eyeglasses.

antepasado, *m.* ancestor.

antepenúltimo, *a.* antepenultimate.

anterior, *a.* previous, former.

antes, *adv.* before; formerly.

anticipación, *f.* anticipation.

anticipar, *v.* anticipate; advance.

anticonceptivo, *a. & n.* contraceptive.

anticongelante, *m.* antifreeze.

anticuado, *a.* antiquated, obsolete.

antídoto, *m.* antidote.

antigüedad, *f.* antiquity; antique.

antiguo, *a.* former; old; antique.

antihistamínico, *m.* antihistamine.

antílope, *m.* antelope.

antinuclear, *a.* antinuclear.

antipatía, *f.* antipathy.

antipático, *a.* disagreeable, nasty.

antiséptico, *a. & m.* antiseptic.

antojarse, *v.* **se me antoja . . .** etc., I desire . . ., take a fancy to . . ., etc.

antojo, *m.* whim, fancy.

antorcha, *f.* torch.

antracita, *f.* anthracite.

anual, *a.* annual, yearly.

anudar, *v.* knot; tie.

anular, *v.* annul, void.

anunciar, v. announce; proclaim, advertise.

anuncio, m. announcement; advertisement.

añadir, v. add.

añil, m. bluing; indigo.

año, m. year.

apacible, a. peaceful, peaceable.

apaciguamiento, m. appeasement.

apaciguar, v. appease; placate.

apagado, a. dull.

apagar, v. extinguish, quench, put out.

aparador, m. buffet, cupboard.

aparato, m. apparatus; machine; appliance, set.

aparcamiento, m. parking lot; parking space.

aparecer, v. appear, show up.

aparejo, m. rig. **—aparejar,** v.

aparentar, v. pretend; profess.

aparente, a. apparent.

apariencia, aparición, f. appearance.

apartado, 1. a. aloof; separate. **2.** m. post-office box.

apartamento, m. apartment. **a. en propiedad,** condominium.

apartar, v. separate; remove.

aparte, adv. apart; aside.

apartheid, m. apartheid.

apasionado, a. passionate.

apatía, f. apathy.

apearse, v. get off, alight.

apedrear, v. stone.

apelación, f. appeal. **—apelar,** v.

apellido, m. family name.

apellido materno, mother's family name.

apellido paterno, father's family name.

apenas, adv. scarcely, hardly.

apéndice, m. appendix.

apercibir, v. prepare, warn.

aperitivo, m. appetizer.

aperos, m.pl. implements.

apetecer, v. desire, have appetite for.

apetito, m. appetite.

ápice, m. apex.

apilar, v. stack.

apio, m. celery.

aplacar, v. appease; placate.

aplastar, v. crush, flatten.

aplaudir, v. applaud, cheer.

aplauso, m. applause.

aplazar, v. postpone, put off.

aplicable, a. applicable.

aplicado, a. industrious, diligent.

aplicar, v. apply.

aplomo, m. aplomb, poise.

apoderado -da, n. attorney.

apoderarse de, v. get hold of, seize.

apodo, m. nickname. — **apodar,** v.

apologético, a. apologetic.

apoplejía, f. apoplexy.

aposento, m. room, flat.

apostar, v. bet, wager.

apóstol, m. apostle.

apoyar, v. support, prop; lean.

apoyo, m. support; prop; aid; approval.

apreciable, a. appreciable.

apreciar, v. appreciate, prize.

aprecio, m. appreciation, regard.

apremio, m. pressure, compulsion.

aprender, v. learn.

aprendiz, m. apprentice.

aprendizaje, m. apprenticeship.

aprensión, f. apprehension.

aprensivo, a. apprehensive.

apresurado, a. hasty, fast.

apresurar, v. hurry, speed up.

apretado, a. tight.

apretar, v. squeeze, press; tighten.

apretón, m. squeeze.

aprieto, m. plight, predicament.

aprobación, f. approbation, approval.

aprobar, v. approve.

apropiación, f. appropriation.

apropiado, a. appropriate. **—apropiar,** v.

aprovechar, v. profit by.

aprovecharse, v. take advantage.

aproximado, a. approximate.

aproximarse a, v. approach.

aptitud, f. aptitude.

apto, a. apt.

apuesta, f. bet, wager, stake.

apuntar, v. point, aim; prompt; write down.

apunte, m. annotation, note; promptings, cue.

apuñalar, v. stab.

apurar, v. hurry; worry.

apuro, m. predicament, scrape, trouble.

aquel, aquella, dem. a. that.

aquél, aquélla, dem. pron. that (one); the former.

aquello, dem. pron. that.

aquí, adv. here. **por a.,** this way.

aquietar, v. allay; lull, pacify.

ara, f. altar.

árabe, a. & n. Arab, Arabic.

arado, m. plow. **—arar,** v.

arándano, m. cranberry.

araña, f. spider. **a. de luces,** chandelier.

arbitración, f. arbitration.

arbitrador -ra, n. arbitrator.

arbitraje, m. arbitration.

arbitrar, v. arbitrate.

arbitrario, a. arbitrary.

árbitro, m. arbiter, umpire, referee.

árbol, m. tree; mast.

árbol genealógico, family tree.

arbusto, m. bush, shrub.

arca, f. chest; ark.

arcada, f. arcade.

arcaico, a. archaic.

arce, m. maple.

arcilla, f. clay.

arco, m. arc; arch; (archer's) bow. **a. iris,** rainbow.

archipiélago, m. archipelago.

archivador, m. file cabinet.

archivo, m. archive; file. — **archivar,** v.

arder, v. burn.

ardid, m. stratagem, cunning.

ardiente, a. ardent, burning, fiery.

ardilla, f. squirrel.

ardor, m. ardor, fervor.

ardor de estómago, heartburn.

arduo, a. arduous.

área, f. area.

arena, *f.* sand; arena.

arenoso, *a.* sandy.

arenque, *m.* herring.

arete, *n.* earring.

argentino -na, *a. & n.* Argentine.

argüir, *v.* dispute, argue.

árido, *a.* arid.

aristocracia, *f.* aristocracy.

aristócrata, *f.* aristocrat.

aristocrático, *a.* aristocratic.

aritmética, *f.* arithmetic.

arma, *f.* weapon, arm.

armadura, *f.* armor; reinforcement; framework.

armamento, *m.* armament.

armar, *v.* arm.

armario, *m.* cabinet, bureau, wardrobe.

armazón, *m.* framework, frame.

armería, *f.* armory.

armisticio, *m.* armistice.

armonía, *f.* harmony.

armonioso, *a.* harmonious.

armonizar, *v.* harmonize.

arnés, *m.* harness.

aroma, *f.* aroma, fragrance.

aromático, *a.* aromatic.

arpa, *f.* harp.

arquear, *v.* arch.

arquitecto, *m.* architect.

arquitectura, *f.* architecture.

arquitectural, *a.* architectural.

arrabal, *m.* suburb.

arraigar, *v.* take root, settle.

arrancar, *v.* pull out, tear out; start up.

arranque, *m.* dash, sudden start; fit of anger.

arrastrar, *v.* drag.

arrebatar, *v.* snatch, grab.

arrebato, *m.* sudden attack, fit of anger.

arrecife, *m.* reef.

arreglar, *v.* arrange; repair, fix; adjust, settle.

arreglárselas, *v.* manage, shift for oneself.

arreglo, *m.* arrangement, settlement.

arremangarse, *v.* roll up one's sleeves; roll up one's pants.

arremeter, *v.* attack.

arrendar, *v.* rent.

arrepentimiento, *m.* repentance.

arrepentirse, *v.* repent.

arrestar, *v.* arrest.

arriba, *adv.* up; upstairs.

arriendo, *m.* lease.

arriero, *m.* muleteer.

arriesgar, *v.* risk.

arrimarse, *v.* lean.

arrodillarse, *v.* kneel.

arrogancia, *f.* arrogance.

arrogante, *a.* arrogant.

arrojar, *v.* throw, hurl; shed.

arrollar, *v.* roll, coil.

arroyo, *m.* brook; gully; gutter.

arroz, *m.* rice.

arruga, *f.* ridge; wrinkle.

arrugar, *v.* wrinkle, crumple.

arruinar, *v.* ruin, destroy, wreck.

arsenal, *m.* arsenal; armory.

arsénico, *m.* arsenic.

arte, *m.* (*f.* in *pl.*) art, craft; wiliness.

arteria, *f.* artery.

artesa, *f.* trough.

artesano -na, *n.* artisan, craftsman.

ártico, *a.* arctic.

articulación, *f.* articulation; joint.

articular, *v.* articulate.

artículo, *m.* article.

artífice, *m. & f.* artisan.

artificial, *a.* artificial.

artificio, *m.* artifice, device.

artificioso, *a.* affected.

artillería, *f.* artillery.

artista, *m. & f.* artist.

artístico, *a.* artistic.

artritis, *f.* arthritis.

arzobispo, *m.* archbishop.

as, *m.* ace.

asado, *a. & n.* roast.

asaltador -ra, *n.* assailant.

asaltante, *m. & f.* mugger.

asaltar, *v.* assail, attack.

asalto, *m.* assault. — **asaltar,** *v.*

asamblea, *f.* assembly.

asar, *v.* roast; broil, cook (meat).

asaz, *adv.* enough; quite.

ascender, *v.* ascend, go up; amount.

ascenso, *m.* ascent.

ascensor, *m.* elevator.

ascensorista, *m. & f.* (elevator) operator.

asco, *m.* nausea; disgusting thing. **qué a.,** how disgusting.

aseado, *a.* tidy. —**asear,** *v.*

asediar, *v.* besiege.

asedio, *m.* siege.

asegurar, *v.* assure; secure.

asegurarse, *v.* make sure.

asemejarse a, *v.* resemble.

asentar, *v.* settle; seat.

asentimiento, *m.* assent. — **asentir,** *v.*

aseo, *m.* neatness, tidiness.

aseos, *m.pl.* restroom.

asequible, *a.* attainable; affordable.

aserción, *f.* assertion.

aserrar, *v.* saw.

asesinar, *v.* assassinate; murder, slay.

asesinato, *m.* assassination, murder.

asesino -na, *n.* murderer, assassin.

aseveración, *f.* assertion.

aseverar, *v.* assert.

asfalto, *m.* asphalt.

así, *adv.* so, thus, this way, that way. **a. como,** as well as. **a. que,** as soon as.

asiático -ca, *a. & n.* Asiatic.

asiduo, *a.* assiduous.

asiento, *m.* seat; chair; site.

asiento delantero, front seat.

asiento trasero, back seat.

asignar, *v.* assign; allot.

asilo, *m.* asylum, sanctuary.

asimilar, *v.* assimilate.

asir, *v.* grasp.

asistencia, *f.* attendance, presence.

asistir, *v.* be present, attend.

asno, *m.* donkey.

asociación, *f.* association.

asociado, *m.* associate, partner.

asociar, *v.* associate.

asolar, *v.* desolate; burn, parch.

asoleado, *a.* sunny.

asomar, *v.* appear, loom up, show up.

asombrar, *v.* astonish, amaze.

asombro, *m.* amazement, astonishment.

aspa, *f.* reel. **—aspar,** *v.*

aspecto, *m.* aspect.

aspereza, *f.* harshness.

áspero, *a.* rough, harsh.

aspiración, *f.* aspiration.

aspirador, *m.* vacuum
cleaner.

aspirar, *v.* aspire.

aspirina, *f.* aspirin.

asqueroso, *a.* dirty, nasty,
filthy.

asta, *f.* shaft.

asterisco, *m.* asterisk.

astilla, *f.* splinter, chip. **—
astillar,** *v.*

astillero, *m.* dry dock.

astro, *m.* star.

astronauta, *m. & f.* astronaut.

astronave, *f.* spaceship.

astronomía, *f.* astronomy.

astucia, *f.* cunning.

astuto, *a.* astute, sly, shrewd.

asumir, *v.* assume.

asunto, *m.* matter, affair,
business; subject.

asustar, *v.* frighten, scare,
startle.

atacar, *v.* attack, charge.

atajo, *m.* shortcut.

ataque, *m.* attack, charge;
spell, stroke.

ataque cardíaco, heart attack.

atar, *v.* tie, bind, fasten.

atareado, *a.* busy.

atascar, *v.* stall, stop, obstruct.

atasco, *m.* traffic jam.

ataúd, *m.* casket, coffin.

atavío, *m.* dress; gear,
equipment.

atemorizar, *v.* frighten.

atención, *f.* attention.

atender, *v.* heed; attend to,
wait on.

atenerse a, *v.* count on, depend on.

atentado, *m.* crime, offense.

atento, *a.* attentive, courteous.

ateo, *m.* atheist.

aterrizaje, *m.* landing (of
aircraft).

aterrizaje forzoso, emergency landing, forced
landing.

aterrizar, *v.* land.

atesorar, *v.* hoard.

atestar, *v.* witness.

atestiguar, *v.* attest, testify.

atinar, *v.* hit upon.

atisbar, *v.* scrutinize, pry.

Atlántico, *m.* Atlantic.

atlántico, *a.* Atlantic.

atlas, *m.* atlas.

atleta, *m. & f.* athlete.

atlético, *a.* athletic.

atletismo, *m.* athletics.

atmósfera, *f.* atmosphere.

atmosférico, *a.* atmospheric.

atolladero, *m.* dead end,
impasse.

atómico, *a.* atomic.

átomo, *m.* atom.

atormentar, *v.* torment,
plague.

atornillar, *v.* screw.

atracción, *f.* attraction.

atractivo, 1. *a.* attractive. **2.**
m. attraction.

atraer, *v.* attract; lure.

atrapar, *v.* trap, catch.

atrás, *adv.* back; behind.

atrasado, *a.* belated; backward; slow (clock).

atrasar, *v.* delay, retard; be
slow.

atraso, *m.* delay; backwardness; (*pl.*) arrears.

atravesar, *v.* cross.

atreverse, *v.* dare.

atrevido, *a.* daring, bold.

atrevimiento, *m.* boldness.

atribuir, *v.* attribute, ascribe.

atributo, *m.* attribute.

atrincherar, *v.* entrench.

atrocidad, *f.* atrocity, outrage.

atronar, *v.* deafen.

atropellar, *v.* trample; fell.

atroz, *a.* atrocious.

aturdir, *v.* daze, stun, bewilder.

atún, *m.* tuna.

audacia, *f.* audacity.

audaz, *a.* audacious, bold.

audible, *a.* audible.

audífono, *m.* hearing aid.

audiovisual, *a.* audiovisual.

auditorio, *m.* audience.

aula, *f.* classroom, hall.

aullar, *v.* howl, bay.

aullido, *m.* howl.

aumentar, *v.* augment; increase, swell.

aun, aún, *adv.* still; even. **a.
cuando,** even though,
even if.

aunque, *conj.* although,
though.

áureo, *a.* golden.

aureola, *f.* halo.

auriculares, *m.pl.* headphones.

aurora, *f.* dawn.

ausencia, *f.* absence.

ausentarse, *v.* stay away.

ausente, *a.* absent.

auspicio, *m.* auspice.

austeridad, *f.* austerity.

austero, *a.* austere.

austriaco -ca, *a. & n.* Austrian.

auténtico, *a.* authentic.

auto, automóvil, *m.* auto,
automobile.

autobús, *m.* bus.

autocine, autocinema, *m.*
drive-in (movie theater).

automático, *a.* automatic.

autonomía, *f.* autonomy.

autopista, *f.* expressway.

autor, *m.* author.

autoridad, *f.* authority.

autoritario, *a.* authoritarian; authoritative.

autorizar, *v.* authorize.

autostop, *m.* hitchhiking.
hacer a., to hitchhike.

auxiliar, 1. *a.* auxiliary. **2.** *v.*
assist, aid.

auxilio, *m.* aid, assistance.

avaluar, *v.* evaluate, appraise.

avance, *m.* advance. **—
avanzar,** *v.*

avaricia, *f.* avarice.

avariento, *a.* miserly, greedy.

avaro -ra, *a. & m.* miser;
miserly.

ave, *f.* bird.

avellana, *f.* hazelnut.

Ave María, *m.* Hail Mary.

avena, *f.* oat.

avenida, *f.* avenue; flood.

avenirse, *v.* compromise;
agree.

aventajar, *v.* surpass, get
ahead of.

aventar, *v.* fan; scatter.

aventura, *f.* adventure.

aventurar, *v.* venture, risk,
gamble.

aventurero -ra, *a. & n.* adventurous; adventurer.

avergonzado, *a.* ashamed, abashed.

avergonzar, *v.* shame, abash.

avería, *f.* damage. —averiar, *v.*

averiguar, *v.* ascertain, find out.

aversión, *f.* aversion.

avestruz, *m.* ostrich.

aviación, *f.* aviation.

aviador -ra, *n.* aviator.

ávido, *a.* avid; eager.

avión, *m.* airplane.

avisar, *v.* notify, let know; warn, advise.

aviso, *m.* notice, announcement; advertisement; warning.

avispa, *f.* wasp.

avivar, *v.* enliven, revive.

axila, *f.* armpit.

aya, *f.* governess.

ayatolá, *m.* ayatollah.

ayer, *adv.* yesterday.

ayuda, *f.* help, aid. —ayudar, *v.*

ayudante, *a.* assistant, helper; adjutant.

ayuno, *m.* fast. —ayunar, *v.*

ayuntamiento, *m.* city hall.

azada, *f.* azadón, *m.* hoe.

azafata, *f.* stewardess, flight attendant.

azar, *m.* hazard, chance. al a., at random.

azotar, *v.* whip, flog; belabor.

azote, *m.* scourge, lash.

azúcar, *m.* sugar.

azucarero, *m.* sugar bowl.

azúcar moreno, brown sugar.

azul, *a.* blue.

azulado, *a.* blue, bluish.

azulejo, *m.* tile; bluebird.

azul marino, navy blue.

B

baba, *f.* drivel. —babear, *v.*

babador, *m.* bib.

babucha, *f.* slipper.

bacalao, *m.* codfish.

bachiller -ra, *n.* bachelor (degree).

bacía, *f.* washbasin.

bacterias, *f.pl.* bacteria.

bacteriología, *f.* bacteriology.

bahía, *f.* bay.

bailador -ra, *n.* dancer.

bailar, *v.* dance.

bailarín -ina, *n.* dancer.

baile, *m.* dance.

baja, *f.* fall (in price); (mil.) casualty.

bajar, *v.* lower; descend.

bajeza, *f.* baseness.

bajo, 1. *prep.* under, below. 2. *a.* low; short; base.

bala, *f.* bullet; ball; bale.

balada, *f.* ballad.

balancear, *v.* balance; roll, swing, sway.

balanza, *f.* balance; scales.

balbuceo, *m.* stammer; babble. —balbucear, *v.*

Balcanes, *m.pl.* Balkans.

balcón, *m.* balcony.

balde, *m.* bucket, pail. de b., gratis. en b., in vain.

balística, *f.* ballistics.

ballena, *f.* whale.

balneario, *m.* bathing resort; spa.

balompié, *m.* football.

balón, *m.* football; (auto.) balloon tire.

baloncesto, *m.* basketball.

balota, *f.* ballot, vote. —balotar, *v.*

balsa, *f.* raft.

bálsamo, *m.* balm.

baluarte, *m.* bulwark.

bambolearse, *v.* sway.

bambú, *n.* bamboo.

banal, *a.* banal, trite.

banana, *f.* banana.

banano, *m.* banana tree.

bancarrota, *f.* bankruptcy.

banco, *m.* bank; bench; school of fish.

banco cooperativo, credit union.

banda, *f.* band.

bandada, *f.* covey; flock.

banda sonora, *f.* soundtrack.

bandeja, *f.* tray.

bandera, *f.* flag; banner; ensign.

bandido -da, *n.* bandit.

bando, *m.* faction.

bandolero -ra, *n.* bandit, robber.

banquero -ra, *n.* banker.

banqueta, *f.* stool; (Mex.) sidewalk.

banquete, *m.* feast, banquet.

banquillo, *m.* stool.

bañar, *v.* bathe.

bañera, *f.* bathtub.

baño, *m.* bath; bathroom.

bar, *m.* bar, pub.

baraja, *f.* pack of cards; game of cards.

baranda, *f.* railing, banister.

barato, *a.* cheap.

barba, *f.* beard; chin.

barbacoa, *f.* barbecue; stretcher.

barbaridad, *f.* barbarity; (Am.) excess (in anything).

bárbaro, *a.* barbarous; crude.

barbería, *f.* barbershop.

barbero, *m.* barber.

barca, *f.* (small) boat.

barcaza, *f.* barge.

barco, *m.* ship, boat.

barniz, *m.* varnish. —barnizar, *v.*

barómetro, *m.* barometer.

barón, *m.* baron.

barquilla, *f.* (naut.) log.

barra, *f.* bar.

barraca, *f.* hut, shed.

barrear, *v.* bar, barricade.

barreno, *m.* blast, blasting. —barrenar, *v.*

barrer, *v.* sweep.

barrera, *f.* barrier.

barricada, *f.* barricade.

barriga, *f.* belly.

barril, *m.* barrel; cask.

barrio, *m.* district, ward, quarter.

barro, *m.* clay, mud.

base, *f.* base; basis. —basar, *v.*

base de datos, database.

bastante, 1. *a.* enough, plenty of. 2. *adv.* enough; rather, quite.

bastar, *v.* suffice, be enough.

bastardo -a, *a.* & *n.* bastard.

bastear, *v.* baste.

bastidor, *m.* wing (in theater).

bastón, *m.* (walking) cane.

bastos, *m.pl.* clubs (cards).

basura, *f.* refuse, dirt; garbage; junk.

basurero -ra, *n.* scavenger.

batalla, *f.* battle. **—batallar,** *v.*

batallón, *m.* batallion.

batata, *f.* sweet potato.

bate, *m.* bat. **—batear,** *v.*

batería, *f.* battery.

batido, *m.* (cooking) batter; milkshake.

batidora, *f.* mixer (for food).

batir, *v.* beat; demolish; conquer.

baúl, *m.* trunk.

bautismo, *m.* baptism.

bautista, *m.* & *f.* Baptist.

bautizar, *v.* christen, baptize.

bautizo, *m.* baptism.

baya, *f.* berry.

bayoneta, *f.* bayonet.

beato, *a.* blessed.

bebé, *m.* baby.

beber, *v.* drink.

bebible, *a.* drinkable.

bebida, *f.* drink, beverage.

beca, *f.* grant, scholarship.

becado -da, *n.* scholar.

becerro, *m.* calf; calfskin.

beldad, *f.* beauty.

belga, *a.* & *n.* Belgian.

Bélgica, *f.* Belgium.

belicoso, *a.* warlike.

beligerante, *a.* & *n.* belligerent.

bellaco, 1. *a.* sly, roguish. **2.** *m.* rogue.

bellas artes, *f.pl.* fine arts.

belleza, *f.* beauty.

bello, *a.* beautiful.

bellota, *f.* acorn.

bendecir, *v.* bless.

bendición, *f.* blessing, benediction.

bendito, *a.* blessed.

beneficio, *m.* benefit. **— beneficiar,** *v.*

beneficioso, *a.* beneficial.

benevolencia, *f.* benevolence.

benévolo, *a.* benevolent.

benigno, *a.* benign.

beodo -da, *a.* & *n.* drunk.

berenjena, *f.* eggplant.

beso, *m.* kiss. **—besar,** *v.*

bestia, *f.* beast, brute.

betabel, *m.* beet.

Biblia, *f.* Bible.

bíblico, *a.* Biblical.

biblioteca, *f.* library.

bicarbonato, *m.* bicarbonate.

bicicleta, *f.* bicycle.

bien, 1. *adv.* well. **2.** *n.* good; (*pl.*) possessions.

bienes inmuebles, *m.pl.* real estate.

bienestar, *m.* well-being, welfare.

bienhechor -ra, *n.* benefactor.

bienvenida, *f.* welcome.

bienvenido, *a.* welcome.

biftec, *m.* steak.

bifurcación, *f.* fork. **—bifurcar,** *v.*

bigamia, *f.* bigamy.

bígamo -a, *n.* bigamist.

bigotes, *m.pl.* mustache.

bikini, *m.* bikini.

bilingüe, *a.* bilingual.

bilingüismo, *m.* bilingualism.

bilis, *f.* bile.

billar, *m.* billiards.

billete, *m.* ticket; bank note; bill.

billete de banco, bank note.

billón, *m.* billion.

bingo, *m.* bingo.

biodegradable, *a.* biodegradable.

biografía, *f.* biography.

biología, *f.* biology.

biombo, *m.* folding screen.

bisabuela, *f.* great-grandmother.

bisabuelo, *m.* great-grandfather.

bisel, *m.* bevel. **—biselar,** *v.*

bisonte, *m.* bison.

bisté, bistec, *m.* steak.

bisutería, *f.* costume jewelry.

bizarro, *a.* brave; generous; smart.

bizcocho, *m.* biscuit, cake.

blanco, 1. *a.* white; blank. **2.** *m.* white; target.

blandir, *v.* brandish, flourish.

blando, *a.* soft.

blanquear, *v.* whiten; bleach.

blasfemar, *v.* blaspheme, curse.

blasfemia, *f.* blasphemy.

blindado, *a.* armored.

blindaje, *m.* armor.

bloque, *m.* block. **—bloquear,** *v.*

bloqueo, *m.* blockade. **— bloquear,** *v.*

blusa, *f.* blouse.

bobo -ba, *a.* & *n.* fool; foolish.

boca, *f.* mouth.

bocado, *m.* bit; bite, mouthful.

bocanada, *f.* puff (of smoke); mouthful (of liquor).

bochorno, *m.* sultry weather; embarrassment.

bocina, *f.* horn.

boda, *f.* wedding.

bodega, *f.* wine cellar; (naut.) hold; (Carib.) grocery store.

bofetada, *f.* **bofetón,** *m.* slap.

boga, *f.* vogue; fad.

bogar, *v.* row (a boat).

bohemio -a, *a.* & *n.* Bohemian.

boicoteo, *m.* boycott. **— boicotear,** *v.*

boina, *f.* beret.

bola, *f.* ball.

bola de nieve, snowball.

bolas de billar, billiard balls.

bolera, *f.* bowling alley.

boletín, *m.* bulletin.

boletín informativo, news bulletin.

boleto, *m.* ticket. **b. de embarque,** boarding pass.

boliche, *m.* bowling alley.

bolígrafo, *m.* ballpoint pen.

boliviano -a, *a.* & *n.* Bolivian.

bollo, *m.* bun, loaf.

bolos, *m.pl.* bowling.

bolsa, *f.* purse; stock exchange.

bolsa de agua caliente, hot-water bottle.

bolsillo, *m.* pocket.

bomba, *f.* pump; bomb; gas station.

bombardear, *v.* bomb; bombard, shell.

bombear, *v.* pump.

bombero, *m.* fireman.
bombilla, *f.* (light) bulb.
bonanza, *f.* prosperity; fair weather.
bondad, *f.* kindness; goodness.
bondadoso, *a.* kind, kindly.
bonito, *a.* pretty.
bono, *m.* bonus; (fin.) bond.
boqueada, *f.* gasp; gape. —**boquear,** *v.*
boquilla, *f.* cigarette holder.
bordado, *m.,* **bordadura,** *f.* embroidery.
bordar, *v.* embroider.
borde, *m.* border, rim, edge, brink, ledge.
borde de la carretera, roadside.
borla, *f.* tassel.
borracho -a, *a.* & *n.* drunk.
borrachón -na, *n.* drunkard.
borrador, *m.* eraser.
borradura, *f.* erasure.
borrar, *v.* erase, rub out.
borrasca, *f.* squall, storm.
borrico, *m.* donkey.
bosque, *m.* forest, wood.
bostezo, *m.* yawn. —**bostezar,** *v.*
bota, *f.* boot.
botalón, *m.* (naut.) boom.
botánica, *f.* botany.
botar, *v.* throw out, throw away.
bote, *m.* boat; can, box.
bote salvavidas, lifeboat.
botica, *f.* pharmacy, drugstore.
boticario, *m.* pharmacist, druggist.
botín, *m.* booty, plunder, spoils.
botiquín, *m.* medicine chest.
boto, *a.* dull, stupid.
botón, *m.* button.
botones, *m.* bellboy (in a hotel).
bóveda, *f.* vault.
boxeador, *m.* boxer.
boxeo, *m.* boxing. —**boxear,** *v.*

boya, *f.* buoy.
boyante, *a.* buoyant.
bozal, *m.* muzzle.
bramido, *m.* roar, bellow. —**bramar,** *v.*
brasileño -ña, *a.* & *n.* Brazilian.
bravata, *f.* bravado.
bravear, *v.* bully.
braza, *f.* fathom.
brazada, *f.* (swimming) stroke.
brazalete, *m.* bracelet.
brazo, *m.* arm.
brea, *f.* tar, pitch.
brecha, *f.* gap, breach.
brécol, *m.* broccoli.
bregar, *v.* scramble.
breña, *f.* rough country with brambly shrubs.
Bretaña, *f.* Britain.
breve, *a.* brief, short. **en b.,** shortly, soon.
brevedad, *f.* brevity.
bribón -na, *n.* rogue, rascal.
brida, *f.* bridle.
brigada, *f.* brigade.
brillante, 1. *a.* brilliant, shiny. **2.** *m.* diamond.
brillo, *m.* shine, glitter. —**brillar,** *v.*
brinco, *m.* jump; bounce, skip. —**brincar,** *v.*
brindis, *m.* toast. —**brindar,** *v.*
brío, *m.* vigor.
brioso, *a.* vigorous, spirited.
brisa, *f.* breeze.
brisa marina, sea breeze.
británico, *a.* British.
brocado -da, *a.* & *n.* brocade.
brocha, *f.* brush.
broche, *m.* brooch, clasp, pin.
broma, *f.* joke. —**bromear,** *v.*
bronce, *m.* bronze; brass.
bronceador, *m.* suntan lotion, suntan oil.
bronquitis, *f.* bronchitis.
brotar, *v.* gush; sprout; bud.

brote, *m.* bud, shoot.
bruja, *f.* witch.
brújula, *f.* compass.
bruma, *f.* mist.
brumoso, *a.* misty.
brusco, *a.* brusque; abrupt, curt.
brutal, *a.* savage, brutal.
brutalidad, *f.* brutality.
bruto -ta, 1. *a.* brutish; ignorant. **2.** *n.* blockhead.
bucear, *v.* dive.
bueno, *a.* good, fair; well (in health).
buey, *m.* ox, steer.
búfalo, *m.* buffalo.
bufanda, *f.* scarf.
bufón -ona, *a.* & *n.* fool, buffoon, clown.
búho, *m.* owl.
buhonero, *m.* peddler, vender.
bujía, *f.* spark plug.
bulevar, *m.* boulevard.
bullicio, *m.* bustle, noise.
bullicioso, *a.* boisterous, noisy.
bulto, *m.* bundle; lump.
buñuelo, *m.* bun.
buque, *m.* ship.
buque de guerra, warship.
buque de pasajeros, passenger ship.
burdo, *a.* coarse.
burgués -esa, *a.* & *n.* bourgeois.
burla, *f.* mockery; fun.
burlador -ra, *n.* trickster, jokester.
burlar, *v.* mock, deride.
burlarse de, *v.* scoff at; make fun of.
burro, *m.* donkey.
busca, *f.* search, pursuit, quest.
buscar, *v.* seek, look for; look up.
busto, *m.* bust.
butaca, *f.* armchair; (theat.) orchestra seat.
buzo, *m.* diver.
buzón, *m.* mailbox.

C

cabal, *a.* exact; thorough.
cabalgar, *v.* ride horseback.
caballeresco, *a.* gentlemanly, chivalrous.
caballería, *f.* cavalry; chivalry.

caballeriza, *f.* stable.

caballero, *m.* gentleman; knight.

caballete, *m.* sawhorse; easel; ridge (of roof).

caballo, *m.* horse.

cabaña, *f.* cabin; booth.

cabaré, *m.* nightclub.

cabaretero -a, *m. & f.* nightclub owner.

cabecear, *v.* pitch (as a ship).

cabecera, *f.* head (of bed, table).

cabello, *m.* hair.

caber, *v.* fit into, be contained in. **no cabe duda,** there is no doubt.

cabeza, *f.* head; warhead.

cabildo, *m.* city hall.

cabildo abierto, town meeting.

cabizbajo, *a.* downcast.

cablegrama, *m.* cablegram.

cabo, *m.* end; (geog.) cape; (mil.) corporal. **llevar a c.,** carry out, accomplish.

cabra, *f.* goat.

cacahuete, *m.* peanut.

cacao, *m.* cocoa; chocolate.

cacerola, *f.* pan, casserole.

cachorro, *m.* cub; puppy.

cada, *a.* each, every.

cadáver, *m.* corpse.

cadena, *f.* chain.

cadera, *f.* hip.

cadete, *m.* cadet.

caer, *v.* fall.

café, *m.* coffee; café.

café exprés, espresso.

café soluble, instant coffee.

cafetal, *m.* coffee plantation.

cafetera, *f.* coffee pot.

caída, *f.* fall, drop; collapse.

caimán, *m.* alligator.

caja, *f.* box, case; checkout counter.

caja de ahorros, savings bank.

caja de cerillos, matchbox.

caja de fósforos, matchbox.

caja torácica, rib cage.

cajero -ra, *n.* cashier.

cajón, *m.* drawer.

cal, *f.* lime.

calabaza, *f.* calabash, pumpkin.

calabozo, *m.* jail, cell.

calambre, *m.* cramp.

calamidad, *f.* calamity, disaster.

calcetín, *m.* sock.

calcio, *m.* calcium.

calcular, *v.* calculate, figure.

cálculo, *m.* calculation, estimate.

caldera, *f.* kettle, caldron; boiler.

caldo, *m.* broth.

calefacción, *f.* heat, heating.

calendario, *m.* calendar.

calentar, *v.* heat, warm.

calidad, *f.* quality, grade.

caliente, *a.* hot, warm.

calificar, *v.* qualify.

callado, *a.* silent, quiet.

callarse, *v.* quiet down; keep still; stop talking.

calle, *f.* street.

calle sin salida, dead end.

callejón, *m.* alley.

callo, *m.* callus, corn.

calma, *f.* calm, quiet.

calmado, *a.* calm.

calmante, *a.* soothing, calming.

calmar, *v.* calm, quiet, lull, soothe.

calor, *n.* heat, warmth. **tener c.,** to be hot, warm; feel hot, warm. **hacer c.,** to be hot, warm (weather).

calorífero, 1. *a.* heat-producing. **2.** *m.* radiator.

calumnia, *f.* slander. **—calumniar,** *v.*

caluroso, *a.* warm, hot.

calvario, *m.* Calvary.

calvo, *a.* bald.

calzado, *m.* footwear.

calzar, *v.* wear (as shoes).

calzoncillos, *m.pl.* shorts.

calzones, *m.pl.* trousers.

cama, *f.* bed.

cámara, *f.* chamber; camera.

camarada, *m. & f.* comrade.

camarera, *f.* chambermaid; waitress.

camarero, *m.* steward; waiter.

camarón, *m.* shrimp.

camarote, *m.* stateroom, berth.

cambiar, *v.* exchange, change, trade; cash.

cambio, *m.* change, exchange. **en c.,** on the other hand.

cambista, *m. & f.* money changer; banker, broker.

cambur, *m.* banana.

camello, *m.* camel.

camilla, *f.* stretcher.

caminar, *v.* walk.

caminata, *f.* tramp, hike.

camino, *m.* road; way.

camión, *m.* truck.

camisa, *f.* shirt.

camisería, *f.* haberdashery.

camiseta, *f.* undershirt; T-shirt.

campamento, *m.* camp.

campana, *f.* bell.

campanario, *m.* bell tower, steeple.

campaneo, *m.* chime.

campaña, *f.* campaign.

campeón -na, *n.* champion.

campeonato, *m.* championship.

campesino -na, *n.* peasant.

campestre, *a.* country, rural.

campo, *m.* field; (the) country.

campo de concentración, concentration camp.

campo de golf, golf course.

Canadá, *m.* Canada.

canadiense, *a. & n.* Canadian.

canal, *m.* canal; channel.

Canal de la Mancha, *m.* English Channel.

canalla, *f.* rabble.

canario, *m.* canary.

canasta, *f.* basket.

cáncer, *m.* cancer.

cancha de tenis, *f.* tennis court.

canciller, *m.* chancellor.

canción, *f.* song.

candado, *m.* padlock.

candela, *f.* fire; light; candle.

candelero, *m.* candlestick.

candidato -ta, *n.* candidate; applicant.

candidatura, *f.* candidacy.

canela, *f.* cinnamon.

cangrejo, *m.* crab.

caníbal, *m.* cannibal.

caniche, *m.* poodle.

canje, *m.* exchange, trade. **—canjear,** *v.*

cano, *a.* gray.

canoa, *f.* canoe.

cansado, *a.* tired, weary.

cansancio, *m.* fatigue.

cansar, *v.* tire, fatigue, wear out.

cantante, *m. & f.* singer.

cantar, 1. *m.* song. 2. *v.* sing.

cántaro, *m.* pitcher.

cantera, *f.* (stone) quarry.

cantidad, *f.* quantity, amount.

cantina, *f.* bar, tavern; restaurant.

canto, *m.* chant, song, singing; edge.

caña, *f.* cane, reed; sugar cane.

cañón, *m.* canyon; cannon; gun barrel.

caoba, *f.* mahogany.

caos, *m.* chaos.

caótico, *a.* chaotic.

capa, *f.* cape, cloak; coat (of paint).

capacidad, *f.* capacity; capability.

capacitar, *v.* enable.

capataz, *m.* foreman.

capaz, *a.* capable, able.

capellán, *m.* chaplain.

caperuza, *f.* hood.

capilla, *f.* chapel.

capital, *m.* capital. *f.* capital (city).

capitalista, *a. & n.* capitalist.

capitán, *m.* captain.

capitular, *v.* yield.

capítulo, *m.* chapter.

capota, *f.* hood.

capricho, *m.* caprice; fancy, whim.

caprichoso, *a.* capricious.

cápsula, *f.* capsule.

capturar, *v.* capture.

capucha, *f.* hood.

capullo, *m.* cocoon.

cara, *f.* face.

caracol, *m.* snail.

carácter, *m.* character.

característica, *f.* characteristic.

característico, *a.* characteristic.

caramba, mild exclamation.

caramelo, *m.* caramel; candy.

carátula, *f.* dial.

caravana, *f.* caravan.

carbón, *m.* carbon; coal.

carbonizar, *v.* char.

carburador, *m.* carburetor.

carcajada, *f.* burst of laughter.

cárcel, *f.* prison, jail.

carcelero, *m.* jailer.

carcinogénico, *a.* carcinogenic.

cardenal, *m.* cardinal.

cardiólogo -a, *m & f.* cardiologist.

carecer, *v.* lack.

carestía, *f.* scarcity; famine.

carga, *f.* cargo; load, burden; freight.

cargar, *v.* carry; load; charge.

cargo, *m.* load; charge, office.

caricatura, *f.* caricature; cartoon.

caricaturista, *m. & f.* caricaturist; cartoonist.

caricia, *f.* caress.

caridad, *f.* charity.

cariño, *m.* affection, fondness.

cariñoso, *a.* affectionate, fond.

carisma, *m.* charisma.

caritativo, *a.* charitable.

carmesí, *a. & m.* crimson.

carnaval, *m.* carnival.

carne, *f.* meat, flesh; pulp.

carne acecinada, *f.* corned beef.

carnero, *m.* ram; mutton.

carnicería, *f.* meat market; massacre.

carnicero -ra, *n.* butcher.

carnívoro, *a.* carnivorous.

caro, *a.* dear, costly, expensive.

carpa, *f.* tent.

carpeta, *f.* folder; briefcase.

carpintero, *m.* carpenter.

carrera, *f.* race; career.

carrera de caballos, horse race.

carreta, *f.* wagon, cart.

carrete, *m.* reel, spool.

carretera, *f.* road, highway.

carril, *m.* rail.

carrillo, *m.* cart (for baggage or shopping).

carro, *m.* car, automobile; cart.

carroza, *f.* chariot.

carruaje, *m.* carriage.

carta, *f.* letter; (*pl.*) cards.

cartel, *m.* placard, poster; cartel.

cartelera, *f.* billboard.

cartera, *f.* pocketbook, handbag, wallet; portfolio.

cartero, *m.* mailman, postman.

cartón, *m.* cardboard.

cartón piedra, *m.* papier-mâché.

cartucho, *m.* cartridge; cassette.

casa, *f.* house, dwelling; home.

casaca, *f.* dress coat.

casa de pisos, apartment house.

casado, *a.* married.

casamiento, *m.* marriage.

casar, *v.* marry, marry off.

casarse, *v.* get married. c. con, marry.

cascabel, *m.* jingle bell.

cascada, *f.* waterfall, cascade.

cascajo, *m.* gravel.

cascanueces, *m.* nutcracker.

cascar, *v.* crack, break, burst.

cáscara, *f.* shell, rind, husk.

casco, *m.* helmet; hull.

casera, *f.* landlady; housekeeper.

caserío, *m.* settlement.

casero, 1. *a.* homemade. 2. *m.* landlord, superintendent.

caseta, *f.* cottage, hut.

casi, *adv.* almost, nearly.

casilla, *f.* booth; ticket office; pigeonhole.

casimir, *m.* cashmere.

casino, *m.* club; clubhouse.

caso, *m.* case. hacer c. a, pay attention to.

casorio, *m.* informal wedding.

caspa, *f.* dandruff.

casta, *f.* caste.

castaña, *f.* chestnut.

castaño, 1. *a.* brown. 2. *m.* chestnut tree.

castañuela, *f.* castanet.

castellano -na, *a. & n.* Castillian.

castidad, f. chastity.
castigar, v. punish, castigate.
castigo, m. punishment.
castillo, m. castle.
castizo, a. pure, genuine; noble.
casto, a. chaste.
castor, m. beaver.
casual, adj. accidental, co-incidental.
casualidad, f. coincidence. **por c.,** by chance.
casuca, f. hut, shanty, hovel.
cataclismo, m. cataclysm.
catacumba, f. catacomb.
catadura, f. act of tasting; appearance.
catalán -na, a. & n. Catalonian.
catálogo, m. catalogue. —**catalogar,** v.
caputta, f. catapult.
catar, v. taste; examine, try; bear in mind.
catarata, f. cataract, waterfall.
catarro, m. head cold, catarrh.
catástrofe, f. catastrophe.
catecismo, m. catechism.
cátedra, f. professorship.
catedral, f. cathedral.
catedrático -ca, n. professor.
categoría, f. category.
categórico, a. categorical.
catequismo, m. catechism.
catequizar, v. catechize.
cátodo, m. cathode.
catolicismo, m. Catholicism.
católico -ca, a. & n. Catholic.
catorce, a. & pron. fourteen.
catre, m. cot.
cauce, m. riverbed; ditch.
caución, f. precaution; security, guarantee.
cauchal, m. rubber plantation.
caucho, m. rubber.
caudal, m. means, fortune; (pl.) holdings.
caudaloso, a. prosperous, rich.
caudillaje, m. leadership; tyranny.
caudillo, m. leader, chief.
causa, f. cause. —**causar,** v.
cautela, f. caution.
cauteloso, m. cautious.

cautivar, v. captivate.
cautiverio, m. captivity.
cautividad, f. captivity.
cautivo -va, a. & n. captive.
cauto, a. cautious.
cavar, v. dig.
caverna, f. cavern, cave.
cavernoso, a. cavernous.
cavidad, f. cavity, hollow.
cavilar, v. criticize, cavil.
cayado, m. shepherd's staff.
cayo, m. small rocky islet, key.
caza, f. hunting, pursuit, game.
cazador, m. hunter.
cazar, v. hunt.
cazatorpedero, m. torpedo-boat, destroyer.
cazo, m. ladle, dipper; pot.
cazuela, f. crock.
cebada, f. barley.
cebo, m. bait. —**cebar,** v.
cebolla, f. onion.
cebolleta, f. spring onion.
ceceo, m. lisp. —**cecear,** v.
cecina, f. dried beef.
cedazo, m. sieve, sifter.
ceder, v. cede; transfer; yield.
cedro, m. cedar.
cédula, f. decree. **c. personal,** identification card.
céfiro, m. zephyr.
cegar, v. blind.
ceguedad, ceguera, f. blindness.
ceja, f. eyebrow.
cejar, v. go backwards; yield, retreat.
celada, f. trap; ambush.
celaje, m. appearance of the sky.
celar, v. watch carefully, guard.
celda, f. cell.
celebración, f. celebration.
celebrante, m. officiating priest.
celebrar, v. celebrate, observe.
célebre, a. celebrated, noted, famous.
celebridad, f. fame; celebrity; pageant.
celeridad, f. speed, rapidity.
celeste, a. celestial.
celestial, a. heavenly.
celibato, m. celibacy.

célibe, 1. a. unmarried. **2.** m. & f. unmarried person.
celista, m. & f. cellist.
celo, m. zeal; (pl.) jealousy.
cellisca, f. sleet. —**cellisquear,** v.
celofán, m. cellophane.
celosía, f. Venetian blind.
celoso, a. jealous; zealous.
céltico, a. Celtic.
célula, f. (biol.) cell.
celuloide, m. celluloid.
cementar, v. cement.
cementerio, m. cemetery.
cemento, m. cement.
cena, f. supper.
cenagal, m. swamp, marsh.
cenagoso, a. swampy, marshy, muddy.
cenar, v. dine, eat.
cencerro, m. cowbell.
cendal, m. thin, light cloth; gauze.
cenicero, m. ashtray.
ceniciento, a. ashen.
cenit, m. zenith.
ceniza, f. ash, ashes.
censo, m. census.
censor, m. censor.
censura, f. reproof, censure; censorship.
censurable, a. objectionable.
censurar, v. censure, criticize.
centavo, m. cent.
centella, f. thunderbolt, lightning.
centellear, v. twinkle, sparkle.
centelleo, m. sparkle.
centenar, m. (a) hundred.
centenario, m. centennial, centenary.
centeno, m. rye.
centígrado, a. centigrade.
centímetro, m. centimeter.
céntimo, m. cent.
centinela, m. sentry, guard.
central, a. central.
centralita, f. switchboard.
centralizar, v. centralize.
centrar, v. center.
céntrico, a. central.
centro, m. center.
centro de mesa, centerpiece.
centroamericano -na, a. & n. Central American.
ceñidor, m. belt, sash; girdle.

ceñir, v. gird.
ceño, m. frown.
ceñudo, a. frowning, grim.
cepa, f. stump.
cepillo, m. brush; plane. —
   cepillar, v.
cera, f. wax.
cerámica, m. ceramics.
cerámico, a. ceramic.
cerca, 1. adv. near. 2. f.
   fence, hedge.
cercado, m. enclosure; garden.
cercamiento, m. enclosure.
cercanía, f. proximity.
cercano, a. near, nearby.
cercar, v. surround.
cercenar, v. clip; lessen, reduce.
cerciorar, v. make sure; affirm.
cerco, m. hoop; siege.
cerda, f. bristle.
cerdo -da, n. hog.
cerdoso, a. bristly.
cereal, a. & m. cereal.
cerebro, m. brain.
ceremonia, f. ceremony.
ceremonial, a. & m. cere-
   monial, ritual.
ceremonioso, a. ceremoni-
   ous.
cereza, f. cherry.
cerilla, f., cerillo, m. match.
cerner, v. sift.
cero, m. zero.
cerrado, a. closed; cloudy;
   obscure; taciturn.
cerradura, f. lock.
cerrajero, m. locksmith.
cerrar, v. close, shut.
cerro, m. hill.
cerrojo, m. latch, bolt.
certamen, m. contest; competition.
certero, a. accurate, exact;
   certain, sure.
certeza, f. certainty.
certidumbre, f. certainty.
certificado, m. certificate.
certificado de compra,
   proof of purchase.
certificar, v. certify; register
   (a letter).
cerúleo, a. cerulean, sky-
   blue.
cervecería, f. brewery; beer
   saloon.

cervecero, m. brewer.
cerveza, f. beer.
cesante, a. unemployed.
cesar, v. cease.
césped, m. sod, lawn.
cesta, f., cesto, m. basket.
cetrino, a. yellow, lemon-
   colored.
cetro, m. scepter.
chabacano, a. vulgar.
chacal, m. jackal.
chacó, m. shako.
chacona, f. chaconne.
chacota, f. fun, mirth.
chacotear, v. joke.
chacra, f. small farm.
chafallar, v. mend badly.
chagra, m. rustic; rural person.
chal, m. shawl.
chalán, m. horse trader.
chaleco, m. vest.
chaleco salvavidas, life
   jacket.
chalet, m. chalet.
challí, m. challis.
chamada, f. brushwood.
chamarillero, m. gambler.
chamarra, f. coarse linen
   jacket.
chambelán, m. chamber-
   lain.
champaña, m. champagne.
champú, m. shampoo.
chamuscar, v. scorch.
chancaco, a. brown.
chancear, v. jest, joke.
chanciller, m. chancellor.
chancillería, f. chancery.
chancla, f. old shoe.
chancleta, f. slipper.
chanclos, m.pl. galoshes.
chancro, m. chancre.
changador, m. porter;
   handyman.
chantaje, m. blackmail.
chantejear, v. blackmail.
chantajista, m. & f. black-
   mailer.
chanto, m. flagstone.
chantre, m. precentor.
chanza, f. joke, jest. —
   chancear, v.
chanzoneta, f. chansonette.
chapa, f. (metal) sheet,
   plate; lock.
chapado en oro, a. gold-
   plated.

chapado en plata, a. silver-
   plated.
chaparrada, f. downpour.
chaparral, m. chaparral.
chaparreras, f.pl. chaps.
chaparrón, m. downpour.
chapear, v. veneer.
chapeo, m. hat.
chapitel, m. spire, steeple;
   (architecture) capital.
chapodar, v. lop.
chapón, m. inkblot.
chapotear, v. paddle or
   splash in the water.
chapoteo, m. splash.
chapucear, v. fumble, bungle.
chapucero, a. sloppy,
   bungling.
chapurrear, v. speak (a language) brokenly.
chapuz, m. dive; ducking.
chapuzar, v. dive; duck.
chaqueta, f. jacket, coat.
chaqueta deportiva, sport
   jacket.
charada, f. charade.
charamusca, f. twisted
   candy stick.
charanga, f. military band.
charanguero, m. peddler.
charca, f. pool, pond.
charco, m. pool, puddle.
charla, f. chat; chatter, prat-
   tle. —charlar, v.
charladuría, f. chatter.
charlatán -ana, n. charlatan.
charlatanismo, m. charla-
   tanism.
charol, m. varnish.
charolar, v. varnish; polish.
charquear, v. jerk (beef).
charquí, m. jerked beef.
charrán, a. roguish.
chascarillo, m. risqué story.
chasco, m. disappointment,
   blow; practical joke.
chasis, m. chassis.
chasquear, v. fool, trick; disappoint; crack (a whip).
chasquido, m. crack (sound).
chata, f. bedpan.
chato, a. flat-nosed, pug-
   nosed.
chauvinismo, m. chauvin-
   ism.
chauvinista, n. & a. chau-
   vinist.

chelín, *m.* shilling.

cheque, *m.* (bank) check.

chica, *f.* girl.

chicana, *f.* chicanery.

chicha, *f.* an alcoholic drink.

chícharo, *f.* pea.

chicharra, *f.* cicada; talkative person.

chicharrón, *m.* crisp fried scrap of meat.

chichear, *v.* hiss in disapproval.

chichón, *m.* bump, bruise, lump.

chicle, *m.* chewing gum.

chico, 1. *a.* little. **2.** *m.* boy.

chicote, *m.* cigar; cigar butt.

chicotear, *v.* whip, flog.

chifladura, *f.* mania; whim; jest.

chiflar, *v.* whistle; become insane.

chiflido, *m.* shrill whistle.

chile, *m.* chili.

chileno -na, *a.* & *n.* Chilean.

chillido, *m.* shriek, scream, screech. **—chillar,** *v.*

chillón, *a.* shrill.

chimenea, *f.* chimney, smokestack; fireplace.

china, *f.* pebble; maid; Chinese woman.

chinarro, *m.* large pebble, stone.

chinche, *f.* bedbug; thumbtack.

chincheta, *f.* thumbtack.

chinchilla, *f.* chinchilla.

chinchorro, *m.* fishing net.

chinela, *f.* slipper.

chinero, *m.* china closet.

chino -na, *a.* & *n.* Chinese.

chipirón, *m.* baby squid.

chiquero, *m.* pen for pigs, goats, etc.

chiquito -ta, 1. *a.* small, tiny. **2.** *m.* & *f.* small child.

chiribitil, *m.* small room, den.

chirimía, *f.* flageolet.

chiripa, *f.* stroke of good luck.

chirla, *f.* mussel.

chirle, *a.* insipid.

chirona, *f.* prison, jail.

chirrido, *m.* squeak, chirp. **—chirriar,** *v.*

chis, *interj.* hush!

chisgarabís, *n.* meddler; unimportant person.

chisguete, *m.* squirt, splash.

chisme, *m.* gossip. **—chismear,** *v.*

chismero -ra, *n.* gossiper.

chismoso, *adj.* gossiping.

chispa, *f.* spark.

chispeante, *a.* sparkling.

chispear, *v.* sparkle.

chisporrotear, *v.* emit sparks.

chistar, *v.* speak.

chiste, *m.* joke, gag; witty saying.

chistera, *f.* fish basket; top hat.

chistoso, *a.* funny, comic, amusing.

chito, *interj.* hush!

chiva, *f.* female goat.

chivato, *m.* kid, young goat.

chivo, *m.* male goat.

chocante, *a.* striking; shocking; unpleasant.

chocar, *v.* collide, clash, crash; shock.

chocarrear, *v.* joke, jest.

choclo, *m.* clog; overshoe; ear of corn.

chocolate, *m.* chocolate.

chocolate con leche, milk chocolate.

chocolatería, *f.* chocolate shop.

chochear, *v.* be in one's dotage.

chochera, *f.* dotage, senility.

chofer, chófer, *m.* chauffeur, driver.

chofeta, *f.* chafing dish.

cholo, *m.* half-breed.

chopo, *m.* black poplar.

choque, *m.* collision, clash, crash; shock.

chorizo, *m.* sausage.

chorrear, *v.* spout; drip.

chorro, *m.* spout; spurt, jet. **llover a chorros,** to pour (rain).

choto, *m.* calf, kid.

choza, *f.* hut, cabin.

chozno -na, *n.* great-great-great-grandchild.

chubasco, *m.* shower, squall.

chubascoso, *a.* squally.

chuchería, *f.* trinket, knickknack.

chulería, *f.* pleasant manner.

chuleta, *f.* chop, cutlet.

chulo, *m.* rascal, rogue; joker.

chupa, *f.* jacket.

chupada, *f.* suck, sip.

chupado, *a.* very thin.

chupaflor, *m.* hummingbird.

chupar, *v.* suck.

churrasco, *m.* roasted meat.

chuscada, *f.* joke, jest.

chusco, *a.* funny, humorous.

chusma, *f.* mob, rabble.

chuzo, *m.* pike.

CI, *abbr.* (**coeficiente intelectual**) IQ (intelligence quotient).

cicatero, *a.* stingy.

cicatriz, *f.* scar.

cicatrizar, *v.* heal.

ciclamato, *m.* cyclamate.

ciclista, *m* & *f.* cyclist.

ciclo, *m.* cycle.

ciclón, *m.* cyclone.

ciego -ga, 1. *a.* blind. **2.** *n.* blind person.

cielo, *m.* heaven; sky, heavens; ceiling.

ciempiés, *m.* centipede.

cien, ciento, *a.* & *pron.* hundred. **por c.,** per cent.

ciénaga, *f.* swamp, marsh.

ciencia, *f.* science.

cieno, *m.* mud.

científico -ca, 1. *a.* scientific. **2.** *n.* scientist.

cierre, *m.* fastener, snap, clasp.

cierto, *a.* certain, sure, true.

ciervo, *m.* deer.

cierzo, *m.* northerly wind.

cifra, *f.* cipher, number. **—cifrar,** *v.*

cigarra, *f.* locust.

cigarrera, cigarrillera, *f.* cigarette case.

cigarrillo, *m.* cigarette.

cigarro, *m.* cigar; cigarette.

cigüeña, *f.* stork.

cilíndrico, *a.* cylindrical.

cilindro, *m.* cylinder.

cima, *f.* summit, peak.

cimarrón, 1. *a.* wild, untamed. **2.** *m.* runaway slave.

címbalo, *m.* cymbal.

cimbrar, *v.* shake, brandish.

cimientos, *m.pl.* foundation.

cinc, *m.* zinc.

cincel, *m.* chisel. —**cincelar**, *v.*

cinco, *a. & pron.* five.

cincuenta, *a. & pron.* fifty.

cincha, *f.* (harness) cinch. —**cinchar**, *v.*

cine, *m.* movies; movie theater.

cíngulo, *m.* cingulum.

cínico -ca, *a. & n.* cynical; cynic.

cinismo, *m.* cynicism.

cinta, *f.* ribbon, tape; (movie) film.

cintilar, *v.* glitter, sparkle.

cinto, *m.* belt; girdle.

cintura, *f.* waist.

cinturón, *m.* belt.

cinturón de seguridad, safety belt.

ciprés, *m.* cypress.

circo, *m.* circus.

circuito, *m.* circuit.

circulación, *f.* circulation.

circular, 1. *a. & m.* circular. 2. *v.* circulate.

círculo, *m.* circle, club.

circundante, *a.* surrounding.

circundar, *v.* encircle, surround.

circunferencia, *f.* circumference.

circunlocución, *n.* circumlocution.

circunscribir, *v.* circumscribe.

circunspección, *n.* decorum, propriety.

circunspecto, *a.* circumspect.

circunstancia, *f.* circumstance.

circunstante, *m.* bystander.

circunvecino, *a.* neighboring, adjacent.

cirio, *m.* candle.

cirrosis, *f.* cirrhosis.

ciruela, *f.* plum; prune.

cirugía, *f.* surgery.

cirujano, *m.* surgeon.

cisne, *m.* swan.

cisterna, *f.* cistern.

cita, *f.* citation; appointment, date.

citación, *f.* citation; (legal) summons.

citar, *v.* cite, quote; summon; make an appointment with.

cítrico, *a.* citric.

ciudad, *f.* city.

ciudadanía, *f.* citizenship.

ciudadano -na, *n.* citizen.

ciudadela, *f.* fortress, citadel.

cívico, *a.* civic.

civil, *a. & n.* civil; civilian.

civilidad, *f.* politeness, civility.

civilización, *f.* civilization.

civilizador, *a.* civilizing.

civilizar, *v.* civilize.

cizallas, *f.pl.* shears. —**cizallar**, *v.*

cizaña, *f.* weed; vice.

clamar, *v.* clamor.

clamor, *m.* clamor.

clamoreo, *m.* persistent clamor.

clamoroso, *a.* clamorous.

clandestino, *a.* secret, clandestine.

clara, *f.* white (of egg).

clara de huevo, egg white.

claraboya, *m.* skylight; bull's-eye.

clarear, *v.* clarify; become light, dawn.

clarete, *m.* claret.

claridad, *f.* clarity.

clarificar, *v.* clarify.

clarín, *m.* bugle, trumpet.

clarinete, *m.* clarinet.

clarividencia, *f.* clairvoyance.

clarividente, *a.* clairvoyant.

claro, *a.* clear; bright; light (in color); of course.

clase, *f.* class; classroom; kind, sort.

clase nocturna, evening class.

clásico, *a.* classic, classical.

clasificar, *v.* classify, rank.

claustro, *m.* cloister.

claustrofobia, *f.* claustrophobia.

cláusula, *f.* clause.

clausura, *f.* cloister; inner sanctum; closing.

clavado, 1. *a.* nailed. 2. *m. & f.* dive.

clavar, *v.* nail, peg, pin.

clave, *f.* code; (mus.) key.

clavel, *m.* carnation.

clavetear, *v.* nail.

clavícula, *f.* collarbone.

clavija, *f.* pin, peg.

clavo, *m.* nail, spike; clove.

clemencia, *f.* clemency.

clemente, *a.* merciful.

clementina, *f.* tangerine.

clerecía, *f.* clergy.

clerical, *a.* clerical.

clérigo, *m.* clergyman.

clero, *m.* clergy.

cliente, *m. & f.* customer, client.

clientela, *f.* clientele, practice.

clima, *m.* climate.

clímax, *m.* climax.

clínica, *f.* clinic.

clínca de reposo, convalescent home.

clínico, *a.* clinical.

clíper, *m.* clipper ship.

cloaca, *f.* sewer.

cloquear, *v.* cluck, cackle.

cloqueo, *m.* cluck.

cloro, *m.* chlorine.

colorformo, *m.* chloroform.

club, *m.* club, association.

club juvenil, youth club.

clueca, *f.* brooding hen.

coacción, *n.* compulsion.

coagular, *v.* coagulate, clot.

coágulo, *m.* clot.

coalición, *f.* coalition.

coartada, *f.* alibi.

coartar, *v.* limit.

cobarde, *a. & n.* cowardly; coward.

cobardía, *f.* cowardice.

cobayo, *m.* guinea pig.

cobertizo, *m.* shed.

cobertor, *m.,* **cobija**, *f.* blanket.

cobertura, *f.* cover, wrapping.

cobijar, *v.* cover; protect.

cobrador, *m.* collector.

cobranza, *f.* collection or recovery of money.

cobrar, *v.* collect; charge; cash.

cobre, *m.* copper.

cobrizo, *a.* coppery.

cobro, *m.* collection or recovery of money.

coca, *f.* coca leaves.

cocaína, *f.* cocaine.

cocal, *m.* coconut plantation.

cocear, v. kick; resist.

cocer, v. cook, boil, bake.

coche, m. coach; car, automobile.

cochecito de niño, baby carriage.

coche de choque, dodgem.

cochera, f. garage.

cochero, m. coachman; cab driver.

cochinada, f. filth; herd of swine.

cochino, m. pig, swine.

cocido, m. stew.

cociente, m. quotient.

cocimiento, m. cooking.

cocina, f. kitchen.

cocinar, v. cook.

cocinero -ra, n. cook.

coco, m. coconut; coconut tree.

cocodrilo, m. crocodile.

cóctel, m. cocktail.

codazo, m. nudge with the elbow.

codicia, f. avarice, greed; lust.

codiciar, v. covet.

codicioso, a. covetous; greedy.

código, m. (law) code.

codo, m. elbow.

codorniz, f. quail.

coeficiente, m. quotient.

coeficiente intelecutal, intelligence quotient.

coetáneo, a. contemporary.

coexistir, v. coexist.

cofrade, m. fellow member of a club, etc.

cofre, m. coffer; chest; trunk.

coger, v. catch; pick; take.

cogote, m. nape.

cohecho, m. bribe. **—cohechar,** v.

coheredero -ra, n. coheir.

coherente, a. coherent.

cohesión, f. cohesion.

cohete, m. fire cracker; rocket.

cohibición, n. restraint; repression.

cohibir, v. restrain; repress.

coincidencia, f. coincidence.

coincidir, v. coincide.

cojear, v. limp.

cojera, m. limp.

cojín, m. cushion.

cojinete, m. small cushion, pad.

cojo -a, 1. a. lame. **2.** n. lame person.

col, f. cabbage.

cola, f. tail; glue; line, queue. **hacer c.,** stand in line.

colaboración, f. collaboration.

colaborar, v. collaborate.

cola de caballo, pony tail.

coladera, f. strainer.

colador, m. colander, strainer.

colapso, m. collapse, prostration.

colar, v. strain; drain.

colateral, a. collateral.

colcha, f. bedspread, quilt.

colchón, m. mattress.

colear, v. wag the tail.

colección, f. collection, set.

coleccionar, v. collect.

colecta, f. collection; collect (a prayer).

colectivo, a. collective.

colector, m. collector.

colega, m. & f. colleague.

colegial, m. college student.

colegiatura, f. scholarship; tuition.

colegio, m. (private) school, college.

colegir, v. infer, deduce.

cólera, f. rage, wrath. m. cholera.

colérico, adj. angry, irritated.

colesterol, m. cholesterol.

coleta, f. pigtail; postscript.

coleto, m. leather jacket.

colgador, m. rack, hanger.

colgaduras, f.pl. drapery.

colgante, a. hanging.

colgar, v. hang up, suspend.

colibrí, m. hummingbird.

coliflor, f. cauliflower.

coligarse, v. band together, unite.

colilla, f. butt of a cigar or cigarette.

colina, f. hill, hillock.

colinabo, m. turnip.

colindante, a. neighboring, adjacent.

colindar, v. neighbor, abut.

coliseo, m. theater; coliseum.

colisión, f. collision.

collado, m. hillock.

collar, m. necklace; collar.

colmar, v. heap up, fill liberally.

colmena, f. hive.

colmillo, m. eyetooth; tusk; fang.

colmo, m. height, peak, extreme.

colocación, f. place, position; employment, job; arrangement.

colocar, v. place, locate, put, set.

colombiano -na, a. & n. Colombian.

colon, m. colon (of intestines).

colonia, f. colony; eau de Cologne.

Colonia, f. Cologne.

colonial, a. colonial.

colonización, f. colonization.

colonizador -ra, n. colonizer.

colonizar, v. colonize.

colono, m. colonist; tenant farmer.

coloquio, m. conversation, talk.

color, m. color. **—colorar,** v.

coloración, f. coloring.

colorado, a. red, ruddy.

colorar, v. color, paint; dye.

colorete, m. rouge.

colorido, m. color, coloring. **—colorir,** v.

colosal, a. colossal.

columbrar, v. discern.

columna, f. column, pillar, shaft.

columpiar, v. swing.

columpio, m. swing.

coma, f. coma; comma.

comadre, f. midwife; gossip; close friend.

comadreja, f. weasel.

comadrona, f. midwife.

comandancia, m. command; command post.

comandante, m. commandant; commander; major.

comandar, v. command.

comandita, f. silent partnership.

comanditario -ra, n. silent partner.

comando, m. command.

comarca, f. region; border, boundary.

comba, f. bulge.

combar, v. bend; bulge.

combate, m. combat. — combatir, v.

combatiente, a. & m. combatant.

combinación, f. combination; slip (garment).

combinar, v. combine.

combustible, 1. a. combustible. 2. m. fuel.

combustión, f. combustion.

comedero, m. trough.

comedia, f. comedy; play.

comediante, m. actor; comedian.

comedido, a. polite, courteous; obliging.

comedirse, v. to be polite or obliging.

comedor, m. dining room. coche c., dining car.

comendador, m. commander.

comensal, m. table companion.

comentador -ra, n. commentator.

comentario, m. commentary.

comento, m. comment. — comentar, v.

comenzar, v. begin, start, commence.

comer, v. eat, dine.

comercial, a. commercial.

comercializar, v. market.

comerciante -ta, n. merchant, trader, businessperson.

comerciar, v. trade, deal, do business.

comercio, m. commerce, trade, business; store.

comestible, 1. a. edible. 2. m. (pl.) groceries, provisions.

cometa, m. comet. f. kite.

cometer, v. commit.

cometido, m. commission; duty; task.

comezón, f. itch.

comicios, m.pl. primary elections.

cómico -ca, a. & n. comic, comical; comedian.

comida, f. food; dinner; meal.

comidilla, f. light meal; gossip.

comienzo, m. beginning.

comilitona, f. spread, feast.

comillas, f.pl. quotation marks.

comilón -na, n. glutton; heavy eater.

comisario, m. commissary.

comisión, f. commission. — comisionar, v.

comisionado -da, n. agent, commissioner.

comisionar, v. commission.

comiso, m. (law) confiscation of illegal goods.

comistrajo, m. mess, hodgepodge.

comité, m. committee.

comitiva, f. retinue.

como, conj. & adv. like, as.

cómo, adv. how.

cómoda, f. bureau, chest (of drawers).

cómodamente, adv. conveniently.

comodidad, f. convenience, comfort; commodity.

comodín, m. joker (playing card).

cómodo, a. comfortable; convenient.

comodoro, m. commodore.

compacto, a. compact.

compadecer, v. be sorry for, pity.

compadraje, m. clique.

compadre, m. close friend.

compaginar, v. put in order; arrange.

compañerismo, m. companionship.

compañero -ra, n. companion, partner.

compañía, f. company.

comparable, a. comparable.

comparación, f. comparison.

comparar, v. compare.

comparativamente, adv. comparatively.

comparativo, a. comparative.

comparecer, v. appear.

comparendo, m. summons.

comparsa, f. carnival masquerade; retinue.

compartimiento, m. compartment.

compartir, v. share.

compás, m. compass; beat, rhythm.

compasar, v. measure exactly.

compasión, f. compassion.

compasivo, a. compassionate.

compatibilidad, f. compatibility.

compatible, a. compatible.

compatriota, m. & f. compatriot.

compeler, v. compel.

compendiar, v. summarize; abridge.

compendiariamente, adv. briefly.

compendio, m. summary; abridgment.

compendiosamente, adv. briefly.

compensación, f. compensation.

compensar, v. compensate.

competencia, f. competence; competition.

competente, a. competent.

competentemente, adv. competently.

competición, f. competition.

competidor -ra, a. & n. competitive; competitor.

competir, v. compete.

compilación, f. compilation.

compilar, v. compile.

compinche, m. pal.

complacencia, f. complacency.

complacer, v. please, oblige, humor.

complaciente, a. pleasing, obliging.

complejidad, f. complexity.

complejo -ja, a. & n. complex.

complemento, m. complement; (gram.) object.

completamente, adv. completely.

completamiento, m. completion, finish.

completar, v. complete.

completo, a. complete, full, perfect.

complexión, f. nature, temperament.

complicación, *f.* complication.

complicado, *a.* complicated.

complicar, *v.* complicate.

cómplice, *m.* & *f.* accomplice, accessory.

complicidad, *f.* complicity.

complot, *m.* conspiracy.

componedor -ra, *n.* typesetter.

componenda, *f.* compromise; settlement.

componente, *a.* & *m.* component.

componer, *v.* compose; fix, repair.

componible, *a.* reparable.

comportable, *a.* endurable.

comportamiento, *m.* behavior.

comportarse, *v.* behave.

comporte, *m.* behavior.

composición, *f.* composition.

compositivo, *a.* synthetic; composite.

compositor -ra, *n.* composer.

compostura, *f.* composure; repair; neatness.

compota, *f.* (fruit) sauce.

compra, *f.* purchase. **ir de compras,** to go shopping.

comprador -ra, *n.* buyer, purchaser.

comprar, *v.* buy, purchase.

comprender, *v.* comprehend, understand; include, comprise.

comprensibilidad, *f.* comprehensibility.

comprensible, *a.* understandable.

comprensión, *f.* comprehension, understanding.

comprensivo, *m.* comprehensive.

compresa, *f.* medical compress.

compresión, *f.* compression.

comprimir, *v.* compress; restrain, control.

comprobación, *f.* proof.

comprobante, 1. *a.* proving. **2.** *m.* proof.

comprobar, *v.* prove; verify, check.

comprometer, *v.* compromise.

comprometerse, *v.* become engaged.

compromiso, *m.* compromise; engagement.

compuerta, *f.* floodgate.

compuesto, *m.* composition; compound.

compulsión, *f.* compulsion.

compulsivo, *a.* compulsive.

compunción, *f.* compunction.

compungirse, *v.* regret, feel remorse.

computación, *f.* computation.

computador, *m.* computer.

computadora de sobremesa, *f.* desktop computer.

computadora doméstica, *f.* home computer.

computar, *v.* compute.

cómputo, *m.* computation.

comulgar, *v.* take communion.

comulgatorio, *m.* communion altar.

común, *a.* common, usual.

comunal, *a.* communal.

comunero, *m.* commoner.

comunicable, *a.* communicable.

comunicación, *f.* communication.

comunicante, *m.* & *f.* communicant.

comunicar, *v.* communicate; convey.

comunicativo, *a.* communicative.

comunidad, *f.* community.

comunión, *f.* communion.

comunismo, *m.* communism.

comunista, *a.* & *n.* communistic; communist.

comúnmente, *adv.* commonly; usually; often.

con, *prep.* with.

concavidad, *f.* concavity.

cóncavo, 1. *a.* concave. **2.** *m.* concavity.

concebible, *a.* conceivable.

concebir, *v.* conceive.

conceder, *v.* concede.

concejal, *m.* councilman.

concejo, *m.* city council.

concento, *m.* harmony (of singing voices).

concentración, *f.* concentration.

concentrar, *v.* concentrate.

concepción, *f.* conception.

conceptible, *a.* conceivable.

concepto, *m.* concept; opinion.

concerniente, *a.* concerning.

concernir, *v.* concern.

concertar, *v.* arrange.

concertina, *f.* concertina.

concesión, *f.* concession.

concha, *f.* (sea) shell.

conciencia, *f.* conscience; consciousness; conscientiousness.

concienzudo, *a.* conscientious.

concierto, *m.* concert.

conciliación, *f.* conciliation.

conciliador -ra, *n.* conciliator.

conciliar, *v.* conciliate.

concilio, *m.* council.

concisión, *f.* conciseness.

conciso, *a.* concise.

concitar, *v.* instigate, stir up.

conciudadano -na, *n.* fellow citizen.

concluir, *v.* conclude.

conclusión, *f.* conclusion.

conclusivo, *a.* conclusive.

concluso, *a.* concluded; closed.

concluyentemente, *adv.* conclusively.

concomitante, *a.* concomitant, attendant.

concordador -ra, *n.* moderator; conciliator.

concordancia, *f.* agreement, concord.

concordar, *v.* agree; put or be in accord.

concordia, *f.* concord, agreement.

concretamente, *adv.* concretely.

concretar, *v.* summarize; make concrete.

concretarse, *v.* limit oneself to.

concreto, *a.* & *m.* concrete.

concubina, *f.* concubine, mistress.

concupiscente, *a.* lustful.

concurrencia, *f.* assembly; attendance; competition.

concurrente, *a.* concurrent.

concurrido, *a.* heavily attended or patronized.

concurrir, *v.* concur; attend.

concurso, *m.* contest, competition; meeting.

conde, *m.* (title) count.

condecente, *a.* appropriate, proper.

condecoración, *f.* decoration; medal; badge.

condecorar, *v.* decorate with a medal.

condena, *f.* prison sentence.

condenación, *f.* condemnation.

condenar, *v.* condemn; damn; sentence.

condensación, *f.* condensation.

condensar, *v.* condense.

condesa, *f.* countess.

condescendencia, *f.* condescension.

condescender, *v.* condescend, deign.

condescendiente, *a.* condescending.

condición, *f.* condition.

condicional, *a.* conditional.

condicionalmente, *adv.* conditionally.

condimentar, *v.* season, flavor.

condimento, *m.* condiment, seasoning, dressing.

condiscípulo -la, *n.* schoolmate.

condolencia, *f.* condolence, sympathy.

condolerse de, *v.* sympathize with.

condominio, *m.* condominium.

condómino, *m.* co-owner.

condonar, *v.* condone.

cóndor, *m.* condor (bird).

conducción, *f.* conveyance.

conducente, *a.* conducive.

conducir, *v.* conduct, escort, lead; drive.

conducta, *f.* conduct, behavior.

conducto, *m.* pipe, conduit; sewer.

conductor -ra, *n.* driver; conductor.

conectar, *v.* connect.

conejera, *f.* rabbit warren; place of ill repute.

conejillo de Indias, guinea pig.

conejo -ja, *n.* rabbit.

conexión, *f.* connection; coupling.

conexivo, *a.* connective.

conexo, *a.* connected, united.

confalón, *m.* ensign, standard.

confección, *f.* workmanship; ready-made article; concoction.

confeccionar, *v.* concoct.

confederación, *f.* confederation.

confederado -da, *a. & n.* confederate.

confederar, *v.* confederate, unite, ally.

conferencia, *f.* lecture; conference. **c. interurbana,** long-distance call.

conferenciante, *m. & f.* lecturer, speaker.

conferenciar, *v.* confer.

conferencista, *m. & f.* lecturer, speaker.

conferir, *v.* confer.

confesar, *v.* confess.

confesión, *f.* confession.

confesionario, *m.* confessional.

confesor -ra, *n.* confessor.

confeti, *m.pl.* confetti.

confiable, *a.* dependable.

confiado, *a.* confident; trusting.

confianza, *f.* confidence, trust, faith.

confiar, *v.* entrust; trust, rely.

confidencia, *f.* confidence, secret.

confidencial, *a.* confidential.

confidente, *m. & f.* confidant.

confidentemente, *adv.* confidently.

confín, *m.* confine.

confinamiento, *m.* confinement.

confinar, *v.* confine, imprison; border on.

confirmación, *f.* confirmation.

confirmar, *v.* confirm.

confiscación, *f.* confiscation.

confiscar, *v.* confiscate.

confitar, *v.* sweeten; make into candy or jam.

confite, *m.* candy.

confitería, *f.* confectionery; candy store.

confitura, *f.* confection.

conflagración, *f.* conflagration.

conflicto, *m.* conflict.

confluencia, *f.* confluence, junction.

confluir, *v.* flow into each other.

conformación, *f.* conformation.

conformar, *v.* conform.

conforme, 1. *a.* acceptable, right, as agreed; in accordance, in agreement. **2.** *conj.* according, as.

conformidad, *f.* conformity; agreement.

conformismo, *m.* conformism.

conformista, *m. & f.* conformist.

confortar, *v.* comfort.

confraternidad, *f.* brotherhood, fraternity.

confricar, *v.* rub vigorously.

confrontación, *f.* confrontation.

confrontar, *v.* confront.

confucianismo, *m.* Confucianism.

confundir, *v.* confuse; puzzle, mix up.

confusamente, *adv.* confusedly.

confusión, *f.* confusion, mix-up; clutter.

confuso, *a.* confused; confusing.

confutación, *f.* disproof.

confutar, *v.* refute, disprove.

congelable, *a.* congealable.

congelación, *f.* congealment; deep freeze.

congelado, *a.* frozen, congealed.

congelar, *v.* congeal, freeze.

congenial, *a.* congenial; analogous.

congeniar, *v.* be congenial.

congestión, *f.* congestion.

conglomeración, *f.* conglomeration.

congoja, *f.* grief, anguish.

congraciamiento, *m.* flattery; ingratiation.

congraciar, *v.* flatter; ingratiate oneself.

congratulación, *f.* congratulation.

congratular, *v.* congratulate.

congregación, *f.* congregation.

congregar, *v.* congregate.

congresista, *m. & f.* congressional representative.

congreso, *m.* congress; conference.

conjetura, *f.* conjecture. — **conjeturar,** *v.*

conjetural, *a.* conjectural.

conjugación, *f.* conjugation.

conjugar, *v.* conjugate.

conjunción, *f.* union; conjunction.

conjuntamente, *adv.* together, jointly.

conjunto. 1. *a.* joint, unified. **2.** *m.* whole.

conjuración, *f.* conspiracy, plot.

conjurado -da, *n.* conspirator, plotter.

conjurar, *v.* conjure.

conllevador, *m.* helper, aide.

conmemoración, *f.* commemoration; remembrance.

conmemorar, *v.* commemorate.

conmemorativo, *a.* commemorative, memorial.

conmensal, *m.* messmate.

conmigo, *adv.* with me.

conmillitón, *m.* fellow soldier.

conminación, *f.* threat, warning.

conminar, *v.* threaten.

conminatorio, *a.* threatening, warning.

coumiseración, *f.* sympathy.

conmoción, *f.* commotion, stir.

conmovedor, *a.* moving, touching.

conmover, *v.* move, affect, touch.

conmutación, *f.* commutation.

conmutador, *m.* electric switch.

conmutar, *v.* exchange.

connotación, *f.* connotation.

connotar, *v.* connote.

connubial, *a.* connubial.

connubio, *m.* matrimony.

cono, *m.* cone.

conocedor -ra, *n.* expert, connoisseur.

conocer, *v.* know, be acquainted with; meet, make the acquaintance of.

conocible, *a.* knowable.

conocido -da, 1. *a.* familiar, well-known. **2.** *n.* acquaintance, person known.

conocimiento, *m.* knowledge, acquaintance; consciousness.

conque, *conj.* so then; and so.

conquista, *f.* conquest.

conquistador -ra, *n.* conqueror.

conquistar, *v.* conquer.

consabido, *a.* aforesaid.

consagración, *f.* consecration.

consagrado, *a.* consecrated.

consagrar, *v.* consecrate, dedicate, devote.

consanguinidad, *f.* consanguinity.

consciente, *a.* conscious, aware.

conscientemente, *adv.* consciously.

conscripción, *f.* conscription for military service.

consecución, *f.* attainment.

consecuencia, *f.* consequence.

consecuente, *a.* consequent; consistent.

consecuentemente, *adv.* consequently.

consecutivamente, *adv.* consecutively.

consecutivo, *a.* consecutive.

conseguir, *v.* obtain, get, secure; succeed in, manage to.

conseja, *f.* fable.

consejero -ra, *n.* adviser, counselor.

consejo, *m.* council; counsel; (piece of) advice. **c. de redacción,** editorial board.

consenso, *m.* consensus.

consentido, *a.* spoiled, bratty.

consentimiento, *m.* consent.

consentir, *v.* allow, permit.

conserje, *m.* superintendent, keeper.

conserva, *f.* conserve, preserve.

conservación, *f.* conservation.

conservador -ra, *a. & n.* conservative.

conservar, *v.* conserve.

conservativo, *a.* conservative, preservative.

conservatorio, *m.* conservatory.

considerable, *a.* considerable, substantial.

considerablemente, *adv.* considerably.

consideración, *f.* consideration.

consideradamente, *adv.* considerably.

considerado, *a.* considerate; considered.

considerando, *conj.* whereas.

considerar, *v.* consider.

consigna, *f.* watchword.

consignación, *f.* consignment.

consignar, *v.* consign.

consignatorio -ria, *n.* consignee; trustee.

consigo, *adv.* with herself, with himself, with oneself, with themselves, with yourself, with yourselves.

consiguiente, 1. *a.* consequent. **2.** *m.* consequence.

consiguientemente, *adv.* consequently.

consistencia, *f.* consistency.

consistente, *a.* consistent.

consistir, *v.* consist.

consistorio, *m.* consistory.

consocio, *m.* associate; partner; comrade.

consola, *f.* console.

consolación, *f.* consolation.

consolar, v. console.
consolativo, a. consolatory.
consolidación, n. consolidation.
consolidado, a. consolidated.
consolidar, v. consolidate.
consonancia, f. agreement, accord, harmony.
consonante, a. & f. consonant.
consonar, v. rhyme.
consorte, m. & f. consort, mate.
conspicuo, a. conspicuous.
conspiración, f. conspiracy, plot.
conspirador -ra, n. conspirator.
conspirar, v. conspire, plot.
constancia, f. perseverance; record.
constante, a. constant.
constantemente, adv. constantly.
constar, v. consist; be clear, be on record.
constelación, f. constellation.
consternación, f. consternation.
consternar, v. dismay.
constipación, f. head cold.
constipado, 1. a. having a head cold. **2.** m. head cold.
constitución, f. constitution.
constitucional, a. constitutional.
constitucionalidad, f. constitutionality.
constituir, v. constitute.
constitutivo, m. constituent.
constituyente, a. constituent.
constreñidamente, adv. compulsively; with constraint.
constreñimiento, m. compulsion; constraint.
constreñir, v. constrain.
constricción, f. constriction.
construcción, f. construction.
constructivo, a. constructive.
constructor -ra, n. builder.
construir, v. construct, build.
consuelo, m. consolation.
cónsul, m. consul.
consulado, m. consulate.
consular, a. consular.
consulta, f. consultation.
consultación, f. consultation.

consultante, m. & f. consultant.
consultar, v. consult.
consultivo, a. consultative.
consultor -ra, n. adviser.
consumación, f. consummation; end.
consumado, a. consummate, down-right.
consumar, v. consummate.
consumidor -ra, n. consumer.
consumir, v. consume.
consumo, m. consumption.
consunción, m. consumption, tuberculosis.
contabilidad, f. accounting bookkeeping.
contabilista, contable, m. & f. accountant.
contacto, m. contact.
contado, m. **al c.,** (for) cash.
contador -ra, n. accountant, bookkeeper; meter.
contagiar, v. infect.
contagio, m. contagion.
contagioso, a. contagious.
contaminación, f. contamination, pollution. **c. del aire, c. atmosférica,** air pollution.
contaminar, v. contaminate, pollute.
contar, v. count; relate, recount, tell. **c. con,** count on.
contemperar, v. moderate.
contemplación, f. contemplation.
contemplador -ra, n. thinker.
contemplar, v. contemplate.
contemplativamente, adv. thoughtfully.
contemplativo, a. contemplative.
contemporáneo -nea, a. & n. contemporary.
contención, f. contention.
contencioso, a. quarrelsome; argumentative.
contender, v. cope, contend; conflict.
contendiente, m. & f. contender.
contenedor, m. container.
contener, v. contain; curb, control.
contenido, m. contents.

contenta, f. endorsement:
contentamiento, m. contentment.
contentar, v. content, satisfy.
contentible, a. contemptible.
contento, 1. a. contented, happy. **2.** m. contentment, satisfaction, pleasure.
contérmino, a. adjacent, abutting.
contestable, a. disputable.
contestación, f. answer. — **contestar,** v.
contestador automático, m. answering machine.
contextura, f. texture.
contienda, f. combat; match; strife.
contigo, adv. with you.
contiguamente, adv. contiguously.
contiguo, a. adjoining, next.
continencia, f. continence, moderation.
continental, a. continental.
continente, m. continent; mainland.
continentemente, adv. in moderation.
contingencia, f. contingency.
contingente, a. contingent; incidental.
continuación, f. continuation. **a c.,** thereupon, hereupon.
continuamente, adv. continuously.
continuar, v. continue, keep on.
continuidad, f. continuity.
continuo, a. continual; continuous.
contorcerse, v. writhe, twist.
contorción, f. contortion.
contorno, m. contour; profile, outline; neighborhood.
contra, prep. against.
contraalmirante, m. rear admiral.
contraataque, m. counterattack.
contrabajo, m. double bass.
contrabalancear, v. counterbalance.
contrabandear, v. smuggle.
contrabandista, m. & f. smuggler.

contrabando, *m.* contraband, smuggling.

contracción, *f.* contraction.

contracepción, *f.* contraception, birth control.

contractual, *a.* contractual.

contradecir, *v.* contradict.

contradicción, *f.* contradiction.

contradictorio, *adj.* contradictory.

contraer, *v.* contract; shrink.

contrahacedor -ra, *n.* imitator.

contrahacer, *v.* forge.

contralor, *m.* comptroller.

contramandar, *v.* countermand.

contraorden, *f.* countermand.

contraparte, *f.* counterpart.

contrapesar, *v.* counterbalance; offset.

contrapeso, *m.* counterweight.

contraproducente, *a.* counterproductive.

contrapunto, *m.* counterpoint.

contrariamente, *adv.* contrarily.

contrariar, *v.* contradict; vex; antagonize; counteract.

contrariedad, *f.* contrariness; opposition; contradiction; disappointment; trouble.

contrario, *a. & m.* contrary, opposite.

contrarrestar, *v.* resist; counteract.

contrasol, *m.* sunshade.

contraste, *m.* contrast. — **contrastar**, *v.*

contratar, *v.* engage, contract.

contratiempo, *m.* accident; misfortune.

contratista, *m. & f.* contractor.

contrato, *m.* contract.

contribución, *f.* contribution; tax.

contribuir, *v.* contribute.

contribuyente, *m. & f.* contributor; taxpayer.

contrición, *f.* contrition.

contristar, *v.* afflict.

contrito, *a.* contrite, remorseful.

control, *m.* control. — **controlar**, *v.*

controlador aéreo, *m.* air traffic controller.

controversia, *f.* controversy.

controversista, *m. & f.* controversialist.

controvertir, *v.* dispute.

contumacia, *f.* stubbornness.

contumaz, *adj.* stubborn.

contumelia, *f.* contumely; abuse.

conturbar, *v.* trouble, disturb.

contusión, *f.* contusion; bruise.

convalecencia, *f.* convalescence.

convalecer, *v.* convalesce.

convaleciente, *a.* convalescent.

convecino -na, 1. *a.* near, close; 2. *n.* neighbor.

convencedor, *adj.* convincing.

convencer, *v.* convince.

convencimiento, *m.* conviction, firm belief.

convención, *f.* convention.

convencional, *a.* conventional.

conveniencia, *f.* suitability; advantage, interest.

conveniente, *a.* suitable; advantageous, opportune.

convenio, *m.* pact, treaty; agreement.

convenir, *v.* assent, agree, concur; be suitable, fitting, convenient.

convento, *m.* convent.

convergencia, *f.* convergence.

convergir, *v.* converge.

conversación, *f.* conversation.

conversar, *v.* converse.

conversión, *f.* conversion.

convertible, *a.* convertible.

convertir, *v.* convert.

convexidad, *f.* convexity.

convexo, *a.* convex.

convicción, *f.* conviction.

convicto, *a.* found guilty.

convidado -da, *n.* guest.

convidar, *v.* invite.

convincente, *a.* convincing.

convite, *m.* invitation, treat.

convocación, *f.* convocation.

convocar, *v.* convoke, assemble.

convoy, *m.* convoy, escort.

convoyar, *v.* convey; escort.

convulsión, *f.* convulsion.

convulsivo, *a.* convulsive.

conyugal, *a.* conjugal.

cónyuge, *m. & f.* spouse, mate.

coñac, *m.* cognac, brandy.

cooperación, *f.* cooperation.

cooperador, *a.* cooperative.

cooperar, *v.* cooperate.

cooperativa, *f.* (food, etc.) cooperative, co-op.

cooperativo, *a.* cooperative.

coordinación, *f.* coordination.

coordinar, *v.* coordinate.

copa, *f.* goblet.

copartícipe, *m & f.* partner.

copete, *m.* tuft; toupee.

copia, *f.* copy. — **copiar**, *v.*

copiadora, *f.* copier.

copioso, *a.* copious.

copista, *m. & f.* copyist.

copla, *f.* popular song.

coplero, *m.* poetaster.

cópula, *f.* connection.

coqueta, *f.* flirt. — **coquetear**, *v.*

coraje, *m.* courage, bravery; anger.

coral, 1. *a.* choral. 2. *m.* coral.

coralino, *a.* coral.

Corán, *m.* Koran.

corazón, *m.* heart.

corazonada, *f.* foreboding.

corbata, *f.* necktie.

corbeta, *f.* corvette.

corcho, *m.* cork.

corcova, *f.* hump, hunchback.

corcovado -da, *a. & n.* hunchback.

cordaje, *m.* rigging.

cordel, *m.* string, cord.

cordero, *m.* lamb.

cordial, *a.* cordial; hearty.

cordialidad, *f.* cordiality.

cordillera, *f.* mountain range.

cordón, *m.* cord; (shoe) lace.

cordura, *f.* sanity.

Corea, f. Korea.
coreano -a, a. & n. Korean.
coreografía, f. choreography.
corista, f. chorus girl.
corneja, f. crow.
córneo, a. horny.
corneta, f. bugle, horn, cornet.
corniforme, a. horn-shaped.
cornisa, f. cornice.
cornucopia, f. cornucopia.
coro, m. chorus; choir.
corola, f. corolla.
corolario, m. corollary.
corona, f. crown; halo; wreath.
coronación, f. coronation.
coronamiento, m. completion of a task.
coronar, v. crown.
coronel, m. colonel.
coronilla, f. crown, top of the head.
corporación, f. corporation.
corporal, adj. corporeal, bodily.
corpóreo, a. corporeal.
corpulencia, f. corpulence.
corpulento, a. corpulent, stout.
corpuscular, a. corpuscular.
corpúsculo, m. corpuscle.
corral, m. corral, pen, yard.
correa, f. belt, strap.
correa transportadora, conveyor belt.
corrección, f. correction.
correcto, a. correct, proper, right.
corrector -ra, n. corrector, proofreader.
corredera, f. race course.
corredizo, a. easily untied.
corredor, m. corridor; runner.
corregible, a. corrigible.
corregidor, m. corrector; magistrate, mayor.
corregir, v. correct.
correlación, f. correlation.
correlacionar, v. correlate.
correlativo, a. correlative.
correo, m. mail.
correoso, a. leathery.
correr, v. run.
correría, f. raid; escapade.
correspondencia, f. correspondence.

corresponder, v. correspond.
correspondiente, a. & m. corresponding; correspondent.
corresponsal, m. correspondent.
corretaje, m. brokerage.
correvedile, m. tale bearer; gossip.
corrida, f. race. **c. (de toros),** bullfight.
corrido, a. abashed; expert.
corriente, 1. a. current, standard. **2.** f. current, stream. m. **al c.,** informed, up to date. **contra la c.,** against the current; upriver, upstream.
corroboración, f. corroboration.
corroborar, v. corroborate.
corroer, v. corrode.
corromper, v. corrupt.
corrompido, a. corrupt.
corrupción, f. corruption.
corruptela, f. corruption; vice.
corruptibilidad, f. corruptibility.
corruptor -ra, n. corrupter.
corsario, m. corsair.
corsé, m. corset.
corso, m. piracy.
cortacésped, m. lawnmower.
cortadillo, m. small glass.
cortado, a. cut.
cortadura, f. cut.
cortante, a. cutting, sharp, keen.
cortapisa, f. obstacle.
cortaplumas, m. penknife.
cortar, v. cut, cut off, cut out.
corte, f. court, m. cut.
cortedad, f. smallness; shyness.
cortejar, v. pay court to, woo.
cortejo, m. court; courtship; sweetheart.
cortés, a. civil, courteous, polite.
cortesana, f. courtesan.
cortesano. 1. a. courtly, courteous. **2.** m. courtier.
cortesía, f. courtesy.
corteza, f. bark; rind; crust.
cortijo, m. farmhouse.
cortina, f. curtain.

corto, a. short.
corva, f. back of the knee.
cosa, f. thing. **c. de,** a matter of, roughly.
cosecha, f. crop, harvest. — **cosechar,** v.
coser, v. sew, stitch.
cosmético, a. & m. cosmetic.
cósmico, a. cosmic.
cosmonauta, m. & f. cosmonaut.
cosmopolita, a. & n. cosmopolitan.
cosmos, m. cosmos.
coso, m. arena for bull fights.
cosquilla, f. tickle. — **cosquillar,** v.
cosquilloso, a. ticklish.
costa, f. coast; cost, expense.
costado, m. side.
costal, m. sack, bag.
costanero, a. coastal.
costar, v. cost.
costarricense, a. & n. Costa Rican.
coste, m. cost, price.
costear, v. defray, sponsor; sail along the coast of.
costilla, f. rib; chop.
costo, m. cost, price.
costoso, a. costly.
costra, f. crust.
costumbre, f. custom, practice, habit.
costura, f. sewing; seam.
costurera, f. seamstress, dressmaker.
costurero, m. sewing basket.
cota de malla, coat of mail.
cotejar, v. compare.
cotidiano, a. daily; everyday.
cotillón, m. cotillion.
cotización, f. quotation.
cotizar, v. quote (a price).
coto, m. enclosure; boundary.
cotón, m. printed cotton cloth.
cotufa, f. Jerusalem artichoke.
coturno, m. buskin.
covacha, f. small cave.
coxal, a. of the hip.
coy, m. hammock.
coyote, m. coyote.
coyuntura, f. joint; juncture.
coz, f. kick.
crac, m. failure.

cráneo, *m.* skull.

craniano, *a.* cranial.

crapuloso, *a.* drunken.

crasiento, *a.* greasy, oily.

craso, *a.* fat; gross.

cráter, *m.* crater.

craza, *f.* crucible.

creación, *f.* creation.

creador -ra, *a. & n.* creative; creator.

crear, *v.* create.

creativo, *a.* creative.

crébol, *m.* holly tree.

crecer, *v.* grow, grow up; increase.

creces, *f.pl.* increase, addition.

crecidamente, *adv.* abundantly.

crecido, *a.* increased, enlarged; swollen.

creciente, 1. *a.* growing. **2.** *m.* crescent.

crecimiento, *m.* growth.

credenciales, *f.pl.* credentials.

credibilidad, *f.* credibility.

crédito, *m.* credit.

credo, *m.* creed, belief.

crédulamente, *adv.* credulously, gullibly.

credulidad, *f.* credulity.

crédulo, *a.* credulous.

creedero, *a.* credible.

creedor, *a.* credulous, believing.

creencia, *f.* belief.

creer, *v.* believe; think.

creíble, *a.* credible, believable.

crema, *f.* cream.

cremación, *f.* cremation.

crema dentífrica, toothpaste.

cremallera, *f.* zipper.

crémor tártaro, *m.* cream of tartar.

cremoso, *a.* creamy.

creosota, *f.* creosote.

crepitar, *v.* crackle.

crepuscular, *a.* of or like the dawn or dusk; crepuscular.

crepúsculo, *m.* dusk, twilight.

crescendo, *m.* crescendo.

crespo, *a.* curly.

crespón, *m.* crepe.

cresta, *f.* crest; heraldic crest.

crestado, *a.* crested.

creta, *f.* chalk.

cretáceo, *a.* chalky.

cretinismo, *m.* cretinism.

cretino -na, *n. & a.* cretin.

cretona, *f.* cretonne.

creyente, 1. *a.* believing. **2.** *n.* believer.

creyón, *m.* crayon.

cría, *f.* (stock) breeding; young (of an animal), litter.

criada, *f.* maid.

criadero, *m.* (agr.) nursery.

criado -da, *n.* servant.

criador, *a.* fruitful, prolific.

crianza, *f.* breeding; upbringing.

criar, *v.* raise, rear; breed.

criatura, *f.* creature; infant.

criba, *f.* sieve.

cribado, *a.* sifted.

cribar, *v.* sift.

crimen, *m.* crime.

criminal, *a. & n.* criminal.

criminalidad, *f.* criminality.

criminalmente, *adv.* criminally.

criminología, *f.* criminology.

criminoso, *a.* criminal.

crines, *f.pl.* mane of a horse.

crinolina, *f.* crinoline.

criocirugía, *f.* cryosurgery.

criollo -lla, *a. & n.* native; Creole.

cripta, *f.* crypt.

criptografía, *f.* cryptography.

crisantemo, *m.* chrysanthemum.

crisis, *f.* crisis.

crisis nerviosa, nervous breakdown.

crisma, *m.* chrism.

crisol, *m.* crucible.

crispamiento, *m.* twitch, contraction.

crispar, *v.* contract (the muscles); twitch.

cristal, *m.* glass; crystal; lens.

cristalería, *f.* glassware.

cristalino, *a.* crystalline.

cristalización, *f.* crystallization.

cristalizar, *v.* crystallize.

cristianar, *v.* baptize.

cristiandad, *f.* Christendom.

cristianismo, *m.* Christianity.

cristiano -na, *a. & n.* Christian.

Cristo, *m.* Christ.

criterio, *m.* criterion; judgment.

crítica, *f.* criticism; critique.

criticable, *a.* blameworthy.

criticador, *a.* critical.

criticar, *v.* criticize.

crítico -ca, *a. & n.* critical; critic.

croar, *v.* croak.

crocante, *m.* almond brittle.

crocitar, *v.* crow.

cromático, *a.* chromatic.

cromo, *m.* chromium.

cromosoma, *m.* chromosome.

cromotipia, *f.* color printing.

crónica, *f.* chronicle.

crónico, *a.* chronic.

cronicón, *m.* concise chronicle.

cronista, *m. & f.* chronicler.

cronología, *f.* chronology.

cronológicamente, *adv.* chronologically.

cronológico, *a.* chronologic.

cronometrar, *v.* time.

cronómetro, *m.* stopwatch; chronometer.

croqueta, *f.* croquette.

croquis, *m.* sketch; rough outline.

crótalo, *m.* rattlesnake; castanet.

cruce, *m.* crossing, crossroads, junction.

crucero, *m.* cruiser.

crucífero, *a.* cross-shaped.

crucificado, *a.* crucified.

crucificar, *v.* crucify.

crucifijo, *m.* crucifix.

crucifixión, *f.* crucifixion.

crucigrama, *m.* crossword puzzle.

crudamente, *adv.* crudely.

crudeza, *f.* crudeness.

crudo, *a.* crude, raw.

cruel, *a.* cruel.

crueldad, *f.* cruelty.

cruelmente, *adv.* cruelly.

cruentamente, *adv.* bloodily.

cruento, *a.* bloody.

crujía, *f.* corridor.

crujido, *m.* creak.

crujir, *v.* crackle; creak; rustle.

cruórico, a. bloody.

crup, m. croup.

crupié, m. & f. croupier.

crustáceo, n. & a. crustacean.

cruz, f. cross.

cruzada, f. crusade.

cruzado -da, n. crusader.

cruzamiento, m. crossing.

cruzar, v. cross.

cruzarse con, v. to (meet and) pass.

cuaderno, m. notebook.

cuadra, f. block; (hospital) ward.

cuadradamente, adv. exactly, precisely; completely, in full.

cuadradillo, m. lump of sugar.

cuadrado -da, a. & n. square.

cuadrafónico, a. quadraphonic.

Cuadragésima, f. Lent.

cuadragesimal, a. Lenten.

cuadrángulo, m. quadrangle.

cuadrante, m. quadrant; dial.

cuadrar, v. square; suit.

cuadricular, a. in squares.

cuadrilátero, a. quadrilateral.

cuadrilla, f. band, troop, gang.

cuadro, m. picture; painting; frame. a cuadros, checked, plaid.

cuadro de servicio, timetable.

cuadrupedal, a. quadruped.

cuádruplo, a. fourfold.

cuajada, f. curd.

cuajamiento, m. coagulation.

cuajar, v. coagulate; overdecorate.

cuajo, m. rennet; coagulation.

cual, rel. pron. which.

cuál, a. & pron. what, which.

cualidad, f. quality.

cualitativo, a. qualitative.

cualquiera, a. & pron. whatever, any; anyone.

cuando, conj. when.

cuando, adv. when. de cuando en cuando, from time to time.

cuantía, f. quantity; amount.

cuantiar, v. estimate.

cuantiosamente, adv. abundantly.

cuantioso, a. abundant.

cuantitativo, a. quantitative.

cuanto, a., adv. & pron. as much as, as many as; all that which. en c., as soon as. en c a, as for. c. antes, as soon as possible. c. más . . . tanto más, the more . . . the more. unos cuantos, a few.

cuánto, a. & adv. how much, how many.

cuaquerismo, m. Quakerism.

cuáquero -ra, n. & a. Quaker.

cuarenta, a. & pron. forty.

cuarentena, f. quarantine.

cuaresma, f. Lent.

cuaresmal, a. Lenten.

cuarta, f. quarter; quadrant; quart.

cuartear, v. divide into quarters.

cuartel, m. (mil.) quarters; barracks; (naut.) hatch. c. general, headquarters. sin c., giving no quarter.

cuartelada, f. military uprising.

cuarterón, n. & a. quadroon.

cuarteto, m. quartet.

cuartillo, m. pint.

cuarto, 1. a. fourth. 2. m. quarter; room.

cuarto de baño, bathroom.

cuarto de dormir, bedroom.

cuarto para invitados, guest room.

cuarzo, m. quartz.

cuasi, adv. almost, nearly.

cuate, a. & n. twin.

cuatrero, m. cattle rustler.

cuatrillón, m. quadrillion.

cuatro, a. & pron. four.

cuatrocientos, a. & pron. four hundred.

cuba, f. cask, tub, vat.

cubano -na, a. & n. Cuban.

cubero, m. cooper.

cubeta, f. small barrel, keg.

cúbico, a. cubic.

cubículo, m. cubicle.

cubierta, f. cover; envelope; wrapping; tread (of a tire); deck.

cubiertamente, adv. secretly, stealthily.

cubierto, m. place (at table).

cubil, m. lair.

cubismo, m. cubism.

cubito de hielo, m. ice cube.

cubo, m. cube; bucket.

cubo de la basura, trash can.

cubrecama, f. bedspread.

cubrir, v. cover.

cubrirse, v. put on one's hat.

cucaracha, f. cockroach.

cuchara, f. spoon, tablespoon.

cucharada, f. spoonful.

cucharita, cucharilla, f. teaspoon.

cucharón, m. dipper, ladle.

cuchicheo, m. whisper. — cuchichear, v.

cuchilla, f. cleaver.

cuchillada, f. slash.

cuchillería, f. cutlery.

cuchillo, m. knife.

cucho, m. fertilizer.

cuchufleta, f. jest.

cuclillo, m. cuckoo.

cuco, a. sly.

cuculla, f. hood, cowl.

cuelga, f. cluster, bunch.

cuelgacapas, m. coat rack.

cuello, m. neck; collar.

cuenca, f. socket; (river) basin; wooden bowl.

cuenco, m. earthen bowl.

cuenta, f. account; bill. darse c., to realize. tener en c., to keep in mind.

cuenta bancaria, bank account.

cuenta de ahorros, savings account.

cuentagotas, m. dropper (for medicine).

cuentista, m. & f. storyteller; informer.

cuento, m. story, tale.

cuerda, f. cord; chord; rope; string; spring (of clock). dar c. a, to wind (clock).

cuerdamente, adv. sanely; prudently.

cuerdo, a. sane; prudent.

cuerno, m. horn.

cuero, m. leather; hide.

cuerpo, m. body; corps.

cuervo, m. crow, raven.

cuesco, m. pit, stone (of fruit).

cuesta, f. hill, slope. llevar a cuestas, to carry on one's back.

cuestación, *f.* solicitation for charity.

cuestión, *f.* question; affair; argument.

cuestionable, *a.* questionable.

cuestionar, *v.* question; discuss; argue.

cuestionario, *m.* questionnaire.

cuete, *m.* firecracker.

cueva, *f.* cave; cellar.

cuguar, *m.* cougar.

cugujada, *f.* lark.

cuidado, *m.* care, caution, worry. **tener c.,** to be careful.

cuidadosamente, *adv.* carefully.

cuidadoso, *a.* careful, painstaking.

cuidante, *n.* caretaker, custodian.

cuidar, *v.* take care of.

cuita, *f.* trouble, care; grief.

cuitado, *a.* unfortunate; shy, timid.

cuitamiento, *m.* timidity.

culata, *f.* haunch, buttock; butt of a gun.

culatada, *f.* recoil.

culatazo, *m.* blow with the butt of a gun; recoil.

culebra, *f.* snake.

culero, *a.* lazy, indolent.

culinario, *a.* culinary.

culminación, *f.* culmination.

culminar, *v.* culminate.

culpa, *f.* fault, guilt, blame. **tener la c.,** to be at fault. **echar la culpa a,** to blame.

culpabilidad, *f.* guilt, fault, blame.

culpable, *a.* at fault, guilty, to blame, culpable.

culpar, *v.* blame, accuse.

cultamente, *adv.* politely, elegantly.

cultivable, *a.* arable.

cultivación, *f.* cultivation.

cultivador -ra, *n.* cultivator.

cultivar, *v.* cultivate.

cultivo, *m.* cultivation; (growing) crop.

culto, 1. *a.* cultured, cultivated. **2.** *m.* cult; worship.

cultura, *f.* culture; refinement.

cultural, *a.* cultural.

culturar, *v.* cultivate.

culturismo, *m.* body building.

culturista, *m. & f.* body builder.

cumbre, *m.* summit, peak.

cumpleaños, *m.pl.* birthday.

cumplidamente, *adv.* courteously, correctly.

cumplido, *a.* polite, polished.

cumplimentar, *v.* compliment.

cumplimiento, *m.* fulfillment; compliment.

cumplir, *v.* comply; carry out, fulfill; reach (years of age).

cumulativo, *a.* cumulative.

cúmulo, *m.* heap, pile.

cuna, *f.* cradle.

cundir, *v.* spread; expand; propagate.

cuneiforme, *a.* cuneiform, wedge-shaped.

cuneo, *m.* rocking.

cuña, *f.* wedge.

cuñada, *f.* sister-in-law.

cuñado, *m.* brother-in-law.

cuñete, *m.* keg.

cuota, *f.* quota; dues.

cuotidiano, *a.* daily.

cupé, *m.* coupé.

Cupido, *m.* Cupid.

cupo, *m.* share; assigned quota.

cupón, *m.* coupon.

cúpula, *f.* dome.

cura, *m.* priest. *f.* treatment, (medical) care. **c. de urgencia,** first aid.

curable, *a.* curable.

curación, *f.* healing; cure; (surgical) dressing.

curado, *a.* cured, healed.

curador -ra, *n.* healer.

curandero -ra, *n.* healer, medicine man.

curar, *v.* cure, heal, treat.

curativo, *a.* curative, healing.

curia, *f.* ecclesiastical court.

curiosear, *v.* snoop, pry, meddle.

curiosidad, *f.* curiosity.

curioso, *a.* curious.

curro, *a.* showy, loud, flashy.

cursante, *n.* student.

cursar, *v.* frequent; attend.

cursi, *a.* vulgar, shoddy, in bad taste.

curso, *m.* course.

curso por correspondencia, *m.* correspondence course.

cursor, *m.* cursor.

curtidor, *m.* tanner.

curtir, *v.* tan.

curva, *f.* curve; bend.

curvatura, *f.* curvature.

cúspide, *f.* top, peak.

custodia, *f.* custody.

custodiar, *v.* guard, watch.

custodio, *m.* custodian.

cutáneo, *a.* cutaneous.

cutícula, *f.* cuticle.

cutis, *m. or f.* skin, complexion.

cuyo, *a.* whose.

D

dable, *a.* possible.

dactilógrafo -fa, *n.* typist.

dádiva, *f.* gift.

dadivosamente, *adv.* generously.

dadivoso, *a.* generous, bountiful.

dado, *m.* die.

dador -ra, *n.* giver.

dados, *m.pl.* dice.

daga, *f.* dagger.

dalia, *f.* dahlia.

dallador, *m.* lawn mower.

dallar, *v.* mow.

daltonismo, *m.* color blindness.

dama, *f.* lady.

damasco, *m.* apricot; damask.

damisela, *f.* young lady, girl.

danés -esa, *a. & n.* Danish, Dane.

danza, *f.* (the) dance. — **danzar,** *v.*

danzante -ta, *n.* dancer.

dañable, *a.* condemnable.

dañar, *v.* hurt, harm; damage.

dañino, *a.* harmful.
daño, *m.* damage; harm.
dañoso, *a.* harmful.
dar, *v.* give; strike (clock). **d. a,** face, open on. **d. con,** find, locate. **¡Dalo por hecho!** Consider it done!
dardo, *m.* dart.
dársena, *f.* dock.
datar, *v.* date.
dátil, *m.* date (fruit).
dativo, *m. & a.* dative.
datos, *m.pl.* data.
de, *prep.* of; from; than.
debajo, *adv.* underneath. **d. de,** under.
debate, *m.* debate.
debatir, *v.* debate, argue.
debe, *m.* debit.
debelación, *f.* conquest.
debelar, *v.* conquer.
deber, 1. *v.* owe; must; be to, be supposed to. **2.** *m.* obligation.
deberes, *m.pl.* homework.
debido, *a.* due.
débil, *a.* weak, faint.
debilidad, *f.* weakness.
debilitación, *f.* weakness.
debilitar, *v.* weaken.
débito, *m.* debit.
debutante, *v.* debutante.
debutar, *v.* make a debut.
década, *f.* decade.
decadencia, *f.* decadence, decline, decay.
decadente, *a.* decadent, declining, decaying.
decaer, *v.* decay, decline.
decalitro, *m.* decaliter.
decálogo, *m.* m. decalogue.
decámetro, *m.* decameter.
decano, *m.* dean.
decantado, *a.* much discussed; overexalted.
decapitación, *f.* beheading.
decapitar, *v.* behead.
decencia, *f.* decency.
decenio, *m.* decade.
decente, *a.* decent.
decentemente, *adv.* decently.
decepción, *f.* disappointment, letdown; delusion.
decepcionar, *v.* disappoint, disillusion.
decibelio, *m.* decibel.
decididamente, *adv.* decidedly.

decidir, *v.* decide.
decigramo, *m.* decigram.
decilitro, *m.* deciliter.
décima, *f.* ten-line stanza.
decimal, *a.* decimal.
décimo, *a.* tenth.
dechado, *m.* model; sample; pattern; example.
decir, *v.* tell, say. **es d.,** that is (to say).
decisión, *f.* decision.
decisivamente, *adv.* decisively.
decisivo, *a.* decisive.
declamación, *f.* declamation, speech.
declamar, *v.* declaim.
declaración, *f.* declaration; statement; plea.
declaración de la renta, tax return.
declarar, *v.* declare, state.
declarativo, *a.* declarative.
declinación, *f.* descent; decay; decline; declension.
declinar, *v.* decline.
declive, *m.* declivity, slope.
decocción, *f.* decoction.
decomiso, *m.* seizure, confiscation.
decoración, *f.* decoration, trimming.
decorado, *m.* (theat.) scenery, set.
decorar, *v.* decorate, trim.
decorativo, *a.* decorative, ornamental.
decoro, *m.* decorum; decency.
decoroso, *a.* decorous.
decrecer, *v.* decrease.
decrépito, *a.* decrepit.
decreto, *m.* decree. **—decretar,** *v.*
dedal, *m.* thimble.
dédalo, *m.* labyrinth.
dedicación, *f.* dedication.
dedicar, *v.* devote; dedicate.
dedicatoria, *f.* dedication, inscription.
dedo, *m.* finger, toe.
dedo anular, ring finger.
dedo índice, index finger.
dedo corazón, middle finger.
dedo meñique, little finger, pinky.
dedo pulgar, thumb.

deducción, *f.* deduction.
deducir, *v.* deduce; subtract.
defectivo, *a.* defective.
defecto, *m.* defect, flaw.
defectuoso, *a.* defective, faulty.
defender, *v.* defend.
defensa, *f.* defense.
defensivo, *a.* defensive.
defensor -ra, *n.* defender.
deferencia, *f.* deference.
deferir, *v.* defer.
deficiente, *a.* deficient.
déficit, *m.* deficit.
definición, *f.* definition.
definido, *a.* definite.
definir, *v.* define; establish.
definitivamente, *adv.* definitely.
definitivo, *a.* definitive.
deformación, *f.* deformation.
deformar, *v.* deform.
deforme, *a.* deformed; ugly.
deformidad, *f.* deformity.
defraudar, *v.* defraud.
defunción, *f.* death.
degeneración, *f.* degeneration.
degenerado, *a.* degenerate. **—degenerar,** *v.*
deglutir, *v.* swallow.
degollar, *v.* behead.
degradación, *f.* degradation.
degradar, *v.* degrade, debase.
deidad, *f.* deity.
deificación, *f.* deification.
deificar, *v.* deify.
deífico, *a.* divine, deific.
deísmo, *m.* deism.
dejadez, *f.* neglect, untidiness; laziness.
dejado, *a.* untidy; lazy.
dejar, *v.* let, allow; leave. **d. de,** stop, leave off. **no d. de,** not fail to.
dejo, *m.* abandonment; negligence; aftertaste; accent.
del, *contr.* of **de** + **el**.
delantal, *m.* apron; pinafore. **delantal de niña,** pinafore.
delante, *adv.* ahead, forward; in front.
delantero, *a.* forward, front, first.
delator, *m.* informer; accuser.
delegación, *f.* delegation.

delegado -da, *n.* delegate. **—delegar,** *v.*

deleite, *m.* delight. — **deleitar,** *v.*

deleitoso, *a.* delightful.

deletrear, *v.* spell; decipher.

delfín, *m.* dolphin; dauphin.

delgadez, *f.* thinness, slenderness.

delgado, *a.* thin, slender, slim, slight.

deliberación, *f.* deliberation.

deliberadamente, *adv.* deliberately.

deliberar, *v.* deliberate.

deliberativo, *a.* deliberative.

delicadamente, *adv.* delicately.

delicadeza, *f.* delicacy.

delicado, *a.* delicate, dainty.

delicia, *f.* delight; deliciousness.

delicioso, *a.* delicious.

delincuencia, *f.* delinquency.

delincuencia de menores, delincuencia juvenil, juvenile delinquency.

delincuente, *a.* & *n.* delinquent; culprit, offender.

delineación, *f.* delineation, sketch.

delinear, *v.* delineate, sketch.

delirante, *a.* delirious.

delirar, *v.* rave, be delirious.

delirio, *m.* delirium; rapture, bliss.

delito, *m.* crime, offense.

delta, *m.* delta (of river); hang glider.

demacrado, *a.* emaciated.

demagogia, *f.* demagogy.

demagogo, *m.* demagogue.

demanda, *f.* demand, claim.

demandador -ra, *n.* plaintiff.

demandar, *v.* sue; demand.

demarcación, *f.* demarcation.

demarcar, *v.* demarcate, limit.

demás, *a.* & *n.* other; (the) rest (of). **por d.,** too much.

demasía, *f.* excess; audacity; iniquity.

demasiado, *a.* & *adv.* too; too much; too many.

demencia, *f.* dementia; insanity.

demente, *a.* demented.

democracia, *f.* democracy.

demócrata, *m.* & *f.* democrat.

democrático, *a.* democratic.

demoler, *v.* demolish, tear down.

demolición, *f.* demolition.

demonio, *m.* demon, devil.

demontre, *m.* devil.

demora, *f.* delay, **—demorar,** *v.*

demostración, *f.* demonstration.

demostrador -ra, *n.* demonstrator.

demostrar, *v.* demonstrate, show.

demostrativo, *a.* demonstrative.

demudar, *v.* change; disguise, conceal.

denegación, *f.* denial; refusal.

denegar, *v.* deny; refuse.

dengue, *m.* prudishness; dengue.

denigración, *f.* defamation, disgrace.

denigrar, *v.* defame, disgrace.

denodado, *a.* brave, dauntless.

denominación, *f.* denomination.

denominar, *v.* name, call.

denotación, *f.* denotation.

denotar, *v.* denote, betoken, express.

densidad, *f.* density.

denso, *a.* dense.

dentado, *a.* toothed; serrated; cogged.

dentadura, *f.* set of teeth.

dentadura postiza, false teeth, dentures.

dental, *a.* dental.

dentífrico, *m.* dentifrice, toothpaste.

dentista, *m.* & *f.* dentist.

dentistería, *f.* dentistry.

dentro, *adv.* within, inside. **d. de poco,** in a short while.

denuedo, *m.* bravery, courage.

denuesto, *m.* insult, offense.

denuncia, *f.* denunciation; declaration; complaint.

denunciación, *f.* denunciation.

denunciar, *v.* denounce.

deparar, *v.* offer; grant.

departamento, *m.* department, section.

departir, *v.* talk, chat.

dependencia, *f.* dependence; branch office.

depender, *v.* depend.

dependiente, *a.* & *m.* dependent; clerk.

depilatorio, *a.* & *n.* depilatory.

deplorable, *a.* deplorable, wretched.

deplorablemente, *adv.* deplorably.

deplorar, *v.* deplore.

deponer, *v.* depose.

deportación, *f.* deportation; exile.

deportar, *v.* deport.

deporte, *m.* sport. **—deportivo,** *a.*

deposición, *f.* assertion, deposition; removal; movement.

depositante, *m.* & *f.* depositor.

depósito, *m.* deposit. **—depositar,** *v.*

depravación, *f.* depravation; depravity.

depravado, *a.* depraved, wicked.

depravar, *v.* deprave, corrupt, pervert.

depreciación, *f.* depreciation.

depreciar, *v.* depreciate.

depredación, *f.* depredation.

depredar, *v.* pillage, depredate.

depresión, *f.* depression.

depresivo, *a.* depressive.

deprimir, *v.* depress.

depurar, *v.* purify.

derecha, *f.* right (hand, side).

derechera, *f.* shortcut.

derecho, 1. *a.* right; straight. **2.** *m.* right; (the) law. **derechos,** (com.) duty.

derechos civiles, *m.pl.* civil rights.

derechos de aduana, *m.pl.* customs duty.

derechura, *f.* straightness.

derelicto, *a.* abandoned, derelict.

deriva, *f.* (naut.) drift.

derivación, *f.* derivation.

derivar, *v.* derive.

dermatólogo -a, *n.* dermatologist, skin doctor.

derogar, *v.* derogate; repeal, abrogate.

derramamiento, *m.* overflow.

derramar, *v.* spill, pour, scatter.

derrame, *m.* overflow; discharge.

derretir, *v.* melt, dissolve.

derribar, *v.* demolish, knock down; bowl over, floor, fell.

derrocamiento, *m.* overthrow.

derrocar, *v.* overthrow; oust; demolish.

derrochar, *v.* waste.

derroche, *m.* waste.

derrota, *f.* rout, defeat. — **derrotar,** *v.*

derrotismo, *m.* defeatism.

derrumbamiento, derrumbe, *m.* collapse; landslide.

derrumbarse, *v.* collapse, tumble.

derviche, *m.* dervish.

desabotonar, *v.* unbutton.

desabrido, *a.* insipid, tasteless.

desabrigar, *v.* uncover.

desabrochar, *v.* unbutton, unclasp.

desacato, *m.* disrespect, lack of respect.

desacierto, *m.* error.

desacobardar, *v.* remove fear; embolden.

desacomodadamente, *adv.* inconveniently.

desacomodado, *a.* unemployed.

desacomodar, *v.* molest; inconvenience; dismiss.

desacomodo, *m.* loss of employment.

desconsejado, *a.* imprudent, ill advised, rash.

desaconsejar, *v.* dissuade (someone); advise against (something).

desacordadamente, *adv.* unadvisedly.

desacordar, *v.* differ, disagree; be forgetful.

desacorde, *a.* discordant.

desacostumbradamente, *adv.* unusually.

desacostumbrado, *a.* unusual, unaccustomed.

desacostumbrar, *v.* give up a habit or custom.

desacreditar, *v.* discredit.

desacuerdo, *m.* disagreement.

desadeudar, *v.* pay one's debts.

desadormecer, *v.* waken, rouse.

desadornar, *v.* divest of ornament.

desadvertidamente, *adv.* inadvertently.

desadvertido, *a.* imprudent.

desadvertimiento, *m.* imprudence, rashness.

desadvertir, *v.* act imprudently.

desafección, *f.* disaffection.

desafecto, *a.* disaffected.

desafiar, *v.* defy; challenge.

desafinar, *v.* be out of tune.

desafío, *m.* defiance; challenge.

desaforar, *v.* infringe one's rights; be outrageous.

desafortunado, *a.* unfortunate.

desafuero, *m.* violation of the law; outrage.

desagraciado, *a.* graceless.

desagradable, *a.* disagreeable, unpleasant.

desagradablemente, *adv.* disagreeably.

desagradecido, *a.* ungrateful.

desagradecimiento, *m.* ingratitude.

desagrado, *m.* displeasure.

desagraviar, *v.* make amends.

desagregar, *v.* separate, disintegrate.

desagriar, *v.* mollify, appease.

desaguadero, *m.* drain, outlet; cesspool; sink.

desaguador, *m.* water pipe.

desaguar, *v.* drain.

desaguisado, *m.* offense; injury.

desahogadamente, *adv.* impudently; brazenly.

desahogado, *a.* impudent, brazen; cheeky.

desahogar, *v.* relieve.

desahogo, *m.* relief; nerve, cheek.

desahuciar, *v.* give up hope for; despair of.

desairado, *a.* graceless.

desaire, *m.* slight; scorn. — **desairar,** *v.*

desajustar, *v.* mismatch, misfit; make unfit.

desalar, *v.* hurry, hasten.

desalentar, *v.* make out of breath; discourage.

desaliento, *m.* discouragement.

desaliñar, *v.* disarrange; make untidy.

desaliño, *m.* slovenliness, untidiness.

desalivar, *v.* remove saliva from.

desalmadamente, *adv.* mercilessly.

desalmado, *a.* merciless.

desalojamiento, *m.* displacement; dislodging.

desalojar, *v.* dislodge.

desalquilado, *a.* vacant, unrented.

desamar, *v.* cease loving.

desamasado, *a.* dissolved, disunited, undone.

desamistarse, *v.* quarrel, disagree.

desamor, *m.* disaffection, dislike; hatred.

desamorado, *a.* cruel; harsh; rude.

desamparador, *m.* deserter.

desamparar, *v.* desert, abandon.

desamparo, *m.* desertion, abandonment.

desamueblado, *a.* unfurnished.

desamueblar, *v.* remove furniture from.

desandrajado, *a.* shabby, ragged.

desanimadamente, *adv.* in a discouraged manner; spiritlessly.

desanimar, v. dishearten, discourage.

desánimo, m. discouragement.

desanudar, v. untie; loosen; disentangle.

desapacible, a. rough, harsh; unpleasant.

desaparecer, v. disappear.

desaparición, f. disappearance.

desapasionadamente, adv. dispassionately.

desapasionado, a. dispassionate.

desapego, m. impartiality.

desapercibido, a. unnoticed; unprepared.

desapiadado, a. merciless, cruel.

desaplicación, f. indolence, laziness; negligence.

desaplicado, a. indolent, lazy; negligent.

desaposesionar, v. dispossess.

desapreciar, v. depreciate.

desapretador, m. screwdriver.

desapretar, v. loosen; relieve, ease.

desaprisionar, v. set free, release.

desaprobación, f. disapproval.

desaprobar, v. disapprove.

desaprovechado, a. useless, profitless; backward.

desaprovechar, v. waste; be backward.

desarbolar, v. unmast.

desarmado, a. disarmed, defenseless.

desarmar, v. disarm.

desarme, m. disarmament.

desarraigado, a. rootless.

desarraigar, v. uproot; eradicate; expel.

desarreglar, v. disarrange, mess up.

desarrollar, v. develop.

desarrollo, m. development.

desarropar, v. undress; uncover.

desarrugar, v. remove wrinkles from.

desaseado, a. dirty; disorderly.

desasear, v. make dirty or disorderly.

desaseo, m. dirtiness; disorder.

desasir, v. loosen; disengage.

desasociable, a. unsociable.

desasosegar, v. disturb.

desasosiego, m. uneasiness.

desastrado, a. ragged, wretched.

desastre, m. disaster.

desastroso, a. disastrous.

desatar, v. untie, undo.

desatención, f. inattention; disrespect; rudeness.

desatender, v. ignore; disregard.

desatentado, a. inconsiderate; imprudent.

desatinado, a. foolish; insane, wild.

desatino, m. blunder. **—desatinar,** v.

desatornillar, v. unscrew.

desautorizado, a. unauthorized.

desautorizar, v. deprive of authority.

desavenencia, f. disagreement, discord.

desaventajado, a. disadvantageous.

desayuno, m. breakfast. **—desayunar,** v.

desazón, f. insipidity; uneasiness.

desazonado, a. insipid; uneasy.

desbandada, f. disbanding.

desbandarse, v. disband.

desbarajuste, m. disorder, confusion.

desbaratar, v. destroy.

desbastar, v. plane, smoothen.

desbocado, a. foul-spoken, indecent.

desbocarse, v. use obscene language.

desbordamiento, m. overflow; flood.

desbordar, v. overflow.

desbrozar, v. clear away rubbish.

descabal, a. incomplete.

descabalar, v. render incomplete; impair.

descabellado, a. absurd, preposterous.

descabezar, v. behead.

descaecimiento, m. weakness; dejection.

descafeinado, a. decaffeinated.

descalabrar, v. injure, wound (esp. the head).

descalabro, m. accident, misfortune.

descalzarse, v. take off one's shoes.

descalzo, a. shoeless; barefoot.

descaminado, a. wrong, misguided.

descaminar, v. mislead; lead into error.

descamisado, a. shirtless; shabby.

descansillo, m. landing (of stairs).

descanso, m. rest. **—descansar,** v.

descarado, a. saucy, fresh.

descarga, f. discharge.

descargar, v. discharge, unload, dump.

descargo, m. unloading; acquittal.

descarnar, v. skin.

descaro, m. gall, effrontery.

descarriar, v. lead or go astray.

descarrilamiento, m. derailment.

descarrilar, v. derail.

descartar, v. discard.

descascarar, v. peel; boast, brag.

descendencia, f. descent, origin; progeny.

descender, v. descend.

descendiente, m. & f. descendant.

descendimiento, m. descent.

descenso, m. descent.

descentralización, f. decentralization.

descifrar, v. decipher, puzzle out.

descoco, m. boldness, brazenness.

descolgar, v. take down.

descollar, v. stand out; excel.

descolorar, v. discolor.

descolorido, a. pale, faded.

descomedido, *a*. disproportionate; rude.

descomedirse, *v*. be rude.

descomponer, *v*. decompose; break down, get out of order.

descomposición, *f*. discomposure; disorder, confusion.

descompuesto, *a*. impudent, rude.

descomulgar, *v*. excommunicate.

descomunal, *a*. extraordinary, huge.

desconcertar, *v*. disconcert, baffle.

desconcierto, *m*. confusion, disarray.

desconectar, *v*. disconnect.

desconfiado, *a*. distrustful.

desconfianza, *f*. distrust.

desconfiar, *v*. distrust, mistrust; suspect.

descongelar, *v*. defrost.

descongestionante, *m*. decongestant.

desconocer, *v*. ignore, fail to recognize.

desconocido -da, *n*. stranger.

desconocimiento, *m*. ingratitude; ignorance.

desconsolado, *a*. disconsolate, wretched.

desconsuelo, *m*. grief.

descontar, *v*. discount, subtract.

descontentar, *v*. dissatisfy.

descontento, *m*. discontent.

descontinuar, *v*. discontinue.

desconvenir, *v*. disagree.

descorazonar, *v*. dishearten.

descorchar, *v*. uncork.

descortés, *a*. discourteous, impolite, rude.

descortesía, *f*. discourtesy, rudeness.

descortezar, *v*. peel.

descoyuntar, *v*. dislocate.

descrédito, *m*. discredit.

describir, *v*. describe.

descripción, *f*. description.

descriptivo, *a*. descriptive.

descuartizar, *v*. dismember, disjoint.

descubridor -ra, *n*. discoverer.

descubrimiento, *m*. discovery.

descubrir, *v*. discover; uncover; disclose.

descubrirse, *v*. take off one's hat.

descuento, *m*. discount.

descuidado, *a*. reckless, careless; slack.

descuido, *m*. neglect. **—descuidar**, *v*.

desde, *prep*. since; from. **d. luego**, of course.

desdén, *m*. disdain. **—desdeñar**, *v*.

desdeñoso, *a*. contemptuous, disdainful, scornful.

desdicha, *f*. misfortune.

deseable, *a*. desirable.

desear, *v*. desire, wish.

desecar, *v*. dry, desiccate.

desechable, *a*. disposable.

desechar, *v*. scrap, reject.

desecho, *m*. remainder, residue; (*pl*.) waste.

desembalar, *v*. unpack.

desembarazado, *a*. free; unrestrained.

desembarazar, *v*. free; extricate; unburden.

desembarcar, *v*. disembark, go ashore.

desembocar, *v*. flow into.

desembolsar, *v*. disburse; expend.

desembolso, *m*. disbursement.

desemejante, *a*. unlike, dissimilar.

desempacar, *v*. unpack.

desempeñar, *v*. carry out; redeem.

desempeño, *m*. fulfillment.

desencajar, *v*. disjoint; disturb.

desencantar, *v*. disillusion.

desencanto, *m*. disillusion.

desencarcelar, *v*. set free; release.

desenchufar, *v*. unplug.

desenfadado, *a*. free; unembarrassed; spacious.

desenfado, *m*. freedom; ease; calmness.

desenfocado, *a*. out of focus.

desengaño, *m*. disillusion. **—des-engañar**, *v*.

desenlace, *m*. outcome, conclusion.

desenredar, *v*. disentangle.

desensartar, *v*. unthread (pearls).

desentenderse, *v*. overlook; avoid noticing.

desenterrar, *v*. disinter, exhume.

desenvainar, *v*. unsheath.

desenvoltura, *f*. confidence; impudence, boldness.

desenvolver, *v*. evolve, unfold.

deseo, *m*. wish, desire, urge.

deseoso, *a*. desirous.

deserción, *f*. desertion.

desertar, *v*. desert.

desertor -ra, *n*. deserter.

desesperación, *f*. despair, desperation.

desesperado, *a*. desperate; hopeless.

desesperar, *v*. despair.

desfachatez, *f*. cheek (gall).

desfalcar, *v*. embezzle.

desfase horario, *m*. jet lag.

desfavorable, *a*. unfavorable.

desfigurar, *v*. disfigure, mar.

desfiladero, *m*. defile.

desfile, *m*. parade. **—desfilar**, *v*.

desfile de modas, fashion show.

desgaire, *m*. slovenliness.

desgana, *f*. lack of appetite; unwillingness; repugnance.

desgarrar, *v*. tear, lacerate.

desgastar, *v*. wear away; waste; erode.

desgaste, *m*. wear; erosion.

desgracia, *f*. misfortune.

desgraciado, *a*. unfortunate.

desgranar, *v*. shell.

desgreñar, *v*. dishevel.

deshacer, *v*. undo, take apart, destroy.

deshacerse de, *v*. get rid of, dispose of.

deshecho, *a*. undone; wasted.

deshelar, *v*. thaw; melt.

desheredamiento, *m*. disinheriting.

desheredar, *v*. disinherit.

deshielo, *m*. thaw, melting.

deshinchar, v. reduce a swelling.

deshojarse, v. shed (leaves).

deshonestidad, f. dishonesty.

deshonesto, a. dishonest.

deshonra, f. dishonor.

deshonrar, v. disgrace; dishonor.

deshonroso, a. dishonorable.

desierto, m. desert, wilderness.

designar, v. appoint, name.

designio, m. purpose, intent.

desigual, a. uneven, unequal.

desigualdad, f. inequality.

desilusión, f. disappointment.

desinfección, f. disinfection.

desinfectar, v. disinfect.

desintegrar, v. disintegrate, zap.

desinterés, m. indifference.

desinteresado, a. disinterested, unselfish.

desistir, v. desist, stop.

desleal, a. disloyal.

deslealtad, f. disloyalty.

desleir, v. dilute, dissolve.

desligar, v. untie, loosen; free, release.

deslindar, v. make the boundaries of.

deslinde, m. demarcation.

desliz, m. slip; false step; weakness.

deslizarse, v. slide; slip; glide; coast.

deslumbramiento, m. dazzling glare; confusion.

deslumbrar, v. dazzle; glare.

deslustre, m. tarnish. — **deslustrar,** v.

desmán, m. mishap; misbehavior; excess.

desmantelar, v. dismantle.

desmañado, a. awkward, clumsy.

desmaquillarse, v. remove one's makeup.

desmayar, v. depress, dishearten.

desmayo, m. faint. **—desmayarse,** v.

desmejorar, v. make worse; decline.

desmembrar, v. dismember.

desmemoria, f. forgetfulness.

desmemoriado, a. forgetful.

desmentir, v. contradict, disprove.

desmenuzable, a. crisp, crumbly.

desmenuzar, v. crumble, break into bits.

desmesurado, a. excessive.

desmobilizar, v. demobilize.

desmonetización, f. demonetization.

desmonetizar, v. demonetize.

desmontado, a. dismounted.

desmontar, v. dismantle.

desmontarse, v. dismount.

desmoralización, f. demoralization.

desmoralizar, v. demoralize.

desmoronar, v. crumble, decay.

desmovilizar, v. demobilize.

desnatar, v. skim.

desnaturalización, f. denaturalization.

desnaturalizar, v. denaturalize.

desnegamiento, m. denial, contradiction.

desnervar, v. enervate.

desnivel, m. unevenness or difference in elevation.

desnudamente, adv. nakedly.

desnudar, v. undress.

desnudez, f. bareness, nudity.

desnudo, a. bare, naked.

desnutrición, f. malnutrition.

desobedecer, v. disobey.

desobediencia, f. disobedience.

desobediente, a. disobedient.

desobedientemente, adv. disobe-diently.

desobligar, v. release from obligation; offend.

desocupado, a. idle, not busy; vacant.

desocupar, v. vacate.

desolación, f. desolation; ruin.

desolado, a. desolate. — **desolar,** v.

desollar, v. skin.

desorden, m. disorder.

desordenar, v. disarrange.

desorganización, f. disorganization.

desorganizar, v. disorganize.

despabilado, a. vigilant, watchful; lively.

despacio, adv. slowly.

despachar, v. dispatch, ship, send.

despacho, m. shipment; dispatch, promptness; office.

desparpajo, m. glibness; fluency of speech.

desparramar, v. scatter.

despavorido, a. terrified.

despecho, m. spite.

despedazar, v. tear up.

despedida, f. farewell; leave-taking; discharge.

despedir, v. dismiss, discharge; see off.

despedirse de, v. say good-bye to, take leave of.

despegar, v. unglue; separate; (aero.) take off.

despego, m. indifference; disinterest.

despejar, v. clear, clear up.

despejo, m. sprightliness; clarity; without obstruction.

despensa, f. pantry.

despensero, m. butler.

despeñar, v. throw down.

desperdicio, m. waste. — **des-perdiciar,** v.

despertador, m. alarm clock.

despertar, v. wake, wake up.

despesar, m. dislike.

despicar, v. satisfy.

despidida, f. gutter.

despierto, a. awake; alert, wide-awake.

despilfarrado, a. wasteful, extravagant.

despilfarrar, v. waste, squander.

despilfarro, m. waste, extravagance.

despique, m. revenge.

desplazamiento, m. displacement.

desplegar, v. display; unfold.

desplome, m. collapse. — **des-plomarse,** v.

desplumar, v. defeather, pluck.

despoblar, v. depopulate.

despojar, v. strip; despoil, plunder.

despojo, m. plunder, spoils; (pl.) remains, debris.

desposado, *a.* newly married.

desposar, *v.* marry.

desposeer, *v.* dispossess.

déspota, *m. & f.* despot.

despótico, *a.* despotic.

despotismo, *m.* despotism, tyranny.

despreciable, *a.* contemptible.

despreciar, *v.* spurn, despise, scorn.

desprecio, *m.* scorn, contempt.

desprender, *v.* detach, unfasten.

desprenderse, *v.* loosen, come apart. **d. de,** part with.

desprendido, *a.* disinterested.

despreocupado, *a.* unconcerned; unprejudiced.

desprevenido, *a.* unprepared, unready.

desproporción, *f.* disproportion.

despropósito, *m.* nonsense.

desprovisto, *a.* devoid.

después, *adv.* afterwards, later; then, next. **d. de, d. que,** after.

despuntar, *v.* blunt; remove the point of.

desquiciar, *v.* unhinge; disturb, unsettle.

desquitar, *v.* get revenge, retaliate.

desquite, *m.* revenge, retaliation.

desrazonable, *a.* unreasonable.

destacamento, *m.* (mil.) detachment.

destacarse, *v.* stand out, be prominent.

destajero -a, *n.* **destajista,** *m. & f.* pieceworker.

destapar, *v.* uncover.

destello, *m.* sparkle, gleam.

destemplar, *v.* (mus.) untune; disturb, upset.

desteñir, *v.* fade, discolor.

desterrado -da, *n.* exile.

desterrar, *v.* banish, exile.

destetar, *v.* wean.

destierro, *m.* banishment, exile.

destilación, *f.* distillation.

destilar, *v.* distill.

destilería, *f.* distillery.

destilería de petróleo, oil refinery.

destinación, *f.* destination.

destinar, *v.* destine, intend.

destinatario -ria, *n.* addressee (mail); payee (money).

destino, *m.* destiny, fate; destination.

destitución, *f.* dismissal; abandonment.

destituido, *a.* destitute.

destorcer, *v.* undo, straighten out.

destornillado, *a.* reckless, careless.

destornillador, *m.* screwdriver.

destraillar, *v.* unleash; set loose.

destral, *m.* hatchet.

destreza, *f.* cleverness; dexterity, skill.

destripar, *v.* eviscerate, disembowel.

destrísimo, *a.* extremely dexterous.

destronamiento, *m.* dethronement.

destronar, *v.* dethrone.

destrozador, *m.* destroyer, wrecker.

destrozar, *v.* destroy, wreck.

destrozo, *m.* destruction, ruin.

destrucción, *f.* destruction.

destructibilidad, *f.* destructibility.

destructible, *a.* destructible.

destructivamente, *adv.* destructively.

destructivo, *a.* destructive.

destruir, *v.* destroy; wipe out.

desuello, *m.* impudence.

desunión, *f.* disunion; discord; separation.

desunir, *v.* disconnect, sever.

desusadamente, *adv.* unusually.

desusado, *a.* archaic; obsolete.

desuso, *m.* disuse.

desvalido, *a.* helpless; destitute.

desvalijador, *m.* highwayman.

desván, *m.* attic.

desvanecerse, *v.* vanish; faint.

desvariado, *a.* delirious; disorderly.

desvarío, *m.* raving. — **desvariar,** *v.*

desvedado, *a.* free; unrestrained.

desveladamente, *adv.* watchfully, alertly.

desvelado, *a.* watchful; alert.

desvelar, *v.* be watchful; keep awake.

desvelo, *m.* vigilance; uneasiness; insomnia.

desventaja, *f.* disadvantage.

desventar, *v.* let air out of.

desventura, *f.* misfortune.

desventurado, *a.* unhappy; unlucky.

desvergonzado, *a.* shameless, brazen.

desvergüenza, *f.* shamelessness.

desvestir, *v.* undress.

desviación, *f.* deviation.

desviado, *a.* deviant; remote.

desviar, *v.* divert; deviate, detour.

desvío, *m.* detour; side track; indifference.

desvirtuar, *v.* decrease the value of.

deszumar, *v.* remove the juice from.

detalle, *m.* detail. —**detallar,** *v.*

detective, *m. & f.* detective.

detención, *f.* detention, arrest.

detenedor -ra, *n.* stopper; catch.

detener, *v.* detain, stop; arrest.

detenidamente, *adv.* carefully, slowly.

detenido, *adv.* stingy; thorough.

detergente, *a.* detergent.

deterioración, *f.* deterioration.

deteriorar, *v.* deteriorate.

determinable, *a.* determinable.

determinación, *f.* determination.

determinar, *v.* determine, settle, decide.

determinismo, *m.* determinism.

determinista, *n.* & *a.* determinist.

detestable, *a.* detestable, hateful.

detestablemente, *adv.* detestably, hatefully, abhorrently.

detestación, *f.* detestation, hatefulness.

detestar, *v.* detest.

detonación, *f.* detonation.

detonar, *v.* detonate, explode.

detracción, *f.* detraction, defamation.

detractar, *v.* detract, defame, vilify.

detraer, *v.* detract.

detrás, *adv.* behind; in back.

detrimento, *m.* detriment, damage.

deuda, *f.* debt.

deudo -da, *n.* relative, kin.

deudor -ra, *n.* debtor.

Deuteronomio, *m.* Deuteronomy.

devalar, *v.* drift off course.

devanar, *v.* to wind, as on a spool.

devanear, *v.* talk deliriously, rave.

devaneo, *m.* frivolity; idle pursuit; delirium.

devastación, *f.* devastation, ruin, havoc.

devastador, *a.* devastating.

devastar, *v.* devastate.

devenir, *v.* happen, occur; become.

devoción, *f.* devotion.

devocionario, *m.* prayer book.

devocionero, *a.* devotional.

devolver, *v.* return, give back.

devorar, *v.* devour.

devotamente, *adv.* devotedly, devoutly, piously.

devoto, *a.* devout; devoted.

deyección, *f.* depression, dejection.

día, *m.* day. **buenos días,** good morning.

diabetes, *f.* diabetes.

diabético, *a.* diabetic.

diablear, *v.* play pranks.

diablo, *m.* devil.

diablura, *f.* mischief.

diabólicamente, *adv.* diabolically.

diabólico, *a.* diabolic, devilish.

diaconato, *m.* deaconship.

diaconía, *f.* deaconry.

diácono, *m.* deacon.

diacrítico, *a.* diacritic.

diadema, *f.* diadem; crown.

diáfano, *a.* transparent.

diafragma, *m.* diaphragm.

diagnosticar, *v.* diagnose.

diagonal, *f.* diagonal.

diagonalmente, *adv.* diagonally.

diagrama, *m.* diagram.

dialectal, *a.* dialectal.

dialéctico, *a.* dialectic.

dialecto, *m.* dialect.

diálogo, *m.* dialogue.

diamante, *m.* diamond.

diamantista, *m.* & *f.* diamond cutter; jeweler.

diametral, *a.* diametric.

diametralmente, *adv.* diametrically.

diámetro, *m.* diameter.

diana, *f.* reveille (mil.); dartboard (game).

diapasón, *m.* standard pitch; tuning fork.

diariamente, *adv.* daily.

diario, *a.* & *m.* daily; daily paper; diary; journal.

diarrea, *f.* diarrhea.

diatriba, *f.* diatribe, harangue.

dibujo, *m.* drawing, sketch. **—dibujar,** *v.*

dicción, *f.* diction.

diccionario, *m.* dictionary.

diccionarista, *m.* & *f.* lexicographer.

dicha, *f.* happiness.

dicho, *m.* saying.

dichoso, *a.* happy; fortunate.

diciembre, *m.* December.

dicotomía, *f.* dichotomy.

dictado, *m.* dictation.

dictador -ra, *n.* dictator.

dictadura, *f.* dictatorship.

dictamen, *m.* dictate.

dictar, *v.* dictate; direct.

dictatorial, dictatorio, *a.* dictatorial.

didáctico, *a.* didactic.

diecinueve, *a.* & *pron.* nineteen.

dieciocho, *a.* & *pron.* eighteen.

dieciseis, *a.* & *pron.* sixteen.

diecisiete, *a.* & *pron.* seventeen.

diente, *m.* tooth.

diestramente, *adv.* skillfully, ably; ingeniously.

diestro, *a.* dexterous, skillful; clever.

dieta, *f.* diet; allowance.

dietética, *f.* dietetics.

dietético, 1. *a.* dietetic; dietary. **2. -ca.** *n.* dietician.

diez, *a.* & *pron.* ten.

diezmal, *a.* decimal.

diezmar, *v.* decimate.

difamación, *f.* defamation, smear.

difamar, *v.* defame, smear, libel.

difamatorio, *a.* defamatory.

diferencia, *f.* difference.

diferencial, *a.* & *f.* differential.

diferenciar, *v.* differentiate, distinguish.

diferente, *a.* different.

diferentemente, *adv.* differently.

diferir, *v.* differ; defer; put off.

difícil, *a.* difficult, hard.

difícilmente, *adv.* with difficulty or hardship.

dificultad, *f.* difficulty.

dificultar, *v.* make difficult.

dificultoso, *a.* difficult, hard.

difidencia, *f.* diffidence.

difidente, *a.* diffident.

difteria, *f.* diphtheria.

difundir, *v.* diffuse, spread.

difunto, 1. *a.* deceased, dead, late. **2. -ta,** *n.* deceased person.

difusamente, *adv.* diffusely.

difusión, *f.* diffusion, spread.

digerible, *a.* digestible.

digerir, *v.* digest.

digestible, *a.* digestible.

digestión, *f.* digestion.

digestivo, *a.* digestive.

digesto, *m.* digest or code of laws.

digitado, *a.* digitate.

digital, 1. *a.* digital. **2.** *f.* foxglove, digitalis.

dignación, *f.* condescension; deigning.

dignamente, *adv.* with dignity.

dignarse, *v.* condescend, deign.

dignatario -ra, *n.* dignitary.

dignidad, *f.* dignity.

dignificar, *v.* dignify.

digno, *a.* worthy; dignified.

digresión, *f.* digression.

digresivo, *a.* digressive.

dij, dije, *m.* trinket, piece of jewelry.

dilación, *f.* delay.

dilapidación, *f.* dilapidation.

dilapidado, *a.* dilapidated.

dilatación, *f.* dilatation, enlargement.

dilatar, *v.* dilate; delay; expand.

dilatoria, *f.* delay.

dilatorio, *a.* dilatory.

dilecto, *a.* loved.

dilema, *m.* dilemma.

diletante, *m. & f.* dilettante.

diligencia, *f.* diligence, industriousness.

diligente, *a.* diligent, industrious.

diligentemente, *adv.* diligently.

dilogía, *f.* ambiguous meaning.

dilución, *f.* dilution.

diluir, *v.* dilute.

diluvial, *a.* diluvial.

diluvio, *m.* flood, deluge.

dimensión, *f.* dimension; measurement.

diminución, *f.* diminution.

diminuto, diminutivo, *a.* diminutive, little.

dimisión, *f.* resignation.

dimitir, *v.* resign.

Dinamarca, *f.* Denmark.

dinamarqués -esa, *a. & n.* Danish, Dane.

dinámico, *a.* dynamic.

dinamita, *f.* dynamite.

dinamitero -ra, *n.* dynamiter.

dínamo, *m.* dynamo.

dinasta, *m.* dynast, king, monarch.

dinastía, *f.* dynasty.

dinástico, *a.* dynastic.

dinero, *m.* money, currency.

dinosauro, *m.* dinosaur.

diócesis, *f.* diocese.

Dios, *m.* God.

dios -sa, *n.* god, goddess.

diploma, *m.* diploma.

diplomacia, *f.* diplomacy.

diplomado -da, *n.* graduate.

diplomarse, *v.* graduate (from a school).

diplomática, *f.* diplomacy.

diplomático -ca, *a. & n.* diplomat; diplomatic.

dipsomanía, *f.* dipsomania.

diptongo, *m.* diphthong.

diputación, *f.* deputation, delegation.

diputado -da, *n.* deputy; delegate.

diputar, *v.* depute, delegate; empower.

dique, *m.* dike; dam.

dirección, *f.* direction; address; guidance; (com.) management.

directamente, *adv.* directly.

directo, *a.* direct.

director -ra, *n.* director; manager.

directorio, *m.* directory.

dirigente, *a.* directing, controlling, managing.

dirigible, *m.* dirigible.

dirigir, *v.* direct; lead; manage.

dirigirse a, *v.* address; approach, turn to; head for.

dirruir, *v.* destroy, devastate.

disanto, *m.* holy day.

discantar, *v.* sing (esp. in counterpoint); discuss.

disceptación, *f.* argument, quarrel.

disceptar, *v.* argue, quarrel.

discernimiento, *m.* discernment.

discernir, *v.* discern.

disciplina, *f.* discipline.

disciplinable, *a.* disciplinable.

disciplinar, *v.* discipline, train, teach.

discípulo -la, *n.* disciple, follower; pupil.

disco, *m.* disk; (phonograph) record.

disco compacto, compact disk.

disco duro, hard disk.

disco flexible, floppy disk.

discontinuación, *f.* discontinuation.

discontinuar, *v.* discontinue, break off, cease.

discordancia, *f.* discordance.

discordar, *v.* disagree, conflict.

discordia, *f.* discord.

discoteca, *f.* disco, discotheque.

discreción, *f.* discretion.

discrecional, *a.* optional.

discrecionalmente, *adv.* optionally.

discrepancia, *f.* discrepancy.

discretamente, *adv.* discreetly.

discreto, *a.* discreet.

discrimen, *m.* risk, hazard.

discriminación, *f.* discrimination.

discriminar, *v.* discriminate.

disculpa, *f.* excuse; apology.

disculpar, *v.* excuse; exonerate.

disculparse, *v.* apologize.

discurrir, *v.* roam; flow; think; plan.

discursante, *n.* lecturer, speaker.

discursivo, *a.* discursive.

discurso, *m.* speech, talk.

discusión, *f.* discussion.

discutible, *a.* debatable.

discutir, *v.* discuss; debate; contest.

disecación, *f.* dissection.

disecar, *v.* dissect.

disección, *f.* dissection.

diseminación, *f.* dissemination.

diseminar, *v.* disseminate, spread.

disensión, *f.* dissension; dissent.

disenso, *m.* dissent.

disentería, *f.* dysentery.

disentir, *v.* disagree, dissent.

diseñador -ra, *n.* designer.

diseño, *m.* design. **—diseñar,** *v.*

disertación, *f.* dissertation.

disforme, *a.* deformed, monstrous, ugly.
disformidad, *f.* deformity.
disfraz, *m.* disguise. **—disfrazar,** *v.*
disfrutar, *v.* enjoy.
disfrute, *m.* enjoyment.
disgustar, *v.* displease; disappoint.
disgusto, *m.* displeasure; disappointment.
disidencia, *f.* dissidence.
disidente, *a.* & *n.* dissident.
disímil, *a.* unlike.
disimilitud, *f.* dissimilarity.
disimulación, *f.* dissimulation.
disimulado, *a.* dissembling, feigning; sly.
disimular, *v.* hide; dissemble.
disimulo, *m.* pretense.
disipación, *f.* dissipation.
disipado, *a.* dissipated; wasted; scattered.
disipar, *v.* waste; scatter.
dislexia, *f.* dyslexia.
disléxico, *a.* dyslexic.
dislocación, *f.* dislocation.
dislocar, *v.* dislocate; displace.
disminuir, *v.* diminish, lessen, reduce.
disociación, *f.* dissociation.
disociar, *v.* dissociate.
disolubilidad, *f.* dissolubility.
disoluble, *a.* dissoluble.
disolución, *f.* dissolution.
disolutamente, *adv.* dissolutely.
disoluto, *a.* dissolute.
disolver, *v.* dissolve.
disonancia, *f.* dissonance; discord.
disonante, *a.* dissonant; discordant.
disonar, *v.* be discordant; clash in sound.
dísono, *a.* dissonant.
dispar, *a.* unlike.
disparadamente, *adv.* hastily, hurriedly.
disparar, *v.* shoot, fire (a weapon).
disparatado, *a.* nonsensical.
disparatar, *v.* talk nonsense.
disparate, *m.* nonsense, tall tale.

disparejo, *a.* uneven, unequal.
disparidad, *f.* disparity.
disparo, *m.* shot.
dispendio, *m.* extravagance.
dispendioso, *a.* expensive; extravagant.
dispensa, dispensación, *f.* dispensation.
dispensable, *a.* dispensable; excusable.
dispensar, *v.* dispense, excuse; grant.
dispensario, *m.* dispensary.
dispepsia, *f.* dyspepsia.
dispéptico, *a.* dyspeptic.
dispersar, *v.* scatter; dispel; disband.
dispersión, *f.* dispersion, dispersal.
disperso, *a.* dispersed.
displicente, *a.* unpleasant.
disponer, *v.* dispose. **d. de,** have at one's disposal.
disponible, *a.* available.
disposición, *f.* disposition; disposal.
dispuesto, *a.* disposed, inclined; attractive.
disputa, *f.* dispute, argument.
disputable, *a.* disputable.
disputador -ra, *n.* disputant.
disputar, *v.* argue; dispute.
disquete, *m.* diskette.
disquetera, *f.* disk drive.
disquisición, *f.* disquisition.
distancia, *f.* distance.
distante, *a.* distant.
distantemente, *adv.* distantly.
distar, *v.* be distant, be far.
distender, *v.* distend, swell, enlarge.
distensión, *f.* distension, swelling.
dístico, *m.* couplet.
distinción, *f.* distinction, difference.
distingo, *m.* restriction.
distinguible, *a.* distinguishable.
distinguido, *a.* distinguished, prominent.
distinguir, *v.* distinguish; make out, spot.

distintamente, *adv.* distinctly, clearly; differently.
distintivo, *a.* distinctive.
distintivo del país, country code.
distinto, *a.* distinct; different.
distracción, *f.* distraction, pastime; absent-mindedness.
distraer, *v.* distract.
distraídamente, *adv.* absentmindedly, distractedly.
distraído, *a.* absentminded; distracted.
distribución, *f.* distribution.
distribuidor -ra, *n.* distributor.
distribuir, *v.* distribute.
distributivo, *a.* distributive.
distributor, *m.* distributor.
distrito, *m.* district.
disturbar, *v.* disturb, trouble.
disturbio, *m.* disturbance, outbreak; turmoil.
disuadir, *v.* dissuade.
disuasión, *f.* dissuasion; deterrence.
disuasivo, *a.* dissuasive.
disyunción, *f.* disjunction.
ditirambo, *m.* dithyramb.
diurno, *a.* diurnal.
diva, *f.* diva, prima donna.
divagación, *f.* digression.
divagar, *v.* digress, ramble.
diván, *m.* couch.
divergencia, *f.* divergence.
divergente, *a.* divergent, differing.
divergir, *v.* diverge.
diversamente, *adv.* diversely.
diversidad, *f.* diversity.
diversificar, *v.* diversify, vary.
diversión, *f.* diversion, pastime.
diverso, *a.* diverse, different; (*pl.*) various, several.
divertido, *a.* humorous, amusing.
divertimiento, *m.* diversion; amusement.
divertir, *v.* entertain, amuse.
divertirse, *v.* enjoy oneself, have a good time.
dividendo, *m.* dividend.
divididero, *a.* to be divided.

dividido, *a.* divided.
dividir, *v.* divide; separate.
divieso, *m.* (med.) boil.
divinamente, *adv.* divinely.
divinidad, *f.* divinity.
divinizar, *v.* deify.
divino, *a.* divine; heavenly.
divisa, *f.* badge, emblem.
divisar, *v.* sight, make out.
divisibilidad, *f.* divisibility.
divisible, *a.* divisible.
división, *f.* division.
divisivo, *a.* divisive.
divo, *m.* movie star.
divorcio, *m.* divorce. **—divorciar,** *v.*
divulgable, *a.* divulgable.
divulgación, *f.* divulgation.
divulgar, *v.* divulge, reveal.
dobladamente, *adv.* doubly.
dobladillo, *m.* hem of a skirt or dress.
dobladura, *f.* fold; bend.
doblar, *v.* fold; bend.
doble, *a.* double.
doblegable, *a.* flexible, foldable.
doblegar, *v.* fold, bend; yield.
doblez, *m.* fold; duplicity.
doblón, *m.* doubloon.
doce, *a.* & *pron.* twelve.
docena, *f.* dozen.
docente, *a.* educational.
dócil, *a.* docile.
docilidad, *f.* docility, tractableness.
dócilmente, *adv.* docilely, meekly.
doctamente, *adv.* learnedly, profoundly.
docto, *a.* learned, expert.
doctor -ra, *n.* doctor.
doctorado, *m.* doctorate.
doctoral, *a.* doctoral.
doctrina, *f.* doctrine.
doctrinador -ra, *n.* teacher.
doctrinal, *m.* doctrinal.
doctrinar, *v.* teach.
documentación, *f.* documentation.
documental, *a.* documentary.
documento, *m.* document.
dogal, *m.* noose.
dogma, *m.* dogma.
dogmáticamente, *adv.* dogmatically.
dogmático, *m.* dogmatic.

dogmatismo, *m.* dogmatism.
dogmatista, *m.* & *f.* dogmatist.
dogo, *m.* bulldog.
dolar, *v.* cut, chop, hew.
dólar, *m.* dollar.
dolencia, *f.* pain; disease.
doler, *v.* ache, hurt, be sore.
doliente, *a.* ill; aching.
dolor, *m.* pain; grief, sorrow, woe.
dolor de cabeza, headache.
dolor de espalda, backache.
dolor de estómago, stomachache.
dolorido, *a.* painful, sorrowful.
dolorosamente, *adv.* painfully, sorrowfully.
doloroso, *a.* painful, sorrowful.
dolosamente, *adv.* deceitfully.
doloso, *a.* deceitful.
domable, *a.* that can be tamed or managed.
domar, *v.* tame; subdue.
dombo, *m.* dome.
domesticable, *a.* that can be domesticated.
domesticación, *f.* domestication.
domésticamente, *adv.* domestically.
domesticar, *v.* tame, domesticate.
domesticidad, *f.* domesticity.
doméstico, *a.* domestic.
domicilio, *m.* dwelling, home, residence, domicile.
dominación, *f.* domination.
dominador, *a.* dominating.
dominante, *a.* dominant.
dominar, *v.* rule, dominate; master.
dómine, *m.* teacher.
domingo, *m.* Sunday.
dominio, *m.* domain; rule; power.
dominó, *m.* domino.
domo, *m.* dome.
Don, *title used before a man's first name.*
don, *m.* gift.
donación, *f.* donation.
donador -ra, *n.* giver, donor.
donaire, *m.* grace.

donairosamente, *adv.* gracefully.
donairoso, *a.* graceful.
donante, *n.* giver, donor.
donar, *v.* donate.
donativo, *m.* donation, contribution; gift.
doncella, *f.* lass; maid.
donde, dónde, *conj.* & *adv.* where.
dondequiera, *adv.* wherever, anywhere.
donosamente, *adv.* gracefully; wittily.
donoso, *a.* graceful; witty.
donosura, *f.* gracefulness; wittiness.
Doña, *title used before a lady's first name.*
dorado, *a.* gilded.
dorador -ra, *n.* gilder.
dorar, *v.* gild.
dórico, *a.* Doric.
dormidero, *a.* sleep-inducing; soporific.
dormido, *a.* asleep.
dormir, *v.* sleep.
dormirse, *v.* fall asleep, go to sleep.
dormitar, *v.* doze.
dormitorio, *m.* dormitory; bedroom.
dorsal, *a.* dorsal.
dorso, *m.* spine.
dos, *a.* & *pron.* two. **los d.,** both.
dosañal, *a.* biennial.
doscientos, *a.* & *pron.* two hundred.
dosel, *m.* canopy; platform, dais.
dosificación, *f.* dosage.
dosis, *f.* dose.
dotación, *f.* endowment; (naut.) crew.
dotador -ra, *n.* donor.
dotar, *v.* endow; give a dowry to.
dote, *f.* dowry; (*pl.*) talents.
dragaminas, *m.* mine sweeper.
dragar, *v.* dredge; sweep.
dragón, *m.* dragon; dragoon.
dragonear, *v.* pretend to be.
drama, *m.* drama; play.
dramática, *f.* drama, dramatic art.

dramáticamente, *adv.* dramatically.

dramático, *a.* dramatic.

dramatizar, *v.* dramatize.

dramaturgo -ga, *n.* playwright, dramatist.

drástico, *a.* drastic.

drenaje, *m.* drainage.

dríada, *f.* dryad.

dril, *m.* denim.

driza, *f.* halyard.

droga, *f.* drug.

drogadicto -ta, *n.* drug addict.

droguería, *f.* drugstore.

droguero, *m.* druggist.

dromedario, *m.* dromedary.

druida, *m. & f.* Druid.

dualidad, *f.* duality.

dubitable, *a.* doubtful.

dubitación, *f.* doubt.

ducado, *m.* duchy.

ducal, *a.* ducal.

ducha, *f.* shower (bath).

ducharse, *v.* take a shower.

dúctil, *a.* ductile.

ductilidad, *f.* ductility.

duda, *f.* doubt.

dudable, *a.* doubtful.

dudar, *v.* doubt; hesitate; question.

dudosamente, *adv.* doubtfully.

dudoso, *a.* dubious; doubtful.

duela, *f.* stave.

duelista, *m. & f.* duelist.

duelo, *m.* duel; grief; mourning.

duende, *m.* elf, hobgoblin.

dueño -ña, *n.* owner; landlord -lady; master, mistress.

dulce, 1. *a.* sweet. **agua d.,** fresh water. **2.** *m.* piece of candy; (*pl.*) candy.

dulcedumbre, *f.* sweetness.

dulcemente, *adv.* sweetly.

dulcería, *f.* confectionery; candy shop.

dulcificar, *v.* sweeten.

dulzura, *f.* sweetness; mildness.

duna, *f.* dune.

dúo, *m.* duo, duet.

duodenal, *a.* duodenal.

duplicación, *f.* duplication; doubling.

duplicadamente, *adv.* doubly.

duplicado, *a. & m.* duplicate.

duplicar, *v.* double, duplicate, repeat.

duplicidad, *f.* duplicity.

duplo, *a.* double.

duque, *m.* duke.

duquesa, *f.* duchess.

durabilidad, *f.* durability.

durable, *a.* durable.

duración, *f.* duration.

duradero, *a.* lasting, durable.

duramente, *adv.* harshly, roughly.

durante, *prep.* during.

durar, *v.* last.

durazno, *m.* peach; peach tree.

dureza, *f.* hardness.

durmiente, *a.* sleeping.

duro, *a.* hard; stiff; stern; stale.

dux, *m.* doge.

E

e, *conj.* and.

ebanista, *m. & f.* cabinetmaker.

ebanizar, *v.* give an ebony finish to.

ébano, *m.* ebony.

ebonita, *f.* ebonite.

ebrio, *a.* drunken, inebriated.

ebullición, *f.* boiling.

echada, *f.* throw.

echadillo, *m.* foundling; orphan.

echar, *v.* throw, toss; pour. **e. a,** start to. **e. a perder,** spoil, ruin. **e. de menos,** miss.

echarse, *v.* lie down.

eclecticismo, *m.* eclecticism.

ecléctico, *n. & a.* eclectic.

eclesiástico, *a. & m.* ecclesiastic.

eclipse, *m.* eclipse. **—eclipsar,** *v.*

écloga, *f.* eclogue.

eco, *m.* echo.

ecología, *f.* ecology.

ecológico, *f.* ecological.

ecologista, *m. & f.* ecologist.

economía, *f.* economy; thrift; economics. **e. política,** political economy.

económicamente, *adv.* economically.

económico, *a.* economic, economical, thrifty; inexpensive.

economista, *m. & f.* economist.

economizar, *v.* save, economize.

ecuación, *f.* equation.

ecuador, *m.* equator.

ecuanimidad, *f.* equanimity.

ecuatorial, *a.* equatorial.

ecuatoriano -na, *a. & n.* Ecuadorian.

ecuestre, *a.* equestrian.

ecuménico. *a.* ecumenical.

edad, *f.* age.

edecán, *m.* aide-de-camp.

Edén, *m.* Eden.

edición, *f.* edition; issue.

edicto, *m.* edict, decree.

edificación, *f.* construction; edification.

edificador, *n.* constructor; builder.

edificar, *v.* build.

edificio, *m.* edifice, building.

editar, *v.* publish, issue; edit.

editor, *m.* publisher; editor.

editorial, *m.* editorial; publishing house.

edredón, *m.* quilt.

educación, *f.* upbringing, breeding; education.

educado, *a.* well-mannered; educated.

educador -ra, *n.* educator.

educar, *v.* educate; bring up; train.

educativo, *a.* educational.

educción, *f.* deduction.

educir, *v.* educe.

efectivamente, *adv.* actually, really.

efectivo, *a.* effective; actual, real. **en e.,** (com.) in cash.

efecto, *m.* effect.

efecto invernáculo, green-house effect.

efectuar, *v.* effect; cash.

eferente, *a.* efferent.

efervescencia, *f.* efferves-cence; zeal.

eficacia, *f.* efficacy.

eficaz, *a.* efficient, effec-tive.

eficazmente, *adv.* effica-ciously.

eficiencia, *f.* efficiency.

eficiente, *a.* efficient.

efigie, *f.* effigy.

efímera, *f.* mayfly.

efímero, *a.* ephemeral, passing.

efluvio, *m.* effluvium.

efundir, *v.* effuse; pour out.

efusión, *f.* effusion.

egipcio -cia, *a. & n.* Egypt-ian.

Egipto, *m.* Egypt.

egoísmo, *m.* egoism, ego-tism, selfishness.

egoísta, *a. & n.* selfish, ego-istic; egoist.

egotismo, *m.* egotism.

egotista, *m. & f.* egotist.

egreso, *m.* expense, outlay.

eje, *m.* axis; axle.

ejecución, *f.* execution; per-formance; enforcement.

ejecutar, *v.* execute; en-force; carry out.

ejecutivo -va, *a. & n.* exec-utive.

ejecutor -ra, *n.* executor.

ejemplar, 1. *a.* exemplary. **2.** *m.* copy.

ejemplificación, *f.* exempli-fication.

ejemplificar, *v.* illustrate.

ejemplo, *m.* example.

ejercer, *v.* exert; practice.

ejercicio, *m.* exercise, drill. **—ejercitar,** *v.*

ejercitación, *f.* exercise, training, drill.

ejercitar, *v.* exercise, train, drill.

ejército, *m.* army.

ejotes, *m.pl.* string beans.

el, *art. & pron.* the; the one.

él, *pron.* he, him; it.

elaboración, *f.* elaboration; working up.

elaborado, *a.* elaborate.

elaborador, *m.* manufac-turer, maker.

elaborar, *v.* elaborate; man-ufacture; brew.

elación, *f.* elation; magna-nimity; turgid style.

elasticidad, *f.* elasticity.

elástico, *m.* elastic.

elección, *f.* election; option, choice.

electivo, *a.* elective.

electo, *a.* elected, chosen, appointed.

electorado, *m.* electorate.

electoral, *a.* electoral.

electricidad, *f.* electricity.

electricista, *m. & f.* electri-cian.

eléctrico, *a.* electric.

electrización, *f.* electrifica-tion.

electrocardiograma, *m.* electrocardiogram.

electrocución, *f.* electrocu-tion.

electrocutar, *v.* electrocute.

electrodo, *m.* electrode.

electrodoméstico, *m.* elec-trical appliance, home appliance.

electroimán, *m.* electro-magnet.

electrólisis, *f.* electrolysis.

electrólito, *m.* electrolyte.

electrón, *m.* electron.

electrónico, *a.* electronic.

elefante, *m.* elephant.

elegancia, *f.* elegance.

elegante, *a.* elegant, smart, stylish, fine.

elegantemente, *adv.* ele-gantly.

elegía, *f.* elegy.

elegibilidad, *f.* eligibility.

elegible, *a.* eligible.

elegir, *v.* select, choose; elect.

elemental, *a.* elementary.

elementalmente, *adv.* ele-mentally; fundamentally.

elemento, *m.* element.

elevación, *f.* elevation; height.

elevador, *m.* elevator.

elevamiento, *m.* elevation.

elevar, *v.* elevate; erect, raise.

elidir, *v.* elide.

eliminación, *f.* elimination.

eliminar, *v.* eliminate.

elipse, *f.* ellipse.

elipsis, *f.* ellipsis.

elíptico, *a.* elliptic.

ella, *pron.* she, her; it.

ello, *pron.* it.

ellos -as, *pron. pl.* they, them.

elocuencia, *f.* eloquence.

elocuente, *a.* eloquent.

elocuentemente, *adv.* elo-quently.

elogio, *m.* praise, compli-ment. **—elogiar,** *v.*

elucidación, *f.* elucidation.

elucidar, *v.* elucidate.

eludir, *v.* elude.

emanar, *v.* emanate, stem.

emancipación, *f.* emancipa-tion; freeing.

emancipador -ra, *n.* eman-cipator.

emancipar, *v.* emancipate; free.

embajada, *f.* embassy; legation; (coll.) errand.

embajador -ra, *n.* ambas-sador.

embalar, *v.* pack, bale.

embaldosado, *m.* tile floor.

embalsamador, *m.* em-balmer.

embalsamar, *v.* embalm.

embarazada, *a.* pregnant.

embarazadamente, *adv.* embarrassedly.

embarazar, *v.* make preg-nant; embarrass.

embarazo, *m.* embarrass-ment; pregnancy.

embarbascado, *a.* difficult; complicated.

embarcación, *f.* boat, ship; embarkation.

embarcadero, *m.* wharf, pier, dock.

embarcador, *m.* shipper, loader, stevedore.

embarcar, *v.* embark, board ship.

embarcarse, *v.* embark; sail.

embargador, *m.* one who impedes; one who orders an embargo.

embargante, *a.* impeding, hindering.

embargar, *v.* impede, re-strain; (leg.) seize, em-bargo.

embargo, *m*. seizure, embargo. **sin e.,** however, nevertheless.

embarnizar, *v*. varnish.

embarque, *m*. shipment.

embarrador -ra, *n*. plasterer.

embarrancar, *v*. get stuck in mud; (naut.) run aground.

embarrar, *v*. plaster; besmear with mud.

embasamiento, *m*. foundation of a building.

embastecer, *v*. get fat.

embaucador -ra, *n*. impostor.

embaucar, *v*. deceive, trick, hoax.

embaular, *v*. pack in a trunk.

embausamiento, *m*. amazement.

embebecer, *v*. amaze, astonish; entertain.

embeber, *v*. absorb; incorporate; saturate.

embelecador -ra, *n*. impostor.

embeleco, *m*. fraud, perpetration.

embeleñar, *v*. fascinate, charm.

embelesamiento, *m*. rapture.

embelesar, *v*. fascinate, charm.

embeleso, *m*. rapture, bliss.

embellecer, *v*. beautify, embellish.

embestida, *f*. violent assault; attack.

emblandecer, *v*. soften; moisten; move to pity.

emblema, *m*. emblem.

emblemático, *a*. emblematic.

embocadura, *f*. narrow entrance; mouth of a river.

embocar, *v*. eat hastily; gorge.

embolia, *f*. embolism.

émbolo, *m*. piston.

embolsar, *v*. pocket.

embonar, *v*. improve, fix, repair.

emborrachador, *a*. intoxicating.

emborrachar, *v*. get drunk.

emboscada, *f*. ambush.

emboscar, *v*. put or lie in ambush.

embotado, *a*. blunt, dull (edged). **—embotar**, *v*.

embotadura, *f*. bluntness; dullness.

embotellamiento, *m*. bottling (liquids); traffic jam.

embotellar, *v*. put in bottles.

embozado, *v*. muzzled; muffled.

embozar, *v*. muzzle; muffle.

embozo, *m*. muffler.

embrague, *m*. (auto.) clutch.

embravecer, *v*. be or make angry.

embriagado, *a*. drunken, intoxicated.

embriagar, *v*. intoxicate.

embriaguez, *f*. drunkenness.

embrión, *m*. embryo.

embrionario, *a*. embryonic.

embrochado, *a*. embroidered.

embrollo, *m*. muddle. **— embrollar**, *v*.

embromar, *v*. tease; joke.

embuchado, *m*. pork sausage.

embudo, *m*. funnel.

embuste, *m*. lie, fib.

embustear, *v*. lie, fib.

embustero -ra, *n*. liar.

embutir, *v*. stuff, cram.

emergencia, *f*. emergency.

emérito, *a*. emeritus.

emético, *m*. & *a*. emetic.

emigración, *f*. emigration.

emigrante, *a*. & *n*. emigrant.

emigrar, *v*. emigrate.

eminencia, *f*. eminence, height.

eminente, *a*. eminent.

emisario -ria, *n*. emissary, spy; outlet.

emisión, *f*. issue; emission.

emisor, *m*. radio transmitter.

emitir, *v*. emit.

emoción, *f*. feeling, emotion, thrill.

emocional, *a*. emotional.

emocionante, *a*. exciting.

emocionar, *v*. touch, move, excite.

emolumento, *m*. emolument; perquisite.

empacar, *v*. pack.

empacho, *m*. shyness, timidity, embarrassment.

empadronamiento, *m*. census; list of taxpayers.

empalizada, *f*. palisade, stockade.

empanada, *f*. meat pie.

empañar, *v*. blur; soil, sully.

empapar, *v*. soak.

empapelado, *m*. wallpaper.

empapelar, *v*. wallpaper.

empaque, *m*. packing; appearance, mien.

empaquetar, *v*. pack, package.

emparedado, *m*. sandwich.

emparejarse, *v*. match, pair off; level, even off.

emparentado, *a*. related by marriage.

emparrado, *m*. arbor.

empastadura, *f*. (dental) filling.

empastar, *v*. fill (a tooth); paste.

empate, *m*. tie, draw. **—empatarse**, *v*.

empecer, *v*. hurt, harm, injure; prevent.

empedernir, *v*. harden.

empeine, *m*. groin; instep; hoof.

empellar, *v*. shove, jostle.

empellón, *m*. hard push, shove.

empeñar, *v*. pledge; pawn.

empeñarse en, *v*. persist in, be bent on.

empeño, *m*. persistence; pledge; pawning.

empeoramiento, *m*. deterioration.

empeorar, *v*. get worse.

emperador, *m*. emperor.

emperatriz, *f*. empress.

empernar, *v*. bolt.

empero, *conj*. however; but.

emperramiento, *m*. stubbornness.

empezar, *v*. begin, start.

empinado, *a*. steep.

empinar, *v*. raise; exalt.

empíreo, *a*. celestial, heavenly; divine.

empíricamente, *adv*. empirically.

empírico, *a*. empirical.

empirismo, *m*. empiricism.

emplastarse, *v*. get smeared.

emplasto, *m*. salve.

emplazamiento, *m.* court summons.

emplazar, *v.* summon to court.

empleado -da, *n.* employee.

emplear, *v.* employ; use.

empleo, *m.* employment, job; use.

empobrecer, *v.* impoverish.

empobrecimiento, *m.* impoverishment.

empollador, *m.* incubator.

empollar, *v.* hatch.

empolvado, *a.* dusty.

empolvar, *v.* powder.

emporcar, *v.* soil, make dirty.

emporio, *m.* emporium.

emprendedor, *a.* enterprising.

emprender, *v.* undertake.

empreñar, *v.* make pregnant; beget.

empresa, *f.* enterprise, undertaking; company.

empresario -ria, *n.* businessperson; impresario.

empréstito, *m.* loan.

empujón, *m.* push; shove. **—empujar,** *v.*

empuñar, *v.* grasp, seize; wield.

emulación, *f.* emulation; envy; rivalry.

emulador, *m.* emulator; rival.

émulo, *a.* rival. **—emular,** *v.*

emulsión, *f.* emulsion.

emulsionar, *v.* emulsify.

en, *prep.* in, on, at.

enaguas, *f.pl.* petticoat; skirt.

enajenable, *a.* alienable.

enajenación, *f.* alienation; derangement, insanity.

enajenar, *v.* alienate.

enamoradamente, *adv.* lovingly.

enamorado, *a.* in love.

enamorador, *m.* wooer; suitor; lover.

enamorarse, *v.* fall in love.

enano -na, *n.* midget; dwarf.

enardecer, *v.* inflame.

enastado, *a.* horned.

encabestrar, *v.* halter.

encabezado, *m.* headline.

encabezamiento, *m.* title; census; tax roll.

encabezar, *v.* head.

encachar, *v.* hide.

encadenamiento, *m.* connection, linkage.

encadenar, *v.* chain; link, connect.

encajar, *v.* fit in, insert.

encaje, *m.* lace.

encalar, *v.* whitewash.

encallarse, *v.* be stranded.

encallecido, *a.* hardened; calloused.

encalvecer, *v.* lose one's hair.

encaminar, *v.* guide; direct; be on the way to.

encandilar, *v.* dazzle; daze.

encantación, *f.* incantation.

encantado, *a.* charmed, fascinated, enchanted.

encantador, *a.* charming, delightful.

encante, *m.* public auction.

encanto, *m.* charm, delight. **—encantar,** *v.*

encapillado, *m.* clothes one is wearing.

encapotar, *v.* cover, cloak; muffle.

encaprichamiento, *m.* infatuation.

encaramarse, *v.* perch; climb.

encararse con, *v.* face.

encarcelación, *f.* imprisonment.

encarcelar, *v.* jail, imprison.

encarecer, *v.* recommend; extol.

encarecidamente, *adv.* extremely; ardently.

encargado -da, *n.* agent; attorney; representative.

encargar, *v.* entrust; order.

encargarse, *v.* take charge, be in charge.

encargo, *m.* errand; assignment; (com.) order.

encarnación, *f.* incarnation.

encarnado, *a.* red.

encarnar, *v.* embody.

encarnecer, *v.* grow fat or heavy.

encarnizado, *a.* bloody, fierce.

encarrilar, *v.* set right; put on the track.

encartar, *v.* ban, outlaw; summon.

encastar, *v.* improve by crossbreeding.

encastillar, *v.* be obstinate or unyielding.

encatarrado, *a.* suffering from a cold.

encausar, *v.* prosecute; take legal action against.

encauzar, *v.* channel; direct.

encefalitis, *f.* encephalitis.

encelamiento, *m.* envy, jealousy.

encenagar, *v.* wallow in mud.

encendedor, *m.* lighter.

encender, *v.* light; set fire to, kindle; turn on.

encendido, *m.* ignition.

encerado, *m.* oilcloth; tarpaulin.

encerar, *v.* wax.

encerrar, *v.* enclose; confine, shut in.

enchapado, *m.* veneer.

enchufe, *m.* (elec.) plug, socket.

encía, *f.* gum.

encíclico, 1. *a.* encyclic. **2.** *f.* encyclical.

enciclopedia, *f.* encyclopedia.

enciclopédico, *a.* encyclopedic.

encierro, *m.* confinement; enclosure.

encima, *adv.* on top. **e. de,** on. **por e. de,** above.

encina, *f.* oak.

encinta, *a.* pregnant.

enclavar, *v.* nail.

enclenque, *a.* frail, weak, sickly.

encogerse, *v.* shrink. **e. de hombros,** shrug the shoulders.

encogido, *a.* shy, bashful, timid.

encojar, *v.* make or become lame; cripple.

encolar, *v.* glue, paste, stick.

encolerizar, *v.* make or become angry.

encomendar, *v.* commend; recommend.

encomiar, *v.* praise, laud, extol.

encomienda, *f.* commission, charge; (postal) package.

encomio, *m.* encomium, eulogy.

enconar, *v.* irritate, annoy, anger.

encono, *m.* rancor, resentment.

enconoso, *a.* rancorous, resentful.

encontrado, *a.* opposite.

encontrar, *v.* find; meet.

encorajar, *v.* encourage; incite.

encorralar, *v.* corral.

encorvadura, *f.* bend, curvature.

encorvar, *v.* arch, bend.

encorvarse, *v.* stoop.

encrucijada, *f.* crossroads.

encuadrar, *v.* frame.

encubierta, 1. *a.* secret, fraudulent. **2.** *f.* fraud.

encubrir, *v.* hide, conceal.

encuentro, *m.* encounter; match, bout.

encurtido, *m.* pickle.

endeble, *a.* rail, weak, sickly.

enderezar, *v.* straighten; redress.

endeudarse, *v.* get into debt.

endiablado, *a.* devilish.

endibia, *f.* endive.

endiosar, *v.* deify.

endorso, endoso, *m.* endorsement.

endosador -ra, *n.* endorser.

endosar, *v.* endorse.

endosatario -ria, *n.* endorsee.

endulzar, *v.* sweeten; soothe.

endurar, *v.* harden.

endurecer, *v.* harden.

enemigo -ga, *n.* foe, enemy.

enemistad, *f.* enmity.

éneo, *a.* brass.

energía, *f.* energy.

energía nuclear, atomic energy, nuclear energy.

energía vital, élan vital, vitality.

enérgicamente, *adv.* energetically.

enérgico, *a.* forceful; energetic.

enero, *m.* January.

enervación, *f.* enervation.

enfadado, *a.* angry.

enfadar, *v.* anger, vex.

enfado, *m.* anger, vexation.

énfasis, *m. or f.* emphasis, stress.

enfáticamente, *adv.* emphatically.

enfático, *a.* emphatic.

enfermar, *v.* make ill; fall ill.

enfermedad, *f.* illness, sickness, disease.

enfermera, *f.* nurse.

enfermería, *f.* sanatorium.

enfermo -ma, *a. & n.* ill, sick; sickly; patient.

enfilar, *v.* line up; put in a row.

enflaquecer, *v.* make thin; grow thin.

enfoque, *m.* focus. **—enfocar,** *v.*

enfrascamiento, *m.* entanglement.

enfrascar, *v.* bottle; entangle oneself.

enfrenar, *v.* bridle, curb; restrain.

enfrentamiento, *m.* clash, confrontation.

enfrente, *adv.* across, opposite; in front.

enfriadera, *f.* icebox; cooler.

enfriar, *v.* chill, cool.

enfurecer, *v.* infuriate, enrage.

engalanar, *v.* adorn, trim.

enganchar, *v.* hook, hitch, attach.

engañar, *v.* deceive, cheat.

engaño, *m.* deceit; delusion.

engañoso, *a.* deceitful.

engarce, *m.* connection, link.

engastar, *v.* to put (gems) in a setting.

engaste, *m.* setting.

engatusar, *v.* deceive, trick.

engendrar, *v.* engender, beget, produce.

engendro, *m.* fetus, embryo.

englobar, *v.* include.

engolfar, *v.* be deeply absorbed.

engolosinar, *v.* allure, charm, entice.

engomar, *v.* gum.

engordador, *a.* fattening.

engordar, *v.* fatten; grow fat.

engranaje, *m.* (mech.) gear.

engranar, *v.* gear; mesh together.

engrandecer, *v.* increase, enlarge; exalt; exaggerate.

engrasación, *f.* lubrication.

engrasar, *v.* grease, lubricate.

engreído, *a.* conceited.

engreimiento, *m.* conceit.

engullidor -ra, *n.* devourer.

engullir, *v.* devour.

enhebrar, *v.* thread.

enhestadura, *f.* raising.

enhestar, *v.* raise, erect, set up.

enhiesto, *a.* erect, upright.

enhorabuena, *f.* congratulations.

enigma, *m.* enigma, puzzle.

enigmáticamente, *adv.* enigmatically.

enigmático, *a.* enigmatic.

enjabonar, *v.* soap, lather.

enjalbegar, *v.* whitewash.

enjambradera, *f.* queen bee.

enjambre, *m.* swarm. **—enjambrar,** *v.*

enjaular, *v.* cage, coop up.

enjebe, *m.* lye.

enjuagar, *v.* rinse.

enjuague bucal, *m.* mouthwash.

enjugar, *v.* wipe, dry off.

enjutez, *f.* dryness.

enjuto, *a.* dried; lean, thin.

enlace, *m.* attachment; involvement; connection.

enladrillador -ra, *n.* bricklayer.

enlardar, *v.* baste.

enlatado -da, *a.* canned (food).

enlatar, *v.* can (food).

enlazar, *v.* lace; join, connect; wed.

enlodar, *v.* cover with mud.

enloquecer, *v.* go insane; drive crazy.

enloquecimiento, *m.* insanity.

enlustrecer, *v.* polish, brighten.

enmarañar, *v.* entangle.

enmendación, *f.* emendation.

enmendador -ra, *n.* emender, reviser.

enmendar, *v.* amend, correct.

enmienda, *f.* amendment; correction.

enmohecer, *v.* rust; mold.

enmohecido, *a.* rusty; moldy.

enmudecer, v. silence; become silent.

ennegrecer, v. blacken.

ennoblecer, v. ennoble.

enodio, m. young deer.

enojado, a. angry, cross.

enojarse, v. get angry.

enojo, m. anger. —**enojar,** v.

enojosamente, adv. angrily.

enorme, a. enormous, huge.

enormemente, adv. enormously; hugely.

enormidad, f. enormity; hugeness.

enraizar, v. take root, sprout.

enramada, f. bower.

enredadera, f. climbing plant.

enredado, a. entangled, snarled.

enredar, v. entangle, snarl; mess up.

enredo, m. tangle, entanglement.

enriquecer, v. enrich.

enrojecerse, v. color; blush.

enrollar, v. wind, coil, roll up.

enromar, v. make dull, blunt.

enronquecimiento, m. hoarseness.

enroscar, v. twist, curl, wind.

ensacar, v. put in a bag.

ensalada, f. salad.

ensaladera, f. salad bowl.

ensalmo, m. charm, enchantment.

ensalzamiento, m. praise.

ensalzar, v. praise, laud, extol.

ensamblar, v. join; unite; connect.

ensanchamiento, m. widening, expansion, extension.

ensanchar, v. widen, expand, extend.

ensangrentado, a. bloody; bloodshot.

ensañar, v. enrage, infuriate; rage.

ensayar, v. try out; rehearse.

ensayista, m. & f. essayist.

ensayo, m. attempt; trial; rehearsal.

ensenada, f. cove.

enseña, f. ensign, standard.

enseñador -ra, n. teacher.

enseñanza, f. education; teaching.

enseñar, v. teach, train; show.

enseres, m.pl. household goods.

ensilaje, m. ensilage.

ensillar, v. saddle.

ensordecer, v. deafen.

ensordecedor, a. deafening.

ensordecimiento, m. deafness.

ensuciar, v. dirty, muddy, soil.

ensueño, m. illusion, dream.

entablar, v. board up; initiate, begin.

entallador, m. sculptor, carver.

entapizar, v. upholster.

ente, m. being.

entenada, f. stepdaughter.

entenado, m. stepson.

entender, v. understand.

entendimiento, m. understanding.

entenebrecer, v. darken.

enterado, a. aware, informed.

enteramente, adv. entirely, completely.

enterar, v. inform.

enterarse, v. find out.

entereza, f. entirety; integrity; firmness.

entero, a. entire, whole, total.

enterramiento, m. burial, interment.

enterrar, v. bury.

entestado, a. stubborn, willful.

entibiar, v. to cool; moderate.

entidad, f. entity.

entierro, m. interment, burial.

entonación, f. intonation.

entonamiento, m. intonation.

entonar, v. chant; harmonize.

entonces, adv. then.

entono, m. intonation; arrogance; affectation.

entortadura, f. crookedness.

entortar, v. make crooked; bend.

entrada, f. entrance; admission, admittance.

entrambos, a. & pron. both.

entrante, a. coming, next.

entrañable, a. affectionate.

entrañas, f.pl. entrails, bowels; womb.

entrar, v. enter, go in, come in.

entre, prep. among; between.

entreabierto, a. ajar, half-open.

entreabrir, v. set ajar.

entreacto, m. intermission.

entrecejo, m. frown; space between the eyebrows.

entrecuesto, m. spine, backbone.

entredicho, m. prohibition.

entrega, f. delivery.

entregar, v. deliver, hand; hand over.

entrelazar, v. intertwine, entwine.

entremedias, adv. meanwhile; halfway.

entremés, m. side dish.

entremeterse, v. meddle, intrude.

entremetido -da, n. meddler.

entrenador -ra, n. coach. —**entrenar,** v.

entrenarse, v. train.

entrepalado, a. variegated; spotted.

entrerenglonar, v. interline.

entresacar, v. select, choose; sift.

entresuelo, m. mezzanine.

entretanto, adv. meanwhile.

entretenedor -ra, n. entertainer.

entretener, v. entertain, amuse; delay.

entretenimiento, m. entertainment, amusement.

entrevista, f. interview. —**entrevistar,** v.

entrevistador -ra, n. interviewer.

entristecedor, a. sad.

entristecer, v. sadden.

entronar, v. enthrone.

entroncar, v. be related or connected.

entronización, f. enthronement.

entronque, m. relationship; connection.

entumecer, *v.* become or be numb; swell.

entusiasmado, *a.* enthusiastic.

entusiasmo, *m.* enthusiasm.

entusiasta, *m. & f.* enthusiast.

entusiástico, *a.* enthusiastic.

enumeración, *f.* enumeration.

enumerar, *v.* enumerate.

enunciación, *f.* enunciation; statement.

enunciar, *v.* enunciate.

envainar, *v.* sheathe.

envalentonar, *v.* encourage, embolden.

envanecimiento, *m.* conceit, vanity.

envasar, *v.* put in a container; bottle.

envase, *m.* container.

envejecer, *v.* age, grow old.

envejecimiento, *m.* oldness, aging.

envenenar, *v.* poison.

envés, *m.* wrong side; back.

envestir, *v.* put in office; invest.

enviada, *f.* shipment.

enviado -da, *n.* envoy.

enviar, *v.* send; ship.

envidia, *f.* envy. **—envidiar,** *v.*

envidiable, *a.* enviable.

envidioso, *a.* envious.

envilecer, *v.* vilify, debase, disgrace.

envío, *m.* shipment.

envión, *m.* shove.

envoltura, *f.* wrapping.

envolver, *v.* wrap, wrap up.

enyesar, *v.* plaster.

enyugar, *v.* yoke.

eperlano, *m.* smelt (fish).

épica, *f.* epic.

épico, *a.* epic.

epicureísmo, *m.* epicureanism.

epicúreo, *n. & a.* epicurean.

epidemia, *f.* epidemic.

epidémico, *a.* epidemic.

epidermis, *f.* epidermis.

epigrama, *m.* epigram.

epigramático -ca, *a.* epigrammatic.

epilepsia, *f.* epilepsy.

epiléptico -ca, *n. & a.* epileptic.

epílogo, *m.* epilogue.

episcopado, *m.* bishopric; episcopate.

episcopal, *a.* episcopal.

episódico, *a.* episodic.

episodio, *m.* episode.

epístola, *f.* epistle, letter.

epitafio, *m.* epitaph.

epitomadamente, *adv.* concisely.

epitomar, *v.* epitomize, summarize.

época, *f.* epoch, age.

epopeya, *f.* epic.

epsomita, *f.* Epsom salts.

equidad, *f.* equity.

equilibrado, *a.* stable.

equilibrio, *m.* equilibrium, balance.

equinoccio, *m.* equinox.

equipaje, *m.* luggage, baggage. **e. de mano,** luggage.

equipar, *v.* equip.

equiparar, *v.* compare.

equipo, *m.* equipment; team.

equitación, *f.* horsemanship; horseback riding, riding.

equitativo, *a.* fair, equitable.

equivalencia, *f.* equivalence.

equivalente, *a.* equivalent.

equivaler, *v.* equal, be equivalent.

equivocación, *f.* mistake.

equivocado, *a.* wrong, mistaken.

equivocarse, *v.* make a mistake, be wrong.

equívoco, *a.* equivocal, ambiguous.

era, *f.* era, age.

erario, *m.* exchequer.

erección, *f.* erection; elevation.

eremita, *m.* hermit.

erguir, *v.* erect; straighten up.

erigir, *v.* erect, build.

erisipela, *f.* erysipelas.

erizado, *a.* bristly.

erizarse, *v.* bristle.

erizo, *m.* hedgehog; sea urchin.

ermita, *f.* hermitage.

ermitaño, *m.* hermit.

erogación, *f.* expenditure. **—erogar,** *v.*

erosión, *f.* erosion.

erótico, *a.* erotic.

erradicación, *f.* eradication.

erradicar, *v.* eradicate.

errado, *a.* mistaken, erroneous.

errante, *a.* wandering, roving.

errar, *v.* be mistaken.

errata, *f.* erratum.

errático, *a.* erratic.

erróneamente, *adv.* erroneously.

erróneo, *a.* erroneous.

error, *m.* error, mistake.

eructo, *m.* belch. **—eructar,** *v.*

erudición, *f.* scholarship, learning.

eruditamente, *adv.* learnedly.

erudito -ta, 1. *n.* scholar. **2.** *a.* scholarly.

erupción, *f.* eruption; rash.

eruptivo, *a.* eruptive.

esbozo, *m.* outline, sketch. **—esbozar,** *v.*

escabechar, *v.* pickle; preserve.

escabeche, *m.* brine.

escabel, *m.* small stool or bench.

escabroso, *a.* rough, irregular; craggy; rude.

escabullirse, *v.* steal away, sneak away.

escala, *f.* scale; ladder. **hacer e.,** to make a stop.

escalada, *f.* escalation.

escalador -ra, *n.* climber.

escalar, *v.* climb; scale.

escaldar, *v.* scald.

escalera, *f.* stairs, staircase; ladder.

escalfado, *a.* poached.

escalofriado, *a.* chilled.

escalofrío, *m.* chill.

escalón, *m.* step.

escalonar, *v.* space out, stagger.

escaloña, *f.* scallion.

escalpar, *v.* scalp.

escalpelo, *m.* scalpel.

escama, *f.* (fish) scale. **— escamar,** *v.*

escamondar, *v.* trim, cut; prune.

escampada, *f.* break in the rain, clear spell.

escandalizar, v. shock, scandalize.

escandalizativo, a. scandalous.

escándalo, m. scandal.

escandaloso, a. scandalous; disgraceful.

escandinavo -va, n. & a. Scandinavian.

escandir, v. scan.

escáner, v. scanner (of a computer).

escanilla, f. cradle.

escañuelo, m. small footstool.

escapada, f. escapade.

escapar, v. escape.

escaparate, m. shop window, store window.

escape, m. escape; (auto.) exhaust.

escápula, f. scapula.

escarabajo, m. black beetle; scarab.

escaramucear, v. skirmish; dispute.

escarbadientes, m. toothpick.

escarbar, v. scratch; poke.

escarcha, f. frost.

escardar, v. weed.

escarlata, f. scarlet.

escarlatina, f. scarlet fever.

escarmentar, v. correct severely.

escarnecedor -ra, n. scoffer; mocker.

escarnecer, v. mock, make fun of.

escarola, f. endive.

escarpa, m. escarpment.

escarpado, 1. a. steep. **2.** m. bluff.

escasamente, adv. scarcely; sparingly; barely.

escasear, v. be scarce.

escasez, f. shortage, scarcity.

escaso, a. scant; scarce.

escatimoso, a. malicious; sly, cunning.

escena, f. scene; stage.

escenario, m. stage (of theater); scenario.

escénico, a. scenic.

escépticamente, adv. skeptically.

escepticismo, m. skepticism.

escéptico -ca, a. & n. skeptic; skeptical.

esclarecer, v. clear up.

esclavitud, f. slavery; bondage.

esclavizar, v. enslave.

esclavo -va, n. slave.

escoba, f. broom.

escocés -esa, a. & n. Scotch, Scottish; Scot.

Escocia, f. Scotland.

escofinar, v. rasp.

escoger, v. choose, select.

escogido, a. chosen, selected.

escogimiento, m. choice.

escolar, 1. a. scholastic, (of) school. **2.** m. & f. student.

escolasticismo, m. scholasticism.

escolta, f. escort. **—escoltar,** v.

escollo, m. reef.

escombro, m. mackerel.

escombros, m.pl. debris, rubbish.

esconce, m. corner.

escondedero, m. hiding place.

esconder, v. hide, conceal.

escondidamente, adv. secretly.

escondimiento, m. concealment.

escondrijo, m. hiding place.

escopeta, f. shotgun.

escopetazo, m. gunshot.

escoplo, m. chisel.

escorbuto, m. scurvy.

escorpena, f. grouper.

escorpión, m. scorpion.

escorzón, m. toad.

escotado, a. low-cut, with a low neckline.

escote, m. low neckline.

escribiente, m. & f. clerk.

escribir, v. write.

escritor -ra, n. writer, author.

escritorio, m. desk.

escritura, f. writing, handwriting.

escrófula, f. scrofula.

escroto, m. scrotum.

escrúpulo, m. scruple.

escrupuloso, a. scrupulous.

escrutinio, m. scrutiny; examination.

escuadra, f. squad; fleet.

escuadrón, m. squadron.

escualidez, f. squalor; poverty; emaciation.

escuálido, a. squalid.

escualo, m. shark.

escuchar, v. listen; listen to.

escudero, m. squire.

escudo, m. shield; protection; coin of certain countries.

escuela, f. school.

escuela nocturna, night school.

escuela por correspondencia, correspondence school.

escuerzo, m. toad.

esculpir, v. carve, sculpture.

escultor -ra, n. sculptor.

escultura, f. sculpture.

escupidera, f. cuspidor.

escupir, v. spit.

escurridero, m. drain board.

escurridor, m. colander, strainer.

escurrir, v. drain off; wring out.

escurrirse, v. slip; sneak away.

ese, esa, dem. a. that.

ése, ésa, dem. pron. that (one).

esencia, f. essence; perfume.

esencial, a. essential.

esencialmente, adv. essentially.

esfera, f. sphere.

esfinge, f. sphinx.

esforzar, v. strengthen.

esforzarse, v. strive, exert oneself.

esfuerzo, m. effort, attempt; vigor.

esgrima, f. fencing.

esguince, m. sprain.

eslabón, m. link (of a chain).

eslabonar, v. link, join, connect.

eslavo -va, a. & n. Slavic; Slav.

esmalte, m. enamel, polish. **—esmaltar,** v.

esmerado, a. careful, thorough.

esmeralda, f. emerald.

esmerarse, v. take pains, do one's best.

esmeril, m. emery.

eso, dem. pron. that.

esófago, m. esophagus.

esotérico, a. esoteric.

espacial, a. spatial.

espacio, m. space. —espaciar, v.

espaciosidad, f. spaciousness.

espacioso, a. spacious.

espada, f. sword; spade (in cards).

espadarte, m. swordfish.

espaguetis, m.pl. spaghetti.

espalda, f. back.

espaldera, f. espalier.

espantar, v. frighten, scare; scare away.

espanto, m. fright.

espantoso, a. frightening, frightful.

España, f. Spain.

español -ola, a. & n. Spanish; Spaniard.

esparcir, v. scatter, disperse.

espárrago, m. asparagus.

espartano -na, n. & a. Spartan.

espasmo, m. spasm.

espasmódico, a. spasmodic.

espata, f. spathe.

espato, m. spar (mineral).

espátula, f. spatula.

especia, f. spice. —especiar, v.

especial, a. special, especial.

especialidad, f. specialty.

especialista, m. & f. specialist.

especialización, f. specialization.

especialmente, adv. especially.

especie, f. species; sort.

especiería, f. grocery store; spice store.

especiero -ra, n. spice dealer; spice box.

especificar, v. specify.

específico, a. specific.

espécimen, m. specimen.

especioso, a. neat; polished; specious.

espectacular, a. spectacular.

espectáculo, m. spectacle, show.

espectador -ra, n. spectator.

espectro, m. specter, ghost.

especulación, f. speculation.

especulador -ra, n. speculator.

especular, v. speculate.

especulativo, a. speculative.

espejo, m. mirror.

espelunca, f. dark cave, cavern.

espera, f. wait.

esperanza, f. hope, expectation.

esperar, v. hope; expect; wait, wait for, watch for.

espesar, v. thicken.

espeso, a. thick, dense, bushy.

espesor, m. thickness, density.

espía, m. & f. spy. —espiar, v.

espigón, m. bee sting.

espina, f. thorn.

espina dorsal, spine.

espinaca, f. spinach.

espinal, a. spinal.

espinazo, m. backbone.

espineta, f. spinet.

espino, m. briar.

espinoso, a. spiny, thorny.

espión, m. spy.

espionaje, m. espionage.

espiral, a. & m. spiral.

espirar, v. expire; breathe, exhale.

espíritu, m. spirit.

espiritual, a. spiritual.

espiritualidad, f. spirituality.

espiritualmente, adv. spiritually.

espita, f. faucet, spigot.

espléndido, a. splendid.

esplendor, m. splendor.

espolear, v. incite, urge on.

espoleta, f. wishbone.

esponja, f. sponge.

esponjoso, a. spongy.

esponsales, m.pl. engagement, betrothal.

esponsalicio, a. nuptial.

espontáneamente, adv. spontaneously.

espontaneidad, f. spontaneity.

espontáneo, a. spontaneous.

espora, f. spore.

esporádico, a. sporadic.

esposa, f. wife.

esposar, v. shackle; handcuff.

esposo, m. husband.

espuela, f. spur. —espolear, v.

espuma, f. foam. —espumar, v.

espumadera, f. whisk; skimmer.

espumajear, v. foam at the mouth.

espumajo, m. foam.

espumar, v. foam, froth; skim.

espumoso, a. foamy; sparkling (wine).

espurio, a. spurious.

esputar, v. spit, expectorate.

esputo, m. spit, saliva.

esquela, f. note.

esqueleto, m. skeleton.

esquema, m. scheme; diagram.

esquero, m. leather sack, leather pouch.

esquiar, v. ski.

esquiciar, v. outline, sketch.

esquicio, m. rough sketch, rough outline.

esquife, m. skiff.

esquilar, v. fleece, shear.

esquilmo, m. harvest.

esquimal, n. & a. Eskimo.

esquina, f. corner.

esquivar, v. evade, shun.

estabilidad, f. stability.

estable, a. stable.

establecedor, m. founder, originator.

establecer, v. establish, set up.

establecimiento, m. establishment.

establero, m. groom.

establo, m. stable.

estaca, f. stake.

estación, f. station; season.

estación de servicio, service station.

estación de trabajo, work station.

estacionamiento, m. parking; parking lot; parking space.

estacionar, v. station; park (a vehicle).

estacionario, a. stationary.

estadista, m. & f. statesman.

estadística, f. statistics.

estadístico, a. statistical.

estado, m. state; condition; status.

Estados Unidos, *m.pl.* United States.

estafa, *f.* swindle, fake. —**estafar,** *v.*

estafeta, *f.* post office.

estagnación, *f.* stagnation.

estallar, *v.* explode; burst; break out.

estallido, *m.* crash; crack; explosion.

estampa, *f.* stamp. —**estampar,** *v.*

estampado, *m.* printed cotton cloth.

estampida, *f.* stampede.

estampilla, *f.* (postage) stamp.

estancado, *a.* stagnant.

estancar, *v.* stanch, stop, check.

estancia, *f.* stay; (S.A.) small farm.

estanciero -ra, *n.* small farmer.

estandarte, *m.* banner.

estanque, *m.* pool; pond.

estante, *m.* shelf.

estaño, *m.* tin. —**estañar,** *v.*

estar, *v.* be; stand; look.

estática, *f.* static.

estático, *a.* static.

estatua, *f.* statue.

estatura, *f.* stature.

estatuto, *m.* statute, law.

este, *m.* east.

este, esta, *dem. a.* this.

éste, ésta, *dem. pron.* this (one); the latter.

estelar, *a.* stellar.

estenografía, *f.* stenography.

estenógrafo -fa, *n.* stenographer.

estera, *f.* mat, matting.

estereofónico, *a.* stereophonic.

estéril, *a.* barren; sterile.

esterilidad, *f.* sterility, fruitlessness.

esterilizar, *v.* sterilize.

esternón, *m.* breastbone.

estética, *f.* esthetics.

estético, *a.* esthetic.

estetoscopio, *m.* stethoscope.

estibador, *m.* stevedore.

estiércol, *m.* dung, manure.

estigma, *m.* stigma; disgrace.

estilarse, *v.* be in fashion, be in vogue.

estilo, *m.* style; sort.

estilográfica, *f.* (fountain) pen.

estima, *f.* esteem.

estimable, *a.* estimable, worthy.

estimación, *f.* estimation.

estimar, *v.* esteem; value; estimate; gauge.

estimular, *v.* stimulate.

estímulo, *m.* stimulus.

estío, *m.* summer.

estipulación, *f.* stipulation.

estipular, *v.* stipulate.

estirar, *v.* stretch.

estirpe, *m.* stock, lineage.

esto, *dem. pron.* this.

estocada, *f.* stab, thrust.

estofado, *m.* stew. —**estofar,** *v.*

estoicismo, *m.* stoicism.

estoico, *n. & a.* stoic.

estómago, *m.* stomach.

estorbar, *v.* bother, hinder, interfere with.

estorbo, *m.* hindrance.

estornudo, *m.* sneeze. —**estornudar,** *v.*

estrabismo, *m.* strabismus.

estrago, *m.* devastation, havoc.

estrangulación, *f.* strangulation.

estrangular, *v.* strangle.

estraperlista, *m. & f.* black marketeer.

estraperlo, *m.* black market.

estratagema, *f.* stratagem.

estrategia, *f.* strategy.

estratégico, *a.* strategic.

estrato, *m.* stratum.

estrechar, *v.* tighten; narrow.

estrechez, *f.* narrowness; tightness.

estrecho, 1. *a.* narrow, tight. **2.** *m.* strait.

estregar, *v.* scour, scrub.

estrella, *f.* star.

estrellamar, *f.* starfish.

estrellar, *v.* shatter, smash.

estremecimiento, *m.* shudder. —**estremecerse,** *v.*

estrenar, *v.* wear for the first time; open (a play).

estreno, *m.* debut, first performance.

estrenuo, *a.* strenuous.

estreñido -da, *a.* constipated.

estreñimiento, *m.* constipation.

estreñir, *v.* constipate.

estrépito, *m.* din.

estreptococo, *m.* streptococcus.

estría, *f.* groove.

estribillo, *m.* refrain.

estribo, *m.* stirrup.

estribor, *m.* starboard.

estrictamente, *adv.* strictly.

estrictez, *f.* strictness.

estricto, *a.* strict.

estrofa, *f.* stanza.

estropajo, *m.* mop.

estropear, *v.* cripple, damage, spoil.

estructura, *f.* structure.

estructural, *a.* structural.

estruendo, *m.* din, clatter.

estuario, *m.* estuary.

estuco, *m.* stucco.

estudiante -ta, *n.* student.

estudiar, *v.* study.

estudio, *m.* study; studio.

estudioso, *a.* studious.

estufa, *f.* stove.

estufa de aire, fan heater.

estulto, *a.* foolish.

estupendo, *a.* wonderful, grand, fine.

estupidez, *f.* stupidity.

estúpido, *a.* stupid.

estupor, *m.* stupor.

estuque, *m.* stucco.

esturión, *m.* sturgeon.

etapa, *f.* stage.

éter, *m.* ether.

etéreo, *a.* ethereal.

eternal, *a.* eternal.

eternidad, *f.* eternity.

eterno, *a.* eternal.

ética, *f.* ethics.

ético, *a.* ethical.

etimología, *f.* etymology.

etiqueta, *f.* etiquette; tag, label.

étnico, *a.* ethnic.

etrusco -ca, *n. & a.* Etruscan.

eucaristía, *f.* Eucharist.

eufemismo, *m.* euphemism.

eufonía, *f.* euphony.

Europa, *f.* Europe.

europeo -pea, *a. & n.* European.

eutanasia, *f.* euthanasia.

evacuación, *f.* evacuation.

evacuar, *v.* evacuate.

evadir, v. evade.
evangélico, a. evangelical.
evangelio, m. gospel.
evangelista, m. evangelist.
evaporación, f. evaporation.
evaporarse, v. evaporate.
evasión, f. evasion.
evasivamente, adv. evasively.
evasivo, a. evasive.
evento, m. event, occurrence.
eventual, a. eventual.
eventualidad, f. eventuality.
evicción, f. eviction.
evidencia, f. evidence.
evidenciar, v. prove, show.
evidente, a. evident.
evitación, f. avoidance.
evitar, v. avoid, shun.
evocación, f. evocation.
evocar, v. evoke.
evolución, f. evolution.
exacerbar, v. irritate deeply; exacerbate.
exactamente, adv. exactly.
exactitud, f. precision, accuracy.
exacto, a. exact, accurate.
exageración, f. exaggeration.
exagerar, v. exaggerate.
exaltación, f. exaltation.
exaltamiento, m. exaltation.
exaltar, v. exalt.
examen, m. test, examination.
examen de ingreso, entrance examination.
examinar, v. test, examine.
exánime, a. spiritless, weak.
exasperación, f. exasperation.
exasperar, v. exasperate.
excavación, f. excavation.
excavar, v. excavate.
exceder, v. exceed, surpass; outrun.
excelencia, f. excellence.
excelente, a. excellent.
excéntrico, a. eccentric.
excepción, f. exception.
excepcional, a. exceptional.
excepto, prep. except, except for.
exceptuar, v. except.
excesivamente, adv. excessively.
excesivo, a. excessive.

exceso, m. excess.
excitabilidad, f. excitability.
excitación, f. excitement.
excitar, v. excite.
exclamación, f. exclamation.
exclamar, v. exclaim.
excluir, v. exclude, bar, shut out.
exclusión, f. exclusion.
exclusivamente, adv. exclusively.
exclusivo, a. exclusive.
excomulgar, v. excommunicate.
excomunión, f. excommunication.
excreción, f. excretion.
excremento, m. excrement.
excretar, v. excrete.
exculpar, v. exonerate.
excursión, f. excursion.
excursionista, m. & f. excursionist; tourist.
excusa, f. excuse. —excusar, v.
excusado, m. toilet.
excusarse, v. apologize.
exención, f. exemption.
exento, a. exempt. —exentar, v.
exhalación, f. exhalation.
exhalar, v. exhale, breathe out.
exhausto, a. exhausted.
exhibición, f. exhibit, exhibition.
exhibir, v. exhibit, display.
exhortación, f. exhortation.
exhortar, v. exhort, admonish.
exhumación, f. exhumation.
exhumar, v. exhume.
exigencia, f. requirement, demand.
exigente, a. exacting, demanding.
exigir, v. require, exact, demand.
eximir, v. exempt.
existencia, f. existence; (econ.) supply.
existente, a. existent.
existir, v. exist.
éxito, m. success.
éxodo, m. exodus.
exoneración, f. exoneration.
exonerar, v. exonerate, acquit.

exorar, v. beg, implore.
exorbitancia, f. exorbitance.
exorbitante, a. exorbitant.
exorcismo, m. exorcism.
exornar, v. adorn, decorate.
exótico, a. exotic.
expansibilidad, f. expansibility.
expansión, f. expansion.
expansivo, a. expansive; effusive.
expatriación, f. expatriation.
expatriar, v. expatriate.
expectación, f. expectation.
expectorar, v. expectorate.
expedición, f. expedition.
expediente, m. expedient; means.
expedir, v. send off, ship; expedite.
expeditivo, a. speedy, prompt.
expedito, a. speedy, prompt.
expeler, v. expel, eject.
expendedor -ra, n. dealer.
expender, v. expend.
expensas, f.pl. expenses, costs.
experiencia, f. experience.
experimentado, a. experienced.
experimental, a. experimental.
experimentar, v. experience.
experimento, m. experiment.
expertamente, adv. expertly.
experto -ta, a. & n. expert.
expiación, f. atonement.
expiar, v. atone for.
expiración, f. expiration.
expirar, v. expire.
explanación, f. explanation.
explanar, v. make level.
expletivo, n. & a. expletive.
explicable, a. explicable.
explicación, f. explanation.
explicar, v. explain.
explicativo, a. explanatory.
explícitamente, adv. explicitly.
explícito, adj. explicit.
exploración, f. exploration.
explorador -ra, n. explorer; scout.
explorar, v. explore; scout.
exploratorio, a. exploratory.
explosión, f. explosion; outburst.

explosivo, *a.* & *m.* explosive.
explotación, *f.* exploitation.
explotar, *v.* exploit.
exponer, *v.* expose; set forth.
exportación, *f.* exportation; export.
exportador -ra, *n.* exporter.
exportar, *v.* export.
exposición, *f.* exhibit; exposition; exposure.
expósito -ta, *n.* foundling; orphan.
expresado, *a.* aforesaid.
expresamente, *adv.* clearly, explicitly.
expresar, *v.* express.
expresión, *f.* expression.
expresivo, *a.* expressive; affectionate.
expreso, *a.* & *m.* express.
exprimidera de naranjas, *f.* orange squeezer.
exprimir, *v.* squeeze.
expropiación, *f.* expropriation.
expropiar, *v.* expropriate.
expulsar, *v.* expel, eject; evict.
expulsión, *f.* expulsion.
expurgación, *f.* expurgation.
expurgar, *v.* expurgate.
exquisitamente, *adv.* exquisitely.
exquisito, *a.* exquisite.

éxtasis, *m.* ecstasy.
extemporáneo, *a.* extemporaneous, impromptu.
extender, *v.* extend; spread; widen; stretch.
extensamente, *adv.* extensively.
extensión, *f.* extension, spread, expanse.
extenso, *a.* extensive, widespread.
extenuación, *f.* weakening; emaciation.
extenuar, *v.* extenuate.
exterior, *a.* & *m.* exterior; foreign.
exterminar, *v.* exterminate.
exterminio, *m.* extermination, ruin.
extinción, *f.* extinction.
extinguir, *v.* extinguish.
extinto, *a.* extinct.
extintor, *m.* fire extinguisher.
extirpar, *v.* eradicate.
extorsión, *f.* extortion.
extra, *n.* extra.
extracción, *f.* extraction.
extractar, *v.* summarize.
extracto, *m.* extract; summary.
extradición, *f.* extradition.
extraer, *v.* extract.
extranjero -ra, **1.** *a.* foreign. **2.** *n.* foreigner; stranger.

extrañar, *v.* surprise; miss.
extraño, *a.* strange, queer.
extraordinariamente, *adv.* extra-ordinarily.
extraordinario, *a.* extraordinary.
extravagancia, *f.* extravagance.
extravagante, *a.* extravagant.
extraviado, *a.* lost, misplaced.
extraviarse, *v.* stray, get lost.
extravío, *m.* misplacement; aberration, deviation.
extremadamente, *adv.* extremely.
extremado, *a.* extreme.
extremaunción, *f.* extreme unction.
extremidad, *f.* extremity.
extremista, *n.* & *a.* extremist.
extremo, *a.* & *m.* extreme, end.
extrínseco, *a.* extrinsic.
exuberancia, *f.* exuberance.
exuberante, *a.* exuberant.
exudación, *f.* exudation.
exudar, *v.* exude, ooze.
exultación, *f.* exultation.
eyaculación, *f.* ejaculation.
eyacular, *v.* ejaculate.
eyección, *f.* ejection.
eyectar, *v.* eject.

F

fábrica, *f.* factory.
fabricación, *f.* manufacture, manufacturing.
fabricante, *m.* & *f.* manufacturer, maker.
fabricar, *v.* manufacture, make.
fabril, *a.* manufacturing, industrial.
fábula, *f.* fable, myth.
fabuloso, *a.* fabulous.
facción, *f.* faction, party; (*pl.*) features.
faccioso, *a.* factious.
fachada, *f.* façade, front.
fácil, *a.* easy.
facilidad, *f.* facility, ease.
facilitar, *v.* facilitate, make easy.
fácilmente, *adv.* easily.

facsímil, *m.* facsimile.
factible, *a.* feasible.
factor, *m.* factor.
factótum, *m.* factotum; jack of all trades.
factura, *f.* invoice, bill.
facturar, *v.* bill; check (baggage).
facultad, *f.* faculty; ability.
facultativo, *a.* optional.
faena, *f.* task; work.
faisán, *m.* pheasant.
faja, *f.* band; sash; zone.
falacia, *f.* fallacy; deceitfulness.
falda, *f.* skirt; lap.
falibilidad, *f.* fallibility.
falla, *f.* failure; fault.
fallar, *v.* fail.
fallecer, *v.* pass away, die.

fallo, *m.* verdict; shortcoming.
falsear, *v.* falsify, counterfeit; forge.
falsedad, *f.* falsehood; lie; falseness.
falsificación, *f.* falsification; forgery.
falsificar, *v.* falsify, counterfeit, forge.
falso, *a.* false; wrong.
falta, *f.* error, mistake; fault; lack. hacer f., to be lacking, to be necessary. sin f., without fail.
faltar, *v.* be lacking, be missing; be absent.
faltriquera, *f.* pocket.
fama, *f.* fame; reputation; glory.

familia, *f.* family; household.

familiar, *a.* familiar; domestic; (of) family.

familiaridad, *f.* familiarity, intimacy.

familiarizar, *v.* familiarize, acquaint.

famoso, *a.* famous.

fanal, *m.* lighthouse; lantern, lamp.

fanático -ca, *a. & n.* fanatic.

fanatismo, *m.* fanaticism.

fanfarria, *f.* bluster. **—fanfarrear,** *v.*

fango, *m.* mud.

fantasía, *f.* fantasy; fancy, whim.

fantasma, *m.* phantom; ghost.

fantástico, *a.* fantastic.

faquín, *m.* porter.

faquir, *m.* fakir.

farallón, *m.* cliff.

Faraón, *m.* Pharaoh.

fardel, *m.* bag; package.

fardo, *m.* bundle.

farináceo, *a.* farinaceous.

faringe, *f.* pharynx.

fariseo, *m.* pharisee, hypocrite.

farmacéutico -ca, 1. *a.* pharmaceutical. **2.** *n.* pharmacist.

farmacia, *f.* pharmacy.

faro, *m.* beacon; lighthouse; headlight.

farol, *m.* lantern; (street) light, street lamp.

farra, *f.* spree.

fárrago, *m.* medley; hodgepodge.

farsa, *f.* farce.

fascinación, *f.* fascination.

fascinar, *v.* fascinate, bewitch.

fase, *f.* phase.

fastidiar, *v.* disgust; irk, annoy.

fastidio, *m.* disgust; annoyance.

fastidioso, *a.* annoying; tedious.

fatal, *a.* fatal.

fatalidad, *f.* fate; calamity, bad luck.

fatalismo, *m.* fatalism.

fatalista, *n. & a.* fatalist.

fatiga, *f.* fatigue. **—fatigar,** *v.*

fauna, *f.* fauna.

fauno, *m.* faun.

favor, *m.* favor; behalf. **por f.,** please.

¡Favor! Puh-lease!

favorable, *a.* favorable.

favorablemente, *adv.* favorably.

favorecer, *v.* favor; flatter.

favoritismo, *m.* favoritism.

favorito -ta, *a. & n.* favorite.

faz, *f.* face.

fe, *f.* faith.

fealdad, *f.* ugliness, homeliness.

febrero, *m.* February.

febril, *a.* feverish.

fecha, *f.* date. **—fechar,** *v.*

fecha de caducidad, expiration date. .

fécula, *f.* starch.

fecundar, *v.* fertilize.

fecundidad, *f.* fecundity, fertility.

fecundo, *a.* fecund, fertile.

federación, *f.* federation.

federal, *a.* federal.

felicidad, *f.* happiness; bliss.

felicitación, *f.* congratulation.

felicitar, *v.* congratulate.

feligrés -esa, *n.* parishioner.

feliz, *a.* happy; fortunate.

felón, *m.* felon.

felonía, *f.* felony.

felpa, *f.* plush.

felpudo, *m.* doormat.

femenino, *a.* feminine.

feminismo, *m.* feminism.

feminista, *m. & f.* feminist.

fenecer, *v.* conclude; die.

fénix, *m.* phoenix; model.

fenomenal, *a.* phenomenal.

fenómeno, *m.* phenomenon.

feo, *a.* ugly, homely.

feracidad, *f.* feracity, fertility.

feraz, *a.* fertile, fruitful; copious.

feria, *f.* fair; market.

feriado, *a.* **día f.,** holiday.

fermentación, *f.* fermentation.

fermento, *m.* ferment. **—fermentar,** *v.*

ferocidad, *f.* ferocity, fierceness.

feroz, *a.* ferocious, fierce.

férreo, *a.* of iron.

ferrería, *f.* ironworks.

ferretería, *f.* hardware; hardware store.

ferrocarril, *m.* railroad.

fértil, *a.* fertile.

fertilidad, *f.* fertility.

fertilizar, *v.* fertilize.

férvido, *a.* fervid, ardent.

ferviente, *a.* fervent.

fervor, *m.* fervor, zeal.

fervoroso, *a.* zealous, eager.

festejar, *v.* entertain, fete.

festejo, *m.* feast.

festín, *m.* feast.

festividad, *f.* festivity.

festivo, *a.* festive.

fétido, *adj.* fetid.

feudal, *a.* feudal.

feudo, *m.* fief; manor.

fiado, *adj.* on trust, on credit.

fiambrera, *f.* lunch box.

fianza, *f.* bail.

fiar, *v.* trust, sell on credit; give credit.

fiarse de, *v.* trust (in), rely on.

fiasco, *m.* fiasco.

fibra, *f.* fiber; vigor.

fibroso, *a.* fibrous.

ficción, *f.* fiction.

ficha, *f.* slip, index card; chip.

ficticio, *a.* fictitious.

fidedigno, *a.* trustworthy.

fideicomisario -ria, *n.* trustee.

fideicomiso, *m.* trust.

fidelidad, *f.* fidelity.

fideo, *m.* noodle.

fiebre, *f.* fever.

fiebre del heno, hayfever.

fiel, *a.* faithful.

fieltro, *m.* felt.

fiera, *f.* wild animal.

fiereza, *f.* fierceness, wildness.

fiero, *a.* fierce; wild.

fiesta, *f.* festival, feast; party.

figura, *f.* figure. **—figurar,** *v.*

figurarse, *v.* imagine.

figurón, *m.* dummy.

fijar, *v.* fix; set, establish; post.

fijarse en, *v.* notice.

fijeza, *f.* firmness.

fijo, *a.* fixed, stationary, permanent, set.

fila, *f.* row, rank, file, line.

filantropía, *f.* philanthropy.

filatelia, *f.* philately, stamp collecting.

filete, *m.* fillet; steak.

film, *m.* film. **—filmar,** *v.*

filo, *m.* (cutting) edge.

filón, *m.* vein (of ore).

filosofía, *f.* philosophy.

filosófico, *a.* philosophical.

filósofo -fa, *n.* philosopher.

filtro, *m.* filter. **—filtrar,** *v.*

fin, *m.* end, purpose, goal. **a f. de que,** in order that. **en f.,** in short. **por f.,** finally, at last.

final, 1. *a.* final. 2. *m.* end.

finalidad, *f.* finality.

finalmente, *adv.* at last.

financiero -ra, 1. *a.* financial. 2. *n.* financier.

finca, *f.* real estate; estate; farm.

finés -esa, *a.* & *n.* Finnish; Finn.

fineza, *f.* courtesy, politeness; fineness.

fingimiento, *m.* pretense.

fingir, *v.* feign, pretend.

fino, *a.* fine; polite, courteous.

firma, *f.* signature; (com.) firm.

firmamento, *m.* firmament, heavens.

firmar, *v.* sign.

firme, *a.* firm, fast, steady, sound.

firmemente, *adv.* firmly.

firmeza, *f.* firmness.

fisco, *m.* exchequer, treasury.

física, *f.* physics.

físico -ca, *a.* & *n.* physical; physicist.

fisiología, *f.* physiology.

fláccido, *a.* flaccid, soft.

flaco, *a.* thin, gaunt.

flagelación, *f.* flagellation.

flagelar, *v.* flagellate, whip.

flagrancia, *f.* flagrancy.

flagrante, *a.* flagrant.

flama, *f.* flame; ardor, zeal.

flamante, *a.* flaming.

flamenco, *m.* flamingo.

flan, *m.* custard.

flanco, *m.* side; (mil.) flank.

flanquear, *v.* flank.

flaqueza, *f.* thinness; weakness.

flauta, *f.* flute.

flautín, *m.* piccolo.

flautista, *m.* & *f.* flutist, piper.

flecha, *f.* arrow.

flechazo, *m.* love at first sight.

flechero -ra, *n.* archer.

fleco, *m.* fringe; flounce.

flema, *f.* phlegm.

flemático, *a.* phlegmatic.

flete, *m.* freight. **—fletar,** *v.*

flexibilidad, *f.* flexibility.

flexible, *a.* flexible, pliable.

flirtear, *v.* flirt.

flojo, *a.* limp; loose, flabby, slack.

flor, *f.* flower; compliment.

flora, *f.* flora.

floral, *a.* floral.

florecer, *v.* flower, bloom; flourish.

floreo, *m.* flourish.

florero, *m.* flower pot; vase.

floresta, *f.* forest.

florido, *a.* flowery; flowering.

florista, *m.* & *f.* florist.

flota, *f.* fleet.

flotante, *a.* floating.

flotar, *v.* float.

flotilla, *f.* flotilla, fleet.

fluctuación, *f.* fluctuation.

fluctuar, *v.* fluctuate.

fluente, *a.* fluent; flowing.

fluidez, *f.* fluency.

flúido, *a.* & *m.* fluid, liquid.

fluir, *v.* flow.

flujo, *m.* flow, flux.

fluor, *m.* fluorine.

fluorescencia, *f.* fluorescence.

fluorescente, *a.* fluorescent.

fobia, *f.* phobia.

foca, *f.* seal.

foco, *m.* focus, center; floodlight.

fogata, *f.* bonfire.

fogón, *m.* hearth, fireplace.

fogosidad, *f.* vehemence, ardor.

fogoso, *a.* vehement, ardent.

folclore, *m.* folklore.

follaje, *m.* foliage.

folleto, *m.* pamphlet, booklet.

fomentar, *v.* develop, promote, further, foster.

fomento, *m.* fomentation.

fonda, *f.* eating house, inn.

fondo, *m.* bottom; back (part); background; (pl.) funds; finances. **a f.,** thoroughly.

fonética, *f.* phonetics.

fonético, *a.* phonetic.

fonógrafo, *m.* phonograph.

fontanero -era, *n.* plumber.

forastero -ra, 1. *a.* foreign, exotic. 2. *n.* stranger.

forjar, *v.* forge.

forma, *f.* form, shape. **—formar,** *v.*

formación, *f.* formation.

formal, *a.* formal.

formaldehido, *m.* formaldehyde.

formalidad, *f.* formality.

formalizar, *v.* finalize; formulate.

formidable, *a.* formidable.

formidablemente, *adv.* formidably.

formón, *m.* chisel.

fórmula, *f.* formula.

formular, *v.* formulate, draw up.

formulario, *m.* form.

foro, *m.* forum.

forraje, *m.* forage, fodder.

forrar, *v.* line.

forro, *m.* lining; condom.

fortalecer, *v.* fortify.

fortaleza, *f.* fort, fortress; fortitude.

fortificación, *f.* fortification.

fortitud, *f.* fortitude.

fortuitamente, *adv.* fortuitously.

fortuito, *a.* fortuitous.

fortuna, *f.* fortune; luck.

forúnculo, *m.* boil.

forzar, *v.* force, compel, coerce.

forzosamente, *adv.* compulsorily; forcibly.

forzoso, *a.* compulsory; necessary. **paro f.,** unemployment.

forzudo, *a.* powerful, vigorous.

fosa, *f.* grave; pit.

fósforo, *m.* match; phosphorus.

fósil, *m.* fossil.

foso, *m.* ditch, trench; moat.

fotocopia, *f.* photocopy.

fotocopiadora, *f.* photocopier.

fotografía, *f.* photograph; photography. **—fotografiar,** *v.*

frac, *m.* dress coat.

fracasar, *v.* fail.

fracaso, *m.* failure.

fracción, *f.* fraction.

fractura, *f.* fracture, break.

fragancia, *f.* fragrance; perfume; aroma.

fragante, *a.* fragrant.

frágil, *a.* fragile, breakable.

fragilidad, *f.* fragility.

fragmentario, *a.* fragmentary.

fragmento, *m.* fragment, bit.

fragor, *m.* noise, clamor.

fragoso, *a.* noisy.

fragua, *f.* forge. **—fraguar,** *v.*

fraile, *m.* monk.

frambuesa, *f.* raspberry.

francamente, *adv.* frankly, candidly.

francés, -esa, *a.* & *n.* French; Frenchman, Frenchwoman.

Francia, *f.* France.

franco, *a.* frank.

franela, *f.* flannel.

frangible, *a.* breakable.

franqueo, *m.* postage.

franqueza, *f.* frankness.

franquicia, *f.* franchise.

frasco, *m.* flask, bottle.

frase, *f.* phrase; sentence.

fraseología, *f.* phraseology; style.

fraternal, *a.* fraternal, brotherly.

fraternidad, *f.* fraternity, brotherhood.

fraude, *m.* fraud.

fraudulento, *a.* fraudulent.

frazada, *f.* blanket.

frecuencia, *f.* frequency.

frecuente, *a.* frequent.

frecuentemente, *adv.* frequently, often.

fregadero, *m.* sink.

fregadura, *f.* scouring, scrubbing.

fregar, *v.* scour, scrub, mop.

fregona, *f.* mop.

freír, *v.* fry.

fréjol, *m.* kidney bean.

frenesí, *m.* frenzy.

frenazo, *m.* sudden braking, slamming on the brakes.

frenéticamente, *adv.* frantically.

frenético, *a.* frantic, frenzied.

freno, *m.* brake. **—frenar,** *v.*

freno de auxilio, emergency brake.

freno de mano, hand brake.

frente, 1. *f.* forehead. **2.** *m.* front. **en f., al f.,** opposite, across. **f. a,** in front of.

fresa, *f.* strawberry.

fresca, *f.* fresh, cool air.

fresco, *a.* fresh; cool; crisp.

frescura, *f.* coolness, freshness.

fresno, *m.* ash tree.

fresquería, *f.* soda fountain.

friabilidad, *f.* brittleness.

friable, *a.* brittle.

frialdad, *f.* coldness.

fríamente, *adv.* coldly; coolly.

frícandó, *m.* fricandeau.

fricar, *v.* rub together.

fricción, *f.* friction.

friccionar, *v.* rub.

friega, *f.* friction; massage.

frigidez, *f.* frigidity.

frígido, *a.* frigid.

frijol, *m.* bean.

frío, *a.* & *n.* cold. **tener f.,** to be cold, feel cold. **hacer f.,** to be cold (weather).

friolento, friolero, *a.* chilly; sensitive to cold.

friolera, *f.* trifle, trinket.

friso, *m.* frieze.

fritillas, *f.pl.* fritters.

frito, *a.* fried.

fritura, *f.* fritter.

frívolamente, *adv.* frivolously.

frivolidad, *f.* frivolity.

frívolo, *a.* frivolous.

frondoso, *a.* leafy.

frontera, *f.* frontier; border.

frotar, *v.* rub.

fructífero, *a.* fruitful.

fructificar, *v.* bear fruit.

fructuosamente, *adv.* fruitfully.

fructuoso, *a.* fruitful.

frugal, *a.* frugal; thrifty.

frugalidad, *f.* frugality; thrift.

frugalmente, *adv.* frugally, thriftily.

fruncir, *v.* gather, contract. **f. el entrecejo,** frown.

fruslería, *f.* trinket.

frustrar, *v.* frustrate, thwart.

fruta, *f.* fruit.

frutería, *f.* fruit store.

fruto, *m.* fruit; product; profit.

fucsia, *f.* fuchsia.

fuego, *m.* fire.

fuelle, *m.* bellows.

fuente, *f.* fountain; source; platter.

fuera, *adv.* without, outside.

fuero, *m.* statute.

fuerte, 1. *a.* strong; loud. **2.** *m.* fort.

fuertemente, *adv.* strongly; loudly.

fuerza, *f.* force, strength.

fuga, *f.* flight, escape.

fugarse, *v.* flee, escape.

fugaz, *a.* fugitive, passing.

fugitivo -va, *a.* & *n.* fugitive.

fulcro, *m.* fulcrum.

fulgor, *m.* gleam, glow. **—fulgurar,** *v.*

fulminante, *a.* explosive.

fumador -ra, *n.* smoker.

fumar, *v.* smoke.

fumigación, *f.* fumigation.

fumigador -ra, *n.* fumigator.

fumigar, *v.* fumigate.

fumoso, *a.* smoky.

función, *f.* function; performance, show.

funcionar, *v.* function; work, run.

funcionario -ria, *n.* official, functionary.

funda, *f.* case, sheath, slipcover.

fundación, *f.* foundation.

fundador -ra, *n.* founder.

fundamental, *a.* fundamental, basic.

fundamentalmente, *adv.* fundamentally.

fundamento, *m.* base, basis, foundation.
fundar, *v.* found, establish.
fundición, *f.* foundry; melting; meltdown.
fundir, *v.* fuse; smelt.
fúnebre, *a.* dismal.
funeral, *m.* funeral.
funeraria, *f.* funeral home, funeral parlor.
funestamente, *adv.* sadly.

fungo, *m.* fungus.
furente, *a.* furious, enraged.
furgoneta, *f.* van.
furia, *f.* fury.
furiosamente, *adv.* furiously.
furioso, *a.* furious.
furor, *m.* furor; fury.
furtivamente, *adv.* furtively.
furtivo, *a.* furtive, sly.
furúnculo, *m.* boil.
fusibilidad, *f.* fusibility.

fusible, *m.* fuse.
fusil, *m.* rifle, gun.
fusilar, *v.* shoot, execute.
fusión, *f.* fusion; merger.
fusionar, *v.* unite, fuse, merge.
fútbol, *m.* football, soccer.
fútil, *a.* trivial.
futilidad, *f.* triviality.
futuro, *a. & m.* future.
futurología, *f.* futurology.

G

gabán, *m.* overcoat.
gabardina, *f.* raincoat.
gabinete, *m.* closet; cabinet; study.
gacela, *f.* gazelle.
gaceta, *f.* gazette, newspaper.
gacetilla, *f.* personal news section of a newspaper.
gaélico, *a.* Gaelic.
gafas, *f.pl.* eyeglasses.
gaguear, *v.* stutter, stammer.
gaita, *f.* bagpipes.
gaje, *m.* salary; fee.
gala, *f.* gala, ceremony; (*pl.*) regalia. **tener a g.,** be proud of.
galán, *m.* gallant.
galano, *a.* stylishly dressed; elegant.
galante, *a.* gallant.
galantería, *f.* gallantry, compliment.
galápago, *m.* fresh-water turtle.
galardón, *m.* prize; reward.
gáleo, *m.* swordfish.
galera, *f.* wagon; shed; galley.
galería, *f.* gallery, (theat.) balcony.
galés -esa, *a. & n.* Welsh; Welshman, Welshwoman.
galgo, *m.* greyhound.
galillo, *m.* uvula.
galimatías, *m.* gibberish.
gallardete, *m.* pennant.
galleta, *f.* cracker.
gallina, *f.* hen.
gallinero, *m.* chicken coop.
gallo, *m.* rooster.
galocha, *f.* galosh.
galón, *m.* gallon; (mil.) stripe.

galope, *m.* gallop. **—galopar,** *v.*
gamba, *f.* prawn.
gamberro -ra, *n.* hooligan.
gambito, *m.* gambit.
gamuza, *f.* chamois.
gana, *f.* desire, wish, mind (to). **de buena g.,** willingly. **tener ganas de,** to feel like.
ganado, *m.* cattle.
ganador -ra, *n.* winner.
ganancia, *f.* gain, profit; (*pl.*) earnings.
ganapán, *m.* drudge.
ganar, *v.* earn; win; beat.
ganchillo, *m.* crochet work.
gancho, *m.* hook, hanger, clip, hairpin.
gandul -la, *n.* idler, tramp, hobo.
ganga, *f.* bargain.
gangrena, *f.* gangrene.
gansarón, *m.* gosling.
ganso, *m.* goose.
garabato, *m.* hook; scrawl, scribble.
garaje, *m.* garage.
garantía, *f.* guarantee; collateral, security.
garantizar, *v.* guarantee, secure, pledge.
garbanzo, *m.* chickpea.
garbo, *m.* grace.
garboso, *a.* graceful, sprightly.
gardenia, *f.* gardenia.
garfa, *f.* claw, talon.
garganta, *f.* throat.
gárgara, *f.* gargle. **—gargarizar,** *v.*
garita, *f.* sentry box.
garito, *m.* gambling house.

garlopa, *f.* carpenter's plane.
garra, *f.* claw.
garrafa, *f.* decanter, carafe.
garrideza, *f.* elegance, handsomeness.
garrido, *a.* elegant, handsome.
garrote, *m.* club, cudgel.
garrotillo, *m.* croup.
garrudo, *a.* powerful, brawny.
garza, *f.* heron.
gas, *m.* gas.
gasa, *f.* gauze.
gaseosa, *f.* carbonated water.
gaseoso, *a.* gaseous.
gasolina, *f.* gasoline.
gasolinera, *f.* gas station.
gastar, *v.* spend; use up; wear out; waste.
gastritis, *f.* gastritis.
gastrómano, *m.* glutton.
gastrónomo -ma, *n.* gourmet, epicure, gastronome.
gatear, *v.* creep.
gatillo, *m.* trigger.
gato -ta, *n.* cat.
gaucho, *m.* Argentine cowboy.
gaveta, *f.* drawer.
gavilla, *f.* sheaf.
gaviota, *f.* seagull.
gayo, *a.* merry, gay.
gazapera, *f.* rabbit warren.
gazapo, *m.* rabbit.
gazmoñada, *f.* prudishness.
gazmoño, *m.* prude.
gaznate, *m.* windpipe.
gelatina, *f.* gelatine.
gemelo -la, *n.* twin.
gemelos, *m.pl.* cuff links; opera glasses; **-as,** twins.

gemido, *m.* moan, groan, wail. **—gemir,** *v.*

genciana, *f.* gentian.

genealogía, *f.* genealogy, pedigree.

generación, *f.* generation.

generador, *m.* generator.

general, *a. & m.* general.

generalidad, *f.* generality.

generalización, *f.* generalization.

generalizar, *v.* generalize.

generalmente, *adv.* generally.

género, *m.* gender; kind; *(pl.)* goods, material.

generosidad, *f.* generosity.

generoso, *a.* generous.

génesis, *f.* genesis.

genético, *a.* genetic.

genial, *a.* genial; brilliant.

genio, *m.* genius; temper; disposition.

genitivo, *m.* genitive.

genocidio, *m.* genocide.

gente, *f.* people, folk.

gentil, *a.* gracious; graceful.

gentileza, *f.* grace, graciousness.

gentío, *m.* mob, crowd.

genuino, *a.* genuine.

geografía, *f.* geography.

geográfico, *a.* geographical.

geométrico, *a.* geometric.

geranio, *m.* geranium.

gerencia, *f.* management.

gerente, *m. & f.* manager, director.

germen, *m.* germ.

germinar, *v.* germinate.

gerundio, *m.* gerund.

gesticulación, *f.* gesticulation.

gesticular, *v.* gesticulate, gesture.

gestión, *f.* conduct; effort; action.

gesto, *m.* gesture, facial expression.

gigante, *a. & n.* gigantic, giant.

gigantesco, *a.* gigantic, huge.

gimnasio, *m.* gymnasium.

gimnástica, *f.* gymnastics.

gimotear, *v.* whine.

ginebra, *f.* gin.

ginecólogo -ga, *n.* gynecologist.

gira, *f.* tour, trip.

girado -da, *n.* (com.) drawee.

girador -ra, *n.* (com.) drawer.

girar, *v.* revolve, turn, spin, whirl.

giratorio, *a.* rotary, revolving.

giro, *m.* whirl, turn, spin; (com.) draft. **g. postal,** money order.

gitano -na, *a. & n.* Gypsy.

glacial, *a.* glacial, icy.

glaciar, *m.* glacier.

gladiador, *m.* gladiator.

glándula, *f.* gland.

glándula endocrina, endocrine gland.

glándula pituitaria, pituitary gland.

glándula prostática, prostate gland.

glasé, *m.* glacé.

glicerina, *f.* glycerine.

globo, *m.* globe; balloon.

gloria, *f.* glory.

glorieta, *f.* bower.

glorificación, *f.* glorification.

glorificar, *v.* glorify.

glorioso, *a.* glorious.

glosa, *f.* gloss. **—glosar,** *v.*

glosario, *m.* glossary.

glotón -ona, *a. & n.* gluttonous; glutton.

glucosa, *f.* glucose.

gluten, *m.* gluten; glue.

gobernación, *f.* government.

gobernador -ra, *n.* governor.

gobernalle, *m.* rudder, tiller, helm.

gobernante, *m. & f.* ruler.

gobernar, *v.* govern.

gobierno, *m.* government.

goce, *m.* enjoyment.

gola, *f.* throat.

golf, *m.* golf.

golfista, *m. & f.* golfer.

golfo, *m.* gulf.

gollete, *m.* upper portion of one's throat.

golondrina, *f.* swallow.

golosina, *f.* delicacy.

goloso, *a.* sweet-toothed.

golpe, *m.* blow, stroke. **de g.,** suddenly.

golpear, *v.* strike, beat, pound.

goma, *f.* rubber; gum; glue; eraser.

góndola, *f.* gondola.

gordo, *a.* fat.

gordura, *f.* fatness.

gorila, *m.* gorilla.

gorja, *f.* gorge.

gorjeo, *m.* warble, chirp. **— gorjear,** *v.*

gorrión, *m.* sparrow.

gorro, *m.* cap.

gota, *f.* drop (of liquid).

gotear, *v.* drip, leak.

goteo, *m.* leak.

gotera, *f.* leak; gutter.

gótico, *a.* Gothic.

gozar, *v.* enjoy.

gozne, *m.* hinge.

gozo, *m.* enjoyment, delight, joy.

gozoso, *a.* joyful, joyous.

grabado, 1. *m.* engraving, cut, print. **2.** *a.* recorded.

grabador, *m.* engraver.

grabadora, *f.* tape recorder.

grabar, *v.* engrave; record.

gracia, *f.* grace; wit, charm. **hacer g.,** to amuse, strike as funny. **tener g.,** to be funny, to be witty.

gracias, *f.pl.* thanks, thank you.

gracioso, *a.* witty, funny.

grada, *f.* step.

gradación, *f.* gradation.

grado, *m.* grade; rank; degree.

graduado -da, *n.* graduate.

gradual, *a.* gradual.

graduar, *v.* grade; graduate.

gráfico, *a.* graphic, vivid.

grafito, *m.* graphite.

grajo, *m.* jackdaw.

gramática, *f.* grammar.

gramo, *m.* gram.

gran, grande, *a.* big, large; great.

granada, *f.* grenade; pomegranate.

granar, *v.* seed.

grandes almacenes, *m.pl.* department store.

grandeza, *f.* greatness.

grandiosidad, *f.* grandeur.

grandioso, *a.* grand, magnificent.

grandor, *m.* size.

granero, *m.* barn; granary.

granito, *m.* granite.

granizada, *f.* hailstorm.

granizo, *m.* hail. **—granizar,** *v.*

granja, *f.* grange; farm; farmhouse.

granjear, v. earn, gain; get.
granjero -era, n. farmer.
grano, m. grain; kernel.
granuja, m. waif, urchin.
grapa, f. clamp, clip.
grapadora, f. stapler.
grasa, f. grease, fat.
grasiento, a. greasy.
gratificación, f. gratification; reward; tip.
gratificar, v. gratify; reward; tip.
gratis, adv. gratis, free.
gratitud, f. gratitude.
grato, a. grateful; pleasant.
gratuito, a. gratuitous; free.
gravamen, m. tax; burden; obligation.
grave, a. grave, serious, severe.
gravedad, f. gravity, seriousness.
gravitación, f. gravitation.
gravitar, v. gravitate.
gravoso, a. burdensome.
graznido, m. croak. —**graznar,** v.
Grecia, f. Greece.
greco -ca, a. & n. Greek.
greda, f. clay.
gresca, f. revelry; quarrel.
griego -ga, a. & n. Greek.
grieta, f. opening; crevice; crack.
grifo, m. faucet.
grillo, m. cricket.
grima, f. fright.
gringo -ga, n. foreigner (usually North American).
gripa, gripe, f. grippe.
gris, a. gray.

grito, m. shout, scream, cry. —**gritar,** v.
grosella, f. currant.
grosería, f. grossness; coarseness.
grosero, a. coarse, vulgar, discourteous.
grotesco, a. grotesque.
grúa, f. crane; tow truck.
gruesa, f. gross.
grueso, 1. a. bulky; stout; coarse, thick. **2.** m. bulk.
grulla, f. crane.
gruñido, m. growl, snarl, mutter. —**gruñir,** v.
grupo, m. group, party.
gruta, f. cavern.
guacamol, guacamole, m. avocado sauce.
guadaña, f. scythe. —**guadañar,** v.
guagua, f. (S.A.) baby; (Carib.) bus.
gualdo, m. yellow, golden.
guano, m. guano (fertilizer).
guante, m. glove.
guantera, f. glove compartment.
guapo, a. handsome.
guarda, m. or f. guard.
guardabarros, m. fender.
guardacostas, m. revenue ship.
guardameta, m. & f. goalkeeper.
guardar, v. keep, store, put away; guard.
guardarropa, f. coat room.
guardarse de, v. beware of, avoid.
guardia, 1. f. guard; watch. **2.** m. policeman.

guardián -na, n. guardian, keeper, watchman.
guardilla, f. attic.
guarida, f. den.
guarismo, m. number, figure.
guarnecer, v. adorn.
guarnición, f. garrison; trimming.
guasa, f. joke, jest.
guayaba, f. guava.
gubernativo, a. governmental.
guerra, f. war.
guerrero -ra, n. warrior.
guía, 1. m. & f. guide. **2.** f. guidebook, directory.
guiar, v. guide; steer, drive.
guija, f. pebble.
guillotina, f. guillotine.
guindar, v. hang.
guinga, f. gingham.
guiñada, f., **guiño,** m. wink. —**guiñar,** v.
guión, m. dash, hyphen; script.
guirnalda, f. garland, wreath.
guisa, f. guise, manner.
guisado, m. stew.
guisante, m. pea.
guisar, v. cook.
guita, f. twine.
guitarra, f. guitar.
guitarrista, m. & f. guitarist.
gula, f. gluttony.
gurú, m. guru.
gusano, m. worm, caterpillar.
gustar, v. please; taste.
gusto, m. pleasure; taste; liking.
gustoso, a. pleasant; tasteful.
gutural, a. guttural.

H

haba, f. bean.
habanera, f. Cuban dance melody.
haber, v. have. **h. de,** be to, be supposed to.
haberes, m.pl. property; worldly goods.
habichuela, f. bean.
hábil, a. skillful; capable; clever.
habilidad, f. ability; skill; talent.

habilidoso, a. able, skillful, talented.
habilitado -da, n. paymaster.
habilitar, v. qualify; supply, equip.
hábilmente, adv. ably.
habitación, f. dwelling; room. **h. individual,** single room.
habitante, m. & f. inhabitant.
habitar, v. inhabit; dwell.
hábito, m. habit; custom.

habitual, a. habitual.
habituar, v. accustom, habituate.
habla, f. speech.
hablador, a. talkative.
hablar, v. talk, speak.
haca, f. pony.
hacedor, m. maker.
hacendado -da, n. hacienda owner; farmer.
hacendoso, a. industrious.

hacer, *v.* do; make. **hace dos años,** etc., two years ago, etc.

hacerse, *v.* become, get to be.

hacha, *f.* ax, hatchet.

hacia, *prep.* toward.

hacienda, *f.* property; estate; ranch; farm; (govt.) treasury.

hada, *f.* fairy.

hado, *m.* fate.

halagar, *v.* flatter.

halar, *v.* haul, pull.

halcón, *m.* hawk, falcon.

haleche, *m.* anchovy.

hallado, *a.* found. **bien h.,** welcome. **mal h.,** uneasy.

hallar, *v.* find, locate.

hallarse, *v.* be located; happen to be.

hallazgo, *m.* find, thing found.

hamaca, *f.* hammock.

hambre, *f.* hunger. **tener h., estar con h.,** to be hungry.

hambrear, *v.* hunger; starve.

hambriento, *a.* starving, hungry.

hamburguesa, *f.* beefburger, hamburger.

haragán -na, *n.* idler, lazy person.

haraganear, *v.* loiter.

harapo, *m.* rag, tatter.

haraposo, *a.* ragged, shabby.

harén, *m.* harem.

harina, *f.* flour, meal.

harnero, *m.* sieve.

hartar, *v.* satiate.

harto, *a.* stuffed; fed up.

hartura, *f.* superabundance, glut.

hasta, 1. *prep.* until, till; as far as, up to. **h. luego,** good-bye, so long. **2.** *adv.* even.

hastío, *m.* distaste, loathing.

hato, *m.* herd.

hay, *v.* there is, there are. **h. que,** it is necessary to. **no h. de qué,** you're welcome, don't mention it.

haya, *f.* beech tree.

haz, *f.* bundle, sheaf; face.

hazaña, *f.* deed; exploit, feat.

hebdomadario, *a.* weekly.

hebilla, *f.* buckle.

hebra, *f.* thread, string.

hebreo -rea, *a.* & *n.* Hebrew.

hechicero -ra, *n.* wizard, witch.

hechizar, *v.* bewitch.

hechizo, *m.* spell.

hecho, *m.* fact; act; deed.

hechura, *f.* workmanship, make.

hediondez, *f.* stench.

hégira, *f.* hegira.

helada, *f.* frost.

heladería, *f.* ice-cream parlor.

helado, *m.* ice cream.

helar, *v.* freeze.

helecho, *m.* fern.

hélice, *f.* propeller; helix.

helicóptero, *m.* helicopter.

helio, *m.* helium.

hembra, *f.* female.

hemisferio, *m.* hemisphere.

hemoglobina, *f.* hemoglobin.

hemorragia, *f.* hemorrhage.

hemorragia nasal, nosebleed.

henchir, *v.* stuff.

hendedura, *f.* crevice, crack.

heno, *m.* hay.

hepática, *f.* liverwort.

hepatitis, *f.* hepatitis.

heraldo, *m.* herald.

herbáceo, *a.* herbaceous.

herbívoro, *a.* herbivorous.

heredar, *v.* inherit.

heredero -ra, *n.* heir; successor.

hereditario, *a.* hereditary.

hereje, *m.* & *f.* heretic.

herejía, *f.* heresy.

herencia, *f.* inheritance; heritage.

herético, *a.* heretical.

herida, *f.* wound, injury.

herir, *v.* wound, injure.

hermafrodita, *a.* & *n.* hermaphrodite.

hermana, *f.* sister.

hermano, *m.* brother.

hermético, *a.* airtight.

hermoso, *a.* beautiful, handsome.

hermosura, *f.* beauty.

hernia, *f.* hernia, rupture.

héroe, *m.* hero.

heroico, *a.* heroic.

heroína, *f.* heroine.

heroísmo, *m.* heroism.

herradura, *f.* horseshoe.

herramienta, *f.* tool; implement.

herrería, *f.* blacksmith's shop.

herrero, *m.* blacksmith.

herrumbre, *f.* rust.

hertzio, *m.* hertz.

hervir, *v.* boil.

hesitación, *f.* hesitation.

heterogéneo, *a.* heterogeneous.

heterosexual, *a.* heterosexual.

hexagonal, *a.* hexagonal.

hexágono, *m.* hexagon.

hez, *f.* dregs, sediment.

híbrido -da, *n.* & *a.* hybrid.

hidalgo -ga, *a.* & *n.* noble.

hidalguía, *f.* nobility; generosity.

hidráulico, *a.* hydraulic.

hidroavión, *m.* seaplane, hydroplane.

hidrofobia, *f.* rabies.

hidrógeno, *m.* hydrogen.

hidropesía, *f.* dropsy.

hiedra, *f.* ivy.

hiel, *f.* gall.

hielo, *m.* ice.

hiena, *f.* hyena.

hierba, *f.* grass; herb; marijuana.

hierbabuena, *f.* mint.

hierro, *m.* iron.

hígado, *m.* liver.

higiene, *f.* hygiene.

higiénico, *a.* sanitary, hygienic.

higo, *m.* fig.

higuera, *f.* fig tree.

hija, *f.* daughter.

hija adoptiva, adopted daughter.

hijastro -tra, *n.* stepchild.

hijo, *m.* son.

hijo adoptivo, *m.* adopted child, adopted son.

hila, *f.* line.

hilandero -ra, *n.* spinner.

hilar, *v.* spin.

hilera, *f.* row, line, tier.

hilo, *m.* thread; string; wire; linen.

himno, *m.* hymn.

hincar, *v.* drive, thrust; sink into.

hincarse, *v.* kneel.

hinchar, v. swell.
hindú, n. & a. Hindu.
hinojo, m. knee.
hipermercado, m. hypermarket.
hipnótico, a. hypnotic.
hipnotismo, m. hypnotism.
hipnotista, m. & f. hypnotist.
hipnotizar, v. hypnotize.
hipo, m. hiccough.
hipocresía, f. hypocrisy.
hipócrita, a. & n. hypocritical; hypocrite.
hipódromo, m. race track.
hipoteca, f. mortgage. —
  hipotecar, v.
hipótesis, f. hypothesis.
hirsuto, a. hairy, hirsute.
hispano, a. Hispanic, Spanish American.
Hispanoamérica, f. Spanish Amer-ica.
hispanoamericano -na, a. & n. Spanish American.
histerectomía, f. hysterectomy.
histeria, f. hysteria.
histérico, a. hysterical.
historia, f. history; story.
historiador -ra, n. historian.
histórico, a. historic, historical.
histrión, m. actor.
hocico, m. snout, muzzle.
hogar, m. hearth; home.
hoguera, f. bonfire, blaze.
hoja, f. leaf; sheet (of paper); pane; blade.
hoja de cálculo, spreadsheet.
hoja de inscripción, entry blank.
hoja de pedidos, order blank.
hoja informativa, newsletter.
hojalata, f. tin.
hojalatero -ra, n. tinsmith.
hojear, v. scan, skim through.
hola, interj. hello.
Holanda, f. Holland, Netherlands.
holandés -esa, a. & n. Dutch; Hollander.
holganza, f. leisure; diversion.
holgazán -ana, 1. a. idle, lazy. **2.** m. idler, loiterer, tramp.
holgazanear, v. idle, loiter.

hollín, m. soot.
holografía, f. holography.
holograma, m. hologram.
hombre, m. man.
hombría, f. manliness.
hombro, m. shoulder.
homenaje, m. homage.
homeópata, m. homeopath.
homicidio, m. homicide.
homilía, f. homily.
homosexual, a. homosexual, gay.
honda, f. sling.
hondo, a. deep.
hondonada, f. ravine.
hondura, f. depth.
honestidad, f. modesty, unpretentiousness.
honesto, a. honest; pure; just.
hongo, m. fungus; mushroom.
honor, m. honor.
honorable, a. honorable.
honorario, 1. a. honorary.
  2. m. honorarium, fee.
honorífico, a. honorary.
honra, f. honor. **—honrar,** v.
honradez, f. honesty.
honrado, a. honest, honorable.
hora, f. hour; time (of day).
horadar, v. perforate.
hora punta, rush hour.
horario, m. timetable, schedule.
horca, f. gallows; pitchfork.
horda, f. horde.
horizontal, a. horizontal.
horizonte, m. horizon.
hormiga, f. ant.
hormiguear, v. itch.
hormiguero, m. ant hill.
hornero -ra, n. baker.
hornillo, m. stove.
horno, m. oven; kiln.
horóscopo, m. horoscope.
horrendo, a. dreadful, horrendous.
horrible, a. horrible, hideous, awful.
hórrido, a. horrid.
horror, m. horror.
horrorizar, v. horrify.
horroroso, a. horrible, frightful.
hortelano, m. horticulturist.
hospedaje, m. lodging.

hospedar, v. give or take lodgings.
hospital, m. hospital.
hospitalario, a. hospitable.
hospitalidad, f. hospitality.
hospitalmente, adv. hospitably.
hostia, f. host.
hostil, a. hostile.
hostilidad, f. hostility.
hotel, m. hotel.
hoy, adv. today. **h. día, h. en día,** nowadays.
hoya, f. dale, valley.
hoyo, m. pit, hole.
hoyuelo, m. dimple.
hoz, f. sickle.
hucha, f. chest, money box; savings.
hueco, 1. a. hollow, empty.
  2. m. hole, hollow.
huelga, f. strike.
huelgista, m. & f. striker.
huella, f. track, trace; footprint.
huérfano -na, a. & n. orphan.
huero, a. empty.
huerta, f. (vegetable) garden.
huerto, m. orchard.
hueso, m. bone; fruit pit.
huésped, m. & f. guest.
huesudo, a. bony.
huevo, m. egg.
huída, f. flight, escape.
huir, v. flee.
hule, m. oilcloth.
humanidad, f. humanity, mankind; humaneness.
humanista, m. & f. humanist.
humanitario, a. humane.
humano, a. human; humane.
humareda, f. dense cloud of smoke.
humedad, f. humidity, moisture, dampness.
humedecer, v. moisten, dampen.
húmedo, a. humid, moist, damp.
humildad, f. humility, meekness.
humilde, a. humble, meek.
humillación, f. humiliation.
humillar, v. humiliate.
humo, m. smoke; (pl.) airs, affectation.
humor, m. humor, mood.

humorista, *m. & f.* humorist.
hundimiento, *m.* collapse.
hundir, *v.* sink; collapse.
húngaro -ra, *a. & n.* Hungarian.
Hungría, *f.* Hungary.

huracán, *m.* hurricane.
huraño, *a.* shy, bashful.
hurgar, *v.* stir.
hurón, *m.* ferret.
hurtadillas, *f.pl.* **a h.,** on the sly.

hurtador -ra, *n.* thief.
hurtar, *v.* steal, rob of; hide.
hurtarse, *v.* hide; withdraw.
husmear, *v.* scent, smell.
huso, *m.* spindle; bobbin.
huso horario, time zone.

I

ibérico, *a.* Iberian.
iberoamericano -na, *a. & n.* Latin American.
ida, *f.* departure; trip out. **i. y vuelta,** round trip.
idea, *f.* idea.
ideal, *a. & m.* ideal.
idealismo, *m.* idealism.
idealista, *m. & f.* idealist.
idear, *v.* plan, conceive.
idéntico, *a.* identical.
identidad, *f.* identity; identification.
identificar, *v.* identify.
idilio, *m.* idyll.
idioma, *m.* language.
idiota, *a. & n.* idiotic; idiot.
idiotismo, *m.* idiom; idiocy.
idolatrar, *v.* idolize, adore.
ídolo, *m.* idol.
idóneo, *a.* suitable, fit, apt.
iglesia, *f.* church.
ignición, *f.* ignition.
ignominia, *f.* ignominy, shame.
ignominioso, *a.* ignominious, shameful.
ignorancia, *f.* ignorance.
ignorante, *a.* ignorant.
ignorar, *v.* be ignorant of, not know.
ignoto, *a.* unknown.
igual, 1. *a.* equal; the same; *(pl.)* alike. **2.** *m.* equal.
igualar, *v.* equal; equalize; match.
igualdad, *f.* equality; sameness.
ijada, *f.* flank (of an animal).
ilegal, *a.* illegal.
ilegítimo, *a.* illegitimate.
ileso, *a.* unharmed.
ilícito, *a.* illicit, unlawful.
iluminación, *f.* illumination.
iluminar, *v.* illuminate.
ilusión, *f.* illusion.
ilusión de óptica, optical illusion.

ilusorio, *a.* illusive.
ilustración, *f.* illustration; learning.
ilustrador -ra, *n.* illustrator.
ilustrar, *v.* illustrate.
ilustre, *a.* illustrious, honorable, distinguished.
imagen, *f.* image.
imaginación, *f.* imagination.
imaginar, *v.* imagine.
imaginario, *a.* imaginary.
imaginativo, *a.* imaginative.
imán, *m.* magnet; imam.
imbécil, *a. & n.* imbecile; stupid, foolish; fool.
imbuir, *v.* imbue, instil.
imitación, *f.* imitation.
imitador -ra, *n.* imitator.
imitar, *v.* imitate.
impaciencia, *f.* impatience.
impaciente, *a.* impatient.
impar, *a.* unequal, uneven, odd.
imparcial, *a.* impartial.
impasible, *a.* impassive, unmoved.
impávido, *adj.* fearless, intrepid.
impedimento, *m.* impediment, obstacle.
impedir, *v.* impede, hinder, stop, obstruct.
impeler, *v.* impel; incite.
impensado, *a.* unexpected.
imperar, *v.* reign; prevail.
imperativo, *a.* imperative.
imperceptible, *a.* imperceptible.
imperdible, *n.* safety pin.
imperecedero, *a.* imperishable.
imperfecto, *a.* imperfect, faulty.
imperial, *a.* imperial.
imperialismo, *m.* imperialism.
impericia, *f.* inexperience.
imperio, *m.* empire.

imperioso, *a.* imperious, domineering.
impermeable, 1. *a.* waterproof. **2.** *m.* raincoat.
impersonal, *a.* impersonal.
impertinencia, *f.* impertinence.
ímpetu, *m.* impulse; impetus.
impetuoso, *a.* impetuous.
impiedad, *f.* impiety.
impío, *a.* impious.
implacable, *a.* implacable, unrelenting.
implicar, *v.* implicate, involve.
implorar, *v.* implore.
imponente, *a.* impressive.
imponer, *v.* impose.
impopular, *a.* unpopular.
importación, *f.* importation, importing.
importador -ra, *n.* importer.
importancia, *f.* importance.
importante, *a.* important.
importar, *v.* be important, matter; import.
importe, *m.* value; amount.
importunar, *v.* beg, importune.
imposibilidad, *f.* impossibility.
imposibilitado, *a.* helpless.
imposible, *a.* impossible.
imposición, *f.* imposition.
impostor -ra, *n.* imposter, faker.
impotencia, *f.* impotence.
impotente, *a.* impotent.
imprecar, *v.* curse.
impreciso, *adj.* inexact.
impregnar, *v.* impregnate.
imprenta, *f.* press; printing house.
imprescindible, *a.* essential.
impresión, *f.* impression.
impresionable, *a.* impressionable.

impresionar, v. impress.

impresor, m. printer.

imprevisión, f. oversight; thoughtlessness.

imprevisto, a. unexpected, unforeseen.

imprimir, v. print; imprint.

improbable, a. improbable.

improbo, a. dishonest.

improductivo, a. unproductive.

improperio, m. insult.

impropio, a. improper.

improvisación, f. improvisation.

improvisar, v. improvise.

improviso, a. unforeseen.

imprudencia, f. imprudence.

imprudente, a. imprudent, reckless.

impuesto, m. tax.

impuesto sobre la renta, income tax.

impulsar, v. prompt, impel.

impulsivo, a. impulsive.

impulso, m. impulse.

impureza, f. impurity.

impuro, a. impure.

imputación, f. imputation.

imputar, v. impute, attribute.

inaccesible, a. inaccessible.

inacción, f. inaction; inactivity.

inaceptable, a. unacceptable.

inactivo, a. inactive; sluggish.

inadecuado, a. inadequate.

inadvertencia, f. oversight.

inadvertido, a. inadvertent, careless; unnoticed.

inagotable, a. inexhaustible.

inalterado, a. unchanged.

inanición, f. starvation.

inanimado, adj. inanimate.

inapetencia, f. lack of appetite.

inaplicable, a. inapplicable; unfit.

inaudito, a. unheard of.

inauguración, f. inauguration.

inaugurar, v. inaugurate, open.

incandescente, a. incandescent.

incansable, a. tireless.

incapacidad, f. incapacity.

incapacitar, v. incapacitate.

incapaz, a. incapable.

incauto, a. unwary.

incendiar, v. set on fire.

incendio, m. fire; conflagration.

incertidumbre, f. uncertainty, suspense.

incesante, a. continual, incessant.

incidente, m. incident, event.

incienso, m. incense.

incierto, a. uncertain, doubtful.

incinerar, v. incinerate; cremate.

incisión, f. incision, cut.

incitamiento, m. incitement, motivation.

incitar, v. incite, instigate.

incivil, a. impolite, rude.

inclemencia, f. inclemency.

inclemente, a. inclement, merciless.

inclinación, f. inclination, bent; slope.

inclinar, v. incline; influence.

inclinarse, v. slope; lean, bend over; bow.

incluir, v. include; enclose.

inclusivo, a. inclusive.

incluso, prep. including.

incógnito, a. unknown.

incoherente, a. incoherent.

incombustible, a. fireproof.

incomible, a. inedible.

incomodar, v. disturb, bother, inconvenience.

incomodidad, f. inconvenience.

incómodo, m. uncomfortable; cumbersome; inconvenient.

incomparable, a. incomparable.

incompatible, a. incompatible.

incompetencia, f. incompetence.

incompetente, a. incompetent.

incompleto, a. incomplete.

incondicional, a. unconditional.

inconexo, a. incoherent; unconnected.

incongruente, a. incongruous.

inconsciencia, f. unconsciousness.

inconsciente, a. unconscious.

inconsecuencia, f. inconsistency.

inconsecuente, a. inconsistent.

inconsiderado, a. inconsiderate.

inconstancia, f. changeableness.

inconstante, a. changeable.

inconveniencia, f. inconvenience; unsuitability.

inconveniente, 1. a. unsuitable. **2.** m. disadvantage; objection.

incorporar, v. incorporate, embody.

incorporarse, v. sit up.

incorrecto, a. incorrect, wrong.

incredulidad, f. incredulity.

incrédulo, a. incredulous.

increíble, a. incredible.

incremento, m. increase.

incubadora, f. incubator.

incubar, v. hatch.

inculto, a. uncultivated.

incumplimento de contrato, m. breach of contract.

incurable, a. incurable.

incurrir, v. incur.

indagación, f. investigation, inquiry.

indagador -ra, n. investigator.

indagar, v. investigate, inquire into.

indebido, a. undue.

indecencia, f. indecency.

indecente, a. indecent.

indeciso, a. undecided.

indefenso, a. defenseless.

indefinido, a. indefinite; undefined.

indeleble, a. indelible.

indemnización de despido, f. severance pay.

indemnizar, v. indemnify.

independencia, f. independence.

independiente, a. independent.

indesmallable, a. runproof.

India, f. India.

indicación, f. indication.

indicar, v. indicate, point out.

indicativo, a. & m. indicative.

índice, *m.* index; forefinger.

índice de materias, table of contents.

indicio, *m.* hint, clue.

indiferencia, *f.* indifference.

indiferente, *a.* indifferent.

indígena, *a. & n.* native.

indigente, *a.* indigent, poor.

indignación, *f.* indignation.

indignado, *a.* indignant, incensed.

indignar, *v.* incense.

indigno, *a.* unworthy.

indio -dia, *a. & n.* Indian.

indirecto, *a.* indirect.

indiscreción, *f.* indiscretion.

indiscreto, *a.* indiscreet.

indiscutible, *a.* unquestionable.

indispensable, *a.* indispensable.

indisposición, *f.* indisposition, ailment; reluctance.

indistinto, *a.* indistinct, unclear.

individual, *a.* individual.

individualidad, *f.* individuality.

individuo, *a. & m.* individual.

indócil, *a.* headstrong, unruly.

índole, *f.* nature, character, disposition.

indolencia, *f.* indolence.

indolente, *a.* indolent.

indómito, *a.* untamed, wild; unruly.

inducir, *v.* induce, persuade.

indudable, *a.* certain, indubitable.

indulgencia, *f.* indulgence.

indulgente, *a.* indulgent.

indultar, *v.* free; pardon.

industria, *f.* industry.

industrial, *a.* industrial.

industrioso, *a.* industrious.

inédito, *a.* unpublished.

ineficaz, *a.* inefficient.

inepto, *a.* incompetent.

inequívoco, *a.* unmistakable.

inercia, *f.* inertia.

inerte, *a.* inert.

inesperado, *a.* unexpected.

inestable, *a.* unstable.

inevitable, *a.* inevitable.

inexacto, *a.* inexact.

inexperto, *a.* unskilled.

inexplicable, *a.* inexplicable, unexplainable.

infalible, *a.* infallible.

infame, *a.* infamous, bad.

infamia, *f.* infamy.

infancia, *f.* infancy; childhood.

infante -ta, *n.* infant.

infantería, *f.* infantry.

infantil, *a.* infantile, childish.

infarto (de miocardio), *m.* heart attack.

infatigable, *a.* untiring.

infausto, *a.* unlucky.

infección, *f.* infection.

infeccioso, *a.* infectious.

infectar, *v.* infect.

infeliz, *a.* unhappy, miserable.

inferior, *a.* inferior; lower.

inferir, *v.* infer; inflict.

infernal, *a.* infernal.

infestar, *v.* infest.

infiel, *a.* unfaithful.

infierno, *m.* hell.

infiltrar, *v.* infiltrate.

infinidad, *f.* infinity.

infinito, *a.* infinite.

inflación, *f.* inflation.

inflamable, *a.* flammable.

inflamación, *f.* inflammation.

inflamar, *v.* inflame, set on fire.

inflar, *v.* inflate, pump up, puff up.

inflexible, *a.* inflexible, rigid.

inflexión, *f.* inflection.

infligir, *v.* inflict.

influencia, *f.* influence.

influenza, *f.* influenza, flu.

influir, *v.* influence, sway.

influyente, *a.* influential.

información, *f.* information.

informal, *a.* informal.

informar, *v.* inform; report.

informática, *f.* computer science; information technology.

informe, *m.* report; (*pl.*) information, data.

infortunio, *m.* misfortune.

infracción, *f.* violation.

infraestructura, *f.* infrastructure.

infrascrito -ta, *n.* signer, undersigned.

infringir, *v.* infringe, violate.

infructuoso, *a.* fruitless.

infundir, *v.* instil, inspire with.

ingeniería, *f.* engineering.

ingeniero -ra, *n.* engineer.

ingenio, *m.* wit; talent.

ingeniosidad, *f.* ingenuity.

ingenioso, *a.* witty; ingenious.

ingenuidad, *f.* candor; naïveté.

ingenuo, *a.* ingenuous, naïve, candid.

Inglaterra, *f.* England.

ingle, *f.* groin.

inglés -esa, *a. & n.* English; Englishman; Englishwoman.

ingratitud, *f.* ingratitude.

ingrato, *a.* ungrateful.

ingravidez, *f.* weightlessness.

ingrávido, *a.* weightless.

ingrediente, *m.* ingredient.

ingresar en, *v.* enter; join.

ingreso, *m.* entrance; (*pl.*) earnings, income.

inhábil, *a.* unskilled; incapable.

inhabilitar, *v.* disqualify.

inherente, *a.* inherent.

inhibir, *v.* inhibit.

inhumano, *a.* cruel, inhuman.

iniciador -ra, *n.* initiator.

inicial, *a.* initial.

iniciar, *v.* initiate, begin.

iniciativa, *f.* initiative.

inicuo, *a.* wicked.

iniquidad, *f.* iniquity; sin.

injuria, *f.* insult. —**injuriar,** *v.*

injusticia, *f.* injustice.

injusto, *a.* unjust, unfair.

inmaculado, *a.* immaculate; pure.

inmediato, *a.* immediate.

inmensidad, *f.* immensity.

inmenso, *a.* immense.

inmersión, *f.* immersion.

inmigración, *f.* immigration.

inmigrante, *a. & n.* immigrant.

inmigrar, *v.* immigrate.

inminente, *a.* imminent.

inmoderado, *a.* immoderate.
inmodesto, *a.* immodest.
inmoral, *a.* immoral.
inmoralidad, *f.* immorality.
inmortal, *a.* immortal.
inmortalidad, *f.* immortality.
inmóvil, *a.* immobile, motionless.
inmundicia, *f.* dirt, filth.
inmune, *a.* immune; exempt.
inmunidad, *f.* immunity.
innato, *a.* innate, inborn.
innecesario, *a.* unnecessary, needless.
innegable, *a.* undeniable.
innoble, *a.* ignoble.
innocuo, *a.* innocuous.
innovación, *f.* innovation.
innumerable, *a.* innumerable, countless.
inocencia, *f.* innocence.
inocentada, *f.* practical joke.
inocente, *a.* innocent.
inocular, *v.* inoculate.
inodoro, *m.* toilet.
inofensivo, *a.* inoffensive, harmless.
inolvidable, *a.* unforgettable.
inoportuno, *a.* inopportune.
inoxidable, *a.* stainless.
inquietante, *a.* disturbing, worrisome, worrying, upsetting.
inquietar, *v.* disturb, worry, trouble.
inquieto, *a.* anxious, uneasy, worried; restless.
inquietud, *f.* concern, anxiety, worry; restlessness.
inquilino -na, *n.* occupant, tenant.
inquirir, *v.* inquire into, investigate.
inquisición, *f.* inquisition, investigation.
insaciable, *a.* insatiable.
insalubre, *a.* unhealthy.
insano, *a.* insane.
inscribir, *v.* inscribe; record.
inscribirse, *v.* register, enroll.
inscripción, *f.* inscription; registration.
insecticida, *m.* insecticide.
insecto, *m.* insect.
inseguro, *a.* unsure, uncertain; insecure, unsafe.
insensato, *a.* stupid, senseless.

insensible, *a.* unfeeling, heartless.
inseparable, *a.* inseparable.
inserción, *f.* insertion.
insertar, *v.* insert.
inservible, *a.* useless.
insidioso, *a.* insidious, crafty.
insigne, *a.* famous, noted.
insignia, *f.* insignia, badge.
insignificante, *a.* insignificant, negligible.
insincero, *a.* insincere.
insinuación, *f.* insinuation; hint.
insinuar, *v.* insinuate, suggest, hint.
insipidez, *f.* insipidity.
insípido, *a.* insipid.
insistencia, *f.* insistence.
insistente, *a.* insistent.
insistir, *v.* insist.
insolación, *f.* sunstroke.
insolencia, *f.* insolence.
insolente, *a.* insolent.
insólito, *a.* unusual.
insolvente, *a.* insolvent.
insomnio, *m.* insomnia.
insonorizado, *a.* soundproof.
insonorizar, *v.* soundproof.
insoportable, *a.* unbearable.
inspección, *f.* inspection.
inspeccionar, *v.* inspect, examine.
inspector -ra, *n.* inspector.
inspiración, *f.* inspiration.
inspirar, *v.* inspire.
instalación, *f.* installation, fixture.
instalar, *v.* install, set up.
instantánea, *f.* snapshot.
instantáneo, *a.* instantaneous.
instante, *a. & m.* instant. **al i.,** at once.
instar, *v.* coax, urge.
instigar, *v.* instigate, urge.
instintivo, *a.* instinctive.
instinto, *m.* instinct. **por i.,** by instinct, instinctively.
institución, *f.* institution.
instituto, *m.* institute. **—instituir,** *v.*
institutriz, *f.* governess.
instrucción, *f.* instruction; education.
instructivo, *a.* instructive.
instructor -ra, *n.* instructor.
instruir, *v.* instruct, teach.
instrumento, *m.* instrument.

insuficiente, *a.* insufficient.
insufrible, *a.* intolerable.
insular, *a.* island, insular.
insulto, *m.* insult. **—insultar,** *v.*
insuperable, *a.* insuperable.
insurgente, *n. & a.* insurgent, rebel.
insurrección, *f.* insurrection, revolt.
insurrecto -ta, *a. & n.* insurgent.
intacto, *a.* intact.
integral, *a.* integral.
integridad, *f.* integrity; entirety.
íntegro, *a.* entire; upright.
intelecto, *m.* intellect.
intelectual, *a. & n.* intellectual.
inteligencia, *f.* intelligence.
inteligente, *a.* intelligent.
inteligible, *a.* intelligible.
intemperie, *f.* bad weather.
intención, *f.* intention.
intendente, *m.* manager.
intensidad, *f.* intensity.
intensificar, *v.* intensify.
intensivo, *a.* intensive.
intenso, *a.* intense.
intentar, *v.* attempt, try.
intento, *m.* intent; attempt.
intercambiable, *a.* interchangeable.
intercambiar, *v.* exchange, interchange.
interceptar, *v.* intercept.
intercesión, *f.* intercession.
interés, *m.* interest; concern; appeal.
interesante, *a.* interesting.
interesar, *v.* interest, appeal to.
interfaz, *f.* interface.
interferencia, *f.* interference.
interino, *a.* temporary.
interior, 1. *a.* interior, inner; **2.** *m.* interior.
interjección, *f.* interjection.
intermedio, 1. *a.* intermediate. **2.** *m.* intermediary; intermission.
interminable, *a.* interminable, endless.
intermisión, *f.* intermission.
intermitente, *a.* intermittent.
internacional, *a.* international.

internarse en, *v.* enter into, go into.

interno, *a.* internal.

interpelar, *v.* ask questions; implore.

interponer, *v.* interpose.

interpretación, *f.* interpretation.

interpretar, *v.* interpret; construe.

intérprete, *m. & f.* interpreter; performer.

interrogación, *f.* interrogation.

interrogar, *v.* question, interrogate.

interrogativo, *a.* interrogative.

interrumpir, *v.* interrupt.

interrupción, *f.* interruption.

intersección, *f.* intersection.

intervalo, *m.* interval.

intervención, *f.* intervention.

intervenir, *v.* intervene, interfere.

intestino, *m.* intestine.

intimación, *f.* intimation, hint.

intimar, *v.* suggest, hint.

intimidad, *f.* intimacy.

intimidar, *v.* intimidate.

íntimo -ma, *a. & n.* intimate.

intolerable, *a.* intolerable.

intolerancia, *f.* intolerance, bigotry.

intolerante, *a.* intolerant.

intoxicación alimenticia, *f.* food poisoning.

intranquilo, *a.* uneasy.

intravenoso, *a.* intravenous.

intrepidez, *f.* daring.

intrépido, *a.* intrepid.

intriga, *f.* intrigue, plot, scheme. **—intrigar,** *v.*

intrincado, *a.* intricate, involved; impenetrable.

introducción, *f.* introduction.

introducir, *v.* introduce.

intruso -sa, *n.* intruder.

intuición, *f.* intuition.

inundación, *f.* flood. **—inundar,** *v.*

inútil, *a.* useless.

invadir, *v.* invade.

inválido -da, *a. & n.* invalid.

invariable, *a.* constant.

invasión, *f.* invasion.

invasor -ra, *n.* invader.

invencible, *a.* invincible.

invención, *f.* invention.

inventar, *v.* invent; devise.

inventario, *m.* inventory.

inventivo, *a.* inventive.

invento, *m.* invention.

inventor -ra, *n.* inventor.

invernáculo, *m.* greenhouse.

invernal, *a.* wintry.

inverosímil, *a.* improbable, unlikely.

inversión, *f.* inversion; (com.) investment.

inverso, *a.* inverse, reverse.

inversor -ra, *n.* investor.

invertir, *v.* invert; reverse; (com.) invest.

investigación, *f.* investigation.

investigador -ra, *n.* investigator; researcher.

investigar, *v.* investigate.

invierno, *m.* winter.

invisible, *a.* invisible.

invitación, *f.* invitation.

invitar, *v.* invite.

invocar, *v.* invoke.

involuntario, *a.* involuntary.

inyección, *f.* injection.

inyectar, *v.* inject.

ir, *v.* go. **irse,** go away, leave.

ira, *f.* anger, ire.

iracundo, *a.* wrathful, irate.

iris, *m.* iris. **arco i.,** rainbow.

Irlanda, *f.* Ireland.

irlandés -esa, *a. & n.* Irish; Irishman, Irishwoman.

ironía, *f.* irony.

irónico, *a.* ironical.

irracional, *a.* irrational; insane.

irradiación, *f.* irradiation.

irradiar, *v.* radiate.

irrazonable, *a.* unreasonable.

irregular, *a.* irregular.

irreligioso, *a.* irreligious.

irremediable, *a.* irremediable, hopeless.

irresistible, *a.* irresistible.

irresoluto, *a.* irresolute, wavering.

irrespetuoso, *a.* disrespectful.

irreverencia, *f.* irreverence.

irreverente, *adj.* irreverent.

irrigación, *f.* irrigation.

irrigar, *v.* irrigate.

irritación, *f.* irritation.

irritar, *v.* irritate.

irrupción, *f.* raid, attack.

isla, *f.* island.

isleño -ña, *n.* islander.

israelita, *n. & a.* Israelite.

Italia, *f.* Italy.

italiano -na, *a. & n.* Italian.

itinerario, *m.* itinerary; timetable.

IVA, *m. abbrev.* **(impuesto sobre el valor añadido)** VAT (value-added tax).

izar, *v.* hoist.

izquierda, *f.* left (hand, side).

izquierdista, *n. & a.* leftist.

izquierdo, *a.* left.

J

jabalí, *m.* wild boar.

jabón, *m.* soap. **j. en polvo,** soap powder.

jabonar, *v.* soap.

jaca, *f.* nag.

jacinto, *m.* hyacinth.

jactancia, *f.* boast. **—jactarse,** *v.*

jactancioso, *a.* boastful.

jadear, *v.* pant, puff.

jaez, *m.* harness; kind.

jalar, *v.* haul, pull.

jalea, *f.* jelly.

jamás, *adv.* never, ever.

jamón, *m.* ham.

Japón, *m.* Japan.

japonés -esa, *a. & n.* Japanese.

jaqueca, *f.* headache.

jarabe, *m.* syrup.

jaranear, *v.* jest; carouse.

jardín, *m.* garden.

jardín de infancia, nursery school.

jardinero -ra, *n.* gardener.

jarra, *f.* jar; pitcher.

jarro, *m.* jug, pitcher.

jaspe, *m.* jasper.
jaula, *f.* cage; coop.
jauría, *f.* pack of hounds.
jazmín, *m.* jasmine.
jefatura, *f.* headquarters.
jefe -fa, *n.* chief, boss.
jefe de comedor, head waiter.
jefe de sala, maître d'.
jefe de taller, foreman.
Jehová, *m.* Jehovah.
jengibre, *m.* ginger.
jerez, *m.* sherry.
jerga, *f.* slang.
jergón, *m.* straw mattress.
jerigonza, *f.* jargon.
jeringa, *f.* syringe.
jeringar, *v.* inject; annoy.
jeroglífico, *m.* hieroglyph.
jersey, *m.* pullover; **j. de cuello alto,** turtleneck sweater.
Jerusalén, *m.* Jerusalem.
jesuita, *m.* Jesuit.
Jesús, *m.* Jesus.
jeta, *f.* snout.
jícara, *f.* cup.
jinete -ta, *n.* horseman.
jingoísmo, *m.* jingoism.
jingoísta, *n. & a.* jingoist.
jira, *f.* picnic; outing.
jirafa, *f.* giraffe.
jiu-jitsu, *m.* jujitsu.
jocundo, *a.* jovial.
jornada, *f.* journey; day's work.
jornal, *m.* day's wage.
jornalero, *m.* day laborer, workman.
joroba, *f.* hump.
jorobado, *a.* humpbacked.

joven, 1. *a.* young. **2.** *m. & f.* young person.
jovial, *a.* jovial, jolly.
jovialidad, *f.* joviality.
joya, *f.* jewel, gem.
joyas de fantasía, *f.pl.* costume jewelry.
joyelero, *m.* jewel box.
joyería, *f.* jewelry; jewelry store.
joyero, *m.* jeweler; jewel case.
juanete, *m.* bunion.
jubilación, *f.* retirement; pension.
jubilar, *v.* retire, pension.
jubileo, *m.* jubilee, public festivity.
júbilo, *m.* glee, rejoicing.
jubiloso, *a.* joyful, gay.
judaico, *a.* Jewish.
judaísmo, *m.* Judaism.
judía, *f.* bean, string bean.
judicial, *a.* judicial.
judío -día, *a. & n.* Jewish; Jew.
juego, *m.* game; play; gambling; set. **j. de damas,** checkers. **j. limpio,** fair play.
Juegos Olímpicos, *m.pl.* Olympic Games.
juerga, *f.* spree.
jueves, *m.* Thursday.
juez, *m.* judge.
jugador -ra, *n.* player.
jugar, *v.* play; gamble.
juglar, *m.* minstrel.
jugo, *m.* juice. **j. de naranja,** orange juice.
jugoso, *a.* juicy.
juguete, *m.* toy, plaything.

juguetear, *v.* trifle.
juguetón, *a.* playful.
juicio, *m.* sense, wisdom, judgment; sanity; trial.
juicioso, *a.* wise, judicious.
julio, *m.* July.
jumento, *m.* donkey.
junco, *m.* reed, rush.
jungla, *f.* jungle.
junio, *m.* June.
junípero, *m.* juniper.
junquillo, *m.* jonquil.
junta, *f.* board, council; joint, coupling.
juntamente, *adv.* jointly.
juntar, *v.* join; connect; assemble.
junto, *a.* together. **j. a,** next to.
juntura, *f.* joint, juncture.
jurado, *m.* jury.
juramento, *m.* oath.
jurar, *v.* swear.
jurisconsulto, *m.* jurist.
jurisdicción, *f.* jurisdiction; territory.
jurisprudencia, *f.* jurisprudence.
justa, *f.* joust. **—justar,** *v.*
justicia, *f.* justice, equity.
justiciero, *a.* just.
justificación, *f.* justification.
justificadamente, *adv.* justifiably.
justificar, *v.* justify, warrant.
justo, *a.* right; exact; just; righteous.
juvenil, *a.* youthful.
juventud, *f.* youth.
juzgado, *m.* court.
juzgar, *v.* judge, estimate.

K, L

káiser, *m.* kaiser.
karate, *m.* karate.
kepis, *m.* military cap.
kerosena, *f.* kerosene.
kilo, kilogramo, *m.* kilogram.
kilohercio, *m.* kilohertz.
kilolitro, *m.* kiloliter.
kilometraje, *m.* mileage.
kilómetro, *m.* kilometer.
kiosco, *m.* newsstand; pavilion.

la, 1. *art. & pron.* the; the one. **2.** *pron.* her, it, you; (*pl.*) them, you.
laberinto, *m.* labyrinth, maze.
labia, *f.* eloquence, fluency.
labio, *m.* lip.
labor, *f.* labor, work.
laborar, *v.* work; till.
laboratorio, *m.* laboratory.
laborioso, *a.* industrious.
labrador, *m.* farmer.

labranza, *f.* farming; farmland.
labrar, *v.* work, till.
labriego -ga, *n.* peasant.
laca, *f.* shellac.
lacio, *a.* withered; limp; straight.
lactar, *v.* nurse, suckle.
lácteo, *a.* milky.
ladear, *v.* tilt, tip; sway.
ladera, *f.* slope.
ladino, *a.* cunning, crafty.

lado, *m.* side. **al l. de,** beside. **de l.,** sideways.

ladra, *f.* barking. **—ladrar,** *v.*

ladrillo, *m.* brick.

ladrón -ona, *n.* thief, robber.

lagarto, *m.* lizard; (Mex.) alligator.

lago, *m.* lake.

lágrima, *f.* tear.

lagrimear, *v.* weep, cry.

laguna, *f.* lagoon; gap.

laico, *a.* lay.

laja, *f.* stone slab.

lamentable, *a.* lamentable.

lamentación, *f.* lamentation.

lamentar, *v.* lament; wail; regret, be sorry.

lamento, *m.* lament, wail.

lamer, *v.* lick; lap.

lámina, *f.* print, illustration.

lámpara, *f.* lamp.

lampiño, *a.* beardless.

lana, *f.* wool.

lanar, *a.* woolen.

lance, *m.* throw; episode; quarrel.

lancha, *f.* launch; small boat.

lanchón, *m.* barge.

langosta, *f.* lobster; locust.

langostino, *m.* king prawn.

languidecer, *v.* languish, pine.

languidez, *f.* languidness.

lánguido, *a.* languid.

lanza, *f.* lance, spear.

lanzada, *f.* thrust, throw.

lanzar, *v.* throw, hurl; launch.

lañar, *v.* cramp; clamp.

lapicero, *m.* mechanical pencil.

lápida, *f.* stone; tombstone.

lápiz, *m.* pencil; crayon.

lápiz de ojos, *m.* eyeliner.

lapso, *m.* lapse.

lardo, *m.* lard.

largar, *v.* loosen; free.

largo, 1. *a.* long. **a lo l. de,** along. **2.** *m.* length.

largometraje, *m.* feature film.

largor, *m.* length.

largueza, *f.* generosity; length.

largura, *f.* length.

laringe, *f.* larynx.

larva, *f.* larva.

lascivia, *f.* lasciviousness.

lascivo, *a.* lascivious.

láser, *m.* laser.

laso, *a.* weary.

lástima, *f.* pity. **ser l.,** to be a pity, to be too bad.

lastimar, *v.* hurt, injure.

lastimoso, *a.* pitiful.

lastre, *m.* ballast. **—lastrar,** *v.*

lata, *f.* tin can; tin (plate); (coll.) annoyance, bore.

latente, *a.* latent.

lateral, *a.* lateral, side.

latigazo, *m.* lash, whipping.

látigo, *m.* whip.

latín, *m.* Latin (language).

latino, *a.* Latin.

latir, *v.* beat, pulsate.

latitud, *f.* latitude.

latón, *m.* brass.

laúd, *m.* lute.

laudable, *a.* laudable.

láudano, *m.* laudanum.

laurel, *m.* laurel.

lava, *f.* lava.

lavabo, lavamanos, *m.* washroom, lavatory.

lavadora, *f.* washing machine.

lavandera, *f.* washerwoman, laundress.

lavandería, *f.* laundry; laundro-mat.

lavaplatos, *m.* dishwasher (machine); *m. & f.* dishwasher (person).

lavar, *v.* wash.

lavatorio, *m.* lavatory.

laya, *f.* spade. **—layar,** *v.*

lazar, *v.* lasso.

lazareto, *m.* isolation hospital; quarantine station.

lazo, *m.* tie, knot; bow; loop.

le, *pron.* him, her, you; (*pl.*) them, you.

leal, *a.* loyal.

lealtad, *f.* loyalty, allegiance.

lebrel, *m.* greyhound.

lección, *f.* lesson.

leche, *f.* milk.

lechería, *f.* dairy.

lechero, *m.* milkman.

lecho, *m.* bed; couch.

lechón, *m.* pig.

lechoso, *a.* milky.

lechuga, *f.* lettuce.

lechuza, *f.* owl.

lecito, *m.* yolk.

lector -ra, *n.* reader.

lectura, *f.* reading.

leer, *v.* read.

legación, *f.* legation.

legado, *m.* bequest.

legal, *a.* legal, lawful.

legalizar, *v.* legalize.

legar, *v.* bequeath, leave, will.

legible, *a.* legible.

legión, *f.* legion.

legislación, *f.* legislation.

legislador -ra, *n.* legislator.

legislar, *v.* legislate.

legislativo, *a.* legislative.

legislatura, *f.* legislature.

legítimo, *a.* legitimate.

lego, *m.* layman.

legua, *f.* league (measure).

legumbre, *f.* vegetable.

lejano, *a.* distant, far-off.

lejía, *f.* lye.

lejos, *adv.* far. **a lo l.,** in the distance.

lelo, *a.* stupid, foolish.

lema, *m.* theme; slogan.

lengua, *f.* tongue; language.

lenguado, *m.* sole, flounder.

lenguaje, *m.* speech; language.

lenguaraz, *a.* talkative.

lente, *m.* or *f.* lens. *m.pl.* eyeglasses.

lenteja, *f.* lentil.

lentilla, *f.* contact lens.

lentitud, *f.* slowness.

lento, *a.* slow.

leña, *f.* wood, firewood.

león, *m.* lion.

leopardo, *m.* leopard.

lerdo, *a.* dull-witted.

lesbiana, *f.* lesbian.

lesión, *f.* wound; damage.

letanía, *f.* litany.

letárgico, *a.* lethargic.

letargo, *m.* lethargy.

letra, *f.* letter (of alphabet); print; words (of a song).

letrado, 1. *a.* learned. **2.** *m.* lawyer.

letrero, *m.* sign, poster.

leva, *f.* (mil.) draft.

levadura, *f.* yeast, leavening, baking powder.

levantador, *m.* lifter; rebel, mutineer.

levantar, *v.* raise, lift.

levantarse, v. rise, get up; stand up.

levar, v. weigh (anchor).

leve, a. slight, light.

levita, f. frock coat.

léxico, m. lexicon, dictionary.

ley, f. law, statute.

leyenda, f. legend.

lezna, f. awl.

libación, f. libation.

libelo, m. libel.

libélula, f. dragonfly.

liberación, f. liberation, release.

liberal, a. liberal.

libertad, f. liberty, freedom.

libertador -ra, n. liberator.

libertar, v. free, liberate.

libertinaje, m. licentiousness.

libertino -na, n. libertine.

libídine, f. licentiousness; lust.

libidinoso, a. libidinous; lustful.

libra, f. pound.

libranza, f. draft, bill of exchange.

librar, v. free, rid.

libre, a. free, unoccupied.

librería, f. bookstore.

librero -ra, n. bookseller.

libreta, f. notebook; booklet.

libreto, m. libretto.

libro, m. book.

libro de texto, textbook.

licencia, f. permission, license, leave; furlough. **l. de armas,** gun permit.

licenciado -da, n. graduate.

licencioso, a. licentious.

lícito, a. lawful.

licor, m. liquor.

licuadora, f. blender (for food).

lid, f. fight. **—lidiar,** v.

líder, m. & f. leader.

liebre, f. hare.

lienzo, m. linen.

liga, f. league, confederacy; garter.

ligadura, f. ligature.

ligar, v. tie, bind, join.

ligero, a. light; fast, nimble.

ligustro, m. privet.

lija, f. sandpaper.

lijar, v. sandpaper.

lima, f. file; lime.

limbo, m. limbo.

limitación, f. limitation.

límite, m. limit. **—limitar,** v.

limo, m. slime.

limón, m. lemon.

limonada, f. lemonade.

limonero, m. lemon tree.

limosna, f. alms.

limosnero -ra, n. beggar.

limpiabotas, m. bootblack.

limpiadientes, m. toothpick.

limpiar, v. clean, wash, wipe.

límpido, a. limpid, clear.

limpieza, f. cleanliness.

limpio, m. clean.

limusina, f. limousine.

linaje, m. lineage, ancestry.

linaza, f. linseed.

lince, a. sharp-sighted, observing.

linchamiento, m. lynching.

linchar, v. lynch.

lindar, v. border, bound.

linde, m. boundary; landmark.

lindero, m. boundary.

lindo, a. pretty, lovely, nice.

línea, f. line.

línea de puntos, dotted line.

lineal, a. lineal.

linfa, f. lymph.

lingüista, m. & f. linguist.

lingüístico, a. linguistic.

linimento, m. liniment.

lino, m. linen; flax.

linóleo, m. linoleum.

linterna, f. lantern; flashlight.

lío, m. pack, bundle; mess, scrape; hassle.

liquidación, f. liquidation.

liquidar, v. liquidate; settle up.

líquido, a. & m. liquid.

lira, f. lyre.

lírico, a. lyric.

lirio, m. lily.

lirismo, m. lyricism.

lis, f. lily.

lisiar, v. cripple, lame.

liso, a. smooth, even.

lisonja, f. flattery.

lisonjear, v. flatter.

lisonjero -ra, n. flatterer.

lista, f. list; stripe; menu.

lista negra, blacklist.

listar, v. list; put on a list.

listo, a. ready; smart, clever.

listón, m. ribbon.

litera, f. litter, bunk, berth.

literal, a. literal.

literario, a. literary.

literato, m. literary person, writer.

literatura, f. literature.

litigación, f. litigation.

litigio, m. litigation; lawsuit.

litoral, m. coast.

litro, m. liter.

liturgia, f. liturgy.

liviano, a. light (in weight).

lívido, a. livid.

llaga, f. sore.

llama, f. flame; llama.

llamada, f. call; knock. **—llamar,** v.

llamarse, v. be called, be named. **se llama . . .** etc., his name is . . . etc.

llamativo, a. gaudy, showy.

llamear, v. blaze.

llaneza, f. simplicity.

llano, 1. a. flat, level; plain. **2.** m. plain.

llanta, f. tire.

llanto, m. crying, weeping.

llanura, f. prairie, plain.

llave, f. key; wrench; faucet; (elec.) switch. **ll. inglesa,** monkey wrench.

llegada, f. arrival.

llegar, v. arrive; reach. **ll. a ser,** become, come to be.

llenar, v. fill.

lleno, a. full.

llenura, f. abundance.

llevadero, a. tolerable.

llevar, v. take, carry, bear; wear (clothes); **ll. a cabo,** carry out.

llevarse, v. take away, run away with. **ll. bien,** get along well.

llorar, v. cry, weep.

lloroso, a. sorrowful, tearful.

llover, v. rain.

llovido, m. stowaway.

llovizna, f. drizzle, sprinkle. **—lloviznar,** v.

lluvia, f. rain.

lluvia ácida, acid rain.

lluvioso, a. rainy.

lo, pron. the; him, it, you; (pl.) them, you.

loar, v. praise, laud.

lobina, f. striped bass.

lobo, *m.* wolf.
lóbrego, *a.* murky; dismal.
local, 1. *a.* local. 2. *m.* site.
localidad, *f.* locality, location; seat (in theater).
localizar, *v.* localize.
loción, *f.* lotion.
loco -ca, 1. *a.* crazy, insane, mad. 2. *n.* lunatic.
locomotora, *f.* locomotive.
locuaz, *a.* loquacious.
locución, *f.* locution, expression.
locura, *f.* folly; madness, insanity.
lodo, *m.* mud.
lodoso, *a.* muddy.
lógica, *f.* logic.
lógico, *a.* logical.
lograr, *v.* achieve; succeed in.
logro, *m.* accomplishment.
lombriz, *f.* earthworm.
lomo, *m.* loin; back (of an animal).
lona, *f.* canvas, tarpaulin.
longevidad, *f.* longevity.

longitud, *f.* longitude; length.
lonja, *f.* shop; market.
lontananza, *f.* distance.
loro, *m.* parrot.
losa, *f.* slab.
lote, *m.* lot, share.
lotería, *f.* lottery.
loza, *f.* china, crockery.
lozanía, *f.* freshness, vigor.
lozano, *a.* fresh, spirited.
lubricación, *f.* lubrication.
lubricar, *v.* lubricate.
lucero, *m.* (bright) star.
lucha, *f.* fight, struggle; wrestling. **—luchar**, *v.*
luchador -ra, *n.* fighter, wrestler.
lúcido, *a.* lucid, clear.
luciente, *a.* shining, bright.
luciérnaga, *f.* firefly.
lucimiento, *m.* success; splendor.
lucir, *v.* shine, sparkle; show off.
lucrativo, *a.* lucrative, profitable.

luego, *adv.* right away; afterwards, next. **l. que**, as soon as. **desde l.**, of course. **hasta l.**, goodbye, so long.
lugar, *m.* place, spot; space, room.
lúgubre, *a.* gloomy; dismal.
lujo, *m.* luxury. **de l.**, deluxe.
lujoso, *a.* luxurious.
lumbre, *f.* fire; light.
luminoso, *a.* luminous.
luna, *f.* moon.
lunar, *m.* beauty mark, mole; polka dot.
lunático -ca, *a.* & *n.* lunatic.
lunes, *m.* Monday.
luneta, *f.* (theat.) orchestra seat.
lupa, *f.* magnifying glass.
lustre, *m.* polish, shine. **— lustrar**, *v.*
lustroso, *a.* shiny.
luto, *m.* mourning.
luz, *f.* light. **dar a l.**, give birth to.

M

maca, *f.* blemish, flaw.
macaco, *a.* ugly, horrid.
macareno, *a.* boasting.
macarrones, *m.pl.* macaroni.
macear, *v.* molest, push around.
macedonia de frutas, *f.* fruit salad.
maceta, *f.* vase; mallet.
machacar, *v.* pound; crush.
machina, *f.* derrick.
machista, *a.* macho.
macho, *m.* male.
machucho, *a.* mature, wise.
macizo, 1. *a.* solid. 2. *m.* bulk; flower bed.
macular, *v.* stain.
madera, *f.* lumber; wood.
madero, *m.* beam, timber.
madrastra, *f.* stepmother.
madre, *f.* mother. **m. política**, mother-in-law.
madreperla, *f.* mother-of-pearl.
madriguera, *f.* burrow; lair, den.
madrina, *f.* godmother.
madroncillo, *m.* strawberry.

madrugada, *f.* daybreak.
madrugar, *v.* get up early.
madurar, *v.* ripen.
madurez, *f.* maturity.
maduro, *a.* ripe; mature.
maestría, *f.* mastery; master's degree.
maestro, *m.* master; teacher.
mafia, *f.* mafia.
maganto, *a.* lethargic, dull.
magia, *f.* magic.
mágico, *a.* & *m.* magic; magician.
magistrado, *m.* magistrate.
magnánimo, *a.* magnanimous.
magnético, *a.* magnetic.
magnetismo, *m.* magnetism.
magnetófono, *m.* tape recorder.
magnificar, *v.* magnify.
magnificencia, *f.* magnificence.
magnífico, *a.* magnificent.
magnitud, *f.* magnitude.
magno, *a.* great, grand.
magnolia, *f.* magnolia.
mago, *m.* magician; wizard.

magosto, *m.* chestnut roast; picnic fire for roasting chestnuts.
magro, *a.* meager; thin.
magullar, *v.* bruise.
mahometano, *n.* & *a.* Mohammedan.
mahometismo, *m.* Mohammedanism.
maíz, *m.* corn.
majadero -ra, *a.* & *n.* foolish; fool.
majar, *v.* mash.
majestad, *f.* majesty.
majestuoso, *a.* majestic.
mal, 1. *adv.* badly; wrong. 2. *m.* evil, ill; illness.
mala, *f.* mail.
malacate, *m.* hoist.
malandanza, *f.* misfortune.
malaventura, *f.* misfortune.
malcomido, *a.* underfed; malnourished.
malcontento, *a.* disssatisfied.
maldad, *f.* badness; wickedness.
maldecir, *v.* curse, damn.
maldición, *f.* curse.

maldito, *a.* accursed, damned.

malecón, *m.* embankment.

maledicencia, *f.* slander.

maleficio, *m.* spell, charm.

malestar, *m.* indisposition.

maleta, *f.* suitcase, valise.

malévolo, *a.* malevolent.

maleza, *f.* weeds; underbrush.

malgastar, *v.* squander.

malhechor -ra, *n.* malefactor, evildoer.

malhumorado, *a.* morose, ill-humored.

malicia, *f.* malice.

maliciar, *v.* suspect.

malicioso, *a.* malicious.

maligno, *a.* malignant, evil.

malla, *f.* mesh, net.

mallas, *f.pl.* leotard.

mallete, *m.* mallet.

malo, *a.* bad; evil, wicked; naughty; ill.

malograr, *v.* miss, lose.

malparto, *m.* abortion, miscarriage.

malquerencia, *f.* hatred.

malquerer, *v.* dislike; bear ill will.

malsano, *a.* unhealthy; unwholesome.

malsín, *m.* malicious gossip.

malta, *f.* malt.

maltratar, *v.* mistreat.

malvado -da, 1. *a.* wicked. **2.** *n.* villain.

malversar, *v.* embezzle.

malvís, *m.* redwing.

mamá, *f.* mama, mother.

mamar, *v.* suckle; suck.

mamífero, *m.* mammal.

mampara, *f.* screen.

mampostería, *f.* masonry.

mamut, *m.* mammoth.

manada, *f.* flock, herd, drove.

manantial, *m.* spring (of water).

manar, *v.* gush, flow out.

mancebo, *m.* young man.

mancha, *f.* stain, smear, blemish, spot. **—manchar,** *v.*

mancilla, *f.* stain; blemish.

manco, *a.* armless; one-armed.

mandadero, *m.* messenger.

mandado, *m.* order, command.

mandamiento, *m.* commandment; command.

mandar, *v.* send; order, command.

mandatario, *m.* attorney; representative.

mandato, *m.* mandate, command.

mandíbula, *f.* jaw; jawbone.

mando, *m.* command, order; leadership.

mando a distancia, remote control.

mandón, *a.* domineering.

mandril, *m.* baboon.

manejar, *v.* handle, manage; drive (a car).

manejo, *m.* management; horsemanship.

manera, *f.* way, manner, means. **de m. que,** so, as a result.

manga, *f.* sleeve.

mangana, *f.* lariat, lasso.

manganeso, *m.* manganese.

mango, *m.* handle; mango (fruit).

mangosta, *f.* mongoose.

manguera, *f.* hose.

manguito, *m.* muff.

maní, *m.* peanut.

manía, *f.* mania, madness; hobby.

maníaco -ca, maniático -ca, *a.* & *n.* maniac.

manicomio, *m.* insane asylum.

manicura, *f.* manicure.

manifactura, *f.* manufacture.

manifestación, *f.* manifestation.

manifestar, *v.* manifest, show.

manifiesto, *a.* & *m.* manifest.

manija, *f.* handle; crank.

maniobra, *f.* maneuver. **—maniobrar,** *v.*

manipulación, *f.* manipulation.

manipular, *v.* manipulate.

maniquí, *m.* mannequin.

manivela, *f.* (mech.) crank.

manjar, *m.* food, dish.

manlieve, *m.* swindle.

mano, *f.* hand.

manojo, *m.* handful; bunch.

manómetro, *m.* gauge.

manopla, *f.* gauntlet.

manosear, *v.* handle, feel, touch.

manotada, *f.* slap, smack. **—manotear,** *v.*

mansedumbre, *f.* meekness, tameness.

mansión, *f.* mansion; abode.

manso, *a.* tame, gentle.

manta, *f.* blanket.

manteca, *f.* fat, lard; butter.

mantecado, *m.* ice cream.

mantecoso, *a.* buttery.

mantel, *m.* tablecloth.

mantener, *v.* maintain, keep; sustain; support.

mantenimiento, *m.* maintenance.

mantequera, *f.* butter dish; churn.

mantequilla, *f.* butter.

mantilla, *f.* mantilla; baby clothes.

mantillo, *m.* humus; manure.

manto, *m.* mantle, cloak.

manual, *a.* & *m.* manual.

manubrio, *m.* handle; crank.

manufacturar, *v.* manufacture; make.

manuscrito, *m.* manuscript.

manzana, *f.* apple; block (of street).

manzano, *m.* apple tree.

maña, *f.* skill; cunning; trick.

mañana, 1. *adv.* tomorrow. **2.** *f.* morning.

mañanear, *v.* rise early in the morning.

mañero, *a.* clever; skillful; lazy.

mapa, *m.* map, chart.

mapache, *m.* raccoon.

mapurito, *m.* skunk.

máquina, *f.* machine. **m. de coser,** sewing machine. **m. de lavar,** washing machine.

maquinación, *f.* machination; plot.

maquinador -ra, *n.* plotter, schemer.

maquinal, *a.* mechanical.

maquinar, *v.* scheme, plot.

maquinaria, *f.* machinery.

maquinista, *m.* machinist; engineer.

mar, *m.* or *f.* sea.

marabú, *m.* marabou.

maraña, *f.* tangle; maze; snarl; plot.

maravilla, *f.* marvel, wonder. **—maravillarse,** *v.*

maravilloso, *a.* marvelous, wonderful.

marbete, *m.* tag, label; check.

marca, *f.* mark, sign; brand, make.

marcador, *m.* highlighter.

marcar, *v.* mark; observe, note.

marcha, *f.* march; progress. **—marchar,** *v.*

marchante, *m.* merchant; customer.

marcharse, *v.* go away, depart.

marchitable, *a.* perishable.

marchitar, *v.* fade, wilt, wither.

marchito, *a.* faded, withered.

marcial, *a.* martial.

marco, *m.* frame.

marea, *f.* tide.

mareado, *a.* seasick.

marearse, *v.* get dizzy; be seasick.

mareo, *m.* dizziness; seasickness.

marfil, *m.* ivory.

margarita, *f.* pearl; daisy.

margen, *m. or f.* margin, edge, rim.

marido, *m.* husband.

marijuana, *f.* marijuana.

marimba, *f.* marimba.

marina, *f.* navy; seascape.

marinero, *m.* sailor, seaman.

marino, *a. & m.* marine, (of) sea; mariner, seaman.

marión, *m.* sturgeon.

mariposa, *f.* butterfly.

mariquita, *f.* ladybird.

mariscal, *m.* marshal.

marisco, *m.* shellfish; mollusk.

marital, *a.* marital.

marítimo, *a.* maritime.

marmita, *f.* pot, kettle.

mármol, *m.* marble.

marmóreo, *a.* marble.

maroma, *f.* rope.

marqués, *m.* marquis.

marquesa, *f.* marquise.

Marruecos, *m.* Morocco.

Marte, *m.* Mars.

martes, *m.* Tuesday.

martillo, *m.* hammer. **—martillar,** *v.*

mártir, *m. & f.* martyr.

martirio, *m.* martyrdom.

martirizar, *v.* martyrize.

marzo, *m.* March.

mas, *conj.* but.

más, *a. & adv.* more, most; plus. **no m.,** only; no more.

masa, *f.* mass; dough.

masaje, *m.* massage.

mascar, *v.* chew.

máscara, *f.* mask.

mascarada, *f.* masquerade.

mascota, *f.* mascot; good-luck charm.

masculino, *a.* masculine.

mascullar, *v.* mumble.

masón, *m.* Freemason.

masticar, *v.* chew.

mástil, *m.* mast; post.

mastín, *m.* mastiff.

mastín danés, Great Dane.

mastuerzo, *m.* fool, ninny.

mata, *f.* plant; bush.

matadero, *m.* slaughterhouse.

matador -ra, *n.* matador.

matafuego, *m.* fire extinguisher.

matanza, *f.* killing, bloodshed, slaughter.

matar, *v.* kill, slay; slaughter.

matasanos, *m.* quack.

mate, *m.* checkmate; Paraguayan tea.

matemáticas, *f.pl.* mathematics.

matemático, *a.* mathematical.

materia, *f.* material; subject (matter).

material, *a. & m.* material.

materialismo, *m.* materialism.

materializar, *v.* materialize.

maternal, materno, *a.* maternal.

maternidad, *f.* maternity; maternity hospital.

matiné, *f.* matinee.

matiz, *m.* hue, shade.

matizar, *v.* blend; tint.

matón, *m.* bully.

matorral, *m.* thicket.

matoso, *a.* weedy.

matraca, *f.* rattle. **—matraquear,** *v.*

matrícula, *f.* registration; tuition.

matricularse, *v.* enroll, register.

matrimonio, *m.* matrimony, marriage; married couple.

matriz, *f.* womb; (mech.) die, mold.

matrona, *f.* matron.

maullar, *v.* mew.

máxima, *f.* maxim.

máxime, *a.* principally.

máximo, *a. & m.* maximum.

maya, *f.* daisy.

mayo, *m.* May.

mayonesa, *f.* mayonnaise.

mayor, 1. *a.* larger, largest; greater, greatest; elder, eldest, senior. **m. de edad,** major, of age. **al por m.,** at wholesale. **2.** *m.* major.

mayoral, *m.* head shepherd; boss; foreman.

mayordomo, *m.* manager; butler, steward.

mayoría, *f.* majority, bulk.

mayorista, *m. & f.* wholesaler.

mayúscula, *f.* capital letter, upper-case letter.

mazmorra, *f.* dungeon.

mazorca, *f.* ear of corn.

me, *pron.* me; myself.

mecánico -ca, *a. & n.* mechanical; mechanic.

mecanismo, *m.* mechanism.

mecanizar, *v.* mechanize.

mecanografía, *f.* typewriting.

mecanógrafo -fa, *n.* typist.

mecedor, *m.* swing.

mecedora, *f.* rocking chair.

mecer, *v.* rock; swing, sway.

mecha, *f.* wick; fuse.

mechón, *m.* lock (of hair).

medalla, *f.* medal.

médano, *m.* sand dune.

media, *f.* stocking.

mediación, *f.* mediation.

mediador -ra, *n.* mediator.

mediados, *m.pl.* **a m. de,** about the middle of (a period of time).

medianero, *m.* mediator.

medianía, *f.* mediocrity.
mediano, *a.* medium; moderate; mediocre.
medianoche, *f.* midnight.
mediante, *prep.* by means of.
mediar, *v.* mediate.
medicamento, *m.* medicine, drug.
medicastro, *m.* quack.
medicina, *f.* medicine.
medicinar, *v.* treat (as a doctor).
médico, 1. *a.* medical. **2.** *m. & f.* doctor, physician.
medida, *f.* measure, step.
medidor, *m.* meter.
medieval, *a.* medieval.
medio, 1. *a.* half; mid, middle of. **2.** *m.* middle; means.
mediocre, *a.* mediocre.
mediocridad, *f.* mediocrity.
mediodía, *m.* midday, noon.
medir, *v.* measure, gauge.
meditación, *f.* meditation.
meditar, *v.* meditate.
mediterráneo, *a.* Mediterranean.
medrar, *v.* thrive; grow.
medroso, *a.* fearful, cowardly.
megáfono, *m.* megaphone.
megahercio, *f.* megahertz.
mejicano -na, *a. & n.* Mexican.
mejilla, *f.* cheek.
mejillón, *m.* mussel.
mejor, *a. & adv.* better; best. **a lo m.,** perhaps.
mejora, *f.,* **mejoramiento,** *m.* improvement.
mejorar, *v.* improve, better.
mejoría, *f.* improvement; superiority.
melancolía, *f.* melancholy.
melancólico, *a.* melancholy.
melaza, *f.* molasses.
melena, *f.* mane; long or loose hair.
melenudo -da, *a.* longhaired.
melindroso, *a.* fussy.
mella, *f.* notch; dent. — **mellar,** *v.*
mellizo -za, *n. & a.* twin.
melocotón, *m.* peach.
melodía, *f.* melody.
melodioso, *a.* melodious.

melón, *m.* melon.
meloso, *a.* like honey.
membrana, *f.* membrane.
membrete, *m.* memorandum; letterhead.
membrillo, *m.* quince.
membrudo, *a.* strong, muscular.
memorable, *a.* memorable.
memorándum, *m.* memorandum; notebook.
memoria, *f.* memory; memoir; memorandum.
mención, *f.* mention. — **mencionar,** *v.*
mendigar, *v.* beg (for alms).
mendigo -a, *n.* beggar.
mendrugo, *m.* (hard) crust, chunk.
menear, *v.* shake, wag; stir.
menester, *m.* need, want; duty, task. **ser m.,** to be necessary.
menesteroso, *a.* needy.
mengua, *f.* decrease; lack; poverty.
menguar, *v.* abate, decrease.
meningitis, *f.* meningitis.
menopausia, *f.* menopause.
menor, *a.* smaller, smallest; lesser, least; younger, youngest, junior. **m. de edad,** minor, under age. **al por m.,** at retail.
menos, *a. & adv.* less, least; minus. **a m. que,** unless. **echar de m.,** to miss.
menospreciar, *v.* cheapen; despise; slight.
mensaje, *m.* message.
mensajero -ra, *n.* messenger.
menstruar, *v.* menstruate.
mensual, *a.* monthly.
mensualidad, *f.* monthly income or allowance; monthly payment.
menta, *f.* mint, peppermint.
menta romana, spearmint.
mentado, *a.* famous.
mental, *a.* mental.
mentalidad, *f.* mentality.
mente, *f.* mind.
mentecato, *a.* foolish, stupid.
mentir, *v.* lie, tell a lie.
mentira, *f.* lie, falsehood. **parece m.,** it seems impossible.

mentiroso, *a.* lying, untruthful.
mentol, *m.* menthol.
menú, *m.* menu.
menudeo, *m.* retail.
menudo, *a.* small, minute. **a m.,** often.
meñique, *a.* tiny.
meple, *m.* maple.
merca, *f.* purchase.
mercader, *m.* merchant.
mercaderías, *f.pl.* merchandise, commodities.
mercado, *m.* market.
Mercado Común, Common Market.
mercado negro, black market.
mercancía, *f.* merchandise; (*pl.*) wares.
mercante, *a.* merchant.
mercantil, *a.* mercantile.
merced, *f.* mercy, grace.
mercenario -ria, *a. & n.* mercenary.
mercurio, *m.* mercury.
merecedor, *a.* worthy.
merecer, *v.* merit, deserve.
merecimiento, *m.* merit.
merendar, *v.* eat lunch; snack.
merendero, *m.* lunchroom.
meridional, *a.* southern.
merienda, *f.* midday meal, lunch; afternoon snack.
mérito, *m.* merit, worth.
meritorio, *a.* meritorious.
merla, *f.* blackbird.
merluza, *f.* haddock.
mermelada, *f.* marmalade.
mero, *a.* mere.
merodeador -ra, *n.* prowler.
mes, *m.* month.
mesa, *f.* table.
meseta, *f.* plateau.
mesón, *m.* inn.
mesonero -ra, *n.* innkeeper.
mestizo -za, *a. & n.* halfcaste.
meta, *f.* goal, objective.
metabolismo, *m.* metabolism.
metafísica, *f.* metaphysics.
metáfora, *f.* metaphor.
metal, *m.* metal.
metálico, *a.* metallic.
metalurgia, *f.* metallurgy.
meteoro, *m.* meteor.

meteorología, *f.* meteorology.

meter, *v.* put (in).

meterse, *v.* interfere, meddle; go into.

metódico, *a.* methodic.

método, *m.* method, approach.

metralla, *f.* shrapnel.

métrico, *a.* metric.

metro, *m.* meter (measure); subway.

metrópoli, *f.* metropolis.

mexicano -na, *a. & n.* Mexican.

mezcla, *f.* mixture; blend.

mezclar, *v.* mix; blend.

mezcolanza, *f.* mixture; hodgepodge.

mezquino, *a.* stingy; petty.

mezquita, *f.* mosque.

mi, *a.* my.

mí, *pron.* me; myself.

microbio, *m.* microbe, germ.

microbús, *m.* minibus.

microchip, *m.* microchip.

microficha, *f.* microfiche.

micrófono, *m.* microphone.

microforma, *f.* microform.

microscópico, *a.* microscopic.

microscopio, *m.* microscope.

microtaxi, *m.* minicab.

miedo, *m.* fear. **tener m.,** fear, be afraid.

miedoso, *a.* fearful.

miel, *f.* honey.

miembro, *m. & f.* member; limb.

mientras, *conj.* while. **m. tanto,** meanwhile. **m. más . . . más,** the more . . . the more.

miércoles, *m.* Wednesday.

miércoles de ceniza, Ash Wednesday.

miga, migaja, *f.* scrap; crumb.

migración, *f.* migration.

migratorio, *a.* migratory.

mil, *a. & pron.* thousand.

milagro, *m.* miracle.

milagroso, *a.* miraculous.

milicia, *f.* militia.

militante, *a.* militant.

militar, 1. *a.* military. **2.** *m.* military man.

militarismo, *m.* militarism.

milla, *f.* mile.

millar, *m.* (a) thousand.

millón, *m.* million.

millonario -ria, *n.* millionaire.

mimar, *v.* pamper, spoil (a child).

mimbre, *m.* willow; wicker.

mímico, *a.* mimic.

mimo, *m.* mime, mimic.

mina, *f.* mine. **—minar,** *v.*

mineral, *a. & m.* mineral.

minero -ra, *n.* miner.

miniatura, *f.* miniature.

miniaturizar, *v.* miniaturize.

mínimo, *a. & m.* minimum.

ministerio, *m.* ministry; cabinet.

ministro -a, *n.* (govt.) minister, secretary.

minoría, *f.* minority.

minoridad, *f.* minority (of age).

minucioso, *a.* minute; thorough.

minúscula, *f.* lower-case letter, small letter.

minué, *m.* minuet.

minuta, *f.* draft.

mío, *a.* mine.

miopía, *f.* myopia.

mira, *f.* gunsight.

mirada, *f.* look; gaze, glance.

miramiento, *m.* consideration; respect.

mirar, *v.* look, look at; watch. **m. a,** face.

miríada, *f.* myriad.

mirlo, *m.* blackbird.

mirón -ona, *n.* bystander, observer.

mirra, *f.* myrrh.

mirto, *m.* myrtle.

misa, *f.* mass, church service.

misceláneo, *a.* miscellaneous.

miserable, *a.* miserable, wretched.

miseria, *f.* misery.

misericordia, *f.* mercy.

misericordioso, *a.* merciful.

misión, *f.* assignment; mission.

misionario -ria, misionero -ra, *n.* missionary.

mismo, 1. *a. & pron.* same; -self, -selves. **2.** *adv.* right, exactly.

misterio, *m.* mystery.

misterioso, *a.* mysterious, weird.

místico -ca, *a. & n.* mystical, mystic.

mitad, *f.* half.

mítico, *a.* mythical.

mitigar, *v.* mitigate.

mitin, *m.* meeting; rally.

mito, *m.* myth.

mitón, *m.* mitten.

mitra, *f.* miter (bishop's).

mixto, *a.* mixed.

mixtura, *f.* mixture.

mobiliario, *m.* household goods.

mocasín, *m.* moccasin.

mocedad, *f.* youthfulness.

mochila, *f.* knapsack, backpack.

mocho, *a.* cropped, trimmed, shorn.

moción, *f.* motion.

mocoso -sa, *n.* brat.

moda, *f.* mode, fashion, style.

modales, *m.pl.* manners.

modelo, *m.* model, pattern.

módem, *m.* modem.

moderación, *f.* moderation.

moderado, *a.* moderate. **—moderar,** *v.*

modernizar, *v.* modernize.

moderno, *a.* modern.

modestia, *f.* modesty.

modesto, *a.* modest.

módico, *a.* reasonable, moderate.

modificación, *f.* modification.

modificar, *v.* modify.

modismo, *m.* (gram.) idiom.

modista, *f.* dressmaker; milliner.

modo, *m.* way, means.

modular, *v.* modulate.

mofarse, *v.* scoff, sneer.

mofletudo, *a.* fat-cheeked.

mohín, *m.* grimace.

moho, *m.* mold, mildew.

mohoso, *a.* moldy.

mojar, *v.* wet.

mojón, *m.* landmark; heap.

molde, *m.* mold, form.

molécula, *f.* molecule.

moler, *v.* grind, mill.

molestar, *v.* molest, bother, disturb, annoy, trouble.

molestia, *f.* bother, annoyance, trouble; hassle.

molesto, *a.* bothersome; annoyed; uncomfortable.

molicie, *f.* softness.

molinero, *m.* miller.

molino, *m.* mill. **m. de viento,** windmill.

mollera, *f.* top of the head.

molusco, *m.* mollusk.

momentáneo, *a.* momentary.

momento, *m.* moment.

mona, *f.* female monkey.

monarca, *m. & f.* monarch.

monarquía, *f.* monarchy.

monarquista, *n. & a.* monarchist.

monasterio, *m.* monastery.

mondadientes, *m.* toothpick.

moneda, *f.* coin; money.

monetario, *a.* monetary.

monición, *m.* warning.

monigote, *m.* puppet.

monja, *f.* nun.

monje, *m.* monk.

mono -na, 1. *a.* (coll.) cute. **2.** *m. & f.* monkey.

monólogo, *m.* monologue.

monopatín, *m.* skateboard.

monopolio, *m.* monopoly.

monopolizar, *v.* monopolize.

monosílabo, *m.* monosyllable.

monotonía, *f.* monotony.

monótono, *a.* monotonous, dreary.

monstruo, *m.* monster.

monstruosidad, *f.* monstrosity.

monstruoso, *a.* monstrous.

monta, *f.* amount; price.

montaña, *f.* mountain.

montañoso, *a.* mountainous.

montar, *v.* mount, climb; amount; (mech.) assemble. **m. a caballo,** ride horseback.

montaraz, *a.* wild, barbaric.

monte, *m.* mountain; forest.

montón, *m.* heap, pile.

montuoso, *a.* mountainous.

montura, *f.* mount; saddle.

monumental, *a.* monumental.

monumento, *m.* monument.

mora, *f.* blackberry.

morada, *f.* residence, dwelling.

morado, *a.* purple.

moral, 1. *a.* moral. **2.** *f.* morale.

moraleja, *f.* moral.

moralidad, *f.* morality, morals.

moralista, *m. & f.* moralist.

morar, *v.* dwell, live, reside.

mórbido, *a.* morbid.

mordaz, *a.* caustic; sarcastic.

mordedura, *f.* bite.

morder, *v.* bite.

moreno -na, *a. & n.* brown; dark-skinned; dark-haired, brunette.

morfina, *f.* morphine.

moribundo, *a.* dying.

morir, *v.* die.

morisco -ca, moro -ra, *a. & n.* Moorish; Moor.

morriña, *f.* sadness.

morro, *m.* bluff; snout.

mortaja, *f.* shroud.

mortal, *a. & n.* mortal.

mortalidad, *f.* mortality.

mortero, *m.* mortar.

mortífero, *a.* fatal, deadly.

mortificar, *v.* mortify.

mortuorio, *a.* funereal.

mosaico, *a. & m.* mosaic.

mosca, *f.* fly.

mosquito, *m.* mosquito.

mostacho, *m.* mustache.

mostaza, *f.* mustard.

mostrador, *m.* counter; showcase.

mostrar, *v.* show, display.

mote, *m.* nickname; alias.

motel, *m.* motel.

motín, *m.* mutiny; riot.

motivo, *m.* motive, reason.

motocicleta, *f.* motorcycle.

motociclista, *m. & f.* motorcyclist.

motor, *m.* motor.

motorista, *m. & f.* motorist.

movedizo, *a.* movable; shaky.

mover, *v.* move; stir.

movible, *a.* movable.

móvil, *a.* mobile.

movilización, *f.* mobilization.

movilizar, *v.* mobilize.

movimiento, *m.* movement, motion.

mozo, *m.* boy; servant, waiter, porter.

muaré, *m.* moiré.

muchacha, *f.* girl, youngster; maid (servant).

muchachez, *m.* boyhood, girlhood.

muchacho, *m.* boy; youngster.

muchedumbre, *f.* crowd, mob.

mucho, 1. *a.* much, many. **2.** *adv.* much.

mucoso, *a.* mucous.

muda, *f.* change.

mudanza, *f.* change; change of residence.

mudar, *v.* change, shift.

mudarse, *v.* change residence, move.

mudo -da, *a. & n.* mute.

mueble, *m.* piece of furniture; (*pl.*) furniture.

mueca, *f.* grimace.

muela, *f.* (back) tooth.

muelle, *m.* pier, wharf; (mech.) spring.

muerte, *f.* death.

muerto -ta, 1. *a.* dead. **2.** *n.* dead person.

muesca, *f.* notch; groove.

muestra, *f.* sample, specimen; sign.

mugido, *m.* lowing; mooing.

mugir, *v.* low, moo.

mugre, *f.* filth, dirt.

mugriento, *a.* dirty.

mujer, *f.* woman; wife. **m. de la lim-pieza,** cleaning lady, charwoman.

mujeril, *a.* womanly, feminine.

mula, *f.* mule.

mulato -ta, *a. & n.* mulatto.

muleta, *f.* crutch; prop.

mulo -la, *n.* mule.

multa, *f.* fine, penalty.

multicolor, *a.* many-colored.

multinacional, *a.* multinational.

múltiple, *a.* multiple.

multiplicación, *f.* multiplication.

multiplicar, *v.* multiply.

multiplicidad, *f.* multiplicity.

multitud, *f.* multitude, crowd.

mundanal, *a.* worldly.
mundano, *a.* worldly, mundane.
mundial, *a.* worldwide; (of the) world.
mundo, *m.* world.
munición, *f.* ammunition.
municipal, *a.* municipal.
municipio, *m.* city hall.
muñeca, *f.* doll; wrist.
muñeco, *m.* doll; puppet.
mural, *a. & m.* mural.
muralla, *f.* wall.

murciélago, *m.* bat.
murga, *f.* musical band.
murmullo, *m.* murmur; rustle.
murmurar, *v.* murmur; rustle; grumble.
musa, *f.* muse.
muscular, *a.* muscular.
músculo, *m.* muscle.
muselina, *f.* muslin.
museo, *m.* museum.
música, *f.* music.
musical, *a.* musical.

músico -ca, *a. & n.* musical; musician.
muslo, *m.* thigh.
mustio, *a.* sad.
musulmano -na, *a. & n.* Muslim.
muta, *f.* pack of hounds.
mutabilidad, *f.* mutability.
mutación, *f.* mutation.
mutilación, *f.* mutilation.
mutilar, *v.* mutilate; mangle.
mutuo, *a.* mutual.
muy, *adv.* very.

N, Ñ

nabo, *m.* turnip.
nácar, *m.* mother-of-pearl.
nacarado, *a.* pearly.
nacer, *v.* be born.
naciente, *a.* rising; nascent.
nacimiento, *m.* birth.
nación, *f.* nation.
nacional, *a.* national.
nacionalidad, *f.* nationality.
nacionalismo, *m.* nationalism.
nacionalista, *n. & a.* nationalist.
nacionalización, *f.* nationalization.
nacionalizar, *v.* nationalize.
Naciones Unidas, *f.pl.* United Nations.
nada, 1. *pron.* nothing; anything. **de n.,** you're welcome. **2.** *adv.* at all.
nadador -ra, *n.* swimmer.
nadar, *v.* swim.
nadie, *pron.* no one, nobody; anyone, anybody.
nafta, *f.* naphtha.
naipe, *m.* (playing) card.
naranja, *f.* orange.
naranjada, *f.* orangeade.
naranjo, *m.* orange tree.
narciso, *m.* daffodil; narcissus.
narcótico, *a. & m.* narcotic.
nardo, *m.* spikenard.
nariz, *f.* nose; (*pl.*) nostrils.
narración, *f.* account.
narrador -ra, *n.* narrator.
narrar, *v.* narrate.
narrativa, *f.* narrative.
nata, *f.* cream.

nata batida, whipped cream.
natación, *f.* swimming.
natal, *a.* native; natal.
natalicio, *m.* birthday.
natalidad, *f.* birth rate.
natillas, *f.pl.* custard.
nativo, *a.* native; innate.
natural, 1. *a.* natural. **2.** *m. & f.* native. *m.* nature, disposition.
naturaleza, *f.* nature.
naturalidad, *f.* naturalness; nationality.
naturalista, *a. & n.* naturalistic; naturalist.
naturalización, *f.* naturalization.
naturalizar, *v.* naturalize.
naufragar, *v.* be shipwrecked; fail.
naufragio, *m.* shipwreck; disaster.
náufrago -ga, *a. & n.* shipwrecked (person).
náusea, *f.* nausea.
nausear, *v.* feel nauseous.
náutico, *a.* nautical.
navaja, *f.* razor; pen knife.
naval, *a.* naval.
nave, *f.* ship.
nave espacial, spaceship.
navegable, *a.* navigable.
navegación, *f.* navigation.
navegador -ra, *n.* navigator.
navegante, *m. & f.* navigator.
navegar, *v.* sail; navigate.
Navidad, *f.* Christmas.
navío, *m.* ship.
neblina, *f.* mist, fog.

nebuloso, *a.* misty; nebulous.
necedad, *f.* stupidity; nonsense.
necesario, *a.* necessary.
necesidad, *f.* necessity, need, want.
necesitado, *a.* needy, poor.
necesitar, *v.* need.
necio -cia, 1. *a.* stupid, silly. **2.** *n.* fool.
néctar, *m.* nectar.
nectarina, *f.* nectarine.
nefando, *a.* nefarious.
negable, *a.* deniable.
negación, *f.* denial, negation.
negar, *v.* deny.
negarse, *v.* refuse, decline.
negativa, *f.* negative, refusal.
negativamente, *adv.* negatively.
negativo, *a.* negative.
negligencia, *f.* negligence, neglect.
negligente, *a.* negligent.
negociación, *f.* negotiation, deal.
negociador -ra, *n.* negotiator.
negociante -ta, *n.* businessperson.
negociar, *v.* negotiate, trade.
negocio, *m.* trade; business.
negro -gra, 1. *a.* black. **2.** *m.* Black.
nene -na, *n.* baby.
neo, neón, *m.* neon.
nervio, *m.* nerve.
nervioso, *a.* nervous.
nerviosamente, *adv.* nervously.

nesciencia, *f.* ignorance.
nesciente, *a.* ignorant.
neto, *a.* net.
neumático, 1. *a.* pneumatic. **2.** *m.* (pneumatic) tire.
neumático de recambio, spare tire.
neumonía, *f.* pneumonia.
neurótico, *a.* neurotic.
neutral, *a.* neutral.
neutralidad, *f.* neutrality.
neutro, *a.* neuter; neutral.
neutrón, *m.* neutron.
nevada, *f.* snowfall.
nevado, *a.* snow-white; snow-capped.
nevar, *v.* snow.
navasca, *f.* blizzard, snowstorm.
nevera, *f.* icebox.
nevoso, *a.* snowy.
ni, 1. *conj.* nor. **ni . . . ni,** neither . . . nor. **2.** *adv.* not even.
nicho, *m.* recess; niche.
nido, *m.* nest.
niebla, *f.* fog; mist.
nieto -ta, *n.* grandchild.
nieve, *f.* snow.
nilón, *m.* nylon.
nimio, *adj.* stingy.
ninfa, *f.* nymph.
ningún -no -na, *a. & pron.* no, none, neither (one); any, either (one).
niñera, *f.* nursemaid, nanny.
niñez, *f.* childhood.
niño -ña 1. *a.* young; childish; childlike. **2.** *n.* child.
níquel, *m.* nickel.
niquelado, *a.* nickel-plated.
nítido, *a.* neat, clean, bright.
nitrato, *m.* nitrate.
nitro, *m.* niter.
nitrógeno, *m.* nitrogen.
nivel, *m.* level; grade. — **nivelar,** *v.*
no, 1. *adv.* not. **no más,** only. **2.** *interj.* no.
noble, *a. & m.* noble; nobleman.
nobleza, *f.* nobility; nobleness.
noche, *f.* night; evening.
Nochebuena, *f.* Christmas Eve.
noción, *f.* notion, idea.
nocivo, *a.* harmful.

noctiluca, *f.* glowworm.
nocturno, *a.* nocturnal.
nodriza, *f.* wet nurse.
no fumador -ra, *m. & f.* nonsmoker.
nogal, *m.* walnut.
nombradía, *f.* fame.
nombramiento, *m.* appointment, nomination.
nombrar, *v.* name, appoint, nominate; mention.
nombre, *m.* name; noun.
nombre y apellidos, (person's) full name.
nómina, *f.* list; payroll.
nominación, *f.* nomination.
nominal, *a.* nominal.
nominar, *v.* nominate.
non, *a.* uneven, odd.
nonada, *f.* trifle.
nordeste, *m.* northeast.
nórdico, *a.* Nordic; northerly.
norma, *f.* norm, standard.
normal, *a.* normal, standard.
normalidad, *f.* normality.
normalizar, *v.* normalize; standardize.
noroeste, *m.* northwest.
norte, *m.* north.
norteamericano -na, *a. & n.* North American.
Noruega, *f.* Norway.
noruego -ga, *a. & n.* Norwegian.
nos, *pron.* us; ourselves.
nosotros -as, *pron.* we, us; ourselves.
nostalgia, *f.* nostalgia, homesickness.
nostálgico, *a.* nostalgic.
nota, *f.* note; grade, mark.
notable, *a.* notable, remarkable.
notación, *f.* notation; note.
notar, *v.* note, notice.
notario -ria, *n.* notary.
noticia, *f.* notice; piece of news; (*pl.*) news.
noticia de última hora, news flash.
notificación, *f.* notification.
notificación de reclutamiento, draft notice.
notificar, *v.* notify.
notorio, *a.* well-known.
novato -ta, *n.* novice.

novecientos, *a. & pron.* nine hundred.
novedad, *f.* novelty; piece of news.
novel, *a.* new; inexperienced.
novela, *f.* novel.
novelista, *m. & f.* novelist.
novena, *f.* novena.
noveno, *a.* ninth.
noventa, *a. & pron.* ninety.
novia, *f.* bride; sweetheart; fiancée.
noviazgo, *m.* engagement.
novicio -cia, *n.* novice, beginner.
noviembre, *m.* November.
novilla, *f.* heifer.
novio, *m.* bridegroom; sweetheart; fiancé.
nube, *f.* cloud.
núbil, *a.* marriageable.
nublado, *a.* cloudy.
nuclear, *a.* nuclear.
núcleo, *m.* nucleus.
nudo, *m.* knot.
nuera, *f.* daughter-in-law.
nuestro, *a.* our, ours.
nueva, *f.* news.
nueve, *a. & pron.* nine.
nuevo, *a.* new. **de n.,** again, anew.
nuez, *f.* nut; walnut.
nulidad, *f.* nonentity; nullity.
nulo, *a.* null, void.
numeración, *f.* numeration.
numerar, *v.* number.
numérico, *a.* numerical.
número, *m.* number; size (of shoe, etc.) **n. impar,** odd number. **n. par,** even number.
numeroso, *a.* numerous.
numismática, *f.* numismatics.
nunca, *adv.* never; ever.
nupcial, *a.* nuptial.
nupcias, *f.pl.* nuptials, wedding.
nutrición, *f.* nutrition.
nutrimento, *m.* nourishment.
nutrir, *v.* nourish.
nutritivo, *a.* nutritious.
nylon, *m.* nylon.
ñame, *m.* yam.
ñapa, *f.* something extra.
ñoñería, *f.* dotage.
ñoño, *a.* feeble-minded, senile.

O

o, *conj.* or. **o . . . o,** either . . . or.

oasis, *m.* oasis.

obedecer, *v.* obey, mind.

obediencia, *f.* obedience.

obediente, *a.* obedient.

obelisco, *m.* obelisk.

obertura, *f.* overture.

obeso, *a.* obese.

obispo, *m.* bishop.

obituario, *m.* obituary.

objeción, *f.* objection.

objetivo, *a. & m.* objective.

objeto, *m.* object. **—obje-tar,** *v.*

objetor de conciencia, *m.* conscientious objector.

oblicuo, *a.* oblique.

obligación, *f.* obligation, duty.

obligar, *v.* oblige, require, compel; obligate.

obligatorio, *a.* obligatory, compulsory.

oblongo, *a.* oblong.

oboe, *m.* oboe.

obra, *f.* work. **—obrar,** *v.*

obrero -ra, *n.* worker, laborer.

obscenidad, *f.* obscenity.

obsceno, *a.* obscene.

obscurecer, *v.* obscure; darken.

obscuridad, *f.* obscurity; darkness.

obscuro, *a.* obscure; dark.

obsequiar, *v.* court; make presents to, fete.

obsequio, *m.* obsequiousness; gift; attention.

observación, *f.* observation.

observador -ra, *n.* observer.

observancia, *f.* observance.

observar, *v.* observe, watch.

observatorio, *m.* observatory.

obsesión, *f.* obsession.

obstáculo, *m.* obstacle.

obstante, *adv.* **no o.,** however, yet, nevertheless.

obstar, *v.* hinder, obstruct.

obstetricia, *f.* obstetrics.

obstinación, *f.* obstinacy.

obstinado, *a.* obstinate, stubborn.

obstinarse, *v.* persist, insist.

obstrucción, *f.* obstruction.

obstruir, *v.* obstruct, clog, block.

obtener, *v.* obtain, get, secure.

obtuso, *a.* obtuse.

obvio, *a.* obvious.

ocasión, *f.* occasion; opportunity, chance. **de o.,** secondhand.

ocasional, *a.* occasional.

ocasionalmente, *adv.* occasionally.

ocasionar, *v.* cause, occasion.

occidental, *a.* western.

occidente, *m.* west.

océano, *m.* ocean.

Océano Atlántico, Atlantic Ocean.

Océano Pacífico, Pacific Ocean.

ocelote, *m.* ocelot.

ochenta, *a. & pron.* eighty.

ocho, *a. & pron.* eight.

ochocientos, *a. & pron.* eight hundred.

ocio, *m.* idleness, leisure.

ociosidad, *f.* idleness, laziness.

ocioso, *a.* idle, lazy.

ocre, *m.* ochre.

octagonal, *a.* octagonal.

octava, *f.* octave.

octavo, *a.* eighth.

octubre, *m.* October.

oculista, *m. & f.* oculist.

ocultación, *f.* concealment.

ocultar, *v.* hide, conceal.

oculto, *a.* hidden.

ocupación, *f.* occupation.

ocupado, *a.* occupied; busy.

ocupante, *m. & f.* occupant.

ocupar, *v.* occupy.

ocuparse de, *v.* take care of, take charge of.

ocurrencia, *f.* occurrence; witticism.

ocurrente, *a.* witty.

ocurrir, *v.* occur, happen.

oda, *f.* ode.

odio, *m.* hate. **—odiar,** *v.*

odiosidad, *f.* odiousness; hatred.

odioso, *a.* obnoxious, odious.

odisea, *f.* odyssey.

OEA, *abbr.* (**Organización de los Estados Americanos**). OAS (**Organization of American States**).

oeste, *m.* west.

ofender, *v.* offend, wrong.

ofenderse, *v.* be offended, take offense.

ofensa, *f.* offense.

ofensiva, *f.* offensive.

ofensivo, *a.* offensive.

ofensor -ra, *n.* offender.

oferta, *f.* offer, proposal.

ofertorio, *m.* offertory.

oficial, *a. & m.* official; officer.

oficialmente, *adv.* officially.

oficiar, *v.* officiate.

oficina, *f.* office.

oficio, *m.* office; trade; church service.

oficioso, *a.* officious.

ofrecer, *v.* offer.

ofrecimiento, *m.* offer, offering. **o. de presentación,** introductory offer.

ofrenda, *f.* offering.

oftalmía, *f.* ophthalmia.

ofuscamiento, *m.* obfuscation; bewilderment.

ofuscar, *v.* obfuscate; bewilder.

ogro, *m.* ogre.

oído, *m.* ear; hearing.

oír, *v.* hear; listen.

ojal, *m.* buttonhole.

ojalá, *interj. expressing wish or hope.* **o. que . . .** would that . . .

ojeada, *f.* glance; peep; look.

ojear, *v.* eye, look at, glance at, stare at.

ojeriza, *f.* spite; grudge.

ojiva, *f.* pointed arch, ogive.

ojo, *m.* eye. **¡Ojo!** Look out!

ola, *f.* wave.

olaje, *m.* surge of waves.

oleada, *f.* swell.

oleo, *m.* oil; holy oil; extreme unction.

oleoducto, *m.* pipeline.

oleomargarina, *f.* oleomargarine.

oleoso, *a.* oily.

oler, *v.* smell.

olfatear, *v.* smell.

olfato, *m.* scent, smell.

oliva, *f.* olive.

olivar, *m.* olive grove.

olivo, *m.* olive tree.

olla, *f.* pot, kettle. **o. podrida,** stew.

olmo, *m.* elm.

olor, *m.* odor, smell, scent.

oloroso, *a.* fragrant, scented.

olvidadizo, *a.* forgetful.

olvidar, *v.* forget.

olvido, *m.* omission; forgetfulness.

ombligo, *m.* navel.

ominar, *v.* foretell.

ominoso, *a.* ominous.

omisión, *f.* omission.

omitir, *v.* omit, leave out.

ómnibus, *m.* bus.

omnipotencia, *f.* omnipotence.

omnipotente, *a.* almighty.

omnipresencia, *f.* omnipresence.

omnisciencia, *f.* omniscience.

omnívoro, *a.* omnivorous.

omóplato, *m.* shoulder blade.

once, *a. & pron.* eleven.

onda, *f.* wave, ripple.

ondear, *v.* ripple.

ondulación, *f.* wave, undulation.

ondular, *v.* undulate, ripple.

onza, *f.* ounce.

opaco, *a.* opaque.

ópalo, *m.* opal.

opción, *f.* option.

ópera, *f.* opera.

operación, *f.* operation.

operar, *v.* operate; operate on.

operario -ria, *n.* operator; (skilled) worker.

operarse, *v.* have an operation.

operativo, *a.* operative.

opereta, *f.* operetta.

opiato, *m.* opiate.

opinar, *v.* opine.

opinión, *f.* opinion, view.

opio, *m.* opium.

oponer, *v.* oppose.

Oporto, *m.* port (wine).

oportunidad, *f.* opportunity.

oportunismo, *m.* opportunism.

oportunista, *n. & a.* opportunist.

oportuno, *a.* opportune, expedient.

oposición, *f.* opposition.

opresión, *f.* oppression.

opresivo, *a.* oppressive.

oprimir, *v.* oppress.

oprobio, *m.* infamy.

optar, *v.* select, choose.

óptica, *f.* optics.

óptico, *a.* optic.

optimismo, *m.* optimism.

optimista, *a. & n.* optimistic; optimist.

óptimo, *a.* best.

opuesto, *a.* opposite; opposed.

opugnar, *v.* attack.

opulencia, *f.* opulence, wealth.

opulento, *a.* opulent, wealthy.

oración, *f.* sentence; prayer; oration.

oráculo, *m.* oracle.

orador -ra, *n.* orator, speaker.

oral, *a.* oral.

orangután, *m.* orangutan.

orar, *v.* pray.

oratoria, *f.* oratory.

oratorio, *a.* oratorical.

orbe, *m.* orb; globe.

órbita, *f.* orbit.

orden, *m. or f.* order.

ordenador, *m.* computer; regulator.

ordenador de sobremesa, desktop computer.

ordenador doméstico, home computer.

ordenanza, *f.* ordinance.

ordenar, *v.* order; put in order; ordain.

ordeñar, *v.* milk.

ordinal, *a. & m.* ordinal.

ordinario, *a.* ordinary; common, usual.

oreja, *f.* ear.

orejera, *f.* earmuff.

orfanato, *m.* orphanage.

organdí, *m.* organdy.

orgánico, *a.* organic.

organigrama, *m.* flow chart.

organismo, *m.* organism.

organista, *m. & f.* organist.

organización, *f.* organization.

organizar, *v.* organize.

órgano, *m.* organ.

orgía, *f.* orgy, revel.

orgullo, *m.* pride.

orgulloso, *a.* proud.

orientación, *f.* orientation.

oriental, *a.* Oriental; eastern.

orientar, *v.* orient.

oriente, *m.* orient, east.

orificación, *f.* gold filling (for tooth).

origen, *m.* origin; parentage, descent.

original, *a.* original.

originalidad, *f.* originality.

originalmente, *adv.* originally.

originar, *v.* originate.

orilla, *f.* shore; bank; edge.

orín, *m.* rust.

orina, *f.* urine.

orinar, *v.* urinate.

orines, *m.pl.* urine.

oriol, *m.* oriole.

orla, *f.* border; edging.

ornado, *a.* ornate.

ornamentación, *f.* ornamentation.

ornamento, *m.* ornament. —**ornamentar,** *v.*

ornar, *v.* ornament, adorn.

oro, *m.* gold.

oropel, *m.* tinsel.

orquesta, *f.* orchestra.

ortiga, *f.* nettle.

ortodoxo, *a.* orthodox.

ortografía, *f.* orthography, spelling.

ortóptero, *a.* orthopterous.

oruga, *f.* caterpillar.

orzuelo, *m.* sty.

os, *pron.* you (*pl.*); yourselves.

osadía, *f.* daring.

osar, *v.* dare.

oscilación, *f.* oscillation.

oscilar, *v.* oscillate, rock.

ósculo, *m.* kiss.

oscurecer, oscuridad, oscuro = obscur-.

oso, osa, *n.* bear.

oso de felpa, teddy bear.

ostentación, *f.* ostentation, showiness.

ostentar, *v.* show off.

ostentoso, *a.* ostentatious, flashy.

ostra, *f.* oyster.

ostracismo, *m.* ostracism.
otalgia, *f.* earache.
otero, *m.* hill, knoll.
otoño, *m.* autumn, fall.
otorgar, *v.* grant, award.
otro, *a. & pron.* other, another. **o. vez,** again. **el uno al o.,** one another, each other.

ovación, *f.* ovation.
oval, ovalado, *a.* oval.
óvalo, *m.* oval.
ovario, *m.* ovary.
oveja, *f.* sheep.
ovejero, *m.* sheep dog.
ovillo, *m.* ball of yarn.
OVNI, *abbr.* (objeto volador no identificado)

UFO (unidentified flying object).
oxidación, *f.* oxidation.
oxidar, *v.* oxidize; rust.
óxido, *m.* oxide.
oxígeno, *m.* oxygen.
oyente, *m. & f.* hearer; (*pl.*) audience.
ozono, *m.* ozone.

P

pabellón, *m.* pavilion. **p. de deportes,** sports center.
pabilo, *m.* wick.
paciencia, *f.* patience.
paciente, *a. & n.* patient.
pacificar, *v.* pacify.
pacífico, *a.* pacific.
pacifismo, *m.* pacifism.
pacifista, *n. & a.* pacifist.
pacto, *m.* pact, treaty.
padecer, *v.* suffer. **p. del corazón,** have heart trouble.
padrastro, *m.* stepfather.
padre, *m.* father; priest; (*pl.*) parents.
padrenuestro, *m.* paternoster, Lord's Prayer.
padrino, *m.* godfather; sponsor.
paella, *f.* dish of rice with meat or chicken.
paga, *f.* pay, wages. **p. extra,** bonus.
pagadero, *a.* payable.
pagador -ra, *n.* payer.
paganismo, *m.* paganism.
pagano -na, *a. & n.* heathen, pagan.
pagar, *v.* pay, pay for. **p. en metálico,** pay cash.
página, *f.* page.
pago, *m.* pay, payment.
país, *m.* country, nation.
paisaje, *m.* landscape, scenery, countryside.
paisano -na, *n.* countryman; compatriot; civilian.
paja, *f.* straw.
pajar, *m.* barn.
pajarita, *f.* bow tie.
pájaro, *m.* bird.
paje, *m.* page (person).
pala, *f.* shovel, spade.
palabra, *f.* word.

palabrero, *a.* talkative; wordy.
palabrista, *m. & f.* talkative person.
palacio, *m.* palace.
paladar, *m.* palate.
paladear, *v.* taste; relish.
palanca, *f.* lever. **p. de cambio,** gearshift.
palangana, *f.* washbasin.
palco, *m.* theater box.
palenque, *m.* palisade.
paleta, *f.* mat, pallet.
paletilla, *f.* shoulder blade.
palidecer, *v.* turn pale.
palidez, *f.* paleness.
pálido, *a.* pale.
paliza, *f.* beating.
palizada, *m.* palisade.
palma, palmera, *f.* palm (tree).
palmada, *f.* slap, clap.
palmear, *v.* applaud.
palo, *m.* pole, stick; suit (in cards); (naut.) mast.
paloma, *f.* dove, pigeon.
palpar, *v.* touch, feel.
palpitación, *f.* palpitation.
palpitar, *v.* palpitate.
paludismo, *m.* malaria.
pampa, *f.* (S.A.) prairie, plain.
pan, *m.* bread; loaf. **p. de centeno,** rye bread.
pana, *f.* corduroy.
panacea, *f.* panacea.
panadería, *f.* bakery.
panadero -ra, *n.* baker.
panameño -ña, *a. & n.* Panamanian, of Panama.
panamericano, *a.* Pan-American.
páncreas, *m.* pancreas.
pandeo, *m.* bulge.
pandilla, *f.* band, gang.

panecillo, *m.* roll, muffin.
panegírico, *m.* panegyric.
pánico, *m.* panic.
panocha, *f.* ear of corn.
panorama, *m.* panorama.
panorámico, *a.* panoramic.
pantalla, *f.* (movie) screen; lamp shade.
pantalones, *m.pl.* trousers, pants.
pantano, *m.* bog, marsh, swamp.
pantanoso, *a.* swampy, marshy.
pantera, *f.* panther.
pantomima, *f.* pantomime.
pantorrilla, *f.* calf (of body).
panza, *f.* belly, paunch.
pañal, *m.* diaper.
paño, *m.* piece of cloth.
pañuelo, *m.* handkerchief.
Papa, *m.* Pope.
papa, *f.* potato.
papá, *m.* papa, father.
papado, *m.* papacy.
papagayo, *m.* parrot.
papal, *a.* papal.
Papá Noel, *m.* Santa Claus.
papel, *m.* paper; role, part. **papel crespón,** crepe paper. **papel de aluminio,** aluminum foil. **papel de escribir,** writing paper. **papel de estaño,** tin foil. **papel de lija,** sandpaper.
papelera, *f.* file cabinet; wastepaper basket.
papelería, *f.* stationery store. **papel moneda,** paper money.
paperas, *f.pl.* mumps.
paquete, *m.* package.
par, 1. *a.* even, equal. **2.** *m.* pair; equal, peer. **abierto de p. en p.,** wide open.

para, *prep.* for; in order to. **p. que,** in order that. **estar p.,** to be about to.

parabién, *m.* congratulation.

parabrisa, *m.* windshield.

paracaídas, *m.* parachute.

parachoques, *m.* (auto.) bumper.

parada, *f.* stop, halt; stopover; parade.

paradero, *m.* whereabouts; stopping place.

paradigma, *m.* paradigm.

paradoja, *f.* paradox.

parafina, *f.* paraffin.

parafrasear, *v.* paraphrase.

paraguas, *m.* umbrella.

paraguayano -na, *n. & a.* Paraguayan.

paraíso, *m.* paradise.

paralelo, *a. & m.* parallel.

parálisis, *f.* paralysis.

paralizar, *v.* paralyze.

paramédico, *m.* paramedic.

parámetro, *m.* parameter.

parapeto, *m.* parapet.

parar, *v.* stop, stem, ward off; stay.

pararse, *v.* stop; stand up.

parasítico, *a.* parasitic.

parásito, *m.* parasite.

parcela, *f.* plot of ground.

parcial, *a.* partial.

parcialidad, *f.* partiality; bias.

parcialmente, *adv.* partially.

pardo, *a.* brown.

parear, *v.* pair; match; mate.

parecer, 1. *m.* opinion. **2.** *v.* seem, appear, look.

parecerse, *v.* look alike. **p. a,** look like.

parecido, *a.* similar.

pared, *f.* wall.

pareja, *f.* pair, couple; (dancing) partner.

parentela, *f.* kinfolk.

parentesco, *m.* parentage, lineage; kin.

paréntesis, *m.* parenthesis.

paria, *m.* outcast, pariah.

paridad, *f.* parity.

pariente, *m. & f.* relative.

parir, *v.* give birth.

parisiense, *n. & a.* Parisian.

parlamentario, *a.* parliamentary.

parlamento, *m.* parliament.

paro, *m.* stoppage; strike. **p. forzoso,** unemployment.

parodia, *f.* parody.

parodista, *m. & f.* parodist.

paroxismo, *m.* paroxysm.

párpado, *m.* eyelid.

parque, *m.* park.

parquímetro, *m.* parking meter.

parra, *f.* grapevine.

párrafo, *m.* paragraph.

parranda, *f.* spree.

parrandear, *v.* carouse.

parrilla, *f.* grill; grillroom.

párroco, *m.* parish priest.

parroquia, *f.* parish.

parroquial, *a.* parochial.

parsimonia, *f.* economy, thrift.

parsimonioso, *a.* economical, thrifty.

parte, *f.* part. **de p. de,** on behalf of. **alguna p.,** somewhere. **por otra p.,** on the other hand. **dar p. a,** to notify.

partera, *f.* midwife.

partición, *f.* distribution.

participación, *f.* participation.

paricipante, *m. & f.* participant.

participar, *v.* participate; announce.

participio, *m.* participle.

partícula, *f.* particle.

particular, 1. *a.* particular; private. **2.** *m.* particular; detail; individual.

particularmente, *adv.* particularly.

partida, *f.* departure; (mil.) party; (sport) game.

partida de defunción, death certificate.

partida de matrimonio, marriage certificate.

partida de nacimiento, birth certificate.

partidario -ria, *n.* partisan.

partido, *m.* side, party, faction; game, match.

partir, *v.* leave, depart; part, cleave, split.

parto, *m.* delivery, childbirth.

pasa, *f.* raisin.

pasado, 1. *a.* past; last. **2.** *m.* past.

pasaje, *m.* passage, fare.

pasajero -ra, 1. *a.* passing, transient. **2.** *n.* passenger.

pasamano, *m.* banister.

pasaporte, *m.* passport.

pasar, *v.* pass; happen; spend (time). **p. por alto,** overlook. **p. lista,** call the roll. **p. sin,** do without.

pasatiempo, *m.* pastime; hobby.

pascua, *f.* religious holiday; (*pl.*) Christmas (season). **P. Florida,** Easter.

pase de modelos, *m.* fashion show.

paseo, *m.* walk, stroll; drive. **—pasear,** *v.*

pasillo, *m.* aisle; hallway.

pasión, *f.* passion.

pasivo, *a.* passive.

pasmar, *v.* astonish, astound, stun.

pasmo, *m.* spasm; wonder.

paso, 1. *a.* dried (fruit). **2.** *m.* pace, step; (mountain) pass.

paso cebra, crosswalk.

paso de ganso, goose step.

paso de peatones, pedestrian crossing.

pasta, *f.* paste; batter; plastic.

pasta dentífrica, toothpaste.

pastar, *v.* graze.

pastel, *m.* pastry; pie.

pastelería, *f.* pastry; pastry shop.

pasteurización, *f.* pasteurization.

pasteurizar, *v.* pasteurize.

pastilla, *f.* tablet, lozenge, coughdrop.

pasto, *m.* pasture; grass.

pastor, *m.* pastor; shepherd.

pastorear, *v.* pasture, tend (a flock).

pastrón, *m.* pastrami.

pastura, *f.* pasture.

pata, *f.* foot (of animal).

patada, *f.* kick.

patán, *m.* boor.

patanada, *f.* rudeness.

patata, *f.* potato. **p. asada,** baked potato.

patear, *v.* stamp, tramp, kick.

patente, *a. & m.* patent. — **patentar**, *v.*

paternal, paterno, *a.* paternal.

paternidad, *f.* paternity, fatherhood.

patético, *a.* pathetic.

patíbulo, *m.* scaffold; gallows.

patín, *m.* skate. — **patinar**, *v.*

patín de ruedas, roller skate.

patio, *m.* yard, court, patio.

pato, *m.* duck.

patria, *f.* native land.

patriarca, *m. & f.* patriarch.

patrimonio, *m.* inheritance.

patriota, *m. & f.* patriot.

patriótico, *a.* patriotic.

patriotismo, *m.* patriotism.

patrocinar, *v.* patronize, sponsor.

patrón -ona, *n.* patron; boss; (dress) pattern.

patrulla, *f.* patrol. — **patrullar**, *v.*

paulatino, *a.* gradual.

pausa, *f.* pause. — **pausar**, *v.*

pausa para el café, coffee break.

pauta, *f.* guideline.

pavesa, *f.* spark, cinder.

pavimentar, *v.* pave.

pavimento, *m.* pavement.

pavo, *m.* turkey. **p. real**, peacock.

pavor, *m.* terror.

payaso -sa, *n.* clown.

paz, *f.* peace.

peatón -na, *n.* pedestrian.

peca, *f.* freckle.

pecado, *m.* sin. — **pecar**, *v.*

pecador -ra, *a. & n.* sinful; sinner.

pecera, *f.* aquarium, fishbowl.

pechera, *f.* shirt front.

pecho, *m.* chest; breast; bosom.

pechuga, *f.* breast (of fowl).

pecoso, *a.* freckled, freckly.

peculiar, *a.* peculiar.

peculiaridad, *f.* peculiarity.

pedagogía, *f.* pedagogy.

pedagogo -ga, *n.* pedagogue, teacher.

pedal, *m.* pedal.

pedantesco, *a.* pedantic.

pedazo, *m.* piece.

pedernal, *m.* flint.

pedestal, *m.* pedestal.

pediatra, *m. & f.* pediatrician.

pediatría, *f.* pediatrics.

pedicuro, *m.* chiropodist.

pedir, *v.* ask, ask for, request; apply for; order.

pedregoso, *a.* rocky.

pegajoso, *a.* sticky.

pegamento, *m.* glue.

pegar, *v.* beat, strike; adhere, fasten, stick.

peinado, *m.* coiffure, hairdo.

peine, *m.* comb. — **peinar**, *v.*

peineta, *f.* (ornamental) comb.

pelagra, *f.* pellagra.

pelar, *v.* skin, pare, peel.

pelea, *f.* fight, row. — **pelearse**, *v.*

pelícano, *m.* pelican.

película, *f.* movie, motion picture, film. **p. de terror** horrow film.

peligrar, *v.* be in danger.

peligro, *m.* peril, danger.

peligroso, *a.* perilous, dangerous.

pelirrojo -ja, *a. & n.* redhead.

pellejo, *m.* skin; peel (of fruit).

pellizco, *m.* pinch. — **pellizcar**, *v.*

pelo, *m.* hair.

pelota, *f.* ball.

peltre, *m.* pewter.

peluca, *f.* wig.

peludo, *a.* hairy.

peluquería, *f.* hairdresser's shop, beauty parlor.

peluquero -ra, *n.* hairdresser.

pena, *f.* pain, grief, trouble, woe; penalty. **valer la p.**, to be worthwhile.

penacho, *m.* plume.

penalidad, *f.* trouble; penalty.

pender, *v.* hang, dangle; be pending.

pendiente, **1.** *a.* hanging; pending. **2.** *m.* incline, slope; earring, pendant.

pendón, *m.* pennant, flag.

penetración, *f.* penetration.

penetrar, *v.* penetrate, pierce.

penicilina, *f.* penicillin.

península, *f.* peninsula.

penitencia, *f.* penitence, penance.

penitenciaría, *f.* penitentiary.

penoso, *a.* painful, troublesome, grievous, distressing.

pensador -ra, *n.* thinker.

pensamiento, *m.* thought.

pensar, *v.* think; intend, plan.

pensativo, *a.* pensive, thoughtful.

pensión, *f.* pension; boardinghouse.

pensionista, *m. & f.* boarder.

pentagonal, *a.* pentagonal.

penúltimo, *a.* next-to-the-last, last but one, penultimate.

penuria, *f.* penury, poverty.

peña, *f.* rock.

peñascoso, *a.* rocky.

peñón, *m.* rock, crag.

Peñón de Gibraltar, Rock of Gibraltar.

peón, *m.* unskilled laborer; infantryman.

peonada, *f.* group of laborers.

peonía, *f.* peony.

peor, *a.* worse, worst.

pepino, *m.* cucumber.

pepita, *f.* seed (in fruit).

pequeñez, *f.* smallness; trifle.

pequeño -ña, **1.** *a.* small, little, short, slight. **2.** *n.* child.

pera, *f.* pear.

peral, *m.* pear tree.

perca, *f.* perch (fish).

percal, *m.* calico, percale.

percance, *m.* mishap, snag, hitch.

percepción, *f.* perception.

perceptivo, *a.* perceptive.

percha, *f.* perch; clothes hanger, rack.

percibir, *v.* perceive, sense; collect.

perder, *v.* lose; miss; waste. **echar a p.**, spoil. **p. el conocimiento**, lose consciousness.

perdición, *f.* perdition, downfall.

pérdida, *f.* loss.

perdiz, *f.* partridge.

perdón, *m.* pardon, forgiveness.

perdonar, *v.* forgive, pardon; spare.

perdurable, *a.* enduring, everlasting.

perdurar, *v.* endure, last.

perecedero, *a.* perishable.

perecer, *v.* perish.

peregrinación, *f.* peregrination; pilgrimage.

peregrino -na, *n.* pilgrim.

perejil, *m.* parsley.

perenne, *a.* perennial.

pereza, *f.* laziness.

perezoso, *a.* lazy, sluggish.

perfección, *f.* perfection.

perfeccionar, *v.* perfect.

perfeccionista, *a. & n.* perfectionist.

perfectamente, *adv.* perfectly.

perfecto, *a.* perfect.

perfidia, *f.* falseness, perfidy.

pérfido, *a.* perfidious.

perfil, *m.* profile.

perforación, *f.* perforation.

perforar, *v.* pierce, perforate.

perfume, *m.* perfume, scent. **—perfumar,** *v.*

pergamino, *m.* parchment.

pericia, *f.* skill, expertness.

perico, *m.* parakeet.

perímetro, *m.* perimeter.

periódico, 1. *a.* periodic. **2.** *m.* newspaper.

periodista, *m. & f.* journalist.

período, *m.* period.

periscopio, *m.* periscope.

perito -ta, *a. & n.* experienced; expert, connoisseur.

perjudicar, *v.* damage, hurt; impair.

perjudicial, *a.* harmful, injurious.

perjuicio, *m.* injury, damage.

perjurar, *v.* commit perjury.

perjurio, *m.* perjury.

perla, *f.* pearl.

permanecer, *v.* remain, stay.

permanencia, *f.* permanence; stay.

permanente, *a.* permanent.

permiso, *m.* permission; permit; furlough.

permitir, *v.* permit, enable, let, allow.

permuta, *f.* exchange, barter.

pernicioso, *a.* pernicious.

perno, *m.* bolt.

pero, *conj.* but.

peróxido, *m.* peroxide.

perpendicular, *m. & a.* perpendicular.

perpetración, *f.* perpetration.

perpetrar, *v.* perpetrate.

perpetuar, *v.* perpetuate.

perpetuidad, *f.* perpetuity.

perpetuo, *a.* perpetual.

perplejo, *a.* perplexed, puzzled.

perrito caliente, *m.* hot dog.

perro -rra, *n.* dog.

persecución, *f.* persecution.

perseguir, *v.* pursue; persecute.

perseverancia, *f.* perseverance.

perseverar, *v.* persevere.

persiana, *f.* shutter, Venetian blind.

persistente, *a.* persistent.

persistir, *v.* persist.

persona, *f.* person.

personaje, *m.* personage; (theat.) character.

personal, 1. *a.* personal. **2.** *m.* personnel, staff.

personalidad, *f.* personality.

personalmente, *adv.* personally.

perspectiva, *f.* perspective; prospect.

perspicaz, *a.* perspicacious, acute.

persuadir, *v.* persuade.

persuasión, *f.* persuasion.

persuasivo, *a.* persuasive.

pertenecer, *v.* pertain; belong.

pertinencia, *f.* pertinence.

pertinente, *a.* pertinent; relevant.

perturbar, *v.* perturb, disturb.

peruano -na, *a. & n.* Peruvian.

perversidad, *f.* perversity.

perverso, *a.* perverse.

pesadez, *f.* dullness.

pesadilla, *f.* nightmare.

pesado, *a.* heavy; dull, dreary, boring.

pésame, *m.* condolence.

pesar, 1. *m.* sorrow; regret. **a p. de,** in spite of. **2.** *v.* weigh.

pesca, *f.* fishing; catch (of fish).

pescadería, *f.* fish store.

pescado, *m.* fish. **—pescar,** *v.*

pescador, *m.* fisherman.

pesebre, *m.* stall, manger; crib.

peseta, *f.* peseta (monetary unit).

pesimismo, *m.* pessimism.

pesimista, *a. & n.* pessimistic; pessimist.

pésimo, *a.* awful, terrible, very bad.

peso, *m.* weight; load; peso (monetary unit).

pesquera, *f.* fishery.

pesquisa, *f.* investigation.

pestaña, *f.* eyelash.

pestañeo, *m.* wink, blink. **—pestañear,** *v.*

peste, *f.* plague.

pesticida, *m.* pesticide.

pestilencia, *f.* pestilence.

pétalo, *m.* petal.

petardo, *m.* firecracker.

petición, *f.* petition.

petirrojo, *m.* robin.

petrel, *m.* petrel.

pétreo, *a.* rocky.

petrificar, *v.* petrify.

petróleo, *m.* petroleum.

petrolero, *m.* oil tanker.

petunia, *f.* petunia.

pez, *m.* fish (in the water). *f.* pitch, tar.

pezuña, *f.* hoof.

piadoso, *a.* pious; merciful.

pianista, *m. & f.* pianist.

piano, *m.* piano.

picadero, *m.* riding school.

picadura, *f.* sting, bite, prick.

picamaderos, *m.* woodpecker.

picante, *a.* hot, spicy.

picaporte, *m.* latch.

picar, *v.* sting, bite, prick; itch; chop up, grind up.

pícaro -ra, 1. *a.* knavish, mischievous. **2.** *n.* rogue, rascal.

picarse, *v.* be offended, piqued.

picazón, *f.* itch.

pícea, f. spruce.

pichón, m. pigeon, squab.

pico, m. peak; pick; beak; spout; small amount.

picotazo, m. peck. **—picotear,** v.

pictórico, a. pictorial.

pie, m. foot. **al p. de la letra,** literally; thoroughly.

piedad, f. piety; pity, mercy.

piedra, f. stone.

piel, f. skin, hide; fur.

pienso, m. fodder.

pierna, f. leg.

pieza, f. piece; room; (theat.) play.

pijama, m. or m.pl. pajamas.

pila, f. pile, stack; battery; sink.

pilar, m. pillar, column.

píldora, f. pill.

piloto, m. & f. pilot.

pillo -a, n. thief; rascal.

pimentón, m. paprika.

pimienta, f. pepper (spice).

pimiento, m. pepper (vegetable).

pináculo, m. pinnacle.

pincel, m. (artist's) brush.

pinchadiscos, m & f. disk jockey.

pinchazo, m. puncture; prick. **—pinchar,** v.

pingajo, m. rag, tatter.

pino, m. pine.

pinta, f. pint.

pintar, v. paint; portray, depict.

pintor -ra, n. painter.

pintoresco, a. picturesque.

pintura, f. paint; painting.

pinzas, f.pl. pincers, tweezers; claws.

piña, f. pineapple.

pío, a. pious; merciful.

piojo, m. louse.

pionero -ra, n. pioneer.

pipa, f. tobacco pipe.

pique, m. resentment, pique. **echar a p.,** sink (ship).

pira, f. pyre.

piragua, f. canoe.

piragüismo, m. canoeing.

piragüista, m. & f. canoeist.

pirámide, f. pyramid.

pirata, m. & f. pirate. **p. de aviones,** hijacker.

pisada, f. tread, step. **—pisar,** v.

pisapapeles, m. paperweight.

piscina, f. fishpond; swimming pool.

piso, m. floor.

pista, f. trace, clue, track; racetrack.

pista de tenis, tennis court.

pistola, f. pistol.

pistón, m. piston.

pitillo, m. cigarette.

pito, m. whistle. **—pitar,** v.

pizarra, f. slate; blackboard.

pizca, f. bit, speck; pinch.

pizza, f. pizza.

placentero, a. pleasant.

placer, 1. m. pleasure. **2.** v. please.

plácido, a. placid.

plaga, f. plague, scourge.

plagio, m. plagiarism; (S.A.) kidnapping.

plan, m. plan. **—planear,** v.

plancha, f. plate; slab, flatiron.

planchar, v. iron, press.

planeta, m. planet.

planificación, f. planning.

planificar, v. plan.

plano, 1. a. level, flat. **2.** m. plan; plane.

planta, f. plant; sole (of foot).

planta baja, f. ground floor.

plantación, f. plantation.

plantar, v. plant.

plantear, v. pose, present.

plantel, m. educational institution; (agr.) nursery.

plasma, m. plasma.

plástico, a. & m. plastic.

plata, f. silver; (coll.) money.

plataforma, f. platform.

plátano, m. plantain; banana.

platel, m. platter.

plática, f. chat, talk. **—platicar,** v.

platillo, m. saucer.

platillo volante, flying saucer.

plato, m. plate, dish.

playa, f. beach, shore.

plaza, f. square. **p. de toros,** bullring.

plazo, m. term, deadline; installment.

plebe, f. common people; masses.

plebiscito, m. plebiscite.

plegable, a. foldable, folding.

plegadura, f. fold, pleat. **—plegar,** v.

pleito, m. lawsuit; dispute.

plenitud, f. fullness; abundance.

pleno, a. full. **en pleno . . .** in the middle of . . .

pliego, m. sheet of paper.

pliegue, m. fold, pleat, crease.

plomería, f. plumbing.

plomero, m. plumber.

plomizo, a. leaden.

plomo, m. lead; fuse.

pluma, f. feather; (writing) pen.

pluma estilográfica, fountain pen.

plumafuente, f. fountain pen.

plumaje, m. plumage.

plumero, m. feather duster; plume.

plumoso, a. feathery.

plural, a. & m. plural.

pluriempleo, m. moonlighting.

PNB, abbr. (producto nacional bruto), GNP (gross national product).

población, f. population; town.

poblador -ra, n. settler.

poblar, v. populate; settle.

pobre, a. & n. poor; poor person.

pobreza, f. poverty, need.

pocilga, f. pigpen.

poción, f. drink; potion.

poco, 1. a. & adv. little, not much, (pl.) few. **por p.,** almost, nearly. **2.** n. **un p. (de),** a little, a bit (of).

poder, 1. m. power. **2.** v. be able to, can; be possible, may, might. **no p. menos de,** not be able to help.

poder adquisitivo, purchasing power.

poderío, m. power, might.

poderoso, a. powerful, mighty, potent.

podrido, a. rotten.

poema, m. poem.

poesía, f. poetry; poem.
poeta, m. & f. poet.
poético, a. poetic.
polaco -ca, a. & n. Polish; Pole.
polar, a. polar.
polaridad, f. polarity.
polea, f. pulley.
polen, m. pollen.
policía, f. police. m. policeman.
polideportivo, m. sports center.
poliéster, m. polyester.
poligamia, f. polygamy.
polígloto -ta, n. polyglot.
polígono industrial, m. industrial park.
polilla, f. moth.
política, f. politics; policy.
político -ca, a. & n. politic; political; politician.
póliza, f. (insurance) policy; permit, ticket.
polizonte, m. policeman.
pollada, f. brood.
pollería, f. poultry shop.
pollino, m. donkey.
pollo, m. chicken.
polo, m. pole; polo; popsicle.
polonés, a. Polish.
Polonia, f. Poland.
polvera, f. powder box; powder puff.
polvo, m. powder; dust.
polvora, f. gunpowder.
pompa, f. pomp.
pomposo, a. pompous.
pómulo, m. cheekbone.
ponche, m. punch (beverage).
ponchera, f. punch bowl.
ponderar, v. ponder.
ponderoso, a. ponderous.
poner, v. put, set, lay, place.
ponerse, v. put on; become, get; set (sun). **p. a,** start to.
poniente, m. west.
pontífice, m. pontiff.
popa, f. stern.
popular, a. popular.
popularidad, f. popularity.
populazo, m. populace; masses.
por, prep. by, through, because of; via; for. **p. qué,** why?

porcelana, f. porcelain, chinaware.
porcentaje, m. percentage.
porche, m. porch; portico.
porción, f. portion, lot.
porfiar, v. persist; argue.
pormenor, m. detail.
pornografía, f. pornography.
poro, m. pore.
poroso, a. porous.
porque, conj. because.
porqué, m. reason, motive.
porra, f. stick, club.
porrazo, m. blow.
portaaviones, m. aircraft carrier.
portador -ra, n. bearer.
portal, m. portal.
portar, v. carry.
portarse, v. behave, act.
portátil, a. portable.
portavoz, m. megaphone; m. & f. spokesperson.
porte, m. bearing; behavior; postage.
portero, m. porter; janitor.
pórtico, m. porch.
portorriqueño -ña, n. & a. Puerto Rican.
portugués -esa, a. & n. Portuguese.
posada, f. lodge, inn.
posar, v. pose.
posdata, f. postscript.
poseer, v. possess, own.
posesión, f. possession.
posibilidad, f. possibility.
posible, a. possible.
posiblemente, adv. possibly.
posición, f. position, stand.
positivo, a. positive.
posponer, v. postpone.
postal, a. postal; postcard.
poste, m. post, pillar.
posteridad, f. posterity.
posterior, a. posterior, rear.
postizo, a. false, artificial.
postrado, a. prostrate. — **postrar,** v.
postre, m. dessert.
póstumo, a. posthumous.
postura, f. posture, pose; bet.
potable, a. drinkable.
potaje, m. porridge; pot stew.
potasa, f. potash.
potasio, m. potassium.
pote, m. pot, jar.

potencia, f. potency, power.
potencial, a. & m. potential.
potentado, m. potentate.
potente, a. potent, powerful.
potestad, f. power.
potro, m. colt.
pozo, m. well.
práctica, f. practice. — **practicar,** v.
práctico, a. practical.
pradera, f. prairie, meadow.
prado, m. meadow; lawn.
pragmatismo, m. pragmatism.
preámbulo, m. preamble.
precario, a. precarious.
precaución, f. precaution.
precaverse, v. beware.
precavido, a. cautious, guarded, wary.
precedencia, f. precedence, priority.
precedente, a. & m. preceding; precedent.
preceder, v. precede.
precepto, m. precept.
preciar, v. value, prize.
preciarse de, v. take pride in.
precio, m. price. **p. del billete de avión** air fare. **p. del cubierto** cover charge.
precioso, a. precious; beautiful, gorgeous.
precipicio, m. precipice, cliff.
precipitación, f. precipitation.
precipitar, v. precipitate, rush; throw headlong.
precipitoso, a. precipitous; rash.
precisar, v. fix, specify; be necessary.
precisión, f. precision; necessity.
preciso, a. precise; necessary.
precocidad, f. precocity.
precocinado, a. precooked, ready-cooked.
precoz, a. precocious.
precursor -ra, **1.** a. preceding. **2.** n. precursor, forerunner.
predecesor, -ra, a. & n. predecessor.
predecir, v. predict, foretell.

predicación, *f.* sermon.
predicador -ra, *n.* preacher.
predicar, *v.* preach.
predicción, *f.* prediction.
predilecto, *a.* favorite, preferred.
predisponer, *v.* predispose.
predisposición, *f.* predisposition; bias.
predominante, *a.* prevailing, prevalent, predominant.
predominar, *v.* prevail, predominate.
predominio, *m.* predominance, sway.
prefacio, *m.* preface.
preferencia, *f.* preference.
preferentemente, *adv.* preferably.
preferible, *a.* preferable.
preferir, *v.* prefer.
prefijo, *m.* prefix; area code, dialing code. — **prefijar,** *v.*
pregón, *m.* proclamation; street cry.
pregonar, *v.* proclaim; cry out.
pregunta, *f.* question, inquiry. **hacer una p.,** to ask a question.
preguntar, *v.* ask, inquire.
preguntarse, *v.* wonder.
prehistórico, *a.* prehistoric.
prejuicio, *m.* prejudice.
prelacía, *f.* prelacy.
preliminar, *a.* & *m.* preliminary.
preludio, *m.* prelude.
prematuro, *a.* premature.
premeditación, *f.* premeditation.
premeditar, *v.* premeditate.
premiar, *v.* reward; award a prize to.
premio, *m.* prize, award; reward. **p. de consuelo,** consolation prize.
premisa, *f.* premise.
premura, *f.* pressure; urgency.
prenda, *f.* jewel; (personal) quality. **p. de vestir,** garment.
prender, *v.* seize, arrest, catch; pin, clip. **p. fuego a,** set fire to.

prensa, *f.* printing press; (the) press.
prensar, *v.* press, compress.
preñado, *a.* pregnant.
preocupación, *f.* worry, preoccupation.
preocupar, *v.* worry, preoccupy.
preparación, *f.* preparation.
preparar, *v.* prepare.
preparativo, *m.* preparation.
preparatorio, *m.* preparatory.
preponderante, *a.* preponderant.
preposición, *f.* preposition.
prerrogativa, *f.* prerogative, privilege.
presa, *f.* capture; (water) dam.
presagiar, *v.* presage, forebode.
presbiteriano -na, *n.* & *a.* Presbyterian.
presbítero, *m.* priest.
prescindir de, *v.* dispense with; omit.
prescribir, *v.* prescribe.
prescripción, *f.* prescription.
presencia, *f.* presence.
presenciar, *v.* witness, be present at.
presentable, *a.* presentable.
presentación, *f.* presentation; introduction.
presentar, *v.* present; introduce.
presente, *a.* & *m.* present.
presentimiento, *m.* premonition.
preservación, *f.* preservation.
preservar, *v.* preserve, keep.
preservativo, *a.* & *m.* preservative; condom.
presidencia, *f.* presidency.
presidencial, *a.* presidential.
presidente -ta, *n.* president.
presidiario -ria, *m.* & *f.* prisoner.
presidio, *m.* prison; garrison.
presidir, *v.* preside.
presión, *f.* pressure.
presión arterial, blood pressure.
preso -sa, *m.* prisoner.
presta, *f.* mint (plant).
prestador -ra, *n.* lender.

prestamista, *m.* & *f.* money lender.
préstamo, *m.* loan.
prestar, *v.* lend.
presteza, *f.* haste, promptness.
prestidigitación, *f.* sleight of hand.
prestigio, *m.* prestige.
presto, 1. *a.* quick, prompt; ready. **2.** *adv.* quickly; at once.
presumido, *a.* conceited, presumptuous.
presumir, *v.* presume; boast; claim; be conceited.
presunción, *f.* presumption; conceit.
presunto, *a.* presumed; prospective.
presuntuoso, *a.* presumptuous.
presupuesto, *m.* premise; budget.
pretender, *v.* pretend; intend; aspire.
pretendiente, *m.* suitor; pretender (to throne).
pretensión, *f.* pretension; claim.
pretérito, *a.* & *m.* preterit, past (tense).
pretexto, *m.* pretext.
prevalecer, *v.* prevail.
prevención, *f.* prevention.
prevenir, *v.* prevent; forewarn; prearrange.
preventivo, *a.* preventive.
prever, *v.* foresee.
previamente, *adv.* previously.
previo, *a.* previous.
previsible, *a.* predictable.
previsión, *f.* foresight. **p. social,** social security.
prieto, *a.* blackish, very dark.
primacía, *f.* primacy.
primario, *a.* primary.
primavera, *f.* spring (season).
primero, *a.* & *adv.* first.
primitivo, *a.* primitive.
primo -ma, *n.* cousin.
primor, *m.* beauty; excellence; lovely thing.
primoroso, *a.* exquisite, elegant; graceful.

princesa, *f.* princess.
principal, 1. *a.* principal, main. **2.** *m.* chief, head, principal.
principalmente, *adv.* principally.
príncipe, *m.* prince.
Príncipe Azul, Prince Charming.
principiar, *v.* begin, initiate.
principio, *m.* beginning, start; principle.
prioridad, *f.* priority.
prisa, *f.* hurry, haste. **darse p.,** hurry, hasten. **tener p.,** be in a hurry.
prisión, *f.* prison; imprisonment.
prisionero -ra, *n.* captive, prisoner.
prisma, *m.* prism.
prismático, *a.* prismatic.
privación, *f.* privation, want.
privado, *a.* private, secret; deprived.
privar, *v.* deprive.
privilegio, *m.* privilege.
pro, *m. or f.* benefit, advantage. **en p. de,** in behalf of. **en p. y en contra,** pro and con.
proa, *f.* prow, bow.
probabilidad, *f.* probability.
probable, *a.* probable, likely.
probablemente, *adv.* probably.
probador, *m.* fitting room.
probar, *v.* try, sample; taste; test; prove.
probarse, *v.* try on.
probidad, *f.* honesty, integrity.
problema, *m.* problem.
probo, *a.* honest.
procaz, *a.* impudent, saucy.
proceder, *v.* proceed.
procedimiento, *m.* procedure.
procesar, *v.* prosecute; sue; process.
procesión, *f.* procession.
proceso, *m.* process; (court) trial.
proclama, proclamación, *f.* proclamation.
proclamar, *v.* proclaim.
procreación, *f.* procreation.
procrear, *v.* procreate.

procurar, *v.* try; see to it; get, procure.
prodigalidad, *f.* prodigality.
prodigar, *v.* lavish; squander, waste.
prodigio, *m.* prodigy.
pródigo, *a.* prodigal; profuse; lavish.
producción, *f.* production.
producir, *v.* produce.
productivo, *a.* productive.
producto, *m.* product.
producto nacional bruto, gross national product.
proeza, *f.* prowess.
profanación, *f.* profanation.
profanar, *v.* defile, desecrate.
profanidad, *f.* profanity.
profano, *a.* profane.
profecía, *f.* prophecy.
proferir, *v.* utter, express.
profesar, *v.* profess.
profesión, *f.* profession.
profesional, *a.* professional.
profesor -ra, *n.* professor, teacher.
profeta, *m.* prophet.
profético, *a.* prophetic.
profetizar, *v.* prophesy.
proficiente, *a.* proficient.
profundamente, *adv.* profoundly, deeply.
profundidad, *f.* profundity, depth.
profundizar, *v.* deepen.
profundo, *a.* profound, deep.
profuso, *a.* profuse.
progenie, *f.* progeny, offspring.
programa, *m.* program; schedule.
programador -ra, *n.* (computer) programmer.
progresar, *v.* progress, advance.
progresión, *f.* progression.
progresista, progresivo, *a.* progressive.
progreso, *m.* progress.
prohibición, *f.* prohibition.
prohibir, *v.* prohibit, forbid.
prohibitivo, *a.* prohibitive.
prole, *f.* progeny.
proletariado, *m.* proletariat.
proliferación, *f.* proliferation.
prolijo, *a.* prolix, tedious; long-winded.

prólogo, *m.* prologue; preface.
prolongar, *v.* prolong.
promedio, *m.* average.
promesa, *f.* promise.
prometer, *v.* promise.
prometido, *a.* promised; engaged (to marry).
prominencia, *f.* prominence.
promiscuamente, *adv.* promiscuously.
promiscuo, *a.* promiscuous.
promisorio, *a.* promissory.
promoción, *f.* promotion.
promocionar, *v.* advertise, promote.
promover, *v.* promote, further.
promulgación, *f.* promulgation.
promulgar, *v.* promulgate.
pronombre, *m.* pronoun.
pronosticación, *f.* prediction, forecast.
pronosticar, *v.* predict, forecast.
pronóstico, *m.* prediction.
prontamente, *adv.* promptly.
prontitud, *f.* promptness.
pronto, 1. *a.* prompt; ready. **2.** *adv.* soon; quickly. **de p.,** abruptly.
pronunciación, *f.* pronunciation.
pronunciar, *v.* pronounce.
propagación, *f.* propagation.
propaganda, *f.* propaganda.
propagandista, *m. & f.* propagandist.
propagar, *v.* propagate.
propicio, *a.* propitious, auspicious, favorable.
propiedad, *f.* property.
propietario -ria, *n.* proprietor; owner; landlord, landlady.
propina, *f.* gratuity, tip.
propio, *a.* proper, suitable; typical; (one's) own; -self.
proponer, *v.* propose.
proporción, *f.* proportion.
proporcionado, *a.* proportionate.
proporcionar, *v.* provide with, supply, afford.
proposición, *f.* proposition, offer; proposal.

propósito, *m.* purpose; plan; **a p.,** by the way, apropos; on purpose.

propuesta, *f.* proposal, motion.

prorrata, *f.* quota.

prórroga, *f.* renewal, extension.

prorrogar, *v.* renew, extend.

prosa, *f.* prose.

prosaico, *a.* prosaic.

proscribir, *v.* prohibit, proscribe, ban.

prosecución, *f.* prosecution.

proseguir, *v.* pursue; proceed, go on.

prosélito -ta, *n.* proselyte.

prospecto, *m.* prospectus.

prosperar, *v.* prosper, thrive, flourish.

prosperidad, *f.* prosperity.

próspero, *a.* prosperous, successful.

prosternado, *a.* prostrate.

prostitución, *f.* prostitution.

prostituir, *v.* prostitute; debase.

prostituta, *f.* prostitute.

protagonista, *m. & f.* protagonist, hero, heroine.

protección, *f.* protection.

protector -ra, *a. & n.* protective; protector.

proteger, *v.* protect, safeguard. **p. contra escritura,** write-protect (diskette).

protegido -da, 1. *n.* protégé. **2.** *a.* protected. **p. contra escritura,** write-protected.

proteína, *f.* protein.

protesta, *f.* protest. — **protes-tar,** *v.*

protestante, *a. & n.* Protestant.

protocolo, *m.* protocol.

protuberancia, *f.* protuberance, lump.

protuberante, *a.* bulging.

provecho, *m.* profit, gain, benefit. **¡Buen provecho!** May you enjoy your meal!

provechoso, *a.* beneficial, advantageous, profitable.

proveer, *v.* provide, furnish.

provenir de, *v.* originate in, be due to, come from.

proverbial, *a.* proverbial.

proverbio, *m.* proverb.

providencia, *f.* providence.

providente, *a.* provident.

provincia, *f.* province.

provincial, *a.* provincial.

provinciano -na, *a. & n.* provincial.

provisión, *f.* provision, supply, stock.

provisional, *a.* provisional.

provocación, *f.* provocation.

provocador -ra, *n.* provoker.

provocar, *v.* provoke, excite.

provocativo, *a.* provocative.

proximidad, *f.* proximity, vicinity.

próximo, *a.* next; near.

proyección, *f.* projection.

proyectar, *v.* plan, project.

proyectil, *m.* projectile, missile, shell.

proyecto, *m.* plan, project, scheme.

proyector, *m.* projector.

prudencia, *f.* prudence.

prudente, *a.* prudent.

prueba, *f.* proof; trial; test.

psicoanálisis, *m.* psychoanalysis.

psicoanalista, *m. & f.* psychoanalyst.

psicodélico, *a.* psychedelic.

psicología, *f.* psychology.

psicológico, *a.* psychological.

psicólogo -ga, *n.* psychologist.

psiquiatra, *m. & f.* psychiatrist.

psiquiatría, *f.* psychiatry.

publicación, *f.* publication.

publicar, *v.* publish.

publicidad, *f.* publicity.

publicista, *m. & f.* publicity agent.

público, *a. & m.* public.

puchero, *m.* pot.

pudiente, *a.* powerful; wealthy.

pudín, *m.* pudding.

pudor, *m.* modesty.

pudoroso, *a.* modest.

pudrirse, *v.* rot.

pueblo, *m.* town, village; (the) people.

puente, *m.* bridge.

puente para peatones, *m.* footbridge.

puerco -ca, *n.* pig.

puericultura, *f.* pediatrics

pueril, *a.* childish.

puerilidad, *f.* puerility.

puerta, *f.* door; gate.

puerta giratoria, revolving door.

puerta principal, front door.

puerto, *m.* port, harbor.

puertorriqueño -ña, *a. & n.* Puerto Rican.

pues, 1. *adv.* well . . . **2.** *conj.* as, since, for.

puesto, *m.* appointment, post, job; place; stand. **p. que,** since.

pugilato, *m.* boxing.

pugna, *f.* conflict.

pugnacidad, *f.* pugnacity.

pugnar, *v.* fight; oppose.

pulcritud, *f.* neatness; exquisitness.

pulga, *f.* flea.

pulgada, *f.* inch.

pulgar, *m.* thumb.

pulir, *v.* polish; beautify.

pulmón, *m.* lung.

pulmonía, *f.* pneumonia.

pulpa, *f.* pulp.

púlpito, *m.* pulpit.

pulque, *m.* pulque (fermented maguey juice).

pulsación, *f.* pulsation, beat.

pulsar, *v.* pulsate, beat.

pulsera, *f.* wristband; bracelet.

pulso, *m.* pulse.

pulverizar, *v.* pulverize.

puma, *m.* puma.

pundonor, *m.* point of honor.

punta, *f.* point, tip, end.

puntada, *f.* stitch.

puntapié, *m.* kick.

puntería, *f.* (marksman's) aim.

puntiagudo, *a.* sharp-pointed.

puntillas, *f.pl.* **de p., en p.,** on tiptoe.

punto, *m.* point; period; spot, dot. **dos puntos,** (punct.) colon. **a p. de,** about to. **al p.,** instantly.

punto de admiración, exclamation mark.

punto de congelación, freezing point.

punto de ebullición, boiling point.

punto de vista, point of view, viewpoint.

puntuación, f. punctuation.

puntual, a. punctual, prompt.

puntuar, v. punctuate.

puñada, f. punch.

puñado, m. handful.

puñal, m. dagger.

puñalada, f. stab.

puñetazo, m. punch, fist blow.

puño, m. fist; cuff; handle.

pupila, f. pupil (of eye).

pupitre, m. writing desk, school desk.

pureza, f. purity; chastity.

purgante, m. laxative.

purgar, v. purge, cleanse.

purgatorio, m. purgatory.

puridad, f. secrecy.

purificación, f. purification.

purificar, v. purify.

purismo, m. purism.

purista, m. & f. purist.

puritanismo, m. puritanism.

puro, 1. a. pure. **2.** m. cigar.

púrpura, f. purple.

purpúreo, a. purple.

purulencia, f. purulence.

purulento, a. purulent.

pus, m. pus.

pusilánime, a. pusillanimous.

puta -to, n. prostitute.

putrefacción, f. putrefaction, rot.

putrefacto, a. putrid, rotten.

pútrido, a. putrid.

puya, f. goad.

Q

que, 1. rel. pron. who, whom; that, which. **2.** conj. than.

qué, 1. a. & pron. what. **por q., para q.,** why? **2.** adv. how.

quebrada, f. ravine, gully, gulch; stream.

quebradizo, a. fragile, brittle.

quebrar, v. break.

queda, f. curfew.

quedar, v. remain, be located; be left. **q. bien a,** be becoming to.

quedarse, v. stay, remain. **q. con,** keep, hold on to; remain with.

quedo, a. quiet; gentle.

quehacer, m. task; chore.

queja, f. complaint.

quejarse, v. complain, grumble.

quejido, m. moan.

quejoso, a. complaining.

quema, f. burning.

quemadura, f. burn.

quemar, v. burn.

querella, f. quarrel; complaint.

querencia, f. affection, liking.

querer, v. want, wish; will; love (a person). **q. decir,** mean. **sin q.,** without meaning to; unwillingly.

querido, a. dear, loved, beloved.

quesería, f. dairy.

queso, m. cheese.

queso crema, cream cheese.

quetzal, m. quetzal.

quiche, f. quiche.

quiebra, f. break, fracture; damage; bankruptcy.

quien, rel. pron. who, whom.

quién, interrog. pron. who, whom.

quienquiera, pron. whoever, whomever.

quietamente, adv. quietly.

quieto, a. quiet, still.

quietud, f. quiet, quietude.

quijada, f. jaw.

quijotesco, a. quixotic.

quilate, m. carat.

quilla, f. keel.

quimera, f. chimera; vision; quarrel.

química, f. chemistry.

químico -ca, a. & n. chemical; chemist.

quimoterapia, f. chemotherapy.

quincallería, f. hardware store.

quince, a. & pron. fifteen.

quinientos, a. & pron. five hundred.

quinina, f. quinine.

quintana, f. country home.

quinto, a. fifth.

quirúrgico, a. surgical.

quiste, m. cyst.

quitamanchas, m. stain remover.

quitanieves, m. snowplow.

quitar, v. take away, remove.

quitarse, v. take off; get rid of.

quitasol, m. parasol, umbrella.

quizá, quizás, adv. perhaps, maybe.

quórum, m. quorum.

R

rábano, m. radish.

rabí, rabino, m. rabbi.

rabia, f. rage; grudge; rabies.

rabiar, v. rage, be furious.

rabieta, f. tantrum.

rabioso, a. furious; rabid.

rabo, m. tail.

racha, f. streak.

racimo, m. bunch, cluster.

ración, f. ration. **—racionar,** v.

racionabilidad, f. rationality.

racional, a. rational.

racionalismo, m. rationalism.

racionalmente, adv. rationally.

radar, m. radar.

radiación, f. radiation.

radiador, m. radiator.

radiante, a. radiant.

radical, a. & n. radical.

radicalismo, *m.* radicalism.
radicoso, *a.* radical.
radio, *m. or f.* radio.
radioactividad, *f.* radioactivity.
radioactivo, *a.* radioactive.
radiocasete, *m.* radio cassette.
radiodifundir, *v.* broadcast.
radiodifusión, *f.* (radio) broadcasting.
radiografía, *f.* X-ray.
radiografiar, *v.* X-ray.
ráfaga, *f.* gust (of wind).
raíz, *f.* root.
raja, *f.* rip; split, crack. — **rajar,** *v.*
ralea, *f.* stock, breed.
ralo, *a.* thin, scattered.
rama, *f.* branch, bough.
ramillete, *m.* bouquet.
ramo, *m.* branch, bough; bouquet.
ramonear, *v.* browse.
rampa, *f.* ramp.
rana, *f.* frog.
rancidez, *f.* rancidity.
rancio, *a.* rancid, rank, stale, sour.
ranchero -ra, *n.* small farmer.
rancho, *m.* ranch.
rango, *m.* rank.
ranúnculo, *m.* ranunculus; buttercup.
ranura, *f.* slot.
ranura de expansión, expansion slot.
rapacidad, *f.* rapacity.
rapaz, 1. *a.* rapacious. **2.** *m.* young boy.
rapé, *m.* snuff.
rápidamente, *adv.* rapidly.
rapidez, *f.* rapidity, speed.
rápido, 1. *a.* rapid, fast, speedy. **2.** *m.* express (train).
rapiña, *f.* robbery, plundering.
rapsodia, *f.* rhapsody.
rapto, *m.* kidnapping.
raquero -ra, *n.* beachcomber.
raqueta, *f.* (tennis) racket.
rareza, *f.* rarity; freak.
raridad, *f.* rarity.
raro, *a.* rare, strange, unusual, odd, queer.

rasar, *v.* skim.
rascacielos, *m.* skyscraper.
rascar, *v.* scrape; scratch.
rasgadura, *f.* tear, rip. — **rasgar,** *v.*
rasgo, *m.* trait.
rasgón, *m.* tear.
rasguño, *m.* scratch. — **rasguñar,** *v.*
raso, 1. *a.* plain. **soldado r.,** (mil.) private. **2.** *m.* satin.
raspar, *v.* scrape; erase.
rastra, *f.* trail, track. — **rastrear,** *v.*
rastrillar, *v.* rake.
rastro, *m.* track, trail, trace; rake; flea market.
rata, *f.* rat.
ratificación, *f.* ratification.
ratificar, *v.* ratify.
rato, *m.* while, spell, short time.
ratón, *m.* mouse.
ratonera, *f.* mousetrap.
raya, *f.* dash, line, streak, stripe.
rayar, *v.* rule, stripe; scratch; cross out.
rayo, *m.* lightning bolt; ray; flash.
rayón, *m.* rayon.
raza, *f.* race; breed, stock.
razón, *f.* reason; ratio. **a r. de,** at the rate of. **tener r.,** to be right.
razonable, *a.* reasonable, sensible.
razonamiento, *m.* argument.
razonar, *v.* reason.
reacción, *f.* reaction.
reaccionar, *v.* react.
reaccionario -ria, *a. & n.* reactionary.
reacondicionar, *v.* recondition.
reactivo, *a. & m.* reactive; (chem.) reagent.
reactor, *m.* reactor.
real, *a.* royal, regal; real, actual.
realdad, *f.* royal authority.
realeza, *f.* royalty.
realidad, *f.* reality.
realista, *a. & n.* realistic; realist.
realización, *f.* achievement, accomplishment.

realizar, *v.* accomplish; fulfill; effect; (com.) realize.
realmente, *adv.* in reality, really.
realzar, *v.* enhance.
reata, *f.* rope; lasso, lariat.
rebaja, *f.* reduction.
rebajar, *v.* cheapen; reduce (in price); lower.
rebanada, *f.* slice. — **rebanar,** *v.*
rebaño, *m.* flock, herd.
rebato, *m.* alarm; sudden attack.
rebelarse, *v.* rebel, revolt.
rebelde, *a. & n.* rebellious; rebel.
rebelión, *f.* rebellion, revolt.
reborde, *m.* border.
rebotar, *v.* rebound.
rebozo, *m.* shawl.
rebuscar, *v.* search thoroughly.
rebuznar, *v.* bray.
recado, *m.* message; errand.
recaída, *f.* relapse. — **recaer,** *v.*
recalcar, *v.* stress, emphasize.
recalentar, *v.* reheat.
recámara, *f.* (Mex.) bedroom.
recapitulación, *f.* recapitulation.
recapitular, *v.* recapitulate.
recatado, *a.* coy; prudent.
recaudador -ra, *n.* tax collector.
recelar, *v.* fear, distrust.
receloso, *a.* distrustful.
recepción, *f.* reception.
recepcionista, *m. & f.* desk clerk.
receptáculo, *m.* receptacle.
receptividad, *f.* receptivity.
receptivo, *a.* receptive.
receptor, *m.* receiver.
receta, *f.* recipe; prescription.
recetar, *v.* prescribe.
rechazar, *v.* reject, spurn, discard.
rechinar, *v.* chatter.
recibimiento, *m.* reception; welcome; anteroom.
recibir, *v.* receive.
recibo, *m.* receipt.
reciclar, *v.* recycle.

recidiva, *f.* relapse.

recién, *adv.* recently, newly, just.

reciente, *a.* recent.

recinto, *m.* enclosure.

recipiente, *m.* recipient.

reciprocación, *f.* reciprocation.

recíprocamente, *adv.* reciprocally.

reciprocar, *v.* reciprocate.

reciprocidad, *f.* reciprocity.

recitación, *f.* recitation.

recitar, *v.* recite.

reclamación, *f.* claim; complaint.

reclamar, *v.* claim; complain.

reclamo, *m.* claim; advertisement, advertising; decoy.

reclinar, *v.* recline, repose, lean.

recluta, *m. & f.* recruit.

reclutar, *v.* recruit, draft.

recobrar, *v.* recover, salvage, regain.

recobro, *m.* recovery.

recoger, *v.* gather; collect; pick up. **r. el conocimiento,** regain consciousness.

recogerse, *v.* retire (for night).

recolectar, *v.* gather, assemble; harvest.

recomendación, *f.* recommendation; commendation.

recomendar, *v.* recommend; commend.

recompensa, *f.* recompense; compensation.

recompensar, *v.* reward; compensate.

reconciliación, *f.* reconciliation.

reconciliar, *v.* reconcile.

reconocer, *v.* recognize; acknowledge; inspect, examine; (mil.) reconnoiter.

reconocimiento, *m.* recognition; appreciation, gratitude.

reconstituir, *v.* reconstitute.

reconstruir, *v.* reconstruct, rebuild.

record, *m.* (sports) record.

recordar, *v.* recall, recollect; remind.

recorrer, *v.* go over; read over; cover (distance).

recorte, *m.* clipping, cutting.

recostarse, *v.* recline, lean back, rest.

recreación, *f.* recreation.

recreo, *m.* recreation.

recriminación, *f.* recrimination.

rectangular, *a.* rectangular.

rectángulo, *m.* rectangle.

rectificación, *f.* rectification.

rectificar, *v.* rectify.

recto, *a.* straight; just, fair. **ángulo r.,** right angle.

recuento, *m.* recount.

recuerdo, *m.* memory; souvenir; remembrance; (*pl.*) regards.

reculada, *f.* recoil. **—recular,** *v.*

recuperación, *f.* recuperation.

recuperar, *v.* recuperate.

recurrir, *v.* revert; resort; have recourse.

recurso, *m.* resource; recourse.

red, *f.* net; trap. **r. local** local area network.

redacción, *f.* (editorial) staff; composition (of written material).

redactar, *v.* draft, draw up; edit.

redactor -ra, *n.* editor.

redada, *f.* netful, catch, haul.

redargución, *f.* retort. **—redargüir,** *v.*

redención, *f.* redemption, salvation.

redentor, *m.* redeemer.

redimir, *v.* redeem.

redoblante, *m.* snare drum; snare dummer.

redonda, *f.* neighborhood, vicinity.

redondo, *a.* round, circular.

reducción, *f.* reduction.

reducir, *v.* reduce.

reembolso, *m.* refund. **—reembolsar,** *v.*

reemplazar, *v.* replace, supersede.

reencarnación, *f.* reincarnation.

reexaminar, *v.* reexamine.

reexpedir, *v.* forward (mail).

referencia, *f.* reference.

referéndum, *m.* referendum.

referir, *v.* relate, report on.

referirse, *v.* refer.

refinamiento, *m.* refinement.

refinar, *v.* refine.

refinería, *f.* refinery.

reflejar, *v.* reflect; think, ponder.

reflejo, *m.* reflection; glare.

reflexión, *f.* reflection, thought.

reflexionar, *v.* reflect, think.

reflujo, *m.* ebb; ebb tide.

reforma, *f.* reform. **—reformar,** *v.*

reformación, *f.* reformation.

reformador -ra, *n.* reformer.

reforma tributaria, tax reform.

reforzar, *v.* reinforce, strengthen; encourage.

refractario, *a.* refractory.

refrán, *m.* proverb, saying.

refrenar, *v.* curb, rein; restrain.

refrescar, *v.* refresh, freshen, cool.

refresco, *m.* refreshment; cold drink.

refrigeración, *f.* refrigeration.

refrigerador, *m.* refrigerator.

refrigerar, *v.* refrigerate.

refuerzo, *m.* reinforcement.

refugiado -da, refugee.

refugiarse, *v.* take refuge.

refugio, *m.* refuge, asylum, shelter.

refulgencia, *f.* refulgence.

refulgente, *a.* refulgent.

refulgir, *v.* shine.

refunfuñar, *v.* mutter, grumble, growl.

refutación, *f.* refutation; rebuttal.

refutar, *v.* refute.

regadera, *f.* watering can.

regadizo, *a.* irrigable.

regadura, *f.* irrigation.

regalar, *v.* give (a gift), give away.

regaliz, *m.* licorice.

regalo, *m.* gift, present, **con r.,** in luxury.

regañar, *v.* reprove; scold.

regaño, *m.* reprimand; scolding.

regar, *v.* water, irrigate.

regatear, *v.* haggle.

regateo, *m.* bargaining, haggling.

regazo, *m.* lap.

regencia, *f.* regency.

regeneración, *f.* regeneration.

regenerar, *v.* regenerate.

regente -ta, *a. & n.* regent.

régimen, *m.* regime; diet.

regimentar, *v.* regiment.

regimiento, *m.* regiment.

región, *f.* region.

regional, *a.* regional, sectional.

regir, *v.* rule; be in effect.

registrar, *v.* register; record; search.

registro, *m.* register; record; search.

regla, *f.* rule, regulation. **en r.,** in order.

reglamento, *m.* code of regulations.

regocijarse, *v.* rejoice, exult.

regocijo, *f.* rejoicing; merriment, joy.

regordete, *a.* chubby, plump.

regresar, *v.* go back, return.

regresión, *f.* regression.

regresivo, *a.* regressive.

regreso, *m.* return.

regulación, *f.* regulation.

regular, 1. *a.* regular; fair, middling. **2.** *v.* regulate.

regularidad, *f.* regularity.

regularmente, *adv.* regularly.

rehabilitación, *f.* rehabilitation.

rehabilitar, *v.* rehabilitate.

rehén, *m.* hostage.

rehogar, *v.* brown.

rehusar, *v.* refuse; decline.

reina, *f.* queen.

reinado, *m.* reign. **—reinar,** *v.*

reino, *m.* kingdom; realm; reign.

reír, *v.* laugh.

reiteración, *f.* reiteration.

reiterar, *v.* reiterate.

reja, *f.* grating, grillwork.

relación, *f.* relation; account, report.

relacionar, *v.* relate, connect.

relajamiento, *m.* laxity, laxness.

relajar, *v.* relax, slacken.

relámpago, *m.* lightning; flash (of lightning).

relatador -ra, *n.* teller.

relatar, *v.* relate, recount.

relativamente, *adv.* relatively.

relatividad, *f.* relativity.

relativo, *a.* relative.

relato, *m.* account, story.

relegación, *f.* relegation.

relegar, *v.* relegate.

relevar, *v.* relieve.

relicario, *m.* reliquary; locket.

relieve, *m.* (sculpture) relief.

religión, *f.* religion.

religiosidad, *f.* religiosity.

religioso -sa, 1. *a.* religious. **2.** *m.* member of a religious order.

reliquia, *f.* relic.

rellenar, *v.* refill; fill up, stuff.

relleno, *m.* filling; stuffing.

reloj, *m.* clock; watch.

reloj de pulsera, wrist watch.

relojería, *f.* watchmaker's shop.

relojero -ra, *n.* watchmaker.

relucir, *v.* glow, shine; excel.

relumbrar, *v.* glitter, sparkle.

remache, *m.* rivet. **—remachar,** *v.*

remar, *v.* row (a boat).

rematado, *a.* finished; sold.

remate, *m.* end, finish; auction. **de r.,** utterly.

remedador -ra, *n.* imitator.

remedar, *v.* imitate.

remedio, *m.* remedy. **—remediar,** *v.*

remendar, *v.* mend, patch.

remesa, *f.* shipment; remittance.

remiendo, *m.* patch.

remilgado, *a.* prudish; affected.

reminiscencia, *f.* reminiscence.

remitir, *v.* remit.

remo, *m.* oar.

remolacha, *f.* beet.

remolcador, *m.* tug (boat); tow truck.

remolino, *m.* whirl; whirlpool; whirlwind.

remolque, *m.* tow. **—remolcar,** *v.*

remontar, *v.* ascend, go up.

remontarse, *v.* get excited; soar. **r. a,** date from; go back to (in time).

remordimiento, *m.* remorse.

remotamente, *adv.* remotely.

remoto, *a.* remote.

remover, *v.* remove; stir; shake; loosen.

rempujar, *v.* jostle.

remuneración, *f.* remuneration.

remunerar, *v.* remunerate.

renacido, *a.* reborn, bornagain.

renacimiento, *m.* rebirth; renaissance.

rencor, *m.* rancor, bitterness, animosity; grudge.

rencoroso, *a.* rancorous, bitter.

rendición, *f.* surrender.

rendido, *a.* weary, worn out.

rendir, *v.* yield; surrender; give up; win over.

renegado -da, *n.* renegade.

renglón, *m.* line; (com.) item.

reno, *m.* reindeer.

renombre, *m.* renown.

renovación, *f.* renovation, renewal.

renovar, *v.* renew; renovate.

renta, *f.* income; rent.

rentar, *v.* yield; rent.

renuencia, *f.* reluctance.

renuente, *a.* reluctant.

renuncia, *f.* resignation; renunciation.

renunciar, *v.* resign; renounce, give up.

reñir, *v.* scold, berate; quarrel, wrangle.

reo, *a. & n.* criminal; convict.

reorganizar, *v.* reorganize.

reparación, *f.* reparation, atonement; repair.

reparar, *v.* repair; mend; stop, stay over. **r. en,** notice; consider.

reparo, *m.* repair; remark; difficulty; objection.

repartición, *f.,* **repartimiento, reparto,** *m.* division, distribution.

repartir, *v.* divide, apportion, distribute; (theat.) cast.

repaso, *m.* review. **—repasar,** *v.*

repatriación, *f.* repatriation.

repatriar, *v.* repatriate.

repeler, *v.* repel.

repente, *m.* **de r.,** suddenly; unexpectedly.

repentinamente, *adv.* suddenly.

repentino, *a.* sudden.

repercusión, *f.* repercussion.

repertorio, *m.* repertoire.

repetición, *f.* repetition; action replay.

repetidamente, *adv.* repeatedly.

repetir, *v.* repeat.

repisa, *f.* shelf.

réplica, *f.* reply; objection; replica.

replicar, *v.* reply; answer back.

repollo, *m.* cabbage.

reponer, *v.* replace; repair.

reponerse, *v.* recover, get well.

reporte, *m.* report; news.

repórter, reportero -ra, *n.* reporter.

reposado, *a.* tranquil, peaceful, quiet.

reposo, *m.* repose, rest. **—reposar,** *v.*

reposte, *f.* pantry.

represalia, *f.* reprisal.

representación, *f.* representation; (theat.) performance.

representante, *m. & f.* representative, agent.

representar, *v.* represent; depict; (theat.) perform.

representativo, *a.* representative.

represión, *f.* repression.

represivo, *a.* repressive.

reprimenda, *f.* reprimand.

reprimir, *v.* repress, quell.

reproche, *m.* reproach. **—reprochar,** *v.*

reproducción, *f.* reproduction.

reproducir, *v.* reproduce.

reptil, *m.* reptile.

república, *f.* republic.

republicano -na, *a. & n.* republican.

repudiación, *f.* repudiation.

repudiar, *v.* repudiate; disown.

repuesto, *m.* spare part. **de r.,** spare.

repugnancia, *f.* repugnance.

repugnante, *a.* disgusting, repugnant, repulsive, revolting.

repugnar, *v.* disgust.

repulsa, *f.* refusal; repulse.

repulsivo, *a.* repulsive.

reputación, *f.* reputation.

reputar, *v.* repute; appreciate.

requerir, *v.* require.

requesón, *m.* cottage cheese.

requisición, *f.* requisition.

requisito, *m.* requisite, requirement.

res, *f.* head of cattle.

resaca, *f.* hangover.

resbalar, *v.* slide; slip.

resbaloso, *a.* slippery.

rescate, *m.* rescue; ransom. **—rescatar,** *v.*

rescindir, *v.* rescind.

resentimiento, *m.* resentment.

resentirse, *v.* resent.

reserva, *f.* reserve. **—reservar,** *v.*

reservación, *f.* reservation.

resfriado, *m.* (med.) cold.

resfriarse, *v.* catch cold.

resguardar, *v.* guard, protect.

residencia, *f.* residence; seat, headquarters.

residente, *a. & n.* resident.

residir, *v.* reside.

residuo, *m.* remainder.

resignación, *f.* resignation.

resignar, *v.* resign.

resina, *f.* resin; rosin.

resistencia, *f.* resistance.

resistir, *v.* resist; endure.

resolución, *f.* resolution.

resolutivamente, *adv.* resolutely.

resolver, *v.* resolve; solve.

resonante, *a.* resonant.

resonar, *v.* resound.

resorte, *m.* (mech.) spring.

respaldar, *v.* endorse; back.

respaldo, *m.* back (of a seat).

respectivo, *a.* respective.

respecto, *m.* relation, proportion; **r. a,** concerning, regarding.

respetabilidad, *f.* respectability.

respetable, *a.* respectable.

respeto, *m.* respect. **—respetar,** *v.*

respetuosamente, *adv.* respectfully.

respetuoso, *a.* respectful.

respiración, *f.* respiration, breath.

respirar, *v.* breathe.

resplandeciente, *a.* resplendent.

resplandor, *m.* brightness, glitter.

responder, *v.* respond, answer.

responsabilidad, *f.* responsibility.

responsable, *a.* responsible.

respuesta, *f.* answer, response, reply.

resquicio, *m.* crack, slit.

resta, *f.* subtraction; remainder.

restablecer, *v.* restore; reestablish.

restablecerse, *v.* recover, get well.

restar, *v.* remain; subtract.

restauración, *f.* restoration.

restaurante, *m.* restaurant.

restaurar, *v.* restore.

restitución, *f.* restitution.

restituir, *v.* restore, give back.

resto, *m.* remainder, rest; (*pl.*) remains.

restorán, *m.* restaurant.

restregar, *v.* rub hard; scrub.

restricción, *f.* restriction.

restrictivo, *a.* restrictive.

restringir, *v.* restrict, curtail.

resucitar, *v.* revive, resuscitate.

resuelto, *a.* resolute.

resultado, *m.* result.

resultar, *v.* result; turn out; ensue.

resumen, *m.* résumé, summary, **en r.,** in brief.

resumir, *v.* sum up.

resurgir, *v.* resurge, reappear.

resurrección, f. resurrection.
retaguardia, f. rear guard.
retal, m. remnant.
retardar, v. retard, slow.
retardo, m. delay.
retención, f. retention.
retener, v. retain, keep; withhold.
reticencia, f. reticence.
reticente, a. reticent.
retirada, f. retreat, retirement.
retirar, v. retire, retreat, withdraw.
retiro, m. retirement.
retorcer, v. wring.
retórica, f. rhetoric.
retórico, a. rhetorical.
retorno, m. return.
retozo, m. frolic, romp. —**retozar,** v.
retozón, a. frisky.
retracción, f. retraction.
retractar, v. retract.
retrasar, v. delay, set back.
retrasarse, v. be slow.
retraso, m. delay, lag, slowness.
retratar, v. portray; photograph.
retrato, m. portrait; picture, photograph.
retreta, f. (mil.) retreat.
retrete, m. toilet.
retribución, f. retribution.
retroactivo, a. retroactive.
retroalimentación, f. feedback.
retroceder, v. recede, go back, draw back, back up.
retumbar, v. resound, rumble.
reumático, a. rheumatic.
reumatismo, m. rheumatism.
reunión, f. gathering, meeting, party; reunion.
reunir, v. gather, collect, bring together.
reunirse, v. meet, assemble, get together.
revelación, f. revelation.
revelar, v. reveal; betray; (phot.) develop.
reventa, f. resale.
reventar, v. burst; split apart.
reventón, m. blowout (of tire).
reverencia, f. reverence.

reverendo, a. reverend.
reverente, a. reverent.
revertir, v. revert.
revés, m. reverse; back, wrong side. **al r.,** just the opposite; inside out.
revisar, v. revise; review.
revisión, f. revision.
revista, f. magazine, periodical; review.
revivir, v. revive.
revocación, f. revocation.
revocar, v. revoke, reverse.
revolotear, v. hover.
revolución, f. revolution.
revolucionario -ria, a. & n. revolutionary.
revolver, v. revolve; stir, agitate.
revólver, m. revolver, pistol.
revuelta, f. revolt; turn.
rey, m. king.
reyerta, f. quarrel, wrangle.
rezar, v. pray.
rezongar, v. grumble; mutter.
ría, f. estuary.
riachuelo, m. creek.
riba, f. embankment.
rico, a. rich, wealthy; delicious.
ridículamente, adv. ridiculously.
ridiculizar, v. ridicule.
ridículo, a. & m. ridiculous; ridicule.
riego, m. irrigation.
rienda, f. rein.
riesgo, m. risk, gamble.
rifa, f. raffle; lottery; scuffle.
rifle, m. rifle.
rígidamente, adv. rigidly.
rigidez, f. rigidity.
rígido, a. rigid, stiff.
rigor, m. rigor.
riguroso, a. rigorous, strict.
rima, f. rhyme. —**rimar,** v.
rimel, m. mascara.
rincón, m. corner, nook.
rinoceronte, m. rhinoceros.
riña, f. quarrel, feud.
riñón, m. kidney.
río, m. river. **r. abajo** downstream, downriver. **r. arriba,** upstream, upriver.
ripio, m. debris.
riqueza, f. wealth.
risa, f. laugh; laughter.
risco, m. cliff.

risibilidad, f. risibility.
risotada, f. peal of laughter.
risueño, a. cheerful, smiling.
rítmico, a. rhythmical.
ritmo, m. rhythm.
rito, m. rite.
ritual, a. & m. ritual.
rivalidad, f. rivalry.
rivera, f. brook.
rizado, a. curly.
rizo, m. curl. —**rizar,** v.
robar, v. rob, steal.
roble, m. oak.
roblón, m. rivet. —**roblar,** v.
robo, m. robbery, theft.
robustamente, adv. robustly.
robusto, a. robust.
roca, f. rock; cliff.
rociada, f. spray, sprinkle. —**rociar,** v.
rocío, m. dew.
rocoso, a. rocky.
rodar, v. roll; roam.
rodear, v. surround, encircle.
rodeo, m. turn, winding; roundup.
rodilla, f. knee.
rodillo, m. roller.
rodio, m. rhodium.
rododendro, m. rhododendron.
roedor, m. rodent.
roer, v. gnaw.
rogación, f. request, entreaty.
rogar, v. beg, plead with, supplicate.
rojizo, a. reddish.
rojo, a. red.
rollizo, a. chubby.
rollo, m. roll; coil.
romadizo, m. head cold.
romance, m. romance; ballad.
románico, a. Romance.
romano -na, a. & n. Roman.
romántico, a. romantic.
romería, f. pilgrimage; picnic.
romero -ra, n. pilgrim.
rompecabezas, m. puzzle (pastime).
romper, v. break, smash, shatter; sever; tear.
rompible, a. breakable.
ron, m. rum.
roncar, v. snore.
ronco, a. hoarse.
ronda, f. round.

rondar, v. prowl.

ronquido, m. snore.

ronronear, v. purr.

ronzal, m. halter.

roña, f. scab; filth.

ropa, f. clothes, clothing. r. blanca, linen. r. interior, underwear.

ropa de marca, designer clothing.

ropero, m. closet.

rosa, f. rose. r. náutica, compass.

rosado, a. pink, rosy.

rosal, m. rose bush.

rosario, m. rosary.

rosbif, m. roast beef.

rosca, f. thread (of screw).

róseo, a. rosy.

rostro, m. face, countenance.

rota, f. defeat; (naut.) course.

rotación, f. rotation.

rotatorio, a. rotary.

rótula, f. kneecap.

rotulador, m. felt-tipped pen.

rótulo, m. label. —rotular, v.

rotundo, a. round; sonorous.

rotura, f. break, fracture, rupture.

rozar, v. rub against, chafe; graze.

rubí, m. ruby.

rubio -bia, a. & n. blond.

rubor, m. blush; bashfulness.

rúbrica, f. caption; scroll.

rucho, m. donkey.

rudeza, f. rudeness; roughness.

rudimentario, a. rudimentary.

rudimento, m. rudiment.

rudo, a. rude, rough.

rueda, f. wheel.

rueda de feria, Ferris wheel.

ruego, m. plea; entreaty.

rufián, m. ruffian.

rufo, a. sandy haired.

rugir, v. bellow, roar.

rugoso, a. wrinkled.

ruibarbo, m. rhubarb.

ruido, m. noise.

ruidoso, a. noisy.

ruina, f. ruin, wreck.

ruinar, v. ruin, destroy.

ruinoso, a. ruinous.

ruiseñor, m. nightingale.

ruleta, f. roulette.

rumba, f. rumba (dance or music).

rumbo, m. course, direction.

rumor, m. rumor; murmur.

runrún, m. rumor.

ruptura, f. rupture, break.

rural, a. rural.

Rusia, f. Russia.

ruso -sa, a. & n. Russian.

rústico -ca, a. & n. rustic. en r., paperback f.

ruta, f. route.

rutina, f. routine.

rutinario, a. routine.

S

sábado, m. Saturday.

sábalo, m. shad.

sábana, f. sheet.

sabañon, m. chilblain.

saber, 1. m. knowledge. 2. v. know; learn, find out; know how to; taste. a s., namely, to wit.

sabiduría, f. wisdom; learning.

sabio -a, 1. a. wise; scholarly. 2. n. sage; scholar.

sable, m. saber.

sabor, m. flavor, taste, savor.

saborear, v. savor, relish.

sabotaje, m. sabotage.

sabroso, a. savory, tasty.

sabueso, m. hound.

sacacorchos, m. corkscrew.

sacapuntas, f. pencil sharpener.

sacar, v. draw out; take out; take.

sacerdocio, m. priesthood.

sacerdote, m. priest.

saciar, v. satiate.

saco, m. sack, bag, pouch; suit coat, jacket.

sacramento, m. sacrament.

sacrificio, m. sacrifice. — sacrificar, v.

sacrilegio, m. sacrilege.

sacristán, m. sexton.

sacro, a. sacred, holy.

sacrosanto, a. sacrosanct.

sacudir, v. shake, jerk, jolt.

sádico, a. sadistic.

sadismo, m. sadism.

sagacidad, f. sagacity.

sagaz, a. sagacious, sage.

sagrado, a. sacred, holy.

sal, f. salt; (coll.) wit.

sala, f. room; living room, parlor; hall, auditorium.

salado, a. salted, salty; (coll.) witty.

salar, v. salt; steep in brine.

salario, m. salary, wages.

salchicha, f. sausage.

sal de la Higuera, Epsom salts.

saldo, m. remainder, balance; (bargain) sale.

saldo acreedor, credit balance.

saldo deudor, debit balance.

salero, m. salt shaker.

salida, f. exit, outlet; departure.

salida de urgencia, emergency exit, fire exit.

salir, v. go out, come out; set out, leave, start; turn out, result.

salirse de, v. get out of. s. con la suya, have one's own way.

salitre, m. saltpeter.

saliva, f. saliva.

salmo, m. psalm.

salmón, m. salmon.

salmonete, m. red mullet.

salmuera, f. pickle; brine.

salobre, a. salty.

salón, m. parlor, living room; hall. s. de baile, dance hall. s. de belleza beauty parlor.

salpicar, v. spatter, splash.

salpullido, m. rash.

salsa, f. sauce; gravy.

saltamontes, m. grasshopper.

salteador, m. highwayman.

salto, m. jump, leap, spring. —saltar, v.

saltón, m. grasshopper.

salubre, *a.* salubrious, healthful.

salubridad, *f.* health.

salud, *f.* health.

saludable, *a.* healthful, wholesome.

saludar, *v.* greet; salute.

saludo, *m.* greeting; salutation; salute.

salutación, *f.* salutation.

salva, *f.* salvo.

salvación, *f.* salvation; deliverance.

salvador -ra, *n.* savior; rescuer.

salvaguardia, *m.* safeguard.

salvaje, *a. & n.* savage, wild (person).

salvamento, *m.* salvation; rescue.

salvar, *v.* save; salvage; rescue; jump over.

salvavidas, *m.* life preserver.

salvia, *f.* sage (plant).

salvo, 1. *a.* safe. **2.** *prep.* except, save (for). **s. que,** unless.

San, *title.* Saint.

sanar, *v.* heal, cure.

sanatorio, *m.* sanatorium.

sanción, *f.* sanction. **—sancionar,** *v.*

sancochar, *v.* parboil.

sandalia, *f.* sandal.

sandez, *f.* stupidity.

sandía, *f.* watermelon.

saneamiento, *m.* sanitation.

sangrar, *v.* bleed.

sangre, *f.* blood.

sangriento, *a.* bloody.

sanguinario, *a.* bloodthirsty.

sanidad, *f.* health.

sanitario, *a.* sanitary.

sano, *a.* healthy, sound, sane; healthful, wholesome.

santidad, *f.* sanctity, holiness.

santificar, *v.* sanctify.

santo -ta, 1. *a.* holy, saintly. **2.** *m.* saint.

Santo -ta, *title.* Saint.

santuario, *m.* sanctuary, shrine.

saña, *f.* rage, anger.

sapiente, *a.* wise.

sapo, *m.* toad.

saquear, *v.* sack; ransack; plunder.

sarampión, *m.* measles.

sarape, *m.* (Mex.) woven blanket; shawl.

sarcasmo, *m.* sarcasm.

sarcástico, *a.* sarcastic.

sardina, *f.* sardine.

sargento, *m.* sergeant.

sarna, *f.* itch.

sartén, *m.* frying pan.

sastre, *m.* tailor.

satánico, *a.* satanic.

satélite, *m.* satellite.

sátira, *f.* satire.

satírico, *a. & m.* satirical; satirist.

satirizar, *v.* satirize.

sátiro, *m.* satyr.

satisfacción, *f.* satisfaction.

satisfacer, *v.* satisfy.

satisfactorio, *a.* satisfactory.

saturación, *f.* saturation.

saturar, *v.* saturate.

sauce, *m.* willow.

sauna, *f.* sauna.

savia, *f.* sap.

saxofón, saxófono, *m.* saxophone.

saya, *f.* skirt.

sazón, *f.* season; seasoning. **a la s.,** at that time.

sazonar, *v.* flavor, season.

se, *pron.* -self, -selves.

seca, *f.* drought.

secador, secador de pelo, *m.* hair dryer.

secante, *a.* **papel s.,** blotting paper.

secar, *v.* dry.

sección, *f.* section.

seco, *a.* dry; curt.

secreción, *f.* secretion.

secretar, *v.* secrete.

secretaría, *f.* secretary's office; secretariat.

secretario -ra, *n.* secretary.

secreto, *a. & m.* secret.

secta, *f.* denomination; sect.

secuela, *f.* result; sequel.

secuestrar, *v.* abduct, kidnap; hijack.

secuestro, *m.* abduction, kidnapping.

secular, *a.* secular.

secundario, *a.* secondary.

sed, *f.* thirst. **tener s., estar con s.,** to be thirsty.

seda, *f.* silk.

sedar, *v.* quiet, allay.

sedativo, *a. & m.* sedative.

sede, *f.* seat, headquarters.

sedentario, *a.* sedentary.

sedición, *f.* sedition.

sedicioso, *a.* seditious.

sediento, *a.* thirsty.

sedimento, *m.* sediment.

sedoso, *a.* silky.

seducir, *v.* seduce.

seductivo, *a.* seductive, alluring.

segar, *v.* reap, harvest; mow.

seglar, *m. & f.* layman, laywoman.

segmento, *m.* segment.

segregar, *v.* segregate.

seguida, *f.* succession. **en s.,** right away, at once.

seguido, *a.* consecutive.

seguir, *v.* follow; continue, keep on, go on.

según, 1. *prep.* according to, **2.** *conj.* as.

segundo, *a. & m.* second. **—segundar,** *v.*

seguridad, *f.* safety, security; assurance.

seguro, 1. *a.* safe, secure; sure, certain. **2.** *m.* insurance.

seis, *a. & pron.* six.

seiscientos, *a. & pron.* six hundred.

selección, *f.* selection, choice.

seleccionar, *v.* select, choose.

selecto, *a.* select, choice, elite.

sello, *m.* seal; stamp. **—sellar,** *v.*

selva, *f.* forest; jungle.

selvoso, *a.* sylvan.

semáforo, *m.* semaphore; traffic light.

semana, *f.* week.

semana inglesa, five-day work week.

semana laboral, work week.

semanal, *a.* weekly.

semántica, *f.* semantics.

semblante, *m.* look, expression.

sembrado, *m.* sown field.

sembrar, *v.* sow, seed.

semejante, 1. *a.* like, similar; such (a). **2.** *m.* fellow man.

semejanza, *f.* similarity, likeness.

semejar, *v.* resemble.

semilla, *f.* seed.

seminario, *m.* seminary.

sémola, *f.* semolina.

senado, *m.* senate.

senador -ra, *n.* senator.

sencillez, *f.* simplicity; naturalness.

sencillo, *a.* simple, natural; single.

senda, *f.* **sendero,** *m.* path, footpath.

senectud, *f.* old age.

senil, *a.* senile.

seno, *m.* breast, bosom.

sensación, *f.* sensation.

sensacional, *a.* sensational.

sensato, *a.* sensible, wise.

sensibilidad, *f.* sensibility; sensitiveness.

sensible, *a.* sensitive; emotional.

sensitivo, *a.* sensitive.

sensual, *a.* sensual.

sensualidad, *f.* sensuality.

sentar, *v.* seat. **s. bien,** fit well, be becoming.

sentarse, *v.* sit, sit down.

sentencia, *f.* (court) sentence.

sentidamente, *adv.* feelingly.

sentido, *m.* meaning, sense; consciousness.

sentido común, common sense.

sentimental, *a.* sentimental.

sentimiento, *m.* sentiment, feeling.

sentir, *v.* feel, sense; hear; regret, be sorry.

seña, *f.* sign, indication; (*pl.*) address.

señal, *f.* sign, signal; mark.

señalar, *v.* designate, point out; mark.

señal de marcar, dial tone.

señor, *m.* gentleman; lord; (title) Mr., Sir.

señora, *f.* lady; wife; (title) Mrs., Madam.

señora de la limpieza, cleaning woman.

señorita, *f.* young lady; (title) Miss.

sépalo, *m.* sepal.

separación, *f.* separation, parting.

separadamente, *adv.* separately.

separado, *a.* separate; separated. **—separar,** *v.*

septentrional, *a.* northern.

septiembre, *m.* September.

séptimo, *a.* seventh.

sepulcro, *m.* sepulcher.

sepultar, *v.* bury, entomb.

sepultura, *f.* grave.

sequedad, *f.* dryness.

sequía, *f.* drought.

ser, *v.* be.

serenata, *f.* serenade.

serenidad, *f.* serenity.

sereno, 1. *a.* serene, calm. **2.** *m.* dew; watchman.

ser humano, *n.* human being.

serie, *f.* series, sequence.

seriedad, *f.* seriousness.

serio, *a.* serious. **en s.,** seriously.

sermón, *m.* sermon.

seroso, *a.* watery.

serpiente, *f.* serpent, snake.

serpiente de cascabel, rattlesnake.

serrano -na, *n.* mountaineer.

serrar, *v.* saw.

serrín, *m.* sawdust.

servicial, *a.* helpful, of service.

servicio, *m.* service; toilet.

servidor -ra, *n.* servant.

servidumbre, *f.* bondage; staff of servants.

servil, *a.* servile, menial.

servilleta, *f.* napkin.

servir, *v.* serve. **s. para,** be good for.

servirse, *v.* help oneself.

sesenta, *a. & pron.* sixty.

sesgo, *m.* slant. **—sesgar,** *v.*

sesión, *f.* session; sitting.

seso, *m.* brain.

seta, *f.* mushroom.

setecientos, *a. & pron.* seven hundred.

setenta, *a. & pron.* seventy.

seto, *m.* hedge.

severamente, *adv.* severely.

severidad, *f.* severity.

severo, *a.* severe, strict, stern.

sexismo, *m.* sexism.

sexista, *a. & n.* sexist.

sexo, *m.* sex.

sexto, *a.* sixth.

sexual, *a.* sexual.

si, *conj.* if; whether.

sí, 1. *pron.* -self, -selves. **2.** *interj.* yes.

sico-. See **psicoanálisis, psicología,** etc.

sicómoro, *m.* sycamore.

SIDA, *m.* AIDS.

sidra, *f.* cider.

siempre, *adv.* always. **para s.,** forever. **s. que,** whenever; provided that.

sierra, *f.* saw; mountain range.

siervo -va, *n.* slave; serf.

siesta, *f.* (afternoon) nap.

siete, *a. & pron.* seven.

sifón, *m.* siphon; siphon bottle.

siglo, *m.* century.

signatura, *f.* (mus.) signature.

significación, *f.* significance.

significado, *m.* meaning.

significante, *a.* significant.

significar, *v.* signify, mean.

significativo, *a.* significant.

signo, *m.* sign, symbol; mark.

siguiente, *a.* following, next.

sílaba, *f.* syllable.

silbar, *v.* whistle; hiss, boo.

silbato, silbido, *m.* whistle.

silencio, *m.* silence, stillness.

silenciosamente, *a.* silently.

silencioso, *a.* silent, still.

silicato, *m.* silicate.

silicio, *m.* silicon.

silla, *f.* chair; saddle.

sillón, *m.* armchair.

silueta, *f.* silhouette.

silvestre, *a.* wild, uncultivated. **fauna s.,** wildlife.

sima, *f.* chasm; cavern.

simbólico, *a.* symbolic.

símbolo, *m.* symbol.

simetría, *f.* symmetry.

simétrico, *a.* symmetrical.

símil, similar, *a.* similar, alike.

similitud, *f.* similarity.

simpatía, *f.* congeniality; friendly feeling.

simpático, *a.* likeable, nice, congenial.

simple, *a.* simple.

simpleza, *f.* silliness; trifle.

simplicidad, *f.* simplicity.

simplificación, *f.* simplification.

simplificar, *v.* simplify.

simular, *v.* simulate.

simultáneo, *a.* simultaneous.

sin, *prep.* without. **s. sentido,** meaningless.

sinagoga, *f.* synagogue.

sinceridad, *f.* sincerity.

sincero, *a.* sincere.

sincronizar, *v.* synchronize.

sindicato, *m.* syndicate; labor union.

síndrome, *m.* syndrome.

sinfonía, *f.* symphony.

sinfónico, *a.* symphonic.

singular, *a. & m.* singular.

siniestro, *a.* sinister, ominous.

sino, *conj.* but.

sinónimo, *m.* synonym.

sinrazón, *f.* wrong, injustice.

sinsabor, *m.* displeasure, distaste; trouble.

sintaxis, *f.* syntax.

síntesis, *f.* synthesis.

sintético, *a.* synthetic.

síntoma, *m.* symptom.

siquiera, *adv.* **ni s.,** not even.

sirena, *f.* siren.

sirviente -ta, *n.* servant.

sistema, *m.* system.

sistemático, *a.* systematic.

sistematizar, *v.* systematize.

sitiar, *v.* besiege.

sitio, *m.* site, location, place, spot.

situación, *f.* situation; location.

situar, *v.* situate; locate.

smoking, *m.* tuxedo, dinner jacket.

so, *prep.* under.

soba, *f.* massage. **—sobar,** *v.*

sobaco, *m.* armpit.

sobaquero, *f.* armhole.

soberano -na, *a. & n.* sovereign.

soberbia, *f.* arrogance.

soberbio, *a.* superb; arrogant.

soborno, *m.* bribe. **—sobornar,** *v.*

sobra, *f.* excess, surplus. **de sobra,** to spare.

sobrado, *m.* attic.

sobrante, *a. & m.* surplus.

sobras, *f. pl.* leftovers.

sobre, 1. *prep.* about; above, over. **2.** *m.* envelope.

sobrecama, *f.* bedspread.

sobrecargo, *m.* supercargo.

sobredicho, *a.* aforesaid.

sobredosis, *f.* overdose.

sobrehumano, *a.* superhuman.

sobrenatural, *a.* supernatural, weird.

sobrepasar, *v.* surpass.

sobresalir, *v.* excel.

sobretodo, *m.* overcoat.

sobrevivir, *v.* survive, outlive.

sobriedad, *f.* sobriety; moderation.

sobrina, *f.* niece.

sobrino, *m.* nephew.

sobrio, *a.* sober, temperate.

socarrén, *m.* eaves.

sociable, *a.* sociable.

social, *a.* social.

socialismo, *m.* socialism.

socialista, *a. & n.* socialist.

sociedad, *f.* society; association.

sociedad de consumo, consumer society.

socio -cia, *n.* associate, partner; member.

sociología, *f.* sociology.

sociológico, *a.* sociological.

sociólogo, -ga, *n.* sociologist.

socorrista, *m. & f.* lifeguard.

socorro, *m.* help, aid. **—socorrer,** *v.*

soda, *f.* soda.

sodio, *m.* sodium.

soez, *a.* vulgar.

sofá, *m.* sofa, couch.

sofisma, *m.* sophism.

sofista, *m. & f.* sophist.

sofocación, *f.* suffocation.

sofocar, *v.* smother, suffocate, stifle, choke.

soga, *f.* rope.

soja, *f.* soya.

sol, *m.* sun.

solada, *f.* dregs.

solanera, *f.* sunburn.

solapa, *f.* lapel.

solar, 1. *a.* solar. **2.** *m.* building lot.

solaz, *m.* solace, comfort. **—solazar,** *v.*

soldado, *m.* soldier.

soldar, *v.* solder, weld.

soledad, *f.* solitude, privacy.

solemne, *a.* solemn.

solemnemente, *adv.* solemnly.

solemnidad, *f.* solemnity.

soler, *v.* be in the habit of.

solicitador -ra, *n.* applicant, petitioner.

solicitar, *v.* solicit; apply for.

solícito, *a.* solicitous.

solicitud, *f.* solicitude; application.

sólidamente, *adv.* solidly.

solidaridad, *f.* solidarity.

solidez, *f.* solidity.

solidificar, *v.* solidify.

sólido, *a. & m.* solid.

soliloquio, *m.* soliloquy.

solitario, *a.* solitary, lone.

sollozo, *m.* sob. **—sollozar,** *v.*

solo, 1. *a.* only; single; alone; lonely. **a solas,** alone. **2.** *m.* (mus.) solo.

sólo, *adv.* only, just.

solomillo, *m.* sirloin.

soltar, *v.* release; loosen.

soltero -ra, *a. & n.* single, unmarried (person).

soltura, *f.* poise, ease, facility.

solubilidad, *f.* solubility.

solución, *f.* solution.

solucionar, *v.* solve, settle.

solvente, *a.* solvent.

sombra, *f.* shade; shadow. **—sombrear,** *v.*

sombra de ojos, eye shadow.

sombrerera, *f.* hatbox.

sombrero, *m.* hat.

sombrilla, *f.* parasol.

sombrío, *a.* somber, bleak, gloomy.

sombroso, *a.* very shady.

someter, *v.* subject; submit.

somnífero, *m.* speeping pill.

somnolencia, *f.* drowsiness.

son, *m.* sound. **—sonar,** *v.*

sonata, *f.* sonata.

sondar, *v.* sound, fathom.

sonido, *m.* sound.

sonoridad, *f.* sonority.

sonoro, *a.* sonorous.

sonrisa, *f.* smile. **—sonreír,** *v.*

sonrojo, *m.* flush, blush. **—sonrojarse,** *v.*

soñador -ra, *a. & n.* dreamy; dreamer.

soñar, *v.* dream.

soñoliento, *a.* sleepy.

sopa, *f.* soup.

soplar, *v.* blow.

soplete, *m.* blowtorch.

soplo, *m.* breath; puff, gust.

soportar, *v.* abide, bear, stand.

soprano, *m. & f.* soprano.

sorbete, *m.* sherbet.

sorbo, *m.* sip. **—sorber,** *v.*

sordera, *f.* deafness.

sórdidamente, *adv.* sordidly.

sordidez, *f.* sordidness.

sórdido, *a.* sordid.

sordo, *a.* deaf; muffled, dull.

sordomudo -da, *a. & n.* deaf-mute.

sorpresa, *f.* surprise. **—sorprender,** *v.*

sorteo, *m.* drawing lots; raffle.

sortija, *f.* ring.

sosa, *f.* (chem.) soda.

soso, *a.* dull, insipid, tasteless.

sospecha, *f.* suspicion.

sospechar, *v.* suspect.

sospechoso, *a.* suspicious.

sostén, *m.* bra, brassiere; support.

sostener, *v.* hold, support; maintain.

sostenimiento, *m.* sustenance.

sota, *f.* jack (in cards).

sótano, *m.* basement, cellar.

soto, *m.* grove.

soviet, *m.* soviet.

soya, *f.* soybean.

su, *a.* his, her, its, their, your.

suave, *a.* smooth; gentle, soft, mild.

suavidad, *f.* smoothness; gentleness, softness, mildness.

suavizar, *v.* soften.

subalterno -na, *a. & n.* subordinate.

subasta, *f.* auction.

subcampeón -na, *n.* runner-up.

subconsciencia, *f.* subconscious.

súbdito -ta, *n.* subject.

subestimar, *v.* underestimate.

subida, *f.* ascent, rise.

subilla, *f.* awl.

subir, *v.* rise, climb, ascend, mount. **s. a,** amount to.

súbito, *a.* sudden.

subjetivo, *a.* subjective.

subjuntivo, *a. & m.* subjunctive.

sublimación, *f.* sublimation.

sublimar, *v.* elevate; sublimate.

sublime, *a.* sublime.

submarinismo, *m.* scuba diving.

submarino, *a. & m.* submarine.

subordinación, *f.* subordination.

subordinado -da, *a. & n.* subordinate. **—subordinar,** *v.*

subrayar, *v.* underline.

subscribirse, *v.* subscribe; sign one's name.

subscripción, *f.* subscription.

subsecuente, *a.* subsequent.

subsidiario, *a.* subsidiary.

subsiguiente, *a.* subsequent.

substancia, *f.* substance.

substancial, *a.* substantial.

substantivo, *a.* substantive, noun.

substitución, *f.* substitution.

substituir, *v.* replace; substitute.

substitutivo, *a.* substitute.

substituto -ta, *n.* substitute.

substraer, *v.* subtract.

subsuelo, *m.* subsoil.

subterfugio, *m.* subterfuge.

subterráneo, 1. *a.* subterranean, underground. **2.** *m.* place underground; subway.

subtítulo, *m.* subtitle.

suburbio, *m.* suburb.

subvención, *f.* subsidy, grant.

subversión, *f.* subversion.

subversivo, *a.* subversive.

subvertir, *v.* subvert.

subyugación, *f.* subjugation.

subyugar, *v.* subjugate, quell.

succión, *f.* suction.

suceder, *v.* happen, occur, befall. **s. a,** succeed, follow.

sucesión, *f.* succession.

sucesivo, *a.* successive. **en lo s.,** in the future.

suceso, *m.* event.

sucesor -ra, *n.* successor.

suciedad, *f.* filth, dirt.

sucio, *a.* filthy, dirty.

suculento, *a.* succulent.

sucumbir, *v.* succumb.

sud, *m.* south.

sudadera, *f.* sweatshirt.

Sudáfrica, *f.* South Africa.

sudafricano -na, *a. & n.* South African..

sudamericano -na, *a. & n.* South American.

sudar, *v.* perspire, sweat.

sudeste, *m.* southeast.

sudoeste, *m.* southwest.

sudor, *m.* perspiration, sweat.

Suecia, *f.* Sweden.

sueco -ca, *a. & n.* Swedish; Swede.

suegra, *f.* mother-in-law.

suegro, *m.* father-in-law.

suela, *f.* sole.

sueldo, *m.* salary, wages.

suelo, *m.* soil; floor; ground.

suelto, 1. *a.* loose; free; odd, separate. **2.** *n.* loose change.

sueño, *m.* sleep; sleepiness; dream. **tener s.,** to be sleepy.

suero, *m.* serum.

suerte, *f.* luck; chance; lot.

suéter, *m.* sweater.

suficiente, *a.* sufficient.

sufragio, *m.* suffrage.

sufrimiento, *m.* suffering, agony.

sufrir, *v.* suffer; undergo; endure.

sugerencia, *f.* suggestion.

sugerir, *v.* suggest.

sugestión, *f.* suggestion.

sugestionar, *v.* influence; hypnotize.

suicida, *m. & f.* suicide (person).

suicidarse, *v.* commit suicide.

suicidio, *m.* (act of) suicide.

Suiza, *f.* Switzerland.

suizo -za, *a. & n.* Swiss.

sujeción, *f.* subjection.

sujetador, *m.* bra, brassiere.

sujetapapeles, *m.* paper clip.

sujetar, v. hold, fasten, clip.
sujeto, 1. a. subject, liable. 2. m. (gram.) subject.
sulfato, m. sulfate.
sulfuro, m. sulfide.
sultán, m. sultan.
suma, f. sum, amount. en s., in short. s. global, lump sum.
sumar, v. add up.
sumaria, f. indictment.
sumario, a. & m. summary.
sumergir, v. submerge.
sumersión, f. submersion.
sumisión, f. submission.
sumiso, a. submissive.
sumo, a. great, high, utmost.
suntuoso, a. sumptuous.
superar, v. overcome, surpass.
superficial, a. superficial, shallow.
superficie, f. surface.
supérfluo, a. superfluous.
superhombre, m. superman.
superintendente, m. & f. superintendent.
superior, 1. a. superior; upper, higher. 2. m. superior.
superioridad, f. superiority.
superlativo, m. & a. superlative.
superstición, f. superstition.

supersticioso, a. superstitious.
supervisar, v. supervise.
supervivencia, f. survival.
suplantar, v. supplant.
suplementario, a. supplementary.
suplemento, m. supplement. —suplementar, v.
suplente, a. & n. substitute.
súplica, f. request, entreaty, plea.
suplicación, f. supplication; request, entreaty.
suplicar, v. request, entreat; implore.
suplicio, m. torture, ordeal.
suplir, v. supply.
suponer, v. suppose, presume, assume.
suposición, f. supposition, assumption.
supositorio, m. suppository.
supremacía, f. supremacy.
supremo, a. supreme.
supresión, f. suppression.
suprimir, v. suppress; abolish.
supuesto, a. supposed. por s., of course.
sur, m. south.
surco, m. furrow. —surcar, v.
surgir, v. arise; appear suddenly.

surtido, m. assortment; supply, stock.
surtir, v. furnish, supply.
susceptibilidad, f. susceptibility.
susceptible, a. susceptible.
suscitar, v. stir up.
suscri- = subscri-
suspender, v. withhold; suspend; fail (in a course).
suspensión, f. suspension.
suspenso, m. failing grade. en s., in suspense.
suspicacia, f. suspicion, distrust.
suspicaz, a. suspicious.
suspicazmente, adv. suspiciously.
suspiro, m. sigh. —suspirar, v.
sustan- = substan-
sustentar, v. sustain, support.
sustento, m. sustenance, support, living.
susti- = substi-
susto, m. fright, scare.
sustraer = substraer.
susurro, m. rustle; whisper. —susurrar, v.
sutil, a. subtle.
sutileza, sutilidad, f. subtlety.
sutura, f. suture.
suyo, a. his, hers, theirs, yours.

T

tabaco, m. tobacco.
tábano, m. horsefly.
tabaquería, f. tobacco shop.
taberna, f. tavern, bar.
tabernáculo, m. tabernacle.
tabique, m. dividing wall, partition.
tabla, f. board, plank; table, list. t. de planchar, ironing board.
tablado, m. stage, platform.
tablero, m. panel.
tableta, f. tablet.
tablilla, f. bulletin board.
tabú, m. taboo.
tabular, a. tabular.
tacaño, a. stingy.
tacha, f. fault, defect.
tachar, v. find fault with; cross out.

tachuela, f. tack.
tácitamente, adv. tacitly.
tácito, a. tacit.
taciturno, a. taciturn.
taco, m. heel (of shoe); billiard cue.
tacón, m. heel (of shoe).
táctico, a. tactical.
tacto, m. (sense of) touch; tact.
tafetán, m. taffeta.
taimado, a. sly.
tajada, n. cut, slice. —tajar, v.
tajea, f. channel.
tal, a. such. con t. que., provided that. t. vez, perhaps.
taladrar, v. drill.
taladro, m. (mech.) drill.

talante, m. humor, disposition.
talco, m. talc.
talega, f. bag, sack.
talento, m. talent.
talla, f. engraving; stature; size (of suit).
tallador -ra, n. engraver; dealer (at cards).
talle, m. figure; waist; fit.
taller, m. workshop, factory.
tallo, m. stem, stalk.
talón, m. heel (of foot); (baggage) check, stub.
tamal, m. tamale.
tamaño, m. size.
tambalear, v. stagger, totter.
también, adv. also, too.
tambor, m. drum.
tamiz, m. sieve, sifter.

tampoco, *adv.* neither, either.

tan, *adv.* so.

tanda, *f.* turn, relay.

tándem, *m.* tandem; pair.

tangencia, *f.* tangency.

tangible, *a.* tangible.

tango, *m.* tango (dance or music).

tanque, *m.* tank.

tanteo, *m.* estimate. **—tantear,** *v.*

tanto, 1. *a. & pron.* so much, so many; as much, as many. **entre t., mientras t.,** meanwhile. **por lo t.,** therefore. **un t.,** somewhat, a bit. **2.** *m.* point (in games); (*pl.*) score. **estar al t.,** to be up to date.

tañer, *v.* play (an instrument); ring (bells).

tapa, *f.* cap, cover. **—tapar,** *v.*

tapadero, *m.* stopper, lid.

tápara, *f.* caper.

tapete, *m.* small rug, mat, cover.

tapia, *f.* wall.

tapicería, *f.* tapestry.

tapioca, *f.* tapioca.

tapiz, *m.* tapestry; carpet.

tapizado (de pared), *m.* (wall) covering.

tapón, *m.* plug; cork.

taquigrafía, *f.* shorthand.

taquilla, *f.* ticket office; box office; ticket window.

tara, *f.* hang-up.

tarántula, *f.* tarantula.

tararear, *v.* hum.

tardanza, *f.* delay; lateness.

tardar, *v.* delay; be late; take (of time). **a más t.,** at the latest.

tarde, 1. *adv.* late. **2.** *f.* afternoon.

tardío, *a.* late, belated.

tarea, *f.* task, assignment.

tarifa, *f.* rate; tariff; price list.

tarjeta, *f.* card.

tarjeta bancaria, bank card.

tarjeta de crédito, credit card.

tarjeta de embarque, boarding pass.

tarta, *f.* tart.

tartamudear, *v.* stammer, falter.

tasa, *f.* rate.

tasación, *f.* valuation.

tasar, *v.* assess, appraise.

tasugo, *m.* badger.

tatuar, *v.* tattoo.

tautología, *f.* tautology.

taxi, taxímetro, *m.* taxi.

taxista, *m. & f.* taxi driver.

taxonomía, *f.* taxonomy.

taza, *f.* cup.

te, *pron.* you; yourself.

té, *m.* tea.

teátrico, *a.* theatrical.

teatro, *m.* theater.

tebeo, *m.* comic book.

techo, *m.* roof. **—techar,** *v.*

tecla, *f.* key (of a piano, etc.).

teclado, *m.* keyboard.

teclado numérico, numeric keypad.

técnica, *f.* technique.

técnicamente, *adv.* technically.

técnico, 1. *a.* technical; **2.** *m.* repairman, technician.

tecnología, *f.* technology.

tedio, *m.* tedium, boredom.

tedioso, *a.* tedious.

teísmo, *m.* theism.

teja, *f.* tile.

tejado, *m.* roof.

tejano -na, *a. & n.* Texan.

tejanos, *m.pl.* jeans.

tejer, *v.* weave; knit.

tejido, *m.* fabric; weaving.

tejón, *m.* badger.

tela, *f.* cloth, fabric, web. **t. metálica,** screen; screening. **t. vaquera,** denim.

telar, *m.* loom.

telaraña, *f.* cobweb, spiderweb.

telefonista, *m. & f.* (telephone) operator.

teléfono, *m.* telephone. **—telefonear,** *v.*

teléfono gratuito, toll-free number.

teléfono público, pay phone, public telephone.

telégrafo, *m.* telegraph. **—telegrafiar,** *v.*

telegrama, *m.* telegram.

telescopio, *m.* telescope.

televisión, *f.* television.

telón, *m.* (theat.) curtain.

telurio, *m.* tellurium.

tema, *m.* theme, subject.

temblar, *v.* tremble, quake; shake, shiver.

temblor, *m.* tremor; shiver.

temer, *v.* fear, be afraid of, dread.

temerario, *a.* rash.

temeridad, *f.* temerity.

temerosamente, *adv.* timorously.

temeroso, *a.* fearful.

temor, *m.* fear.

témpano, *m.* kettledrum; iceberg.

temperamento, *m.* temperament.

temperancia, *f.* temperance.

temperatura, *f.* temperature.

tempestad, *f.* tempest, storm.

tempestuoso, *a.* tempestuous, stormy.

templado, *a.* temperate, mild, moderate.

templanza, *f.* temperance; mildness.

templar, *v.* temper; tune (an instrument).

templo, *m.* temple.

temporada, *f.* season, time, spell.

temporal, temporáneo, *a.* temporary.

temprano, *a. & adv.* early.

tenacidad, *f.* tenacity.

tenaz, *a.* tenacious, stubborn.

tenazmente, *adv.* tenaciously.

tendencia, *f.* tendency, trend.

tender, *v.* stretch, stretch out.

tendero -ra, *n.* shopkeeper, storekeeper.

tendón, *m.* tendon, sinew.

tenebrosidad, *f.* gloom.

tenebroso, *a.* dark, gloomy.

tenedor, *m. & f.* keeper; holder; *m.* fork.

tener, *v.* have; own; hold. **t. que,** have to, must.

teniente, *m.* lieutenant.

tenis, *m.* tennis; (*pl.*) sneakers.

tenor, *m.* tenor.

tensión, *f.* tension, stress, strain.

tenso, *a.* tense.

tentación, *f.* temptation.

tentáculo, *m.* tentacle.

tentador, *a.* alluring, tempting.

tentar, *v.* tempt, lure; grope, probe.

tentativa, *f.* attempt.

tentativo, *a.* tentative.

teñir, *v.* tint, dye.

teología, *f.* theology.

teológico, *a.* theological.

teoría, *f.* theory.

teórico, *a.* theoretical.

terapéutico, *a.* therapeutic.

tercero, *a.* third.

tercio, *m.* third.

terciopelo, *m.* velvet.

terco, *a.* obstinate, stubborn.

termal, *a.* thermal.

terminación, *f.* termination; completion.

terminal aérea, *f.* air terminal.

terminar, *v.* terminate, finish.

término, *m.* term; end.

terminología, *f.* terminology.

termómetro, *m.* thermometer.

termos, *m.* thermos.

termostato, *m.* thermostat.

ternero -ra, *n.* calf.

ternura, *f.* tenderness.

terquedad, *f.* stubbornness.

terraza, *f.* terrace.

terremoto, *m.* earthquake.

terreno, **1.** *a.* earthly, terrestrial. **2.** *m.* ground, terrain; lot, plot.

terrible, *a.* terrible, awful.

terrífico, *a.* terrifying.

territorio, *m.* territory.

terrón, *m.* clod, lump; mound.

terror, *m.* terror.

terso, *a.* smooth, glossy; terse.

tertulia, *f.* social gathering, party.

tesis, *f.* thesis.

tesorería, *f.* treasury.

tesorero -ra, *n.* treasurer.

tesoro, *m.* treasure.

testamento, *m.* will, testament.

testarudo, *a.* stubborn.

testificar, *v.* testify.

testigo, *m.* & *f.* witness.

testimonial, *a.* testimonial.

testimonio, *m.* testimony.

teta, *f.* teat.

tetera, *f.* teapot.

tétrico, *a.* sad; gloomy.

texto, *m.* text.

textura, *f.* texture.

tez, *f.* complexion.

ti, *pron.* you; yourself.

tía, *f.* aunt.

tibio, *a.* lukewarm.

tiburón, *m.* shark.

tiemblo, *m.* aspen.

tiempo, *m.* time; weather; (gram.) tense.

tienda, *f.* shop, store; tent.

tientas, *f.pl.* **andar a t.**, to grope (in the dark).

tierno, *a.* tender.

tierra, *f.* land; ground; earth, dirt, soil.

tieso, *a.* taut, stiff, hard, strong.

tiesto, *m.* flower pot.

tiesura, *f.* stiffness; harshness.

tifo, *m.* typhus.

tifoideo, *m.* typhoid fever.

tigre, *m.* tiger.

tijeras, *f.pl.* scissors.

tila, *f.* linden.

timbre, *m.* seal, stamp; tone; (electric) bell.

tímidamente, *adv.* timidly.

timidez, *f.* timidity.

tímido, *a.* timid, shy.

timón, *m.* rudder, helm.

tímpano, *m.* kettledrum; eardrum.

tina, *f.* tub, vat.

tinaja, *f.* jar.

tinta, *f.* ink.

tinte, *m.* tint, shade.

tintero, *m.* inkwell.

tinto, *a.* wine-colored; red (of wine).

tintorería, *f.* dry cleaning shop.

tintorero -ra, *n.* dyer; dry cleaner.

tintura, *f.* tincture; dye.

tiñoso, *a.* scabby; stingy.

tío, *m.* uncle.

tiovivo, *m.* merry-go-round.

típico, *a.* typical.

tipo, *m.* type, sort; (interest) rate; (coll.) guy, fellow.

tipo de cambio, exchange rate.

tipo de interés, interest rate.

tira, *f.* strip.

tirabuzón, *m.* corkscrew.

tirada, *f.* edition.

tirado -da, *a.* dirt-cheap.

tiranía, *f.* tyranny.

tiránico, *m.* tyrannical.

tirano -na, *n.* tyrant.

tirante, **1.** *a.* tight, taut; tense. **2.** *m.pl.* suspenders.

tirar, *v.* throw; draw; pull; fire (a weapon).

tiritar, *v.* shiver.

tiro, *m.* throw; shot.

tirón, *m.* pull. **de un t.**, at a stretch, at one stroke.

tísico, *n.* & *a.* consumptive.

tisis, *f.* consumption, tuberculosis.

titanio, *m.* titanium.

títere, *m.* puppet.

titilación, *f.* twinkle.

titubear, *v.* stagger; totter; waver.

titulado, *a.* entitled; so-called.

titular, **1.** *a.* titular. **2.** *v.* entitle.

título, *m.* title, headline.

tiza, *f.* chalk.

tiznar, *v.* smudge; stain.

toalla, *f.* towel. **t. sanitaria**, sanitary napkin.

toalleta, *f.* small towel.

tobillo, *m.* ankle.

tobogán, *m.* toboggan.

tocadiscos, *m.* record player.

tocadiscos compacto, tocadiscos digital, CD player.

tocado, *m.* hairdo.

tocador, *m.* boudoir; dressing table.

tocante, *a.* touching. **t. a**, concerning, relative to.

tocar, *v.* touch; play (an instrument). **t. a uno**, be one's turn; be up to one.

tocayo -ya, *n.* namesake.

tocino, *m.* bacon.

tocólogo -ga, *n.* obstetrician.

todavía, *adv.* yet, still.

todo, **1.** *a.* all, whole. **todos los**, every. **2.** *pron.* all, everything. **con t.**, still, however. **del t.**, wholly; at all.

todopoderoso, *a.* almighty.

toldo, *m.* awning.

tolerancia, *f.* tolerance.

tolerante, *a.* tolerant.

tolerar, *v.* tolerate.

toma, *f.* taking, capture, seizure.

tomaína, *f.* ptomaine.

tomar, *v.* take; drink. **t. el sol**, sunbathe.

tomate, *m.* tomato.

tomillo, *m.* thyme.

tomo, *m.* volume.

tonada, *f.* tune.

tonel, *m.* barrel, cask.

tonelada, *f.* ton.

tonelaje, *m.* tonnage.

tónico, *a. & m.* tonic.

tono, *m.* tone, pitch, shade. **darse t.**, to put on airs.

tonsila, *f.* tonsil.

tonsilitis, *f.* tonsilitis.

tontería, *f.* nonsense, foolishness.

tonto -ta, *a. & n.* foolish, silly; fool.

topacio, *m.* topaz.

topar, *v.* run into. **t. con**, come upon.

tópico, **1.** *a.* topical. **2.** *m.* cliché.

topo, *m.* mole (animal).

toque, *m.* touch.

tórax, *m.* thorax.

torbellino, *m.* whirlwind.

torcer, *v.* twist; wind; distort.

toreador -a, *n.* toreador.

torero -ra, *n.* bullfighter.

torio, *m.* thorium.

tormenta, *f.* storm.

tormento, *m.* torment.

tornado, *m.* tornado.

tornar, *v.* return; turn.

tornarse en, *v.* turn into, become.

torneo, *m.* tournament.

tornillo, *m.* screw.

toro, *m.* bull.

toronja, *f.* grapefruit.

torpe, *a.* awkward, clumsy; sluggish.

torpedero, *m.* torpedo boat.

torpedo, *m.* torpedo.

torre, *f.* tower.

torre de mando, control tower.

torrente, *m.* torrent.

tórrido, *a.* torrid.

torta, *f.* cake; loaf.

tortilla, *f.* omelet; (Mex.) tortilla, pancake.

tórtola, *f.* dove.

tortuga, *f.* turtle.

tortuoso, *a.* tortuous.

tortura, *f.* torture. **—torturar**, *v.*

tos, *m.* cough. **—toser**, *v.*

tosco, *a.* coarse, rough, uncouth.

tosquedad, *f.* coarseness, roughness.

tostador, *m.* toaster.

tostar, *v.* toast; tan.

total, *a. & m.* total.

totalidad, *f.* totality, entirety, whole.

totalitario, *a.* totalitarian.

totalmente, *adv.* totally; entirely.

tótem, *m.* totem.

tóxico, *a.* toxic.

toxicómano -na, *m. & f.* drug addict.

trabajador -ra, **1.** *a.* hardworking. **2.** *n.* worker.

trabajo, *m.* work; labor. **—trabajar**, *v.*

trabar, *v.* fasten, shackle; grasp; strike up.

tracción, *f.* traction.

tracto, *m.* tract.

tractor, *m.* tractor.

tradición, *f.* tradition.

tradicional, *a.* traditional.

traducción, *f.* translation.

traducir, *v.* translate.

traductor -ra, *n.* translator.

traer, *v.* bring; carry; wear.

tráfico, *m.* traffic. **—traficar**, *v.*

tragaperras, *f.* slot machine, one-armed bandit.

tragar, *v.* swallow.

tragedia, *f.* tragedy.

trágicamente, *adv.* tragically.

trágico -ca, **1.** *a.* tragic. **2.** *n.* tragedian.

trago, *m.* swallow; drink.

traición, *f.* treason, betrayal.

traicionar, *v.* betray.

traidor -ra, *a. & n.* traitorous; traitor.

traje, *m.* suit; dress; garb, apparel.

traje de baño, bathing suit.

trama, *v.* plot (of a story).

tramador -ra, *n.* weaver; plotter.

tramar, *v.* weave; plot, scheme.

trámite, *m.* (business) deal, transaction.

tramo, *m.* span, stretch, section.

trampa, *f.* trap, snare.

trampista, *m. & f.* cheater; swindler.

trance, *m.* critical moment or stage. **a todo t.**, at any cost.

tranco, *m.* stride.

tranquilidad, *f.* tranquility, calm, quiet.

tranquilizante, *m.* tranquilizer.

tranquilizar, *v.* quiet, calm down.

tranquilo, *a.* tranquil, calm.

transacción, *f.* transaction.

transbordador, *m.* ferry.

transbordador espacial, space, shuttle.

transcribir, *v.* transcribe.

transcripción, *f.* transcription.

transcurrir, *v.* elapse.

transeúnte, *a. & n.* transient; passerby.

transexual, *a.* transsexual.

transferencia, *f.* transference.

transferir, *v.* transfer.

transformación, *f.* transformation.

transformar, *v.* transform.

transfusión, *f.* transfusion.

transgresión, *f.* transgression.

transgresor -ra, *n.* transgressor.

transición, *f.* transition.

transigir, *v.* compromise, settle; agree.

transistor, *m.* transistor.

transitivo, *a.* transitive.

tránsito, *m.* transit, passage.

transitorio, *a.* transitory.

transmisión, *f.* transmission; broadcast.

transmisora, *f.* broadcasting station.

transmitir, *v.* transmit; broadcast.

transparencia, *f.* transparency.

transparente, 1. *a.* transparent. **2.** *m.* (window) shade.

transportación, *f.* transportation.

transportar, *v.* transport, convey.

transporte, *m.* transportation; transport.

tranvía, *m.* streetcar, trolley.

trapacero -ra, *n.* cheat; swindler.

trapo, *m.* rag.

tráquea, *f.* trachea.

tras, *prep.* after; behind.

trasegar, *v.* upset, overturn.

trasero, *a.* rear, back.

traslado, *m.* transfer. **—trasladar,** *v.*

traslapo, *m.* overlap. **—traslapar,** *v.*

trasnochar, *v.* stay up all night.

traspalar, *v.* shovel.

traspasar, *v.* go beyond; cross; violate; pierce.

trasquilar, *v.* shear; clip.

trastornar, *v.* overturn, overthrow, upset.

trastorno, *m.* overthrow; up-heaval.

trastorno mental, mental disorder.

tratado, *m.* treaty; treatise.

tratamiento, *m.* treatment.

tratar, *v.* treat, handle. **t. de,** deal with; try to; call (a name).

tratarse de, *v.* be a question of.

trato, *m.* treatment; manners; (com.) deal.

través, *adv.* **a t. de,** through, across. **de t.,** sideways.

travesía, *f.* crossing; voyage:

travesti, *m.* transvestite.

travestido, *a.* disguised.

travesura, *f.* prank; mischief.

travieso, *a.* naughty, mischievous.

trayectoria, *f.* trajectory.

trazar, *v.* plan, devise; trace; draw.

trazo, *n.* plan, outline; line, stroke.

trébol, *m.* clover.

trece, *a.* & *pron.* thirteen.

trecho, *m.* space, distance, stretch.

tregua, *f.* truce; respite, lull.

treinta, *a.* & *pron.* thirty.

tremendo, *a.* tremendous.

tremer, *v.* tremble.

tren, *m.* train.

trenza, *f.* braid. **—trenzar,** *v.*

trepar, *v.* climb, mount.

trepidación, *f.* trepidation.

tres, *a.* & *pron.* three.

trescientos, *a.* & *pron.* three hundred.

triángulo, *m.* triangle.

tribu, *f.* tribe.

tribulación, *f.* tribulation.

tribuna, *f.* rostrum, stand; (*pl.*) grandstand.

tribunal, *m.* court, tribunal.

tributario, *a.* & *m.* tributary.

tributo, *m.* tribute.

triciclo, *m.* tricycle.

trigo, *m.* wheat.

trigonometría, *f.* trigonometry.

trigueño, *a.* swarthy, dark.

trilogía, *f.* trilogy.

trimestral, *a.* quarterly.

trinchar, *v.* carve (meat).

trinchera, *f.* trench, ditch.

trineo, *m.* sled; sleigh.

trinidad, *f.* trinity.

tripa, *f.* tripe, entrails.

triple, *a.* triple. **—triplicar,** *v.*

trípode, *m.* tripod.

tripulación, *f.* crew.

tripulante, *m* & *f.* crew member.

tripular, *v.* man.

triste, *a.* sad, sorrowful; dreary.

tristemente, *adv.* sadly.

tristeza, *f.* sadness; gloom.

triunfal, *a.* triumphal.

triunfante, *a.* triumphant.

triunfo, *m.* triumph; trump. **—triunfar,** *v.*

trivial, *a.* trivial, commonplace.

trivialidad, *f.* triviality.

trocar, *v.* exchange, switch; barter.

trofeo, *m.* trophy.

trombón, *m.* trombone.

trompa, trompeta, *f.* trumpet, horn.

tronada, *f.* thunderstorm.

tronar, *v.* thunder.

tronco, *m.* trunk, stump.

trono, *m.* throne.

tropa, *f.* troop.

tropel, *m.* crowd, throng.

tropezar, *v.* trip, stumble, **t. con,** come upon, run into.

trópico, *a.* & *m.* tropical; tropics.

tropiezo, *m.* stumble; obstacle; slip, error.

trote, *m.* trot. **—trotar,** *v.*

trovador, *m.* troubadour.

trozo, *m.* piece, portion, fragment; selection, passage.

trucha, *f.* trout.

trueco, trueque, *m.* exchange, barter.

trueno, *m.* thunder.

trufa, *f.* truffle.

tu, *a.* your.

tú, *pron.* you.

tuberculosis, *f.* tuberculosis.

tubo, *m.* tube, pipe.

tubo de ensayo, test tube.

tubo de escape, exhaust pipe.

tuerca, *f.* (mech.) nut.

tulipán, *m.* tulip.

tumba, *f.* tomb, grave.

tumbar, *v.* knock down.

tumbarse, *v.* lie down.

tumbo, *m.* tumble; somersault.

tumbona, *f.* deck chair.

tumor, *m.* tumor; growth.

tumulto, *m.* tumult, commotion.

tumultuoso, *a.* tumultuous, boisterous.

tunante, *m.* rascal, rogue.

tunda, *f.* spanking, whipping.

túnel, *m.* tunnel.

túnel del Canal de la Mancha, Channel Tunnel. (informal) Chunnel.

tungsteno, *m.* tungsten.

túnica, *f.* tunic, robe.

tupir, *v.* pack tight, stuff; stop up.

turbación, *f.* confusion, turmoil.

turbamulta, *f.* mob, disorderly crowd.

turbar, *v.* disturb, upset; embarrass.

turbina, f. turbine.
turbio, a. turbid; muddy.
turco -ca, a. & n. Turkish;
   Turk.
turismo, m. touring, (foreign) travel, tourism.

turista, m. & f. tourist.
turno, m. turn; (work) shift.
turquesa, f. turquoise.
Turquía, f. Turkey.
turrón, m. nougat.
tusa, f. corncob; corn.

tutear, v. use the pronoun
   tú, etc., in addressing a
   person.
tutela, f. guardianship; aegis.
tutor -ra, n. tutor; guardian.
tuyo, a. your, yours.

U

u, conj. or.
ubre, f. udder.
Ucrania, f. Ukraine.
ucranio -ia, a. & n. Ukrain-
   ian.
ufano, a. proud, haughty.
úlcera, f. ulcer.
ulterior, a. ulterior.
último, a. last, final; ulti-
   mate; latest. **por ú.,** finally. **ú. minuto,** last
   minute, eleventh hour.
ultraje, m. outrage. **—ultrajar,** v.
ultrasónico, a. ultrasonic.
umbral, m. threshold.
umbroso, a. shady.
un, una, art. & a. a, an;
   one; (pl.) some.
unánime, a. unanimous.
unanimidad, f. unanimity.
unción, f. unction.
ungüento, m. ointment, salve.
único, a. only, sole; unique.
unicornio, m. unicorn.
unidad, f. unit; unity.

**unidad de cuidados inten-
   sivos, unidad de vigilancia intensiva,** intensive-
   care unit.
unificar, v. unify.
uniforme, a. & m. uniform.
uniformidad, f. uniformity.
unión, f. union; joining.
unir, v. unite, join.
universal, a. universal.
universalidad, f. universal-
   ity.
universidad, f. university;
   college.
universo, m. universe.
uno, una, pron. one; (pl.)
   some.
untar, v. spread; grease;
   anoint.
uña, f. fingernail.
urbanidad, f. urbanity;
   good breeding.
urbanismo, m. city planning.
urbano, a. urban; urbane;
   well-bred.
urbe, f. large city.

urgencia, f. urgency.
urgente, a. urgent, pressing.
   entrega u., special delivery.
urgir, v. be urgent.
urna, f. urn; ballot box;
   (pl.) polls.
urraca, f. magpie.
usanza, f. usage, custom.
usar, v. use; wear.
uso, m. use; usage; wear.
usted, pron. you.
usual, a. usual.
usualmente, adv. usually.
usura, f. usury.
usurero -ra, n. usurer.
usurpación, f. usurpation.
usurpar, v. usurp.
utensilio, m. utensil.
útero, m. uterus.
útil, a. useful, handy.
utilidad, f. utility, usefulness.
utilizar, v. use, utilize.
útilmente, adv. usefully.
utópico, a. utopian.
uva, f. grape.

V

vaca, f. cow; beef.
vacaciones, f.pl. vacation,
   holidays.
vacancia, f. vacancy.
vacante, 1. a. vacant. **2.** f.
   vacancy.
vaciar, v. empty; pour out.
vacilación, f. vacillation,
   hesitation.
vacilante, a. vacillating.
vacilar, v. falter, hesitate;
   waver; stagger.
vacío, 1. a. empty. **2.** m.
   void, empty space.
vacuna, f. vaccine.
vacunación, f. vaccination.
vacunar, v. vaccinate.

vacuo, 1. a. empty, vacant.
   2. m. vacuum.
vadear, v. wade through,
   ford.
vado, m. ford.
vagabundo -da, a. & n.
   vagabond.
vagar, v. wander, rove,
   roam; loiter.
vago -ga, 1. a. vague, hazy;
   wandering, vagrant. **2.** n.
   vagrant, tramp.
vagón, m. railroad car.
vahído, m. dizziness.
vaina, f. sheath; pod.
vainilla, f. vanilla.
vaivén, m. vibration, sway.
vajilla, f. (dinner) dishes.

valentía, f. valor, courage.
valer, 1. m. worth. **2.** v. be
   worth.
valerse de, v. make use of,
   avail oneself of.
valía, f. value.
validez, f. validity.
válido, a. valid.
valiente, a. valiant, brave,
   courageous.
valija, f. valise.
valioso, a. valuable.
valla, f. fence, barrier.
valle, m. valley.
valor, m. value, worth;
   bravery, valor; (pl.,
   com.) securities.
valoración, f. appraisal.

valorar, *v.* value, appraise.

vals, *m.* waltz.

valsar, *v.* waltz.

valuación, *f.* valuation.

valuar, *v.* value; rate.

válvula, *f.* valve.

válvula de seguridad, safety valve.

vandalismo, *m.* vandalism.

vándalo -la, *n.* vandal.

vanidad, *f.* vanity.

vanidoso, *a.* vain, conceited.

vano, *a.* vain; inane.

vapor, *m.* vapor; steam; steamer, steamship.

vaquero -ra, *n.* cowboy.

vara, *f.* wand, stick, switch.

varadero, *m.* shipyard.

varar, *v.* launch; be stranded; run aground.

variable, *a.* variable.

variación, *f.* variation.

variar, *v.* vary.

varicela, *f.* chicken pox.

variedad, *f.* variety.

varios, *a. & pron. pl.* various; several.

variz, *f.* varicose vein.

varón, *m.* man; male.

varonil, *a.* manly, virile.

vasallo, *m.* vassal.

vasectomía, *f.* vasectomy.

vasija, *f.* bowl, container (for liquids).

vaso, *m.* water glass; vase. **v. de papel**, paper cup.

vástago, *m.* bud, shoot; twig; offspring.

vasto, *a.* vast.

vecindad, *f.* **vecindario**, *m.* neighborhood, vicinity.

vecino -na, *a. & n.* neighboring; neighbor.

vedar, *v.* forbid; impede.

vega, *f.* meadow.

vegetación, *f.* vegetation.

vegetal, *m.* vegetable.

vehemente, *a.* vehement.

vehículo, *m.* vehicle; conveyance.

veinte, *a. & pron.* twenty.

vejez, *f.* old age.

vejiga, *f.* bladder.

vela, *f.* vigil, watch; candle; sail.

velar, *v.* stay up, sit up; watch over.

vellón, *m.* fleece.

velloso, *a.* hairy; fuzzy.

velludo, *a.* downy.

velo, *m.* veil.

velocidad, *f.* velocity, speed; rate. **v. máxima**, speed limit.

velomotor, *m.* motorbike, moped.

veloz, *a.* speedy, fast, swift.

vena, *f.* vein.

venado, *m.* deer.

vencedor -ra, *n.* victor.

vencer, *v.* defeat, overcome, conquer; (com.) become due, expire.

vencimiento, *m.* defeat; expiration.

venda, *f.* **vendaje**, *m.* bandage. **—vendar**, *v.*

vendedor -ra, *n.* seller, trader; sales clerk.

vender, *v.* sell.

vendimia, *f.* vintage; grape harvest.

Venecia, *f.* Venice.

veneciano -na, *a. & n.* Venetian.

veneno, *m.* poison.

venenoso, *a.* poisonous.

veneración, *f.* veneration.

venerar, *v.* venerate, revere.

venero, *m.* spring; origin.

véneto, *a.* Venetian.

venezolano -na, *a. & n.* Venezuelan.

vengador -ra, *n.* avenger.

venganza, *f.* vengeance, revenge.

vengar, *v.* avenge.

venida, *f.* arrival, advent, coming.

venidero, *a.* future; coming.

venir, *v.* come.

venta, *f.* sale; sales.

ventaja, *f.* advantage; profit.

ventajoso, *a.* advantageous; profitable.

ventana, *f.* window.

ventero -ra, *n.* innkeeper.

ventilación, *m.* ventilation.

ventilador, *m.* ventilator, fan.

ventilar, *v.* ventilate, air.

ventisquero, *m.* snowdrift; glacier.

ventoso, *a.* windy.

ventura, *f.* venture; happiness; luck.

ver, *v.* see. **tener que v. con**, have to do with.

vera, *f.* edge.

veracidad, *f.* truthfulness, veracity.

verano, *m.* summer. **—veranear**, *v.*

veras, *f.pl.* **de v.**, really, truly.

veraz, *a.* truthful.

verbigracia, *adv.* for example.

verbo, *m.* verb.

verboso, *a.* verbose.

verdad, *f.* truth. **ser v.**, to be true.

verdadero, *a.* true, real.

verde, *a.* green; risqué, off-color.

verdor, *m.* greenness, verdure.

verdugo, *m.* hangman.

verdura, *f.* verdure, vegetation; (*pl.*) vegetables.

vereda, *f.* path.

veredicto, *m.* verdict.

vergonzoso, *a.* shameful, embarrassing; shy, bashful.

vergüenza, *f.* shame; disgrace; embarrassment.

verificar, *v.* verify, check.

verja, *f.* grating, railing.

verosímil, *a.* likely, plausible.

verraco, *m.* boar.

verruga, *f.* wart.

versátil, *a.* versatile.

verse, *v.* look, appear.

versión, *f.* version.

verso, *m.* verse, stanza; line (of poetry).

verter, *v.* pour, spill; shed; empty.

vertical, *a.* vertical.

vertiente, *f.* slope; watershed.

vertiginoso, *a.* dizzy.

vértigo, *m.* vertigo, dizziness.

vestíbulo, *m.* vestibule, lobby.

vestido, *m.* dress; clothing.

vestigio, *m.* vestige, trace.

vestir, *v.* dress, clothe.

veterano -na, *a. & n.* veteran.

veterinario -ria, **1.** *a.* veterinary. **2.** *n.* veterinarian.

veto, *m.* veto.

vetusto, *a.* ancient, very old.

vez, *f.* time; turn. **tal v.,** perhaps. **a la v.,** at the same time. **en v. de,** instead of. **una v.,** once. **otra v.,** again.

vía, *f.* track; route, way.

viaducto, *m.* viaduct.

viajante, *a.* & *n.* traveling; traveler.

viajar, *v.* travel; journey; tour.

viaje, *m.* trip, journey, voyage; (*pl.*) travels.

viaje de estudios, field trip.

viaje todo incluido, package tour.

viajero -ra, *n.* traveler; passenger.

viandas, *f.pl.* victuals, food.

víbora, *f.* viper.

vibración, *f.* vibration.

vibrar, *v.* vibrate.

vicepresidente -ta, *n.* vice president.

vicio, *m.* vice.

vicioso, *a.* vicious; licentious.

víctima, *f.* victim.

victoria, *f.* victory.

victorioso, *a.* victorious.

vid, *f.* grapevine.

vida, *f.* life; living.

vídeo, *m.* videotape.

videocámara, *f.* video camera.

videodisco, *m.* videodisc.

videojuego, *m.* video game.

vidrio, *m.* glass.

viejo -ja, *a.* & *n.* old; old person.

viento, *m.* wind. **hacer v.,** to be windy.

vientre, *m.* belly.

viernes, *m.* Friday.

viga, *f.* beam, rafter.

vigente, *a.* in effect (prices, etc.).

vigilante, *a.* & *m.* vigilant, watchful; watchman.

vigilante nocturno, night watchman.

vigilar, *v.* guard, watch over.

vigilia, *f.* vigil, watchfulness; (rel.) fast.

vigor, *m.* vigor. **en v.,** in effect, in force.

vil, *a.* vile, low, contemptible.

vileza, *f.* baseness; vileness.

villa, *f.* town; country house.

villancico, *m.* Christmas carol.

villanía, *f.* villainy.

villano, *m.* boor.

vinagre, *m.* vinegar.

vinagrera, *f.* cruet.

vínculo, *m.* link. **—vincular,** *v.*

vindicar, *v.* vindicate.

vino, *m.* wine.

viña, *f.* vineyard.

violación, *f.* violation; rape.

violador -ra, *m.* & *f.* rapist.

violar, *v.* violate; rape.

violencia, *f.* violence.

violento, *a.* violent; impulsive.

violeta, *f.* violet.

violín, *m.* violin.

violón, *m.* bass viol.

virar, *v.* veer, change course.

virgen, *f.* virgin.

viril, *a.* virile, manly.

virilidad, *f.* virility, manhood.

virtual, *a.* virtual.

virtud, *f.* virtue; efficacy, power.

virtuoso, *a.* virtuous.

viruela, *f.* smallpox.

viruelas locas, *f.pl.* chicken pox.

visa, *f.* visa.

visaje, *m.* grimace.

visera, *f.* visor.

visible, *a.* visible.

visión, *f.* vision.

visionario -ria, *a.* & *n.* visionary.

visita, *f.* visit; *m.* & *f.* visitor, caller. **v. con guía, v. explicada, v. programada,** guided tour.

visitación, *f.* visitation.

visitante, *a.* & *n.* visiting; visitor.

visitar, *v.* visit; inspect, examine.

vislumbrar, *v.* glimpse.

vislumbre, *f.* glimpse.

viso, *m.* looks; outlook.

víspera, *f.* eve, day before.

vista, *f.* view; scene; sight.

vista de pájaro, bird's-eye view.

vistazo, *m.* glance, glimpse.

vistoso, *a.* beautiful; showy.

visual, *a.* visual.

vital, *a.* vital.

vitalidad, *f.* vitality.

vitamina, *f.* vitamin.

vitando, *a.* hateful.

vituperar, *v.* vituperate; revile.

viuda, *f.* widow.

viudo, *m.* widower.

vivaz, *a.* vivacious, buoyant; clever.

víveres, *m.pl.* provisions.

viveza, *f.* animation, liveliness.

vívido, *a.* vivid, bright.

vivienda, *f.* (living) quarters, dwelling.

vivificar, *v.* vivify, enliven.

vivir, *v.* live.

vivo, *a.* live, alive, living; vivid; animated, brisk.

vocablo, *m.* word.

vocabulario, *m.* vocabulary.

vocación, *f.* vocation, calling.

vocal, 1. *a.* vocal. **2.** *f.* vowel.

vocear, *v.* vociferate.

vodca, *m.* vodka.

vodevil, *m.* vaudeville.

volante, 1. *a.* flying. **2.** *m.* memorandum; (steering) wheel.

volar, *v.* fly; explode.

volcán, *m.* volcano.

volcar, *v.* upset, capsize.

voltaje, *m.* voltage.

voltear, *v.* turn, whirl; overturn.

voltio, *m.* volt.

volumen, *m.* volume.

voluminoso, *a.* voluminous.

voluntad, *f.* will. **buena v.** goodwill.

voluntario -ria, *a.* & *n.* voluntary; volunteer.

voluntarioso, *a.* willful.

volver, *v.* turn; return, go back, come back. **v. a hacer** (etc.), do (etc.) again.

volverse, *v.* turn around; turn, become.

vómito, *m.* vomit. **—vomitar,** *v.*

voracidad, *f.* voracity; greed.

voraz, *a.* greedy, ravenous.

vórtice, *m.* whirlpool.

vosotros -as, *pron.pl.* you; yourselves.

votación, *f.* voting; vote.

voto, *m.* vote; vow. **—votar,** *v.*

voz, *f.* voice; word. **a voces,** by shouting. **en v. alta,** aloud.
vuelco, *m.* upset.
vuelo, *m.* flight. **v. libre,** hang gliding.

vuelo chárter, charter flight.
vuelo regular, scheduled flight.
vuelta, *f.* turn, bend; return. **a la v. de,** around. **dar una v.,** to take a walk.

vuestro, *a.* your, yours.
vulgar, *a.* vulgar, common.
vulgaridad, *f.* vulgarity.
vulgo, *m.* (the) masses, (the) common people.
vulnerable, *a.* vulnerable.

Y, Z

y, *conj.* and.
ya, *adv.* already; now; at once. **y. no,** no longer, any more. **y. que,** since.
yacer, *v.* lie.
yacimiento, *m.* deposit.
yanqui, *a. & n.* North American.
yate, *m.* yacht.
yegua, *f.* mare.
yelmo, *m.* helmet.
yema, *f.* yolk (of an egg).
yerba, *f.* grass; herb.
yerno, *m.* son-in-law.
yerro, *m.* error, mistake.
yeso, *m.* plaster.
yídish, *m.* Yiddish.
yo, *pron.* I.
yodo, *m.* iodine.

yoduro, *m.* iodide.
yugo, *m.* yoke.
yunque, *m.* anvil.
yunta, *f.* team (of animals).
zafarse, *v.* run away, escape. **z. de,** get rid of.
zafio, *a.* coarse, uncivil.
zafiro, *m.* sapphire.
zaguán, *m.* vestibule, hall.
zalamero -ra, *n.* flatterer, wheedler.
zambullir, *v.* plunge, dive.
zanahoria, *f.* carrot.
zanja, *f.* ditch, trench.
zapatería, *f.* shoe store; shoemaker's shop.
zapatero, *m.* shoemaker.
zapato, *m.* shoe.
zar, *m.* czar.

zaraza, *f.* calico; chintz.
zarza, *f.* bramble.
zarzuela, *f.* musical comedy.
zodíaco, *m.* zodiac.
zona, *f.* zone.
zoología, *f.* zoology.
zoológico, *a.* zoological.
zorro -rra, *n.* fox.
zozobra, *f.* worry, anxiety; capsizing.
zozobrar, *v.* capsize; worry.
zumba, *f.* spanking.
zumbido, *m.* buzz, hum. — **zumbar,** *v.*
zumo, *m.* juice. **z. de naranja,** orange juice.
zurcir, *v.* darn, mend.
zurdo, *a.* left-handed.
zurrar, *v.* flog, drub.

ENGLISH-SPANISH

A

a, *art.* un, una.

abacus, *n.* ábaco *m.*

abandon, 1. *n.* desenfreno, abandono *m.* **2.** *v.* abandonar, desamparar.

abandoned, *a.* abandonado.

abandonment, *n.* abandono, desamparo *m.*

abase, *v.* degradar, humillar.

abasement, *n.* degradación, humillación *f.*

abash, *v.* avergonzar.

abate, *v.* menguar, moderarse.

abatement, *n.* disminución *f.*

abbess, *n.* abadesa *f.*

abbey, *n.* abadía *f.*

abbot, *n.* abad *m.*

abbreviate, *v.* abreviar.

abbreviation, *n.* abreviatura *f.*

abdicate, *v.* abdicar.

abdication, *n.* abdicación *f.*

abdomen, *n.* abdomen *m.*

abdominal, *a.* abdominal.

abduct, *v.* secuestrar.

abduction, *n.* secuestración *f.*

abductor, *n.* secuestrador - ra.

aberrant, *a.* aberrante.

aberration, *n.* aberración *f.*

abet, *v.* apoyar, favorecer.

abetment, *n.* apoyo *m.*

abettor, *n.* cómplice *m. & f.*

abeyance, *n.* suspensión *f.*

abhor, *v.* abominar, odiar.

abhorrence, *n.* detestación *f.;* aborrecimiento *m.*

abhorrent, *a.* detestable, aborrecible.

abide, *v.* soportar. **to a. by,** cumplir con.

abiding, *a.* perdurable.

ability, *n.* habilidad *f.*

abject, *a.* abyecto; desanimado.

abjuration, *n.* renuncia *f.*

abjure, *v.* renunciar.

ablative, *a. & n.* (gram.) ablativo *m.*

ablaze, *a.* en llamas.

able, *a.* capaz; competente. **to be a.,** poder.

able-bodied, *a.* robusto.

ablution, *n.* ablución *f.*

ably, *adv.* hábilmente.

abnegate, *v.* repudiar; negar.

abnegation, *n.* abnegación; repudiación *f.*

abnormal, *a.* anormal.

abnormality, *n.* anormalidad, deformidad *f.*

abnormally, *adv.* anormalmente.

aboard, *adv.* a bordo.

abode, *n.* residencia *f.*

abolish, *v.* suprimir.

abolishment, *n.* abolición *f.*

abolition, *n.* abolición *f.*

abominable, *a.* abominable.

abominate, *v.* abominar, detestar.

abomination, *n.* abominación *f.*

aboriginal, *a. & n.* aborigen *f.*

abortion, *n.* aborto *m.*

abortive, *a.* abortivo.

abound, *v.* abundar.

about, 1. *adv.* como. **about to,** para; a punto de. **2.** *prep.* de, sobre, acerca de.

about-face, *n.* (mil.) media vuelta.

above, 1. *adv.* arriba. **2.** *prep.* sobre; por encima de.

aboveboard, *a. & adv.* sincero, franco.

abrasion, *n.* raspadura *f.;* (med.) abrasión *f.*

abrasive, 1. *a.* raspante. **2.** *n.* abrasivo *m.*

abreast, *adv.* de frente.

abridge, *v.* abreviar.

abridgment, *n.* abreviación *f.;* compendio *m.*

abroad, *adv.* en el extranjero, al extranjero.

abrogate, *v.* abrogar, revocar.

abrogation, *n.* abrogación, revocación *f.*

abrupt, *a.* repentino; brusco.

abruptly, *adv.* bruscamente, precipitadamente.

abruptness, *n.* precipitación; brusquedad *f.*

abscess, *n.* absceso *m.*

abscond, *v.* fugarse.

absence, *n.* ausencia, falta *f.*

absent, *a.* ausente.

absentee, *a. & n.* ausente *m. & f.*

absent-minded, *a.* distraído.

absinthe, *n.* absenta *f.*

absolute, *a.* absoluto.

absolutely, *adv.* absolutamente.

absoluteness, *n.* absolutismo *m.*

absolution, *n.* absolución *f.*

absolutism, *n.* absolutismo, despotismo *m.*

absolve, *v.* absolver.

absorb, *v.* absorber; preocupar.

absorbed, *a.* absorbido; absorto.

absorbent, *a.* absorbente.

absorbent cotton, algodón hidrófilo *m.*

absorbing, *a.* interesante.

absorption, *n.* absorción; preocupación *f.*

abstain, *v.* abstenerse.

abstemious, *a.* abstemio, sobrio.

abstinence, *n.* abstinencia *f.*

abstract, 1. *n.* resumen *m.* **2.** *v.* abstraer.

abstracted, *a.* distraído.

abstraction, *n.* abstracción *f.*

abstruse, *a.* abstruso.

absurd, *a.* absurdo, ridículo.

absurdity, *n.* absurdo *m.*

absurdly, *adv.* absurdamente.

abundance, *n.* abundancia *f.*

abundant, *a.* abundante.

abundantly, *adv.* abundantemente.

abuse, 1. *n.* abuso *m.* **2.** *v.* abusar de; maltratar.

abusive, *a.* abusivo.

abusively, *adv.* abusivamente, ofensivamente.

abut (on), *v.* terminar (en); lindar (con).

abutment, *n.* (building) estribo, contrafuerte *m.*

abyss, *n.* abismo *m.*

Abyssinian, *a. & n.* abisinio -nia.

acacia, *n.* acacia *f.*

academic, *a.* académico.

academy, *n.* academia *f.*

acanthus, *n.* (bot.) acanto *m.*

accede, *v.* acceder; consentir.

accelerate, *v.* acelerar.

acceleration, *n.* aceleración *f.*

accelerator, *n.* (auto.) acelerador *m.*

accent, 1. *n.* acento *m.* **2.** *v.* acentuar.

accentuate, *v.* acentuar.

accept, *v.* aceptar.

acceptability, *n.* aceptabilidad *f.*

acceptable, *a.* aceptable.

acceptably, *adv.* aceptablemente.

acceptance, *n.* aceptación *f.*

access, *n.* acceso *m.*, entrada *f.*

accessible, *a.* accesible.

accessory, 1. *a.* accesorio. **2.** *n.* cómplice *m. & f.*

accident, *n.* accidente *m.* **by a.,** por casualidad.

accidental, *a.* accidental.

accidentally, *adv.* accidentalmente, casualmente.

acclaim, *v.* aclamar.

acclamation, *n.* aclamación *f.*

acclimate, *v.* aclimatar.

acclivity, *n.* subida *f.*

accolade, *n.* acolada *f.*

accommodate, *v.* acomodar.

accommodating, *a.* bondadoso, complaciente.

accommodation, *n.* servicio *m.; (pl.)* alojamiento *m.*

accompaniment, *n.* acompañamiento *m.*

accompanist, *n.* acompañante *m. & f.*

accompany, *v.* acompañar.

accomplice, *n.* cómplice *m. & f.*

accomplish, *v.* llevar a cabo; realizar.

accomplished, *a.* acabado, cumplido; culto.

accomplishment, *n.* realización *f.;* logro *m.*

accord, 1. *n.* acuerdo *m.* **2.** *v.* otorgar.

accordance, *n.:* **in a. with,** de acuerdo con.

accordion, *n.* acordeón *m.*

accordingly, *adv.* en conformidad.

according to, *prep.* según.

accordion, *n.* (mus.) acordeón *m.*

accost, *v.* dirigirse a.

account, 1. *n.* relato *m.;* (com.) cuenta *f.* **on a. of,** a causa de. **on no a.,** de ninguna manera. **2.** *v.* **a. for,** explicar.

accountable, *a.* responsable.

accountant, *n.* contador -ra.

accounting, *n.* contabilidad *f.*

accouter, *v.* equipar, ataviar.

accouterments, *n.* equipo, atavío *m.*

accredit, *v.* acreditar.

accretion, *n.* aumento *m.*

accrual, *n.* aumento, incremento *m.*

accrue, *v.* provenir; acumularse.

accumulate, *v.* acumular.

accumulation, *n.* acumulación *f.*

accumulative, *a.* acumulativo.

accumulator, *n.* acumulador *m.*

accuracy, *n.* exactitud, precisión *f.*

accurate, *a.* exacto.

accursed, *a.* maldito.

accusation, *n.* acusación *f.*, cargo *m.*

accusative, *a. & n.* acusativo *m.*

accuse, *v.* acusar.

accused, *a. & n.* acusado -da, procesado -da.

accuser, *n.* acusador -ra.

accustom, *v.* acostumbrar.

accustomed, *a.* acostumbrado.

ace, 1. *a.* sobresaliente. **2.** *n.* as *m.*

acerbity, *n.* acerbidad, amargura *f.*

acetate, *n.* (chem.) acetato *m.*

acetic, *a.* acético.

acetylene, 1. *a.* acetilénico. **2.** *n.* (chem.) acetileno *m.*

ache, 1. *n.* dolor *m.* **2.** *v.* doler.

achieve, *v.* lograr, llevar a cabo.

achievement, *n.* realización *f.;* hecho notable *m.*

acid, *a. & n.* ácido *m.*

acidify, *v.* acidificar.

acidity, *n.* acidez *f.*

acidosis, *n.* (med.) acidismo *m.*

acid rain, lluvia ácida *f.*

acid test, prueba decisiva.

acidulous, *a.* agrio, acídulo.

acknowledge, *v.* admitir; (receipt) acusar.

acme, *n.* apogeo, colmo *m.*

acne, *n.* (med.) acné *m. & f.*

acolyte, *n.* acólito *m.*

acorn, *n.* bellota *f.*

acoustics, *n.* acústica *f.*

acquaint, *v.* familiarizar. **to be acquainted with,** conocer.

acquaintance, *n.* conocimiento *m.;* (person known) conocido -da. **to make the a. of,** conocer.

acquainted, be acquainted with, *v.* conocer.

acquiesce, *v.* consentir.

acquiescence, *n.* consentimiento *m.*

acquire, *v.* adquirir.

acquirement, *n.* adquisición *f.; (pl.)* conocimientos *m.pl.*

acquisition, *n.* adquisición *f.*

acquisitive, *a.* adquisitivo.

acquit, *v.* exonerar, absolver.

acquittal, *n.* absolución *f.*

acre, *n.* acre *m.*

acreage, número de acres.

acrid, *a.* acre, punzante.

acrimonious, *a.* acrimonioso, mordaz.

acrimony, *n.* acrimonia, aspereza *f.*

acrobat, *n.* acróbata *m. & f.*

acrobatic, *a.* acrobático.

across, 1. *adv.* a través, al otro lado. **2.** *prep.* al otro lado de, a través de.

acrostic, *n.* acróstico *m.*

act, 1. *n.* acción *f.;* acto *m.* **2.** *v.* actuar, portarse. **act as,** hacer de. **act on,** decidir sobre.

acting, 1. *a.* interino. **2.** *n.* acción *f.;* (theat.) representación *f.*

actinism, *n.* actinismo *m.*

actinium, *n.* (chem.) actinio *m.*

action, *n.* acción *f.* **take a.,** tomar medidas.

action replay, repetición *f.*

activate, *v.* activar.

activation, *n.* activación *f.*

activator, *n.* (chem.) activador *m.*

active, *a.* activo.

activity, *n.* actividad *f.*

actor, *n.* actor *m.*

actress, *n.* actriz *f.*

actual, *a.* real, efectivo.

actuality, *n.* realidad, actualidad *f.*

actually, *adv.* en realidad.

actuary, *n.* actuario *m.*

actuate, *v.* impulsar, mover.

acumen, *n.* cacumen *m.,* perspicacia *f.*

acupuncture, *n.* acupuntura *f.*

acute, *a.* agudo; perspicaz.

acutely, *adv.* agudamente.

acuteness, *n.* agudeza *f.*

adage, *n.* refrán, proverbio *m.*

adamant, *a.* firme.

Adam's apple, nuez de la garganta.

adapt, *v.* adaptar.

adaptable, *a.* adaptable.

adaptability, *n.* adaptabilidad *f.*

adaptation, *n.* adaptación *f.*

adapter, *n.* (tech.) adaptador *m.;* (mech.) ajustador *m.*

adaptive, *a.* adaptable, acomodable.

add, *v.* agregar, añadir. **a. up,** sumar.

adder, *n.* víbora; serpiente *f.*

addict, *n.* adicto -ta; ('fan') aficionado -da.

addition, *n.* adición *f.* **in a. to,** además de.

additional, *a.* adicional.

addle, *v.* confundir.

address, 1. *n.* dirección *f.;* señas *f.pl.;* (speech) discurso. **2.** *v.* dirigirse a.

addressee, *n.* destinatario -ia.

adduce, *v.* aducir.

adenoid, *a.* adenoidea.

adept, *a.* adepto.

adeptly, *adv.* diestramente.

adeptness, *n.* destreza *f.*

adequacy, *n.* suficiencia *f.*

adequate, *a.* adecuado.

adequately, *adv.* adecuadamente.

adhere, *v.* adherirse, pegarse.

adherence, *n.* adhesión *f.;* apego *m.*

adherent, *n.* adherente *m.,* partidario -ria.

adhesion, *n.* adhesión *f.*

adhesive, *a.* adhesivo. **a. tape,** esparadrapo *m.*

adhesiveness, *n.* adhesividad *f.*

adieu, 1. *interj.* adiós. **2.** *n.* despedida *f.*

adjacent, *a.* adyacente.

adjective, *n.* adjetivo *m.*

adjoin, *v.* lindar (con).

adjoining, *a.* contiguo.

adjourn, *v.* suspender, levantar.

adjournment, *n.* suspensión *f.;* (leg.) espera *f.*

adjunct, *n.* adjunto *m.;* (gram.) atributo *m.*

adjust, *v.* ajustar, acomodar; arreglar.

adjuster, *n.* ajustador -ra.

adjustment, *n.* ajuste; arreglo *m.*

adjutant, *n.* (mil.) ayudante *m.*

administer, *v.* administrar.

administration, *n.* administración *f.;* gobierno *m.*

administrative, *a.* administrativo.

administrator, *n.* administrador -ra.

admirable, *a.* admirable.

admirably, *adv.* admirablemente.

admiral, *n.* almirante *m.*

admiralty, *n.* Ministerio de Marina.

admiration, *n.* admiración *f.*

admire, *v.* admirar.

admirer, *n.* admirador -ra; enamorado -da.

admiringly, *adv.* admirativamente.

admissible, *a.* admisible, aceptable.

admission, *n.* admisión; entrada *f.*

admit, *v.* admitir.

admittance, *n.* entrada *f.*

admittedly, *adv.* reconocidamente.

admixture, *n.* mezcla *f.*

admonish, *v.* amonestar.

admonition, *n.* admonición *f.*

adolescence, *n.* adolescencia *f.*

adolescent, *n.* & *a.* adolescente.

adopt, *v.* adoptar.

adopted child, hija adoptiva *f.,* hijo adoptivo *m.*

adoption, *n.* adopción *f.*

adorable, *a.* adorable.

adoration, *n.* adoración *f.*

adore, *v.* adorar.

adorn, *v.* adornar.

adornment, *n.* adorno *m.*

adrenalin, *n.* adrenalina *f.*

adrift, *adv.* a la ventura.

adroit, *a.* diestro.

adulate, *v.* adular.

adulation, *n.* adulación *f.*

adult, *a.* & *n.* adulto -a.

adulterant, *a.* & *n.* adulterante *m.*

adulterate, *v.* adulterar.

adulterer, *n.* adúltero -ra.

adulteress, *n.* adúltera *f.*

adultery, *n.* adulterio *m.*

advance, 1. *n.* avance; adelanto *m.* **in a.,** de antemano, antes. **2.** *v.* avanzar, adelantar.

advanced, *a.* avanzado, adelantado.

advancement, *n.* adelantamiento *m.;* promoción *f.*

advantage, *n.* ventaja *f.* **take a. of,** aprovecharse de.

advantageous, *a.* provechoso, ventajoso.

advantageously, *adv.* ventajosamente.

advent, *n.* venida, llegada *f.*

adventitious, *a.* adventicio, espontáneo.

adventure, *n.* aventura *f.*

adventurer, *n.* aventurero -ra.

adventurous, *a.* aventurero, intrépido.

adventurously, *adv.* arriesgadamente.

adverb, *n.* adverbio *m.*

adverbial, *a.* adverbial.

adversary, *n.* adversario -a.

adverse, *a.* adverso.

adversely, *adv.* adversamente.

adversity, *n.* adversidad *f.*

advert, *v.* hacer referencia a.

advertise, *v.* avisar, anunciar; (promote) promocionar.

advertisement, *n.* aviso, anuncio *m.*

advertiser, *n.* anunciante *m. & f.,* avisador -ra.

advertising, *n.* publicidad *f.*

advice, *n.* consejos *m.pl.*

advisability, *n.* prudencia, propiedad *f.*

advisable, *a.* aconsejable, prudente.

advisably, *adv.* prudentemente.

advise, *v.* aconsejar. **a. against,** desaconsejar.

advisedly, *adv.* avisadamente, prudentemente.

advisement, *n.* consideración *f.;* **take under a.,** someter a estudio.

adviser, *n.* consejero -ra.

advocacy, *n.* abogacía; defensa *f.*

advocate, 1. *n.* abogado -da. **2.** *v.* apoyar.

aegis, *n.* amparo *m.*

aerate, *v.* airear, ventilar.

aeration, *n.* aeración, ventilación *f.*

aerial, *a.* aéreo.

aerie, *n.* nido de águila.

aeronautics, *n.* aeronáutica *f.*

aerosol bomb, bomba insecticida.

afar, *adv.* lejos. **from a.,** de lejos, desde lejos.

affability, *n.* afabilidad, amabilidad *f.*

affable, *a.* afable.

affably, *adv.* afablemente.

affair, *n.* asunto *m.* **love a.,** aventura amorosa.

affect, *v.* afectar; (emotionally) conmover.

affectation, *n.* afectación *f.*

affected, *a.* artificioso.

affecting, *a.* conmovedor.

affection, *n.* cariño *m.*

affectionate, *a.* afectuoso, cariñoso.

affectionately, *adv.* afectuosamente, con cariño.

affiance, *v.* dar palabra de casamiento; **become affianced,** comprometerse.

affidavit, *n.* (leg.) declaración, deposición *f.*

affiliate, 1. *n.* afiliado -da. **2.** *v.* afiliar.

affiliation, *n.* afiliación *f.*

affinity, *n.* afinidad *f.*

affirm, *v.* afirmar.

affirmation, *n.* afirmación, aserción *f.*

affirmative, 1. *n.* afirmativa *f.* **2.** *a.* afirmativo.

affirmatively, *adv.* afirmativamente, aseveradamente.

affix, 1. *n.* (gram.) afijo *m.* **2.** *v.* fijar, pegar, poner.

afflict, *v.* afligir.

affliction, *n.* aflicción *f.;* mal *m.*

affluence, *n.* abundancia, opulencia *f.*

affluent, *a.* opulento, afluente.

afford, *v.* proporcionar. **be able to a.,** tener con que comprar.

affordable, *a.* asequible.

affront, 1. *n.* afrenta *f.* **2.** *v.* afrentar, insultar.

afield, *adv.* lejos de casa; lejos del camino; lejos del asunto.

afire, *adv.* ardiendo.

afloat, *adv.* (naut.) a flote.

aforementioned, aforesaid, *a.* dicho, susodicho.

afraid, *a.* **to be a.,** tener miedo, temer.

African, *n. & a.* africano -na.

aft, *adv.* (naut.) a popa, en popa.

after, 1. *prep.* después de. **2.** *conj.* después que.

aftermath, *n.* resultados *m.pl.,* consecuencias *f.pl.*

afternoon, *n.* tarde *f.* **good a.,** buenas tardes.

afterthought, *n.* idea tardía.

afterward(s), *adv.* después.

again, *adv.* otra vez, de nuevo. **to do a.,** volver a hacer.

against, *prep.* contra; en contra de.

agape, *adv.* con la boca abierta.

agate, *n.* ágata *f.*

age, 1. *n.* edad *f.* **of a.,** mayor de edad. **old a.,** vejez *f.* **2.** *v.* envejecer.

aged, *a.* viejo, anciano, añejo.

ageism, *n.* discriminación contra las personas de edad.

ageless, *a.* sempiterno.

agency, *n.* agencia *f.*

agenda, *n.* agenda *f.,* orden *m.*

agent, *n.* agente; representante *m. & f.*

agglutinate, *v.* aglutinar.

agglutination, *n.* aglutinación *f.*

aggrandize, *v.* agrandar; elevar.

aggrandizement, *n.* engrandecimiento *m.*

aggravate, *v.* agravar; irritar.

aggravation, *n.* agravamiento; empeoramiento *m.*

aggregate, *a. & n.* agregado *m.*

aggregation, *n.* agregación *f.*

aggression, *n.* agresión *f.*

aggressive, *a.* agresivo -va.

aggressively, *adv.* agresivamente.

aggressiveness, *n.* agresividad *f.*

aggressor, *n.* agresor -ra.

aghast, *a.* horrorizado.

agile, *a.* ágil.

agility, *n.* agilidad, ligereza, prontitud *f.*

agitate, *v.* agitar.

agitation, *n.* agitación *f.*

agitator, *n.* agitador -ra.

agnostic, *a. & n.* agnóstico -ca.

ago, *adv.* hace. **two days a.,** hace dos días.

agonized, *a.* angustioso.

agony, *n.* sufrimiento *m.;* angustia *f.*

agrarian, *a.* agrario.

agree, *v.* estar de acuerdo; convenir. **a. with one,** sentar bien.

agreeable, *a.* agradable.

agreeably, *adv.* agradablemente.

agreement, *n.* acuerdo *m.*

agriculture, *n.* agricultura *f.*

ahead, *adv.* adelante.

aid, 1. *n.* ayuda *f.* 2. *v.* ayudar.

aide, *n.* ayudante -ta.

AIDS, *n.* SIDA *m.*

ailing, *adj.* enfermo.

ailment, *n.* enfermedad *f.*

aim, 1. *n.* puntería *f.;* (purpose) propósito *m.* 2. *v.* apuntar.

aimless, *a.* sin objeto.

air, *n.* aire *m.* **by a.** por avión. 2. *v.* ventilar, airear.

airbag, *n.* (in automobiles) saco de aire *m.*

air-conditioned, *a.* con aire acondicionado.

air-conditioning, acondicionamiento del aire.

aircraft, *n.* avión *m.*

aircraft carrier, portaaviones *m.*

airfare, *n.* precio del billete de avión *m.*

airing, *n.* ventilación *f.*

airline, *n.* línea aérea *f.*

airliner, *n.* avión de pasajeros.

airmail, *n.* correo aéreo.

airplane, *n.* avión, aeroplano *m.*

air pollution, contaminación atmosférica, contaminación del aire.

airport, *n.* aeropuerto *m.*

air pressure, presión atmosférica.

air raid, ataque aéreo.

airsick, *a.* mareado.

air terminal, terminal aérea *f.*

airtight, *a.* hermético.

air traffic controller, controlador aéreo *m.*

aisle, *n.* pasillo *m.*

ajar, *a.* entreabierto.

akin, *a.* emparentado, semejante.

alacrity, *n.* alacridad, presteza *f.*

alarm, 1. *n.* alarma *f.* 2. *v.* alarmar.

alarmist, *n.* alarmista *m.* & *f.*

albino, *n.* albino -na.

album, *n.* álbum *m.*

alcohol, *n.* alcohol *m.*

alcoholic, *a.* alcohólico.

alcove, *n.* alcoba *f.*

ale, *n.* cerveza inglesa.

alert, 1. *n.* alarma *f.* **on the a.,** alerta, sobre aviso. 2. *a.* listo, vivo. 3. *v.* poner sobre aviso.

alfalfa, *n.* alfalfa *f.*

algebra, *n.* álgebra *f.*

alias, *n.* alias *m.*

alibi, *n.* excusa *f.;* (leg.) coartada *f.*

alien, 1. *a.* ajeno, extranjero. 2. *n.* extranjero -ra.

alienate, *v.* enajenar.

alight, *v.* bajar, apearse.

align, *v.* alinear.

alike, 1. *a.* semejante, igual. 2. *adv.* del mismo modo, igualmente.

alimentary canal, *n.* tubo digestivo *m.*

alive, *a.* vivo; animado.

alkali, *n.* (chem.) álcali, cali *m.*

alkaline, *a.* alcalino.

all, *a.* & *pron.* todo. **not at a.,** de ninguna manera, nada.

allay, *v.* aquietar.

allegation, *n.* alegación *f.*

allege, *v.* alegar; pretender.

allegiance, *n.* lealtad *f.;* (to country) homenaje *m.*

allegory, *n.* alegoría *f.*

allergy, *n.* alergia *f.*

alleviate, *v.* aliviar.

alley, *n.* callejón *m.* **bowling a.,** bolera *f.,* boliche *m.*

alliance, *n.* alianza *f.*

allied, *a.* aliado.

alligator, *n.* caimán *m.;* (Mex.) lagarto *m.* **a. pear,** aguacate *m.*

allocate, *v.* colocar, asignar.

allot, *v.* asignar.

allotment, *n.* lote, porción *f.*

allow, *v.* permitir, dejar.

allowance, *n.* abono *m.;* dieta *f.* **make a. for,** tener en cuenta.

alloy, *n.* mezcla *f.* (metal) aleación *f.*

all right, está bien.

allude, *v.* aludir.

allure, 1. *n.* atracción *f.* 2. *v.* atraer, tentar.

alluring, *a.* tentador, seductivo.

allusion, *n.* alusión *f.*

ally, 1. *n.* aliado -da. 2. *v.* aliar.

almanac, *n.* almanaque *m.*

almighty, *a.* todopoderoso.

almond, *n.* almendra *f.*

almost, *adv.* casi.

alms, *n.* limosna *f.*

aloft, *adv.* arriba, en alto.

alone, *adv.* solo, a solas. **to leave a.,** dejar en paz.

along, *prep.* por; a lo largo de. **a. with,** junto con.

alongside, 1. *adv.* al lado. 2. *prep.* junto a.

aloof, *a.* apartado.

aloud, *adv.* en voz alta.

alpaca, *n.* alpaca *f.*

alphabet, *n.* alfabeto *m.*

alphabetical, *a.* alfabético.

alphabetize, *v.* alfabetizar.

already, *adv.* ya.

also, *adv.* también.

altar, *n.* altar *m.*

alter, *v.* alterar.

alteration, *n.* alteración *f.*

alternate, 1. *a.* alterno. 2. *n.* substituto -ta. 3. *v.* alternar.

alternative, 1. *a.* alternativo. 2. *n.* alternativa *f.*

although, *conj.* aunque.

altitude, *n.* altura *f.*

alto, *n.* contralto *m.*

altogether, *adv.* en junto; enteramente.

altruism, *n.* altruismo *m.*

alum, *n.* alumbre *m.*

aluminum, *n.* aluminio *m.*

aluminum foil, papel de aluminio *m.*

always, *adv.* siempre.

amalgam, *n.* amalgama *f.*

amalgamate, *v.* amalgamar.

amass, *v.* amontonar.

amateur, *n.* aficionado -da.

amaze, v. asombrar; sorprender.

amazement, n. asombro m.

amazing, a. asombroso, pasmoso.

ambassador, n. embajador -ra.

amber, 1. a. ambarino. **2.** n. ámbar m.

ambidextrous, a. ambidextro.

ambiguity, n. ambigüedad f.

ambiguous, a. ambiguo.

ambition, n. ambición f.

ambitious, a. ambicioso.

ambulance, n. ambulancia f.

ambush, 1. n. emboscada f. **2.** v. acechar.

ameliorate, v. mejorar.

amenable, a. tratable, dócil.

amend, v. enmendar.

amendment, n. enmienda f.

amenity, n. amenidad f.

American, a. & n. americano -na, norteamericano -na.

amethyst, n. amatista f.

amiable, a. amable.

amicable, a. amigable.

amid, prep. entre, en medio de.

amidships, adv. (naut.) en medio del navío.

amiss, adv. mal. **to take a.,** llevar a mal.

amity, n. amistad, armonía f.

ammonia, n. amoníaco m.

ammunition, n. municiones f.pl.

amnesia, n. (med.) amnesia f.

amnesty, n. amnistía f., indulto m.

amniocentesis, n. amniocéntesis f.

amoeba, n. amiba f.

among, prep. entre.

amoral, a. amoral.

amorous, a. amoroso.

amorphous, a. amorfo.

amortize, v. (com.) amortizar.

amount, 1. n. cantidad, suma f. **2.** v. **a. to,** subir a.

ampere, n. (elec.) amperio m.

amphibian, a. & n. anfibio m.

amphitheater, n. anfiteatro, circo m.

ample, a. amplio; suficiente.

amplify, v. amplificar.

amputate, v. amputar.

amuse, v. entretener, divertir.

amusement, n. diversión f.

an, art. un, una.

anachronism, n. anacronismo, m.

analogous, a. análogo, parecido.

analogy, n. analogía f.

analysis, n. análisis m.

analyst, n. analista m. & f.

analytic, a. analítico.

analyze, v. analizar.

anarchy, n. anarquía f.

anatomy, n. anatomía f.

ancestor, n. antepasado m.

ancestral, a. de los antepasados, hereditario.

ancestry, n. linaje, abolengo m.

anchor, 1. n. ancla f. **weigh a.,** levar el ancla. **2.** v. anclar.

anchorage, n. (naut.) ancladero, anclaje m.

anchovy, n. anchoa f.

ancient, a. & n. antiguo -ua.

and, conj. y, (before i-, hi-) e.

anecdote, n. anécdota f.

anemia, n. (med.) anemia f.

anesthetic, n. anestesia f.

anew, adv. de nuevo.

angel, n. ángel m.

anger, 1. n. ira f., enojo m. **2.** v. enfadar, enojar.

angle, n. ángulo m.

angry, a. enojado, enfadado.

anguish, n. angustia f.

angular, a. angular.

aniline, n. (chem.) anilina f.

animal, a. & n. animal m.

animate, 1. adj. animado. **2.** v. animar.

animated, a. vivo, animado.

animation, n. animación, viveza f.

animosity, n. rencor m.

anise, n. anís m.

ankle, n. tobillo m.

annals, n.pl. anales m.pl.

annex, 1. n. anexo m., adición f. **2.** v. anexar.

annexation, n. anexión, adición f.

annihilate, v. aniquilar, destruir.

anniversary, n. aniversario m.

annotate, v. anotar.

annotation, n. anotación f., apunte m.

announce, v. anunciar.

announcement, n. anuncio, aviso m.

announcer, n. anunciador -ra; (radio) locutor -ra.

annoy, v. molestar.

annoyance, n. molestia, incomodidad f.

annual, a. anual.

annuity, n. anualidad, pensión f.

annul, v. anular, invalidar.

anode, n. (elec.) ánodo m.

anoint, v. untar; (rel.) ungir.

anomalous, a. anómalo, irregular.

anonymous, a. anónimo.

another, a. & pron. otro.

answer, 1. n. contestación, respuesta f. **2.** v. contestar, responder. **a. for,** ser responsable de.

answerable, a. discutible, refutable.

answering machine, contestador automático m.

ant, n. hormiga f.

antacid, a. & n. antiácido m.

antagonism, n. antagonismo m.

antagonist, n. antagonista m. & f.

antagonistic, a. antagónico, hostil.

antagonize, v. contrariar.

antarctic, a. & n. antártico m.

antecedent, a. & n. antecedente m.

antedate, v. antedatar.

antelope, n. antílope m., gacela f.

antenna, n. antena f.

antepenultimate, a. antepenúltimo.

anterior, a. anterior.

anteroom, n. antecámara f.

anthem, n. himno m.; (religious) antífona f.

anthology, *n.* antología *f.*

anthracite, *n.* antracita *f.*

anthrax, *n.* (med.) ántrax *m.*

anthropology, *n.* antropología *f.*

antiaircraft, *a.* antiaéreo.

antibody, *n.* anticuerpo *m.*

anticipate, *v.* esperar, anticipar.

anticipation, *n.* anticipación *f.*

anticlerical, *a.* anticlerical.

anticlimax, *n.* anticlímax *m.*

antidote, *n.* antídoto *m.*

antifreeze, *n.* anticongelante *m.*

antihistamine, *n.* antihistamínico *m.*

antimony, *n.* antimonio *m.*

antinuclear, *a.* antinuclear.

antipathy, *n.* antipatía *f.*

antiquated, *a.* anticuado.

antique, 1. *a.* antiguo. **2.** *n.* antigüedad *f.*

antiquity, *n.* antigüedad *f.*

antiseptic, *a.* & *n.* antiséptico *m.*

antisocial, *a.* antisocial.

antitoxin, *n.* (med.) antitoxina *f.*

antler, *n.* asta *f.*

anvil, *n.* yunque *m.*

anxiety, *n.* ansia, ansiedad *f.*

anxious, *a.* inquieto, ansioso.

any, *a.* alguno; (at all) cualquiera; (after *not*) ninguno.

anybody, *pron.* alguien; (at all) cualquiera; (after *not*) nadie.

anyhow, *adv.* de todos modos; en todo caso.

anyone, *pron.* = anybody.

anything, *pron.* algo; (at all) cualquier cosa; (after *not*) nada.

anyway, *adv.* = anyhow.

anywhere, *adv.* en alguna parte; (at all) dondequiera; (after *not*) en ninguna parte.

apart, *adv.* aparte. **to take a.,** deshacer.

apartheid, *n.* apartheid *m.*

apartment, *n.* apartamento, piso *m.*

apartment house, casa de pisos *f.*

apathetic, *a.* apático.

apathy, *n.* apatía *f.*

ape, 1. *n.* mono -na. **2.** *v.* imitar.

aperture, *n.* abertura *f.*

apex, *n.* ápice *m.*

aphorism, *n.* aforismo *m.*

apiary, *n.* colmenario, abejar *m.*

apiece, *adv.* por persona; cada uno.

apologetic, *a.* apologético.

apologist, *n.* apologista *m.* & *f.*

apologize, *v.* excusarse, disculparse.

apology, *n.* excusa; apología *f.*

apoplectic, *a.* apopléctico.

apoplexy, *n.* apoplejía *f.*

apostate, *n.* apóstata *m.* & *f.*

apostle, *n.* apóstol *m.*

apostolic, *a.* apostólico.

apall, *v.* horrorizar; consternar.

apparatus, *n.* aparato *m.*

apparel, *n.* ropa *f.*

apparent, *a.* aparente; claro.

apparition, *n.* aparición *f.*; fantasma *m.*

appeal, 1. *n.* súplica *f.*; interés *m.*; (leg.) apelación *f.* **2.** *v.* apelar, suplicar; interesar.

appear, *v.* aparecer, asomar; (seem) parecer; (leg.) comparecer.

appearance, *n.* apariencia *f.*, aspecto *m.*; aparición *f.*

appease, *v.* aplacar, apaciguar.

appeasement, *n.* apaciguamiento *m.*

appeaser, *n.* apaciguador -ra, pacificador -ra.

appellant, *n.* apelante, demandante *m.* & *f.*

appellate, *a.* (leg.) de apelación.

appendage, *n.* añadidura *f.*

appendectomy, *n.* (med.) apendectomía *f.*

appendicitis, *n.* (med.) apendicitis *f.*

appendix, *n.* apéndice *m.*

appetite, *n.* apetito *m.*

appetizer, *n.* aperitivo *m.*

appetizing, *a.* apetitoso.

applaud, *v.* aplaudir.

applause, *n.* aplauso *m.*

apple, *n.* manzana *f.* **a. tree,** manzano *m.*

applesauce, *n.* compota de manzana.

appliance, *n.* aparato *m.*

applicable, *a.* aplicable.

applicant, *n.* suplicante *m.* & *f.*; candidato -ta.

application, *n.* solicitud *f.*

applied, *a.* aplicado. **a. for,** pedido.

appliqué, *n.* (sewing) aplicación *f.*

apply, *v.* aplicar. **a. for,** solicitar, pedir.

appoint, *v.* nombrar.

appointment, *n.* nombramiento *m.*; puesto *m.*

apportion, *v.* repartir.

apposition, *n.* (gram.) aposición *f.*

appraisal, *n.* valoración *f.*

appraise, *v.* evaluar; tasar; estimar.

appreciable, *a.* apreciable; notable.

appreciate, *v.* apreciar, estimar.

appreciation, *n.* aprecio; reconocimiento *m.*

apprehend, *v.* prender, capturar.

apprehension, *n.* aprensión *f.*; detención *f.*

apprehensive, *a.* aprensivo.

apprentice, *n.* aprendiz -iza.

apprenticeship, *n.* aprendizaje *m.*

apprise, *v.* informar.

approach, 1. *n.* acceso; método *m.* **2.** *v.* acercarse.

approachable, *a.* accesible.

approbation, *n.* aprobación *f.*

appropriate, 1. *a.* apropiado. **2.** *v.* apropiar.

appropriation, *n.* apropiación *f.*

approval, *n.* aprobación *f.*

approve, *v.* aprobar.

approximate, 1. *a.* aproximado. **2.** *v.* aproximar.

approximately, *adv.* aproximadamente.

approximation, *n.* aproximación *f.*

appurtenance, *n.* dependencia *f.*

apricot, *n.* albaricoque, damasco *m.*

April, *n.* abril *m.*

apron, *n.* delantal *m.*

apropos, *adv.* a propósito.

apt, *a.* apto; capaz.

aptitude, *n.* aptitud; facilidad *f.*

aquarium, *n.* acuario *m.,* pecera *f.*

aquatic, *a.* acuático.

aqueduct, *n.* acueducto *m.*

aqueous, *a.* ácueo, acuoso, aguoso.

aquiline, *a.* aquilino, aguileño.

Arab, *a. & n.* árabe *m. & f.*

arable, *a.* cultivable.

arbitrary, *a.* arbitrario.

arbitrate, *v.* arbitrar.

arbitration, *n.* arbitraje *m.,* arbitración *f.*

arbitrator, *n.* arbitrador -ra.

arbor, *n.* emparrado *m.*

arboreal, *a.* arbóreo.

arc, *n.* arco *m.*

arch, 1. *n.* arco *m.* **2.** *v.* arquear, encorvar.

archaeology, *n.* arqueología *f.*

archaic, *a.* arcaico.

archbishop, *n.* arzobispo *m.*

archdiocese, *n.* archidiócesis *f.*

archduke, *n.* archiduque *m.*

archer, *n.* arquero *m.*

archery, *n.* ballestería *f.*

archipelago, *n.* archipiélago *m.*

architect, *n.* arquitecto -ta.

architectural, *a.* arquitectural.

architecture, *n.* arquitectura *f.*

archive, *n.* archivo *m.*

archway, *n.* arcada *f.*

arctic, *a.* ártico.

ardent, *a.* ardiente.

ardor, *n.* ardor *m.,* pasión *f.*

arduous, *a.* arduo, difícil.

area, *n.* área; extensión *f.*

area code, prefijo *m.*

arena, *n.* arena *f.*

Argentine, *a. & n.* argentino -na.

argue, *v.* disputar; sostener.

argument, *n.* disputa *f.;* razonamiento *m.*

argumentative, *a.* argumentoso.

aria, *n.* (mus.) aria *f.*

arid, *a.* árido, seco.

arise, *v.* surgir; alzarse.

aristocracy, *n.* aristocracia *f.*

aristocrat, *n.* aristócrata *m.*

aristocratic, *a.* aristocrático.

arithmetic, *n.* aritmética *f.*

ark, *n.* arca *f.*

arm, 1. *n.* brazo *m.;* (weapon) arma *f.* **2.** *v.* armar.

armament, *n.* armamento *m.*

armchair, *n.* sillón *m.,* butaca *f.*

armed forces, fuerzas militares.

armful, *n.* brazada *f.*

armhole, *n.* (sew.) sobaquera *f.*

armistice, *n.* armisticio *m.*

armor, *n.* armadura *f.,* blindaje *m.*

armored, *a.* blindado.

armory, *n.* armería *f.,* arsenal *m.*

armpit, *n.* axila *f.,* sobaco *m.*

army, *n.* ejército *m.*

arnica, *n.* árnica *f.*

aroma, *n.* fragancia *f.*

aromatic, *a.* aromático.

around, *prep.* alrededor de, a la vuelta de; cerca de **a. here,** por aquí.

arouse, *v.* despertar; excitar.

arraign, *v.* (leg.) procesar criminalmente.

arrange, *v.* arreglar; concertar; (mus.) adaptar.

arrangement, *n.* arreglo; orden *m.*

array, 1. *n.* orden; adorno *m.* **2.** *v.* adornar.

arrears, *n.* atrasos *m.pl.*

arrest, 1. *n.* detención *f.* **2.** *v.* detener, arrestar.

arrival, *n.* llegada *f.*

arrive, *v.* llegar.

arrogance, *n.* arrogancia *f.*

arrogant, *a.* arrogante.

arrogate, *v.* arrogarse, usurpar.

arrow, *n.* flecha *f.*

arrowhead, *n.* punta de flecha *f.*

arsenal, *n.* arsenal *m.*

arsenic, *n.* arsénico *m.*

arson, *n.* incendio premeditado.

art, *n.* arte *m.* (*f.* in *pl.*); (skill) maña *f.*

arterial, *a.* arterial.

arteriosclerosis, *n.* arteriosclerosis *f.*

artery, *n.* arteria *f.*

artesian well, pozo artesiano *m.*

artful, *a.* astuto.

arthritis, *n.* artritis *f.*

artichoke, *n.* alcachofa *f.*

article, *n.* artículo *m.*

articulate, *v.* articular.

articulation, *n.* articulación *f.*

artifice, *n.* artificio *m.*

artificial, *a.* artificial.

artificially, *adv.* artificialmente.

artillery, *n.* artillería *f.*

artisan, *n.* artesano -na.

artist, *n.* artista *m. & f.*

artistic, *a.* artístico.

artistry, *n.* arte *m. & f.*

artless, *a.* natural, cándido.

as, *adv. & conj.* como; **as . . . as** tan . . . como.

asbestos, *n.* asbesto *m.*

ascend, *v.* ascender.

ascendancy, *n.* ascendiente *m.*

ascendant, *a.* ascendente.

ascent, *n.* subida *f.,* ascenso *m.*

ascertain, *v.* averiguar.

ascetic, 1. *a.* ascético. **2.** *n.* asceta *m. & f.*

ascribe, *v.* atribuir.

ash, *n.* ceniza *f.*

ashamed, *a.* avergonzado.

ashen, *a.* pálido.

ashore, *adv.* a tierra. **go a.,** desembarcar.

ashtray, *n.* cenicero *m.*

Ash Wednesday, miércoles de ceniza *m.*

Asiatic, *a. & n.* asiático -ca.

aside, *adv.* al lado. **a. from,** aparte de.

ask, *v.* preguntar; invitar; (request) pedir. **a. for,** pedir. **a. a question,** hacer una pregunta.

askance, *adv.* de soslayo; con recelo.

asleep, *a.* dormido. **to fall a.,** dormirse.

asparagus, *n.* espárrago *m.*

aspect, *n.* aspecto *m.,* apariencia *f.*

asperity, *n.* aspereza *f.*

aspersion, *n.* calumnia *f.*

asphalt, *n.* asfalto *m.*

asphyxia, *n.* asfixia *f.*

asphyxiate, *v.* asfixiar, sofocar.

aspirant, *a. & n.* aspirante *m. & f.*

aspirate, *v.* aspirar.

aspiration, *n.* aspiración *f.*

aspirator, *n.* aspirador *m.*

aspire, *v.* aspirar. **a. to,** ambicionar.

aspirin, *n.* aspirina *f.*

ass, *n.* asno, burro *m.*

assail, *v.* asaltar, acometer.

assailant, *n.* asaltador -ra.

assassin, *n.* asesino -na.

assassinate, *v.* asesinar.

assassination, *n.* asesinato *m.*

assault, 1. *n.* asalto *m.* **2.** *v.* asaltar, atacar.

assay, *v.* examinar; ensayar.

assemblage, *n.* asamblea *f.*

assemble, *v.* juntar, convocar; (mechanism) montar.

assembly, *n.* asamblea, concurrencia *f.*

assent, 1. *n.* asentimiento *m.* **2.** *v.* asentir, convenir.

assert, *v.* afirmar, aseverar. **a. oneself,** hacerse sentir.

assertion, *n.* aserción, aseveración *f.*

assertive, *a.* asertivo.

assess, *v.* tasar, evaluar.

assessor, *n.* asesor -ra.

asset, *n.* ventaja *f.* **assets,** (com.) capital *m.*

asseverate, *v.* aseverar, afirmar.

asseveration, *n.* aseveración *f.*

assiduous, *a.* asiduo.

assiduously, *adv.* asiduamente.

assign, *v.* asignar; destinar.

assignable, *a.* asignable, transferible.

assignation, *n.* asignación *f.*

assignment, *n.* misión; tarea *f.*

assimilate, *v.* asimilar.

assimilation, *n.* asimilación *f.*

assimilative, *a.* asimilativo.

assist, *v.* ayudar, auxiliar.

assistance, *n.* ayuda *f.,* auxilio *m.*

assistant, *n.* ayudante -ta, asistente -ta.

associate, 1. *n.* socio -cia. **2.** *v.* asociar.

association, *n.* asociación; sociedad *f.*

assonance, *n.* asonancia *f.*

assort, *v.* surtir con variedad.

assorted, *a.* variado, surtido.

assortment, *n.* surtido *m.*

assuage, *v.* mitigar, aliviar.

assume, *v.* suponer; asumir.

assuming, *a.* presuntuoso. **a. that,** dado que.

assumption, *n.* suposición; (rel.) asunción *f.*

assurance, *n.* seguridad; confianza *f.;* garantía *f.*

assure, *v.* asegurar; dar confianza.

assured, 1. *a.* seguro. **2.** *a. & n.* (com.) asegurado -da.

assuredly, *adv.* ciertamente.

aster, *n.* (bot.) aster *f.*

asterisk, *n.* asterisco *m.*

astern, *adv.* (naut.) a popa.

asteroid, *n.* asteroide *m.*

asthma, *n.* (med.) asma *f.*

astigmatism, *n.* astigmatismo *m.*

astir, *adv.* en movimiento.

astonish, *v.* asombrar, pasmar.

astonishment, *n.* asombro *m.,* sorpresa *f.*

astound, *v.* pasmar, sorprender.

astral, *a.* astral, estelar.

astray, *a.* desviado.

astride, *adv.* a horcajadas.

astringent, *a. & n.* astringente *m.*

astrology, *n.* astrología *f.*

astronaut, *n.* astronauta *m. & f.*

astronomy, *n.* astronomía *f.*

astute, *a.* astuto; agudo.

asunder, *adv.* en dos.

asylum, *n.* asilo, refugio *m.*

asymmetry, *n.* asimetría *f.*

at, *prep,* a, en; cerca de.

ataxia, *n.* (med.) ataxia *f.*

atheist, *n.* ateo -tea.

athlete, *n.* atleta *m. & f.*

athletic, *a.* atlético.

athletics, *n.* atletismo *m.,* deportes *m.pl.*

athwart, *prep,* a través de.

Atlantic, 1. *a.* atlántico. **2.** *n.* Atlántico *m.*

Atlantic Ocean, Océano Atlántico *m.*

atlas, *n.* atlas *m.*

atmosphere, *n.* atmósfera *f.;* (fig.) ambiente *m.*

atmospheric, *a.* atmosférico.

atoll, *n.* atolón *m.*

atom, *n.* átomo *m.*

atomic, *a.* atómico.

atomic bomb, bomba atómica *f.*

atomic energy, energía atómica, energía nuclear *f.*

atomic theory, teoría atómica. *f.*

atomic weight, peso atómico *m.*

atonal, *a.* (mus.) atonal.

atone, *v.* expiar, compensar.

atonement, *n.* expiación; reparación *f.*

atrocious, *a.* atroz.

atrocity, *n.* atrocidad *f.*

atrophy, 1. *n.* (med.) atrofia *f.* **2.** *v.* atrofiar.

atropine, *n.* (chem.) atropina *f.*

attach, *v.* juntar; prender; (hook) enganchar; (fig.) atribuir.

attaché, *n.* agregado -da.

attachment, 1. enlace *m.;* accesorio *m.;* (emotional) afecto, cariño *m.*

attack, 1. *n.* ataque *m.* **2.** *v.* atacar.

attacker, *n.* asaltador -ra.

attain, *v.* lograr, alcanzar.

attainable, *a.* accesible, realizable.

attainment, *n.* logro; *(pl.)* dotes *f.pl.*

attempt, 1. *n.* ensayo; esfuerzo *m.;* tentativa *f.* **2.** *v.* ensayar, intentar.

attend, *v.* atender; (a meeting) asistir a.

attendance, *n.* asistencia; presencia *f.*

attendant, 1. *a.* concomitante. **2.** *n.* servidor -ra.

attention, *n.* atención *f.;* obsequio *m.* **to pay a. to,** hacer caso a.

attentive, *a.* atento.

attentively, *adv.* atentamente.

attenuate, *v.* atenuar, adelgazar.

attest, *v.* confirmar, atestiguar.

attic, *n.* desván *m.,* guardilla *f.*

attire, 1. *n.* traje *m.* **2.** *v.* vestir.

attitude, *n.* actitud *f.,* ademán *m.*

attorney, *n.* abogado -da, apoderado -da.

attract, *v.* atraer. **a. attention,** llamar la atención.

attraction, *n.* atracción *f.,* atractivo *m.*

attractive, *a.* atractivo; simpático.

attributable, *a.* atribuible, imputable.

attribute, 1. *n.* atributo *m.* **2.** *v.* atribuir.

attrition, *n.* roce, desgaste *m.;* atrición *f.*

attune, *v.* armonizar.

auction, *n.* subasta *f.,* (S.A.) venduta *f.*

auctioneer, *n.* subastador -ra. (S.A.) martillero -ra.

audacious, *a.* audaz.

audacity, *n.* audacia *f.*

audible, *a.* audible.

audience, *n.* auditorio, público *m.;* entrevista *f.*

audiovisual, *a.* audiovisual.

audit, 1. *n.* revisión de cuentas *f.* **2.** *v.* revisar cuentas.

audition, *n.* audición *f.*

auditor, *n.* interventor -ora, revisor -ora.

auditorium, *n.* sala *f.;* teatro *m.*

auditory, *a. & n.* auditorio *m.*

augment, *v.* aumentar.

augur, *v.* augurar, pronosticar.

August, *n.* agosto *m.*

aunt, *n.* tía *f.*

auspice, *n.* auspicio *m.*

auspicious, *a.* favorable; propicio.

austere, *a.* austero.

austerity, *n.* austeridad, severidad *f.*

Austrian, *a. & n.* austríaco -ca.

authentic, *a.* auténtico.

authenticate, *v.* autenticar.

authenticity, *n.* autenticidad *f.*

author, *n.* autor -ra, escritor -ra.

authoritarian, *a. & n.* autoritario -ria.

authoritative, *a.* autoritativo; autorizado.

authoritatively, *adv.* autoritativamente.

authority, *n.* autoridad *f.*

authorization, *n.* autorización *f.*

authorize, *v.* autorizar.

auto, *n.* auto, automóvil *m.*

autobiography, *n.* autobiografía *f.*

autocracy, *n.* autocracia *f.*

autocrat, *n.* autócrata *m. & f.*

autograph, *n.* autógrafo *m.*

automatic, *a.* automático.

automatically, *adv.* automáticamente.

automobile, *n.* automóvil, coche *m.*

automotive, *a.* automotriz.

autonomy, *n.* autonomía *f.*

autopsy, *n.* autopsia *f.*

autumn, *n.* otoño *m.*

auxiliary, *a.* auxiliar.

avail, 1. *n.* **of no a.,** en vano. **2.** *v.* **a. oneself of,** aprovecharse.

available, *a.* disponible.

avalanche, *n.* alud *m.*

avarice, *n.* avaricia, codicia *f.*

avariciously, *adv.* avaramente.

avenge, *v.* vengar.

avenger, *n.* vengador -ra.

avenue, *n.* avenida *f.*

average, 1. *a.* medio; común. **2.** *n.* promedio, término medio *m.* **3.** *v.* calcular el promedio.

averse, *a.* **to be a. to,** tener antipatía a, opuesto a.

aversion, *n.* aversión *f.*

avert, *v.* desviar; impedir.

aviary, *n.* pajarera, avería *f.*

aviation, *n.* aviación *f.*

aviator, *n.* aviador -ra.

aviatrix, *n.* aviatriz *f.*

avid, *a.* ávido.

avocado, *n.* aguacate *m.*

avocado sauce, guacamol, guacamole *m.*

avocation, *n.* pasatiempo *f.*

avoid, *v.* evitar.

avoidable, *a.* evitable.

avoidance, *n.* evitación *f.;* (leg.) anulación *f.*

avow, *v.* declarar; admitir.

avowal, *n.* admisión *f.*

avowed, *a.* reconocido; admitido.

avowedly, *adv.* reconocidamente; confesadamente.

await, *v.* esperar, aguardar.

awake, *a.* despierto.

awaken, *v.* despertar.

award, 1. *n.* premio *m.* **2.** *v.* otorgar.

aware, *a.* enterado, consciente.

awash, *a. & adv.* (naut.) a flor de agua.

away, *adv. (*see under verb: **go away, put away, take away,** etc.)

awe, *n.* pavor *m.*

awesome, *a.* pavoroso; aterrador.

awful, *a.* horrible, terrible, muy malo, pésimo.

awhile, *adv.* por un rato.

awkward, *a.* torpe, desmañado; (fig.) delicado, embarazoso.

awning, *n.* toldo *m.*

awry, *a.* oblicuo, torcido.

ax, axe, *n.* hacha *f.*

axiom, *n.* axioma *m.*

axis, *n.* eje *m.*

axle, *n.* eje *m.*

ayatollah, *n.* ayatolá *m.*

azure, *a.* azul.

B

babble, 1. *n.* balbuceo, murmullo *m.* **2** *v.* balbucear.

babbler, *n.* hablador -ra, charlador -ra.

baboon, *n.* mandril *m.*

baby, *n.* nene, bebé *m.*

baby carriage, cochecito de niño *m.*

babyish, *a.* infantil.

baby squid, chipirón *m.*

bachelor, *n.* soltero *m.*

bacillus, *n.* bacilo, microbio *m.*

back, 1. *adv.* atrás. **to be b.,** estar de vuelta. **b. of,** detrás de. **2.** *n.* espalda *f.;* (of animal) lomo *m.*

backache, *n.* dolor de espalda *m.*

backbone, *n.* espinazo *m.;* (fig.) firmeza *f.*

backer, *n.* sostenedor -ra.

background, *n.* fondo *m.* antecedentes *m.pl.*

backing, *n.* apoyo *m.,* garantía *f.*

backlash, *n.* repercusión negativa.

backlog, *n.* atrasos *m.pl.*

backpack, *n.* mochila *f.*

back seat, asiento trasero *m.*

backstage, *n.* entre bastidores *m.*

backward, 1. *a.* atrasado. **2.** *adv.* hacia atrás.

backwardness, *n.* atraso *m.*

backwater, *n.* parte de río estancada *f.*

backwoods, *n.* región del monte apartada *f.*

bacon, *n.* tocino *m.*

bacteria, *n.* bacterias *f.pl.*

bacteriologist, *n.* bacteriólogo -a.

bacteriology, *n.* bacteriología *f.*

bad, *a.* malo.

badge, *n.* insignia, divisa *f.*

badger, 1. *n.* tejón *m.* **2.** *v.* atormentar.

badly, *adv.* mal.

badness, *n.* maldad *f.*

bad-tempered, *a.* de mal humor.

baffle, *v.* desconcertar.

bafflement, *n.* contrariedad; confusión *f.*

bag, 1. *n.* saco *m.;* bolsa *f.* **2.** *v.* ensacar, cazar.

baggage, *n.* equipaje *m.* **b. check,** talón *m.*

baggage cart (airport), carrillo para llevar equipaje.

baggy, *a.* abotagado; bolsudo; hinchado.

bagpipe, *n.* gaita *f.*

bail, 1. *n.* fianza *f.* **2.** *v.* desaguar.

bailiff, *n.* alguacil *m.*

bait, 1. *n.* cebo *m.* **2.** *v.* cebar.

bake, *v.* cocer en horno.

baked potato, patata asada *f.*

baker, *n.* panadero -ra, hornero -ra.

bakery, *n.* panadería *f.*

baking, *n.* hornada *f.* **b. powder,** levadura *f.*

balance, 1. *n.* balanza *f.;* equilibrio *m.;* (com.) saldo *m.*

balcony, *n.* balcón *m.;* (theat.) galería *f.*

bald, *a.* calvo.

baldness, *n.* calvicie *f.*

bale, 1. *n.* bala *f.* **2.** *v.* embalar.

balk, *v.* frustrar; rebelarse.

Balkans, *npl.* Balcanes *mpl.*

balky, *a.* rebelón.

ball, *n.* bola, pelota *f.;* (dance) baile *m.*

ballad, *n.* romance, *m.;* balada *f.*

ballast, 1. *n.* lastre *m.* **2.** *v.* lastrar.

ball bearing, cojinete de bolas *m.*

ballerina, *n.* bailarina *f.*

ballet, *n.* danza *f.;* ballet *m.*

ballistics, *n.* balística *f.*

balloon, *n.* globo *m.* **b. tire,** neumático de balón.

ballot, 1. *n.* balota *f.,* voto *m.* **2.** *v.* balotar, votar.

ballpoint pen, bolígrafo *m.*

ballroom, *n.* salón de baile *m.*

balm, *n.* bálsamo; ungüento *m.*

balmy, *a.* fragante; reparador; calmante.

balsa, *n.* balsa *f.*

balsam, *n.* bálsamo *m.*

balustrade, *n.* barandilla *f.*

bamboo, *n.* bambú *m.,* caña *f.*

ban, 1. *n.* prohibición *f.* **2.** *v.* prohibir; proscribir.

banal, *a.* trivial; vulgar.

banana, *n.* banana *f.,* cambur *m.* **b. tree,** banano, plátano *m.*

band, 1. *n.* banda *f.;* (of men) banda, cuadrilla, partida *f.* **2.** *v.* asociarse.

bandage, 1. *n.* vendaje *m.* **2.** *v.* vendar.

bandanna, *n.* pañuelo (grande) *m.;* bandana *f.*

bandbox, *n.* caja de cartón.

bandit, *n.* bandido -da.

bandmaster, *n.* director de una banda musical *m.*

bandstand, *n.* kiosco de música.

bang, 1. *interj.* ¡pum! **2.** *n.* ruido de un golpe. **3.** *v.* golpear ruidosamente.

banish, *v.* desterrar.

banishment, *n.* destierro *m.*

banister, *n.* pasamanos *m.pl.*

bank, 1. *n.* banco *m.;* (of a river) margen *f.* **2.** *v.* depositar.

bank account, cuenta bancaria *f.*

bankbook, *n.* libreta de depósitos *f.*

bank card, tarjeta bancaria *f.*

banker, *n.* banquero -ra.

banking, 1. *a.* bancaria. **2.** *n.* banca *f.*

bank note, billete de banco *m.*

bankrupt, *n.* insolvente.

bankruptcy, *n.* bancarrota *f.*

banner, *n.* bandera *f.;* estandarte *m.*

banquet, *n.* banquete *m.*

banter, 1. *n.* choteo *m.;* zumba; burla *f.* **2.** *v.* chotear; zumbar; burlarse.

baptism, *n.* bautismo, bautizo *m.*

baptismal, *a.* bautismal.

Baptist, *n.* bautista *m. & f.*

baptize, *v.* bautizar.
bar, 1. *n.* barra *f.;* obstáculo *m.;* (tavern) taberna *f.,* bar *m.* **2.** *v.* barrear; prohibir, excluir.
barbarian, 1. *a.* bárbaro. **2.** *n.* bárbaro -ra.
barbarism, *n.* barbarismo *m.,* barbarie *f.*
barbarous, *n.* bárbaro, cruel.
barbecue, *n.* animal asado entero; (Mex.) barbacoa *f.*
barber, *n.* barbero *m.* **b. shop,** barbería *f.*
barbiturate, *n.* barbitúrico *m.*
bare, 1. *a.* desnudo; descubierto. **2.** *v.* desnudar; descubrir.
bareback, *adv.* sin silla.
barefoot(ed), *a.* descalzo.
barely, *adv.* escasamente, apenas.
bareness, *n.* desnudez *f.;* pobreza *f.*
bargain, 1. *n.* ganga *f.,* compra ventajosa *f.;* contrato *m.* **2.** *v.* regatear; negociar.
barge, *n.* lanchón *m.,* barcaza *f.*
baritone, *n.* barítono *m.*
barium, *n.* bario *m.*
bark, 1. *n.* corteza *f.;* (of dog) ladrido *f.* **2.** *v.* ladrar.
barley, *n.* cebada *f.*
barn, *n.* granero *m.*
barnacle, *n.* lapa *f.*
barnyard, *n.* corral *m.*
barometer, *n.* barómetro *m.*
barometric, *a.* barométrico.
baron, *n.* barón *m.*
baroness, *n.* baronesa *f.*
baronial, *a.* baronial.
baroque, *a.* barroco.
barracks, *n.* cuartel *m.*
barrage, *n.* cortina de fuego *f.*
barred, *a.* excluído; prohibido.
barrel, *n.* barril *m.;* (of gun) cañón *m.*
barren, *a.* estéril.
barrenness, *n.* esterilidad *f.*
barricade, *n.* barricada, barrera *f.*
barrier, *n.* barrera *f.;* obstáculo *m.*
barroom, *n.* cantina *f.*

bartender, *n.* tabernero; cantinero *m.*
barter, 1. *n.* cambio, trueque *m.* **2.** *v.* cambiar, trocar.
base, 1. *a.* bajo, vil. **2.** *n.* base *f.* **3.** *v.* basar.
baseball, *n.* béisbol *m.*
baseboard, *n.* tabla de resguardo.
basement, *n.* sótano *m.*
baseness, *n.* bajeza, vileza *f.*
bashful, *a.* vergonzoso, tímido.
bashfully, *adv.* tímidamente; vergonzosamente.
bashfulness, *n.* vergüenza; timidez *f.*
basic, *a.* fundamental, básico.
basin, *n.* bacía *f.;* (of river) cuenca *f.*
basis, *n.* base *f.*
bask, *v.* tomar el sol.
basket, *n.* cesta, canasta *f.*
bass, *n.* (fish) lobina *f.;* (mus.) bajo profundo *m.* **b. viol.** violón *m.*
bassinet, *n.* bacinete *m.*
bassoon, *n.* bajón *m.*
bastard, *a.* & *n.* bastardo -da; hijo -a natural.
baste, *v.* (sew) bastear; (cooking) pringar.
bat, 1. *n.* (animal) murciélago *m.;* (baseball) bate *m.* **2.** *v.* batear.
batch, *n.* cantidad de cosas.
bath, *n.* baño *m.*
bathe, *v.* bañar, bañarse.
bather, *n.* bañista *m.* & *f.*
bathing resort, balneario *m.*
bathing suit, traje de baño.
bathrobe, *n.* bata de baño *f.*
bathroom, *n.* cuarto de baño.
bathtub, *n.* bañera *f.*
baton, *n.* bastón *m.;* (mus.) batuta *f.*
battalion, *n.* batallón *m.*
batter, 1. *n.* (cooking) batido *m.;* (baseball) voleador *m.* **2.** *v.* batir; derribar.
battery, *n.* batería; (elec.) pila *f.*
batting, *n.* agramaje, moldeaje *m.*
battle, 1. *n.* batalla *f.;* combate *m.* **2.** *v.* batallar.

battlefield, *n.* campo de batalla.
battleship, *n.* acorazado *m.*
bauxite, *n.* bauxita *f.*
bawl, *v.* gritar; vocear.
bay, 1. *n.* bahía *f.* **2.** *v.* aullar.
bayonet, *n.* bayoneta *f.*
bazaar, *n.* bazar *m.,* feria *f.*
BC, *abbr.* (**before Christ**) a.C. (antes de Cristo).
be, *v.* ser; estar. (See **hacer; hay; tener** in Sp.-Eng. section.)
beach, *n.* playa *f.*
beachcomber, *n.* raquero -ra *m.* & *f.*
beacon, *n.* faro *m.*
bead, *n.* cuenta *f.;* *pl.* (rel.) rosario *m.*
beading, *n.* abalorio *m.*
beady, *a.* globuloso; burbujoso.
beak, *n.* pico *m.*
beaker, *n.* vaso con pico *m.*
beam, *n.* viga *f.;* (of wood) madero *m.;* (of light) rayo *m.*
beaming, *a.* radiante.
bean, *n.* haba, habichuela *f.,* frijol *m.*
bear, 1. *n.* oso -sa. **2.** *v.* llevar; (endure) aguantar.
bearable, *a.* sufrible; soportable.
beard, *n.* barba *f.*
bearded, *a.* barbado; barbudo.
beardless, *a.* lampiño; imberbe.
bearer, *n.* portador -ra.
bearing, *n.* porte, aguante *m.*
bearskin, *n.* piel de oso *f.*
beast, *n.* bestia *f.;* bruto -ta.
beat, *v.* golpear; batir; pulsar; (in games) ganar, vencer.
beaten, *a.* vencido; batido.
beatify, *v.* beatificar.
beating, *n.* paliza *f.*
beau, *n.* novio *m.*
beautiful, *a.* hermoso, bello.
beautifully, *adv.* bellamente.
beautify, *v.* embellecer.
beauty, *n.* hermosura, belleza *f.* **b. parlor,** salón de belleza *f.*
beaver, *n.* castor *m.*

becalm, v. calmar; sosegar; encalmarse.

because, conj. porque. b. of, a causa de.

beckon, v. hacer señas.

become, v. hacerse; ponerse.

becoming, a. propio, correcto; be b., quedar bien, sentar bien.

bed, n. cama f.; lecho m.; (of river) cauce m.

bedbug, n. chinche m.

bedclothes, n. ropa de cama f.

bedding, n. colchones m.pl.

bedfellow, n. compañero -ra de cama.

bedizen, v. adornar; aderezar.

bedridden, a. postrado (en cama).

bedrock, n. (mining) lecho de roca m.; (fig.) fundamento m.

bedroom, n. alcoba f.; (Mex.) recámara f.

bedside, n. al lado de una cama m.

bedspread, n. cubrecama, sobrecama f.

bedstead, n. armadura de cama f.

bedtime, n. hora de acostarse.

bee, n. abeja f.

beef, n. carne de vaca.

beefburger, n. hamburguesa f.

beefsteak, n. bistec, bisté m.

beehive, n. colmena f.

beer, n. cerveza f.

beeswax, n. cera de abejas.

beet, n. remolacha f.; (Mex.) betabel m.

beetle, n. escarabajo m.

befall, v. suceder, sobrevenir.

befitting, a. conveniente; propio; digno.

before, 1. adv. antes. 2. prep. antes de; (in front of) delante de. 3. conj. antes que.

beforehand, adv. de antemano.

befriend, v. amparar.

befuddle, v. confundir; aturdir.

beg, v. rogar, suplicar; (for alms) mendigar.

beget, v. engendrar; producir.

beggar, n. mendigo -ga; (Sp. Am.) limosnero -ra.

beggarly, a. pobre, miserable.

begin, v. empezar, comenzar, principiar.

beginner, n. principiante -ta.

beginning, n. principio, comienzo m.

begrudge, v. envidiar.

behalf: in, on b. of, a favor de, en pro de.

behave, v. portarse, comportarse.

behavior, n. conducta f.; comportamiento m.

behead, v. decapitar.

behind, 1. adv. atrás, detrás. 2. prep. detrás de.

behold, v. contemplar.

beige, a. beige.

being, n. existencia f.; (person) ser m.

bejewel, v. adornar con joyas.

belated, a. atrasado, tardío.

belch, 1. n. eructo m. 2. v. vomitar; eructar.

belfry, n. campanario m.

Belgian, a. & n. belga m. & f.

Belgium, n. Bélgica f.

belie, v. desmentir.

belief, n. creencia f.; parecer m.

believable, a. creíble.

believe, v. creer.

believer, n. creyente m. & f.

belittle, v. dar poca importancia a.

bell, n. campana f.; (of house) campanilla f.; (electric) timbre m.

bellboy, n. mozo, botones m.

bellicose, a. guerrero.

belligerence, n. beligerancia f.

belligerent, a. & n. beligerante m. & f.

belligerently, adv. belicosamente.

bellow, v. bramar, rugir.

bellows, n. fuelle m.

belly, n. vientre m.; panza, barriga f.

belong, v. pertenecer.

belongings, n. propiedad f.

beloved, a. querido, amado.

below, 1. adv. debajo, abajo. 2. prep. debajo de.

belt, n. cinturón m.

bench, n. banco m.

bend, 1. n. vuelta; curva f. 2. v. encorvar, doblar.

beneath, 1. adv. debajo, abajo. 2. prep. debajo de.

benediction, n. bendición f.

benefactor, n. bienhechor -ra.

benefactress, n. bienhechora f.

beneficial, a. provechoso, beneficioso.

beneficiary, n. beneficiario -ria, beneficiado -da.

benefit, 1. n. provecho, beneficio m. 2. v. beneficiar.

benevolence, n. benevolencia f.

benevolent, a. benévolo.

benevolently, adv. benignamente.

benign, a. benigno.

benignity, n. benignidad; bondad f.

bent, 1. a. encorvado. b. on, resuelto a. 2. n. inclinación f.

benzene, n. benceno m.

bequeath, v. legar.

bequest, n. legado m.

berate, v. reñir, regañar.

bereave, v. despojar; desolar.

bereavement, n. privación f.; despojo m.; (mourning) luto m.

berry, n. baya f.

berth, n. camarote m.; (naut.) litera f.; (for vessel) amarradero m.

beseech, v. suplicar; implorar.

beseechingly, adv. suplicantemente.

beset, v. acosar; rodear.

beside, prep. al lado de.

besides, adv. además, por otra parte.

besiege, v. sitiar; asediar.

besieged, a. sitiado.

besieger, n. sitiador -ra.

besmirch, v. manchar; deshonrar.

best, a. & adv. mejor. at b., a lo más.

bestial, *a.* bestial; brutal.

bestir, *v.* incitar; intrigar.

best man, *n.* padrino de boda.

bestow, *v.* conferir.

bestowal, *n.* dádiva; presentación *f.*

bet, 1. *n.* apuesta *f.* **2.** *v.* apostar.

betoken, *v.* presagiar, anunciar.

betray, *v.* traicionar; revelar.

betrayal, *n.* traición *f.*

betroth, *v.* contraer esponsales; prometerse.

betrothal, *n.* esponsales *m.pl.*

better, 1. *a. & adv.* mejor. **2.** *v.* mejorar.

between, *prep.* entre, en medio de.

bevel, 1. *n.* cartabón *m.* **2.** *v.* cortar al sesgo.

beverage, *n.* bebida *f.;* (cold) refresco *m.*

bewail, *v.* llorar; lamentar.

beware, *v.* guardarse, precaverse.

bewilder, *v.* aturdir.

bewildered, *a.* descarriado.

bewildering, *a.* aturdente.

bewilderment, *n.* aturdimiento *m.;* perplejidad *f.*

bewitch, *v.* hechizar; embrujar.

beyond, *prep.* más allá de.

biannual, *a.* semianual; semestral.

bias, 1. *n.* parcialidad *f.;* prejuicio *m.* **on the b.,** al sesgo. **2.** *v.* predisponer, influir.

bib, *n.* babador *m.*

Bible, *n.* Biblia *f.*

Biblical, *a.* bíblico.

bibliography, *n.* bibliografía *f.*

bicarbonate, *n.* bicarbonato *m.*

bicentennial, *a. & n.* bicentenario *m.*

biceps, *n.* bíceps *m.*

bicker, *v.* altercar.

bicycle, *n.* bicicleta *f.*

bicyclist, *n.* biciclista *m. & f.*

bid, 1. *n.* proposición, oferta *f.* **2.** *v.* mandar; ofrecer.

bidder, *n.* postor -ra.

bide, *v.* aguardar; esperar.

bier, *n.* ataúd *m.*

bifocal, *a.* bifocal.

big, *a.* grande.

bigamist, *n.* bígamo -ma.

bigamy, *n.* bigamia *f.*

bigot, *n.* persona intolerante.

bigotry, *n.* intolerancia *f.*

bikini, *n.* bikini *m.*

bilateral, *a.* bilateral.

bile, *n.* bilis *f.*

bilingual, *a.* bilingüe.

bilingualism, *n.* bilingüismo *m.*

bilious, *a.* bilioso.

bill, 1. *n.* cuenta, factura *f.;* (money) billete *m.;* (of bird) pico *m.* **2.** *v.* facturar.

billboard, *n.* cartelera *f.*

billet, 1. *n.* billete *m.;* (mil.) boleta *f.* **2.** *v.* aposentar.

billfold, *n.* cartera *f.*

billiard balls, bolas de billar.

billiards, *n.* billar *m.*

billion, *n.* billón *m.*

bill of health, *n.* certificado de sanidad.

bill of lading, *n.* conocimiento de embarque.

bill of sale, *n.* escritura de venta.

billow, *n.* ola; oleada *f.*

bimetallic, *a.* bimetálico.

bimonthly, *a. & adv.* bimestral.

bin, *n.* hucha *f.;* depósito *m.*

bind, *v.* atar; obligar; (book) encuadernar.

bindery, *n.* taller de encuadernación *m.*

binding, *n.* encuadernación *f.*

bingo, *n.* bingo *m.*

binocular, 1. *a.* binocular. **2.** *n.pl.* gemelos *m.pl.*

biochemistry, *n.* bioquímica *f.*

biodegradable, *a.* biodegradable.

biofeedback, *n.* biofeedback.

biographer, *n.* biógrafo -fa.

biographical, *a.* biográfico.

biography, *n.* biografía *f.*

biological, *a.* biológico.

biologically, *adv.* biológicamente.

biology, *n.* biología *f.*

bipartisan, *a.* bipartito.

biped, *n.* bípedo *m.*

bird, *n.* pájaro *m.;* ave *f.*

bird of prey, *n.* ave de rapiña *f.*

bird's-eye view, *n.* vista de pájaro *f.*

birth, *n.* nacimiento *m.* **give b. to,** dar a luz.

birth certificate, partida de nacimiento *f.*

birth control, *n.* contracepción *f.*

birthday, *n.* cumpleaños *m.*

birthmark, *n.* marca de nacimiento *f.*

birthplace, *n.* natalicio *m.*

birth rate, *n.* natalidad *f.*

birthright, *n.* primogenitura *f.*

biscuit, *n.* bizcocho *m.*

bisect, *v.* bisecar.

bishop, *n.* obispo *m.;* (chess) alfil *m.*

bishopric, *n.* obispado *m.*

bismuth, *n.* bismuto *m.*

bison, *n.* bisonte *m.*

bit, *n.* pedacito *m.;* (mech.) taladro *m.;* (for horse) bocado *m.;* (computer) bit *m.*

bitch, *n.* perra *f.*

bite, 1. *n.* bocado *m.;* picada *f.* **2.** *v.* morder; picar.

biting, *a.* penetrante; mordaz.

bitter, *a.* amargo.

bitterly, *adv.* amargamente; agriamente.

bitterness, *n.* amargura *f.;* rencor *m.*

bivouac, 1. *n.* vivaque *m.* **2.** *v.* vivaquear.

biweekly, *a.* quincenal.

black, *a.* negro.

Black, *n.* (person) negro -gra; persona de color.

blackberry, *n.* mora *f.*

blackbird, *n.* mirlo *m.*

blackboard, *n.* pizarra *f.*

blacken, *v.* ennegrecer.

black eye, *n.* ojo amoratado.

blackguard, *n.* tunante; pillo *m.*

blacklist, lista negra *f.*

blackmail, 1. *n.* chantaje *m.*
2. *v.* amenazar con chantaje, chantajear.

black market, mercado negro, estraperlo *m.*

black marketeer, estraperlista *mf.*

blackout, *n.* oscurecimiento, apagamiento *m.*

blacksmith, *n.* herrero -ra.

bladder, *n.* vejiga *f.*

blade, *n.* (sword) hoja *f.;* (oar) pala *f.;* (grass) brizna *f.*

blame, *v.* culpar, echar la culpa a.

blameless, *a.* inculpable.

blanch, *v.* blanquear; escaldar.

bland, *a.* blando.

blank, *a.* & *n.* en blanco.

blanket, *n.* manta *f.;* cobertor *m.*

blare, 1. *n.* sonido de trompeta. **2.** *v.* sonar como trompeta.

blaspheme, *v.* blasfemar.

blasphemer, *n.* blasfemo -ma, blasfemador -ra.

blasphemous, *a.* blasfemo, impío.

blasphemy, *n.* blasfemia *f.*

blast, 1. *n.* barreno *m.;* (wind) ráfaga *f.* **2.** *v.* barrenar.

blatant, *a.* bramante; descarado.

blaze, 1. *n.* llama, hoguera *f.* **2.** *v.* encenderse en llama.

blazing, *a.* flameante.

bleach, 1. *n.* lejía, blanqueador. *v.* blanquear.

bleachers, *n.* asientos al aire libre.

bleak, *a.* frío y sombrío.

bleakness, *n.* desolación *f.*

bleed, *v.* sangrar.

blemish, 1. *n.* mancha *f.;* lunar *m.* **2.** *v.* manchar.

blend, 1. *n.* mezcla *f.* **2.** *v.* mezclar, combinar.

blended, *a.* mezclado.

blender (for food), *n.* licuadora *f.*

bless, *v.* bendecir.

blessed, *a.* bendito.

blessing, *a.* bendición *f.*

blight, 1. *n.* plaga *f.;* tizón *m.* **2.** *v.* atizonar.

blind, *a.* ciego.

blindfold, *v.* vendar los ojos.

blinding, *a.* deslumbrante; ofuscante.

blindly, *adv.* ciegamente.

blindness, *n.* ceguedad, ceguera *f.*

blink, 1. *n.* guiñada *f.* **2.** *v.* guiñar.

bliss, *n.* felicidad *f.*

blissful, *a.* dichoso; bienaventurado.

blissfully, *adv.* felizmente.

blister, *n.* ampolla *f.*

blithe, *a.* alegre; jovial; gozoso.

blizzard, *n.* nevasca *f.*

bloat, *v.* hinchar.

bloc, *n.* grupo (político); bloc.

block, 1. *n.* bloque *m.;* (street) manzana, cuadra *f.* **2.** *v.* bloquear.

blockade, 1. *n.* bloqueo *m.* **2.** *v.* bloquear.

blond, *a.* & *n.* rubio -ia.

blood, *n.* sangre *f.;* parentesco, linaje *m.*

bloodhound, *n.* sabueso *m.*

bloodless, *a.* exangüe; desangrado.

blood poisoning, envenenamiento de sangre.

blood pressure, presión arterial.

bloodshed, *n.* matanza *f.*

bloodthirsty, *a.* cruel, sanguinario.

bloody, *a.* ensangrentado, sangriento.

bloom, 1. *n.* flor *f.* **2.** *v.* florecer.

blooming, *a.* lozano; fresco; floreciente.

blossom, 1. *n.* flor *f.* **2.** *v.* florecer.

blot, 1. *n.* mancha *f.* **2.** *v.* manchar.

blotch, 1. *n.* mancha, roncha *f.* **2.** *v.* manchar.

blotter, *n.* papel secante.

blouse, *n.* blusa *f.*

blow, 1. *n.* golpe *m.;* (fig.) chasco *m.* **2.** *v.* soplar.

blowout, *n.* reventón de neumático *m.*

blubber, *n.* grasa de ballena.

bludgeon, 1. *n.* porra *f.* **2.** *v.* apalear.

blue, *a.* azul; triste, melancólico.

bluebird, *n.* azulejo *m.*

blue jeans, jeans; vaqueros *m.pl.*

blueprint, *n.* heliografía *f.*

bluff, 1. *n.* risco *m.* **2.** *v.* alardear; baladronar.

bluing, *n.* añil *m.*

blunder, 1. *n.* desatino *m.* **2.** *v.* desatinar.

blunderer, *n.* desatinado -da.

blunt, 1. *a.* embotado; descortés. **2.** *v.* embotar.

bluntly, *a.* bruscamente.

bluntness, *n.* grosería *f.;* brusquedad.

blur, 1. *n.* trazo confuso. **2.** *v.* hacer indistinto.

blush, 1. *n.* rubor, sonrojo *m.* **2.** *v.* sonrojarse.

bluster, 1. *n.* fanfarria *f.* **2.** *v.* fanfarrear.

boar, *n.* verraco *m.* **wild b.,** jabalí.

board, 1. *n.* tabla; (govt.) consejo *m.;* junta *f.* **b. and room,** cuarto y comida, casa y comida. **2.** *v.* (ship) abordar.

boarder, *n.* pensionista *m.* & *f.*

boardinghouse, *n.* pensión *f.,* casa de huéspedes.

boarding pass, boleto de embarque *m.,* tarjeta de embarque *f.*

boast, 1. *n.* jactancia *f.* **2.** *v.* jactarse.

boaster, *n.* fanfarrón -na.

boastful, *a.* jactancioso.

boastfulness, *n.* jactancia *f.*

boat, *n.* barco, buque, bote *m.*

boathouse, *n.* casilla de botes *f.*

boatswain, *n.* contramaestre *m.*

bob, *v.* menear.

bobbin, *n.* bobina *f.*

bobby pin, *n.* gancho *m.,* horquilla.

bodice, *n.* corpiño *m.*

bodily, *a.* corporal.

body, *n.* cuerpo *m.*

body builder, culturista *mf.*

body building, culturismo *m.*

bodyguard, *n.* guardaespaldas.

bog, *n.* pantano *m.*

Bohemian, *a. & n.* bohemio -mia.

boil, 1. *n.* hervor *m.;* (med.) divieso *m.* **2.** *v.* hervir.

boiler, *n.* marmita; caldera *f.*

boiling point, punto de ebullición *m.*

boisterous, *a.* tumultuoso.

boisterously, *adv.* tumultuosamente.

bold, *a.* atrevido, audaz.

boldface, *n.* (type) letra negra.

boldly, *adv.* audazmente; descaradamente.

boldness, *n.* atrevimiento *m.;* osadía *f.*

Bolivian, *a. & n.* boliviano -na.

bologna, *n.* salchicha *f.,* mortadela.

bolster, 1. *n.* travesero, cojín *m.* **2.** *v.* apoyar, sostener.

bolt, 1. *n.* perno *m.;* (of door) cerrojo *m.;* (lightning) rayo *m.* **2.** *v.* acerrojar.

bomb, 1. *n.* bomba *f.* **2.** *v.* bombardear.

bombard, *v.* bombardear.

bombardier, *n.* bombardero -ra.

bombardment, *n.* bombardeo *m.*

bomber, *n.* avión de bombardeo.

bombproof, *a.* a prueba de granadas.

bombshell, *n.* bomba *f.*

bonbon, *n.* dulce, bombón *m.*

bond, *n.* lazo *m.;* (com.) bono *m.*

bondage, *n.* esclavitud, servidumbre *f.*

bonded, *a.* garantizado.

bone, *n.* hueso *m.*

boneless, *a.* sin huesos.

bonfire, *n.* hoguera, fogata *f.*

bonnet, *n.* gorra *f.*

bonus, *n.* sobrepaga *f.*

bony, *a.* huesudo.

boo, *v.* abuchear.

book, *n.* libro *m.*

bookbinder, *n.* encuadernador -ora.

bookcase, *n.* armario para libros.

bookkeeper, *n.* tenedor -ra de libros.

bookkeeping, *n.* contabilidad *f.*

booklet, *n.* folleto *m.*, libreta *f.*

bookseller, *n.* librero -ra.

bookstore, *n.* librería *f.*

boom, *n.* (naut.) botalón *m.;* prosperidad repentina.

boon, *n.* dádiva *f.*

boor, *n.* patán, rústico *m.*

boorish, *a.* villano.

boost, 1. *n.* alza; ayuda *f.* **2.** *v.* levantar, alzar; fomentar.

booster, *n.* fomentador *m.*

boot, *n.* bota *f.*

bootblack, *n.* limpiabotas *m.*

booth, *n.* cabaña; casilla *f.*

booty, *n.* botín *f.*

border, 1. *n.* borde *m.;* frontera *f.* **2.** *v.* **b. on,** lindar con.

borderline, 1. *a.* marginal. **2.** *n.* margen *m.*

bore, 1. *n.* lata *f.;* persona pesada. **2.** *v.* aburrir, fastidiar; (mech.) taladrar.

boredom, *n.* aburrimiento *m.*

boric acid, *n.* ácido bórico *m.*

boring, *a.* aburrido, pesado.

born, *a.* nacido. **be born,** nacer.

born-again, *a.* renacido.

borrow, *v.* pedir prestado.

bosom, *n.* seno, pecho *m.*

boss, *n.* jefe, patrón *m.*

botany, *n.* botánica *f.*

both, *pron. & a.* ambos, los dos.

bother, 1. *n.* molestia *f.* **2.** *v.* molestar, incomodar.

bothersome, *a.* molesto.

bottle, 1. *n.* botella *f.* **2.** *v.* embotellar.

bottling, *n.* embotellamiento *m.*

bottom, *n.* fondo *m.*

boudoir, *n.* tocador *m.*

bough, *n.* rama *f.*

boulder, *n.* canto rodado.

boulevard, *n.* bulevar *m.*

bounce, 1. *n.* brinco *m.* **2.** *v.* brincar; hacer saltar.

bound, 1. *n.* salto *m.* **2.** *v.* limitar.

boundary, *n.* límite, lindero *m.*

bouquet, *n.* ramillete de flores.

bourgeois, *a. & n.* burgués -esa.

bout, *n.* encuentro; combate *m.*

bow, 1. *n.* saludo *m.;* (of ship) proa *f.;* (archery) arco *m.;* (ribbon) lazo *m.* **2.** *v.* saludar, inclinar.

bowels, *n.* intestinos *m.pl.;* entrañas *f.pl.*

bowl, 1. *n.* vasija *f.;* platón *m.* **2.** *v.* jugar a los bolos. **b. over,** derribar.

bowlegged, *a.* perniabierto.

bowling, *n.* bolos *m.pl.*

bow tie, pajarita *f.*

box, 1. *n.* caja *f.;* (theat.) palco *m.* **2.** *v.* (sports) boxear.

boxcar, *n.* vagón *m.*

boxer, *n.* boxeador -ra, pugilista *m. & f.*

boxing, *n.* boxeo *m.*

box office, *n.* taquilla *f.*

boy, *n.* muchacho, chico, niño *m.*

boycott, 1. *n.* boicoteo *m.* **2.** *v.* boicotear.

boyhood, *n.* muchachez *f.*

boyish, *a.* pueril.

boyishly, *adv.* puerilmente.

bra, *n.* sujetador, sostén *m.*

brace, 1. *n.* grapón *m.; pl.* tirantes *m.pl.* **2.** *v.* reforzar.

bracelet, *n.* brazalete *m.*, pulsera *f.*

bracket, *n.* ménsula *f.*

brag, *v.* jactarse.

braggart, 1. *a.* jactancioso. **2.** *n.* jaque *m.*

braid, 1. *n.* trenza *f.* **2.** *v.* trenzar.

brain, *n.* cerebro, seso *m.*

brainy, *a.* sesudo, inteligente.

brake, 1. *n.* freno *m.* **2.** *v.* frenar.

bran, *n.* salvado *m.*

branch, n. ramo m.; (of tree) rama f.

brand, n. marca f.

brandish, v. blandir.

brand-new, a. enteramente nuevo.

brandy, n. aguardiente, coñac m.

brash, a. impetuoso.

brass, n. bronce, latón m.

brassiere, n. corpiño, sujetador, sostén m.

brat, n. mocoso m.

bravado, n. bravata f.

brave, a. valiente.

bravery, n. valor m.

brawl, 1. n. alboroto m. **2.** v. alborotar.

brawn, n. músculo m.

bray, n. rebuznar.

brazen, a. desvergonzado.

Brazil, n. Brasil m.

Brazilian, a. & n. brasileño -ña.

breach, n. rotura; infracción f.

breach of contract, incumplimiento de contrato m.

bread, n. pan m.

breadth, n. anchura f.

break, 1. n. rotura; pausa f. **2.** v. quebrar, romper.

breakable, a. rompible, frágil.

breakage, n. rotura f., destrozo m.

breakfast, 1. n. desayuno, almuerzo m. **2.** v. desayunar, almorzar.

breakneck, a. rápido, precipitado, atropellado.

breast, n. (of human) pecho, seno m.; (of fowl) pechuga f.

breastbone, n. esternón m.

breath, n. aliento; soplo m.

breathe, v. respirar.

breathless, a. desalentado.

breathlessly, adv. jadeantemente, intensamente.

bred, a. criado; educado.

breeches, n.pl. calzones; pantalones, m.pl.

breed, 1. n. raza f. **2.** v. engendrar; criar.

breeder, n. criador -ra.

breeding, n. cría f.

breeze, n. brisa f.

breezy, a.: **it is b.,** hace brisa.

brevity, n. brevedad f.

brew, v. fraguar; elaborar.

brewer, n. cervecero -ra.

brewery, n. cervecería f.

bribe, 1. n. soborno, cohecho m. **2.** v. sobornar, cohechar.

briber, n. sobornador -ra.

bribery, n. soborno, cohecho m.

brick, n. ladrillo m.

bricklayer, n. albañil m.

bridal, a. nupcial.

bride, n. novia f.

bridegroom, n. novio m.

bridesmaid, n. madrina de boda.

bridge, n. puente m.

bridged, a. conectado.

bridgehead, n. (mil.) cabeza de puente.

bridle, n. brida f.

brief, a. breve.

briefcase, n. maletín m.

briefly, adv. brevemente.

briefness, n. brevedad f.

brier, n. zarza f.

brig, n. bergantín m.

brigade, n. brigada f.

bright, a. claro, brillante.

brighten, v. abrillantar; alegrar.

brightness, n. resplandor m.

brilliance, n. brillantez f.

brilliant, a. brillante.

brim, n. borde m.; (of hat) ala f.

brine, n. escabeche, m. salmuera f.

bring, v. traer. **b. about,** efectuar, llevar a cabo.

brink, n. borde m.

briny, a. salado.

brisk, a. vivo; enérgico.

briskly, adv. vivamente.

briskness, n. viveza f.

bristle, n. cerda f.

bristly, a. hirsuto.

Britain, n. **Great B.,** Gran Bretaña f.

British, a. británico.

British Empire, imperio británico m.

British Isles, islas británicas f.

Briton, n. inglés m.

brittle, a. quebradizo, frágil.

broad, a. ancho.

broadcast, 1. n. radiodifusión n. **2.** v. radiodifundir.

broadcaster, n. locutor -ra.

broadcloth, n. paño fino.

broaden, v. ensanchar.

broadly, adv. ampliamente.

broadminded, a. tolerante, liberal.

brocade, n. brocado m.

brocaded, a. espolinado.

broccoli, n. brécol m.

broil, v. asar.

broiler, n. parrilla f.

broken, a. roto, quebrado.

broken-hearted, a. angustiado.

broker, n. corredor -ra, bolsista m. & f.

brokerage, n. corretaje m.

bronchial, a. bronquial.

bronchitis, n. bronquitis f.

bronze, n. bronce m.

brooch, n. broche m.

brood, 1. n. cría, progenie f. **2.** v. empollar; cobijar.

brook, n. arroyo m., quebrada f.

broom, n. escoba f.

broomstick, n. palo de escoba.

broth, n. caldo m.

brothel, n. burdel m.

brother, n. hermano m.

brotherhood, n. fraternidad f.

brother-in-law, n. cuñado m.

brotherly, a. fraternal.

brow, n. ceja; frente f.

brown, a. pardo, moreno; marrón. v. rehogar.

brown sugar, azúcar moreno m.

browse, v. curiosear; ramonear.

bruise, 1. n. contusión f. **2.** v. magullar.

brunette, a. & n. moreno -na, trigueño -ña.

brush, 1. n. cepillo m.; brocha f. **2.** v. cepillar.

brushwood, n. matorral m.

brusque, a. brusco.

brusquely, adv. bruscamente.

brutal, a. brutal.

brutality, *n.* brutalidad *f.*
brutalize, *v.* embrutecer.
brute, *n.* bruto -ta, bestia *f.*
bubble, *n.* ampolla *f.*
bucket, *n.* cubo *m.*
buckle, *n.* hebilla *f.*
buckram, *n.* bucarán *m.*
bucksaw, *n.* sierra de bastidor.
buckshot, *n.* posta *f.*
buckwheat, *n.* trigo sarraceno.
bud, 1. *n.* brote *m.* **2.** *v.* brotar.
budding, *a.* en capullo.
budge, *v.* moverse.
budget, *n.* presupuesto *m.*
buffalo, *n.* búfalo *m.*
buffer, *n.* parachoques *m.*
buffet, *n.* bufet *m.;* (furniture) aparador *m.*
buffoon, *n.* bufón *m.*
bug, *n.* insecto *m.*
bugle, *n.* clarín *m.;* corneta *f.*
build, *v.* construir.
builder, *n.* constructor -ra.
building, *n.* edificio *m.*
bulb, *n.* bulbo *m.;* (of lamp) bombilla, ampolla *f.*
bulge, 1. *n.* abultamiento *m.* **2.** *v.* abultar.
bulging, *a.* protuberante.
bulk, *n.* masa *f.;* grueso *m.;* mayoría *f.*
bulkhead, *n.* frontón *m.*
bulky, *a.* grueso, abultado.
bull, *n.* toro *m.*
bulldog, *n.* perro de presa.
bullet, *n.* bala *f.*
bulletin, *n.* boletín *m.*
bulletproof, *a.* a prueba de bala.
bullfight, *n.* corrida de toros.
bullfighter, *n.* torero -ra.
bullfinch, *n.* pinzón real *m.*
bully, 1. *n.* rufián *m.* **2.** *v.* bravear.
bulwark, *n.* baluarte *m.*

bum, *n.* holgazán *m.*
bump, 1. *n.* golpe, choque *m.* **2.** *v.* **b. into,** chocar contra.
bumper, *n.* parachoques *m.*
bun, *n.* bollo *m.*
bunch, *n.* racimo; montón *m.*
bundle, 1. *n.* bulto *m.* **2.** *v.* **b. up,** abrigar.
bungalow, *n.* casa de un solo piso.
bungle, *v.* estropear.
bunion, *n.* juanete *m.*
bunk, *n.* litera *f.*
bunny, *n.* conejito -ta.
bunting, *n.* lanilla; banderas *f.*
buoy, *n.* boya *f.*
buoyant, *a.* boyante; vivaz.
burden, 1. *n.* carga *f.* **2.** *v.* cargar.
burdensome, *a.* gravoso.
bureau, *n.* (furniture) cómoda *f.;* departamento *m.*
burglar, *n.* ladrón -ona.
burglarize, *v.* robar.
burglary, *n.* robo *m.*
burial, *n.* entierro *m.*
burlap, *n.* arpillera *f.*
burly, *a.* corpulento.
burn, *v.* quemar; arder.
burner, *n.* mechero *m.*
burning, *a.* ardiente.
burnish, *v.* pulir; acicalar.
burrow, *v.* minar; horadar.
burst, *v.* reventar.
bury, *v.* enterrar.
bus, *n.* autobús *m.*
bush, *n.* arbusto *m.*
bushy, *a.* matoso; peludo.
business, *n.* negocios *m.pl.;* comercio *m.*
businesslike, *a.* directo, práctico.
businessman, *n.* hombre de negocios, comerciante *m.*
businesswoman, *n.* mujer de negocios.

bust, *n.* busto; pecho *m.*
bustle, *n.* bullicio *m.;* animación *f.*
busy, *a.* ocupado, atareado.
busybody, *n.* entremetido -da.
but, *conj.* pero; sino.
butcher, *n.* carnicero -ra.
butchery, *n.* carnicería; matanza *f.*
butler, *n.* mayordomo *m.*
butt, *n.* punta *f.;* cabo extremo *m.*
butter, *n.* manteca, mantequilla *f.*
buttercup, *n.* ranúnculo *m.*
butterfat, *n.* mantequilla *f.*
butterfly, *n.* mariposa *f.*
buttermilk, *n.* suero (de leche) *m.*
button, *n.* botón *m.*
buttonhole, *n.* ojal *m.*
buttress, *n.* sostén; refuerzo *m.*
buxom, *a.* regordete.
buy, *v.* comprar.
buyer, *n.* comprador -ra.
buzz, 1. *n.* zumbido *m.* **2.** *v.* zumbar.
buzzard, *n.* gallinazo *m.*
buzzer, *n.* zumbador *m.;* timbre *m.*
buzz saw, *n.* sierra circular *f.*
by, *prep.* por; (near) cerca de, al lado de; (time) para.
by-and-by, *adv.* pronto; luego.
bygone, *a.* pasado.
bylaw, *n.* estatuto, reglamento *m.*
bypass, *n.* desvío *m.*
byproduct, *n.* subproducto *m.*
bystander, *n.* espectador -ra; mirón -na.
byte, *n.* en teoría de la información: ocho bits, byte *m.*
byway, *n.* camino desviado *m.*

C

cab, *n.* taxi, coche de alquiler *m.*
cabaret, *n.* cabaret *m.*
cabbage, *n.* repollo *m.*
cabin, *n.* cabaña *f.*

cabinet, *n.* gabinete; ministerio *m.*
cabinetmaker, *n.* ebanista *m.*
cable, *n.* cable *m.*
cablegram, *n.* cablegrama *m.*

cache, *n.* escondite *m.*
cackle, 1. *n.* charla *f.;* cacareo *m.* **2.** *v.* cacarear.
cacophony, *n.* cacofonía *f.*
cactus, *n.* cacto *m.*

cad, *n.* persona vil.

cadaver, *n.* cadáver *m.*

cadaverous, *a.* cadavérico.

cadence, *n.* cadencia *f.*

cadet, *n.* cadete *m.*

cadmium, *n.* cadmio *m.*

cadre, *n.* núcleo; (mil.) cuadro *m.*

café, *n.* café *m.,* cantina *f.*

cafeteria, *n.* cafetería *f.*

caffeine, *n.* cafeína *f.*

cage, 1. *n.* jaula *f.* **2.** *v.* enjaular.

caged, *a.* enjaulado.

caisson, *n.* arcón *m.;* (mil.) furgón *m.*

cajole, *v.* lisonjear; adular.

cake, *n.* torta *f.;* bizcocho *m.*

calamitous, *a.* calamitoso.

calamity, *n.* calamidad *f.*

calcify, *v.* calcificar.

calcium, *n.* calcio *m.*

calculable, *a.* calculable.

calculate, *v.* calcular.

calculating, *a.* interesado.

calculation, *n.* calculación *f.;* cálculo *m.*

calculus, *n.* cálculo *m.*

caldron, *n.* caldera *f.*

calendar, *n.* calendario *m.*

calf, *n.* ternero *m.* (animal); pantorrilla *f.* (of the body).

calfskin, *n.* piel de becerro.

caliber, *n.* calibre *m.*

calico, *n.* calicó *m.*

caliper, *n.* calibrador *m.*

calisthenics, *n.* calistenia, gimnasia *f.*

calk, *v.* calafatear; rellenar.

calker, *n.* calafate -ta.

call, 1. *n.* llamada *f.* **2.** *v.* llamar.

calligraphy, *n.* caligrafía *f.*

calling, *n.* vocación *f.*

calling card, tarjeta (de visita) *f.*

callously, *adv.* insensiblemente.

callow, *a.* sin experiencia.

callus, *n.* callo *m.*

calm, 1. *a.* tranquilo, calmado. **2.** *n.* calma *f.* **3.** *v.* calmar.

calmly, *adv.* serenamente.

calmness, *n.* calma *f.*

caloric, *a.* calórico.

calorie, *n.* caloría *f.*

calorimeter, *n.* calorímetro *m.*

calumniate, *v.* calumniar.

calumny, *n.* calumnia *f.*

Calvary, *n.* Calvario *m.*

calve, *v.* parir (la vaca).

calyx, *n.* cáliz *m.*

camaraderie, *n.* compañerismo *m.,* compadrería *f.*

cambric, *n.* batista *f.*

camcorder, *n.* videocámara *f.*

camel, *n.* camello -lla.

camellia, *n.* camelia *f.*

camel's hair, pelo de camello.

cameo, *n.* camafeo *m.*

camera, *n.* cámara *f.*

camouflage, *n.* camuflaje *m.*

camouflaging, *n.* simulacro, disfraz *m.*

camp, 1. *n.* campamento *m.* **2.** *v.* acampar.

campaign, *n.* campaña *f.*

camper, *n.* acampado *m.*

campfire, *n.* fogata de campamento.

camphor, *n.* alcanfor *m.*

camphor ball, bola de alcanfor.

campus, *n.* campo de colegio (o universidad), campus *m.*

can, *v.* (be able) poder.

can, 1. *n.* lata *f.* **2.** *v.* conservar en latas, enlatar.

Canada, *n.* Canadá *m.*

Canadian, *a.* & *n.* canadiense.

canal, *n.* canal *m.*

canalize, *v.* canalizar.

canard, *n.* embuste *m.*

canary, *n.* canario -ria.

cancel, *v.* cancelar.

cancellation, *n.* cancelación *f.*

cancer, *n.* cáncer *m.*

candelabrum, *n.* candelabro *m.*

candid, *a.* cándido, sincero.

candidacy, *n.* candidatura *f.*

candidate, *n.* candidato -ta.

candidly, *adv.* cándidamente.

candidness, *n.* candidez; sinceridad *f.*

candied, *a.* garapiñado.

candle, *n.* vela *f.*

candlestick, *n.* candelero *m.*

candor, *n.* candor *m.;* sinceridad *f.*

candy, *n.* dulces *m.pl.*

cane, *n.* caña *f.;* (for walking) bastón *m.*

canine, *a.* canino.

canister, *n.* frasco *m.;* lata *f.*

canker, *n.* llaga; úlcera *f.*

cankerworm, *n.* oruga *f.*

canned, *a.* envasado, enlatado.

canner, *n.* envasador *m.*

cannery, *n.* fábrica de conservas alimenticias *f.*

cannibal, *n.* caníbal *m.* & *f.*

cannon, *n.* cañón *m.*

cannonade, *n.* cañoneo *m.*

cannoneer, *n.* cañonero -ra.

canny, *a.* sagaz; prudente.

canoe, *n.* canoa, piragua *f.*

canoeing, *n.* piragüismo *m.*

canoeist, *n.* piragüista *m.* & *f.*

canon, *n.* canon *m.;* (rel.) canónigo *m.*

canonical, *a.* canónico.

canonize, *v.* canonizar.

can opener, abrelatas *m.*

canopy, *n.* dosel *m.*

cant, *n.* hipocresía *f.*

cantaloupe, *n.* melón *m.*

canteen, *n.* cantina *f.*

canter, 1. *n.* medio galope *m.* **2.** *v.* galopar.

cantonment, *n.* (mil.) acuartelamiento *m.*

canvas, *n.* lona *f.*

canyon, *n.* cañón, desfiladero *m.*

cap, 1. *n.* tapa *f.;* (headwear) gorro *m.* **2.** *v.* tapar.

capability, *n.* capacidad *f.*

capable, *a.* capaz.

capably, *adv.* hábilmente.

capacious, *a.* espacioso.

capacity, *n.* capacidad *f.*

cape, *n.* capa *f.,* (geog.) cabo *m.*

caper, *n.* zapateta *f.;* (bot.) alcaparra *f.*

capillary, *a.* capilar.

capital, *n.* capital *m.;* (govt.) capital *f.*

capitalism, *n.* capitalismo *m.*

capitalist, *n.* capitalista *m.* & *f.*

capitalistic, *a.* capitalista.

capitalization, *n.* capitalización *f.*

capitalize, *v.* capitalizar.

capital letter, *n.* mayúscula *f.*

capitulate, *v.* capitular.

capon, *n.* capón *m.*

caprice, *n.* capricho *m.*

capricious, *a.* caprichoso.

capriciously, *adv.* caprichosamente.

capriciousness, *n.* capricho *m.*

capsize, *v.* zozobrar, volcar.

capsule, *n.* cápsula *f.*

captain, *n.* capitán -tana.

caption, *n.* título *m.*; (motion pictures) subtítulo *m.*

captious, *a.* capcioso.

captivate, *v.* cautivar.

captivating, *a.* encantador.

captive, *n.* cautivo -va, prisionero -ra.

captivity, *n.* cautividad *f.*

captor, *n.* apresador -ra.

capture, 1. *n.* captura *f.* **2.** *v.* capturar.

car, *n.* coche, carro *m.*; (of train) vagón, coche *m.* **baggage c.,** vagón de equipajes. **parlor c.,** coche salón.

carafe, *n.* garrafa *f.*

caramel, *n.* caramelo *m.*

carat, *n.* quilate *m.*

caravan, *n.* caravana *f.*

caraway, *n.* alcaravea *f.*

carbide, *n.* carburo *m.*

carbine, *n.* carabina *f.*

carbohydrate, *n.* hidrato de carbono.

carbon, *n.* carbón *m.*

carbon dioxide, anhídrido carbónico.

carbon monoxide, monóxido de carbono.

carbon paper, papel carbón *m.*

carbuncle, *n.* carbúnculo *m.*

carburetor, *n.* carburador *m.*

carcinogenic, *a.* carcinogénico.

card, *n.* tarjeta *f.* **playing c.,** naipe *m.*

cardboard, *n.* cartón *m.*

cardiac, *a.* cardíaco.

cardigan, *n.* chaqueta de punto.

cardinal, 1. *a.* cardinal. **2.** *n.* cardenal *m.*

cardiologist, *n.* cardiólogo, -ga *m. & f.*

care, 1. *n.* cuidado. **2.** *v.* **c. for,** cuidar.

careen, *v.* carenar; echarse de costado.

career, *n.* carrera *f.*

carefree, *a.* descuidado.

careful, *a.* cuidadoso. **be. c.,** tener cuidado.

carefully, *adv.* cuidadosamente.

carefulness, *n.* esmero; cuidado *m.*; cautela *f.*

careless, *a.* descuidado.

carelessly, *adv.* descuidadamente; negligentemente.

carelessness, *n.* descuido *m.*

caress, 1. *n.* caricia *f.* **2.** *v.* acariciar.

caretaker, *n.* guardián -ana.

cargo, *n.* carga *f.*

caricature, *n.* caricatura *f.*

caricaturist, *n.* caricaturista *m. & f.*

caries, *n.* caries *f.*

carload, *n.* furgonada, vagonada.

carnal, *a.* carnal.

carnation, *n.* clavel *m.*

carnival, *n.* carnaval *m.*

carnivorous, *a.* carnívoro.

carol, *n.* villancico *m.*

carouse, *v.* parrandear.

carpenter, *n.* carpintero -ra.

carpet, *n.* alfombra *f.*

carpeting, *n.* alfombrado *m.*

car pool, uso habitual, por varias personas, de un automóvil perteneciente a una de ellas.

carriage, *n.* carruaje; (bearing) porte *m.*

carrier, *n.* portador -ra.

carrier pigeon, paloma mensajera.

carrot, *n.* zanahoria *f.*

carrousel, *n.* volantín, carrusel *m.*

carry, *v.* llevar, cargar. **c. out,** cumplir, llevar a cabo.

cart, *n.* carreta *f.*

cartage, *n.* acarreo, carretaje *m.*

cartel, *n.* cartel *m.*

cartilage, *n.* cartílago *m.*

carton, *n.* caja de cartón.

cartoon, *n.* caricatura *f.*

cartoonist, *n.* caricaturista *m. & f.*

cartridge, *n.* cartucho *m.*

carve, *v.* esculpir; (meat) trinchar.

carver, *n.* tallador -ra; grabador -ra.

carving, *n.* entalladura *f.*; arte de trinchar. **c. knife,** trinchante *m.*

cascade, *n.* cascada *f.*

case, *n.* caso *m.*; (box) caja *f.* **in any c.,** sea como sea.

cash, 1. *n.* dinero contante. **2.** *v.* efectuar, cambiar.

cashier, *n.* cajero -ra.

cashmere, *n.* casimir *m.*

casino, *n.* casino *m.*

cask, *n.* barril *m.*

casket, *n.* ataúd *m.*

casserole, *n.* cacerola *f.*

cassette, *n.* cassette *m.*; cartucho *m.*

cast, 1. *n.* (theat.) reparto de papeles. **2.** *v.* echar; (theat.) repartir.

castanet, *n.* castañuela *f.*

castaway, *n.* náufrago -ga.

caste, *n.* casta *f.*

caster, *n.* tirador *m.*

castigate, *v.* castigar.

Castilian, *a.* castellano.

cast iron, *n.* hierro colado *m.*

castle, *n.* castillo *m.*

castoff, *a.* descartado.

casual, *a.* casual.

casually, *adv.* casualmente.

casualness, *n.* casualidad *f.*

casualty, *n.* víctima *f.*; (mil.) baja *f.*

cat, *n.* gato -ta.

cataclysm, *n.* cataclismo *m.*

catacomb, *n.* catacumba *f.*

catalogue, *n.* catálogo *m.*

catapult, *n.* catapulta *f.*

cataract, *n.* catarata *f.*

catarrh, *n.* catarro *m.*

catastrophe, *n.* catástrofe *f.*

catch, *v.* alcanzar, atrapar, coger.

catchy, *a.* contagioso.

catechism, *n.* catequismo *m.*

catechize, *v.* catequizar.

categorical, *a.* categórico.

category, *n.* categoría *f.*

cater, v. abastecer; proveer.
c. to, complacer.
caterpillar, n. gusano m.
catgut, n. cuerda (de tripa).
catharsis, n. catarsis, purga f.
cathartic, 1. a. catártico; purgante. 2. n. purgante m.
cathedral, n. catedral f.
cathode, n. cátodo m.
Catholic, a. católico & n. católico -ca.
Catholicism, n. catolicismo m.
catnap, n. siesta corta.
catsup, n. salsa de tomate.
cattle, n. ganado m.
cattleman, n. ganadero m.
cauliflower, n. coliflor m.
causation, n. causalidad f.
cause, n. causa f.
causeway, n. calzada elevada f.; terraplén m.
caustic, a. cáustico.
cauterize, v. cauterizar.
cautery, n. cauterio m.
caution, n. cautela f.
cautious, a. cauteloso.
cavalcade, n. cabalgata f.
cavalier, n. caballero m.
cavalry, n. caballería f.
cave, cavern, n. caverna, gruta f.
cave-in, n. hundimiento m.
caviar, n. caviar m.
cavity, n. hueco m.
cayman, n. caimán m.
CD player, tocadiscos compacto, tocadiscos digital m.
cease, v. cesar.
ceaseless, a. incesante.
cedar, n. cedro m.
cede, v. ceder.
ceiling, n. techo; cielo m.
celebrant, n. celebrante -ta.
celebrate, v. celebrar.
celebration, n. celebración f.
celebrity, n. celebridad.
celerity, n. celeridad; prontitud f.
celery, n. apio m.
celestial, a. celeste.
celibacy, n. celibato -ta.
celibate, a. & n. célibe m. & f.
cell, n. celda f.; (biol.) célula f.
cellar, n. sótano m.

cellist, a. celista m. & f.
cello, n. violonchelo m.
cellophane, n. celofán m.
cellular, a. celular.
celluloid, n. celuloide m.
cellulose, 1. a. celuloso. 2. n. celulosa f.
Celtic, a. céltico.
cement, n. cemento m.
cemetery, n. cementerio m.; campo santo m.
censor, n. censor -ra.
censorious, a. severo; crítico.
censorship, n. censura f.
censure, 1. n. censura f. 2. v. censurar.
census, n. censo m.
cent, n. centavo, céntimo m.
centenary, a. & n. centenario m.
centennial, a. & n. centenario m.
center, n. centro m.
centerfold, n. página central desplegable en una revista.
centerpiece, n. centro de mesa.
centigrade, a. centígrado.
centigrade thermometer, termómetro centígrado.
central, a. central.
Central American, a. & n. centroamericano -na.
centralize, v. centralizar.
century, n. siglo m.
century plant, maguey m.
ceramic, a. cerámico.
ceramics, n. cerámica f.
cereal, n. cereal m.
cerebral, a. cerebral.
ceremonial, a. ceremonial.
ceremonious, a. ceremonioso.
ceremony, n. ceremonia f.
certain, a. cierto, seguro.
certainly, adv. sin duda, seguramente.
certainty, n. certeza f.
certificate, n. certificado m.
certification, n. certificación f.
certified, a. certificado.
certify, v. certificar.
certitude, n. certeza f.
cessation, n. cesación, descontinuación f.

cession, n. cesión f.
chafe, v. irritar.
chafing dish, n. escalfador m.
chagrin, n. disgusto m.
chain, 1. n. cadena f. 2. v. encadenar.
chair, n. silla f.
chairman, n. presidente -ta.
chairperson, n. presidente -ta; persona que preside.
chalk, n. tiza f.
challenge, 1. n. desafío m. 2. v. desafiar.
challenger, n. desafiador -ra.
chamber, n. cámara f.
chamberlain, n. camarero m.
chambermaid, n. camarera f.
chameleon, n. camaleón m.
chamois, n. gamuza f.
champagne, n. champán m., champaña f.
champion, 1. n. campeón -na 2. v. defender.
championship, n. campeonato m.
chance, n. oportunidad, ocasión f. by c., por casualidad, por acaso. take a c., aventurarse.
chancel, n. antealtar m.
chancellery, n. cancillería f.
chancellor, n. canciller m.
chandelier, n. araña de luces.
change, 1. n. cambio; (from a bill) moneda f. 2. v. cambiar.
changeability, n. mutabilidad f.
changeable, a. variable, inconstante.
changer, n. cambiador -ra.
channel, 1. n. canal m. 2. v. encauzar.
Channel Tunnel, túnel del Canal de la Mancha m.
chant, 1. n. canto llano m. 2. v. cantar.
chaos, n. caos m.
chaotic, a. caótico.
chap, 1. n. (coll.) tipo m. 2. v. rajar.
chapel, n. capilla f.
chaperon, n. acompañante -ta de señorita.
chaplain, n. capellán m.
chapter, n. capítulo m.
char, v. carbonizar.

character, *n.* carácter *m.*

characteristic, 1. *a.* característico. **2.** *n.* característica *f.*

characterization, *n.* caracterización *f.*

characterize, *v.* caracterizar.

charcoal, *n.* carbón leña.

charge, 1. *n.* acusación *f.;* ataque *m.* **2.** *v.* cargar; acusar; atacar.

chariot, *n.* carroza *f.*

charisma, *n.* carisma *m.*

charitable, *a.* caritativo.

charitableness, *n.* caridad *f.*

charitably, *adv.* caritativamente.

charity, *n.* caridad *f.;* (alms) limosna *f.*

charlatan, *n.* charlatán -na.

charlatanism, *n.* charlatanería *f.*

charm, 1. *n.* encanto *m.;* (witchcraft) hechizo *m.* **2.** *v.* encantar; hechizar.

charming, *a.* encantador.

charred, *a.* carbonizado.

chart, *n.* tabla, esquema *f.*

charter, 1. *n.* carta *f.* **2.** *v.* alquilar.

charter flight, vuelo chárter *m.*

charwoman, *n.* mujer de la limpieza *f.*

chase, 1. *n.* caza *f.* **2.** *v.* cazar; perseguir.

chaser, *n.* perseguidor -ra.

chasm, *n.* abismo *m.*

chassis, *n.* chasis *m.*

chaste, *a.* casto.

chasten, *v.* corregir, castigar.

chastise, *v.* castigar.

chastisement, *n.* castigo *m.*

chastity, *n.* castidad, pureza *f.*

chat, 1. *n.* plática, charla *f.* **2.** *v.* platicar, charlar.

chateau, *n.* castillo *m.*

chattels, *n.pl.* bienes *m.*

chatter, 1. *v.* cotorrear; (teeth) rechinar. **2.** *n.* cotorreo *m.*

chatterbox, *n.* charlador -ra.

chauffeur, *n.* chofer *m.*

cheap, *a.* barato.

cheapen, *v.* rebajar, menospreciar.

cheaply, *adv.* barato.

cheapness, *n.* baratura *f.*

cheat, *v.* engañar.

cheater, *n.* engañador -ra.

check, 1. *n.* verificación *f.;* (bank) cheque *m.;* (restaurant) cuenta *f.;* (chess) jaque *m.* **2.** *v.* verificar.

checkers, *n.* juego de damas.

checkmate, *v.* dar mate.

checkout counter, caja *f.*

cheek, *n.* mejilla *f.* (of face), desfachatez *f.* (gall).

cheekbone, *n.* pómulo *m.*

cheer, 1. *n.* alegría *f.;* aplauso *m.* **2.** *v.* alegrar; aplaudir.

cheerful, *a.* alegre.

cheerfully, *adv.* alegremente.

cheerfulness, *n.* alegría *f.*

cheerless, *a.* triste.

cheery, *a.* alegre.

cheese, *n.* queso *m.* **cottage c.,** requesón *m.*

chef, *n.* cocinero en jefe.

chemical, 1. *a.* químico. **2.** *n.* reactivo *m.*

chemically, *adv.* químicamente.

chemist, *n.* químico -ca.

chemistry, *n.* química *f.*

chemotherapy, *n.* quimioterapia *f.*

chenille, *n.* felpilla *f.*

cherish, *v.* apreciar.

cherry, *n.* cereza *f.*

cherub, *n.* querubín *m.*

chess, *n.* ajedrez *m.*

chest, *n.* arca *f.;* (physiology) pecho *m.*

chestnut, *n.* castaña *f.*

chevron, *n.* sardineta *f.*

chew, *v.* mascar, masticar.

chewer, *n.* mascador -ra.

chic, *a.* elegante, paquete.

chicanery, *n.* trampería *f.*

chick, *n.* pollito -ta.

chicken, *n.* pollo *m.,* gallina *f.*

chicken-hearted, *a.* cobarde.

chicken pox, viruelas locas, varicela *f.*

chicle, *n.* chicle *m.*

chicory, *n.* achicoria *f.*

chide, *v.* regañar, reprender.

chief, 1. *a.* principal. **2.** *n.* jefe -fa.

chiefly, *adv.* principalmente, mayormente.

chieftain, *n.* caudillo *m.;* (Indian c.) cacique *m.*

chiffon, *n.* chifón *m.,* gasa *f.*

chilblain, *n.* sabañón *m.*

child, *n.* niño -ña; hijo -ja.

childbirth, *n.* parto *m.*

childhood, *n.* niñez *f.*

childish, *a.* pueril.

childishness, *n.* puerilidad *f.*

childless, *a.* sin hijos.

childlike, *a.* infantil.

Chilean, *a.* & *n.* chileno -na.

chili, *n.* chile, ají *m.*

chill, 1. *n.* frío; escalofrío *m.* **2.** *v.* enfriar.

chilliness, *n.* frialdad *f.*

chilly, *a.* frío; friolento.

chimes, *n.* juego de campanas.

chimney, *n.* chimenea *f.*

chimpanzee, *n.* chimpancé *m.*

chin, *n.* barba *f.*

china, *n.* loza *f.*

chinchilla, *n.* chinchilla *f.*

Chinese, *a.* & *n.* chino -na.

chink, *n.* grieta *f.*

chintz, *n.* zaraza *f.*

chip, 1. *n.* astilla *f.* **2.** *v.* astillar.

chiropodist, *n.* pedicuro -ra.

chiropractor, *n.* quiropráctico -ca.

chirp, 1. *n.* chirrido *m.* **2.** *v.* chirriar, piar.

chisel, 1. *n.* cincel *m.* **2.** *v.* cincelar, talar.

chivalrous, *a.* caballeroso.

chivalry, *n.* caballería *f.*

chive, *n.* cebollino *m.*

chloride, *n.* cloruro *m.*

chlorine, *n.* cloro *m.*

chloroform, *n.* cloroformo *m.*

chlorophyll, *n.* clorofila *f.*

chock-full, *a.* repleto, colmado.

chocolate, *n.* chocolate *m.*

choice, 1. *a.* selecto, escogido. **2.** *n.* selección *f.;* escogimiento *m.*

choir, *n.* coro *m.*

choke, *v.* sofocar, ahogar.

cholera, *n.* cólera *f.*

choleric, *a.* colérico, irascible.

cholesterol, *n.* colesterol *m.*

choose, *v.* elegir, escoger.

chop, 1. *n.* chuleta, costilla *f.* **2.** *v.* tajar; cortar.

chopper, *n.* tajador -ra.

choppy, *a.* agitado.

choral, *a.* coral.

chord, *n.* cuerda *f.;* acorde *m.*

chore, *n.* tarea *f.,* quehacer *m.*

choreography, *n.* coreografía *f.*

chorister, *n.* corista *m.*

chorus, *n.* coro *m.*

christen, *v.* bautizar.

Christendom, *n.* cristiandad *f.*

Christian, *a. & n.* cristiano -na.

Christianity, *n.* cristianismo *m.*

Christmas, *n.* Navidad, Pascua *f.* **Merry C.,** felices Pascuas. **C. Eve,** Nochebuena *f.*

chromatic, *a.* cromático.

chromium, *n.* cromo *m.*

chromosome, *n.* cromosoma *m.*

chronic, *a.* crónico.

chronicle, *n.* crónica *f.*

chronological, *a.* cronológico.

chronology, *n.* cronología *f.*

chrysalis, *n.* crisálida *f.*

chrysanthemum, *n.* crisantemo *m.*

chubby, *a.* regordete, rollizo.

chuck, *v.* (cluck) cloquear; (throw) echar, tirar.

chuckle, *v.* reír entre dientes.

chum, *n.* amigo -ga; compinche *m.*

chummy, *a.* íntimo.

chunk, *n.* trozo *m.*

chunky, *a.* fornido, trabado.

Chunnel, *n.* túnel del Canal de la Mancha *m.*

church, *n.* iglesia *f.*

churchman, *n.* eclesiástico *m.*

churchyard, *n.* cementerio *m.*

churn, 1. *n.* mantequera *f.* **2.** *v.* agitar, revolver.

chute, *n.* conducto; canal *m.*

cicada, *n.* cigarra, chicharra *f.*

cider, *n.* sidra *f.*

cigar, *n.* cigarro, puro *m.*

cigarette, *n.* cigarrillo, cigarro, pitillo *m.* **c. case,** cigarrillera *f.* **c. lighter,** encendedor *m.*

cinchona, *n.* cinchona *f.*

cinder, *n.* ceniza *f.*

cinema, *n.* cine *m.*

cinnamon, *n.* canela *f.*

cipher, *n.* cifra *f.*

circle, *n.* círculo *m.*

circuit, *n.* circuito *m.*

circuitous, *a.* tortuoso.

circuitously, *adv.* tortuosamente.

circular, *a.* circular, redondo.

circularize, *v.* hacer circular.

circulate, *v.* circular.

circulation, *n.* circulación *f.*

circulator, *n.* diseminador -ra.

circulatory, *a.* circulatorio.

circumcise, *v.* circuncidar.

circumcision, *n.* circuncisión *f.*

circumference, *n.* circunferencia *f.*

circumlocution, *n.* circunlocución *f.*

circumscribe, *v.* circunscribir; limitar.

circumspect, *a.* discreto.

circumstance, *n.* circunstancia *f.*

circumstantial, *a.* circunstancial, indirecto.

circumstantially, *adv.* minuciosamente.

circumvent, *v.* evadir, evitar.

circumvention, *n.* trampa *f.*

circus, *n.* circo *m.*

cirrhosis, *n.* cirrosis *f.*

cistern, *n.* cisterna *f.*

citadel, *n.* ciudadela *f.*

citation, *n.* citación *f.*

cite, *v.* citar.

citizen, *n.* ciudadano -na.

citizenship, *n.* ciudadanía *f.*

citric, *a.* cítrico.

city, *n.* ciudad *f.*

city hall, ayuntamiento, municipio *m.*

city planning, urbanismo *m.*

civic, *a.* cívico.

civics, *n.* ciencia del gobierno civil.

civil, *a.* civil; cortés.

civilian, *a. & n.* civil *m. & f.*

civility, *n.* cortesía *f.*

civilization, *n.* civilización *f.*

civilize, *v.* civilizar.

civil rights, derechos civiles *m. pl.*

civil service, *n.* servicio civil oficial *m.*

civil war, *n.* guerra civil *f.*

clabber, 1. *n.* cuajo *m.* **2.** *v.* cuajarse.

clad, *a.* vestido.

claim, 1. *n.* demanda; pretensión *f.* **2.** *v.* demandar, reclamar.

claimant, *n.* reclamante -ta.

clairvoyance, *n.* clarividencia *f.*

clairvoyant, *a.* clarividente.

clam, *n.* almeja *f.*

clamber, *v.* trepar.

clamor, 1. *n.* clamor *m.* **2.** *v.* clamar.

clamorous, *a.* clamoroso.

clamp, 1. *n.* prensa de sujeción *f.* **2.** *v.* asegurar, sujetar.

clan, *n.* tribu *f.,* clan *m.*

clandestine, *a.* clandestino.

clandestinely, *adv.* clandestinamente.

clangor, *n.* estruendo *m.,* estrépito *m.*

clannish, *a.* unido; exclusivista.

clap, *v.* aplaudir.

clapboard, *n.* chilla *f.*

claque, *n.* claque *f.*

claret, *n.* clarete *m.*

clarification, *n.* clarificación *f.*

clarify, *v.* clarificar.

clarinet, *n.* clarinete *m.*

clarinetist, *n.* clarinetista *m. & f.*

clarity, *n.* claridad *f.*

clash, 1. *n.* choque, enfrentamiento *m.* **2.** *v.* chocar.

clasp, 1. *n.* broche *m.* **2.** *v.* abrochar.

class, *n.* clase *f.*

classic, classical, *a.* clásico.

classicism, *n.* clasicismo *m.*

classifiable, *a.* clasificable, calificable.

classification, *n.* clasificación *f.*

classify, *v.* clasificar.

classmate, *n.* compañero -ra
de clase.

classroom, *n.* sala de clase.

clatter, 1. *n.* alboroto *m.* **2.**
v. alborotar.

clause, *n.* cláusula *f.*

claustrophobia, *n.* claustrofobia *f.*

claw, *n.* garra *f.*

clay, *n.* arcilla *f.*; barro *m.*

clean, 1. *a.* limpio. **2.** *v.*
limpiar.

cleaner, *n.* limpiador -ra.

**cleaning lady, cleaning
woman,** señora de la
limpieza, mujer de la
limpieza *f.*

cleanliness, *n.* limpieza *f.*

cleanse, *v.* limpiar, purificar.

cleanser, *n.* limpiador *m.*,
purificador *m.*

clear, *a.* claro.

clearance, *n.* espacio libre. **c.
sale,** venta de liquidación.

clearing, *n.* despejo *m.*;
desmonte *m.*

clearly, *adv.* claramente,
evidentemente.

clearness, *n.* claridad *f.*

cleavage, *n.* resquebradura *f.*

cleaver, *n.* partidor *m.*,
hacha *f.*

clef, *n.* clave, llave *f.*

clemency, *n.* clemencia *f.*

clench, *v.* agarrar.

clergy, *n.* clero *m.*

clergyman, *n.* clérigo *m.*

clerical, *a.* clerical. **c.
work,** trabajo de oficina.

clericalism, *n.* clericalismo
m.

clerk, *n.* dependiente, escribiente *m.*

clerkship, *n.* escribanía *f.*,
secretaría *f.*

clever, *a.* diestro, hábil.

cleverly, *adv.* diestramente,
hábilmente.

cleverness, *n.* destreza *f.*

cliché, *n.* tópico *m.*

client, *n.* cliente -ta.

clientele, *n.* clientela *f.*

cliff, *n.* precipicio, risco *m.*

climate, *n.* clima *m.*

climatic, *a.* climático.

climax, *n.* colmo *m.*, culminación *f.*

climb, *v.* escalar; subir.

climber, *n.* trepador -ra, escalador -ra; (bot.)
enredadera *f.*

climbing plant, enredadera *f.*

clinch, *v.* afirmar.

cling, *v.* pegarse.

clinic, *n.* clínica *f.*

clinical, *a.* clínico.

clinically, *adv.* clínicamente.

clip, 1. *n.* grapa *f.* **paper c.,**
gancho *m.* **2.** *v.* prender;
(shear) trasquilar.

clipper, *n.* recortador *m.*;
(aero.) clíper *m.*

clipping, *n.* recorte *m.*

clique, *n.* camarilla *f.*, compadraje *m.*

cloak, 1. *n.* capa *f.*, manto *m.*

clock, *n.* reloj *m.* **alarm c.,**
despertador *m.*

clod, *n.* terrón *m.*; césped *m.*

clog, *v.* obstruir.

cloister, *n.* claustro *m.*

clone, 1. *n.* clon *m.* & *f.* **2.**
v. clonar.

close, 1. *a.* cercano. **2.** *adv.*
cerca. **c. to,** cerca de. **3.**
v. cerrar; tapar.

closely, *adv.* (near) de
cerca; (tight) es-
trechamente; (care)
cuidadosamente.

closeness, *n.* contigüidad *f.*,
apretamiento *m.*; (airless)
falta de ventilación *f.*

closet, *n.* gabinete *m.*
clothes c., ropero *m.*

clot, 1. *n.* coágulo *f.* **2.** *v.*
coagularse.

cloth, *n.* paño *m.*; tela *f.*

clothe, *v.* vestir.

clothes, clothing, *n.* ropa *f.*

clothing, *n.* vestidos *m.*,
ropa *f.*

cloud, *n.* nube *f.*

cloudburst, *n.* chaparrón *m.*

cloudiness, *n.* nebulosidad
f.; obscuridad *f.*

cloudless, *a.* despejado, sin
nubes.

cloudy, *a.* nublado.

clove, *n.* clavo *m.*

clover, *n.* trébol *m.*

clown, *n.* bufón -na, payaso
-sa.

clownish, *a.* grosero; bu-
fonesco.

cloy, *v.* saciar, empalagar.

club, 1. *n.* porra *f.*; (social)
círculo, club *m.*; (cards)
basto *m.* **2.** *v.* golpear
con una porra.

clubfoot, *n.* pateta *m.*, pie
zambo *m.*

clue, *n.* seña, pista *f.*

clump, *n.* grupo *m.*, masa *f.*

clumsiness, *n.* tosquedad *f.*;
desmaña *f.*

clumsy, *a.* torpe, desmañado.

cluster, 1. *n.* grupo *m.*; (fruit)
racimo *m.* **2.** *v.* agrupar.

clutch, 1. *n.* (auto.) embrague *m.* **2.** *v.* agarrar.

clutter, 1. *n.* confusión *f.* **2.**
v. poner en desorden.

coach, 1. *n.* coche, vagón
m.; coche ordinario;
(sports) entrenador *m.* **2.**
v. entrenar.

coachman, *n.* cochero -ra.

coagulate, *v.* coagular.

coagulation, *n.* coagulación
f.

coal, *n.* carbón *m.*

coalesce, *v.* unirse, soldarse.

coalition, *n.* coalición *f.*

coal oil, *n.* petróleo *m.*

coal tar, *n.* alquitrán *m.*

coarse, *a.* grosero, burdo;
(material) tosco, grueso.

coarsen, *v.* vulgarizar.

coarseness, *n.* grosería;
tosquedad *f.*

coast, 1. *n.* costa *f.*, litoral
m. **2.** *v.* deslizarse.

coastal, *a.* costanero.

coast guard, guardacostas
m. & *f.*

coat, 1. *n.* saco *m.*, chaqueta *f.*; (paint) capa *f.* **2.**
v. cubrir.

coat of arms, *n.* escudo *m.*

coax, *v.* instar.

cobalt, *n.* cobalto *m.*

cobbler, *n.* zapatero -ra.

cobblestone, *n.* guijarro *m.*

cobra, *n.* cobra *f.*

cobweb, *n.* telaraña *f.*

cocaine, *n.* cocaína *f.*

cock, *n.* (rooster) gallo *m.*;
(water, etc.) llave *f.*;
(gun) martillo *m.*

cockfight, *n.* riña de gallos *f.*

cockpit, *n.* gallera *f.*;
reñidero de gallos *m.*;
(aero.) cabina *f.*

cockroach, *n.* cucaracha *f.*

cocktail, *n.* cóctel *m.*

cocky, *a.* confiado, atrevido.

cocoa, *n.* cacao *m.*

coconut, *n.* coco *m.*

cocoon, *n.* capullo *m.*

cod, *n.* bacalao *m.*

code, *n.* código *m.*; clave *f.*

codeine, *n.* codeína *f.*

codfish, *n.* bacalao *m.*

codify, *v.* compilar.

cod-liver oil, aceite de hígado de bacalao *m.*

coeducation, *n.* coeducación *f.*

coequal, *a.* mutuamente igual.

coerce, *v.* forzar.

coercion, *n.* coerción *f.*

coercive, *a.* coercitivo.

coexist, *v.* coexistir.

coffee, *n.* café *m.* **c. plantation,** cafetal *m.* **c. shop,** café *m.*

coffee break, pausa para el café *f.*

coffer, *n.* cofre *m.*

coffin, *n.* ataúd *m.*

cog, *n.* diente de rueda *m.*

cogent, *a.* convincente.

cogitate, *v.* pensar, reflexionar.

cognizance, *n.* conocimiento *m.*, comprensión *f.*

cognizant, *a.* conocedor, informado.

cogwheel, *n.* rueda dentada *f.*

cohere, *v.* pegarse.

coherent, *a.* coherente.

cohesion, *n.* cohesión *f.*

cohesive, *a.* cohesivo.

cohort, *n.* cohorte *f.*

coiffure, *n.* peinado, tocado *m.*

coil, 1. *n.* rollo *m.*; (naut.) adujada *f.* **2.** *v.* enrollar.

coin, *n.* moneda *f.*

coinage, *n.* sistema monetario *m.*

coincide, *v.* coincidir.

coincidence, *n.* coincidencia; casualidad *f.*

coincident, *a.* coincidente.

coincidental, *a.* coincidental.

coincidentally, *adv.* coincidentalmente, al mismo tiempo.

colander, *n.* colador *m.*

cold, *a.* & *n.* frío -a; (med.) resfriado *m.* **to be c.,** tener frío; (weather) hacer frío.

coldly, *adv.* fríamente.

coldness, *n.* frialdad *f.*

collaborate, *v.* colaborar.

collaboration, *n.* colaboración *f.*

collaborator, *n.* colaborador -ra.

collapse, 1. *n.* desplome *m.*; (med.) colapso *m.* **2.** *v.* desplomarse.

collar, *n.* cuello *m.*

collarbone, *n.* clavícula *f.*

collate, *v.* comparar.

collateral, 1. *a.* colateral. **2.** *n.* garantía *f.*

collation, *n.* comparación *f.*; (food) colación *f.*, merienda *f.*

colleague, *n.* colega *m.* & *f.*

collect, *v.* cobrar; recoger; coleccionar.

collection, *n.* colección *f.*

collective, *a.* colectivo.

collectively, *adv.* colectivamente, en masa.

collector, *n.* colector -ra; coleccionista *m.* & *f.*

college, *n.* colegio *m.*; universidad *f.*

collegiate, *a.* colegiado *m.*

collide, *v.* chocar.

collision, *n.* choque *m.*

colloquial, *a.* familiar.

colloquially, *adv.* familiarmente.

colloquy, *n.* conversación *f.*, coloquio *m.*

collusion, *n.* colusión *f.*, connivencia *f.*

Cologne, *n.* Colonia *f.*

Colombian, *a.* & *n.* colombiano -na.

colon, *n.* colon *m.*; (punct.) dos puntos.

colonel, *n.* coronel *m.*

colonial, *a.* colonial.

colonist, *n.* colono -na.

colonization, *n.* colonización *f.*

colonize, *v.* colonizar.

colony, *n.* colonia *f.*

color, 1. *n.* color; colorido *m.* **2.** *v.* colorar; colorir.

coloration, *n.* colorido *m.*

colored, *a.* de color.

colorful, *a.* vívido.

colorless, *a.* descolorido, sin color.

colossal, *a.* colosal.

colt, *n.* potro *m.*

column, *n.* columna *f.*

coma, *n.* coma *m.*

comb, 1. *n.* peine *m.* **2.** *v.* peinar.

combat, 1. *n.* combate *m.* **2.** *v.* combatir.

combatant, *n.* combatiente -ta.

combative, *a.* combativo.

combination, *n.* combinación *f.*

combine, *v.* combinar.

combustible, *a.* & *n.* combustible *m.*

combustion, *n.* combustión *f.*

come, *v.* venir. **c. back,** volver. **c. in,** entrar. **c. out,** salir. **c. up,** subir. **c. upon,** encontrarse con.

comedian, *n.* cómico -ca.

comedienne, *n.* cómica *f.*, actriz *f.*

comedy, *n.* comedia *f.*

comet, *n.* cometa *m.*

comfort, 1. *n.* confort *m.*; solaz *m.* **2.** *v.* confortar; solazar.

comfortable, *a.* cómodo.

comfortably, *adv.* cómodamente.

comforter, *n.* colcha *f.*

comfortingly, *adv.* confortantemente.

comfortless, *a.* sin consuelo; sin comodidades.

comic, comical, *a.* cómico.

comic book, *n.* tebeo *m.*

coming, 1. *n.* venida *f.*, llegada *f.* **2.** *a.* próximo, que viene, entrante.

comma, *n.* coma *f.*

command, 1. *n.* mando *m.* **2.** *v.* mandar.

commandeer, *v.* reclutar forzosamente, expropiar.

commander, *n.* comandante -ta.

commander in chief, *n.* generalísimo, jefe supremo.

commandment, *n.* mandato; mandamiento *m.*

commemorate, *v.* conmemorar.

commemoration, *n.* conmemoración *f.*

commemorative, *a.* conmemorativo.

commence, *v.* comenzar, principiar.

commencement, *n.* comienzo *m.;* graduación *f.*

commend, *v.* encomendar; elogiar.

commendable, *a.* recomendable.

commendably, *adv.* loablemente.

commendation, *n.* recomendación *f.;* elogio *m.*

commensurate, *a.* proporcionado.

comment, 1. *n.* comentario *m.* 2. *v.* comentar.

commentary, *n.* comentario *m.*

commentator, *n.* comentador -ra.

commerce, *n.* comercio *m.*

commercial, *a.* comercial.

commercialism, *n.* comercialismo *m.*

commercialize, *v.* mercantilizar, explotar.

commercially, *a. & adv.* comercialmente.

commiserate, *v.* compadecerse.

commissary, *n.* comisario *m.*

commission, 1. *n.* comisión *f.* 2. *v.* comisionar.

commissioner, *n.* comisario -ria.

commit, *v.* cometer.

commitment, *n.* compromiso *m.*

committee, *n.* comité *m.*

commodious, *a.* cómodo.

commodity, *n.* mercadería *f.*

common, *a.* común; ordinario.

commonly, *adv.* comúnmente, vulgarmente.

Common Market, Mercado Común *m.*

commonplace, *a.* trivial, banal.

common sense, sentido común *m.*

commonwealth, *n.* estado *m.;* nación *f.*

commotion, *n.* tumulto *m.*

communal, *a.* comunal, público.

commune, 1. *n.* distrito municipal *m.;* comuna *f.* 2. *v.* conversar.

communicable, *a.* comunicable; (med.) transmisible.

communicate, *v.* comunicar.

communication, *n.* comunicación *f.*

communicative, *a.* comunicativo.

communion, *n.* comunión *f.* **take c.,** comulgar.

communiqué, *n.* comunicación *f.*

communism, *n.* comunismo *m.*

communist, *n.* comunista *m. & f.*

communistic, *a.* comunístico.

community, *n.* comunidad *f.*

commutation, *n.* conmutación *f.*

commuter, *n.* empleado que viaja diariamente desde su domicilio hasta la ciudad donde trabaja.

compact, 1. *a.* compacto. 2. *n.* pacto *m.;* (lady's) polvera *f.*

compact disk, disco compacto *m.*

companion, *n.* compañero -ra.

companionable, *a.* sociable.

companionship, *n.* compañerismo *m.*

company, *n.* compañía *f.*

comparable, *a.* comparable.

comparative, *a.* comparativo.

comparatively, *a.* relativamente.

compare, *v.* comparar.

comparison, *n.* comparación *f.*

compartment, *n.* compartimiento *m.*

compass, *n.* compás *m.;* (naut.) brújula *f.*

compassion, *n.* compasión *f.*

compassionate, *a.* compasivo.

compassionately, *adv.* compasivamente.

compatible, *a.* compatible.

compatriot, *n.* compatriota *m. & f.*

compel, *v.* obligar.

compensate, *v.* compensar.

compensation, *n.* compensación *f.*

compensatory, *a.* compensatorio.

compete, *v.* competir.

competence, *n.* competencia *f.*

competent, *a.* competente, capaz.

competently, *adv.* competentemente.

competition, *n.* concurrencia *f.;* concurso *m.*

competitive, *a.* competidor.

competitor, *n.* competidor -ra.

compile, *v.* compilar.

complacency, *n.* complacencia *f.*

complacent, *a.* complaciente.

complacently, *adv.* complacientemente.

complain, *v.* quejarse.

complaint, *n.* queja *f.*

complement, *n.* complemento *m.*

complete, 1. *a.* completo 2. *v.* completar.

completely, *adv.* completamente, enteramente.

completeness, *n.* integridad *f.*

completion, *n.* terminación *f.*

complex, *a.* complejo.

complexion, *n.* tez *f.*

complexity, *n.* complejidad *f.*

compliance, *n.* consentimiento *m.* **in c. with,** de acuerdo con.

compliant, *a.* dócil; complaciente.

complicate, *v.* complicar.

complicated, *a.* complicado.

complication, *n.* complicación *f.*

complicity, *n.* complicidad *f.*

compliment, 1. *n.* elogio *m.* (fig.) **2.** *v.* felicitar; echar flores.

complimentary, *a.* galante, obsequioso, regaloso.

comply, *v.* cumplir.

component, *a.* & *n.* componente *m.*

comport, *v.* portarse.

compose, *v.* componer.

composed, *a.* tranquilo; (made up) compuesto.

composer, *n.* compositor -ra.

composite, *a.* compuesto.

composition, *n.* composición *f.*

composure, *n.* serenidad *f.*; calma *f.*

compote, *n.* compota *f.*

compound, *a.* & *n.* compuesto *m.*

comprehend, *v.* comprender.

comprehensible, *a.* comprensible.

comprehension, *n.* comprensión *f.*

comprehensive, *a.* comprensivo.

compress, 1. *n.* cabezal *m.* **2.** *v.* comprimir.

compressed, *a.* comprimido.

compression, *n.* compresión *f.*

compressor, *n.* compresor *m.*

comprise, *v.* comprender; abarcar.

compromise, 1. *n.* compromiso *m.* **2.** *v.* comprometer.

compromiser, *n.* compromisario *m.*

compulsion, *n.* compulsión *f.*

compulsive, *a.* compulsivo.

compulsory, *a.* obligatorio.

compunction, *n.* compunción *f.*; escrúpulo *m.*

computation, *n.* computación *f.*

compute, *v.* computar, calcular.

computer, *n.* computadora *f.*, ordenador *m.*

computerize, *v.* procesar en computadora, computerizar.

computer programmer, programador -ra de ordenadores.

computer science, informática *f.*

comrade, *n.* camarada *m.* & *f.*; compañero -ra.

comradeship, *n.* camaradería *f.*

concave, *a.* cóncavo.

conceal, *v.* ocultar, esconder.

concealment, *n.* ocultación *f.*

concede, *v.* conceder.

conceit, *n.* amor propio; engreimiento *m.*

conceited, *a.* engreído.

conceivable, *a.* concebible.

conceive, *v.* concebir.

concentrate, *v.* concentrar.

concentration, *n.* concentración *f.*

concentration camp, campo de concentración *m.*

concept, *n.* concepto *m.*

conception, *n.* concepción *f.*; concepto *m.*

concern, 1. *n.* interés *m.*; inquietud *f.*; (com.) negocio *m.* **2.** *v.* concernir.

concerning, *prep.* respecto a.

concert, *n.* concierto *m.*

concerted, *a.* convenido.

concession, *n.* concesión *f.*

conciliate, *v.* conciliar.

conciliation, *n.* conciliación *f.*

conciliator, *n.* conciliador -ra.

conciliatory, *a.* conciliatorio.

concise, *a.* conciso.

concisely, *adv.* concisamente.

conciseness, *n.* concisión *f.*

conclave, *n.* conclave *m.*

conclude, *v.* concluir.

conclusion, *n.* conclusión *f.*

conclusive, *a.* conclusivo, decisivo.

conclusively, *adv.* concluyentemente.

concoct, *v.* confeccionar.

concomitant, *n.* & *a.* concomitante *m.*

concord, *n.* concordia *f.*

concordat, *n.* concordato *m.*

concourse, *n.* concurso *m.*; confluencia *f.*

concrete, *a.* concreto.

concretely, *adv.* concretamente.

concubine, *n.* concubina, amiga *f.*

concur, *v.* concurrir.

concurrence, *n.* concurrencia *f.*; casualidad *f.*

concurrent, *a.* concurrente.

concussion, *n.* concusión *f.*; (c. of the brain) conmoción cerebral *f.*

condemn, *v.* condenar.

condemnable, *a.* culpable, condenable.

condemnation, *n.* condenación *f.*

condensation, *n.* condensación *f.*

condense, *v.* condensar.

condenser, *n.* condensador *m.*

condescend, *v.* condescender.

condescension, *n.* condescendencia *f.*

condiment, *n.* condimento *m.*

condition, 1. *n.* condición *f.*; estado *m.* **2.** *v.* acondicionar.

conditional, *a.* condicional.

conditionally, *adv.* condicionalmente.

condole, *v.* condolerse.

condolence, *n.* pésame *m.*

condom, *n.* forro, preservativo *m.*

condominium, *n.* condominio *m.*

condone, *v.* condonar.

conducive, *a.* conducente.

conduct, 1. *n.* conducta *f.* **2.** *v.* conducir.

conductivity, *n.* conductividad *f.*

conductor, *n.* conductor *m.*

conduit, *n.* caño *m.*, canal *f.*; conducto *m.*

cone, *n.* cono *m.* **ice-cream c.,** barquillo de helado.

confection, *n.* confitura *f.*

confectioner, *n.* confitero -ra.

confectionery, *n.* dulcería *f.*

confederacy, *n.* federación *f.*

confederate, *a.* & *n.* confederado *n.*

confederation, *n.* confederación *f.*

confer, *v.* conferenciar; conferir.

conference, *n.* conferencia *f.*; congreso *m.*

confess, *v.* confesar.

confession, *n.* confesión *f.*

confessional, **1.** *n.* confesionario *m.* **2.** *a.* confesional.

confessor, *n.* confesor *m.*

confetti, *n.* confetti *m.*

confidant, confidante, *n.* confidente *m.* & *f.*

confide, *v.* confiar.

confidence, *n.* confianza *f.*

confident, *a.* confiado; cierto.

confidential, *a.* confidencial.

confidentially, *adv.* confidencialmente, en secreto.

confidently, *adv.* confiadamente.

confine, **1.** *n.* confín *m.* **2.** *v.* confinar; encerrar.

confirm, *v.* confirmar.

confirmation, *n.* confirmación *f.*

confiscate, *v.* confiscar.

confiscation, *n.* confiscación *f.*

conflagration, *n.* incendio *m.*

conflict, **1.** *n.* conflicto *m.* **2.** *v.* oponerse; estar en conflicto.

conform, *v.* conformar.

conformation, *n.* conformación *f.*

conformer, *n.* conformista *m.* & *f.*

conformist, *n.* conformista *m.* & *f.*

conformity, *n.* conformidad *f.*

confound, *v.* confundir.

confront, *v.* confrontar.

confrontation, *n.* enfrentamiento *m.*

confuse, *v.* confundir.

confusion, *n.* confusión *f.*

congeal, *v.* congelar, helar.

congealment, *n.* congelación *f.*

congenial, *a.* congenial.

congenital, *a.* congénito.

congenitally, *adv.* congenitalmente.

congestion, *n.* congestión *f.*

conglomerate, **1.** *v.* conglomerar. **2.** *a.* & *n.* conglomerado.

conglomeration, *n.* conglomeración *f.*

congratulate, *v.* felicitar.

congratulation, *n.* felicitación *f.*

congratulatory, *a.* congratulatorio.

congregate, *v.* congregar.

congregation, *n.* congregación *f.*

congress, *n.* congreso *m.*

conic, **1.** *n.* cónica *f.* **2.** *a.* cónico.

conjecture, **1.** *n.* conjetura *f.* **2.** *v.* conjeturar.

conjugal, *a.* conyugal, matrimonial.

conjugate, *v.* conjugar.

conjugation, *n.* conjugación *f.*

conjunction, *n.* conjunción *f.*

conjunctive, **1.** *n.* (gram.) conjunción *f.* **2.** *a.* conjuntivo.

conjunctivitis, *n.* conjuntivitis *f.*

conjure, *v.* conjurar.

connect, *v.* juntar; relacionar.

connection, *n.* conexión *f.*

connivance, *n.* consentimiento *m.*

connive, *v.* disimular.

connoisseur, *n.* perito -ta.

connotation, *n.* connotación *f.*

connote, *v.* connotar.

connubial, *a.* conyugal.

conquer, *v.* conquistar.

conquerable, *a.* conquistable, vencible.

conqueror, *n.* conquistador -ra.

conquest, *n.* conquista *f.*

conscience, *n.* conciencia *f.*

conscientious, *a.* concienzudo.

conscientiously, *adv.* escrupulosamente.

conscientious objector, objetor de conciencia *m.*

conscious, *a.* consciente.

consciously, *adv.* con conocimiento.

consciousness, *n.* consciencia *f.*

conscript, **1.** *n.* conscripto *m.*, recluta *m.* **2.** *v.* reclutar, alistar.

conscription, *n.* conscripción *f.*, alistamiento *m.*

consecrate, *v.* consagrar.

consecration, *n.* consagración *f.*

consecutive, *a.* consecutivo, seguido.

consecutively, *adv.* consecutivamente, de seguida.

consensus, *n.* consenso *m.*, acuerdo general *m.*

consent, **1.** *n.* consentimiento *m.* **2.** *v.* consentir.

consequence, *n.* consecuencia *f.*

consequent, *a.* consiguiente.

consequential, *a.* importante.

consequently, *adv.* por lo tanto, por consiguiente.

conservation, *n.* conservación *f.*

conservatism, *n.* conservatismo *m.*

conservative, *a.* conservador, conservativo.

conservatory, *n.* (plants) invernáculo *m.*; (school) conservatorio *m.*

conserve, *v.* conservar.

consider, *v.* considerar. **C. it done!** ¡Dalo por hecho!

considerable, *a.* considerable.

considerably, *adv.* considerablemente.

considerate, *a.* considerado.

considerately, *adv.* consideradamente.

consideration, *n.* consideración *f.*

considering, *prep.* visto que, en vista de.

consign, *v.* consignar.

consignment, *n.* consignación *f.*, envío *m.*

consist, *v.* consistir.

consistency, *n.* consistencia *f.*

consistent, *a.* consistente.

consolation, *n.* consolación *f.*

consolation prize, premio de consuelo *m.*

console, *v.* consolar.

consolidate, *v.* consolidar.

consommé, *n.* caldo *m.*

consonant, *n.* consonante *f.*

consort, 1. *n.* cónyuge *m.* & *f.*; socio. **2.** *v.* asociarse.

conspicuous, *a.* conspicuo.

conspicuously, *adv.* visiblemente, llamativamente.

conspicuousness, *n.* visibilidad *f.*; evidencia *f.*; fama *f.*

conspiracy, *n.* conspiración *f.*; complot *m.*

conspirator, *n.* conspirador -ra.

conspire, *v.* conspirar.

conspirer, *n.* conspirante *m.* & *f.*

constancy, *n.* constancia *f.*, lealtad *f.*

constant, *a.* constante.

constantly, *adv.* constantemente, de continuo.

constellation, *n.* constelación *f.*

consternation, *n.* consternación *f.*

constipate, *v.* estreñir.

constipated, *a.* estreñido, *m.*

constipation, *n.* estreñimiento, *m.*

constituency, *n.* distrito electoral *m.*

constituent, 1. *a.* constituyente. **2.** *n.* elector *m.*

constitute, *v.* constituir.

constitution, *n.* constitución *f.*

constitutional, *a.* constitucional.

constrain, *v.* constreñir.

constraint, *n.* constreñimiento *m.*, compulsión *f.*

constrict, *v.* apretar, estrechar.

construct, *v.* construir.

construction, *n.* construcción *f.*

constructive, *a.* constructivo.

constructively, *adv.* constructivamente; por deducción.

constructor, *n.* constructor *m.*

construe, *v.* interpretar.

consul, *n.* cónsul *m.*

consular, *a.* consular.

consulate, *n.* consulado *m.*

consult, *v.* consultar.

consultant, *n.* consultor -ora.

consultation, *n.* consulta *f.*

consume, *v.* consumir.

consumer, *n.* consumidor -ra.

consumer society, sociedad de consumo *f.*

consummation, *n.* consumación *f.*

consumption, *n.* consumo *m.;* (med.) tisis.

consumptive, 1. *n.* tísico *m.* **2.** *a.* consuntivo.

contact, 1. *n.* contacto *m.* **2.** *v.* ponerse en contacto con.

contact lens, lentilla *f.*

contagion, *n.* contagio *m.*

contagious, *a.* contagioso.

contain, *v.* contener.

container, *n.* envase *m.*

contaminate, *v.* contaminar.

contemplate, *v.* contemplar.

contemplation, *n.* contemplación *f.*

contemplative, *a.* contemplativo.

contemporary, *n.* & *a.* contemporáneo -nea.

contempt, *n.* desprecio *m.*

contemptible, *v.* vil, despreciable.

contemptuous, *a.* desdeñoso.

contemptuously, *adv.* desdeñosamente.

contend, *v.* contender; competir.

contender, *n.* competidor -ra.

content, 1. *a.* contento. **2.** *n.* contenido *m.* **3.** *v.* contentar.

contented, *a.* contento.

contention, *n.* contención *f.*

contentment, *n.* contentamiento *m.*

contest, 1. *n.* concurso *m.* **2.** *v.* disputar.

contestable, *a.* contestable.

context, *n.* contexto *m.*

contiguous, *a.* contiguo.

continence, *n.* continencia *f.*, castidad *f.*

continent, *n.* continente *m.*

continental, *a.* continental.

contingency, *n.* eventualidad *f.*, casualidad *f.*

contingent, *a.* contingente.

continual, *a.* continuo.

continuation, *n.* continuación *f.*

continue, *v.* continuar.

continuity, *n.* continuidad *f.*

continuous, *a.* continuo.

continuously, *adv.* continuamente.

contour, *n.* contorno *m.*

contraband, *n.* contrabando *m.*

contraception, *n.* contracepción *f.*

contraceptive, *n.* & *a.* anticeptivo *m.*

contract, 1. *n.* contrato *m.* **2.** *v.* contraer.

contraction, *n.* contracción *f.*

contractor, *n.* contratista *m.* & *f.*

contradict, *v.* contradecir.

contradiction, *n.* contradicción *f.*

contradictory, *a.* contradictorio.

contralto, *n.* contralto *m.*

contrary, *a.* & *n.* contrario -ria.

contrast, 1. *n.* contraste *m.* **2.** *v.* contrastar.

contribute, *v.* contribuir.

contribution, *n.* contribución *f.*

contributive, contributory, *a.* contribuyente.

contributor, *n.* contribuidor -ra.

contrite, *a.* contrito.

contrition, *n.* contrición *f.*

contrivance, *n.* aparato *m.;* estratagema *f.*

contrive, *v.* inventar, tramar; darse maña.

control, 1. *n.* control *m.* **2.** *v.* controlar.

controllable, *a.* controlable, dominable.

controller, *n.* interventor -ra; contralor -ra.

control tower, torre de mando *f.*

controversial, *a.* contencioso.

controversy, *n.* controversia *f.*

contusion, *n.* contusión *f.*

convalesce, *v.* convalecer.

convalescence, *n.* convalecencia *f.*

convalescent, *n.* convaleciente *m. & f.*
convalescent home, clínica
de reposo *f.*
convene, *v.* juntarse; convocar.
convenience, *n.* comodidad *f.*
convenient, *a.* cómodo;
oportuno.
conveniently, *adv.* cómodamente.
convent, *n.* convento *m.*
convention, *n.* convención *f.*
conventional, *a.* convencional.
conventionally, *adv.* con-
vencionalmente.
converge, *v.* convergir.
convergence, *n.* convergencia *f.*
convergent, *a.* convergente.
conversant, *a.* versado; en-
tendido (de).
conversation, *n.* conversación, plática *f.*
conversational, *a.* de conversación.
conversationalist, *n.* con-
versador -ra.
converse, *v.* conversar.
conversely, *adv.* a la inversa.
convert, 1. *n.* convertido
da-. 2. *v.* convertir.
converter, *n.* convertidor *m.*
convertible, *a.* convertible.
convex, *a.* convexo.
convey, *v.* transportar; comunicar.
conveyance, *n.* transporte;
vehículo *m.*
conveyor, *n.* conductor *m.;*
(mech.) transportador *m.*
conveyor belt, correa transportadora *f.*
convict, 1. *n.* reo *m.* 2. *v.*
declarar culpable.
conviction, *n.* convicción *f.*
convince, *v.* convencer.
convincing, *a.* convincente.
convivial, *a.* convival.
convocation, *n.* convocación; asamblea *f.*
convoke, *v.* convocar, citar.
convoy, *n.* convoy *m.;* escolta *f.*
convulse, *v.* convulsionar;
agitar violentamente.
convulsion, *n.* convulsión *f.*

convulsive, *a.* convulsivo.
cook, 1. *n.* cocinero -ra. 2.
v. cocinar, cocer.
cookbook, *n.* libro de
cocina *m.*
cooky, *n.* galleta dulce *f.*
cool, 1. *a.* fresco. 2. *v.* refrescar.
cooler, *n.* enfriadera *f.*
coolness, *n.* frescura *f.*
coop, 1. *n.* jaula *f.* **chicken
c.,** gallinero *m.* 2. *v.* enjaular.
cooperate, *v.* cooperar.
cooperation, *n.* cooperación
f.
cooperative, *a.* cooperativo.
cooperatively, *adv.* coopera-
tivamente.
coordinate, *v.* coordinar.
coordination, *n.* coordinación *f.*
coordinator, *n.* coordinador
-ra.
cope, *v.* contender. **c. with,**
superar, hacer frente a.
copier, *n.* copiadora *f.*
copious, *a.* copioso, abundante.
copiously, *adv.* copiosa-
mente.
copiousness, *n.* abundancia *f.*
copper, *n.* cobre *m.*
copy, 1. *n.* copia *f.;* ejemplar *m.* 2. *v.* copiar.
copyist, *n.* copista *m. & f.*
copyright, *n.* derechos de
propiedad literaria *m.pl.*
coquetry, *n.* coquetería *f.*
coquette, *n.* coqueta *f.*
coral, *n.* coral *m.*
cord, *n.* cuerda *f.*
cordial, *a.* cordial.
cordiality, *n.* cordialidad *f.*
cordially, *adv.* cordialmente.
cordon off, *v.* acordonar.
cordovan, *n.* cordobán *m.*
corduroy, *n.* pana *f.*
core, *n.* corazón; centro *m.*
cork, *n.* corcho *m.*
corkscrew, *n.* tirabuzón *m.*
corn, *n.* maíz *m.*
cornea, *n.* córnea *f.*
corned beef, carne acecinada *f.*
corner, *n.* rincón *m.;* (of
street) esquina *f.*
cornet, *n.* corneta *f.*

cornetist, *n.* cornetín *m.*
cornice, *n.* cornisa *f.*
cornstarch, *n.* maicena *f.*
corollary, *n.* corolario *m.*
coronary, *a.* coronario.
coronation, *n.* coronación *f.*
corporal, 1. *a.* corpóreo. 2.
n. cabo *m.*
corporate, *a.* corporativo.
corporation, *n.* corporación
f.
corps, *n.* cuerpo *m.*
corpse, *n.* cadáver *m.*
corpulent, *a.* corpulento.
corpuscle, *n.* corpúsculo *m.*
corral, 1. *n.* corral *m.* 2. *v.*
acorralar.
correct, 1. *a.* correcto. 2. *v.*
corregir.
correction, *n.* corrección;
enmienda *f.*
corrective, *n. & a.* correc-
tivo.
correctly, *adv.* correctamente.
correctness, *n.* exactitud *f.*
correlate, *v.* correlacionar.
correlation, *n.* correlación *f.*
correspond, *v.* corresponder.
correspondence, *n.* correspondencia *f.*
correspondence course,
curso por correspondencia *m.*
correspondence school, escuela por correspondencia *f.*
correspondent, *a. & n.* correspondiente *m. & f.*
corresponding, *a.* correspondiente.
corridor, *n.* corredor,
pasillo *m.*
corroborate, *v.* corroborar.
corroboration, *n.* corroboración *f.*
corroborative, *a.* corrobo-
rante.
corrode, *v.* corroer.
corrosion, *n.* corrosión *f.*
corrugate, *v.* arrugar; ondular.
corrupt, 1. *a.* corrompido.
2. *v.* corromper.
corruptible, *a.* corruptible.
corruption, *n.* corrupción *f.*
corruptive, *a.* corruptivo.

corset, *n.* corsé *m.*, (girdle) faja *f.*

cortege, *n.* comitiva *f.*, séquito *m.*

corvette, *n.* corbeta *f.*

cosmetic, *a.* & *n.* cosmético *m.*

cosmic, *a.* cósmico.

cosmonaut, *n.* cosmonauta *m.* & *f.*

cosmopolitan, *a.* & *n.* cosmopolita *m.* & *f.*

cosmos, *n.* cosmos *m.*

cost, 1. *n.* coste *m.*; costa *f.* **2.** *v.* costar.

Costa Rican, *a.* & *n.* costarricense *m.* & *f.*

costly, *a.* costoso, caro.

costume, *n.* traje; disfraz *m.*

costume jewelry, bisutería *f.*, joyas de fantasía *f.pl.*

cot, *n.* catre *m.*

coterie, *n.* camarilla *f.*

cotillion, *n.* cotillón *m.*

cottage, *n.* casita *f.*

cottage cheese, *n.* requesón *m.*

cotton, *n.* algodón *m.*

cottonseed, *n.* semilla del algodón *f.*

couch, *n.* sofá *m.*

cougar, *n.* puma *m.*

cough, 1. *n.* tos *f.* **2.** *v.* toser.

council, *n.* consejo, concilio *m.*

counsel, 1. *n.* consejo; (law) abogado -da. **2.** *v.* aconsejar. **to keep one's c.,** no decir nada.

counselor, *n.* consejero -ra; (law) abogado -da.

count, 1. *n.* cuenta *f.*; (title) conde *m.* **2.** *v.* contar.

countenance, 1. *n.* aspecto *m.*; cara *f.* **2.** *v.* aprobar.

counter, 1. *adv.* **c. to,** contra, en contra de. **2.** *n.* mostrador *m.*

counteract, *v.* contrarrestar.

counteraction, *n.* neutralización *f.*

counterbalance, 1. *n.* contrapeso *m.* **2.** *v.* contrapesar.

counterfeit, 1. *a.* falsificado. **2.** *v.* falsear.

countermand, *v.* contramandar.

counteroffensive, *n.* contraofensiva *f.*

counterpart, *n.* contraparte *f.*

counterproductive, *a.* contraproductive.

countess, *n.* condesa *f.*

countless, *a.* innumerable.

country, *n.* campo *m.*; (pol.) país *m.*; (homeland) patria *f.*

country code, distintivo del país *m.*

countryman, *n.* paisano *m.* **fellow c.,** compatriota *m.*

countryside, *n.* campo, paisaje *m.*

county, *n.* condado *m.*

coupé, *n.* cupé *m.*

couple, 1. *n.* par *m.* **2.** *v.* unir.

coupon, *n.* cupón, talón *m.*

courage, *n.* valor *m.*

courageous, *a.* valiente.

course, *n.* curso *m.* **of c.,** por supuesto, desde luego.

court, 1. *n.* corte *f.*; cortejo *m.*; (of law) tribunal *m.* **2.** *v.* cortejar.

courteous, *a.* cortés.

courtesy, *n.* cortesía *f.*

courthouse, *n.* palacio de justicia *m.*, tribunal *m.*

courtier, *n.* cortesano *m.*

courtly, *a.* cortés, galante.

courtroom, *n.* sala de justicia *f.*

courtship, *n.* cortejo *m.*

courtyard, *n.* patio *m.*

cousin, *n.* primo -ma.

covenant, *n.* contrato, convenio *m.*

cover, 1. *n.* cubierta, tapa *f.* **2.** *v.* cubrir, tapar.

cover charge, precio del cubierto *m.*

covet, *v.* ambicionar, suspirar por.

covetous, *a.* codicioso.

cow, *n.* vaca *f.*

coward, *n.* cobarde *m.* & *f.*

cowardice, *n.* cobardía *f.*

cowardly, *a.* cobarde.

cowboy, *n.* vaquero, gaucho *m.*

cower, *v.* agacharse (de miedo).

cowhide, *n.* cuero *m.*

coy, *a.* recatado, modesto.

coyote, *n.* coyote *m.*

cozy, *a.* cómodo y agradable.

crab, *n.* cangrejo *m.*

crab apple, *n.* manzana silvestre *f.*

crack, 1. *n.* hendedura *f.*; (noise) crujido *m.* **2.** *v.* hender; crujir.

cracker, *n.* galleta *f.*

cradle, *n.* cuna *f.*

craft, *n.* arte *m.*

craftsman, *n.* artesano -na.

craftsmanship, *n.* artesanía *f.*

crafty, *a.* ladino.

crag, *n.* despeñadero *m.*; peña *f.*

cram, *v.* rellenar, hartar.

cramp, *n.* calambre *m.*

cranberry, *n.* arándano *m.*

crane, 1. *n.* (bird) grulla *f.*; (mech.) **2.** *n.* grúa *f.*

cranium, *n.* cráneo *m.*

crank, *n.* (mech.) manivela *f.*

cranky, *a.* chiflado, caprichoso.

crash, 1. *n.* choque; estallido *m.* **2.** *v.* estallar.

crate, *n.* canasto *m.*

crater, *n.* cráter *m.*

crave, *v.* desear; anhelar.

craven, *a.* cobarde.

craving, *n.* sed *m.*, anhelo *m.*

crawl, *v.* andar a gatas, arrastrarse.

crayon, *n.* creyón; lápiz *m.*

crazy, *a.* loco.

creak, *v.* crujir.

creaky, *a.* crujiente.

cream, *n.* crema *f.*

cream cheese, queso crema *m.*

creamery, *n.* lechería *f.*

creamy, *a.* cremoso.

crease, 1. *n.* pliegue *m.* **2.** *v.* plegar.

create, *v.* crear.

creation, *n.* creación *f.*

creative, *a.* creativo, creador.

creator, *n.* creador -ra.

creature, *n.* criatura *f.*

credence, *n.* creencia *f.*

credentials, *n.* credenciales *f.pl.*

credibility, *n.* credibilidad *f.*

credible, *a.* creíble.

credit, 1. *n.* crédito *m.* **on c.,** al fiado. **2.** *v.* (com.) abonar.

creditable, *a.* fidedigno.

credit balance, saldo acreedor.

credit card, *n.* tarjeta de crédito *f.*

creditor, *n.* acreedor -ra.

credit union, banco cooperativo *m.*

credo, *n.* credo *m.*

credulity, *n.* credulidad *f.*

credulous, *a.* crédulo.

creed, *n.* credo *m.*

creek, *n.* riachuelo *m.*

creep, *v.* gatear.

cremate, *v.* incinerar.

crematory, *n.* crematorio *m.*

creosote, *n.* creosota *f.*

crepe, *n.* crespón *m.*

crepe paper, papel crespón *m.*

crescent, *a. & n.* creciente *f.*

crest, *n.* cresta; cima *f.;* (heraldry) timbre *m.*

cretonne, *n.* cretona *f.*

crevice, *n.* grieta *f.*

crew, *n.* tripulación *f.*

crew member, tripulante *m. & f.*

crib, *n.* pesebre *m.;* cuna.

cricket, *n.* grillo *m.*

crime, *n.* crimen *m.*

criminal, *a. & n.* criminal *m. & f.*

criminologist, *n.* criminólogo -ga, criminalista *m. & f.*

criminology, *n.* criminología *f.*

crimson, *a. & n.* carmesí *m.*

cringe, *v.* encogerse, temblar.

cripple, 1. *n.* lisiado -da. **2.** *v.* estropear, lisiar.

crisis, *n.* crisis *f.*

crisp, *a.* crespo, fresco.

crispness, *n.* encrespadura *f.*

crisscross, *a.* entrelazado.

criterion, *n.* criterio *m.*

critic, *n.* crítico -ca.

critical, *a.* crítico.

criticism, *n.* crítica; censura *f.*

criticize, *v.* criticar; censurar.

critique, *n.* crítica *f.*

croak, 1. *n.* graznido *m.* **2.** *v.* graznar.

crochet, 1. *n.* crochet *m.* **2.** *v.* hacer crochet.

crochet work, ganchillo *m.*

crock, *n.* cazuela *f.;* olla de barro.

crockery, *n.* loza *f.*

crocodile, *n.* cocodrilo *m.*

crony, *n.* compinche *m.*

crooked, *a.* encorvado; deshonesto.

croon, *v.* canturrear.

crop, *n.* cosecha *f.*

croquet, *n.* juego de croquet *m.*

croquette, *n.* croqueta *f.*

cross, 1. *a.* enojado, mal humorado. **2.** *n.* cruz *f.* **3.** *v.* cruzar, atravesar.

crossbreed, 1. *n.* mestizo *m.* **2.** *v.* cruzar (animales o plantas).

cross-examine, *v.* interrogar.

cross-eyed, *a.* bizco.

cross-fertilization, *n.* alogamia *f.*

crossing, crossroads, *n.* cruce *m.*

cross section, corte transversal *m.*

crosswalk, *n.* paso cebra *m.*

crossword, crossword puzzle, *n.* crucigrama *m.*

crotch, *n.* bifurcación *f.;* (anat.) bragadura *f.*

crouch, *v.* agacharse.

croup, *n.* (med.) crup *m.*

croupier, *n.* crupié *m. & f.*

crow, *n.* cuervo *m.*

crowd, 1. *n.* muchedumbre *f.;* tropel *m.* **2.** *v.* apretar.

crowded, *a.* lleno de gente.

crown, 1. *n.* corona *f.* **2.** *v.* coronar.

crown prince, príncipe heredero *m.*

crucial, *a.* crucial.

crucible, *n.* crisol *f.*

crucifix, *n.* crucifijo *m.*

crucifixion, *n.* crucifixión *f.*

crucify, *v.* crucificar.

crude, *a.* crudo; (oil) bruto.

crudeness, *a.* crudeza *f.*

cruel, *a.* cruel.

cruelty, *n.* crueldad *f.*

cruet, *n.* vinagrera *f.*

cruise, 1. *n.* viaje por mar. **2.** *v.* navegar.

cruiser, *n.* crucero *m.*

crumb, *n.* miga; migaja *f.*

crumble, *v.* desmigajar; desmoronar.

crumple, *v.* arrugar; encogerse.

crusade, *n.* cruzada *f.*

crusader, *n.* cruzado *m.*

crush, *v.* aplastar.

crust, *n.* costra; corteza *f.*

crustacean, *n.* crustáceo *m.*

crutch, *n.* muleta *f.*

cry, 1. *n.* grito *m.* **2.** *v.* gritar; (weep) llorar.

cryosurgery, *n.* criocirugía *f.*

crypt, *n.* gruta *f.,* cripta *f.*

cryptic, *a.* secreto.

cryptography, *n.* criptografía *f.*

crystal, *n.* cristal *m.*

crystalline, *a.* cristalino, transparente.

crystallize, *v.* cristalizar.

cub, *n.* cachorro *m.*

Cuban, *n. & a.* cubano -na.

cube, *n.* cubo *m.*

cubic, *a.* cúbico.

cubicle, *n.* cubículo *m.*

cubic measure, medida de capacidad *f.*

cubism, *n.* cubismo *m.*

cuckoo, *n.* cuco *m.*

cucumber, *n.* pepino *m.*

cuddle, *v.* abrazar.

cudgel, *n.* palo *m.*

cue, *n.* apunte *m.;* (billiards) taco *m.*

cuff, *n.* puño de camisa. **c. links,** gemelos.

cuisine, *n.* arte culinario *m.*

culinary, *a.* culinario.

culminate, *v.* culminar.

culmination, *n.* culminación *f.*

culpable, *a.* culpable.

culprit, *n.* criminal; delincuente *m. & f.*

cult, *n.* culto *m.*

cultivate, *v.* cultivar.

cultivated, *a.* cultivado.

cultivation, *n.* cultivo *m.;* cultivación *f.*

cultivator, *n.* cultivador -ra.

cultural, *a.* cultural.

culture, *n.* cultura *f.*

cultured, *a.* culto.

cumbersome, *a.* pesado, incómodo.

cumulative, *a.* acumulativo.

cunning, 1. *a.* astuto. **2.** *n.* astucia *f.*

cup, *n.* taza, jícara *f.*

cupboard, *n.* armario, aparador *m.*

cupidity, *n.* avaricia *f.*

curable, *a.* curable.

curator, *n.* guardián -ana.

curb, 1. *n.* freno *m.* **2.** *v.* refrenar.

curd, *n.* cuajada *f.*

curdle, *v.* cuajarse, coagularse.

cure, 1. *n.* remedio *m.* **2.** *v.* curar, sanar.

curfew, *n.* toque de queda *m.*

curio, *n.* objeto curioso.

curiosity, *n.* curiosidad *f.*

curious, *a.* curioso.

curl, 1. *n.* rizo *m.* **2.** *v.* rizar.

curly, *a.* rizado.

currant, *n.* grosella *f.*

currency, *n.* circulación *f.;* dinero *m.*

current, *a. & n.* corriente *f.*

current events, actualidades *f.pl.*

currently, *adv.* corrientemente.

curriculum, *n.* plan de estudio *m.*

curse, 1. *n.* maldición *f.* **2.** *v.* maldecir.

cursor, *n.* cursor *m.*

cursory, *a.* sumario.

curt, *a.* brusco.

curtail, *v.* reducir; restringir.

curtain, *n.* cortina *f.;* (theat.) telón *m.*

curtsy, 1. *n.* reverencia *f.* **2.** *v.* hacer una reverencia.

curvature, *n.* curvatura *f.*

curve, 1. *n.* curva *f.* **2.** *v.* encorvar.

cushion, *n.* cojín *m.;* almohada *f.*

cuspidor, *n.* escupidera *f.*

custard, *n.* flan *m.;* natillas *f.pl.*

custodian, *n.* custodio *m.*

custody, *n.* custodia *f.*

custom, *n.* costumbre *f.*

customary, *a.* acostumbrado, usual.

customer, *n.* cliente *m. & f.*

customhouse, customs, *n.* aduana *f.*

customs duty, derechos de aduana *m.pl.*

customs officer, agente de aduana *m. & f.*

cut, 1. *n.* corte *m.;* cortada *f.;* tajada *f.;* (printing) grabado *m.* **2.** *v.* cortar; tajar.

cute, *a.* mono, lindo.

cut glass, cristal tallado *m.*

cuticle, *n.* cutícula *f.*

cutlery, *n.* cuchillería *f.*

cutlet, *n.* chuleta *f.*

cutter, *n.* cortador -ra; (naut.) cúter *m.*

cutthroat, *n.* asesino -na.

cyclamate, *n.* ciclamato *m.*

cycle, *n.* ciclo *m.*

cyclist, *n.* ciclista *m. & f.*

cyclone, *n.* ciclón, huracán *m.*

cyclotron, *n.* ciclotrón *m.*

cylinder, *n.* cilindro *m.*

cylindrical, *a.* cilíndrico.

cymbal, *n.* címbalo *m.*

cynic, *n.* cínico -ca.

cynical, *a.* cínico.

cynicism, *n.* cinismo *m.*

cypress, *n.* ciprés *m.* **c. nut,** piñuela *f.*

cyst, *n.* quiste *m.*

D

dad, *n.* papá *m.,* papito *m.*

daffodil, *n.* narciso *m.*

dagger, *n.* puñal *m.*

dahlia, *n.* dalia *f.*

daily, *a.* diario, cotidiano.

daintiness, *n.* delicadeza *f.*

dainty, *a.* delicado.

dairy, *n.* lechería, quesería *f.*

dais, *n.* tablado *m.*

daisy, *n.* margarita *f.*

dale, *n.* valle *m.*

dally, *v.* holgar; perder el tiempo.

dam, *n.* presa *f.;* dique *m.*

damage, 1. *n.* daño *m.* **2.** *v.* dañar.

damask, *n.* damasco *m.*

damn, *v.* condenar.

damnation, *n.* condenación *f.*

damp, *a.* húmedo.

dampen, *v.* humedecer.

dampness, *n.* humedad *f.*

damsel, *n.* doncella *f.*

dance, 1. *n.* baile *m.;* danza *f.* **2.** *v.* bailar.

dance hall, salón de baile *m.*

dancer, *n.* bailador -ra; (professional) bailarín -na.

dancing, *n.* baile *m.*

dandelion, *n.* amargón *m.*

dandruff, *n.* caspa *f.*

dandy, *n.* petimetre *m.*

danger, *n.* peligro *m.*

dangerous, *a.* peligroso.

dangle, *v.* colgar.

Danish, *a. & n.* danés -sa; dinamarqués -sa.

dapper, *a.* gallardo.

dare, *v.* atreverse, osar.

daredevil, *n.* atrevido *m.,* -da *f.*

daring, 1. *a.* atrevido. **2.** *n.* osadía *f.*

dark, 1. *a.* obscuro; moreno. **2.** *n.* obscuridad *f.*

darken, *v.* obscurecer.

darkness, *n.* obscuridad *f.*

darkroom, *n.* cámara obscura *f.*

darling, *a. & n.* querido -da, amado -da.

darn, *v.* zurcir.

darning needle, aguja de zurcir *m.*

dart, *n.* dardo *m.*

dartboard, *n.* diana *f.*

dash, *n.* arranque *m.;* (punct.) guión *m.*

data, *n.* datos *m.*

database, *n.* base de datos *m.*

data processing, proceso de datos *m.*

date, *n.* fecha *f.;* (engagement) cita *f.;* (fruit) dátil *m.*

daughter, *n.* hija *f.*

daughter-in-law, *n.* nuera *f.*

daunt, *v.* intimidar.

dauntless, *a.* intrépido.

davenport, *n.* sofá *m.*

dawn, 1. *n.* alba, madrugada *f.* **2.** *v.* amanecer.

day, *n.* día *m.* **good d.,** buenos días.

daybreak, *n.* alba, madrugada *f.*

daydream, *n.* fantasía *f.*

daylight, n. luz del día.
daze, v. aturdir.
dazzle, v. deslumbrar.
deacon, n. diácono m.
dead, a. muerto.
deaden, v. amortecer.
dead end, atolladero m. (impasse); callejón sin salida m. (street).
deadline, n. fecha límite f.
deadlock, n. paro m.
deadly, a. mortal.
deaf, a. sordo.
deafen, v. ensordecer.
deafening, a. ensordecedor.
deaf-mute, n. sordomudo -da.
deafness, n. sordera f.
deal, 1. n. trato m.; negociación f. **a great d., a good d.,** mucho. 2. v. tratar; negociar.
dealer, n. comerciante m., (at cards) tallador -ra.
dean, n. decano -na.
dear, a. querido; caro.
dearth, n. escasez f.
death, n. muerte f.
death certificate, partida de defunción f.
deathless, a. inmortal.
debacle, n. desastre m.
debase, v. degradar.
debatable, a. discutible.
debate, 1. n. debate m. 2. v. disputar, deliberar.
debauch, v. corromper.
debilitate, v. debilitar.
debit, n. débito m.
debit balance, saldo deudor m.
debonair, a. cortés; alegre, vivo.
debris, n. escombros m.pl.
debt, n. deuda f. **get into d.** endeudarse.
debtor, n. deudor -ra.
debunk, v. desacreditar; desenmascarar.
debut, n. debut, estreno m.
debutante, n. debutante f.
decade, n. década f.
decadence, n. decadencia f.
decadent, a. decadente.
decaffeinated, a. descafeinado.
decalcomania, n. calcomanía f.

decanter, n. garrafa f.
decapitate, v. descabezar.
decay, 1. n. descaecimiento m.; (dental) caries f. 2. v. decaer; (dental) cariarse.
deceased, a. muerto, difunto.
deceit, n. engaño m.
deceitful, a. engañoso.
deceive, v. engañar.
December, n. diciembre m.
decency, n. decencia f.; decoro m.
decent, a. decente.
decentralize, v. descentralizar.
deception, n. decepción f.
deceptive, a. deceptivo.
decibel, n. decibelio m.
decimal, a. decimal.
decide, v. decidir.
decipher, v. descifrar.
decision, n. decisión f.
decisive, a. decisivo.
deck, n. cubierta f.
deckchair, m. tumbona f.
declamation, n. declamación f.
declaration, n. declaración f.
declarative, a. declarativo.
declare, v. declarar.
declension, n. declinación f.
decline, 1. n. decadencia f. 2. v. decaer; negarse; (gram.) declinar.
decompose, v. descomponer.
decongestant, n. descongestionante m.
decorate, v. decorar, adornar.
decoration, n. decoración f.
decorative, a. decorativo.
decorator, n. decorador -ra.
decorous, a. correcto.
decorum, n. decoro m.
decrease, v. disminuir.
decree, n. decreto m.
decrepit, a. decrépito.
decry, v. desacreditar.
dedicate, v. dedicar; consagrar.
dedication, n. dedicación; dedicatoria f.
deduce, deduct, v. deducir.
deduction, n. rebaja; deducción f.
deductive, a. deductivo.
deed, n. acción; hazaña f.
deem, v. estimar.
deep, a. hondo, profundo.

deepen, v. profundizar, ahondar.
deep freeze, congelación f.
deeply, adv. profundamente.
deer, n. venado, ciervo m.
deface, v. mutilar.
defamation, n. calumnia f.
defame, v. difamar.
default, 1. n. defecto m. 2. v. faltar.
defeat, 1. n. derrota f. 2. v. derrotar.
defeatism, n. derrotismo m.
defect, n. defecto m.
defective, a. defectivo.
defend, v. defender.
defendant, n. acusado -da.
defender, n. defensor -ra.
defense, n. defensa f.
defensive, a. defensivo.
defer, v. aplazar; diferir.
deference, n. deferencia f.
defiance, n. desafío m.
defiant, a. desafiador.
deficiency, n. defecto m.
deficient, a. deficiente.
deficit, n. déficit, descubierto m.
defile, 1. n. desfiladero m. 2. v. profanar.
define, v. definir.
definite, a. exacto; definitivo.
definitely, adv. definitivamente.
definition, n. definición f.
definitive, a. definitivo.
deflation, n. desinflación f.
deflect, v. desviar.
deform, v. deformar.
deformity, n. deformidad f.
defraud, v. defraudar.
defray, v. costear.
defrost, v. descongelar.
deft, a. diestro.
defy, v. desafiar.
degenerate, 1. a. degenerado. 2. v. degenerar.
degeneration, n. degeneración f.
degradation, n. degradación f.
degrade, v. degradar.
degree, n. grado m.
deign. v. condescender.
deity, n. deidad f.
dejected, a. abatido.
dejection, n. tristeza f.

delay, 1. *n.* retardo *m.*, demora *f.* **2.** *v.* tardar, demorar.

delegate, 1. *n.* delegado -da. **2.** *v.* delegar.

delegation, *n.* delegación *f.*

delete, *v.* suprimir, tachar.

deliberate, 1. *a.* premeditado. **2.** *v.* deliberar.

deliberately, *adv.* deliberadamente.

deliberation, *n.* deliberación *f.*

deliberative, *a.* deliberativo.

delicacy, *n.* delicadeza *f.*

delicate, *a.* delicado.

delicious, *a.* delicioso.

delight, *n.* deleite *m.*

delightful, *a.* deleitoso.

delinquency, *a.* delincuencia *f.*

delinquent, *a.* & *n.* delincuente. *m.* & *f.*

delirious, *a.* delirante.

deliver, *v.* entregar.

deliverance, *n.* liberación; salvación *f.*

delivery, *n.* entrega *f.*; (med.) parto *m.*

delude, *v.* engañar.

deluge, *n.* inundación *f.*

delusion, *n.* decepción *f.*; engaño *m.*

delve, *v.* cavar, sondear.

demagogue, *n.* demagogo -ga.

demand, 1. *n.* demanda *f.* **2.** *v.* demandar; exigir.

demarcation, *n.* demarcación *f.*

demeanor, *n.* conducta *f.*

demented, *a.* demente, loco.

demilitarize, *v.* desmilitarizar.

demobilize, *v.* desmovilizar.

democracy, *n.* democracia *f.*

democrat, *n.* demócrata *m.* & *f.*

democratic, *a.* democrático.

demolish, *v.* demoler.

demon, *n.* demonio *m.*

demonstrate, *v.* demostrar.

demonstration, *n.* demostración *f.*

demonstrative, *a.* demostrativo.

demoralize, *v.* desmoralizar.

demure, *a.* modesto, serio.

den, *n.* madriguera, caverna *f.*

denature, *v.* alterar.

denial, *n.* negación *f.*

denim, *n.* dril, tela vaquera.

Denmark, *n.* Dinamarca *f.*

denomination, *n.* denominación; secta *f.*

denote, *v.* denotar.

denounce, *v.* denunciar.

dense, *a.* denso, espeso; estúpido.

density, *n.* densidad *f.*

dent, 1. *n.* abolladura *f.* **2.** *v.* abollar.

dental, *a.* dental.

dentist, *n.* dentista *m.* & *f.*

dentistry, *n.* odontología *f.*

denture, *n.* dentadura *f.*

denunciation, *n.* denunciación *f.*

deny, *v.* negar, rehusar.

deodorant, *n.* desodorante *m.*

depart, *v.* partir; irse, marcharse.

department, *n.* departamento *m.*

department store, grandes almacenes *m.pl.*

departmental, *a.* departamental.

departure, *n.* salida; desviación *f.*

depend, *v.* depender.

dependability, *n.* confiabilidad *f.*

dependable, *a.* confiable.

dependence, *n.* dependencia *f.*

dependent, *a.* & *n.* dependiente *m.* & *f.*

depict, *v.* pintar; representar.

deplete, *v.* agotar.

deplorable, *a.* deplorable.

deplore, *v.* deplorar.

deport, *v.* deportar.

deportation, *n.* deportación *f.*

deportment, *n.* conducta *f.*

depose, *v.* deponer.

deposit, 1. *n.* depósito *m.* (of money); yacimiento (of ore, etc.) *m.* **2.** *v.* depositar.

depositor, *n.* depositante *m.* & *f.*

depot, *n.* depósito *m.*; (railway) estación *f.*

depravity, *n.* depravación *f.*

deprecate, *v.* deprecar.

depreciate, *v.* depreciar.

depreciation, *n.* depreciación *f.*

depredation, *n.* depredación *f.*

depress, *v.* deprimir; desanimar.

depression, *n.* depresión *f.*

deprive, *v.* privar.

depth, *n.* profundidad, hondura *f.*

depth charge, carga de profundidad *f.*

deputy, *n.* diputado -da.

deride, *v.* burlar.

derision, *n.* burla *f.*

derivation, *n.* derivación *f.*

derivative, *a.* derivativo.

derive, *v.* derivar.

dermatologist, *n.* dermatólogo -ga.

derogatory, *a.* derogatorio.

derrick, *n.* grúa *f.*

descend, *v.* descender, bajar.

descendant, *n.* descendiente *m.* & *f.*

descent, *n.* descenso *m.*; origen *m.*

describe, *v.* describir.

description, *n.* descripción *f.*

descriptive, *a.* descriptivo.

desecrate, *v.* profanar.

desert, 1. *n.* desierto *m.* **2.** *v.* abandonar.

deserter, *n.* desertor -ra.

desertion, *n.* deserción *f.*

deserve, *v.* merecer.

design, 1. *n.* diseño *m.* **2.** *v.* diseñar.

designate, *v.* señalar, apuntar; designar.

designation, *n.* designación *f.*

designer, *n.* diseñador -ra; (technical) proyectista *m.* & *f.*

designer clothes, designer clothing, ropa de marca *f.*

desirability, *n.* conveniencia *f.*

desirable, *a.* deseable.

desire, 1. *n.* deseo *m.* **2.** *v.* desear.

desirous, *a.* deseoso.

desist, v. desistir.

desk, n. escritorio m.

desk clerk, recepcionista m. & f.

desktop computer, computadora de sobremesa f., ordenador de sobremesa f.

desolate, 1. a. desolado. **2.** v. desolar.

desolation, n. desolación, ruina f.

despair, 1. n. desesperación f. **2.** v. desesperar.

despatch, dispatch, 1. n. despacho m.; prontitud f. **2.** v. despachar.

desperado, n. bandido m.

desperate, a. desesperado.

desperation, n. desesperación f.

despicable, a. vil.

despise, v. despreciar.

despite, prep. a pesar de.

despondent, a. abatido; desanimado.

despot, n. déspota m. & f.

despotic, a. despótico.

dessert, n. postre m.

destination, n. destinación f.

destine, v. destinar.

destiny, n. destino m.

destitute, a. destituído, indigente.

destitution, n. destitución f.

destroy, v. destrozar, destruir.

destroyer, n. destruidor -ra; (naval) destructor m.

destruction, n. destrucción f.

destructive, a. destructivo.

desultory, a. inconexo; casual.

detach, v. separar, desprender.

detachment, n. (mil.) destacamento; desprendimiento m.

detail, 1. n. detalle m. **2.** v. detallar.

detain, v. detener.

detect, v. descubrir.

detection, n. detección f.

detective, n. detective m. & f.

détente, n. distensión f.; (pd.) deténte.

detention, n. detención; cautividad f.

deter, v. disuadir.

detergent, n. & a. detergente m.

deteriorate, v. deteriorar.

deterioration, n. deterioración f.

determination, n. determinación f.

determine, v. determinar.

deterrence, n. disuasión f.

detest, v. detestar.

detonate, v. detonar.

detour, 1. n. desvío m. **2.** v. desviar.

detract, v. disminuir.

detriment, n. detrimento m., daño m.

detrimental, a. dañoso.

devaluate, v. depreciar.

devastate, v. devastar.

develop, v. desarrollar; (phot.) revelar.

developing nation, nación en desarrollo.

development, n. desarrollo m.

deviate, v. desviar.

deviation, n. desviación f.

device, n. aparato; artificio m.

devil, n. diablo, demonio m.

devious, a. desviado.

devise, v. inventar.

devoid, a. desprovisto.

devote, v. dedicar, consagrar.

devoted, a. devoto.

devotee, n. aficionado -da.

devotion, n. devoción f.

devour, v. devorar.

devout, a. devoto.

dew, n. rocío, sereno m.

dexterity, n. destreza f.

dexterous, a. diestro.

diabetes, n. diabetes f.

diabolic, a. diabólico.

diadem, n. diadema f.

diagnose, v. diagnosticar.

diagnosis, n. diagnóstico m.

diagonal, n. diagonal f.

diagram, n. diagrama m.

dial, n. cuadrante m., carátula f.

dialect, n. dialecto m.

dialing code, prefijo m.

dialogue, n. diálogo m.

dial tone, señal de marcar f.

diameter, n. diámetro m.

diamond, n. diamante, brillante m.

diaper, n. pañal m.

diarrhea, n. diarrea f.

diary, n. diario m.

diathermy, n. diatermia f.

dice, n. dados m.pl.

dictate, 1. n. mandato m. **2.** v. dictar.

dictation, n. dictado m.

dictator, n. dictador -ra.

dictatorship, n. dictadura f.

diction, n. dicción f.

dictionary, n. diccionario m.

die, 1. n. matriz f.; (game) dado m. **2.** v. morir.

diet, n. dieta f.

dietary, a. dietético.

dietitian, n. & a. dietético - ca.

differ, v. diferir.

difference, n. diferencia f. **to make no d.,** no importar.

different, a. diferente, distinto.

differential, n. diferencial f.

differentiate, v. diferenciar.

difficult, a. difícil.

difficulty, n. dificultad f.

diffident, a. tímido.

diffuse, v. difundir.

diffusion, n. difusión f.

dig, v. cavar.

digest, 1. n. extracto m. **2.** v. digerir.

digestible, a. digerible.

digestion, n. digestión f.

digestive, a. digestivo.

digital, a. digital.

digitalis, n. digital f.

dignified, a. digno.

dignify, v. dignificar.

dignitary, n. dignatario -ria.

dignity, n. dignidad f.

digress, v. divagar.

digression, n. digresión f.

dike, n. dique m.

dilapidated, a. dilapidado.

dilapidation, n. dilapidación f.

dilate, v. dilatar.

dilatory, a. dilatorio.

dilemma, n. dilema m.

dilettante, n. diletante m. & f.

diligence, n. diligencia f.

diligent, a. diligente, aplicado.

dilute, v. diluir.

dim, 1. *a.* oscuro. **2.** *v.* oscurecer.

dimension, *n.* dimensión *f.*

diminish, *v.* disminuir.

diminution, *n.* disminución *f.*

diminutive, *a.* diminutivo.

dimness, *n.* oscuridad *f.*

dimple, *n.* hoyuelo *m.*

din, *n.* alboroto, estrépito *m.*

dine, *v.* comer, cenar.

diner, *n.* coche comedor *m.*

dingy, *a.* deslucido, deslustrado.

dining room, comedor *m.*

dinner, *n.* comida, cena *f.*

dinosaur, *n.* dinosauro *m.*

diocese, *n.* diócesis *f.*

dip, *v.* sumergir, hundir.

diphtheria, *n.* difteria *f.*

diploma, *n.* diploma *m.*

diplomacy, *n.* diplomacia *f.*

diplomat, *n.* diplomático -ca.

diplomatic, *a.* diplomático.

dipper, *n.* cucharón *m.*

dire, *a.* horrendo.

direct, 1. *a.* directo. **2.** *v.* dirigir.

direction, *n.* dirección *f.*

directive, *n.* directiva *f.*

directly, *adv.* directamente.

director, *n.* director -ra.

directory, *n.* directorio *m.,* guía *f.*

dirigible, *n.* dirigible *m.*

dirt, *n.* basura *f.;* (earth) tierra *f.*

dirt-cheap, *a.* tirado.

dirty, *a.* sucio.

disability, *n.* inhabilidad *f.*

disable, *v.* incapacitar.

disabuse, *v.* desengañar.

disadvantage, *n.* desventaja *f.*

disagree, *v.* desconvenir; disentir.

disagreeable, *a.* desagradable.

disagreement, *n.* desacuerdo *m.*

disappear, *v.* desaparecer.

disappearance, *n.* desaparición *f.*

disappoint, *v.* disgustar, desilusionar.

disappointment, *n.* disgusto *m.,* desilusión *f.*

disapproval, *n.* desaprobación *f.*

disapprove, *v.* desaprobar.

disarm, *v.* desarmar.

disarmament, *n.* desarme *m.*

disarrange, *v.* desordenar; desarreglar.

disaster, *n.* desastre *m.*

disastrous, *a.* desastroso.

disavow, *v.* repudiar.

disavowal, *n.* repudiación *f.*

disband, *v.* dispersarse.

disbelieve, *v.* descreer.

disburse, *v.* desembolsar, pagar.

discard, *v.* descartar.

discern, *v.* discernir.

discerning, *a.* discernidor, perspicaz.

discernment, *n.* discernimiento *m.*

discharge, *v.* descargar; despedir.

disciple, *n.* discípulo -la.

disciplinary, *a.* disciplinario.

discipline, *n.* disciplina *f.*

disclaim, *v.* repudiar.

disclaimer, *n.* negación *f.*

disclose, *v.* revelar.

disclosure, *n.* revelación *f.*

disco, *n.* discoteca *f.*

discolor, *v.* descolorar.

discomfort, *n.* incomodidad *f.*

disconcert, *v.* desconcertar.

disconnect, *v.* desunir; desconectar.

disconnected, *a.* desunido.

disconsolate, *a.* desconsolado.

discontent, *n.* descontento *m.*

discontented, *a.* descontento.

discontinue, *v.* descontinuar.

discord, *n.* discordia *f.*

discordant, *a.* disonante.

discotheque, *n.* discoteca *f.*

discount, *n.* descuento *m.*

discourage, *v.* desalentar, desanimar.

discouragement, *n.* desaliento, desánimo *m.*

discourse, *n.* discurso *m.*

discourteous, *a.* descortés.

discourtesy, *n.* descortesía *f.*

discover, *v.* descubrir.

discoverer, *n.* descubridor -ra.

discovery, *n.* descubrimiento *m.*

discreet, *a.* discreto.

discrepancy, *n.* discrepancia *f.*

discretion, *n.* discreción *f.*

discriminate, *v.* distinguir. **d. against** discriminar contra.

discrimination, *n.* discernimiento *m.; discriminación *f.*

discuss, *v.* discutir.

discussion, *n.* discusión *f.*

disdain, 1. *n.* desdén *m.* **2.** *v.* desdeñar.

disdainful, *a.* desdeñoso.

disease, *n.* enfermedad *f.,* mal *m.*

disembark, *v.* desembarcar.

disentangle, *v.* desenredar.

disfigure, *v.* desfigurar.

disgrace, 1. *n.* vergüenza; deshonra *f.* **2.** *v.* deshonrar.

disgraceful, *a.* vergonzoso.

disguise, 1. *n.* disfraz *m.* **2.** *v.* disfrazar.

disgust, 1. *n.* repugnancia **2.** *v.* fastidiar; repugnar.

dish, *n.* plato *m.*

dishearten, *v.* desanimar; descorazonar.

dishonest, *a.* deshonesto.

dishonesty, *n.* deshonestidad *f.*

dishonor, 1. *n.* deshonra *f.* **2.** *v.* deshonrar.

dishonorable, *a.* deshonroso.

dishwasher, *n.* lavaplatos *m.*

disillusion, 1. *n.* desengaño *m.* **2.** *v.* desengañar.

disinfect, *v.* desinfectar.

disinfectant, *n.* desinfectante *m.*

disinherit, *v.* desheredar.

disintegrate, *v.* desintegrar.

disinterested, *a.* desinteresado.

disk, *n.* disco *m.*

disk drive, disquetera *f.*

diskette, *n.* disquete *m.*

disk jockey, pinchadiscos *m. & f.*

dislike, 1. *n.* antipatía *f.* **2.** *v.* no gustar de.

dislocate, *v.* dislocar.

dislodge, v. desalojar; desprender.

disloyal, a. desleal; infiel.

disloyalty, n. deslealtad f.

dismal, a. lúgubre.

dismantle, v. desmantelar, desmontar.

dismay, 1. n. consternación f. **2.** v. consternar.

dismiss, v. despedir.

dismissal, n. despedida f.

dismount, v. apearse, desmontarse.

disobedience, n. desobediencia f.

disobedient, a. desobediente.

disobey, v. desobedecer.

disorder, n. desorden m.

disorderly, a. desarreglado, desordenado.

disown, v. repudiar.

dispassionate, a. desapasionado; templado.

dispatch, 1. n. despacho m. **2.** v. despachar.

dispel, v. dispersar.

dispensary, n. dispensario m.

dispensation, n. dispensación f.

dispense, v. dispensar.

dispersal, n. dispersión f.

disperse, v. dispersar.

displace, v. dislocar.

display, 1. n. despliegue m., exhibición f. **2.** v. desplegar, exhibir.

displease, v. disgustar; ofender.

displeasure, n. disgusto, sinsabor m.

disposable, a. disponible; desechable.

disposal, n. disposición f.

dispose, v. disponer.

disposition, n. disposición f.; índole f., genio m.

dispossess, v. desposeer.

disproportionate, a. desproporcionado.

disprove, v. confutar.

dispute, 1. n. disputa f. **2.** v. disputar.

disqualify, v. inhabilitar.

disregard, 1. n. desatención f. **2.** v. desatender.

disrepair, n. descompostura f.

disreputable, a. desacreditado.

disrespect, n. falta de respeto, f., desacato m.

disrespectful, a. irrespetuoso.

disrobe, v. desvestir.

disrupt, v. romper; desbaratar.

dissatisfaction, n. descontento m.

dissatisfy, v. descontentar.

dissect, v. disecar.

dissemble, v. disimular.

disseminate, v. diseminar.

dissension, n. disensión f.

dissent, 1. n. disensión f. **2.** v. disentir.

dissertation, n. disertación f.

dissimilar, a. desemejante.

dissipate, v. disipar.

dissipation, n. disipación f.; libertinaje m.

dissolute, a. disoluto.

dissolution, n. disolución f.

dissolve, v. disolver; derretirse.

dissonant, a. disonante.

dissuade, v. disuadir.

distance, n. distancia f. **at a d., in the d.,** a lo lejos.

distant, a. distante, lejano.

distaste, n. disgusto, sinsabor m.

distasteful, a. desagradable.

distill, v. destilar.

distillation, n. destilación f.

distillery, n. destilería f.

distinct, a. distinto.

distinctive, a. distintivo; característico.

distinctly, adv. distintamente.

distinction, n. distinción f.

distinguish, v. distinguir.

distinguished, a. distinguido.

distort, v. falsear; torcer.

distract, v. distraer.

distraction, n. distracción f.

distraught, a. aturrullado; demente.

distress, 1. n. dolor m. **2.** v. afligir.

distressing, a. penoso.

distribute, v. distribuir.

distribution, n. distribución f.; reparto m.

distributor, n. distribuidor - ra.

district, n. distrito m.

distrust, 1. n. desconfianza f. **2.** v. desconfiar.

distrustful, a. desconfiado; sospechoso.

disturb, v. incomodar; inquietar.

disturbance, n. disturbio m.

disturbing, a. inquietante.

ditch, n. zanja f.; foso m.

divan, n. diván m.

dive, 1. n. clavado m.; (coll.) leonera f. **2.** v. echar un clavado; bucear.

diver, n. buzo m.

diverge, v. divergir.

divergence, n. divergencia f.

divergent, a. divergente.

diverse, a. diverso.

diversion, n. diversión f.; pasatiempo m.

diversity, n. diversidad f.

divert, v. desviar; divertir.

divest, v. desnudar, despojar.

divide, v. dividir.

dividend, n. dividendo m.

divine, a. divino.

divinity, n. divinidad f.

division, n. división f.

divorce, 1. n. divorcio m. **2.** v. divorciar.

divorcee, n. divorciado -da.

divulge, v. divulgar, revelar.

dizziness, n. vértigo, mareo m.

dizzy, a. mareado.

DNA, abbr. (deoxyribonucleic acid) ADN (ácido deoxirribonucleico) m.

do, v. hacer.

docile, a. dócil.

dock, 1. n. muelle m. **dry d.,** astillero m. **2.** v. entrar en muelle.

doctor, n. médico m.; doctor -ra.

doctorate, n. doctorado m.

doctrine, n. doctrina f.

document, n. documento m.

documentary, a. documental.

documentation, n. documentación f.

dodge, 1. n. evasión f. **2.** v. evadir.

dodgem, *n.* coche de choque *m.*

doe, *n.* gama *f.*

dog, *n.* perro -a.

dogma, *n.* dogma *m.*

dogmatic, *a.* dogmático.

dogmatism, *n.* dogmatismo *m.*

doily, *n.* servilletita *f.*

doleful, *a.* triste.

doll, *n.* muñeca -co.

dollar, *n.* dólar *m.*

dolorous, *a.* lastimoso.

dolphin, *n.* delⁿⁿ *m.*

domain, *n.* dominio *m.*

dome, *n.* domo *m.*

domestic, *a.* doméstico.

domesticate, *v.* domesticar.

domicile, *n.* domicilio *m.*

dominance, *n.* dominación *f.*

dominant, *a.* dominante.

dominate, *v.* dominar.

domination, *n.* dominación *f.*

domineer, *v.* dominar.

domineering, *a.* tiránico, mandón.

dominion, *n.* dominio; territorio *m.*

domino, *n.* dominó *m.*

donate, *v.* donar; contribuir.

donation, *n.* donación *f.*

donkey, *n.* asno, burro *m.*

doom, **1.** *n.* perdición, ruina *f.* **2.** *v.* perder, ruinar.

door, *n.* puerta *f.*

doorman, *n.* portero *m.*

doormat, *n.* felpudo *m.*

doorway, *n.* entrada *f.*

dope, *n.* (coll.) narcótico *m.*; idiota *m.*

dormant, *a.* durmiente; inactivo.

dormitory, *n.* dormitorio *m.*

dosage, *n.* dosificación *f.*

dose, *n.* dosis *f.*

dot, *n.* punto *m.*

dotted line, línea de puntos *f.*

double, **1.** *a.* doble. **2.** *v.* duplicar.

double bass, contrabajo *m.*

double-breasted, *a.* cruzado.

double-cross, *v.* traicionar.

doubly, *adv.* doblemente.

doubt, **1.** *n.* duda *f.* **2.** *v.* dudar.

doubtful, *a.* dudoso, incierto.

doubtless, **1.** *a.* indudable. **2.** *adv.* sin duda.

dough, *n.* pasta, masa *f.*

doughnut, *n.* buñuelo *m.*

dove, *n.* paloma *f.*

dowager, *n.* viuda (con título) *f.*

down, **1.** *adv.* abajo. **2.** *prep.* **d. the street,** *etc.* calle abajo, *etc.*

downcast, *a.* cabizbajo.

downfall, *n.* ruina, perdición *f.*

downhearted, *a.* descorazonado.

downpour, *n.* chaparrón *m.*

downright, *a.* absoluto, completo.

downriver, *adv.* aguas abajo, río abajo.

downstairs, **1.** *adv.* abajo. **2.** *n.* primer piso.

downstream, *adv.* aguas abajo, río abajo.

downtown, *adv.* al centro, en el centro.

downward, **1.** *a.* descendente. **2.** *adv.* hacia abajo.

dowry, *n.* dote *f.*

doze, *v.* dormitar.

dozen, *n.* docena *f.*

draft, **1.** *n.* dibujo *m.*; (com.) giro *m.*; (mil.) conscripción *f.* **2.** *v.* dibujar; (mil.) reclutar.

draftee, *n.* conscripto *m.*

draft notice, notificación de reclutamiento *f.*

drag, *v.* arrastrar.

dragon, *n.* dragón *m.*

drain, **1.** *n.* desaguadero *m.* **2.** *v.* desaguar.

drainage, *n.* drenaje *m.*

drain board, escurridero *m.*

drama, *n.* drama *m.*

dramatic, *a.* dramático.

dramatics, *n.* dramática *f.*

dramatist, *n.* dramaturgo -ga.

dramatize, *v.* dramatizar.

drape, **1.** *n.* cortinas *f.pl.* **2.** *v.* vestir; adornar.

drapery, *n.* colgaduras *f.pl.*; ropaje *m.*

drastic, *a.* drástico.

draw, *v.* dibujar; atraer. **d. up,** formular.

drawback, *n.* desventaja *f.*

drawer, *n.* cajón *m.*

drawing, *n.* dibujo *m.*; rifa *f.*

dread, **1.** *n.* terror *m.* **2.** *v.* temer.

dreadful, *a.* terrible.

dreadfully, *adv.* horrendamente.

dream, **1.** *n.* sueño, ensueño *m.* **2.** *v.* soñar.

dreamer, *n.* soñador -ra; visionario -ia.

dreamy, *a.* soñador, contemplativo.

dreary, *a.* monótono y pesado.

dredge, **1.** *n.* rastra *f.* **2.** *v.* rastrear.

dregs, *n.* sedimento *m.*

drench, *v.* mojar.

dress, **1.** *n.* vestido; traje *m.* **2.** *v.* vestir.

dresser, *n.* (furniture) tocador.

dressing, *n.* (med.) curación *f.*; (cookery) relleno *m.*, salsa *f.*

dressing gown, bata *f.*

dressing table, tocador *m.*

dressmaker, *n.* modista *m.* & *f.*

drift, **1.** *n.* tendencia *f.*; (naut.) deriva *f.* **2.** *v.* (naut.) derivar; (snow) amontonarse.

drill, **1.** *n.* ejercicio *m.*; (mech.) taladro *m.* **2.** *v.* (mech.) taladrar.

drink, **1.** *n.* bebida *f.* **2.** *v.* beber, tomar.

drinkable, *a.* potable, bebible.

drip, *v.* gotear.

drive, **1.** *n.* paseo *m.* **2.** *v.* impeler; (auto.) guiar, conducir.

driver, *n.* conductor -ra; chofer *m.* **d.'s license,** permiso de conducir.

drive-in (movie theater), *n.* autocine, autocinema *m.*

driveway, *n.* entrada para coches.

drizzle, **1.** *n.* llovizna *f.* **2.** *v.* lloviznar.

dromedary, *n.* dromedario *m.*

droop, *v.* inclinarse.

drop, 1. *n.* gota *f.* **2.** *v.* soltar; dejar caer.

dropout, *n.* joven que abandona sus estudios.

dropper, *n.* cuentagotas *f.*

dropsy, *n.* hidropesía *f.*

drought, *n.* sequía *f.*

drove, *n.* manada *f.*

drown, *v.* ahogar.

drowse, *v.* adormecer.

drowsiness, *n.* somnolencia *f.*

drowsy, *a.* soñoliento.

drudge, *n.* ganapán *m.*

drudgery, *n.* trabajo penoso.

drug, 1. *n.* droga *f.* **2.** *v.* narcotizar.

drug addict, drogadicto -ta, toxicómano -na *m. & f.*

druggist, *n.* farmacéutico -ca, boticario -ria.

drugstore, *n.* farmacia, botica, droguería *f.*

drum, *n.* tambor *m.*

drummer, *n.* tambor *m.*

drumstick, *n.* palillo *m.;* (leg) pierna *f.*

drunk, *a. & n.* borracho, -a.

drunkard, *n.* borrachón *m.*

drunken, *a.* borracho; ebrio.

drunkenness, *n.* embriaguez *f.*

dry, 1. *a.* seco, árido. **2.** *v.* secar.

dry cell, *n.* pila seca *f.*

dry-cleaner, *n.* tintorero -ra.

dryness, *n.* sequedad *f.*

dual, *a.* doble.

dubious, *a.* dudoso.

duchess, *n.* duquesa *f.*

duck, 1. *n.* pato *m.* **2.** *v.* zambullir; (avoid) esquivar.

duct, *n.* canal *m.*

due, 1. *n.* debido; (com.) vencido. **2. dues,** *n.* cuota *f.*

duel, *n.* duelo *m.*

duelist, *n.* duelista *m.*

duet, *n.* dúo *m.*

duke, *n.* duque *m.*

dull, *a.* apagado, desteñido; sin punta; (fig.) pesado, soso.

dullness, *n.* estupidez; pesadez *f.;* deslustre *m.*

duly, *adv.* debidamente.

dumb, *a.* mudo; (coll.) estúpido.

dumbwaiter, *n.* montaplatos *m.*

dumfound, *v.* confundir.

dummy, *n.* maniquí *m.*

dump, 1. *n.* depósito *m.* **2.** *v.* descargar.

dune, *n.* duna *f.*

dungeon, *n.* calabozo *m.*

dunk, *v.* mojar.

dupe, *v.* engañar.

duplicate, 1. *a. & n.* duplicado *m.* **2.** *v.* duplicar.

duplication, *n.* duplicación *f.*

duplicity, *n.* duplicidad *f.*

durability, *n.* durabilidad *f.*

durable, *a.* durable, duradero.

duration, *n.* duración *f.*

duress, *n.* compulsión *f.;* encierro *m.*

during, *prep.* durante.

dusk, *n.* crepúsculo *m.*

dusky, *a.* oscuro; moreno.

dust, 1. *n.* polvo *m.* **2.** *v.* polvorear; despolvorear.

dusty, *a.* empolvado.

Dutch, *a.* holandés -sa.

dutiful, *a.* respetuoso.

dutifully, *adv.* respetuosamente, obedientemente.

duty, *n.* deber *m.;* (com.) derechos *m.pl.*

duty-free, *a.* libre de derechos.

dwarf, 1. *n.* enano -na. **2.** *v.* achicar.

dwell, *v.* habitar, residir. **d. on,** espaciarse en.

dwelling, *n.* morada, casa *f.*

dwindle, *v.* disminuirse.

dye, 1. *n.* tintura *f.* **2.** *v.* teñir.

dyer, *n.* tintorero -ra.

dynamic, *a.* dinámico.

dynamite, *n.* dinamita *f.*

dynamo, *n.* dínamo *m.*

dynasty, *n.* dinastía *f.*

dysentery, *n.* disentería *f.*

dyslexia, *n.* dislexia *f.*

dyslexic, *a.* disléxico.

dyspepsia, *n.* dispepsia *f.*

E

each, 1. *a.* cada. **2.** *pron.* cada una -na. **e. other,** el uno al otro.

eager, *a.* ansioso.

eagerly, *adv.* ansiosamente.

eagerness, *n.* ansia *f.*

eagle, *n.* águila *f.*

ear, *n.* oído *m.;* (outer) oreja *f.;* (of corn) mazorca *f.*

earache, *n.* dolor de oído *m.*

earl, *n.* conde *m.*

early, *a. & adv.* temprano.

earn, *v.* ganar.

earnest, *a.* serio.

earnestly, *adv.* seriamente.

earnings, *n.* ganancias *f.pl.;* (com.) ingresos *m.pl.*

earphone, *n.* auricular *m.*

earring, *n.* pendiente, arete *m.*

earth, *n.* tierra *f.*

earthquake, *n.* terremoto *m.*

ease, 1. *n.* reposo *m.;* facilidad *f.* **2.** *v.* aliviar.

easel, *n.* caballete *m.*

easily, *adv.* fácilmente.

east, *n.* oriente, este *m.*

Easter, *n.* Pascua Florida.

eastern, *a.* oriental.

eastward, *adv.* hacia el este.

easy, *a.* fácil.

eat, *v.* comer.

eau de Cologne, colonia *f.*

eaves, *n.* socarrén *m.*

ebb, 1. *n.* menguante *f.* **2.** *v.* menguar.

ebony, *n.* ébano *m.*

eccentric, *a.* excéntrico.

eccentricity, *n.* excentricidad *f.*

ecclesiastic, *a. & n.* eclesiástico *m.*

echelon, *n.* escalón *m.*

echo, *n.* eco *m.*

eclipse, 1. *n.* eclipse *m.* **2.** *v.* eclipsar.

ecological, *a.* ecológico.

ecology, *n.* ecología *f.*

economic, *a.* económico.

economical, *a.* económico.

economics, *n.* economía política.

economist, *n.* economista *m. & f.*

economize, *v.* economizar.

economy, *n.* economía *f.*

ecstasy, *n.* éxtasis *m.*

Ecuadorian, *a. & n.* ecuatoriano -na.

ecumenical, *a.* ecuménico.

eczema, *n.* eczema *f.*

eddy, 1. *n.* remolino *m.* **2.** *v.* remolinar.

edge, 1. *n.* filo; borde *m.* **2.** *v.* **e. one's way,** abrirse paso.

edible, *a.* comestible.

edict, *n.* edicto *m.*

edifice, *n.* edificio *m.*

edify, *v.* edificar.

edition, *n.* edición *f.*

editor, *n.* redactor -ra.

editorial, *n.* editorial *m.* **e. board,** consejo de redacción *m.* **e. staff,** redacción *f.*

educate, *v.* educar.

education, *n.* instrucción; enseñanza *f.*

educational, *a.* educativo.

educator, *n.* educador -ra, pedagogo -ga.

eel, *n.* anguila *f.*

efface, *v.* tachar.

effect, 1. *n.* efecto *m.* **in e.,** en vigor. **2.** *v.* efectuar, realizar.

effective, *a.* eficaz; efectivo; en vigor.

effectively, *adv.* eficazmente.

effectiveness, *n.* efectividad *f.*

effectual, *a.* eficaz.

effeminate, *a.* afeminado.

efficacy, *n.* eficacia *f.*

efficiency, *n.* eficiencia *f.*

efficient, *a.* eficaz.

efficiently, *adv.* eficazmente.

effigy, *n.* efigie *f.*

effort, *n.* esfuerzo *m.*

effrontery, *n.* impudencia *f.*

effusive, *a.* efusivo.

egg, 1. *n.* huevo *m.* **fried e.,** huevo frito. **soft-boiled e.,** h. pasado por agua. **scrambled eggs,** huevos revueltos.

eggplant, *n.* berenjena *f.*

egg white, clara de huevo *f.*

egoism, egotism, *n.* egoísmo *m.*

egoist, egotist, *n.* egoísta *m. & f.*

egotism, *n.* egotismo *m.*

egotist, *n.* egotista *m. & f.*

Egypt, *n.* Egipto *m.*

Egyptian, *a. & n.* egipcio -ia.

eight, *a. & pron.* ocho.

eighteen, *a. & pron.* dieciocho.

eighth, *a.* octavo.

eightieth, *n.* octogésimo *m.*

eighty, *a. & pron.* ochenta.

either, 1. *a. & pron.* cualquiera de los dos. **2.** *adv.* tampoco. **3.** *conj.* **either . . . or,** o . . . o.

ejaculate, *v.* exclamar; eyacular.

ejaculation, *n.* eyaculación *f.*

eject, *v.* expeler; eyectar.

ejection, *n.* expulsión *f.;* eyección *f.*

elaborate, 1. *a.* elaborado. **2.** *v.* elaborar; ampliar.

élan vital, energía vital *f.*

elapse, *v.* transcurrir; pasar.

elastic, *a. & n.* elástico *m.*

elasticity, *n.* elasticidad *f.*

elate, *v.* exaltar.

elation, *n.* exaltación *f.*

elbow, *n.* codo *m.*

elder, 1. *a.* mayor. **2.** *n.* anciano -na.

elderly, *a.* de edad.

eldest, *a.* mayor.

elect, *v.* elegir.

election, *n.* elección *f.*

elective, *a.* electivo.

electorate, *n.* electorado *m.*

electric, electrical, *a.* eléctrico.

electrician, *n.* electricista *m. & f.*

electricity, *n.* electricidad *f.*

electrocardiogram, *n.* electrocardiograma *m.*

electrocute, *v.* electrocutar.

electrode, *n.* electrodo *m.*

electrolysis, *n.* electrólisis *f.*

electron, *n.* electrón *m.*

electronic, *a.* electrónico.

electronics, *n.* electrónica *f.*

elegance, *n.* elegancia *f.*

elegant, *a.* elegante.

elegy, *n.* elegía *f.*

element, *n.* elemento *m.*

elemental, *a.* elemental.

elementary, *a.* elemental.

elephant, *n.* elefante -ta.

elevate, *v.* elevar.

elevation, *n.* elevación *f.*

elevator, *n.* ascensor *f.*

eleven, *a. & pron.* once.

eleventh, *a.* undécimo.

eleventh hour, último minuto *m.*

elf, *n.* duende *m.*

elicit, *v.* sacar; despertar.

eligibility, *n.* elegibilidad *f.*

eligible, *a.* elegible.

eliminate, *v.* eliminar.

elimination, *n.* eliminación *f.*

elixir, *n.* elixir *m.*

elk, *n.* alce *m.,* anta *m.*

elm, *n.* olmo *m.*

elocution, *n.* elocución *f.*

elongate, *v.* alargar.

elope, *v.* fugarse.

eloquence, *n.* elocuencia *f.*

eloquent, *a.* elocuente.

eloquently, *adv.* elocuentemente.

else, *adv.* más. **someone e.,** otra persona. **something e.,** otra cosa. **or e.,** de otro modo.

elsewhere, *adv.* en otra parte.

elucidate, *v.* elucidar.

elude, *v.* eludir.

elusive, *a.* evasivo.

emaciated, *a.* demacrado, enflaquecido.

emanate, *v.* emanar.

emancipate, *v.* emancipar.

emancipation, *n.* emancipación *f.*

emancipator, *n.* libertador -ra.

embalm, *v.* embalsamar.

embankment, *n.* malecón, dique *m.*

embargo, *n.* embargo *m.*

embark, *v.* embarcar.

embarrass, *v.* avergonzar; turbar.

embarrassing, *a.* penoso, vergonzoso.

embarrassment, *n.* turbación; vergüenza *f.*

embassy, *n.* embajada *f.*

embellish, *v.* hermosear, embellecer.

embellishment, *n.* embellecimiento *m.*

embezzle, *v.* desfalcar, malversar.

emblem, *n.* emblema *m.*

embody, *v.* incorporar; personificar.

embrace, 1. *n.* abrazo *m.* **2.** *v.* abrazar.

embroider, *v.* bordar.

embroidery, *n.* bordado *m.*

embryo, *n.* embrión *m.*

embryonic, *a.* embrionario.

emerald, *n.* esmeralda *f.*

emerge, *v.* salir.

emergency, *n.* emergencia *f.*

emergency brake, freno de auxilio *m.*

emergency exit, salida de urgencia *f.*

emergency landing, aterrizaje forzoso *m.*

emergent, *a.* emergente.

emery, *n.* esmeril *m.*

emetic, *n.* emético *m.*

emigrant, *a. & n.* emigrante *m. & f.*

emigrate, *v.* emigrar.

emigration, *n.* emigración *f.*

eminence, *n.* altura; eminencia *f.*

eminent, *a.* eminente.

emissary, *n.* emisario *m.*

emission, *n.* emisión *f.*

emit, *v.* emitir.

emolument, *n.* emolumento *m.*

emotion, *n.* emoción *f.*

emotional, *a.* emocional; sentimental.

emperor, *n.* emperador *m.*

emphasis, *n.* énfasis *m. or f.*

emphasize, *v.* acentuar, recalcar.

emphatic, *a.* enfático.

empire, *n.* imperio *m.*

empirical, *a.* empírico.

employ, *v.* emplear.

employee, *n.* empleado -da.

employer, *n.* patrón -ona.

employment, *n.* empleo *m.*

employment agency, agencia de colocaciones *f.*

empower, *v.* autorizar.

emptiness, *n.* vaciedad; futilidad *f.*

empty, 1. *a.* vacío. **2.** *v.* vaciar.

emulate, *v.* emular.

emulsion, *n.* emulsión *f.*

enable, *v.* capacitar; permitir.

enact, *v.* promulgar, decretar.

enactment, *n.* ley *f.,* estatuto *m.*

enamel, 1. *n.* esmalte *m.* **2.** *v.* esmaltar.

enamored, *a.* enamorado.

enchant, *v.* encantar.

enchantment, *n.* encanto *m.*

encircle, *v.* circundar.

enclose, *v.* encerrar. **enclosed,** (in letter) adjunto.

enclosure, *n.* recinto *m.; (in letter)* incluso *m.*

encompass, *v.* circundar.

encounter, 1. *n.* encuentro *m.* **2.** *v.* encontrar.

encourage, *v.* animar.

encouragement, *n.* estímulo *m.*

encroach, *v.* usurpar; meterse.

encyclical, *n.* encíclica *f.*

encyclopedia, *n.* enciclopedia *f.*

end, 1. *n.* fin, término, cabo; extremo; (aim) propósito *m.* **2.** *v.* acabar; terminar.

endanger, *v.* poner en peligro.

endear, *v.* hacer querer.

endeavor, 1. *n.* esfuerzo *m.* **2.** *v.* esforzarse.

ending, *n.* conclusión *f.*

endless, *a.* sin fin.

endocrine gland, glándula endocrina *f.*

endorse, *v.* endosar; apoyar.

endorsement, *n.* endoso *m.*

endow, *v.* dotar, fundar.

endowment, *n.* dotación *f.,* fundación *f.*

endurance, *n.* resistencia *f.*

endure, *v.* soportar, resistir, aguantar.

enema, *n.* enema; lavativa *f.*

enemy, *n.* enemigo -ga.

energetic, *a.* enérgico.

energy, *n.* energía *f.*

enervate, *v.* enervar.

enervation, *n.* enervación *f.*

enfold, *v.* envolver.

enforce, *v.* ejecutar.

enforcement, *n.* ejecución *f.*

engage, *v.* emplear; ocupar.

engaged, *a.* (to marry) prometido.

engagement, *n.* combate; compromiso; contrato *m.; cita f.*

engine, *n.* máquina *f.* (railroad) locomotora *f.*

engineer, *n.* ingeniero -ra; maquinista *m.*

engineering, *n.* ingeniería *f.*

England, *n.* Inglaterra *f.*

English, *a. & n.* inglés -esa.

English Channel, Canal de la Mancha *m.*

Englishman, *n.* inglés *m.*

Englishwoman, *n.* inglesa *f.*

engrave, *v.* grabar.

engraver, *n.* grabador *m.*

engraving, *n.* grabado *m.*

engross, *v.* absorber.

enhance, *v.* aumentar en valor; realzar.

enigma, *n.* enigma *m.*

enigmatic, *a.* enigmático.

enjoy, *v.* gozar de; disfrutar de. **e. oneself,** divertirse.

enjoyable, *a.* agradable.

enjoyment, *n.* goce *m.*

enlarge, *v.* agrandar; ampliar.

enlargement, *n.* ensanchamiento *m.,* ampliación *f.*

enlarger, *n.* amplificador *m.*

enlighten, *v.* informar.

enlightenment, *n.* esclarecimiento *m.; cultura f.*

enlist, *v.* reclutar; alistarse.

enlistment, *n.* alistamiento *m.*

enliven, *v.* avivar.

enmesh, *v.* entrampar.

enmity, *n.* enemistad *f.*

enormity, *n.* enormidad *f.*

enormous, *a.* enorme.

enough, *a. & adv.* bastante. **to be e.,** bastar.

enrage, *v.* enfurecer.

enrich, *v.* enriquecer.

enroll, *v.* registrar; matricularse.

enrollment, *n.* matriculación *f.*

ensign, *n.* bandera *f.;* (naval) subteniente *m.*

enslave, *v.* esclavizar.

ensue, *v.* seguir, resultar.

entail, *v.* acarrear, ocasionar.

entangle, *v.* enredar.

enter, *v.* entrar.

enterprise, *n.* empresa *f.*

enterprising, *a.* emprendedor.

entertain, *v.* entretener; divertir.

entertainment, *n.* entretenimiento *m.;* diversión *f.*

enthrall, *v.* esclavizar; cautivar.

enthusiasm, *n.* entusiasmo *m.*

enthusiast, *n.* entusiasta *m. & f.*

enthusiastic, *a.* entusiasmado.

entice, *v.* inducir.

entire, *a.* entero.

entirely, *adv.* enteramente.

entirety, *n.* totalidad *f.*

entitle, *v.* autorizar; (book) titular.

entity, *n.* entidad *f.*

entrails, *n.* entrañas *f.pl.*

entrance, *n.* entrada *f.*

entrance examination, examen de ingreso *m.*

entrant, *n.* competidor -ra.

entreat, *v.* rogar, suplicar.

entreaty, *n.* ruego *m.,* súplica *f.*

entrench, *v.* atrincherar.

entrust, *v.* confiar.

entry, *n.* entrada *f.;* (com.) partida *f.*

entry blank, hoja de inscripción *f.*

enumerate, *v.* enumerar.

enumeration, *n.* enumeración *f.*

enunciate, *v.* enunciar.

enunciation, *n.* enunciación *f.*

envelop, *v.* envolver.

envelope, *n.* sobre *m.;* cubierta *f.*

enviable, *a.* envidiable.

envious, *a.* envidioso.

environment, *n.* ambiente *m.*

environmentalist, *n.* ambientalista, ecologista *m. & f.*

environmental protection, protección del ambiente.

environs, *n.* alrededores *m.*

envoy, *n.* enviado *m.*

envy, 1. *n.* envidia *f.* **2.** *v.* envidiar.

eon, *n.* eón *m.*

ephemeral, *a.* efímero.

epic, 1. *a.* épico. **2.** *n.* epopeya *f.*

epicure, *n.* epicúreo *m.*

epidemic, 1. *a.* epidémico. **2.** *n.* epidemia *f.*

epidermis, *n.* epidermis *f.*

epigram, *n.* epigrama *m.*

epilepsy, *n.* epilepsia *f.*

epilogue, *n.* epílogo *m.*

episode, *n.* episodio *m.*

epistle, *n.* epístola *f.*

epitaph, *n.* epitafio *m.*

epithet, *n.* epíteto *m.*

epitome, *n.* epítome *m.*

epoch, *n.* época, era *f.*

Epsom salts, *n.pl.* sal de la Higuera *f.*

equal, 1. *a. & n.* igual *m.* **2.** *v.* igualar; equivaler.

equality, *n.* igualdad *f.*

equalize, *v.* igualar.

equanimity, *n.* ecuanimidad *f.*

equate, *v.* igualar.

equation, *n.* ecuación *f.*

equator, *n.* ecuador *m.*

equatorial, *a.* ecuatorial

equestrian, 1. *n.* jinete *m.* **2.** *a.* ecuestre.

equilibrium, *n.* equilibrio *m.*

equinox, *n.* equinoccio *m.*

equip, *v.* equipar.

equipment, *n.* equipo *m.*

equitable, *a.* equitativo.

equity, *n.* equidad, justicia *f.*

equivalent, *a. & n.* equivalente *m.*

equivocal, *a.* equívoco, ambiguo.

era, *n.* era, época, edad *f.*

eradicate, *v.* extirpar.

erase, *v.* borrar.

eraser, *n.* borrador *m.*

erasure, *n.* borradura *f.*

erect, 1. *a.* derecho, erguido. **2.** *v.* erigir.

erection, erectness, *n.* erección *f.*

ermine, *n.* armiño *m.*

erode, *v.* corroer.

erosion, *n.* erosión *f.*

erotic, *a.* erótico.

err, *v.* equivocarse.

errand, *n.* encargo, recado *m.*

errant, *a.* errante.

erratic, *a.* errático.

erroneous, *a.* erróneo.

error, *n.* error *m.*

erudite, *a.* erudito.

erudition, *n.* erudición *f.*

eruption, *n.* erupción, irrupción *f.*

erysipelas, *n.* erisipela *f.*

escalate, *v.* escalar; intensificarse.

escalator, *n.* escalera mecánica *f.*

escapade, *n.* escapada; correría *f.*

escape, 1. *n.* fuga, huída *f.* **fire e.,** escalera de salvamento. **2.** *v.* escapar; fugarse.

eschew, *v.* evadir.

escort, 1. *n.* escolta *f.* **2.** *v.* escoltar.

escrow, *n.* plica *f.*

escutcheon, *n.* escudo de armas *m.*

esophagus, *n.* esófago *m.*

esoteric, *a.* esotérico.

especially, *adv.* especialmente.

espionage, *n.* espionaje *m.*

espresso, *n.* café exprés, *m.*

essay, *n.* ensayo *m.*

essayist, *n.* ensayista *m. & f.*

essence, *n.* esencia *f.;* perfume *m.*

essential, *a.* esencial.

essentially, *adv.* esencialmente.

establish, *v.* establecer.

establishment, *n.* establecimiento *m.*

estate, *n.* estado *m.;* hacienda *f.;* bienes *m.pl.*

esteem, 1. *n.* estima *f.* **2.** *v.* estimar.

estimable, *a.* estimable.

estimate, 1. *n.* cálculo; presupuesto *m.* **2.** *v.* estimar.

estimation, *n.* estimación *f.;* cálculo *m.*

estrange, *v.* extrañar; enajenar.

estuary, *n.* estuario *m.*

etch, *v.* grabar al agua fuerte.

etching, *n.* aguafuerte.

eternal, *a.* eterno.

eternity, *n.* eternidad *f.*

ether, *n.* éter *m.*

ethereal, *a.* etéreo.

ethical, *a.* ético.

ethics, *n.* ética *f.*

ethnic, *a.* étnico.

etiquette, *n.* etiqueta *f.*

etymology, *n.* etimología *f.*

eucalyptus, *n.* eucalipto *m.*

eugenic, *a.* eugenésico.

eugenics, *n.* eugenesia *f.*

eulogize, *v.* elogiar.
eulogy, *n.* elogio *m.*
eunuch, *n.* eunuco *m.*
euphonious, *a.* eufónico.
Europe, *n.* Europa *f.*
European, *a.* & *n.* europeo - pea.
euthanasia, *n.* eutanasia *f.*
evacuate, *v.* evacuar.
evade, *v.* evadir.
evaluate, *v.* evaluar.
evaluation, *n.* valoración *f.*
evangelist, *n.* evangelista *m.* & *f.*
evaporate, *v.* evaporarse.
evaporation, *n.* evaporación *f.*
evasion, *n.* evasión *f.*
evasive, *a.* evasivo.
eve, *n.* víspera *f.*
even, 1. *a.* llano; igual. **2.** *adv.* aun; hasta. **not e.,** ni siquiera.
evening, *n.* noche, tarde *f.* **good e.!** ¡buenas tardes! ¡buenas noches!
evening class, clase nocturna *f.*
evenness, *n.* uniformidad *f.*
even number, número par. *m.*
event, *n.* acontecimiento, suceso *m.*
eventful, *a.* memorable.
eventual, *a.* eventual.
ever, *adv.* alguna vez; (after *not*) nunca. **e. since,** desde que.
everlasting, *a.* eterno.
every, *a.* cada, todos los.
everybody, *pron.* todo el mundo; cada uno.
everyday, *a.* ordinario, de cada día.
everyone, *pron.* todo el mundo; cada uno; cada cual.
everything, *pron.* todo *m.*
everywhere, *adv.* por todas partes, en todas partes.
evict, *v.* expulsar.
eviction, *n.* evicción *f.*
evidence, *n.* evidencia *f.*
evident, *a.* evidente.
evidently, *adv.* evidentemente.
evil, 1. *a.* malo; maligno. **2.** *n.* mal *m.*
evince, *v.* revelar.

evoke, *v.* evocar.
evolution, *n.* evolución *f.*
evolve, *v.* desenvolver; desarrollar.
ewe, *v.* oveja *f.*
exact, 1. *a.* exacto. **2.** *v.* exigir.
exacting, *a.* exigente.
exactly, *adv.* exactamente.
exaggerate, *v.* exagerar.
exaggeration, *n.* exageración *f.*
exalt, *v.* exaltar.
exaltation, *n.* exaltación *f.*
examination, *n.* examen *m.*; (legal) interrogatorio *m.*
examine, *v.* examinar.
example, *n.* ejemplo *m.*
exasperate, *v.* exasperar.
exasperation, *n.* exasperación *f.*
excavate, *v.* excavar, cavar.
exceed, *v.* exceder.
exceedingly, *adv.* sumamente, extremadamente.
excel, *v.* sobresalir.
excellence, *n.* excelencia *f.*
Excellency, *n.* (title) Excelencia *f.*
excellent, *a.* excelente.
except, 1. *prep.* salvo, excepto. **2.** *v.* exceptuar.
exception, *n.* excepción *f.*
exceptional, *a.* excepcional.
excerpt, *n.* extracto.
excess, *n.* exceso *m.*
excessive, *a.* excesivo.
exchange, 1. *n.* cambio; canje *m.* **stock e.,** bolsa *f.* **telephone e.,** central telefónica. **2.** *v.* cambiar, canjear, intercambiar.
exchangeable, *a.* cambiable.
exchange rate, tipo de cambio *m.*
excise, 1. *n.* sisa *f.* **2.** *v.* extirpar.
excite, *v.* agitar; provocar; emocionar.
excitement, *n.* agitación, conmoción *f.*
exciting, *a.* emocionante.
exclaim, *v.* exclamar.
exclamation, *n.* exclamación *f.*
exclamation mark or **point,** punto de admiración *m.*
exclude, *v.* excluir.

exclusion, *n.* exclusión *f.*
exclusive, *a.* exclusivo.
excommunicate, *v.* excomulgar, descomulgar.
excommunication, *n.* excomunión *f.*
excrement, *n.* excremento *m.*
excruciating, *a.* penosísimo.
exculpate, *v.* exculpar.
excursion, *n.* excursión, jira *f.*
excuse, 1. *n.* excusa *f.* **2.** *v.* excusar, perdonar, disculpar; dispensar.
execrable, *a.* execrable.
execute, *v.* ejecutar.
execution, *n.* ejecución *f.*
executioner, *n.* verdugo *m.*
executive, *a.* & *n.* ejecutivo -va.
executor, *n.* testamentario *m.*
exemplary, *a.* ejemplar.
exemplify, *v.* ejemplificar.
exempt, 1. *a.* exento. **2.** *v.* exentar.
exercise, 1. *n.* ejercicio *m.* **2.** *v.* ejercitar.
exert, *v.* esforzar.
exertion, *n.* esfuerzo *m.*
exhale, *v.* exhalar.
exhaust, 1. *n.* (auto.) escape *m.* **2.** *v.* agotar.
exhaust pipe, tubo de escape *m.*
exhaustion, *n.* agotamiento *m.*
exhaustive, *a.* exhaustivo.
exhibit, 1. *n.* exhibición, exposición *f.* **2.** *v.* exhibir.
exhibition, *n.* exhibición *f.*
exhilarate, *v.* alegrar; estimular.
exhort, *v.* exhortar.
exhortation, *n.* exhortación *f.*
exhume, *v.* exhumar.
exigency, *n.* exigencia *f.*, urgencia *f.*
exile, 1. *n.* destierro *m.*, (person) desterrado *m.* **2.** *v.* desterrar.
exist, *v.* existir.
existence, *n.* existencia *f.*
existent, *a.* existente.
exit, *n.* salida *f.*
exodus, *n.* éxodo *m.*
exonerate, *v.* exonerar.
exorbitant, *a.* exorbitante.
exorcise, *v.* exorcizar.
exotic, *a.* exótico.
expand, *v.* dilatar; ensanchar.

expanse, *n.* espacio *m.;* extensión *f.*

expansion, *n.* expansión *f.*

expansion slot, ranura de expansión *f.*

expansive, *a.* expansivo.

expatiate, *v.* espaciarse.

expatriate, 1. *n.* & *a.* expatriado *m.* **2.** *v.* expatriar.

expect, *v.* esperar; contar con.

expectancy, *n.* esperanza *f.*

expectation, *n.* esperanza *f.*

expectorate, *v.* expectorar.

expediency, *n.* conveniencia *f.*

expedient, 1. *a.* oportuno. **2.** *n.* expediente *m.*

expedite, *v.* acelerar, despachar.

expedition, *n.* expedición *f.*

expel, *v.* expeler; expulsar.

expend, *v.* desembolsar, expender.

expenditure, *n.* desembolso; gasto *m.*

expense, *n.* gasto *m.;* costa *f.*

expensive, *a.* caro, costoso.

expensively, *adv.* costosamente.

experience, 1. *n.* experiencia *f.* **2.** *v.* experimentar.

experienced, *a.* experimentado, perito.

experiment, 1. *n.* experimento *m.* **2.** *v.* experimentar.

experimental, *a.* experimental.

expert, *a.* & *n.* experto -ta.

expertise, *n.* pericia *f.*

expiate, *v.* expiar.

expiration, *n.* expiración *f.*

expiration date, fecha de caducidad *f.*

expire, *v.* expirar; (com.) vencerse.

explain, *v.* explicar.

explanation, *n.* explicación *f.*

explanatory, *a.* explicativo.

expletive, 1. *n.* interjección *f.* **2.** *a.* expletivo.

explicit, *a.* explícito, claro.

explode, *v.* estallar, volar; refutar.

exploit, 1. *n.* hazaña *f.* **2.** *v.* explotar.

exploitation, *n.* explotación *f.*

exploration, *n.* exploración *f.*

exploratory, *a.* exploratorio.

explore, *v.* explorar.

explorer, *n.* explorador -ra.

explosion, *n.* explosión *f.*

explosive, *a.* explosivo.

export, 1. *n.* exportación *f.* **2.** *v.* exportar.

exportation, *n.* exportación *f.*

expose, *v.* exponer; descubrir.

exposition, *n.* exposición *f.*

expository, *a.* expositivo.

expostulate, *v.* altercar.

exposure, *n.* exposición *f.*

expound, *v.* exponer, explicar.

express, 1. *a.* & *n.* expreso *m.* **e. company,** compañía de porteo. **2.** *v.* expresar.

expression, *n.* expresión *f.*

expressive, *a.* expresivo.

expressly, *adv.* expresamente.

expressman, *n.* empresario de expresos *m.*

expressway, *n.* autopista *f.*

expropriate, *v.* expropiar.

expulsion, *n.* expulsión *f.*

expunge, *v.* borrar, expurgar.

expurgate, *v.* expurgar.

exquisite, *a.* exquisito.

extant, *a.* existente.

extemporaneous, *a.* improvisado.

extend, *v.* extender.

extension, *n.* extensión *f.*

extensive, *a.* extenso.

extensively, *adv.* extensamente.

extent, *n.* extensión *f.;* grado *m.* **to a certain e.,** hasta cierto punto.

extenuate, *v.* extenuar.

exterior, *a.* & *n.* exterior *m.*

exterminate, *v.* exterminar.

extermination, *n.* exterminio *m.*

external, *a.* externo, exterior.

extinct, *a.* extinto.

extinction, *n.* extinción *f.*

extinguish, *v.* extinguir, apagar.

extol, *v.* alabar.

extort, *v.* exigir dinero sin derecho.

extortion, *n.* extorsión *f.*

extra, 1. *a.* extraordinario; adicional. **2.** *n.* (newspaper) extra *m.*

extract, 1. *n.* extracto *m.* **2.** *v.* extraer.

extraction, *n.* extracción *f.*

extraneous, *a.* extraño; ajeno.

extraordinary, *a.* extraordinario.

extravagance, *n.* extravagancia *f.*

extravagant, *a.* extravagante.

extreme, *a.* & *n.* extremo *m.*

extremity, *n.* extremidad *f.*

extricate, *v.* desenredar.

exuberant, *a.* exuberante.

exude, *v.* exudar.

exult, *v.* regocijarse.

exultant, *a.* triunfante.

eye, 1. *n.* ojo *m.* **2.** *v.* ojear.

eyeball, *n.* globo del ojo.

eyebrow, *n.* ceja *f.*

eyeglasses, *n.* lentes *m.pl.*

eyelash, *n.* pestaña *f.*

eyelid, *n.* párpado *m.*

eyeliner, *n.* lápiz de ojos *m.*

eye shadow, *n.* sombra de ojos *f.*

eyesight, *n.* vista *f.*

F

fable, *n.* fábula; ficción *f.*

fabric, *n.* tejido *m.,* tela *f.*

fabricate, *v.* fabricar.

fabulous, *a.* fabuloso.

façade, *n.* fachada *f.*

face, 1. *n.* cara *f.* **make faces,** hacer muecas. **2.** encararse con. **f. the street,** dar a la calle.

facet, *n.* faceta *f.*

facetious, *a.* chistoso.

facial, 1. *n.* masaje facial *m.* **2.** *a.* facial.

facile, *a.* fácil.

facilitate, *v.* facilitar.

facility, *n.* facilidad *f.*

facsimile, *n.* facsímile *m.*

fact, *n.* hecho *m.* **in f.,** en realidad.

faction, *n.* facción *f.*

factor, *n.* factor *m.*

factory, *n.* fábrica *f.*

factual, *a.* verdadero.

faculty, *n.* facultad *f.*

fad, *n.* boga; novedad *f.*

fade, *v.* desteñirse; (flowers) marchitarse.

fail, 1. *n.* **without f.,** sin falla. **2.** *v.* fallar; fracasar. **not to f. to,** no dejar de.

failure, *n.* fracaso *m.*

faint, 1. *a.* débil; vago; pálido. **2.** *n.* desmayo *m.* **3.** *v.* desmayarse.

faintly, *adv.* débilmente; indistintamente.

fair, 1. *a.* razonable, justo; (hair) rubio; (weather) bueno. **2.** *n.* feria *f.*

fairly, *adv.* imparcialmente; regularmente; claramente; bellamente.

fairness, *n.* justicia *f.*

fair play, juego limpio *m.*

fairy, *n.* hada *f.*, duende *m.*

faith, *n.* fe; confianza *f.*

faithful, *a.* fiel.

fake, 1. *a.* falso; postizo. **2.** *n.* imitación; estafa *f.* **3.** *v.* imitar; fingir.

faker, *n.* imitador *m.*; farsante *m.*

falcon, *n.* halcón *m.*

fall, 1. *n.* caída; catarata *f.*; (season) otoño *m.*; (in price) baja *f.* **2.** *v.* caer; bajar. **f. asleep,** dormirse; **f. in love,** enamorarse.

fallacious, *a.* falaz.

fallacy, *n.* falacia *f.*

fallible, *a.* falible.

fallout, *n.* lluvia radiactiva, polvillo radiactivo.

fallow, *a.* sin cultivar; barbecho.

false, *a.* falso; postizo.

falsehood, *n.* falsedad; mentira *f.*

falseness, *n.* falsedad, perfidia *f.*

false teeth, dentadura postiza *f.*

falsetto, *n.* falsete *m.*

falsification, *n.* falsificación *f.*

falsify, *v.* falsificar.

falter, *v.* vacilar; (in speech) tartamudear.

fame, *n.* fama *f.*

familiar, *a.* familiar; conocido. **be f. with,** estar familiarizado con.

familiarity, *n.* familiaridad *f.*

familiarize, *v.* familiarizar.

family, *n.* familia; especie *f.*

family name, apellido *m.*

family tree, árbol genealógico *m.*

famine, *n.* hambre; carestía *f.*

famished, *a.* hambriento.

famous, *a.* famoso, célebre.

fan, *n.* abanico; ventilador *m.* (sports) aficionado -da.

fanatic, *a.* & *n.* fanático -ca.

fanatical, *a.* fanático.

fanaticism, *n.* fanatismo *m.*

fanciful, *a.* caprichoso; fantástico.

fancy, 1. *a.* fino, elegante. **f. foods,** novedades *f.pl.* **2.** *n.* fantasía *f.*; capricho *m.* **3.** *v.* imaginar.

fanfare, *n.* fanfarria *f.*

fang, *n.* colmillo *m.*

fan heater, estufa de aire *f.*

fantastic, *a.* fantástico.

fantasy, *n.* fantasía *f.*

far, 1. *a.* lejano, distante. **2.** *adv.* lejos. **how f.,** a qué distancia. **as f. as,** hasta. **so f., thus f.,** hasta aquí.

farce, *n.* farsa *f.*

fare, *n.* pasaje *m.*

farewell, 1. *n.* despedida *f.* **to say f.** despedirse. **2.** *interj.* ¡adiós!

farfetched, *a.* forzado, inverosímil.

farm, 1. *n.* granja; hacienda *f.* **2.** *v.* cultivar, labrar la tierra.

farmer, *n.* labrador, agricultor *m.*

farmhouse, *n.* hacienda, alquería *f.*

farming, *n.* agricultura *f.*; cultivo *m.*

fascinate, *v.* fascinar, embelesar.

fascination, *n.* fascinación *f.*

fascism, *n.* fascismo *m.*

fashion, 1. *n.* moda; costumbre; guisa *f.* **be in f.,** estilarse. **2.** *v.* formar.

fashionable, *a.* de moda, en boga.

fashion show, desfile de modas, pase de modelos *m.*

fast, 1. *a.* rápido, veloz; (watch) adelantado; (color) firme. **2.** *adv.* ligero, de prisa. **3.** *n.* ayuno *m.* **4.** *v.* ayunar.

fasten, *v.* afirmar; atar; fijar.

fastener, *n.* asegurador *m.*

fastidious, *a.* melindroso.

fat, 1. *a.* gordo. **2.** *n.* grasa, manteca *f.*

fatal, *a.* fatal.

fatality, *n.* fatalidad *f.*

fatally, *adv.* fatalmente.

fate, *n.* destino *m.*; suerte *f.*

fateful, *a.* fatal; ominoso.

father, *n.* padre *m.*

fatherhood, *n.* paternidad *f.*

father-in-law, *n.* suegro *m.*

fatherland, *n.* patria *f.*

fatherly, 1. *a.* paternal. **2.** *adv.* paternalmente.

fathom, 1. *n.* braza *f.* **2.** *v.* sondar; (fig.) penetrar en.

fatigue, 1. *n.* fatiga *f.*, cansancio *m.* **2.** *v.* fatigar, cansar.

fatten, *v.* engordar, cebar.

faucet, *n.* grifo *m.*, llave *f.*

fault, *n.* culpa *f.*; defecto *m.* **at f.,** culpable.

faultless, *a.* sin tacha, perfecto.

faultlessly, *adv.* perfectamente.

faulty, *a.* defectuoso, imperfecto.

fauna, *n.* fauna *f.*

favor, 1. *n.* favor *m.* **2.** *v.* favorecer.

favorable, *a.* favorable.

favorite, *a.* & *n.* favorito -ta.

favoritism, *n.* favoritismo *m.*

fawn, 1. *n.* cervato *m.* **2.** *v.* halagar, adular.

faze, *v.* desconcertar.

fear, 1. *n.* miedo, temor *m.* **2.** *v.* temer.

fearful, *a.* temeroso, medroso.

fearless, *a.* intrépido; sin temor.

fearlessness, *n.* intrepidez *f.*

feasible, *a.* factible.

feast, *n.* banquete *m.;* fiesta *f.*

feat, *n.* hazaña *f.;* hecho *m.*

feather, *n.* pluma *f.*

feature, 1. *n.* facción *f.;* rasgo *m.;* (movies) película principal *f.,* largometraje *m.* **2.** *v.* presentar como atracción especial.

February, *n.* febrero *m.*

federal, *a.* federal.

federation, *n.* confederación, federación *f.*

fee, *n.* honorarios *m.pl.*

feeble, *a.* débil.

feebleminded, *a.* imbécil.

feebleness, *a.* debilidad *f.*

feed, 1. *n.* pasto *m.* **2.** *v.* alimentar; dar de comer. **fed up with,** harto de.

feedback, *n.* feedback *m.,* retroalimentación *f.*

feel, 1. *n.* sensación *f.* **2.** *v.* sentir; palpar. **f. like,** tener ganas de.

feeling, *n.* sensación; sentimiento *f.*

feign, *v.* fingir.

felicitate, *v.* felicitar.

felicitous, *a.* feliz.

felicity, *n.* felicidad *f.,* dicha *f.*

feline, *a.* felino.

fellow, *n.* compañero; socio *m.;* (coll.) tipo *m.*

fellowship, *n.* compañerismo; (for study) beca *f.*

felon, *n.* reo *m.* & *f.,* felón -ona.

felony, *n.* felonía *f.*

felt, *n.* fieltro *m.*

felt-tipped pen, rotulador *m.*

female, *a.* & *n.* hembra *f.*

feminine, *a.* femenino.

feminist, *a.* & *n.* feminista *m.* & *f.*

fence, 1. *n.* cerca *f.* **2.** *v.* cercar.

fender, *n.* guardabarros *m.pl.*

ferment, 1. *n.* fermento *m.;* (fig.) agitación *f.* **2.** *v.* fermentar.

fermentation, *n.* fermentación *f.*

fern, *n.* helecho *m.*

ferocious, *a.* feroz, fiero.

ferociously, *adv.* ferozmente.

ferocity, *n.* ferocidad, fiereza *f.*

Ferris wheel, rueda de feria *f.*

ferry, *n.* transbordador *m.,* barca de transporte.

fertile, *a.* fecundo; (land) fértil.

fertility, *n.* fertilidad *f.*

fertilization, *n.* fertilización *f.*

fertilize, *v.* fertilizar, abonar.

fertilizer, *n.* abono *m.*

fervency, *n.* ardor *m.*

fervent, *a.* fervoroso.

fervently, *adv.* fervorosamente.

fervid, *a.* férvido.

fervor, *n.* fervor *m.*

fester, *v.* ulcerarse.

festival, *n.* fiesta *f.*

festive, *a.* festivo.

festivity, *n.* festividad *f.*

festoon, 1. *n.* festón *m.* **2.** *v.* festonear.

fetch, *v.* ir por; traer.

fete, 1. *n.* fiesta *f.* **2.** *v.* festejar.

fetid, *a.* fétido.

fetish, *n.* fetiche *m.*

fetter, 1. *n.* grillete *m.* **2.** *v.* engrillar.

fetus, *n.* feto *m.*

feud, *n.* riña *f.*

feudal, *a.* feudal.

feudalism, *n.* feudalismo *m.*

fever, *n.* fiebre *f.*

feverish, *a.* febril.

feverishly, *adv.* febrilmente.

few, *a.* pocos. **a. f.,** algunos, unos cuantos.

fiancé, fiancée, *n.* novio -via.

fiasco, *n.* fiasco *m.*

fiat, *n.* fiat *m.,* orden *f.*

fib, 1. *n.* mentira *f.* **2.** *v.* mentir.

fiber, *n.* fibra *f.*

fibrous, *a.* fibroso.

fickle, *a.* caprichoso.

fickleness, *n.* inconstancia *f.*

fiction, *n.* ficción *f.;* (literature) novelas *f.pl.*

fictitious, *a.* ficticio.

fidelity, *n.* fidelidad *f.*

fidget, *v.* inquietar.

field, *n.* campo *m.*

field trip, viaje de estudios *m.*

fiend, *n.* demonio *m.*

fiendish, *a.* diabólico, malvado.

fierce, *a.* fiero, feroz.

fiery, *a.* ardiente.

fiesta, *n.* fiesta *f.*

fife, *n.* pífano *m.*

fifteen, *n.* & *a. & pron.* quince.

fifteenth, *n.* & *a.* décimoquinto.

fifth, *a.* quinto.

fifty, *a. & pron.* cincuenta.

fig, *n.* higo *m.* **f. tree,** higuera *f.*

fight, 1. *n.* lucha, pelea *f.* **2.** *v.* luchar, pelear.

fighter, *n.* peleador -ra, luchador -ra.

figment, *n.* invención *f.*

figurative, *a.* metafórico.

figuratively, *adv.* figuradamente.

figure, 1. *n.* figura; cifra *f.* **2.** *v.* figurar; calcular.

filament, *n.* filamento *m.*

file, 1. *n.* archivo *m.;* (instrument) lima *f.;* (row) fila *f.* **2.** *v.* archivar; limar.

file cabinet, archivador *m.*

filial, *a.* filial.

filigree, *n.* filigrana *f.*

fill, *v.* llenar.

fillet, *n.* filete *m.*

filling, *n.* relleno *m.;* (dental) empastadura *f.* **f. station,** gasolinera *f.*

film, 1. *n.* película *f.,* film *m.* **2.** *v.* filmar.

filter, 1. *n.* filtro *m.* **2.** *v.* filtrar.

filth, *n.* suciedad, mugre *f.*

filthy, *a.* sucio.

fin, *n.* aleta *f.*

final, 1. *a.* final, último. **2.** *n.* examen final. **finals** (sports) final *f.*

finalist, *n.* finalista *m.* & *f.*

finally, *adv.* finalmente.

finances, *n.* recursos, fondos *m.pl.*

financial, *a.* financiero.

financier, *n.* financiero -ra.

find, 1. *n.* hallazgo *m.* **2.** *v.* hallar; encontrar. **f. out,** averiguar, enterarse, saber.

fine, 1. *a.* fino; bueno. **2.** *adv.* muy bien. **3.** *n.* multa *f.* **4.** *v.* multar.

fine arts, bellas artes *fpl.*

finery, *n.* gala *f.,* adorno *m.*

finesse, 1. *n.* artificio *m.* **2.** *v.* valerse de artificio.

finger, *n.* dedo *m.*

finger bowl, *n.* enjuagatorio *m.*

fingernail, *n.* uña *f.*

fingerprint, 1. *n.* impresión digital *f.* **2.** *v.* tomar las impresiones digitales.

finicky, *a.* melindroso.

finish, 1. *n.* conclusión *f.* **2.** *v.* acabar, terminar.

finished, *a.* acabado.

finite, *a.* finito.

fir, *n.* abeto *m.*

fire, 1. *n.* fuego; incendio *m.* **2.** *v.* disparar, tirar; (coll.) despedir.

fire alarm, *n.* alarma de incendio *f.*

firearm, *n.* arma de fuego.

firecracker, *n.* triquitraque *m.,* buscapiés *m.,* petardo *m.*

fire engine, bomba de incendios *f.*

fire escape, escalera de incendios *f.*

fire exit, salida de urgencia *f.*

fire extinguisher, matafuego *m.*

firefly, *n.* luciérnaga *f.*

fireman, *n.* bombero *m.;* (railway) fogonero *m.*

fireplace, *n.* hogar, fogón *m.*

fireproof, *a.* incombustible.

fireside, *n.* hogar, fogón *m.*

fireworks, *n.* fuegos artificiales.

firm, 1. *a.* firme. **2.** *n.* firma, empresa *f.*

firmness, *n.* firmeza *f.*

first, *a. & adv.* primero. **at f.,** al principio.

first aid, primeros auxilios.

first-class, *a.* de primera clase.

fiscal, *a.* fiscal.

fish, 1. *n.* (food) pescado *m.;* (alive) pez *m.* **2.** *v.* pescar.

fisherman, *n.* pescador *m.*

fishhook, *n.* anzuelo *m.*

fishing, *n.* pesca *f.* **go f.,** ir de pesca.

fishmonger, *n.* pescadero *m.*

fish store, pescadería *f.*

fission, *n.* fisión *f.*

fissure, *n.* grieta *f.,* quebradura *f.;* fisura.

fist, *n.* puño *m.*

fit, 1. *a.* capaz; justo. **2.** *n.* corte, talle *m.;* (med.) convulsión *f.* **3.** *v.* caber; quedar bien, sentar bien.

fitful, *a.* espasmódico; caprichoso.

fitness, *n.* aptitud; conveniencia *f.*

fitting, 1. *a.* conveniente. **be f.,** convenir. **2.** *n.* ajuste *m.*

fitting room, probador *m.*

five, *a. & pron.* cinco.

five-day work week, semana inglesa *f.*

fix, 1. *n.* apuro *m.* **2.** *v.* fijar; arreglar; componer, reparar.

fixation, *n.* fijación *f.;* fijeza *f.*

fixed, *a.* fijo.

fixture, *n.* instalación; guarnición *f.*

flabby, *a.* flojo.

flaccid, *a.* flojo; flácido.

flag, *n.* bandera *f.*

flagellant, *n. &. a.* flagelante *m.*

flagon, *n.* frasco *m.*

flagrant, *a.* flagrante.

flagrantly, *adv.* notoriamente.

flair, *n.* aptitud especial *f.*

flake, 1. *n.* escama *f.;* copo de nieve. **2.** *v.* romperse en láminas.

flamboyant, *a.* flamante, llamativo.

flame, 1. *n.* llama *f.* **2.** *v.* llamear.

flaming, *a.* llameante, flamante.

flamingo, *n.* flamenco *m.*

flammable, *a.* inflamable.

flank, 1. *n.* ijada *f.;* (mil.) flanco *m.* **2.** *v.* flanquear.

flannel, *n.* franela *f.*

flap, 1. *n.* cartera *f.* **2.** *v.* aletear; sacudirse.

flare, 1. *n.* llamarada *f.* **2.** *v.* brillar; (fig.) enojarse.

flash, 1. *n.* resplandor *m.;* (lightning) rayo, relámpago *m.;* (fig.) instante *m.* **2.** *v.* brillar.

flashcube, *n.* cubo de flash *m.*

flashlight, *n.* linterna (eléctrica).

flashy, *a.* ostentoso.

flask, *n.* frasco *m.*

flat, 1. *a.* llano; (tire) desinflado. **2.** *n.* llanura *f.;* apartamento *m.*

flatness, *n.* llanura *f.*

flatten, *v.* aplastar, allanar; abatir.

flatter, *v.* adular, lisonjear.

flatterer, *n.* lisonjero -ra; zalamero -ra.

flattery, *n.* adulación, lisonja *f.*

flaunt, *v.* ostentar.

flavor, 1. *n.* sabor *m.* **2.** *v.* sazonar.

flavoring, *n.* condimento *m.*

flaw, *n.* defecto *m.*

flax, *n.* lino *m.*

flay, *v.* despellejar; excoriar.

flea, *n.* pulga *f.*

flea market, rastro *m.*

fleck, 1. *n.* mancha *f.* **2.** *v.* varetear.

flee, *v.* huir.

fleece, 1. *n.* vellón *m.* **2.** *v.* esquilar.

fleet, 1. *a.* veloz. **2.** *n.* flota *f.*

fleeting, *a.* fugaz, pasajero.

flesh, *n.* carne *f.*

fleshy, *a.* gordo; carnoso.

flex, 1. *n.* doblez *m.* **2.** *v.* doblar.

flexibility, *n.* flexibilidad *f.*

flexible, *a.* flexible.

flier, *n.* aviador -ra.

flight, *n.* vuelo *m.;* fuga *f.*

flight attendant, *n.* azafata *f.;* ayudante de vuelo *m.*

flimsy, *a.* débil.

flinch, *v.* acobardarse.

fling, *v.* lanzar.

flint, *n.* pedernal *m.*

flip, *v.* lanzar.

flippant, *a.* impertinente.

flippantly, *adv.* impertinentemente.

flirt, 1. *n.* coqueta *f.* **2.** *v.* coquetear, flirtear.

flirtation, *n.* coqueteo *m.*

float, *v.* flotar.

flock, 1. *n.* rebaño *m.* **2.** *v.* congregarse.

flog, *v.* azotar.

flood, 1. *n.* inundación *f.* **2.** *v.* inundar.

floor, 1. *n.* suelo, piso *m.* **2.** *v.* derribar.

floppy disk, disco flexible *m.*

floral, *a.* floral.

florid, *a.* florido.

florist, *n.* florista *m. & f.*

flounce, 1. *n.* (sewing) volante *m.* **2.** *v.* pernear.

flounder, *n.* rodaballo *m.*

flour, *n.* harina *f.*

flourish, 1. *n.* (mus.) floreo *m.* **2.** *v.* florecer; prosperar; blandir.

flow, 1. *n.* flujo *m.* **2.** *v.* fluir.

flow chart, organigrama *m.*

flower, 1. *n.* flor *f.* **2.** *v.* florecer.

flowerpot, *n.* maceta *f.*

flowery, *a.* florido.

fluctuate, *v.* fluctuar.

fluctuation, *n.* fluctuación *f.*

flue, *n.* humero *m.*

fluency, *n.* fluidez *f.*

fluent, *a.* fluido; competente.

fluffy, *a.* velloso.

fluid, *a. & n.* fluido *m.*

fluidity, *n.* fluidez *f.*

fluoroscope, *n.* fluoroscopio *m.*

flurry, *n.* agitación *f.*

flush, 1. *a.* bien provisto. **2.** *n.* sonrojo *m.* **3.** *v.* limpiar con un chorro de agua; sonrojarse.

flute, *n.* flauta *f.*

flutter, 1. *n.* agitación *f.* **2.** *v.* agitarse.

flux, *n.* flujo *m.*

fly, 1. *n.* mosca *f.* **2.** *v.* volar.

flying saucer, platillo volante *m.*

foam, 1. *n.* espuma *f.* **2.** *v.* espumar.

focal, *a.* focal.

focus, 1. *n.* enfoque *m.* **2.** *v.* enfocar.

fodder, *n.* forraje *m.*, pienso *m.*

foe, *n.* adversario -ria, enemigo -ga.

fog, *n.* niebla *f.*

foggy, *a.* brumoso.

foil, *v.* frustrar.

foist, *v.* imponer.

fold, 1. *n.* pliegue *m.* **2.** *v.* doblar, plegar.

foldable, *a.* plegable.

folder, *n.* circular *m.;* (for filing) carpeta *f.*

folding, *a.* plegable.

foliage, *n.* follaje *m.*

folio, *n.* infolio; folio *m.*

folklore, *n.* folklore *m.*

folks, *n.* gente; familia *f.*

follicle, *n.* folículo *m.*

follow, *v.* seguir.

follower, *n.* partidario -ria.

folly, *n.* locura *f.*

foment, *v.* fomentar.

fond, *a.* cariñoso, tierno. **be f. of,** ser aficionado a.

fondle, *v.* acariciar.

fondly, *adv.* tiernamente.

fondness, *n.* afición *f.;* cariño *m.*

food, *n.* alimento *m.;* comida *f.*

food poisoning, intoxicación alimenticia *f.*

foodstuffs, *n.pl.* comestibles, víveres *m.pl.*

fool, 1. *n.* tonto -ta; bobo -ba; bufón -ona. **2.** *v.* engañar.

foolhardy, *a.* temerario.

foolish, *a.* bobo, tonto, majadero.

foolproof, *a.* seguro.

foot, *n.* pie *m.*

footage, *n.* longitud en pies.

football, *n.* fútbol, balompié *m.*

footbridge, *n.* puente para peatones *m.*

foothold, *n.* posición establecida.

footing, *n.* base *f.*, fundamento *m.*

footlights, *n.pl.* luces del proscenio.

footnote, *n.* nota al pie de una página.

footpath, *n.* sendero *m.*

footprint, *n.* huella *f.*

footstep, *n.* paso *m.*

footstool, *n.* escañuelo *m.*, banqueta *f.*

fop, *n.* petimetre *m.*

for, 1. *prep.* para; por. **as f.,** en cuanto a. **what f.,** ¿para qué? **2.** *conj.* porque, pues.

forage, 1. *n.* forraje *m.* **2.** *v.* forrajear.

foray, *n.* correría *f.*

forbear, *v.* cesar; abstenerse.

forbearance, *n.* paciencia *f.*

forbid, *v.* prohibir.

forbidding, *a.* repugnante.

force, 1. *n.* fuerza *f.* **2.** *v.* forzar.

forced landing, aterrizaje forzoso *m.*

forceful, *a.* fuerte; enérgico.

forcible, *a.* a la fuerza; enérgico.

ford, 1. *n.* vado *m.* **2.** *v.* vadear.

fore, 1. *a.* delantero. **2.** *n.* delantera *f.*

fore and aft, de popa a proa.

forearm, *n.* antebrazo *m.*

forebears, *n.pl.* antepasados *m.pl.*

forebode, *v.* presagiar.

foreboding, *n.* presentimiento *m.*

forecast, 1. *n.* pronóstico *m.;* profecía *f.* **2.** *v.* pronosticar.

forecastle, *n.* (naut.) castillo de proa.

forefathers, *n.* antepasados *m.pl.*

forefinger, *n.* índice *m.*

forego, *v.* renunciar.

foregone, *a.* predeterminado.

foreground, *n.* primer plano.

forehead, *n.* frente *f.*

foreign, *a.* extranjero.

foreign aid, *n.* ayuda exterior *f.*

foreigner, *n.* extranjero -ra; forastero -ra.

foreleg, *n.* pierna delantera.

foreman, *n.* capataz, jefe de taller *m.*

foremost, 1. *a.* primero. **2.** *adv.* en primer lugar.

forenoon, *n.* mañana *f.*

forensic, *a.* forense.

forerunner, *n.* precursor -ra.

foresee, *v.* prever.

foreshadow, v. prefigurar, anunciar.

foresight, n. previsión f.

forest, n. bosque m.; selva f.

forestall, v. anticipar; prevenir.

forester, n. silvicultor -ra; guardamontes m.pl. & f.pl.

forestry, n. silvicultura f.

foretell, v. predecir.

forever, adv. por siempre, para siempre.

forevermore, adv. siempre.

forewarn, v. advertir, avisar.

foreword, n. prefacio m.

forfeit, 1. n. prenda; multa f. **2.** v. perder.

forfeiture, n. decomiso m., multa f.; pérdida.

forgather, v. reunirse.

forge, 1. n. fragua f. **2.** v. forjar; falsear.

forger, n. forjador -ra; falsificador -ra.

forgery, n. falsificación f.

forget, v. olvidar.

forgetful, a. olvidadizo.

forgive, v. perdonar.

forgiveness, n. perdón m.

fork, 1. n. tenedor m.; bifurcación f. **2.** v. bifurcarse.

forlorn, a. triste.

form, 1. n. forma f.; (document) formulario m. **2.** v. formar.

formal, a. formal; ceremonioso. **f. dance,** baile de etiqueta. **f. dress,** traje de etiqueta.

formality, n. formalidad f.

formally, adv. formalmente.

format, n. formato m.

formation, n. formación f.

formative, a. formativo.

former, a. anterior; antiguo. **the f.,** aquél.

formerly, adv. antiguamente.

formidable, a. formidable.

formless, a. sin forma.

formula, n. fórmula f.

formulate, v. formular.

formulation, n. formulación f.; expresión f.

forsake, v. abandonar.

fort, n. fortaleza f.; fuerte m.

forte, a. & adv. (mus.) forte; fuerte.

forth, adv. adelante. **back and f.,** de aquí allá. **and so f.,** etcétera.

forthcoming, a. futuro, próximo.

forthright, a. franco.

forthwith, adv. inmediatamente.

fortification, n. fortificación f.

fortify, v. fortificar.

fortissimo, a. & adv. (mus.) fortísimo.

fortitude, n. fortaleza; fortitud f.

fortnight, n. quincena f.

fortress, n. fuerte m., fortaleza f.

fortuitous, a. fortuito.

fortunate, a. afortunado.

fortune, n. fortuna; suerte f.

fortune-teller, n. sortílego -ga, adivino -na.

forty, a. & pron. cuarenta.

forum, n. foro m.

forward, 1. a. delantero; atrevido. **2.** adv. adelante. **3.** v. trasmitir, reexpedir.

foster, 1. n. **f. child,** hijo adoptivo. **2.** v. fomentar; criar.

foul, a. sucio; impuro.

found, v. fundar.

foundation, n. fundación f.; (of building) cimientos m.pl.

founder, 1. n. fundador -ra. **2.** v. irse a pique.

foundry, n. fundición f.

fountain, n. fuente f.

fountain pen, pluma estilográfica, plumafuente f.

four, a. & pron. cuatro.

fourteen, a. & pron. catorce.

fourth, a. & n. cuarto m.

fowl, n. ave f.

fox, n. zorro -rra.

fox-trot, n. foxtrot m.

foxy, a. astuto.

foyer, n. salón de entrada.

fracas, n. riña f.

fraction, n. fracción f.

fracture, 1. n. fractura, rotura f. **2.** v. fracturar, romper.

fragile, a. frágil.

fragment, n. fragmento, trozo m.

fragmentary, a. fragmentario.

fragrance, n. fragancia f.

fragrant, a. fragante.

frail, a. débil, frágil.

frailty, n. debilidad, fragilidad f.

frame, 1. n. marco; armazón; cuadro; cuerpo m. **2.** v. fabricar; formar; encuadrar.

frame-up, n. (coll.) conspiración f.

framework, n. armazón m.

France, n. Francia f.

franchise, n. franquicia f.

frank, 1. a. franco. **2.** n. carta franca. **3.** v. franquear.

frankfurter, n. salchicha f.

frankly, adv. francamente.

frankness, n. franqueza f.

frantic, a. frenético.

fraternal, a. fraternal.

fraternity, n. fraternidad f.

fraternization, n. fraternización f.

fraternize, v. confraternizar.

fratricide, n. fratricida m. & f.; fratricidio m.

fraud, n. fraude m.

fraudulent, a. fraudulento.

fraudulently, adv. fraudulentamente.

fraught, a. cargado.

freak, n. rareza f.; monstruosidad f.

freckle, n. peca f.

freckled, freckly, a. pecoso.

free, 1. a. libre; gratis. **2.** v. libertar, librar.

freedom, n. libertad f.

freeze, v. helar, congelar.

freezer, n. heladora f.

freezing point, punto de congelación m.

freight, 1. n. carga f.; flete m. **2.** v. cargar; fletar.

freighter, n. (naut.) fletador m.

French, a. & n. francés -esa.

Frenchman, n. francés m.

Frenchwoman, n. francesa f.

frenzied, a. frenético.

frenzy, n. frenesí m.

frequency, n. frecuencia f.

frequency modulation, modulación de frecuencia.

frequent, a. frecuente.

frequently, *adv.* frecuentemente.

fresco, *n.* fresco.

fresh, *a.* fresco. **f. water,**
agua dulce.

freshen, *v.* refrescar.

freshness, *n.* frescura *f.*

fret, *v.* quejarse, irritarse;
(mus.) traste *m.*

fretful, *a.* irritable.

fretfully, *adv.* de mala gana.

fretfulness, *n.* mal humor.

friar, *n.* fraile *m.*

fricassee, *n.* fricasé *m.*

friction, *n.* fricción *f.*

Friday, *n.* viernes *m.* **Good
F.,** Viernes Santo *m.*

fried, *a.* frito.

friend, *n.* amigo -ga.

friendless, *a.* sin amigos.

friendliness, *n.* amistad *f.*

friendly, *a.* amistoso.

friendship, *n.* amistad *f.*

fright, *n.* susto *m.*

frighten, *v.* asustar, espantar.

frightful, *a.* espantoso.

frigid, *a.* frígido; frío.

frill, *n.* (sewing) lechuga *f.*

fringe, *n.* fleco; borde *m.*

frisky, *a.* retozón.

fritter, *n.* fritura *f.*

frivolity, *n.* frivolidad *f.*

frivolous, *a.* frívolo.

frivolousness, *n.* frivolidad *f.*

frock, *n.* vestido de mujer.
f. coat, levita *f.*

frog, *n.* rana *f.*

frolic, 1. *n.* retozo *m.* **2.** *v.*
retozar.

from, *prep.* de; desde.

front, *n.* frente; (of building) fachada *f.* **in f. of,**
delante de.

frontal, *a.* frontal.

front door, puerta principal
f.

frontier, *n.* frontera *f.*

front seat, asiento delantero
m.

frost, *n.* helada, escarcha *f.*

frosty, *a.* helado.

froth, *n.* espuma *f.*

frown, 1. *n.* ceño *m.* **2.** *v.*
fruncir el entrecejo.

frowzy, *a.* desaliñado.

frozen, *a.* helado; congelado.

fructify, *v.* fructificar.

frugal, *a.* frugal.

frugality, *n.* frugalidad *f.*

fruit, *n.* fruta *f.;* (benefits)
frutos *m.pl.* **f. tree,** árbol
frutal.

fruitful, *a.* productivo.

fruition, *n.* fruición *f.*

fruitless, *a.* inútil, en vano.

fruit salad, macedonia de
frutas *f.*

fruit store, fruit shop, *n.*
frutería *f.*

frustrate, *v.* frustrar.

frustration, *n.* frustración *f.*

fry, *v.* freír.

fuel, *n.* combustible *m.*

fugitive, *a. & n.* fugitivo -va.

fugue, *n.* (mus.) fuga *f.*

fulcrum, *n.* fulcro *m.*

fulfill, *v.* cumplir.

fulfillment, *n.* cumplimiento *m.;* realización *f.*

full, *a.* lleno; completo;
pleno.

full name, nombre y apellidos.

fullness, *n.* plenitud *f.*

fulminate, *v.* volar; fulminar.

fulmination, *n.* fulmi-
nación; detonación *f.*

fumble, *v.* chapucear.

fume, 1. *n.* humo *m.* **2.** *v.*
humear.

fumigate, *v.* fumigar.

fumigator, *n.* fumigador *m.*

fun, *n.* diversión *f.* **to make
f. of,** burlarse de. **to
have f.,** divertirse.

function, 1. *n.* función *f.* **2.**
v. funcionar.

functional, *a.* funcional.

fund, *n.* fondo *m.*

fundamental, *a.* fundamental.

funeral, *n.* funeral *m.*

**funeral home, funeral par-
lor,** funeraria *f.*

fungus, *n.* hongo *m.*

funnel, *n.* embudo *m.;* (of
ship) chimenea *f.*

funny, *a.* divertido, gracioso.
to be f., tener gracia.

fur, *n.* piel *f.*

furious, *a.* furioso.

furlough, *n.* permiso *m.*

furnace, *n.* horno *m.*

furnish, *v.* surtir, proveer;
(a house) amueblar.

furniture, *n.* muebles *m.pl.*

furrow, 1. *n.* surco *m.* **2.** *v.*
surcar.

further, 1. *a. & adv.* más. **2.**
v. adelantar, fomentar.

furthermore, *adv.* además.

fury, *n.* furor *m.;* furia *f.*

fuse, 1. *n.* fusible *m.* **2.** *v.*
fundir.

fuss, 1. *n.* alboroto *m.* **2.** *v.*
preocuparse por pe-
queñeces.

fussy, *a.* melindroso.

futile, *a.* fútil.

future, 1. *a.* futuro. **2.** *n.*
porvenir *m.*

futurology, *n.* futurología *f.*

G

gag, *n.* chiste *m.;* mordaza *f.*

gaiety, *n.* alegría *f.*

gain, 1. *n.* ganancia *f.* **2.** *v.*
ganar.

gait, *n.* paso *m.*

gale, *n.* ventarrón *m.*

gall, *n.* hiel *f.;* (fig.) amargura *f.;* descaro *m.*

gallant, 1. *a.* galante. **2.** *n.*
galán *m.*

gallery, *n.* galería *f.;* (theat.)
paraíso *m.*

gallon, *n.* galón *m.*

gallop, 1. *n.* galope *m.* **2.** *v.*
galopar.

gallows, *n.* horca *f.*

gamble, 1. *n.* riesgo *m.* **2.** *v.*
jugar, aventurar.

game, *n.* juego *m.;* (match)

partida *f.;* (hunting) caza
f.

gang, *n.* cuadrilla; pandilla *f.*

gangster, *n.* rufián *m.*

gap, *n.* raja *f.*

gape, *v.* boquear.

garage, *n.* garaje *m.*

garbage, *n.* basura *f.*

garden, *n.* jardín *m.;* (vegetable) huerta *f.*

gardener, *n.* jardinero -ra.
gargle, 1. *n.* gárgara *f.* **2.** *v.* gargarizar.
garland, *n.* guirnalda *f.*
garlic, *n.* ajo *m.*
garment, *n.* prenda de vestir.
garrison, *n.* guarnición *f.*
garter, *n.* liga *f.;* ataderas *f.pl.*
gas, *n.* gas *m.*
gasohol, *n.* gasohol *m.*
gasoline, *n.* gasolina *f.*
gasp, 1. *n.* boqueada *f.* **2.** *v.* boquear.
gas station, gasolinera *f.*
gate, *n.* puerta; entrada; verja *f.*
gather, *v.* recoger; inferir; reunir.
gaudy, *a.* brillante; llamativo.
gauge, 1. *n.* manómetro, indicador *m.* **2.** *v.* medir; estimar.
gaunt, *a.* flaco.
gauze, *n.* gasa *f.*
gay, 1. *a.* alegre; homosexual. **2.** *n.* homosexual.
gaze, 1. *n.* mirada *f.* **2.** *v.* mirar con fijeza.
gear, *n.* engranaje *m.* **in g.,** en juego.
gearshift, *n.* palanca de cambio *f.*
gem, *n.* joya *f.*
gender, *n.* género *m.*
general, *a.* & *n.* general *m.*
generality, *n.* generalidad *f.*
generalize, *v.* generalizar.
generation, *n.* generación *f.*
generator, *n.* generador *m.*
generosity, *n.* generosidad *f.*
generous, *a.* generoso.
genetic, *a.* genético.
genial, *a.* genial.
genius, *n.* genio *m.*
genocide, *n.* genocidio *m.*
gentle, *a.* suave; manso; benigno.
gentleman, *n.* señor; caballero *m.*
gentleness, *n.* suavidad *f.*
genuine, *a.* genuino.
genuineness, *n.* pureza *f.*
geographical, *a.* geográfico.
geography, *n.* geografía *f.*
geometric, *a.* geométrico.
geranium, *n.* geranio *f.*

germ, *n.* germen; microbio *m.*
German, *a.* & *n.* alemán -mana.
Germany, *n.* Alemania *f.*
gesticulate, *v.* gesticular.
gesture, 1. *n.* gesto *m.* **2.** *v.* gesticular, hacer gestos.
get, *v.* obtener; conseguir; (become) ponerse. **go and g.,** ir a buscar; **g. away,** irse; escaparse; **g. together,** reunirse; **g. on,** subirse; **g. off,** bajarse; **g. up,** levantarse; **g. there,** llegar.
ghastly, *a.* pálido; espantoso.
ghost, *n.* espectro, fantasma *m.*
giant, *n.* gigante *m.*
gibberish, *n.* galimatías, *m.*
gift, *n.* regalo, don; talento *m.*
gild, *v.* dorar.
gin, *n.* ginebra *f.*
ginger, *n.* jengibre *m.*
gingerbread, *n.* pan de jengibre.
gingham, *n.* guinga *f.*
gird, *v.* ceñir.
girdle, *n.* faja *f.*
girl, *n.* muchacha, niña, chica *f.*
give, *v.* dar; regalar. **g. back,** devolver. **g. up,** rendirse; renunciar.
giver, *n.* dador -ra; donador -ra.
glacier, *n.* glaciar; ventisquero *m.*
glad, *a.* alegre, contento. **be g.,** alegrarse.
gladly, *adj.* con mucho gusto.
gladness, *n.* alegría *f.;* placer *m.*
glamor, *n.* encanto *m.;* elegancia *f.*
glamorous, *a.* encantador; elegante.
glance, 1. *n.* vistazo *m.,* ojeada *f.* **2.** *v.* ojear.
gland, *n.* glándula *f.*
glare, 1. *n.* reflejo; brillo *m.* **2.** *v.* deslumbrar; echar miradas indignadas.

glass, *n.* vidrio; vaso *m.;* **(eyeglasses),** lentes, anteojos *m.pl.*
gleam, 1. *n.* fulgor *m.* **2.** *v.* fulgurar.
glee, *n.* alegría *f.;* júbilo *m.*
glide, *v.* deslizarse.
glimpse, 1. *n.* vislumbre, vistazo *m.* **2.** *v.* vislumbrar, ojear.
glisten, 1. *n.* brillo *m.* **2.** *v.* brillar.
glitter, 1. *n.* resplandor *m.* **2.** *v.* brillar.
globe, *n.* globo; orbe *m.*
gloom, *n.* oscuridad; tristeza *f.*
gloomy, *a.* oscuro; sombrío; triste.
glorify, *v.* glorificar.
glorious, *a.* glorioso.
glory, *n.* gloria, fama *f.*
glossary, *n.* glosario *m.*
glove, *n.* guante *m.*
glove compartment, guantera *f.*
glow, 1. *n.* fulgor *m.* **2.** *v.* relucir; arder.
glucose, *f.* glucosa.
glue, 1. *n.* cola *f.,* pegamento *m.* **2.** *v.* encolar, pegar.
glum, *a.* de mal humor.
glutton, *n.* glotón -ona.
gnaw, *v.* roer.
GNP *(abbr.* **gross national product), PNB** (producto nacional bruto).
go, *v.* ir, irse. **g. away,** irse, marcharse. **g. back,** volver, regresar. **g. down,** bajar. **g. in,** entrar. **g. on,** seguir. **g. out,** salir. **g. up,** subir.
goal, *n.* meta *f.;* objeto *m.*
goalkeeper, *n.* guardameta *mf.*
goat, *n.* cabra *f.*
goblet, *n.* copa *f.*
God, *n.* Dios *m.*
gold, *n.* oro *m.*
golden, *a.* áureo.
gold-plated, *a.* chapado en oro.
golf, *n.* golf *m.*
golf course, campo de golf *m.*
golfer, *n.* golfista *m.* & *f.*

good, 1. *a.* bueno. **2.** *n.* bienes *m.pl.;* (com.) géneros *m.pl.*

good-bye, 1. *n.* adiós *m.* **2.** *interj.* ¡adiós!, ¡hasta la vista!, ¡hasta luego! **say g. to,** despedirse de.

goodness, *n.* bondad *f.*

goodwill, *n.* buena voluntad. *f.*

goose, *n.* ganso *m.*

gooseberry, *n.* uva crespa *f.*

gooseneck, 1. *n.* cuello de cisne *m.* **2.** *a.* curvo.

goose step, paso de ganso *m.*

gore, 1. *n.* sangre *f.* **2.** *v.* acornear.

gorge, 1. *n.* gorja *f.* **2.** *v.* engullir.

gorgeous, *a.* magnífico; precioso.

gorilla, *n.* gorila *m.*

gory, *a.* sangriento.

gosling, *n.* gansarón *m.*

gospel, *n.* evangelio *m.*

gossamer, 1. *n.* telaraña *f.* **2.** *a.* delgado.

gossip, 1. *n.* chisme *m.* **2.** *v.* chismear.

Gothic, *a.* gótico.

gouge, 1. *n.* gubia *f.* **2.** *v.* escoplear.

gourd, *n.* calabaza *f.*

gourmand, *n.* glotón *m.*

gourmet, *a.* gastrónomo - ma.

govern, *v.* gobernar.

governess, *n.* aya, institutriz *f.*

government, *n.* gobierno *m.*

governmental, *a.* gubernamental.

governor, *n.* gobernador - ra.

governorship, *n.* gobernatura *f.*

gown, *n.* vestido *m.* **dressing g.,** bata *f.*

grab, *v.* agarrar, arrebatar.

grace, *n.* gracia; gentileza; merced *f.*

graceful, *a.* agraciado.

graceless, *a.* réprobo; torpe.

gracious, *a.* gentil, cortés.

grackle, *n.* grajo *m.*

grade, 1. *n.* grado; nivel *m.;* pendiente; nota; calidad *f.* **2.** *v.* graduar.

grade crossing, *n.* paso a nivel *m.*

gradual, *a.* gradual, paulatino.

gradually, *adv.* gradualmente.

graduate, 1. *n.* graduado - da, diplomado -da. **2.** *v.* graduar; diplomarse.

graft, 1. *n.* injerto *m.;* soborno público. **2.** *v.* injertar.

graham, *a.* centeno; acemita.

grail, *n.* grial *m.*

grain, *n.* grano; cereal *m.*

grain alcohol, *n.* alcohol de madera *m.*

gram, *n.* gramo *m.*

grammar, *n.* gramática *f.*

grammarian, *n.* gramático - ca.

grammar school, *n.* escuela elemental *f.*

grammatical, *a.* gramatical.

gramophone, *n.* gramófono *m.*

granary, *n.* granero *m.*

grand, *a.* grande, ilustre; estupendo.

grandchild, *n.* nieto -ta.

granddaughter, *n.* nieta *f.*

grandee, *n.* noble *m.*

grandeur, *n.* grandeza *f.*

grandfather, *n.* abuelo *m.*

grandiloquent, *a.* grandílocuo.

grandiose, *a.* grandioso.

grand jury, jurado de acusación, jurado de juicio *m.*

grandly, *adv.* grandiosamente.

grandmother, *n.* abuela *f.*

grand opera, ópera grande *f.*

grandparents, *n.* abuelos *m.pl.*

grandson, *n.* nieto *m.*

grandstand, *n.* andanada *f.,* tribuna *f.*

grange, *n.* granja *f.*

granger, *n.* labriego *m.*

granite, *n.* granito *m.*

granny, *n.* abuelita *f.*

grant, 1. *n.* concesión; subvención *f.* **2.** *v.* otorgar; conceder; conferir. **take**

for granted, tomar por cierto.

granular, *a.* granular.

granulate, *v.* granular.

granulation, *n.* granulación *f.*

granule, *n.* gránulo *m.*

grape, *n.* uva *f.*

grapefruit, *n.* toronja *f.*

grape harvest, vendimia *f.*

grapeshot, *n.* metralla *f.*

grapevine, *n.* vid; parra *f.*

graph, *n.* gráfica *f.*

graphic, *a.* gráfico.

graphite, *n.* grafito *m.*

graphology, *n.* grafología *f.*

grapple, *v.* agarrar.

grasp, 1. *n.* puño; poder; conocimiento *m.* **2.** *v.* empuñar, agarrar; comprender.

grasping, *a.* codicioso.

grass, *n.* hierba *f.;* (marijuana) marijuana *f.*

grasshopper, *n.* saltamontes *m.*

grassy, *a.* herboso.

grate, *n.* reja *f.*

grateful, *a.* agradecido.

gratify, *v.* satisfacer.

grating, 1. *n.* enrejado *m.* **2.** *a.* discordante.

gratis, *adv. & a.* gratis.

gratitude, *n.* agradecimiento *m.*

gratuitous, *adj.* gratuito.

gratuity, *n.* propina *f.*

grave, 1. *a.* grave. **2.** *n.* sepultura; tumba *f.*

gravel, *n.* cascajo *m.*

gravely, *adv.* gravemente.

gravestone, *n.* lápida sepulcral *f.*

graveyard, *n.* cementerio *m.*

gravitate, *v.* gravitar.

gravitation, *n.* gravitación *f.*

gravity, *n.* gravedad; seriedad *f.*

gravure, *n.* fotograbado *m.*

gravy, *n.* salsa *f.*

gray, *a.* gris; (hair) cano.

grayish, *a.* pardusco.

gray matter, substancia gris *f.*

graze, *v.* rozar; (cattle) pastar.

grazing, *a.* pastando.

grease, 1. *n.* grasa *f.* **2.** *v.* engrasar.

greasy, *a.* grasiento.

great, *a.* grande, ilustre; estupendo.

Great Dane, mastín danés *m.*

great-grandfather, *n.* bisabuelo.

great-grandmother, *f.* bisabuela.

greatness, *n.* grandeza *f.*

Greece, *n.* Grecia *f.*

greed, greediness, *n.* codicia, voracidad *f.*

greedy, *a.* voraz.

Greek, *a.* & *n.* griego -ga.

green, *a.* & *n.* verde *m.*
greens, *n.* verduras *f.pl.*

greenery, *n.* verdor *m.*

greenhouse, *n.* invernáculo *m.*

greenhouse effect, *n.* efecto invernáculo *m.*

greet, *v.* saludar.

greeting, *n.* saludo *m.*

gregarious, *a.* gregario; sociable.

grenade, *n.* granada; bomba *f.*

greyhound, *n.* galgo *m.*

grid, *n.* parrilla *f.*

griddle, *n.* tortera *f.*

griddlecake, *n.* tortita de harina *f.*

gridiron, *n.* parrilla *f.*; campo de fútbol *m.*

grief, *n.* dolor *m.*; pena *f.*

grievance, *n.* pesar; agravio *m.*

grieve, *v.* afligir.

grievous, *a.* penoso.

grill, 1. *n.* parrilla *f.* **2.** *v.* asar a la parrilla.

grillroom, *n.* parrilla *f.*

grim, *a.* ceñudo.

grimace, 1. *n.* mueca *f.* **2.** *v.* hacer muecas.

grime, *n.* mugre *f.*

grimy, *a.* sucio; mugroso.

grin, 1. *n.* sonrisa *f.* **2.** *v.* sonreír.

grind, *v.* moler; afilar.

grindstone, *n.* amoladera *f.*

gringo, *n.* gringo; yanqui *m.*

grip, 1. *n.* maleta *f.* **2.** *v.* agarrar.

gripe, 1. *v.* agarrar. **2.** *n.* asimiento *m.*, opresión *f.*

grippe, *n.* gripe *f.*

grisly, *a.* espantoso.

grist, *n.* molienda *f.*

gristle, *n.* cartílago *m.*

grit, *n.* arena *f.*; entereza *f.*

grizzled, *a.* tordillo.

groan, 1. *n.* gemido *m.* **2.** *v.* gemir.

grocer, *n.* abacero *m.*

grocery, *n.* tienda de comestibles, abacería; (Carib.) bodega *f.*

grog, *n.* brebaje *m.*

groggy, *a.* medio borracho; vacilante.

groin, *n.* ingle *f.*

groom, 1. *n.* (of horses) establero; (at wedding) novio *m.*

groove, 1. *n.* estría *f.* **2.** *v.* acanalar.

grope, *v.* tentar; andar a tientas.

gross, 1. *a.* grueso; grosero. **2.** *n.* gruesa *f.*

grossly, *adv.* groseramente.

gross national product, producto nacional bruto *m.*

grossness, *n.* grosería *f.*

grotesque, *a.* grotesco.

grotto, *n.* gruta *f.*

grouch, *n.* gruñón; descontento *m.*

ground, *n.* tierra *f.*; terreno; suelo; campo; fundamento *m.*

ground floor, planta baja *f.*

groundhog, *n.* marmota *f.*

groundless, *a.* infundado.

groundwork, *n.* base *f.*, fundamento *m.*

group, 1. *n.* grupo *m.* **2.** *v.* agrupar.

groupie, *n.* persona aficionada que acompaña a un grupo de música moderna.

grouse, *v.* quejarse.

grove, *n.* arboleda *f.*

grovel, *v.* rebajarse; envilecerse.

grow, *v.* crecer; cultivar.

growl, 1. *n.* gruñido *m.* **2.** *v.* gruñir.

grown, *a.* crecido; desarrollado.

grownup, *n.* adulto -ta.

growth, *n.* crecimiento *m.*; vegetación *f.*; (med.) tumor *m.*

grub, *n.* gorgojo *m.*, larva *f.*

grubby, *a.* gorgojoso, mugriento.

grudge, *n.* rencor *m.* **bear a g.,** guardar rencor.

gruel, 1. *n.* atole *m.* **2.** *v.* agotar.

gruesome, *a.* horripilante.

gruff, *a.* ceñudo.

grumble, *v.* quejarse.

grumpy, *a.* gruñón; quejoso.

grunt, *v.* gruñir.

guarantee, 1. *n.* garantía *f.* **2.** *v.* garantizar.

guarantor, *n.* fiador -ra.

guaranty, *n.* garantía *f.*

guard, 1. *n.* guardia *m.* & *f.* **2.** *v.* vigilar.

guarded, *a.* cauteloso.

guardhouse, *n.* prisión militar *f.*

guardian, *n.* guardián -ana.

guardianship, *n.* tutela *f.*

guardsman, *n.* centinela *m.*

guava, *n.* guayaba *f.*

gubernatorial, *a.* gubernativo.

guerrilla, *n.* guerrilla *f.*; guerrillero -ra.

guess, 1. *n.* conjetura *f.* **2.** *v.* adivinar; (coll.) creer.

guesswork, *n.* conjetura *f.*

guest, *n.* huésped *m.* & *f.*

guest room, alcoba de huéspedes *f.*, alcoba de respeto *f.*, cuarto para invitados *m.*

guffaw, *n.* risotada *f.*

guidance, *n.* dirección *f.*

guide, 1. *n.* guía *m.* & *f.* **2.** *v.* guiar.

guidebook, *n.* guía *f.*

guided tour, visita explicada, visita programada, visita con guía *f.*

guideline, *n.* pauta *f.*

guidepost, *n.* poste indicador *m.*

guild, *n.* gremio *m.*

guile, *n.* engaño *m.*

guillotine, 1. *n.* guillotina *f.* **2.** *v.* guillotinar.

guilt, *n.* culpa *f.*

guiltily, *adv.* culpablemente.

guiltless, *a.* inocente.

guilty, *a.* culpable.

guinea fowl, gallina de
Guinea *f.*
guinea pig, cobayo *m.,*
conejillo de Indias *m.*
guise, *n.* modo *m.*
guitar, *n.* guitarra *f.*
guitarist, *n.* guitarrista *m. & f.*
gulch, *n.* quebrada *f.*
gulf, *n.* golfo *m.*
gull, *n.* gaviota *f.*
gullet, *n.* esófago *m.; zanja f.*
gullible, *a.* crédulo.
gully, *n.* barranca *f.*
gulp, 1. *n.* trago *m.* **2.** *v.* tragar.
gum, 1. *n.* goma *f.;* (anat.)
encía *f.,* chewing g., chicle *m.* **2.** *v.* engomar.
gumbo, *n.* quimbombó *m.*

gummy, *a.* gomoso.
gun, *n.* fusil; cañón *m.;*
revólver.
gunboat, *n.* cañonero *m.*
gunman, *n.* bandido *m.*
gunner, *n.* artillero *m.*
gun permit, licencia de
armas *f.*
gunpowder, *n.* pólvora *f.*
gunshot, *n.* escopetazo *m.*
gunwale, *n.* borda *f.*
gurgle, 1. *n.* gorgoteo *m.* **2.**
v. gorgotear.
guru, *n.* gurú *m.*
gush, 1. *n.* chorro *m.* **2.** *v.*
brotar, chorrear.
gusher, *n.* pozo de petróleo *m.*
gust, *n.* soplo *m.; ráfaga f.*
gustatory, *a.* gustativo.

gusto, *n.* gusto; placer *m.*
gusty, *a.* borrascoso.
gut, *n.* intestino *m.,* tripa *f.*
gutter, *n.* canal; zanja *f.*
guttural, *a.* gutural.
guy, *n.* tipo *m.*
guzzle, *v.* engullir; tragar.
gym, *n.* gimnasio *m.*
gymnasium, *n.* gimnasio *m.*
gymnast, *n.* gimnasta *m. & f.*
gymnastic, *a.* gimnástico.
gymnastics, *n.* gimnasia *f.*
gynecologist, *n.* ginecólogo,
-ga *m. & f.*
gynecology, *n.* ginecología *f.*
gypsum, *n.* yeso *m.*
Gypsy, *a. & n.* gitano -na.
gyrate, *v.* girar.
gyroscope, *n.* giroscopio *m.*

H

habeas corpus, habeas corpus *m.*
haberdasher, *n.* camisero *m.*
haberdashery, *n.* camisería *f.*
habiliment, *n.* vestuario *m.*
habit, *n.* costumbre *f.,* hábito
m. **be in the h. of,** estar
acostumbrado a; soler.
habitable, *a.* habitable.
habitat, *n.* habitación *f.,*
ambiente *m.*
habitation, *n.* habitación *f.*
habitual, *a.* habitual.
habituate, *v.* habituar.
habitué, *n.* parroquiano *m.*
hack, 1. *n.* coche de
alquiler. **2.** *v.* tajar.
hackneyed, *a.* trillado.
hacksaw, *n.* sierra para cortar metal *f.*
haddock, *n.* merluza *f.*
haft, *n.* mango *m.*
hag, *n.* bruja *f.*
haggard, *a.* trasnochado.
haggle, *v.* regatear.
hail, 1. *n.* granizo; (greeting) saludo *m.* **2.** *v.*
granizar; saludar.
Hail Mary, Ave María *m.*
hailstone, *n.* piedra de
granizo *f.*
hailstorm, *n.* granizada *f.*
hair, *n.* pelo; cabello *m.*
haircut, *n.* corte de pelo.
hairdo, *n.* peinado *m.*

hairdresser, *n.* peluquero *m.*
hair dryer, secador de pelo,
secador *m.*
hairpin, *n.* horquilla *f.;*
gancho *m.*
hair's-breadth, *n.* ancho de
un pelo *m.*
hairspray, *n.* aerosol para
cabello.
hairy, *a.* peludo.
halcyon, 1. *n.* alcedón *m.* **2.**
a. tranquilo.
hale, *a.* sano.
half, 1. *a.* medio. **2.** *n.* mitad
f.
half-and-half, *a.* mitad y
mitad.
half-baked, *a.* medio crudo.
half-breed, *n.* mestizo *m.*
half brother, *n.* medio hermano *m.*
half-hearted, *a.* sin entusiasmo.
half-mast, *a. & n.* media
asta *m.*
halfpenny, *n.* medio
penique *m.*
halfway, *adv.* a medio
camino.
half-wit, *n.* bobo *m.*
halibut, *n.* hipogloso *m.*
hall, *n.* corredor *m.;* (for assembling) sala *f.* **city h.,**
ayuntamiento *m.*

hallmark, *n.* marca del contraste *f.*
hallow, *v.* consagrar.
Halloween, *n.* víspera de
Todos los Santos *f.*
hallucination, *n.* alucinación *f.*
hallway, *n.* pasadizo *m.*
halo, *n.* halo *m.;* corona *f.*
halt, 1. *a.* cojo. **2.** *n.* parada
f. **3.** *v.* parar. **4.** *interj.*
¡alto!
halter, *n.* cabestro *m.*
halve, *v.* dividir en dos
partes.
halyard, *n.* driza *f.*
ham, *n.* jamón *m.*
hamburger, *n.* albóndiga *f.*
hamlet, *n.* aldea *f.*
hammer, 1. *n.* martillo *m.* **2.**
v. martillar.
hammock, *n.* hamaca *f.*
hamper, *n.* canasta *f.,* cesto
m.
hamstring, 1. *n.* tendón de
la corva *m.* **2.** *v.* desjarretar.
hand, 1. *n.* mano *f.* **on the
other h.,** en cambio. **2.** *v.*
pasar. **h. over,** entregar.
handbag, *n.* cartera *f..*
handball, *n.* pelota *f.*
handbook, *n.* manual *m.*
handbrake, *n.* freno de
mano *m.*

handcuff, 1. *n.* esposa **2.** *v.* esposar.

handful, *n.* puñado *m.*

handicap, *n.* desventaja *f.*

handicraft, *n.* artífice *m.;* destreza manual.

handiwork, *n.* artefacto *m.*

handkerchief, *n.* pañuelo *m.*

handle, 1. *n.* mango *m.* **2.** *v.* manejar.

hand luggage, equipaje de mano *m.*

handmade, *a.* hecho a mano.

handmaid, *n.* criada de mano, sirvienta *f.*

hand organ, organillo *m.*

handsome, *a.* guapo; hermoso.

hand-to-hand, *adv.* de mano a mano.

handwriting, *n.* escritura *f.*

handy, *a.* diestro; útil; a la mano.

hang, *v.* colgar; ahorcar.

hangar, *n.* hangar *m.*

hangdog, *a. & n.* camastrón *m.*

hanger, *n.* colgador, gancho *m.*

hanger-on, *n.* dependiente; mogollón *m.*

hang glider, aparato para vuelo libre, delta, ala delta.

hanging, 1. *n.* ahorcadura *f.* **2.** *a.* colgante.

hangman, *n.* verdugo *m.*

hangnail, *n.* padrastro *m.*

hang out, *v.* enarbolar.

hangover, *n.* resaca *f.*

hangup, *n.* tara (psicológica) *f.*

hank, *n.* madeja *f.*

hanker, *v.* ansiar; apetecer.

haphazard, *a.* casual.

happen, *v.* acontecer, suceder, pasar.

happening, *n.* acontecimiento *m.*

happiness, *n.* felicidad; dicha *f.*

happy, *a.* feliz; contento; dichoso.

happy-go-lucky, *a. & n.* descuidado *m.*

harakiri, *n.* harakiri (suicidio japonés) *m.*

harangue, 1. *n.* arenga *f.* **2.** *v.* arengar.

harass, *v.* acosar; atormentar.

harbinger, *n.* presagio *m.*

harbor, 1. *n.* puerto; albergue *m.* **2.** *v.* abrigar.

hard, 1. *a.* duro; difícil. **2.** *adv.* mucho.

hard coal, antracita *m.*

hard disk, disco duro *m.*

harden, *v.* endurecer.

hard-headed, *a.* terco.

hard-hearted, *a.* empedernido.

hardiness, *n.* vigor *m.*

hardly, *adv.* apenas.

hardness, *n.* dureza; dificultad *f.*

hardship, *n.* penalidad *f.;* trabajo *m.*

hardware, *n.* ferretería *f.*

hardwood, *n.* madera dura *f.*

hardy, *a.* fuerte, robusto.

hare, *n.* liebre *f.*

harebrained, *a.* tolondro.

harelip, 1. *n.* labio leporino *m.* **2.** *a.* labihendido.

harem, *n.* harén *m.*

hark, *v.* escuchar; atender.

Harlequin, *n.* arlequín *m.*

harlot, *n.* ramera *f.*

harm, 1. *n.* mal, daño; perjuicio *m.* **2.** *v.* dañar.

harmful, *a.* dañoso.

harmless, *a.* inocente.

harmonic, *n.* armónico *m.*

harmonica, *n.* armónica *f.*

harmonious, *a.* armonioso.

harmonize, *v.* armonizar.

harmony, *n.* armonía *f.*

harness, *n.* arnés *m.*

harp, *n.* arpa *f.*

harpoon, *n.* arpón *m.*

harridan, *n.* vieja regañona *f.*

harrow, 1. *n.* rastro *m.;* grada *f.* **2.** *v.* gradar.

harry, *v.* acosar.

harsh, *a.* áspero.

harshness, *n.* aspereza *f.*

harvest, 1. *n.* cosecha *f.* **2.** *v.* cosechar.

hash, *n.* picadillo *m.*

hashish, *n.* haxis *m.*

hasn't, *v.* no tiene (neg. + tener).

hassle, *n.* lío *m.*, molestia *f.;* controversia *f.*

hassock, *n.* cojín *m.*

haste, *n.* prisa *f.*

hasten, *v.* apresurarse, darse prisa.

hasty, *a.* apresurado.

hat, *n.* sombrero *m.*

hat box, sombrerera *f.*

hatch, 1. *n.* (naut.) cuartel *m.* **2.** *v.* incubar; (fig.) tramar.

hatchery, *n.* criadero *m.*

hatchet, *n.* hacha pequeña.

hate, 1. *n.* odio *m.* **2.** *v.* odiar, detestar.

hateful, *a.* detestable.

hatred, *n.* odio *m.*

haughtiness, *n.* arrogancia *f.*

haughty, *a.* altivo.

haul, 1. *n.* (fishery) redada *f.* **2.** *v.* tirar, halar.

haunch, *n.* anca *f.*

haunt, 1. *n.* lugar frecuentado. **2.** *v.* frecuentar, andar por.

have, *v.* tener; haber.

haven, *n.* puerto; asilo *m.*

haven't, *v.* no tiene (neg. + tener).

havoc, *n.* ruina *f.*

hawk, *n.* halcón *m.*

hawker, *n.* buhonero *m.*

hawser, *n.* cable *m.*

hawthorn, *n.* espino *m.*

hay, *n.* heno *m.*

hay fever, *n.* fiebre del heno *f.*

hayfield, *n.* henar *m.*

hayloft, *n.* henil *m.*

haystack, *n.* hacina de heno *f.*

hazard, 1. *n.* azar *m.* **2.** *v.* aventurar.

hazardous, *a.* peligroso.

haze, *n.* niebla *f.*

hazel, *n.* avellano *m.*

hazelnut, avellana *f.*

hazy, *a.* brumoso.

he, *pron.* él *m.*

head, 1. *n.* cabeza *f.;* jefe *m.* **2.** *v.* dirigir; encabezar.

headache, *n.* dolor de cabeza *m.*

headband, *n.* venda para cabeza *f.*

headfirst, *adv.* de cabeza.

headgear, *n.* tocado *m.*

headlight, *n.* linterna delantera *f.,* farol de tope *m.*

headline, *n.* encabezado *m.*

headlong, *a.* precipitoso.

head-on, *adv.* de frente.

headphones, *n.pl.* auriculares *m.pl.*

headquarters, *n.* jefatura *f.;* (mil.) cuartel general.

headstone, *n.* lápida mortuoria *f.*

headstrong, *a.* terco.

headwaters, *n.* cabeceras *f.pl.*

head waiter, jefe de comedor *m. & f.*

headway, *n.* avance *m.,* progreso *m.*

headwork, *n.* trabajo mental *m.*

heady, *a.* impetuoso.

heal, *v.* curar, sanar.

health, *n.* salud *f.*

healthful, *a.* saludable.

healthy, *a.* sano; salubre.

heap, *n.* montón *m.*

hear, *v.* oír. **h. from,** tener noticias de. **h. about, h. of,** oír hablar de.

hearing, *n.* oído *m.*

hearing aid, audífono *m.*

hearsay, *n.* rumor *m.*

hearse, *n.* ataúd *m.*

heart, *n.* corazón; ánimo *m.* **by h.,** de memoria. **have h. trouble** padecer del corazón.

heartache, *n.* angustia *f.*

heart attack, ataque cardíaco, infarto, infarto de miocardio *m.*

heartbreak, *n.* angustia *f.;* pesar *m.*

heartbroken, *a.* acongojado.

heartburn, *n.* acedía *f.,* ardor de estómago *m.*

heartfelt, *a.* sentido.

hearth, *n.* hogar *m.,* chimenea *f.*

heartless, *a.* empedernido.

heartsick, *a.* desconsolado.

heart-stricken, *a.* afligido.

heart-to-heart, *adv.* franco; sincero.

hearty, *a.* cordial; vigoroso.

heat, 1. *n.* calor; ardor *m.;* calefacción *f.* **2.** *v.* calentar.

heated, *a.* acalorado.

heater, *n.* calentador *m.*

heath, *n.* matorral *m.*

heathen, *a. & n.* pagano -na.

heather, *n.* brezo *m.*

heating, *n.* calefacción *f.*

heatstroke, *n.* insolación *f.*

heat wave, onda de calor *f.*

heave, *v.* tirar.

heaven, *n.* cielo *m.*

heavenly, *a.* divino.

heavy, *a.* pesado; oneroso.

Hebrew, *a. & n.* hebreo -ea.

hectic, *a.* turbulento.

hedge, *n.* seto *m.*

hedgehog, *n.* erizo *m.*

hedonism, *n.* hedonismo *m.*

heed, 1. *n.* cuidado *m.* **2.** *v.* atender.

heedless, *a.* desatento; incauto.

heel, *n.* talón *m.;* (of shoe) tacón *m.*

heifer, *n.* novilla *f.*

height, *n.* altura *f.*

heighten, *n.* elevar; exaltar.

heinous, *a.* nefando.

heir, heiress, *n.* heredero -ra.

helicopter, *n.* helicóptero *m.*

heliotrope, *n.* heliotropo *m.*

helium, *n.* helio *m.*

hell, *n.* infierno *m.*

Hellenism, *n.* helenismo *m.*

hellish, *a.* infernal.

hello, *interj.* ¡hola!; (on telephone) aló; bueno.

helm, *n.* timón *m.*

helmet, *n.* yelmo, casco *m.*

helmsman, *n.* limonero *m.*

help, 1. *n.* ayuda *f.* **help!** ¡socorro! **2.** *v.* ayudar. **h. oneself,** servirse. **can't help (but),** no poder menos de.

helper, *n.* ayudante *m.*

helpful, *a.* útil; servicial.

helpfulness, *n.* utilidad *f.*

helpless, *a.* imposibilitado.

hem, 1. *n.* ribete *m.* **2.** *v.* ribetear.

hemisphere, *n.* hemisferio *m.*

hemlock, *n.* abeto *m.*

hemoglobin, *n.* hemoglobina *f.*

hemophilia, *n.* hemofilia *f.*

hemorrhage, *n.* hemorragia *f.*

hemorrhoid, *n.* hemorroides *f.pl.*

hemp, *n.* cáñamo *m.*

hemstitch, 1. *n.* vainica *f.* **2.** *v.* hacer una vainica.

hen, *n.* gallina *f.*

hence, *adv.* por lo tanto.

henceforth, *adv.* de aquí en adelante.

henchman, *n.* paniaguado *m.*

henna, *n.* alheña *f.*

hepatitis, *n.* hepatitis *f.*

her, 1. *a.* su. **2.** *pron.* ella; la; le.

herald, *n.* heraldo *m.*

heraldic, *a.* heráldico.

heraldry, *n.* heráldica *f.*

herb, *n.* yerba, hierba *f.*

herbaceous, *a.* herbáceo.

herbarium, *n.* herbario *m.*

herd, 1. *n.* hato, rebaño *m.* **2.** *v.* reunir en hatos.

here, *adv.* aquí; acá.

hereafter, *adv.* en lo futuro.

hereby, *adv.* por éstas, por la presente.

hereditary, *a.* hereditario.

heredity, *n.* herencia *f.*

herein, *adv.* aquí dentro; incluso.

heresy, *n.* herejía *f.*

heretic, 1. *a.* herético. **2.** *n.* hereje *m. & f.*

heretical, *a.* herético.

heretofore, *adv.* hasta ahora.

herewith, *adv.* con esto, adjunto.

heritage, *n.* herencia *f.*

hermetic, *a.* hermético.

hermit, *n.* ermitaño *m.*

hernia, *n.* hernia *f.*

hero, *n.* héroe *m.*

heroic, *a.* heroico.

heroically, *adv.* heroicamente.

heroin, *n.* heroína *f.*

heroine, *n.* heroína *f.*

heroism, *n.* heroísmo *m.*

heron, *n.* garza *f.*

herring, *n.* arenque *m.*

hers, *pron.* suyo, de ella.

herself, *pron.* sí, sí misma, se. **she h.,** ella misma. **with h.,** consigo.

hertz, *n.* hertzio *m.*

hesitancy, *n.* hesitación *f.*

hesitant, *a.* indeciso.

hesitate, *v.* vacilar.

hesitation, *n.* duda; vacilación *f.*

heterogeneous, a. heterogéneo.

heterosexual, a. heterosexual.

hexagon, n. hexágono m.

hibernate, v. invernar.

hibernation, n. invernada f.

hibiscus, n. hibisco m.

hiccup, 1. n. hipo m. **2.** v. tener hipo.

hickory, n. nogal americano m.

hidden, a. oculto; escondido.

hide, 1. n. cuero m.; piel f. **2.** v. esconder; ocultar.

hideous, a. horrible.

hide-out, n. escondite m.

hiding place, escondrijo m.

hierarchy, n. jerarquía f.

high, a. alto, elevado; (in price) caro.

highbrow, n. erudito m.

high fidelity, de alta fidelidad.

highlighter, n. marcador m.

highly, adv. altamente; sumamente.

high school, escuela secundaria f.

highway, n. carretera f.; camino real m.

hijacker, n. secuestrador, pirata de aviones m.

hike, n. caminata f.

hilarious, a. alegre, bullicioso.

hilariousness, hilarity, n. hilaridad f.

hill, n. colina f.; cerro m.; **down h.,** cuesta abajo. **up h.,** cuesta arriba.

hilly, a. accidentado.

hilt, n. puño m. **up to the h.,** a fondo.

him, pron. él; lo; le.

himself, pron. sí, sí mismo; se. **he h.,** él mismo. **with h.,** consigo.

hinder, v. impedir.

hindmost, a. último.

hindquarter, n. cuarto trasero m.

hindrance, n. obstáculo m.

hinge, 1. n. gozne m. **2.** v. engoznar. **h. on,** depender de.

hint, 1. n. insinuación f.; indicio m. **2.** v. insinuar.

hip, n. cadera f.

hippopotamus, n. hipopótamo m.

hire, v. alquilar.

his, 1. a. su. **2.** pron. suyo, de él.

Hispanic, a. hispano.

hiss, v. silbar, sisear.

historian, n. historiador m.

historic, historical, a. histórico.

history, n. historia f.

histrionic, a. histriónico.

hit, 1. n. golpe m.; (coll.) éxito m. **2.** v. golpear, dar.

hitch, v. amarrar; enganchar.

hitchhike, v. hacer autostop.

hitchhiker, n. autostopista f.

hitchhiking, n. autostop m.

hither, adv. acá, hacia acá.

hitherto, adv. hasta ahora.

hive, n. colmena f.

hives, n. urticaria f.

hoard, 1. n. acumulación f. **2.** v. acaparar; atesorar.

hoarse, a. ronco.

hoax, 1. n. engaño m. **2.** v. engañar.

hobby, n. afición f., pasatiempo m.

hobgoblin, n. trasgo m.

hobnob, v. tener intimidad.

hobo, n. vagabundo m.

hockey, n. hockey m. **ice-h.,** hockey sobre hielo.

hod, n. esparavel m.

hodgepodge, n. baturrillo m.; mezcolanza f.

hoe, 1. n. azada f. **2.** v. cultivar con azada.

hog, n. cerdo, puerco m.

hoist, 1. n. grúa f., elevador m. **2.** v. elevar, enarbolar.

hold, 1. n. presa f.; agarro m.; (naut.) bodega f. **to get h. of,** conseguir, apoderarse de. **2.** v. tener; detener; sujetar; celebrar.

holder, n. tenedor m. **cigarette h.,** boquilla f.

holdup, n. salteamiento m.

hole, n. agujero; hoyo; hueco m.

holiday, n. día de fiesta.

holiness, n. santidad f.

Holland, n. Holanda f.

hollow, 1. a. hueco. **2.** n. cavidad f. **3.** v. ahuecar; excavar.

holly, n. acebo m.

hollyhock, n. malva real f.

holocaust, n. holocausto m.

hologram, n. holograma m.

holography, n. holografía f.

holster, n. pistolera f.

holy, a. santo.

holy day, disanto m.

Holy See, Santa Sede f.

Holy Spirit, Espíritu Santo m.

Holy Week, Semana Santa f.

homage, n. homenaje m.

home, n. casa, morada f; hogar m. **at h.,** en casa. **to go h.,** ir a casa.

home appliance, electrodoméstica m.

home computer, ordenador doméstico m., computadora doméstica f.

homeland, n. patria f.

homely, a. feo; casero.

home rule, n. autonomía f.

homesick, a. nostálgico.

homespun, a. casero; tocho.

homeward, adv. hacia casa.

homework, n. deberes mpl.

homicide, n. homicida m. & f.

homily, n. homilía f.

homogeneous, a. homogéneo.

homogenize, v. homogenizar.

homosexual, n. & a. homosexual m.

Honduras, n. Honduras f.

hone, 1. n. piedra de afilar f. **2.** v. afilar.

honest, a. honrado, honesto; sincero.

honestly, adv. honradamente; de veras.

honesty, n. honradez, honestidad f.

honey, n. miel f.

honeybee, n. abeja obrera f.

honeymoon, n. luna de miel.

honeysuckle, n. madreselva f.

honor, 1. n. honra f.; honor m. **2.** v. honrar.

honorable, a. honorable; ilustre.

honorary, *a.* honorario.

hood, *n.* capota; capucha *f.;* (auto.) cubierta del motor.

hoodlum, *n.* pillo *m.*, rufián *m.*

hoof, *n.* pezuña *f.*

hook, 1. *n.* gancho *m.* **2.** *v.* enganchar.

hooligan, *n.* gamberro -rra.

hoop, *n.* cerco *m.*

hop, 1. *n.* salto *m.* **2.** *v.* saltar.

hope, 1. *n.* esperanza *f.* **2.** *v.* esperar.

hopeful, *a.* lleno de esperanzas.

hopeless, *a.* desesperado; sin remedio.

horde, *n.* horda *f.*

horehound, *n.* marrubio *m.*

horizon, *n.* horizonte *m.*

horizontal, *a.* horizontal.

hormone, *n.* hormón *m.*

horn, *n.* cuerno *m.;* (music) trompa *f.;* (auto.) bocina *f.*

hornet, *n.* avispón *m.*

horny, *a.* córneo; calloso.

horoscope, *n.* horóscopo *m.*

horrendous, *a.* horrendo.

horrible, *a.* horrible.

horrid, *a.* horrible.

horrify, *v.* horrorizar.

horror, *n.* horror *m.*

horror film, película de terror *f.*

horse, *n.* caballo *m.* **to ride a h.,** cabalgar.

horseback, *n.* **on h.,** a caballo. **to ride h.,** montar a caballo.

horseback riding, equitación *f.*

horsefly, *n.* tábano *m.*

horsehair, *n.* pelo de caballo *m.;* tela de crin *f.*

horseman, *n.* jinete *m.*

horsemanship, *n.* manejo *m.*, equitación *f.*

horsepower, *n.* caballo de fuerza *m.*

horse race, carrera de caballos *f.*

horseradish, *n.* rábano picante *m.*

horseshoe, *n.* herradura *f.*

hortatory, *a.* exhortatorio.

horticulture, *n.* horticultura *f.*

hose, *n.* medias *f.pl;* (garden) manguera *f.*

hosiery, *n.* calcetería *f.*

hospitable, *a.* hospitalario.

hospital, *n.* hospital *m.*

hospitality, *n.* hospitalidad *f.*

hospitalization, *n.* hospitalización *f.*

hospitalize, *v.* hospitalizar.

host, *n.* anfitrión *m.*, dueño de la casa; (rel.) hostia *f.*

hostage, *n.* rehén *m.*

hostel, *n.* hostería *f.*

hostelry, *n.* fonda *f.*, parador *m.*

hostess, *n.* anfitriona *f.*, dueña de la casa.

hostile, *a.* hostil.

hostility, *n.* hostilidad *f.*

hot, *a.* caliente; (sauce) picante. **to be h.,** tener calor; (weather) hacer calor.

hotbed, *n.* estercolero *m.* (fig.) foco *m.*

hot dog, perrito caliente *m.*

hotel, *n.* hotel *m.*

hot-headed, *a.* turbulento, alborotadizo.

hothouse, *n.* invernáculo *m.*

hot-water bottle, bolsa de agua caliente *f.*

hound, 1. *n.* sabueso *m.* **2.** *v.* perseguir; seguir la pista.

hour, *n.* hora *f.*

hourglass, *n.* reloj de arena *m.*

hourly, 1. *a.* por horas. **2.** *adv.* a cada hora.

house, 1. *n.* casa *f.;* (theat.) público *m.* **2.** *v.* alojar, albergar.

housefly, *n.* mosca ordinaria *f.*

household, *n.* familia; casa *f.*

housekeeper, *n.* ama de llaves.

housemaid, *n.* criada *f.*, sirvienta *f.*

housewife, *n.* ama de casa.

housework, *n.* tareas domésticas.

hovel, *n.* choza *f.*

hover, *v.* revolotear.

hovercraft, *n.* aerodeslizador *m.*

how, *adv.* cómo. **h. much,** cuánto. **h. many,** cuántos. **h. far,** a qué distancia.

however, *adv.* como quiera; sin embargo.

howl, 1. *n.* aullido *m.* **2.** *v.* aullar.

hub, *n.* centro *m.;* eje *m.* **h. of a wheel,** cubo de la rueda *m.*

hubbub, *n.* alboroto *m.*, bulla *f.*

hue, *n.* matiz; color *m.*

hug, 1. *n.* abrazo *m.* **2.** *v.* abrazar.

huge, *a.* enorme.

hulk, *n.* casco de buque *m.*

hull, 1. *n.* cáscara *f.;* (naval) casco *m.* **2.** *v.* decascarar.

hum, 1. *n.* zumbido *m.* **2.** *v.* tararear; zumbar.

human, *a.* & *n.* humano -na.

human being, ser humano *m.*

humane, *a.* humano, humanitario.

humanism, *n.* humanidad *f.;* benevolencia *f.*

humanitarian, *a.* humanitario.

humanity, *n.* humanidad *f.*

humanly, *a.* humanamente.

humble, *a.* humilde.

humbug, *n.* farsa *f.*, embaucador *m.*

humdrum, *a.* monótono.

humid, *a.* húmedo.

humidity, *n.* humedad *f.*

humiliate, *v.* humillar.

humiliation, *n.* mortificación *f.;* bochorno *m.*

humility, *n.* humildad *f.*

humor, *1. n.* humor; capricho *m.* **2.** *v.* complacer.

humorist, *n.* humorista *m.*

humorous, *a.* divertido.

hump, *n.* joroba *f.*

humpback, *n.* jorobado *m.*

humus, *n.* humus *m.*

hunch, *n.* giba *f.;* (idea) corazonada *f.*

hunchback, *n.* jorobado *m.*

hundred, 1. *a.* & *pron.* cien, ciento. **200,** doscientos. **300,** trescientos. **400,** cuatrocientos. **500,** quinientos. **600,** seiscientos. **700,** setecientos. **800,** ochocientos. **900,** novecientos. **2.** *n.* centenar *m.*

hundredth, *n. & a.* centésimo *m.*

Hungarian, *a. & n.* húngaro -ra.

Hungary, Hungría *f.*

hunger, *n.* hambre *f.*

hungry, *a.* hambriento. **to be h.,** tener hambre.

hunt, 1. *n.* caza *f.* **2.** *v.* cazar. **h. up,** buscar.

hunter, *n.* cazador *m.*

hunting, *n.* caza *f.* **to go h.,** ir de caza.

hurdle, *n.* zarzo *m.,* valla *f.;* dificultad *f.*

hurl, *v.* arrojar.

hurricane, *n.* huracán *m.*

hurry, 1. *n.* prisa *f.* **to be in a h.,** tener prisa. **2.** *v.* apresurar; darse prisa.

hurt, 1. *n.* daño, perjuicio *m.* **2.** *v.* dañar; lastimar; doler; ofender.

hurtful, *a.* perjudicial, dañino.

hurtle, *v.* lanzar.

husband, *n.* marido, esposo *m.*

husk, 1. *n.* cáscara *f.* **2.** *v.* descascarar.

husky, *a.* fornido.

hustle, *v.* empujar.

hustle and bustle, ajetreo *m.*

hut, *n.* choza *f.*

hyacinth, *n.* jacinto *m.*

hybrid, *a.* híbrido.

hydrangea, *n.* hortensia *f.*

hydraulic, *a.* hidráulico.

hydroelectric, *a.* hidroeléctrico.

hydrogen, *n.* hidrógeno *m.*

hydrophobia, *n.* hidrofobia. *f.*

hydroplane, *n.* hidroavión *m.*

hydrotherapy, *n.* hidroterapia *f.*

hyena, *n.* hiena *f.*

hygiene, *n.* higiene *f.*

hygienic, *a.* higiénico.

hymn, *n.* himno *m.*

hymnal, *n.* himnario *m.*

hypercritical, *a.* hipercrítico.

hypermarket, *n.* hipermercado *m.*

hyphen, *n.* guión *m.*

hyphenate, *v.* separar con guión.

hypnosis, *n.* hipnosis *f.*

hypnotic, *a.* hipnótico.

hypnotism, *n.* hipnotismo *m.*

hypnotize, *v.* hipnotizar.

hypochondria, *n.* hipocondría *f.*

hypochondriac, *n. & a.* hipocondríaco *m.*

hypocrisy, *n.* hipocresía *f.*

hypocrite, *n.* hipócrita *m. & f.*

hypocritical, *a.* hipócrita.

hypodermic, *a.* hipodérmico.

hypotenuse, *n.* hipotenusa *f.*

hypothesis, *n.* hipótesis *f.*

hypothetical, *a.* hipotético.

hysterectomy, *n.* histerectomía *f.*

hysteria, hysterics, *n.* histeria *f.*

hysterical, *a.* histérico.

I

I, *pron.* yo.

iambic, *a.* yámbico.

ice, *n.* hielo *m.*

iceberg, *n.* iceberg *m.*

icebox, *n.* refrigerador *m.*

ice cream, helado, mantecado *m.;* **i.-c. cone,** barquillo de helado; **i.-c. parlor** heladería *f.*

ice cube, cubito de hielo.

ice skate, patín de cuchilla *m.*

icon, *n.* icón *m.*

icy, *a.* helado; indiferente.

idea, *n.* idea *f.*

ideal, *a.* ideal.

idealism, *n.* idealismo *m.*

idealist, *n.* idealista *m. & f.*

idealistic, *a.* idealista.

idealize, *v.* idealizar.

ideally, *adv.* idealmente.

identical, *a.* idéntico.

identifiable, *a.* identificable.

identification, *n.* identificación *f.* **i. papers,** cédula de identidad *f.*

identify, *v.* identificar.

identity, *n.* identidad *f.*

ideology, *n.* ideología *f.*

idiocy, *n.* idiotez *f.*

idiom, *n.* modismo *m.;* idioma *m.*

idiot, *n.* idiota *m. & f.*

idiotic, *a.* idiota, tonto.

idle, *a.* desocupado; perezoso.

idleness, *n.* ociosidad, pereza *f.*

idol, *n.* ídolo *m.*

idolatry, *n.* idolatría *f.*

idolize, *v.* idolatrar.

idyl, *n.* idilio *m.*

idyllic, *a.* idílico.

if, *conj.* si. **even if,** aunque.

ignite, *v.* encender.

ignition, *n.* ignición *f.*

ignoble, *a.* innoble, indigno.

ignominious, *a.* ignominioso.

ignoramus, *n.* ignorante *m.*

ignorance, *n.* ignorancia *f.*

ignorant, *a.* ignorante. **to be i. of,** ignorar.

ignore, *v.* desconocer, pasar por alto.

ill, *a.* enfermo, malo.

illegal, *a.* ilegal.

illegible, *a.* ilegible.

illegibly, *a.* ilegiblemente.

illegitimacy, *n.* ilegitimidad *f.*

illegitimate, *a.* ilegítimo; desautorizado.

illicit, *a.* ilícito.

illiteracy, *n.* analfabetismo *m.*

illiterate, *a. & n.* analfabeto -ta.

illness, *n.* enfermedad, maldad *f.*

illogical, *a.* ilógico.

illuminate, *v.* iluminar.

illumination, *n.* iluminación *f.*

illusion, *n.* ilusión *f.;* ensueño *m.*

illusive, *a.* ilusivo.

illustrate, *v.* ilustrar; ejemplificar.

illustration, *n.* ilustración
f.; ejemplo; grabado *m.*
illustrative, *a.* ilustrativo.
illustrious, *a.* ilustre.
ill will, *n.* malevolencia f.
image, *n.* imagen, estatua f.
imagery, *n.* imaginación f.
imaginable, *a.* imaginable.
imaginary, *a.* imaginario.
imagination, *n.* imaginación
f.
imaginative, *a.* imaginativo.
imagine, *v.* imaginarse, figurarse.
imam, *n.* imán *m.*
imbecile, *n. & a.* imbécil *m.*
imitate, *v.* imitar.
imitation, *n.* imitación f.
imitative, *a.* imitativo.
immaculate, *a.* inmaculado.
immanent, *a.* inmanente.
immaterial, *a.* inmaterial;
sin importancia.
immature, *a.* inmaturo.
immediate, *a.* inmediato.
immediately, *adv.* inmediatamente.
immense, *a.* inmenso.
immerse, *v.* sumergir.
immigrant, *n. & a.* inmigrante *m. & f.*
immigrate, *v.* inmigrar.
imminent, *a.* inminente.
immobile, *a.* inmóvil.
immoderate, *a.* inmoderado.
immodest, *a.* inmodesto;
atrevido.
immoral, *a.* inmoral.
immorality, *n.* inmoralidad f.
immorally, *adv.* licenciosa-
mente.
immortal, *a.* inmortal.
immortality, *n.* inmortalidad f.
immortalize, *v.* inmortalizar.
immune, *a.* inmune.
immunity, *n.* inmunidad f.
immunize, *v.* inmunizar.
impact, *n.* impacto *m.*
impair, *v.* empeorar, perjudicar.
impale, *v.* empalar.
impart, *v.* impartir, comunicar.
impartial, *a.* imparcial.
impatience, *n.* impaciencia f.
impatient, *a.* impaciente.
impede, *v.* impedir, estorbar.

impediment, *n.* impedimento *m.*
impel, *v.* impeler.
impenetrable, *a.* impenetrable.
impenitent, *n. & a.* impeni-
tente *m.*
imperative, *a.* imperativo.
imperceptible, *a.* imperceptible.
imperfect, *a.* imperfecto.
imperfection, *n.* imperfec-
ción f.
imperial, *a.* imperial.
imperialism, *n.* imperialismo *m.*
imperious, *a.* imperioso.
impersonal, *a.* impersonal.
impersonate, *v.* personificar; imitar.
impersonation, *n.* personifi-
cación f.; imitación f.
impertinence, *n.* impertinencia f.
impervious, *a.* impermeable.
impetuous, *a.* impetuoso.
impetus, *n.* ímpetu *m.*, impulso *m.*
impinge, *v.* tropezar; infringir.
implacable, *a.* implacable.
implant, *v.* implantar; inculcar.
implement, *n.* herramienta f.
implicate, *v.* implicar; embrollar.
implication, *n.* inferencia f.;
complicidad f.
implicit, *a.* implícito.
implied, *a.* implícito.
implore, *v.* implorar.
imply, *v.* significar; dar a
entender.
impolite, *a.* descortés.
import, 1. *n.* importación f.
2. *v.* importar.
importance, *n.* importancia
f.
important, *a.* importante.
importation, *n.* importación
f.
importune, *v.* importunar.
impose, *v.* imponer.
imposition, *n.* imposición f.
impossibility, *n.* imposibilidad f.
impossible, *a.* imposible.
impotence, *n.* impotencia f.

impotent, *a.* impotente.
impregnable, *a.* impregnable.
impregnate, *v.* impregnar;
fecundizar.
impresario, *n.* empresario *m.*
impress, *v.* impresionar.
impression, *n.* impresión f.
impressive, *a.* imponente.
imprison, *v.* encarcelar.
imprisonment, *n.* prisión f.,
encarcelación f.
improbable, *a.* improbable.
impromptu, *a.* extemporáneo.
improper, *a.* impropio.
improve, *v.* mejorar; progresar.
improvement, *n.* mejoramiento; progreso *m.*
improvise, *v.* improvisar.
impudent, *a.* descarado.
impugn, *v.* impugnar.
impulse, *n.* impulso *m.*
impulsive, *a.* impulsivo.
impunity, *n.* impunidad f.
impure, *a.* impuro.
impurity, *n.* impureza f.;
deshonestidad f.
impute, *v.* imputar.
in, 1. *prep.* en; dentro de. **2.**
adv. adentro.
inadvertent, *a.* inadvertido.
inalienable, *a.* inalienable.
inane, *a.* mentecato.
inaugural, *a.* inaugural.
inaugurate, *v.* inaugurar.
inauguration, *n.* inauguración f.
Inca, *n.* inca *m.*
incandescent, *a.* incandescente.
incantation, *n.* encantación
f., conjuro *m.*
incapacitate, *v.* incapacitar.
incarcerate, *v.* encarcelar.
incarnate, *a.* encarnado;
personificado.
incarnation, *n.* encarnación
f.
incendiary, *a.* incendario.
incense, 1. *n.* incienso *m.* **2.**
v. indignar.
incentive, *n.* incentivo *m.*
inception, *n.* comienzo *m.*
incessant, *a.* incesante.
incest, *n.* incesto *m.*
inch, *n.* pulgada f.

incidence, *n.* incidencia *f.*

incident, *n.* incidente *m.*

incidental, *a.* incidental.

incidentally, *adv.* incidentalmente; entre paréntesis.

incinerate, *v.* incinerar.

incinerator, *n.* incinerador *m.*

incipient, *a.* incipiente.

incision, *n.* incisión *f.;* cortadura *f.*

incisive, *a.* incisivo; mordaz.

incisor, *n.* incisivo *m.*

incite, *v.* incitar, instigar.

inclination, *n.* inclinación *f.;* declive *m.*

incline, 1. *n.* pendiente *m.* **2.** *v.* inclinar.

inclose, *v.* incluir.

include, *v.* incluir, englobar.

including, *prep.* incluso.

inclusive, *a.* inclusivo.

incognito, *n. & adv.* incógnito *m.*

income, *n.* renta *f.;* ingresos *m.pl.*

income tax, impuesto sobre la renta *m.*

incomparable, *a.* incomparable.

inconvenience, 1. *n.* incomodidad *f.* **2.** *v.* incomodar.

inconvenient, *a.* incómodo.

incorporate, *v.* incorporar; dar cuerpo.

incorrigible, *a.* incorregible.

increase, *v.* crecer; aumentar.

incredible, *a.* increíble.

incredulity, *n.* incredulidad *f.*

incredulous, *a.* incrédulo.

increment, *n.* incremento *m.,* aumento *m.*

incriminate, *v.* incriminar.

incrimination, *n.* incriminación *f.*

incrust, *v.* incrustar.

incubator, *n.* incubadora *f.*

inculcate, *v.* inculcar.

incumbency, *n.* incumbencia *f.*

incumbent, *a.* obligatorio; colocado sobre.

incur, *v.* incurrir.

incurable, *a.* incurable.

indebted, *a.* obligado; adeudado.

indeed, *adv.* verdaderamente, de veras. **no i.,** de ninguna manera.

indefatigable, *a.* incansable.

indefinite, *a.* indefinido.

indefinitely, *adv.* indefinidamente.

indelible, *a.* indeleble.

indemnify, *v.* indemnizar.

indemnity, *n.* indemnificación *f.*

indent, 1. *n.* diente *f.,* mella *f.* **2.** *v.* indentar, mellar.

indentation, *n.* indentación *f.*

independence, *n.* independencia *f.*

independent, *a.* independiente.

in-depth, *adj.* en profundidad.

index, *n.* índice *m.;* (of book) tabla *f.*

index card, ficha *f.*

index finger, dedo índice *m.*

India, *n.* India *f.*

Indian, *a. & n.* indio -dia.

indicate, *v.* indicar.

indication, *n.* indicación *f.*

indicative, *a. & n.* indicativo *m.*

indict, *v.* encausar.

indictment, *n.* (law) sumaria; denuncia *f.*

indifference, *n.* indiferencia *f.*

indifferent, *a.* indiferente.

indigenous, *a.* indígena.

indigent, *a.* indigente, pobre.

indigestion, *n.* indigestión *f.*

indignant, *a.* indignado.

indignation, *n.* indignación *f.*

indignity, *n.* indignidad *f.*

indirect, *a.* indirecto.

indiscreet, *a.* indiscreto.

indiscretion, *n.* indiscreción *f.*

indiscriminate, *a.* promiscuo.

indispensable, *a.* indispensable.

indisposed, *a.* indispuesto.

individual, *a. & n.* individuo *m.*

individuality, *n.* individualidad *f.*

individually, *adv.* individualmente.

indivisible, *a.* indivisible.

indoctrinate, *v.* doctrinar, enseñar.

indolent, *a.* indolente.

indoor, *a.* interior. **indoors,** *adv.* en casa; bajo techo.

indorse, *v.* endosar.

induce, *v.* inducir, persuadir.

induct, *v.* instalar, iniciar.

induction, *n.* introducción *f.;* instalación *f.*

inductive, *a.* inductivo; introductor.

indulge, *v.* favorecer. **i. in,** entregarse a.

indulgence, *n.* indulgencia *f.*

indulgent, *a.* indulgente.

industrial, *a.* industrial.

industrialist, *n.* industrial *m.*

industrial park, polígono industrial *m.*

industrious, *a.* industrioso, trabajador.

industry, *n.* industria *f.*

inedible, *a.* incomible.

ineligible, *a.* inelegible.

inept, *a.* inepto.

inert, *a.* inerte.

inertia, *n.* inercia *f.*

inevitable, *a.* inevitable.

inexpensive, *a.* económico.

inexplicable, *a.* inexplicable.

infallible, *a.* infalible.

infamous, *a.* infame.

infamy, *n.* infamia *f.*

infancy, *n.* infancia *f.*

infant, *n.* nene *m.;* criatura *f.*

infantile, *a.* infantil.

infantry, *n.* infantería *f.*

infatuated, *a.* infatuado.

infatuation, *a.* encaprichamiento *m.*

infect, *v.* infectar.

infection, *n.* infección *f.*

infectious, *a.* infeccioso.

infer, *v.* inferir.

inference, *n.* inferencia *f.*

inferior, *a.* inferior.

infernal, *a.* infernal.

inferno, *n.* infierno *m.*

infest, *v.* infestar.

infidel, 1. *n.* infiel *m. & f.;* pagano -na. **2.** *a.* infiel.

infidelity, *n.* infidelidad *f.*

infiltrate, *v.* infiltrar.

infinite, *a.* infinito.

infinitesimal, *a.* infinitesimal.

infinitive, *n. & a.* infinitivo *m.*

infinity, *n.* infinidad *f.*

infirm, *a.* enfermizo.

infirmary, *n.* hospital *m.,* enfermería *f.*

infirmity, *n.* enfermedad *f.*

inflame, *v.* inflamar.

inflammable, *a.* inflamable.

inflammation, *n.* inflamación *f.*

inflammatory, *a.* inflamante; (med.) inflamatorio.

inflate, *v.* inflar.

inflation, *n.* inflación *f.*

inflection, *n.* inflexión *f.;* (of the voice) modulación de la voz *f.*

inflict, *v.* infligir.

infliction, *n.* imposición *f.*

influence, 1. *n.* influencia *f.* **2.** *v.* influir en.

influential, *a.* influyente.

influenza, *n.* gripe *f.*

influx, *n.* afluencia *f.*

inform, *v.* informar. **i. one-self,** enterarse.

informal, *a.* informal.

information, *n.* informaciones *f.pl.*

information technology, *n.* informática *f.*

infrastructure, *n.* infraestructura *f.*

infringe, *v.* infringir.

infuriate, *v.* enfurecer.

ingenious, *a.* ingenioso.

ingenuity, *n.* ingeniosidad; destreza *f.*

ingredient, *n.* ingrediente *m.*

inhabit, *v.* habitar.

inhabitant, *n.* habitante *m. & f.*

inhale, *v.* inhalar.

inherent, *a.* inherente.

inherit, *v.* heredar.

inheritance, *n.* herencia *f.*

inhibit, *v.* inhibir.

inhibition, *n.* inhibición *f.*

inhuman, *a.* inhumano.

inimical, *a.* hostil.

inimitable, *a.* inimitable.

iniquity, *n.* iniquidad *f.*

initial, *a. & n.* inicial *f.*

initiate, *v.* iniciar.

initiation, *n.* iniciación *f.*

initiative, *n.* iniciativa *f.*

inject, *v.* inyectar.

injection, *n.* inyección *f.*

injunction, *n.* mandato *m.;* (law) embargo *m.*

injure, *v.* herir; lastimar; ofender.

injurious, *a.* perjudicial.

injury, *n.* herida; afrenta *f.;* perjuicio *m.*

injustice, *n.* injusticia *f.*

ink, *n.* tinta *f.*

inland, 1. *a.* interior. **2.** *adv.* tierra adentro.

inlet, *n.* entrada *f.;* ensenada *f.;* estuario *m.*

inmate, *n.* residente *m. & f.;* (of a prison) preso -sa.

inn, *n.* posada *f.;* mesón *m.*

inner, *a.* interior. **i. tube,** cámara de aire.

innocence, *n.* inocencia *f.*

innocent, *a.* inocente.

innocuous, *a.* innocuo.

innovation, *n.* innovación *f.*

innuendo, *n.* insinuación *f.*

innumerable, *a.* innumerable.

inoculate, *v.* inocular.

inoculation, *n.* inoculación *f.*

input, *n.* aducto *m.*

inquest, *n.* indagación *f.*

inquire, *v.* preguntar; inquirir.

inquiry, *n.* pregunta; investigación *f.*

inquisition, *n.* escudriñamiento *m.;* (church) Inquisición *f.*

insane, *a.* loco. **to go i.,** perder la razón; volverse loco.

insanity, *n.* locura *f.,* demencia *f.*

inscribe, *v.* inscribir.

inscription, *n.* inscripción; dedicatoria *f.*

insect, *n.* insecto *m.*

insecticide, *n. & a.* insecticida *m.*

inseparable, *a.* inseparable.

insert, *v.* insertar, meter.

insertion, *n.* inserción *f.*

inside, 1. *a. & n.* interior *m.* **2.** *adv.* adentro, por dentro. **i. out,** al revés. **3.** *prep.* dentro de.

insidious, *a.* insidioso.

insight, *n.* perspicacia *f.;* comprensión *f.*

insignia, *n.* insignias *f.pl.*

insignificance, *n.* insignificancia *f.*

insignificant, *a.* insignificante.

insinuate, *v.* insinuar.

insinuation, *n.* insinuación *f.*

insipid, *a.* insípido.

insist, *v.* insistir.

insistence, *n.* insistencia *f.*

insistent, *a.* insistente.

insolence, *n.* insolencia *f.*

insolent, *a.* insolente.

insomnia, *n.* insomnio *m.*

inspect, *v.* inspeccionar, examinar.

inspection, *n.* inspección *f.*

inspector, *n.* inspector -ora.

inspiration, *n.* inspiración *f.*

inspire, *v.* inspirar.

install, *v.* instalar.

installation, *n.* instalación *f.*

installment, *n.* plazo *m.*

instance, *n.* ocasión *f.* **for i.,** por ejemplo.

instant, *a. & n.* instante *m.*

instantaneous, *a.* instantáneo.

instant coffee, café soluble *m.*

instantly, *adv.* al instante.

instead, *adv.* en lugar de eso. **i. of,** en vez de, en lugar de.

instigate, *v.* instigar.

instill, *v.* instilar.

instinct, *n.* instinto *m.* **by i.,** por instinto.

instinctive, *a.* instintivo.

instinctively, *adv.* por instinto.

institute, 1. *n.* instituto *m.* **2.** *v.* instituir.

institution, *n.* institución *f.*

instruct, *v.* instruir.

instruction, *n.* instrucción *f.*

instructive, *a.* instructivo.

instructor, *n.* instructor -ora.

instrument, *n.* instrumento *m.*

instrumental, *a.* instrumental.

insufficient, *a.* insuficiente.

insular, *a.* insular; estrecho de miras.

insulate, *v.* aislar.

insulation, *n.* aislamiento *m.*

insulator, *n.* aislador *m.*

insulin, *n.* insulina *f.*

insult, 1. *n.* insulto *m.* **2.** *v.* insultar.

insuperable, *a.* insuperable.

insurance, *n.* seguro *m.*

insure, *v.* asegurar.

insurgent, *a.* & *n.* insurgente *m.* & *f.*

insurrection, *n.* insurrección *f.*

intact, *a.* intacto.

intangible, *a.* intangible, impalpable.

integral, *a.* íntegro.

integrate, *v.* integrar.

integrity, *n.* integridad *f.*

intellect, *n.* intelecto *m.*

intellectual, *a.* & *n.* intelectual *m.* & *f.*

intelligence, *n.* inteligencia *f.*

intelligence quotient, coeficiente intelectual *m.*

intelligent, *a.* inteligente.

intelligible, *a.* inteligible.

intend, *v.* pensar; intentar; destinar.

intense, *a.* intenso.

intensify, *v.* intensificar.

intensity, *n.* intensidad *f.*

intensive, *a.* intensivo.

intensive-care unit, unidad de cuidados intensivos, unidad de vigilancia intensiva *f.*

intent, *n.* intento *m.*

intention, *n.* intención *f.*

intentional, *a.* intencional.

intercede, *v.* interceder.

intercept, *v.* interceptar; detener.

interchange, *v.* intercambiar.

interchangeable, *a.* intercambiable.

intercourse, *n.* tráfico *m.*; comunicación *f.*; coito *m.*

interest, 1. *n.* interés *m.* **2.** *v.* interesar.

interesting, *a.* interesante.

interest rate, *n.* tipo de interés *m.*

interface, *n.* interfaz.

interfere, *v.* entrometerse, intervenir. **i. with,** estorbar.

interference, *n.* intervención *f.*; obstáculo *m.*

interior, *a.* interior.

interject, *v.* interponer; intervenir.

interjection, *n.* interjección *f.*; interposición *f.*

interlude, *n.* intervalo *m.*; (theat.) intermedio *m.*; (music) interludio *m.*

intermediary, *n.* intermediario -ria.

intermediate, *a.* intermedio.

interment, *n.* entierro.

intermission, *n.* intermisión *f.*; (theat.) entreacto *m.*

intermittent, *a.* intermitente.

intern, 1. *n.* interno -na, internado -da. **2.** *v.* internar.

internal, *a.* interno.

international, *a.* internacional.

internationalism, *n.* internacionalismo *m.*

interpose, *v.* interponer.

interpret, *v.* interpretar.

interpretation, *n.* interpretación *f.*

interpreter, *n.* intérprete *m.* & *f.*

interrogate, *v.* interrogar.

interrogation, *n.* interrogación; pregunta *f.*

interrogative, *a.* interrogativo.

interrupt, *v.* interrumpir.

interruption, *n.* interrupción *f.*

intersect, *v.* cortar.

intersection, *n.* intersección *f.*; (street) bocacalle *f.*

intersperse, *v.* entremezclar.

interval, *n.* intervalo *m.*

intervene, *v.* intervenir.

intervention, *n.* intervención *f.*

interview, 1. *n.* entrevista *f.* **2.** *v.* entrevistar.

interviewer, *n.* entrevistador -ora *m.* & *f.*

intestine, *n.* intestino *m.*

intimacy, *n.* intimidad; familiaridad *f.*

intimate, 1. *a.* íntimo, familiar. **2.** *n.* amigo -ga íntimo -ma. **3.** *v.* insinuar.

intimidate, *v.* intimidar.

intimidation, *n.* intimidación *f.*

into, *prep.* en, dentro de.

intonation, *n.* entonación *f.*

intone, *v.* entonar.

intoxicate, *v.* embriagar.

intoxication, *n.* embriaguez *f.*

intravenous, *a.* intravenoso.

intrepid, *a.* intrépido.

intricacy, *n.* complejidad *f.*; enredo *m.*

intricate, *a.* intrincado; complejo.

intrigue, 1. *n.* intriga *f.* **2.** *v.* intrigar.

intrinsic, *a.* intrínseco.

introduce, *v.* introducir; (a person) presentar.

introduction, *n.* presentación; introducción *f.*

introductory, *a.* introductor; preliminar. **i. offer,** ofrecimiento de presentación *m.*

introvert, *n.* & *a.* introvertido -da.

intrude, *v.* entremeterse.

intruder, *n.* intruso -sa.

intuition, *n.* intuición *f.*

intuitive, *a.* intuitivo.

inundate, *v.* inundar.

invade, *v.* invadir.

invader, *n.* invasor -ra.

invalid, *a.* & *n.* inválido -da.

invariable, *a.* invariable.

invasion, *n.* invasión *f.*

invective, 1. *n.* invectiva *f.* **2.** *a.* ultrajante.

inveigle, *v.* seducir.

invent, *v.* inventar.

invention, *n.* invención *f.*

inventive, *a.* inventivo.

inventor, *n.* inventor -ra.

inventory, *n.* inventario *m.*

invertebrate, *n.* & *a.* invertebrado *m.*

invest, *v.* investir; (com.) invertir.

investigate, *v.* investigar.

investigation, *n.* investigación *f.*

investment, *n.* inversión *f.*

investor, *n.* inversor, -ra.

inveterate, *a.* inveterado.

invidious, *a.* abominable, odioso, injusto.

invigorate, *v.* vigorizar, fortificar.

invincible, *a.* invencible.

invisible, *a.* invisible.

invitation, *n.* invitación *f.*

invite, *v.* invitar, convidar.

invocation, *n.* invocación *f.*

invoice, *n.* factura *f.*

invoke, *v.* invocar.

involuntary, *a.* involuntario.

involve, *v.* envolver; implicar.

involved, *a.* complicado.

invulnerable, *a.* invulnerable.

inward, *adv.* hacia adentro.

inwardly, *adv.* interiormente.

iodine, *n.* iodo *m.*

IQ, *abbr.* CI (coeficiente intelectual) *m.*

irate, *a.* encolerizado.

Ireland, *n.* Irlanda *f.*

iris, *n.* (anat.) iris *m.*; (botany) flor de lis *f.*

Irish, *a.* irlandés.

irk, *v.* fastidiar.

iron, 1. *n.* hierro *m.*; (appliance) plancha *f.* **2.** *v.* planchar.

ironical, *a.* irónico.

ironing board, tabla de planchar *f.*

irony, *n.* ironía *f.*

irrational, *a.* irracional; ilógico.

irregular, *a.* irregular.

irregularity, *n.* irregularidad *f.*

irrelevant, *a.* ajeno.

irresistible, *a.* irresistible.

irresponsible, *a.* irresponsable.

irreverent, *a.* irreverente.

irrevocable, *a.* irrevocable.

irrigate, *v.* regar; (med.) irrigar.

irrigation, *n.* riego *m.*

irritability, *n.* irritabilidad *f.*

irritable, *a.* irritable.

irritant, *n. & a.* irritante *m.*

irritate, *v.* irritar.

irritation, *n.* irritación *f.*

island, *n.* isla *f.*

isolate, *v.* aislar.

isolation, *n.* aislamiento *m.*

isosceles, *a.* isósceles.

issuance, *n.* emisión *f.*; publicación *f.*

issue, 1. *n.* emisión; edición; progenie *f.*; número *m.*; punto en disputa. **2.** *v.* emitir; publicar.

isthmus, *n.* istmo *m.*

it, *pron.* ello; él, ella; lo, la.

Italian, *a. & n.* italiano -na.

Italy, *n.* Italia *f.*

itch, 1. *n.* picazón *f.* **2.** *v.* picar.

item, *n.* artículo; detalle *m.*; inserción *f.*; (com.) renglón *m.*

itemize, *v.* detallar.

itinerant, 1. *n.* viandante *m.* **2.** *a.* ambulante.

itinerary, *n.* itinerario *m.*

its, *a.* su.

itself, *pron.* sí; se.

ivory, *n.* marfil *m.*

ivy, *n.* hiedra *f.*

J

jab, 1. *n.* pinchazo *m.* **2.** *v.* pinchar.

jack, *n.* (for lifting) gato *m.*; (cards) sota *f.*

jackal, *n.* chacal *m.*

jackass, *n.* asno *m.*

jacket, *n.* chaqueta *f.*; saco *m.*

jack-of-all-trades, *n.* estuche *m.*

jade, *n.* (horse) rocín *m.*; (woman) picarona *f.*; (mineral) jade *m.*

jaded, *a.* rendido.

jagged, *a.* mellado.

jaguar, *n.* jaguar *m.*

jail, *n.* cárcel *f.*

jailer, *n.* carcelero *m.*

jam, 1. *n.* conserva *f.*; aprieto, apretón *m.* **2.** *v.* apiñar, apretar; trabar.

janitor, *n.* portero *m.*

January, *n.* enero *m.*

Japan, *n.* Japón *m.*

Japanese, *a. & n.* japonés -esa.

jar, 1. *n.* jarro *m.* **2.** *v.* chocar; agitar.

jargon, *n.* jerga *f.*

jasmine, *n.* jazmín *m.*

jaundice, *n.* ictericia *f.*

jaunt, *n.* paseo *m.*

javelin, *n.* jabalina *f.*

jaw, *n.* quijada *f.*

jay, *n.* grajo *m.*

jazz, *n.* jazz *m.*

jealous, *a.* celoso. **to be j.,** tener celos.

jealousy, *n.* celos *m.pl.*

jeans, *n.* vaqueros, tejanos *m.pl.*

jeer, 1. *n.* burla *f.*, mofa *f.* **2.** *v.* burlar, mofar.

jelly, *n.* jalea *f.*

jellyfish, *n.* aguamar *m.*

jeopardize, *v.* arriesgar.

jeopardy, *n.* riesgo *m.*

jerk, 1. *n.* sacudida *f.* **2.** *v.* sacudir.

jerky, *a.* espasmódico.

Jerusalem, *n.* Jerusalén *m.*

jest, 1. *n.* broma *f.* **2.** *v.* bromear.

jester, *n.* bufón -ona; burlón -ona.

Jesuit, *a. & n.* jesuíta *m.*

Jesus Christ, *n.* Jesucristo *m.*

jet, *n.* chorro *m.*; (gas) mechero *m.*

jet lag, *n.* defase horario *m.*

jetsam, *n.* echazón *f.*

jettison, *v.* echar al mar.

jetty, *n.* muelle *m.*

Jew, *n.* judío -día.

jewel, *n.* joya *f.*

jeweler, *n.* joyero -ra.

jewelry, *n.* joyas *f.pl.* **j. store,** joyería *f.*

Jewish, *a.* judío.

jib, *n.* (naut.) foque *m.*

jiffy, *n.* instante *m.*

jig, *n.* jiga *f.* **j-saw,** sierra de vaivén *f.*

jilt, *v.* dar calabazas.

jingle, 1. *n.* retintín *m.*; rima pueril *f.* **2.** *v.* retiñir.

jinx, 1. *n.* aojo *m.* **2.** *v.* aojar.

jittery, *a.* nervioso.

job, *n.* empleo *m.*

jobber, *n.* destajista *m. & f.*, corredor *m.*

jockey, *n.* jockey *m.*

jocular, *a.* jocoso.

jog, 1. *n.* empujoncito *m.* **2.** *v.* empujar; estimular. **j. along,** ir a un trote corto.

join, *v.* juntar; unir.

joiner, *n.* ebanista *m.*

joint, *n.* juntura *f.*

jointly, *adv.* conjuntamente.

joke, 1. *n.* broma, chanza *f.;* chiste *m.* **2.** *v.* bromear.

joker, *n.* bromista *m.* & *f.;* comodín *m.*

jolly, *a.* alegre, jovial.

jolt, 1. *n.* sacudido *m.* **2.** *v.* sacudir.

jonquil, *n.* junquillo *m.*

jostle, *v.* empujar.

journal, *n.* diario *m.;* revista *f.*

journalism, *n.* periodismo *m.*

journalist, *n.* periodista *m.* & *f.*

journey, 1. *n.* viaje *m.;* jornada *f.* **2.** *v.* viajar.

journeyman, *n.* jornalero *m.,* oficial *m.*

jovial, *a.* jovial.

jowl, *n.* carrillo *m.*

joy, *n.* alegría *f.*

joyful, joyous, *a.* alegre, gozoso.

jubilant, *a.* jubiloso.

jubilee, *n.* jubileo *m.*

Judaism, *n.* judaísmo *m.*

judge, 1. *n.* juez *m.* & *f.* **2.** *v.* juzgar.

judgment, *n.* juicio *m.*

judicial, *a.* judicial.

judiciary, *a.* judiciario.

judicious, *a.* juicioso.

jug, *n.* jarro *m.*

juggle, *v.* escamotear.

juice, *n.* jugo, zumo *m.*

juicy, *a.* jugoso.

July, *n.* julio *m.*

jumble, 1. *n.* revoltillo *m.* **2.** *v.* arrebujar, revolver.

jump, 1. *n.* salto *m.* **2.** *v.* saltar, brincar.

junction, *n.* confluencia *f.;* (railway) empalme *m.*

juncture, *n.* juntura *f.;* coyuntura *f.*

June, *n.* junio *m.*

jungle, *n.* jungla, selva *f.*

junior, *a.* menor; más joven. **Jr.,** hijo.

juniper, *n.* enebro *m.*

junk, *n.* basura *f.*

junket, 1. *n.* leche cuajada *f.* **2.** *v.* festejar.

jurisdiction, *n.* jurisdicción *f.*

jurisprudence, *n.* jurisprudencia *f.*

jurist, *n.* jurista *m.* & *f.*

juror, *n.* jurado -da.

jury, *n.* jurado *m.*

just, 1. *a.* justo; exacto. **2.** *adv.* exactamente; (only) sólo. **j. now,** ahora mismo. **to have j.,** acabar de.

justice, *n.* justicia *f.;* (person) juez *m.* & *f.*

justifiable, *a.* justificable.

justification, *n.* justificación *f.*

justify, *v.* justificar.

jut, *v.* sobresalir.

jute, *n.* yute *m.*

juvenile, *a.* juvenil.

juvenile delinquency, delincuencia de menores, delincuencia juvenil *f.*

K

kaleidoscope, *n.* calidoscopio *m.*

kangaroo, *n.* canguro *m.*

karakul, *n.* caracul *m.*

karat, *n.* quilate *m.*

karate, *n.* karate *m.*

keel, 1. *n.* quilla *f.* **2.** *v.* **to k. over,** volcarse.

keen, *a.* agudo; penetrante.

keep, *v.* mantener, retener; guardar; preservar. **k. on,** seguir, continuar.

keeper, *n.* guardián *m.*

keepsake, *n.* recuerdo *m.*

keg, *n.* barrilito *m.*

kennel, *n.* perrera *f.*

kerchief, *n.* pañuelo *m.*

kernel, *n.* pepita *f.;* grano *m.*

kerosene, *n.* kerosén *m.*

ketchup, *n.* salsa de tomate *f.*

kettle, *n.* caldera, olla *f.*

kettledrum, *n.* tímpano *m.*

key, *n.* llave *f.;* (music) clave *f.;* (piano) tecla *f.*

keyboard, *n.* teclado *m.*

keyhole, *n.* bocallave *f.*

keypad, *n.* teclado *m.*

khaki, *a.* caqui.

kick, 1. *n.* patada *f.* **2.** *v.* patear; (coll.) quejarse.

kid, 1. *n.* cabrito *m.;* (coll.) niño -ña, chico -ca. **2.** *v.* (coll.) bromear.

kidnap, *v.* secuestrar.

kidnaper, *n.* secuestrador -ora.

kidnaping, *n.* rapto, secuestro *m.*

kidney, *n.* riñón *m.*

kidney bean, *n.* frijol *m.*

kill, *v.* matar.

killer, *n.* matador -ora.

kiln, *n.* horno *m.*

kilogram, *n.* kilogramo *m.*

kilohertz, *n.* kilohercio *m.*

kilometer, *n.* kilómetro *m.*

kilowatt, *n.* kilovatio *m.*

kin, *n.* parentesco *m.;* parientes *m.pl.*

kind, 1. *a.* bondadoso, amable. **2.** *n.* género *m.;* clase *f.* **k. of,** algo, un poco.

kindergarten, *n.* kindergarten *m.*

kindle, *v.* encender.

kindling, *n.* encendimiento *m.* **k.-wood,** leña menuda *f.*

kindly, *a.* bondadoso.

kindness, *n.* bondad *f.*

kindred, *n.* parentesco *m.*

kinetic, *a.* cinético.

king, *n.* rey *m.*

kingdom, *n.* reino *m.*

king prawn, langostino *m.*

kink, *n.* retorcimiento *m.*

kiosk, *n.* kiosco *m.*

kiss, 1. *n.* beso *m.* **2.** *v.* besar.

kitchen, *n.* cocina *f.*

kite, *n.* cometa *f.*

kitten, *n.* gatito -ta.

kleptomania, *n.* cleptomanía *f.*

kleptomaniac, *n.* cleptómano -na.

knack, *n.* don *m.,* destreza *f.*

knapsack, *n.* alforja *f.*

knead, *v.* amasar.

knee, *n.* rodilla *f.*

kneecap, *n.* rodillera, rótula *f.*

kneel, *v.* arrodillarse.

knickers, *n.* calzón corto *m.;* pantalones *m.pl.*

knife, *n.* cuchillo *m.*

knight, *n.* caballero *m.;* (chess) caballo *m.*

knit, *v.* tejer.

knob, *n.* tirador *m.*

knock, 1. *n.* golpe *m.;* llamada *f.* **2.** *v.* golpear; tocar, llamar.

knot, 1. *n.* nudo; lazo *m.* **2.** *v.* anudar.

knotty, *a.* nudoso.

know, *v.* saber; (a person) conocer.

knowledge, *n.* conocimiento, saber *m.*

knuckle, *n.* nudillo *m.* **k. bone,** jarrete *m.* **to k. under,** ceder a.

Koran, *n.* Corán *m.*

Korea, *n.* Corea *f.*

Korean, *a.* & *n.* coreano.

L

label, 1. *n.* rótulo *m.* **2.** *v.* rotular; designar.

labor, 1. *n.* trabajo *m.;* la clase obrera. **2.** *v.* trabajar.

laboratory, *n.* laboratorio *m.*

laborer, *n.* trabajador, obrero *m.*

laborious, *a.* laborioso, difícil.

labor union, gremio obrero, sindicato *m.*

labyrinth, *n.* laberinto *m.*

lace, 1. *n.* encaje *m.;* (of shoe) lazo *m.* **2.** *v.* amarrar.

lacerate, *v.* lacerar, lastimar.

laceration, *n.* laceración *f.,* desgarro *m.*

lack, 1. *n.* falta *f.* **l. of respect,** desacato *m.* **2.** *v.* faltar, carecer.

lackadaisical, *a.* indiferente; soñador.

laconic, *a.* lacónico.

lacquer, 1. *n.* laca *f.,* barniz *m.* **2.** *v.* laquear, barnizar.

lactic, *a.* láctico.

lactose, *n.* lactosa *f.*

ladder, *n.* escalera *f.*

ladle, 1. *n.* cucharón *m.* **2.** *v.* servir con cucharón.

lady, *n.* señora, dama *f.*

ladybug, *n.* mariquita *f.*

lag, 1. *n.* retraso *m.* **2.** *v.* quedarse atrás.

lagoon, *n.* laguna *f.*

laid-back, *a.* de buen talante, ecuánime, pacífico.

laity, *n.* laicado *m.*

lake, *n.* lago *m.*

lamb, *n.* cordero *m.*

lame, 1. *a.* cojo; estropeado. **2.** *v.* estropear, lisiar; incapacitar.

lament, 1. *n.* lamento *m.* **2.** *v.* lamentar.

lamentable, *a.* lamentable.

lamentation, *n.* lamento *m.;* lamentación *f.*

laminate, 1. *a.* laminado. **2.** *v.* laminar.

lamp, *n.* lámpara *f.*

lampoon, 1. *n.* pasquín *m.* **2.** *v.* pasquinar.

lance, 1. *n.* lanza *f.* **2.** *v.* (med.) abrir.

land, 1. *n.* país *m.;* tierra *f.* **native l.,** patria *f.* **2.** *v.* desembarcar; (plane) aterrizar.

landholder, *n.* hacendado - da.

landing, *n.* (of stairs) descanso, descansillo *m.;* (ship) desembarcadero *m.;* (airplane) aterrizaje *m.*

landlady, landlord, *n.* propietario -ria.

landmark, *n.* mojón *m.,* señal *f.;* rasgo sobresaliente *m.*

landscape, *n.* paisaje *m.*

landslide, *n.* derrumbe *m.*

lane, *n.* senda *f.*

language, *n.* lengua *f.,* idioma; lenguaje *m.*

languid, *a.* lánguido.

languish, *v.* languidecer.

languor, *n.* languidez *f.*

lanolin, *n.* lanolina *f.*

lantern, *n.* linterna *f.;* farol *m.*

lap, 1. *n.* regazo *m.;* falda *f.* **2.** *v.* lamer.

lapel, *n.* solapa *f.*

lapse, 1. *n.* lapso *m.* **2.** *v.* pasar; decaer; caer en error.

larceny, *n.* ratería *f.*

lard, *n.* manteca de cerdo *f.*

large, *a.* grande.

largely, *v.* ampliamente; mayormente; muy.

largo, *n.* & *a.* (mus.) largo *m.*

lariat, *n.* lazo *m.*

lark, *n.* (bird) alondra *f.*

larva, *n.* larva *f.*

laryngitis, *n.* laringitis *f.*

larynx, *n.* laringe *f.*

lascivious, *a.* lascivo.

laser, *n.* láser *m.*

lash, 1. *n.* azote, latigazo *m.* **2.** *v.* azotar.

lass, *n.* doncella *f.*

lassitude, *n.* lasitud *f.*

lasso, 1. *n.* lazo *m.* **2.** *v.* enlazar.

last, 1. *a.* pasado; (final) último. **at l.,** por fin. **l. but one,** penúltimo. **l. but two,** antepenúltimo. **2.** *v.* durar.

lasting, *a.* duradero.

latch, *n.* aldaba *f.*

late, 1. *a.* tardío; (deceased) difunto. **to be l.,** llegar tarde. **2.** *adv.* tarde.

lately, *adv.* recientemente.

latent, *a.* latente.

lateral, *a.* lateral.

lather, 1. *n.* espuma de jabón. **2.** *v.* enjabonar.

Latin, *n.* latín *m.*

Latin America, Hispanoamérica, América Latina *f.*

Latin American, hispanoamericano -na.

latitude, *n.* latitud *f.*

latrine, *n.* letrina *f.*

latter, *a.* posterior. **the l.,** éste.

lattice, *n.* celosía *f.*

laud, *v.* loar.

laudable, *a.* laudable.

laudanum, *n.* láudano *m.*

laudatory, *a.* laudatorio.
laugh, 1. *n.* risa, risotada *f.*
2. *v.* reír. **l. at,** reírse de.
laughable, *a.* risible.
laughter, *n.* risa *f.*
launch, 1. *n.* (naut.) lancha
f. **2.** *v.* lanzar.
launder, *v.* lavar y planchar
la ropa.
laundry, *n.* lavandería *f.*
laundryman, *n.* lavandero -
ra.
laureate, *n.* & *a.* laureado -
da.
laurel, *n.* laurel *m.*
lava, *n.* lava *f.*
lavatory, *n.* lavatorio *m.*
lavender, *n.* lavándula *f.*
lavish, 1. *a.* pródigo. **2.** *v.*
prodigar.
law, *n.* ley *f.; derecho *m.*
lawful, *a.* legal.
lawless, *a.* sin ley.
lawn, *n.* césped; prado *m.*
lawn mower, *n.* cortacésped
m. & *f.*
lawsuit, *n.* pleito *m.*
lawyer, *n.* abogado *m.* & *f.*
lax, *a.* flojo, laxo.
laxative, *n.* purgante *m.*
laxity, *n.* laxidad *f.; flojedad
f.
lay, 1. *a.* secular. **2.** *v.*
poner.
layer, *n.* capa *f.*
layman, *n.* lego, seglar *m.*
lazy, *a.* perezoso.
lead, 1. *n.* plomo *m.; (theat.)
papel principal. **to take
the l.,** tomar la delantera.
2. *v.* conducir; dirigir.
leaden, *a.* plomizo; pesado;
abatido.
leader, *n.* líder *m.* & *f.; jefe
m. & *f.; director -ora.
leadership, *n.* dirección *f.*
leaf, *n.* hoja *f.*
leaflet, *n.* (bot.) hojilla *f.;
folleto *m.*
league, *n.* liga; (measure)
legua *f.*
leak, 1. *n.* escape; goteo *m.*
2. *v.* gotear; (naut.) hacer
agua.
leakage, *n.* goteo *m.*, escape
m., pérdida *f.*
leaky, *a.* llovedizo, resque-
brajado.

lean, 1. *a.* flaco, magro. **2.**
v. apoyarse, arrimarse.
leap, 1. *n.* salto *m.* **2.** *v.* saltar.
leap year, *n.* año bisiesto *m.*
learn, *v.* aprender; saber.
learned, *a.* erudito.
learning, *n.* erudición *f.,* instrucción *f.*
lease, 1. *n.* arriendo *m.* **2.** *v.*
arrendar.
leash, 1. *n.* correa *f.* **2.** *v.*
atraillar.
least, *a.* menor; mínimo.
the l., lo menos. **at l.,**
por lo menos.
leather, *n.* cuero *m.*
leathery, *a.* coriáceo.
leave, 1. *n.* licencia *f.* **to
take l.,** despedirse. **2.** *v.*
dejar; (depart) salir, irse.
l. out, omitir.
leaven, 1. *n.* levadura *f.* **2.** *v.*
fermentar, imbuir.
lecherous, *a.* lujurioso.
lecture, *n.* conferencia *f.*
lecturer, *n.* conferencista *m.*
& *f.; catedrático -ca.
ledge, *n.* borde *m.; capa *f.*
ledger, *n.* libro mayor *m.*
lee, *n.* sotavento *m.*
leech, *n.* sanguijuela *f.*
leek, *n.* puerro *m.*
leer, *v.* mirar de soslayo.
leeward, *a.* sotavento.
left, *a.* izquierdo. **the l.,** la
izquierda. **to be left,**
quedarse.
left-handed, *a.* zurdo.
leftist, *n.* izquierdista *m.* &
f.
leftovers, *m.pl.* sobros *f.pl.*
leg, *n.* pierna *f.*
legacy, *n.* legado *m.,* herencia *f.*
legal, *a.* legal.
legalize, *v.* legalizar.
legation, *n.* legación, embajada *f.*
legend, *n.* leyenda *f.*
legendary, *a.* legendario.
legible, *a.* legible.
legion, *n.* legión *f.*
legislate, *v.* legislar.
legislation, *n.* legislación *f.*
legislator, *n.* legislador -ra.
legislature, *n.* legislatura *f.*
legitimate, *a.* legítimo.
legume, *n.* legumbre *f.*

leisure, *n.* desocupación *f.;
horas libres.
leisurely, 1. *a.* deliberado.
2. *adv.* despacio.
lemon, *n.* limón *m.*
lemonade, *n.* limonada *f.*
lend, *v.* prestar.
length, *n.* largo *m.; duración
f.
lengthen, *v.* alargar.
lengthwise, *adv.* a lo largo.
lengthy, *a.* largo.
lenient, *a.* indulgente.
lens, *n.* lente *m.* or *f.*
Lent, *n.* cuaresma *f.*
Lenten, *a.* cuaresmal.
lentil, *n.* lenteja *f.*
leopard, *n.* leopardo *m.*
leotard, *n.* mallas *f.pl.*
leper, *n.* leproso -sa.
leprosy, *n.* lepra *f.*
lesbian, *n.* lesbiana *f.*
lesion, *n.* lesión *f.*
less, *a.* & *adv.* menos.
lessen, *v.* disminuir.
lesser, *a.* menor; más pequeño.
lesson, *n.* lección *f.*
lest, *conj.* para que no.
let, *v.* dejar; permitir; arrendar.
letdown, *n.* decepción *f.*
lethal, *a.* letal.
lethargic, *a.* letárgico.
lethargy, *n.* letargo *m.*
letter, *n.* carta; (of alphabet)
letra *f.*
letterhead, *n.* membrete *m.*
lettuce, *n.* lechuga *f.*
leukemia, *n.* leucemia *f.*
levee, *n.* recepción *f.*
level, 1. *a.* llano, nivelado.
2. *n.* nivel *m.; llanura *f.*
3. *v.* allanar; nivelar.
lever, *n.* palanca *f.*
levity, *n.* levedad *f.*
levy, 1. *n.* leva *f.* **2.** *v.* imponer.
lewd, *a.* lascivo.
lexicon, *n.* léxico *m.*
liability, *n.* riesgo *m.;
obligación *f.*
liable, *a.* sujeto; responsable.
liaison, *n.* vinculación *f.,* enlace *m.; concubinaje *m.*
liar, *n.* embustero -ra.
libel, 1. *n.* libelo *m.* **2.** *v.*
difamar.

libelous, *a.* difamatorio.

liberal, *a.* liberal; generoso.

liberalism, *n.* liberalismo *m.*

liberality, *n.* liberalidad *f.*

liberate, *v.* libertar.

liberty, *n.* libertad *f.*

libidinous, *a.* libidinoso.

librarian, *n.* bibliotecario - ria.

library, *n.* biblioteca *f.*

libretto, *n.* libreto *m.*

license, *n.* licencia *f.;* permiso *m.*

licentious, *a.* licencioso.

lick, *v.* lamer.

licorice, *n.* regaliz *m.*

lid, *n.* tapa *f.*

lie, 1. *n.* mentira *f.* 2. *v.* mentir. **l. down,** acostarse, echarse.

lieutenant, *n.* teniente *m.*

life, *n.* vida *f.*

lifeboat, *n.* bote salvavidas *m.*

life buoy, boya *f.*

lifeguard, socorrista *m. & f.*

life insurance, seguro de vida *m.*

life jacket, chaleco salvavidas *m.*

lifeless, *a.* sin vida.

life preserver, salvavidas *m.*

life style, modo de vida *m.*

lift, *v.* levantar, alzar, elevar.

ligament, *n.* ligamento *m.*

ligature, *n.* ligadura *f.*

light, 1. *a.* ligero; liviano; (in color) claro. 2. *n.* luz; candela *f.* 3. *v.* encender; iluminar.

light bulb, bombilla *f.*

lighten, *v.* aligerar; aclarar; iluminar.

lighter, *n.* encendedor *m.*

lighthouse, *n.* faro *m.*

lightness, *n.* ligereza; agilidad *f.*

lightning, *n.* relámpago *m.*

like, 1. *a.* semejante. 2. *prep.* como. 3. *v.* **I like . . .** me gusta, me gustan . . . **I should like,** quisiera.

likeable, *a.* simpático, agradable.

likelihood, *n.* probabilidad *f.*

likely, *a.* probable; verosímil.

liken, *v.* comparar; asemejar.

likeness, *n.* semejanza *f.*

likewise, *adv.* igualmente.

lilac, *n.* lila *f.*

lilt, 1. *n.* cadencia alegre *f.* 2. *v.* cantar alegremente.

lily, *n.* lirio *m.*

lily of the valley, muguete *m.*

limb, *n.* rama *f.*

limber, *a.* flexible. **to l. up,** ponerse flexible.

limbo, *n.* limbo *m.*

lime, *n.* cal *f.;* (fruit) limoncito *m.,* lima *f.*

limestone, *n.* piedra caliza *f.*

limewater, *n.* agua de cal *f.*

limit, 1. *n.* límite *m.* 2. *v.* limitar.

limitation, *n.* limitación *f.*

limitless, *a.* ilimitado.

limousine, *n.* limusina *f.*

limp, 1. *n.* cojera *f.* 2. *a.* flojo. 3. *v.* cojear.

limpid, *a.* límpido.

line, 1. *n.* línea; fila; raya *f.;* (of print) renglón *m.* 2. *v.* forrar; rayar.

lineage, *n.* linaje *m.*

lineal, *a.* lineal.

linear, *a.* linear, longitudinal.

linen, *n.* lienzo, lino *m.;* ropa blanca.

liner, *n.* vapor *m.*

linger, *v.* demorarse.

lingerie, *n.* ropa blanca *f.*

linguist, *n.* lingüista *m. & f.*

linguistic, *a.* lingüístico.

liniment, *n.* linimento *m.*

lining, *n.* forro *m.*

link, 1. *n.* eslabón; vínculo *m.* 2. *v.* vincular.

linoleum, *n.* linóleo *m.*

linseed, *n.* linaza *f.;* simiente de lino *f.*

lint, *n.* hilacha *f.*

lion, *n.* león *m.*

lip, *n.* labio *m.*

lipstick, *n.* lápiz de labios.

liqueur, *n.* licor *m.*

liquid, *a. & n.* líquido *m.*

liquidate, *v.* liquidar.

liquidation, *n.* liquidación *f.*

liquor, *n.* licor *m.*

lisp, 1. *n.* ceceo *m.* 2. *v.* cecear.

list, 1. *n.* lista *f.* 2. *v.* registrar.

listen (to), *v.* escuchar.

listless, *a.* indiferente.

litany, *n.* letanía *f.*

liter, *n.* litro *m.*

literal, *a.* literal.

literary, *a.* literario.

literate, *a.* alfabetizado.

literature, *n.* literatura *f.*

litigant, *n. & a.* litigante *m. & f.*

litigation, *n.* litigio, pleito *m.*

litter, 1. *n.* litera *f.;* cama de paja. 2. *v.* poner en desorden.

little, *a.* pequeño; (quantity) poco.

little finger, meñique *m.*

liturgical, *a.* litúrgico.

liturgy, *n.* liturgia *f.*

live, 1. *a.* vivo. 2. *v.* vivir.

livelihood, *n.* subsistencia *f.*

lively, *a.* vivo; rápido; animado.

liver, *n.* hígado *m.*

livery, *n.* librea *f.*

livestock, *n.* ganadería *f.*

livid, *a.* lívido.

living, 1. *a.* vivo. 2. *n.* sustento *m.* **to earn (make) a living,** ganarse la vida.

living room, salón *m.*

lizard, *n.* lagarto *m.,* lagartija *f.*

llama, *n.* llama *f.*

load, 1. *n.* carga *f.* 2. *v.* cargar.

loaf, 1. *n.* pan *m.* 2. *v.* holgazanear.

loam, *n.* marga *f.*

loan, 1. *n.* préstamo *m.* 2. *v.* prestar.

loathe, *v.* aborrecer, detestar.

lobby, *n.* vestíbulo *m.*

lobe, *n.* lóbulo *m.*

lobster, *n.* langosta *f.*

local, *a.* local.

local area network, red local *f.*

locale, *n.* localidad *f.*

locality, *n.* localidad *f.,* lugar *m.*

localize, *v.* localizar.

locate, *v.* situar; hallar.

location, *n.* sitio *m.;* posición *f.*

lock, 1. *n.* cerradura *f.;* (pl.) cabellos *m.pl.* 2. *v.* cerrar con llave.

locker, *n.* cajón *m.;* ropero *m.*

locket, *n.* guardapelo *m.;* medallón *m.*

lockjaw, *n.* trismo *m.*

locksmith, *n.* cerrajero -ra.
locomotive, *n.* locomotora *f.*
locust, *n.* cigarra *f.,* saltamontes *m.*
locution, *n.* locución *f.*
lode, *n.* filón *m.,* veta *f.*
lodge, 1. *n.* logia; (inn) posada *f.* **2.** *v.* fijar; alojar, morar.
lodger, *n.* inquilino *m.*
lodging, *n.* alojamiento *m.*
loft, *n.* desván, sobrado *m.*
lofty, *a.* alto; altivo.
log, *n.* tronco de árbol; (naut.) barquilla *f.*
loge, *n.* palco *m.*
logic, *n.* lógica *f.*
logical, *a.* lógico.
loin, *n.* lomo *m.*
loiter, *v.* haraganear.
lone, *a.* solitario.
loneliness, *n.* soledad *f.*
lonely, lonesome, *a.* solo y triste.
lonesome, *a.* solitario, aislado.
long, 1. *a.* largo. **a l. time,** mucho tiempo. **2.** *adv.* mucho tiempo. **how l.,** cuánto tiempo. **no longer,** ya no. **3.** *v.* **l. for,** anhelar.
long-distance call, conferencia interurbana *f.*
longevity, *n.* longevidad *f.*
long-haired, *a.* melenudo.
longing, *n.* anhelo *m.*
longitude, *n.* longitud *m.*
look, 1. *n.* mirada *f.;* aspecto *m.* **2.** *v.* parecer; mirar. **l. at,** mirar. **l. for,** buscar. **l. like,** parecerse a. **l. out!,** ¡cuidado! **l. up,** buscar; ir a ver, venir a ver.
looking glass, espejo *m.*
loom, 1. *n.* telar *m.* **2.** *v.* asomar.
loop, *n.* vuelta *f.*
loophole, *n.* aspillera *f.;* (fig.) callejuela, evasiva *f.,* efugio *m.*

loose, *a.* suelto; flojo.
loose change, suelto *m.*
loosen, *v.* soltar; aflojar.
loot, 1. *n.* botín *m.,* saqueo *m.* **2.** *v.* saquear.
lopsided, *a.* desequilibrado.
loquacious, *a.* locuaz.
lord, *n.* señor *m.;* (Brit. title) lord *m.*
lordship, *n.* señorío *m.*
lose, *v.* perder. **l. consciousness,** perder el concimiento.
loss, *n.* pérdida *f.*
lost, *a.* perdido.
lot, *n.* suerte *f.* **building l.,** solar *m.* **a lot (of), lots of,** mucho.
lotion, *n.* loción *f.*
lottery, *n.* lotería *f.*
loud, 1. *a.* fuerte; ruidoso. **2.** *adv.* alto.
loudspeaker, *n.* altavoz *m.*
lounge, *n.* sofá *m.;* salón de fumar *m.*
louse, *n.* piojo *m.*
love, 1. *n.* amor *m.* **in l.,** enamorado. **to fall in l.,** enamorarse. **l. at first sight,** flechazo *m.* **2.** *v.* querer; amar; adorar.
lovely, *a.* hermoso.
lover, *n.* amante *m.* & *f.*
low, *a.* bajo; vil.
low-cut, *a.* escotado.
lower, *v.* bajar; (in price) rebajar.
lower-case letter, minúscula *f.*
lowly, *a.* humilde.
low neckline, escote *m.*
loyal, *a.* leal, fiel.
loyalist, *n.* lealista *m.* & *f.*
loyalty, *n.* lealtad *f.*
lozenge, *n.* pastilla *f.*
lubricant, *n.* lubricante *m.*
lubricate, *v.* engrasar, lubricar.
lucid, *a.* claro, lúcido.
luck, *n.* suerte; fortuna *f.*

lucky, *a.* afortunado. **to be l.,** tener suerte.
lucrative, *a.* lucrativo.
ludicrous, *a.* rídiculo.
luggage, *n.* equipaje *m.*
lukewarm, *a.* tibio.
lull, 1. *n.* momento de calma. **2.** *v.* calmar.
lullaby, *n.* arrullo *m.*
lumbago, *n.* lumbago *m.*
lumber, *n.* madera *f.*
luminous, *a.* luminoso.
lump, *n.* protuberancia *f.;* (of sugar) terrón *m.*
lump sum, suma global *f.*
lunacy, *n.* locura *f.*
lunar, *a.* lunar.
lunatic, *a.* & *n.* loco -ca.
lunch, luncheon, 1. *n.* merienda *f.,* almuerzo *m.* **2.** *v.* merendar, almorzar.
lunch box, fiambrera *f.*
lung, *n.* pulmón *m.*
lunge, 1. *n.* estocada, arremetida *f.* **2.** *v.* dar un estocada, arremeter.
lure, *v.* atraer.
lurid, *a.* sensacional; espeluznante.
lurk, *v.* esconderse; espiar.
luscious, *a.* sabroso, delicioso.
lust, *n.* sensualidad; codicia *f.*
luster, *n.* lustre *m.*
lustful, *a.* sensual, lascivo.
lusty, *a.* vigoroso.
lute, *n.* laúd *m.*
Lutheran, *n.* & *a.* luterano -na.
luxuriant, *a.* exuberante, frondoso.
luxurious, *a.* lujoso.
luxury, *n.* lujo *m.*
lying, *a.* mentiroso.
lymph, *n.* linfa *f.*
lynch, *v.* linchar.
lyre, *n.* lira *f.*
lyric, *a.* lírico.
lyricism, *n.* lirismo *m.*

M

macabre, *a.* macabro.
macaroni, *n.* macarrones *m.*
machine, *n.* máquina *f.*

machine gun, *n.* ametralladora *f.*
machinery, *n.* maquinaria *f.*

machinist, *n.* maquinista *m.* & *f.,* mecánico *m.*
macho, *a.* machista.

mackerel, *n.* escombro *m.*

mad, *a.* loco; furioso.

madam, *n.* señora *f.*

mafia, *n.* mafia *f.*

magazine, *n.* revista *f.*

magic, 1. *a.* mágico. **2.** *n.* magia *f.*

magician, *n.* mágico *m.*

magistrate, *n.* magistrado - da.

magnanimous, *a.* magnánimo.

magnate, *n.* magnate *m.*

magnesium, *n.* magnesio *m.*

magnet, *n.* imán *m.*

magnetic, *a.* magnético.

magnificence, *n.* magnificencia *f.*

magnificent, *a.* magnífico.

magnify, *v.* magnificar.

magnifying glass, lupa *f.*

magnitude, *n.* magnitud *f.*

mahogany, *n.* caoba *f.*

magpie, *n.* hurraca *f.*

maid, *n.* criada *f.* **old m.,** solterona *f.*

maiden, *a.* soltera.

mail, 1. *n.* correo *m.* **air m.,** correo aéreo. **by return m.,** a vuelta de correo. **2.** *v.* echar al correo.

mailbox, *n.* buzón *m.*

mailman, *n.* cartero *m.*

maim, *v.* mutilar.

main, *a.* principal.

mainframe, *n.* componente central de una computadora.

mainland, *n.* continente *m.*

maintain, *v.* mantener; sostener.

maintenance, *n.* mantenimiento; sustento *m.;* conservación *f.*

maître d', *n.* jefe de sala *m.* & *f.*

maize, *n.* maíz *m.*

majestic, *a.* majestuoso.

majesty, *n.* majestad *f.*

major, 1. *a.* mayor. **2.** *n.* (mil.) comandante *m.;* (study) especialidad *f.*

majority, *n.* mayoría *f.*

make, 1. *n.* marca *f.* **2.** *v.* hacer; fabricar; (earn) ganar.

maker, *n.* fabricante *m.*

makeshift, *a.* provisional.

make-up, *n.* cosméticos *m.pl.*

malady, *n.* mal *m.,* enfermedad *f.*

malaria, *n.* paludismo *m.*

male, *a.* & *n.* macho *m.*

malevolent, *a.* malévolo.

malice, *n.* malicia *f.*

malicious, *a.* malicioso.

malign, 1. *v.* difamar. **2.** *a.* maligno.

malignant, *a.* maligno.

malnutrition, *n.* desnutrición *f.*

malt, *n.* malta *f.*

mammal, *n.* mamífero *m.*

man, 1. *n.* hombre; varón *m.* **2.** *v.* tripular.

manage, *v.* manejar; dirigir; administrar; arreglárselas. **m. to,** lograr.

management, *n.* dirección, administración *f.*

manager, *n.* director -ora.

mandate, *n.* mandato *m.*

mandatory, *a.* obligatorio.

mandolin, *n.* mandolina *f.*

mane, *n.* crines *f.pl.*

maneuver, 1. *n.* maniobra *f.* **2.** *v.* maniobrar.

manganese, *n.* manganeso *m.*

manger, *n.* pesebre *m.*

mangle, 1. *n.* rodillo, exprimidor *m.* **2.** *v.* mutilar.

manhood, *n.* virilidad *f.*

mania, *n.* manía *f.*

maniac, *a.* & *n.* maniático -ca; maníaco -ca.

manicure, *n.* manicura *f.*

manifest, 1. *a.* & *n.* manifiesto *m.* **2.** *v.* manifestar.

manifesto, *n.* manifiesto *m.*

manifold, 1. *a.* muchos. **2.** *n.* (auto.) tubo múltiple.

manipulate, *v.* manipular.

mankind, *n.* humanidad *f.*

manly, *a.* varonil.

manner, *n.* manera *f.,* modo *m.* **manners,** modales *m.pl.*

mannerism, *n.* manerismo *m.*

mansion, *n.* mansión *f.*

mantel, *n.* manto de chimenea.

mantle, *n.* manto *m.*

manual, *a.* & *n.* manual *m.*

manufacture, *v.* fabricar.

manufacturer, *n.* fabricante *m.*

manufacturing, *n.* fabricación *f.*

manure, *n.* abono, estiércol *m.*

manuscript, *n.* manuscrito *m.*

many, *a.* muchos. **how m.,** cuántos. **so m.,** tantos. **too m.,** demasiados. **as m. as,** tantos como.

map, *n.* mapa *m.*

maple, *n.* arce *m.*

mar, *v.* estropear; desfigurar.

marble, *n.* mármol *m.*

march, 1. *n.* marcha *f.* **2.** *v.* marchar.

March, *n.* marzo *m.*

mare, *n.* yegua *f.*

margarine, *n.* margarina *f.*

margin, *n.* margen *m.* or *f.*

marijuana, *n.* marijuana *f.*

marine, 1. *a.* marino. **2.** *n.* soldado de marina.

mariner, *n.* marinero *m.*

marionette, *n.* marioneta *f.*

marital, *a.* marital.

maritime, *a.* marítimo.

mark, 1. *n.* marca *f.* **2.** *v.* marcar.

market, *n.* mercado *m.* **meat m.,** carnicería *f.* **stock m.,** bolsa *f.* *v.* comercializar.

marmalade, *n.* mermelada *f.*

maroon, 1. *a.* & *n.* color rojo oscuro. **2.** *v.* dejar abandonado.

marquis, *n.* marqués *m.*

marriage, *n.* matrimonio *m.*

marriage certificate, partida de matrimonio *f.*

married, *a.* casado. **to get m.,** casarse.

marrow, *n.* médula *f.;* substancia *f.*

marry, *v.* casarse con; casar.

marsh, *n.* pantano *m.*

marshal, *n.* mariscal *m.*

marshmallow, *n.* malvarisco *m.;* bombón de altea *m.*

martial, *a.* marcial. **m. law,** gobierno militar.

martyr, *n.* mártir *m.* & *f.*

martyrdom, *n.* martirio *m.*

marvel, 1. *n.* maravilla *f.* **2.** *v.* maravillarse.

marvelous, *a.* maravilloso.

mascara, *n.* rimel *m.*

mascot, *n.* mascota *f.*

masculine, *a.* masculino.

mash, *v.* majar. **mashed potatoes,** puré de papas *m.*

mask, *n.* máscara *f.*

mason, *n.* albañil *m.*

masquerade, *n.* mascarada *f.*

mass, *n.* masa *f.;* (rel.) misa *f.* **to say m.,** cantar misa. **m. production,** producción en serie.

massacre, 1. *n.* carnicería, matanza *f.* **2.** *v.* matar atrozmente, destrozar.

massage, 1. *n.* masaje *m.;* soba *f.* **2.** *v.* sobar.

masseur, *n.* masajista *m.* & *f.*

massive, *a.* macizo, sólido.

mast, *n.* palo, árbol *m.*

master, 1. *n.* amo; maestro *m.* **2.** *v.* domar, dominar.

masterpiece, *n.* obra maestra *f.*

master's degree, maestría *f.*

mastery, *n.* maestría *f.*

mat, 1. *n.* estera; palleta *f.* **2.** *v.* enredar.

match, 1. *n.* igual *m;* fósforo *m.;* (sport) partida, contienda *f.;* (marriage) noviazgo; casamiento. **2.** *v.* ser igual a; igualar.

matchbox, caja de cerillas, caja de fósforos *f.*

mate, 1. *n.* consorte *m.* & *f.;* compañero -ra. **2.** *v.* igualar; casar.

material, *a.* & *n.* material *m.* **raw materials,** materias primas.

materialism, *n.* materialismo *m.*

materialize, *v.* materializar.

maternal, *a.* materno.

maternity, *n.* maternidad *f.*

maternity hospital, maternidad *f.*

mathematical, *a.* matemático.

mathematics, *n.* matemáticas *f.pl.*

matinee, *n.* matiné *f.*

matrimony, *n.* matrimonio *m.*

matron, *n.* matrona; directora *f.*

matter, 1. *n.* materia *f.;* asunto *m.* **what's the m.?,** ¿qué pasa? **2.** *v.* importar.

mattress, *n.* colchón *m.*

mature, 1. *a.* maduro. **2.** *v.* madurar.

maturity, *n.* madurez *f.*

maudlin, *a.* sentimental en exceso; sensiblero.

maul, *v.* aporrear.

maxim, *n.* máxima *f.*

maximum, *a.* & *n.* máximo.

may, *v.* poder.

May, *n.* mayo *m.*

maybe, *adv.* quizá, quizás, tal vez.

mayonnaise, *n.* mayonesa *f.*

mayor, *n.* alcalde *m.* alcaldesa *f.*

maze, *n.* laberinto *m.*

me, *pron.* mí; me. **with me,** conmigo.

meadow, *n.* prado *m.;* vega *f.*

meager, *a.* magro; pobre.

meal, *n.* comida; (flour) harina *f.*

mean, 1. *a.* bajo; malo. **2.** *n.* medio (see also **means**). **3.** *v.* significar; querer decir.

meaning, *n.* sentido, significado *m.*

meaningless, *a.* sin sentido.

means, *n.pl.* medios, recursos *m.* **by all m.,** sin falta. **by no m.,** de ningún modo. **by m. of,** por medio de.

meanwhile, *adv.* mientras tanto.

measles, *n.* sarampión *m.*

measure, 1. *n.* medida *f.;* (music) compás *m.* **2.** *v.* medir.

measurement, *n.* medida, dimensión *f.*

meat, *n.* carne *f.*

mechanic, *n.* mecánico *m.* & *f.*

mechanical, *a.* mecánico.

mechanism, *n.* mecanismo *m.*

mechanize, *v.* mecanizar.

medal, *n.* medalla *f.*

meddle, *v.* meterse, entremeterse.

mediate, *v.* mediar.

medical, *a.* médico.

medicine, *n.* medicina *f.*

medicine chest, botiquín *m.*

medieval, *a.* medieval.

mediocre, *a.* mediocre.

mediocrity, *n.* mediocridad *f.*

meditate, *v.* meditar.

meditation, *n.* meditación *f.*

Mediterranean, *n.* Mediterráneo *m.*

medium, 1. *a.* mediano, medio. **2.** *n.* medio *m.*

medley, *n.* mezcla *f.,* ensalada *f.*

meek, *a.* manso; humilde.

meekness, *n.* modestia; humildad *f.*

meet, 1. *a.* apropiado. **2.** *n.* concurso *m.* **3.** *v.* encontrar; reunirse; conocer.

meeting, *n.* reunión *f.;* mitin *m.*

megahertz, *n.* megahercio *m.*

megaphone, *n.* megáfono *m.*

melancholy, 1. *a.* melancólico. **2.** *n.* melancolía *f.*

mellow, *a.* suave; blando; maduro.

melodious, *a.* melodioso.

melodrama, *n.* melodrama *m.*

melody, *n.* melodía *f.*

melon, *n.* melón *m.*

melt, *v.* derretir.

meltdown, *n.* fundición resultante de un accidente en un reactor nuclear.

member, *n.* socio -ia; miembro *m.* **m. of the crew,** tripulante *m.* & *f.*

membership, *n.* número de miembros.

membrane, *n.* membrana *f.*

memento, *n.* recuerdo *m.*

memoir, *n.* memoria *f.*

memorable, *a.* memorable.

memorandum, *n.* memorándum, volante *m.*

memorial, 1. *a.* conmemorativo. **2.** *n.* memorial *m.*

memorize, *v.* aprender de memoria.

memory, *n.* memoria *f.;* recuerdo *m.*

menace, 1. *n.* amenaza *f.* **2.** *v.* amenazar.

mend, *v.* reparar, remendar.

menial, 1. *a.* servil. **2.** *n.* sirviente -ta.

meningitis, *n.* meningitis *f.*

menopause, *n.* menopausia *f.*

menstruation, *n.* menstruación *f.*

menswear, *n.* ropa de caballeros *f.*

mental, *a.* mental.

mental disorder, trastorno mental *m.*

mentality, *n.* mentalidad *f.*

menthol, *n.* mentol *m.*

mention, 1. *n.* mención *f.* **2.** *v.* mencionar.

menu, *n.* menú *m.*, lista *f.*

mercantile, *a.* mercantil.

mercenary, *a.* & *n.* mercenario -ria.

merchandise, *n.* mercancía *f.*

merchant, 1. *a.* mercante. **2.** *n.* comerciante *m.*

merciful, *a.* misericordioso, compasivo.

merciless, *a.* cruel, inhumano.

mercury, *n.* mercurio *m.*

mercy, *n.* misericordia; merced *f.*

mere, *a.* mero, puro.

merely, *adv.* solamente; simplemente.

merge, *v.* unir, combinar.

merger, *n.* consolidación, fusión *f.*

meringue, *n.* merengue *m.*

merit, 1. *n.* mérito *m.* **2.** *v.* merecer.

meritorious, *a.* meritorio.

mermaid, *n.* sirena *f.*

merriment, *n.* regocijo *m.*

merry, *a.* alegre, festivo.

merry-go-round, *n.* caballitos *m. pl.*; tiovivo *m.*

mesh, *n.* malla *f.*

mess, 1. *n.* lío *m.*; confusión *f.*; (mil.) salón comedor; rancho *m.* **2.** *v.* **m. up,** ensuciar; enredar.

message, *n.* mensaje, recado *m.*

messenger, *n.* mensajero -ra.

messy, *a.* confuso; desarreglado.

metabolism, *n.* metabolismo *m.*

metal, *n.* metal *m.*

metallic, *a.* metálico.

metaphysics, *n.* metafísica *f.*

meteor, *n.* meteoro *m.*

meteorology, *n.* meteorología *f.*

meter, *n.* contador, medidor; (measure) metro *m.*

method, *n.* método *m.*

meticulous, *a.* meticuloso.

metric, *a.* métrico.

metropolis, *n.* metrópoli *f.*

metropolitan, *a.* metropolitano.

Mexican, *a.* & *n.* mexicano -na.

Mexico, *n.* México *m.*

mezzanine, *n.* entresuelo *m.*

microbe, *n.* microbio *m.*

microchip, *n.* microchip *m.*

microfiche, *n.* microficha *f.*

microfilm, *n.* microfilm *m.*

microform, *n.* microforma *f.*

microphone, *n.* micrófono *m.*

microscope, *n.* microscopio *m.*

microscopic, *a.* microscópico.

mid, *a.* medio.

middle, *a.* & *n.* medio *m.* **in the m. of,** en medio de, a mediados de.

middle-aged, *a.* de edad madura.

Middle East, Medio Oriente *m.*

middle finger, dedo corazón *m.*

midget, *n.* enano -na.

midnight, *n.* medianoche *f.*

midwife, *n.* comadrona, partera *f.*

might, *n.* poder *m.*, fuerza *f.*

mighty, *a.* poderoso.

migraine, *n.* migraña *f.*; jaqueca *f.*

migrate, *v.* emigrar.

migration, *n.* emigración *f.*

migratory, *a.* migratorio.

mild, *a.* moderado, suave; templado.

mildew, *n.* añublo *m.*, moho *m.*

mile, *n.* milla *f.*

mileage, *n.* kilometraje *m.*

militant, *a.* militante.

militarism, *n.* militarismo *m.*

military, *a.* militar.

militia, *n.* milicia *f.*

milk, 1. *n.* leche *f.* **2.** *v.* ordeñar.

milk chocolate, chocolate con leche *m.*

milkman, *n.* lechero *m.*

milk shake, batido *m.*

milky, *a.* lácteo; lechoso.

mill, 1. *n.* molino *m.*; fábrica *f.* **2.** *v.* moler.

miller, *n.* molinero -ra.

millimeter, *n.* milímetro *m.*

milliner, *n.* sombrerero -ra.

millinery, *n.* sombrerería *f.*

million, *n.* millón *m.*

millionaire, *n.* millonario -ria.

mimic, 1. *n.* mimo -ma. **2.** *v.* imitar.

mind, 1. *n.* mente; opinión *f.* **2.** *v.* obedecer. **never m.,** no se ocupe.

mindful, *a.* atento.

mine, 1. *pron.* mío. **2.** *n.* mina *f.* **3.** *v.* minar.

miner, *n.* minero *m.*

mineral, *a.* & *n.* mineral *m.*

mineral water, agua mineral *f.*

mine sweeper, dragaminas *f.*

mingle, *v.* mezclar.

miniature, *n.* miniatura *f.*

miniaturize, *v.* miniaturizar.

minibus, *n.* microbús *m.*

minicab, *n.* microtaxi *m.*

minimize, *v.* menospreciar.

minimum, *a.* & *n.* mínimo *m.*

mining, *n.* minería *f.*

minister, 1. *n.* ministro -tra; (rel.) pastor *m.* **2.** *v.* ministrar.

ministry, *n.* ministerio *m.*

mink, *n.* visón *m.*; (fur) piel de visón *m.*

minor, 1. *a.* menor. **2.** *n.* menor de edad.

minority, *n.* minoría *f.*

minstrel, *n.* juglar *m.*

mint, 1. *n.* menta *f.*; casa de moneda. **2.** *v.* acuñar.

minus, *prep.* menos.

minute, 1. *a.* minucioso. **2.** *n.* minuto, momento *m.*

miracle, *n.* milagro *m.*

miraculous, *a.* milagroso.

mirage, *n.* espejismo *m.*

mire, *n.* lodo *m.*

mirror, n. espejo m.
mirth, n. alegría; risa f.
misbehave, v. portarse mal.
miscellaneous, a. misceláneo.
mischief, n. travesura, diablura f.
mischievous, a. travieso, dañino.
miser, n. avaro -ra.
miserable, a. miserable; infeliz.
miserly, a. avariento, tacaño.
misfortune, n. desgracia f., infortunio, revés m.
misgiving, n. recelo m., desconfianza f.
mishap, n. desgracia f., contratiempo m.
mislead, v. extraviar, despistar; pervertir.
misplaced, a. extraviado.
mispronounce, v. pronunciar mal.
miss, 1. n. señorita f. **2.** v. perder; echar de menos, extrañar. **be missing,** faltar.
missile, n. proyectil m.
mission, n. misión f.
missionary, n. misionero -ra.
mist, n. niebla, bruma f.
mistake, n. equivocación f.; error m. **to make a m.,** equivocarse.
mistaken, a. equivocado.
mister, n. señor m.
mistletoe, n. muérdago m.
mistreat, v. maltratar.
mistress, n. ama; señora; concubina f.
mistrust, v. desconfiar; sospechar.
misty, a. nebuloso, brumoso.
misunderstand, v. entender mal.
misuse, v. maltratar; abusar.
mite, n. pizca f., blanca f.
mitten, n. mitón, confortante m.
mix, v. mezclar. **m. up,** confundir.
mixer (for food), n. batidora f.
mixture, n. mezcla, mixtura f.
mix-up, n. confusión f.

moan, 1. n. quejido, gemido m. **2.** v. gemir.
mob, n. muchedumbre f.; gentío m.
mobilization, n. movilización f.
mobilize, v. movilizar.
mock, v. burlar.
mockery, n. burla f.
mod, a. a la última; en boga.
mode, n. modo m.
model, 1. n. modelo m. **2.** v. modelar.
modem, n. módem m.
moderate, 1. a. moderado. **2.** v. moderar.
moderation, n. moderación; sobriedad f.
modern, a. moderno.
modernize, v. modernizar.
modest, a. modesto.
modesty, n. modestia f.
modify, v. modificar.
modulate, v. modular.
moist, a. húmedo.
moisten, v. humedecer.
moisture, n. humedad f.
molar, n. molar m.
molasses, n. melaza f.
mold, 1. n. molde; moho m. **2.** v. moldar, formar; enmohecerse.
moldy, a. mohoso.
mole, n. lunar m.; (animal) topo m.
molecule, n. molécula f.
molest, v. molestar.
mollify, v. mollificar.
moment, n. momento m.
momentary, a. momentáneo.
momentous, a. importante.
monarch, n. monarca m. & f.
monarchy, n. monarquía f.
monastery, n. monasterio m.
Monday, n. lunes m.
monetary, a. monetario.
money, n. dinero m. **m. order,** giro postal.
mongrel, 1. n. mestizo m. **2.** a. mestizo, cruzado.
monitor, n. amonestador m.
monk, n. monje m.
monkey, n. mono -na.
monocle, n. monóculo m.
monologue, n. monólogo m.
monopolize, v. monopolizar.
monopoly, n. monopolio m.

monosyllable, n. monosílabo m.
monotone, n. monotonía f.
monotonous, a. monótono.
monotony, n. monotonía f.
monsoon, n. monzón m.
monster, n. monstruo m.
monstrosity, n. monstruosidad f.
monstrous, a. monstruoso.
month, n. mes m.
monthly, a. mensual.
monument, n. momumento m.
monumental, a. monumental.
mood, n. humor m.; (gram.) modo m.
moody, a. caprichoso, taciturno.
moon, n. luna f.
moonlight, n. luz de la luna.
moonlighting, n. pluriempleo m.
moor, 1. n. párano m. **2.** v. anclar.
Moor, n. moro -ra.
mop, 1. n. fregasuelos m., fregona f., (S.A.) trapeador m. **2.** v. fregar, (S.A.) trapear.
moped, n. (vehicle) velomotor m.
moral, 1. a. moral. **2.** n. moraleja f. **morals,** moralidad f.
morale, n. espíritu m.
moralist, n. moralista m. & f.
morality, n. moralidad, ética f.
morbid, a. mórbido.
more, a. & adv. más. **m. and m.,** cada vez más.
moreover, adv. además.
morgue, n. necrocomio m.
morning, n. mañana f. **good m.,** buenos días.
Morocco, n. Marruecos m.
morose, a. malhumorado.
morphine, n. morfina f.
morsel, n. bocado m.
mortal, a. & n. mortal m. & f.
mortality, n. mortalidad f.
mortar, n. mortero m.
mortgage, 1. n. hipoteca f. **2.** v. hipotecar.
mortify, v. mortificar.
mosaic, n. & a. mosaico m.

mosque, *n.* mezquita *f.*

mosquito, *n.* mosquito *m.*

moss, *n.* musgo *m.*

most, 1. *a.* más. 2. *adv.* más; sumamente. 3. *pron.* **m. of,** la mayor parte de.

mostly, *adv.* principalmente; en su mayor parte.

motel, *n.* motel *m.*

moth, *n.* polilla *f.*

mother, *n.* madre *f.*

mother-in-law, *n.* suegra *f.*

motif, *n.* tema *m.*

motion, 1. *n.* moción *f.;* movimiento *m.* 2. *v.* hacer señas.

motionless, *a.* inmóvil.

motion picture, película *f.*

motivate, *v.* motivar.

motive, *n.* motivo *m.*

motor, *n.* motor *m.*

motorboat, *n.* lancha motora *f.,* autobote, motorbote *m.,* gasolinera *f.*

motorcycle, *n.* motocicleta *f.*

motorcyclist, *n.* motociclista *m. & f.*

motorist, *n.* motorista *m. & f.*

motto, *n.* lema *m.*

mound, *n.* terrón; montón *m.*

mount, 1. *n.* monte *m.;* (horse) montura *f.* 2. *v.* montar; subir.

mountain, *n.* montaña *f.*

mountaineer, *n.* montañés *m.*

mountainous, *a.* montañoso.

mourn, *v.* lamentar, llorar; llevar luto.

mournful, *a.* triste.

mourning, *n.* luto; lamento *m.*

mouse, *n.* ratón, ratoncito *m.*

mouth, *n.* boca *f.;* (of river) desembocadura *f.*

mouthwash, *n.* enjuague bucal *m.*

movable, *a.* movible, movedizo.

move, 1. *n.* movimiento *m.;* mudanza *f.* 2. *v.* mover; mudarse; emocionar, conmover. **m. away,** quitar; alejarse; mudarse.

movement, *n.* movimiento *m.*

movie, *n.* película *f.* **m. theater, movies,** cine *m.*

moving, *a.* conmovedor; persuasivo.

mow, *v.* guadañar, segar.

Mr., *title.* Señor (Sr.).

Mrs., *title.* Señora (Sra.).

much, *a. & adv.* mucho. **how m.,** cuánto. **so m.,** tanto. **too m.,** demasiado. **as m. as,** tanto como.

mucilage, *n.* mucílago *f.*

mucous, *a.* mucoso.

mucous membrane, *n.* membrana mucosa *f.*

mud, *n.* fango, lodo *m.*

muddy, 1. *a.* lodoso; turbio. 2. *v.* ensuciar; enturbiar.

muff, *n.* manguito *m.*

muffin, *n.* panecillo *m.*

mug, *n.* cubilete *m.*

mugger, *n.* asaltante *m. & f.*

mulatto, *n.* mulato *m.*

mule, *n.* mula *f.*

mullah, *n.* mullah *m.*

multicultural, *a.* multicultural.

multinational, *a.* multinacional.

multiple, *a.* múltiple.

multiplication, *n.* multiplicación *f.*

multiplicity, *n.* multiplicidad *f.*

multiply, *v.* multiplicar.

multitude, *n.* multitud *f.*

mummy, *n.* momia *f.*

mumps, *n.* paperas *f.pl.*

municipal, *a.* municipal.

munificent, *a.* munífico.

munitions, *n.* municiones *m.pl.*

mural, *a. & n.* mural *m.*

murder, 1. *n.* asesinato; homicidio *m.* 2. *v.* asesinar.

murderer, *n.* asesino -na.

murmur, 1. *n.* murmullo *m.* 2. *v.* murmurar.

muscle, *n.* músculo *m.*

muscular, *a.* muscular.

muse, 1. *n.* musa *f.* 2. *v.* meditar.

museum, *n.* museo *m.*

mushroom, *n.* seta *f.,* hongo *m.*

music, *n.* música *f.*

musical, *a.* musical; melodioso.

musician, *n.* músico -ca.

Muslim, *a. & n.* musulmano.

muslin, *n.* muselina *f.;* percal *m.*

mussel, *n.* mejillón *m.*

must, *v.* deber; tener que.

mustache, *n.* bigotes *m.pl.*

mustard, *n.* mostaza *f.*

muster, 1. *n.* (mil.) revista *f.* 2. *v.* reunir, juntar.

mute, *a. & n.* mudo -da.

mutilate, *v.* mutilar.

mutiny, 1. *n.* motín *m.* 2. *v.* amotinarse.

mutter, *v.* refunfuñar, gruñir.

mutton, *n.* carnero *m.*

mutual, *a.* mutuo.

muzzle, 1. *n.* hocico *m.;* bozal *m.* 2. *v.* embozar.

my, *a.* mi.

myriad, *n.* miríada *f.*

myrtle, *n.* mirto *m.*

myself, *pron.* mí, mí mismo; me. **I m.,** yo mismo.

mysterious, *a.* misterioso.

mystery, *n.* misterio *m.*

mystic, *a.* místico.

mystify, *v.* confundir.

myth, *n.* mito *m.*

mythical, *a.* mítico.

mythology, *n.* mitología *f.*

N

nag, 1. *n.* jaca *f.* 2. *v.* regañar; sermonear.

nail, 1. *n.* clavo *m.;* (finger) uña *f.* **n. polish,** esmalte para las uñas. 2. *v.* clavar.

naïve, *a.* ingenuo.

naked, *a.* desnudo.

name, 1. *n.* nombre *m.;* reputación *f.* 2. *v.* nombrar, mencionar.

namely, *adv.* a saber; es decir.

namesake, *n.* tocayo *m.*

nanny, *n.* niñera *f.*

nap, *n.* siesta *f.* **to take a n.,** echar una siesta.

naphtha, *n.* nafta *f.*

napkin, *n.* servilleta *f.*

narcissus, *n.* narciso *m.*

narcotic, *a.* & *n.* narcótico *m.*

narrate, *v.* narrar.

narrative, 1. *a.* narrativo. **2.** *n.* cuento, relato *m.*

narrow, *a.* estrecho, angosto. **n.-minded,** intolerante.

nasal, *a.* nasal.

nasty, *a.* desagradable.

nation, *n.* nación *f.*

national, *a.* nacional.

nationalism, *n.* nacionalismo *m.*

nationality, *n.* nacionalidad *f.*

nationalization, *n.* nacionalización *f.*

nationalize, *v.* nacionalizar.

native, 1. *a.* nativo. **2.** *n.* natural; indígena *m.* & *f.*

nativity, *n.* natividad *f.*

natural, *a.* natural.

naturalist, *n.* naturalista *m.* & *f.*

naturalize, *v.* naturalizar.

naturalness, *n.* naturalidad *f.*

nature, *n.* naturaleza *f.;* índole *f.;* humor *m.*

naughty, *a.* travieso, desobediente.

nausea, *n.* náusea *f.*

nauseous, *a.* nauseoso.

nautical, *a.* náutico.

naval, *a.* naval.

nave, *n.* nave *f.*

navel, *n.* ombligo *m.*

navigable, *a.* navegable.

navigate, *v.* navegar.

navigation, *n.* navegación *f.*

navigator, *n.* navegante *m.* & *f.*

navy, *n.* marina *f.*

navy blue, azul marino *m.*

near, 1. *a.* cercano, próximo. **2.** *adv.* cerca. **3.** *prep.* cerca de.

nearby, 1. *a.* cercano. **2.** *adv.* cerca.

nearly, *adv.* casi.

nearsighted, *a.* corto de vista.

neat, *a.* aseado; ordenado.

neatness, *n.* aseo *m.*

nebulous, *a.* nebuloso.

necessary, *a.* necesario.

necessity, *n.* necesidad *f.*

neck, *n.* cuello *m.*

necklace, *n.* collar *m.*

necktie, *n.* corbata *f.*

nectar, *n.* néctar *m.*

nectarine, *n.* nectarina *f.*

need, 1. *n.* necesidad; (poverty) pobreza *f.* **2.** *v.* necesitar.

needle, *n.* aguja *f.*

needless, *a.* innecesario, inútil.

needy, *a.* indigente, necesitado, pobre.

nefarious, *a.* nefario.

negative, 1. *a.* negativo. **2.** *n.* negativa *f.*

neglect, 1. *n.* negligencia *f.;* descuido *m.* **2.** *v.* descuidar.

negligee, *n.* negligé *m.*, bata de casa *f.*

negligent, *a.* negligente, descuidado.

negligible, *a.* insignificante.

negotiate, *v.* negociar.

negotiation, *n.* negociación *f.*

Negro, *n.* negro -ra.

neighbor, *n.* vecino -na.

neighborhood, *n.* vecindad *f.*

neither, 1. *a.* & *pron.* ninguno de los dos. **2.** *adv.* tampoco. **3.** *conj.* **neither . . . nor,** ni . . . ni.

neon, *n.* neón *m.* **n. light,** tubo neón *m.*

nephew, *n.* sobrino *m.*

nerve, *n.* nervio *m.;* (coll.) audacia *f.*

nervous, *a.* nervioso.

nervous breakdown, crisis nerviosa *f.*

nest, *n.* nido *m.*

net, 1. *a.* neto. **2.** *n.* red *f.* **hair n.,** albanega, redecilla *f.* **3.** *v.* redar; (com.) ganar.

netting, *n.* red *m.;* obra de malla *f.*

network, *n.* (radio) red radiodifusora.

neuralgia, *n.* neuralgia *f.*

neurology, *n.* neurología *f.*

neurotic, *a.* neurótico.

neutral, *a.* neutral.

neutrality, *n.* neutralidad *f.*

neutron, *n.* neutrón *m.*

neutron bomb, bomba de neutrones *f.*

never, *adv.* nunca, jamás; **n. mind,** no importa.

nevertheless, *adv.* no obstante, sin embargo.

new, *a.* nuevo.

news, *n.* noticias *f.pl.*

newsboy, *n.* vendedor -ra de periódicos.

news bulletin, boletín informativo *m.*

news flash, *n.* noticia de última hora *f.*

newsletter, *n.* hoja informativa *f.*

newspaper, *n.* periódico *m.*

New Testament, Nuevo Testamento *m.*

new year, *n.* año nuevo *m.*

next, 1. *a.* próximo; siguiente; contiguo. **2.** *adv.* luego, después. **n. door,** al lado. **n. to,** al lado de.

next-to-the-last, *a.* penúltimo.

nibble, *v.* picar.

nice, *a.* simpático, agradable; amable; hermoso; exacto.

nick, *n.* muesca *f.*, picadura *f.* **in the n. of time,** a punto.

nickel, *n.* níquel *m.*

nickname, 1. *n.* apodo, mote *m.* **2.** *v.* apodar.

nicotine, *n.* nicotina *f.*

niece, *n.* sobrina *f.*

niggardly, *a.* mezquino.

night, *n.* noche *f.* **good n.,** buenas noches. **last n.,** anoche. **n. club,** cabaret *m.*

nightclub, *n.* cabaret *m.*

nightclub owner, cabaretero -ra *m.* & *f.*

nightgown, *n.* camisa de dormir.

nightingale, *n.* ruiseñor *m.*

nightly, *adv.* todas las noches.

nightmare, *n.* pesadilla *f.*

night school, escuela nocturna *f.*

night watchman, vigilante nocturno *m.*

nimble, *a.* ágil.

nine, *a.* & *pron.* nueve.

nineteen, *a.* & *pron.* diecinueve.

ninety, *a.* & *pron.* noventa.

ninth, *a.* noveno.

nipple, *n.* teta *f.;* pezón *m.*

nitrogen, *n.* nitrógeno *m.*

no, 1. *a.* ninguno. **no one,** nadie. **2.** *adv.* no.

nobility, *n.* nobleza *f.*

noble, *a.* & *n.* noble *m.*

nobleman, *n.* noble *m.*

nobody, *pron.* nadie.

nocturnal, *a.* nocturno.

nocturne, *n.* nocturno *m.*

nod, 1. *n.* seña con la cabeza. **2.** *v.* inclinar la cabeza; (doze) dormitar.

no-frills, *a.* sin extras.

noise, *n.* ruido *m.*

noiseless, *a.* silencioso.

noisy, *a.* ruidoso.

nominal, *a.* nominal.

nominate, *v.* nombrar.

nomination, *n.* nombramiento *m.*, nominación *f.*

nominee, *n.* candidato -ta.

nonaligned (in political sense), *a.* no alineado.

nonchalant, *a.* indiferente.

noncombatant, *n.* no combatiente *m.*

noncommittal, *a.* evasivo; reservado.

nondescript, *a.* difícil de describir.

none, *pron.* ninguno.

nonentity, *n.* nulidad *f.*

nonpartisan, *a.* sin afiliación.

non-proliferation, *n.* no proliferación *m.*

nonsense, *n.* tontería *f.*

nonsmoker, *n.* no fumador -dora.

noodle, *n.* fideo *m.*

noon, *n.* mediodía *m.*

noose, *n.* lazo corredizo *m.*; dogal *m.*

nor, *conj.* ni.

normal, *a.* normal.

north, *n.* norte *m.*

North America, Norte América *f.*

North American, *a.* & *n.* norteamericano -na.

northeast, *n.* nordeste *m.*

northern, *a.* septentrional.

North Pole, *n.* Polo Norte *m.*

northwest, *n.* noroeste *m.*

Norway, *n.* Noruega *f.*

Norwegian, *a.* & *n.* noruego -ga.

nose, *n.* nariz *f.*

nosebleed, *n.* hemorragia nasal *f.*

nostalgia, *n.* nostalgia *f.*

nostril, *n.* ventana de la nariz; (pl.) narices *f.pl.*

not, *adv.* no. **n. at all,** de ninguna manera. **n. even,** ni siquiera.

notable, *a.* notable.

notary, *n.* notario *m.*

notation, *a.* notación *f.*

notch, *n.* muesca *f.*; corte *m.*

note, 1. *n.* nota *f.*; apunte *m.* **2.** *v.* notar.

notebook, *n.* libreta *f.*, cuaderno *m.*

noted, *a.* célebre.

notepaper, *n.* papel de notas *m.*

noteworthy, *a.* notable.

nothing, *pron.* nada.

notice, 1. *n.* aviso *m.*; noticia *f.* **2.** *v.* observar, fijarse en.

noticeable, *a.* notable.

notification, *n.* notificación *f.*

notify, *v.* notificar.

notion, *n.* noción; idea *f.*; (pl.) novedades *f.pl.*

notoriety, *n.* notoriedad *f.*

notorious, *a.* notorio.

noun, *n.* nombre, sustantivo *m.*

nourish, *v.* nutrir, alimentar.

nourishment, *n.* nutrimento; alimento *m.*

novel, 1. *a.* nuevo, original. **2.** *n.* novela *f.*

novelist, *n.* novelista *m.* & *f.*

novelty, *n.* novedad *f.*

November, *n.* noviembre *m.*

novena, *n.* novena *f.*

novice, *n.* novicio -cia, novato -ta.

novocaine, *n.* novocaína *f.*

now, *adv.* ahora. **n. and then,** de vez en cuando.

by n., ya. **from n. on,** de ahora en adelante. **just n.,** ahorita. **right n.,** ahora mismo.

nowadays, *adv.* hoy día, hoy en día, actualmente.

nowhere, *adv.* en ninguna parte.

nozzle, *n.* boquilla *f.*

nuance, *n.* matiz *m.*

nuclear, *a.* nuclear.

nuclear energy, energía nuclear *f.*

nuclear warhead, cabeza nuclear *f.*

nuclear waste, desechos nucleares *m.pl.*

nucleus, *n.* núcleo *m.*

nude, *a.* desnudo.

nuisance, *n.* molestia *f.*

nuke, *n.* bomba atómica *f.*

nullify, *v.* anular.

number, 1. *n.* número *m.*; cifra *f.* **license n.,** matrícula *f.* **2.** *v.* numerar, contar.

numeric, numerical, *a.* numérico.

numeric keypad, teclado numérico *m.*

numerous, *a.* numeroso.

nun, *n.* monja *f.*

nuptial, *a.* nupcial.

nurse, 1. *n.* enfermera *f.*; (child's) ama, niñera *f.* **2.** *v.* criar, alimentar, amamantar; cuidar.

nursery, *n.* cuarto destinado a los niños; (agr.) plantel, criadero *m.*

nursery school, jardín de infancia *m.*

nurture, *v.* nutrir.

nut, *n.* nuez *f.*; (mech.) tuerca *f.*

nutcracker, *n.* cascanueces *m.*

nutrition, *n.* nutrición *f.*

nutritious, *a.* nutritivo.

nylon, *n.* nilón *m.*

nymph, *n.* ninfa *f.*

O

oak, *n.* roble *m.*

oar, *n.* remo *m.*

OAS, *abbr.* (Organization of American States) OEA (Organización de los Estados Americanos) *f.*

oasis, *n.* oasis *m.*

oat, *n.* avena *f.*

oath, *n.* juramento *m.*

oatmeal, n. harina de avena f.

obedience, n. obediencia f.

obedient, a. obediente.

obese, a. obeso, gordo.

obey, v. obedecer.

obituary, n. obituario m.

object, 1. n. objeto m.; (gram.) complemento m. **2.** v. oponerse; objetar.

objection, n. objeción f.

objectionable, a. censurable.

objective, a. & n. objetivo m.

obligation, n. obligación f.

obligatory, a. obligatorio.

oblige, v. obligar; complacer.

oblique, a. oblicuo.

obliterate, v. borrar; destruir.

oblivion, n. olvido m.

oblong, a. oblongo.

obnoxious, a. ofensivo, odioso.

obscene, a. obsceno, indecente.

obscure, 1. a. obscuro. **2.** v. obscurecer.

observance, n. observancia; ceremonia f.

observation, n. observación f.

observatory, n. observatorio m.

observe, v. observar; celebrar.

observer, n. observador -ra.

obsession, n. obsesión f.

obsolete, a. anticuado.

obstacle, n. obstáculo m.

obstetrician, n. obstétrico -ca, tocólogo -ga m. & f.

obstinate, a. obstinado, terco.

obstruct, v. obstruir, impedir.

obstruction, n. obstrucción f.

obtain, v. obtener, conseguir.

obtuse, a. obtuso.

obviate, v. obviar.

obvious, a. evidente, obvio.

occasion, 1. n. ocasión f. **2.** v. ocasionar.

occasional, a. ocasional.

occult, a. oculto.

occupant, n. ocupante m. & f.; inquilino -na.

occupation, n. ocupación f.; empleo m.

occupy, v. ocupar; emplear.

occur, v. ocurrir.

occurrence, n. ocurrencia f.

ocean, n. océano m.

o'clock: it's one o., es la una. **it's two o.,** son las dos, etc. **at . . . o.,** a las . . .

octagon, n. octágono m.

octave, n. octava f.

October, n. octubre m.

octopus, n. pulpo m.

oculist, n. oculista m. & f.

odd, a. impar; suelto; raro.

odd number, número impar m.

odious, a. odioso.

odor, n. olor m.; fragancia f.

of, prep. de.

off, adv. (see under verb: **stop off, take off,** etc.)

offend, v. ofender.

offender, n. ofensor -ra; delincuente m. & f.

offense, n. ofensa f.; crimen m.

offensive, 1. a. ofensivo. **2.** n. ofensiva f.

offer, 1. n. oferta f. **2.** v. ofrecer.

offering, n. oferta f.

office, n. oficina f.; despacho m.; oficio, cargo m.

officer, n. oficial m. & f. **police o.,** agente de policía m. & f.

official, 1. a. oficial. **2.** n. oficial m. & f., funcionario -ria.

officiate, v. oficiar.

officious, a. oficioso.

offspring, n. hijos m.pl.; progenie f.

often, adv. muchas veces, a menudo. **how o.,** con qué frecuencia.

oil, 1. n. aceite; óleo; petróleo m. **2.** v. aceitar; engrasar.

oil refinery, destilería de petróleo f.

oil tanker, petrolero m.

oily, a. aceitoso.

ointment, n. ungüento m.

okay, adv. bien; de acuerdo.

old, a. viejo; antiguo. **o. man, o. woman,** viejo -ja.

old-fashioned, a. fuera de moda, anticuado.

Old Testament, Antiguo Testamento m.

olive, n. aceituna, oliva f.

ombudsman, n. ombudsman m.

omelet, n. tortilla de huevos.

omen, n. agüero m.

ominous, a. ominoso, siniestro.

omission, n. omisión f.; olvido m.

omit, v. omitir.

omnibus, n. ómnibus m.

omnipotent, a. omnipotente.

on, prep. en, sobre, encima de. **2.** adv. adelante.

once, adv. una vez. **at o.,** en seguida. **o. in a while,** de vez en cuando.

one, a. & pron. uno -na.

one-armed bandit, tragaperras f.

oneself, pron. sí mismo -ma; se. **with o.,** consigo.

onion, n. cebolla f.

only, 1. a. único, solo. **2.** adv. sólo, solamente.

onward, adv. adelante.

opal, n. ópalo m.

opaque, a. opaco.

open, 1. a. abierto; franco. **o. air,** aire libre. **2.** v. abrir.

opening, n. abertura f.

opera, n. ópera f. **o. glasses,** anteojos de ópera; gemelos m.pl.

operate, v. operar.

operation, n. operación f. **to have an o.,** operarse, ser operado.

operative, a. eficaz, operativo.

operator, n. operario -ria. **elevator o.,** ascensorista m. & f. **telephone o.,** telefonista m. & f.

operetta, n. opereta f.

ophthalmic, a. oftálmico.

opinion, n. opinión f.

opponent, n. antagonista m. & f.

opportunism, n. oportunismo m.

opportunity, n. ocasión, oportunidad f.

oppose, v. oponer.

opposite, 1. *a.* opuesto, contrario. **2.** *prep.* al frente de. **3.** *n.* contrario *m.*

opposition, *n.* oposición *f.*

oppress, *v.* oprimir.

oppression, *n.* opresión *f.*

oppressive, *a.* opresivo.

optic, *a.* óptico.

optical illusion, ilusión de óptica *f.*

optician, *n.* óptico -ca.

optics, *n.* óptica *f.*

optimism, *n.* optimismo.

optimistic, *a.* optimista.

option, *n.* opción, elección *f.*

optional, *a.* discrecional, facultativo.

optometry, *n.* optometría *f.*

opulent, *a.* opulento.

or, *conj.* o, (before o-, ho-) u.

oracle, *n.* oráculo *m.*

oral, *a.* oral, vocal.

orange, *n.* naranja *f.*

orange juice, jugo de naranja, zumo de naranja *m.*

orange squeezer, *n.* exprimidora de naranjas *f.*

oration, *n.* discurso *m.*; oración *f.*

orator, *n.* orador -ra.

oratory, *n.* oratoria *f.*; (church) oratorio *m.*

orbit, *n.* órbita *f.*

orchard, *n.* huerto *m.*

orchestra, *n.* orquesta *f.* **o. seat,** butaca *f.*

orchid, *n.* orquídea *f.*

ordain, *v.* ordenar.

ordeal, *n.* prueba *f.*

order, 1. *n.* orden, *m. or f.*; clase *f.*; (com.) pedido *m.* **in o. that,** para que. **2.** *v.* ordenar; mandar; pedir.

order blank, hoja de pedidos *f.*

orderly, *a.* ordenado.

ordinance, *n.* ordenanza *f.*

ordinary, *a.* ordinario.

ordination, *n.* ordenación *f.*

ore, *n.* mineral *m.*

organ, *n.* órgano *m.*

organdy, *n.* organdí *m.*

organic, *a.* orgánico.

organism, *n.* organismo *m.*

organist, *n.* organista *m. & f.*

organization, *n.* organización *f.*

organize, *v.* organizar.

orgy, *n.* orgía *f.*

orient, 1. *n.* oriente *m.* **2.** *v.* orientar.

Orient, *n.* Oriente *m.*

Oriental, *a.* oriental.

orientation, *n.* orientación *f.*

origin, *n.* origen *m.*

original, *a. & n.* original *m.*

originality, *n.* originalidad *f.*

ornament, 1. *n.* ornamento *m.* **2.** *v.* ornamentar.

ornamental, *a.* ornamental, decorativo.

ornate, *a.* ornado.

ornithology, *n.* ornitología *f.*

orphan, *a. & n.* huérfano -na.

orphanage, *n.* orfanato *m.*

orthodox, *a.* ortodoxo.

ostentation, *n.* ostentación *f.*

ostentatious, *a.* ostentoso.

ostrich, *n.* avestruz *f.*

other, *a. & pron.* otro. **every o. day,** un día sí otro no.

otherwise, *adv.* de otra manera.

ought, *v.* deber.

ounce, *n.* onza *f.*

our, ours, *a. & pron.* nuestro.

ourselves, *pron.* nosotros -as; mismos -as; nos.

oust, *v.* desalojar.

ouster, *n.* desahucio *m.*

out, 1. *adv.* fuera, afuera. **out of,** fuera de. **2.** *prep.* por.

outbreak, *n.* erupción *f.*

outcast, *n.* paria *m. & f.*

outcome, *n.* resultado *m.*

outdoors, *adv.* fuera de casa; al aire libre.

outer, *a.* exterior, externo.

outfit, 1. *n.* equipo; traje *m.* **2.** *v.* equipar.

outgrowth, *n.* resultado *m.*

outing, *n.* paseo *m.*

outlaw, 1. *n.* bandido *m.* **2.** *v.* proscribir.

outlet, *n.* salida *f.*

outline, 1. *n.* contorno; esbozo *m.*; silueta *f.* **2.** *v.* esbozar.

outlive, *v.* sobrevivir.

out-of-court settlement, arreglo pacífico *m.*

out-of-date, *a.* anticuado.

out of focus, *a.* desenfocado.

outpost, *n.* puesto avanzado.

output, *n.* capacidad *f.*; producción *f.*

outrage, 1. *n.* ultraje *m.*; atrocidad *f.* **2.** *v.* ultrajar.

outrageous, *a.* atroz.

outrun, *v.* exceder.

outside, 1. *a. & n.* exterior *m.* **2.** *adv.* afuera, por fuera. **3.** *prep.* fuera de.

outskirt, *n.* borde *m.*

outward, *adv.* hacia afuera.

outwardly, *adv.* exteriormente.

oval, 1. *a.* oval, ovalado. **2.** *n.* óvalo *m.*

ovary, *n.* ovario *m.*

ovation, *n.* ovación *f.*

oven, *n.* horno *m.*

over, 1. *prep.* sobre, encima de; por. **2.** *adv.* **o. here,** aquí. **o. there,** allí, por allí. **to be o.,** estar terminado.

overcoat, *n.* abrigo, sobretodo *m.*

overcome, *v.* superar, vencer.

overdose, *n.* sobredosis *f.*

overdue, *a.* retrasado.

overflow, 1. *n.* inundación *f.* **2.** *v.* inundar.

overhaul, *v.* repasar.

overhead, *adv.* arriba, en lo alto.

overkill, *n.* efecto mayor que el pretendido.

overlook, *v.* pasar por alto.

overnight, *adv.* **to stay or stop o.,** pasar la noche.

overpower, *v.* vencer.

overrule, *v.* predominar.

overrun, *v.* invadir.

oversee, *v.* superentender.

oversight, *n.* descuido *m.*

overt, *a.* abierto.

overtake, *v.* alcanzar.

overthrow, 1. *n.* trastorno *m.* **2.** *v.* trastornar.

overture, *n.* (mus.) obertura *f.*

overturn, *v.* trastornar.

overview, *n.* visión de conjunto *f.*

overweight, *a.* demasiado pesado.

overwhelm, *v.* abrumar.

overwork, v. trabajar demasiado.

owe, v. deber. **owing to,** debido a.

owl, n. búho m., lechuza f.

own, 1. a. propio. **2.** v. poseer.

owner, n. dueño -ña.

ox, n. buey m.

oxygen, n. oxígeno m.

oxygen tent, tienda de oxígeno f.

oyster, n. ostra f.

P

pace, 1. n. paso m. **2.** v. pasearse. **p. off,** medir a pasos.

pacific, a. pacífico.

Pacific Ocean, Océano Pacífico m.

pacifier, n. pacificador m.; (baby p.) chupete m.

pacifism, n. pacifismo m.

pacifist, n. pacifista m. & f.

pacify, v. pacificar.

pack, 1. n. fardo; paquete m.; (animals) muta f. **p. of cards,** baraja f. **2.** v. empaquetar; (baggage) empacar.

package, n. paquete, bulto m.

package tour, viaje todo incluido m.

pact, n. pacto m.

pad, 1. n. colchoncillo m. **p. of paper,** bloc de papel. **2.** v. rellenar.

paddle, 1. n. canalete m. **2.** v. remar.

padlock, n. candado m.

pagan, a. & n. pagano -na.

page, n. página f.; (boy) paje m.

pageant, n. espectáculo m.; procesión f.

pail, n. cubo m.

pain, n. dolor m. **to take pains,** esmerarse.

painful, a. doloroso; penoso.

pain killer, analgésico m.

paint, 1. n. pintura f. **2.** v. pintar.

painter, n. pintor -ra.

painting, n. pintura f.; cuadro m.

pair, 1. n. par m.; pareja f. **2.** v. parear. **p. off,** emparejarse.

pajamas, n. pijama m.

palace, n. palacio m.

palatable, a. sabroso, agradable.

palate, n. paladar m.

palatial, a. palaciego, suntuoso.

pale, a. pálido. **to turn pale,** palidecer.

paleness, n. palidez f.

palette, n. paleta f.

pallbearer, n. portador del féretro, portaféretro m.

pallid, a. pálido.

palm, n. palma f. **p. tree,** palmera f.

palpitate, v. palpitar.

paltry, a. miserable.

pamper, v. mimar.

pamphlet, n. folleto m.

pan, n. cacerola f.

panacea, n. panacea f.

Pan-American, a. panamericano.

pane, n. hoja de vidrio f., cuadro m.

panel, n. tablero m.

pang, n. dolor; remordimiento m.

panic, n. pánico m.

panorama, n. panorama m.

pant, v. jadear.

panther, n. pantera f.

pantomime, n. pantomima f.; mímica f.

pantry, n. despensa f.

pants, n. pantalones, m.pl.

panty hose, n. pantys, pantimedias f.pl. (medias hasta la cintura).

papal, a. papal.

paper, n. papel; periódico; artículo m.

paperback, n. libro en rústica m.

paper clip, sujetapapeles m.

paper cup, vaso de papel m.

paper hanger, empapelador -ra.

paper money, papel moneda m.

paperweight, pisapapeles m.

papier-mâché, n. cartón piedra m.

paprika, n. pimentón m.

par, n. paridad f.; (com.) par f.

parable, n. parábola f.

parachute, n. paracaídas m.

parade, 1. n. desfile m., procesión f. **2.** v. desfilar.

paradise, n. paraíso m.

paradox, n. paradoja f.

paraffin, n. parafina f.

paragraph, n. párrafo m.

parakeet, n. perico m.

parallel, 1. a. paralelo. **2.** v. correr parejas con.

paralysis, n. parálisis f.

paralyze, v. paralizar.

paramedic, n. paramédico -ca.

parameter, n. parámetro m.

paramount, a. supremo.

paraphrase, 1. n. paráfrasis f. **2.** v. parafrasear.

parasite, n. parásito m.

parboil, v. sancochar.

parcel, n. paquete m. **p. of land,** lote de terreno.

parchment, n. pergamino m.

pardon, 1. n. perdón m. **2.** v. perdonar.

pare, v. pelar.

parentage, n. origen m.; extracción f.

parenthesis, n. paréntesis m.

parents, n. padres m.pl.

parish, n. parroquia f.

Parisian, a. & n. parisiense m. & f.

park, 1. n. parque m. **2.** v. estacionar.

parking lot, n. estacionamiento, aparcamiento m.

parking meter, parquímetro m.

parking space, estacionamiento, aparcamiento m.

parkway, n. bulevar m.; autopista f.

parley, n. conferencia f.; (mil.) parlamento m.

parliament, n. parlamento m.

parliamentary, a. parlamentario.

parlor, n. sala f., salón m.

parochial, a. parroquial.

parody, 1. n. parodia f. **2.** v. parodiar.

parole, 1. n. palabra de honor f.; (mil.) santo y seña. **2.** v. poner en libertad bajo palabra.

paroxysm, n. paroxismo m.

parrot, n. loro, papagayo m.

parsimony, n. parsimonia f.

parsley, n. perejil m.

parson, n. párroco m.

part, 1. n. parte f.; (theat.) papel m. **2.** v. separarse, partirse. **p. with,** desprenderse de.

partake, v. tomar parte.

partial, a. parcial.

participant, n. participante m. & f.

participate, v. participar.

participation, n. participación f.

participle, n. participio m.

particle, n. partícula f.

particular, a. & n. particular m.

parting, n. despedida f.

partisan, a. & n. partidario -ria.

partition, 1. n. tabique m. **2.** v. dividir, partir.

partly, adv. en parte.

partner, n. socio -cia; compañero -ra.

partridge, n. perdiz f.

party, n. tertulia, fiesta f.; grupo m.; (political) partido m.

pass, 1. n. pase; (mountain) paso m. **2.** v. pasar. **p. away,** fallecer.

passable, a. transitable; regular.

passage, n. pasaje; (corridor) pasillo m.

passé, a. anticuado.

passenger, n. pasajero -ra.

passenger ship, buque de pasajeros m.

passerby, n. transeúnte m. & f.

passion, n. pasión f.

passionate, a. apasionado.

passive, a. pasivo.

passport, n. pasaporte m.

past, 1. a. & n. pasado m. **2.** prep. más allá de; después de.

paste, 1. n. pasta f. **2.** v. empastar; pegar.

pasteurize, v. pasteurizar.

pastime, n. pasatiempo m.; diversión f.

pastor, n. pastor m.

pastrami, n. pastrón m.

pastry, n. pastelería f.

pasture, 1. n. pasto m.; pradera f. **2.** v. pastar.

pat, 1. n. golpecillo m. **to stand p.,** mantenerse firme. **2.** v. dar golpecillos.

patch, 1. n. remiendo m. **2.** v. remendar.

patent, 1. a. & n. patente m. **2.** v. patentar.

patent leather, charol m.

paternal, a. paterno, paternal.

paternity, n. paternidad f.

path, n. senda f.

pathetic, a. patético.

pathology, n. patología f.

pathos, n. rasgo conmovedor m.

patience, n. paciencia f.

patient, 1. a. paciente. **2.** n. enfermo -ma, paciente m. & f.

patio, n. patio m.

patriarch, n. patriarca m.

patriot, n. patriota m. & f.

patriotic, a. patriótico.

patriotism, n. patriotismo m.

patrol, 1. n. patrulla f. **2.** v. patrullar.

patrolman, n. vigilante m.; patrullador m.

patron, n. patrón m.

patronize, v. condescender; patrocinar; ser cliente de.

pattern, n. modelo m.

pauper, n. indigente m. & f.

pause, 1. n. pausa f. **2.** v. pausar.

pave, v. pavimentar. **p. the way,** preparar el camino.

pavement, n. pavimento m.

pavilion, n. pabellón m.

paw, 1. n. pata f. **2.** v. patear.

pawn, 1. n. prenda f.; (chess) peón de ajedrez m. **2.** v. empeñar.

pay, 1. n. pago; sueldo, salario m.; **2.** v. pagar. **p. back,** pagar; vengarse de. **p. cash,** pagar en metálico.

payee, n. destinatario -ria m. & f.

payment, n. pago m.; recompensa f.

pay phone, teléfono público m.

pea, n. guisante m.

peace, n. paz f.

peaceable, a. pacífico.

peaceful, a. tranquilo.

peach, n. durazno, melocotón m.

peacock, n. pavo real m.

peak, n. pico, cumbre; máximo m.

peal, n. repique; estruendo m. **p. of laughter,** risotada f.

peanut, n. maní, cacahuete m.

pear, n. pera f.

pearl, n. perla f.

peasant, n. campesino -na.

pebble, n. guija f.

peck, 1. n. picotazo m. **2.** v. picotear.

peculiar, a. peculiar.

pecuniary, a. pecuniario.

pedagogue, n. pedagogo -ga.

pedagogy, n. pedagogía f.

pedal, n. pedal m.

pedant, n. pedante m. & f.

peddler, n. buhonero m.

pedestal, n. pedestal m.

pedestrian, n. peatón -na.

pedestrian crossing, paso de peatones m.

pediatrician, n. pediatra m. & f.

pediatrics, n. puericultura f.

pedigree, n. genealogía f.

peek, 1. n. atisbo m. **2.** v. atisbar.

peel, 1. n. corteza f.; (fruit) pellejo m. **2.** v. descortezar; pelar.

peep, 1. *n.* ojeada *f.* **2.** *v.* mirar, atisbar.

peer, 1. *n.* par *m.* **2.** *v.* mirar fijamente.

peg, *n.* clavija; estaquilla *f.;* gancho *m.*

pelt, 1. *n.* pellejo *m.* **2.** *v.* apedrear; (rain) caer con fuerza.

pelvis, *n.* pelvis *f.*

pen, *n.* pluma *f.;* corral *m.* **fountain p.,** pluma fuente.

penalty, *n.* pena; multa *f.;* castigo *m.*

penance, *n.* penitencia *f.* **to do p.,** penar.

penchant, *n.* propensión *f.*

pencil, *n.* lápiz *m.*

pencil sharpener, sacapuntas *m.*

pending, *a.* pendiente. **to be p.,** pender.

penetrate, *v.* penetrar.

penetration, *n.* penetración *f.*

penicillin, *n.* penicilina *f.*

peninsula, *n.* península *f.*

penitent, *n. & a.* penitente *m. & f.*

penknife, *n.* cortaplumas *f.*

penniless, *a.* indigente.

penny, *n.* penique *m.*

pension, *n.* pensión *f.*

pensive, *a.* pensativo.

penultimate, *a.* penúltimo.

penury, *n.* penuria *f.*

people, 1. *n.* gente *f.;* (of a nation) pueblo *m.* **2.** *v.* poblar.

pepper, *n.* pimienta *f.;* (plant) pimiento *m.*

per, *prep.* por.

perambulator, *n.* cochecillo de niño *m.*

perceive, *v.* percibir.

percent, *adv.* por ciento.

percentage, *n.* porcentaje *m.*

perceptible, *a.* perceptible.

perception, *n.* percepción *f.*

perch, *n.* percha *f.;* (fish) perca *f.*

perdition, *n.* perdición *f.*

peremptory, *a.* perentorio, terminante.

perennial, *a.* perenne.

perfect, 1. *a.* perfecto. **2.** *v.* perfeccionar.

perfection, *n.* perfección *f.*

perfectionist, *a. & n.* perfeccionista *m. & f.*

perforation, *n.* perforación *f.*

perform, *v.* hacer; ejecutar; (theat.) representar.

performance, *n.* ejecución *f.;* (theat.) representación *f.*

perfume, 1. *n.* perfume *m.;* fragancia *f.* **2.** *v.* perfumar.

perfunctory, *a.* perfunctorio, superficial.

perhaps, *adv.* quizá, quizás, tal vez.

peril, *n.* peligro *m.*

perilous, *a.* peligroso.

perimeter, *n.* perímetro *m.*

period, *n.* período *m.;* (punct.) punto *m.*

periodic, *a.* periódico.

periodical, *n.* revista *f.*

periphery, *n.* periferia *f.*

perish, *v.* perecer.

perishable, *a.* perecedero.

perjury, *n.* perjurio *m.*

permanent, *a.* permanente. **p. wave,** ondulado permanente.

permeate, *v.* penetrar.

permissible, *a.* permisible.

permission, *n.* permiso *m.*

permit, 1. *n.* permiso *m.* **2.** *v.* permitir.

pernicious, *a.* pernicioso.

perpendicular, *n. & a.* perpendicular *f.*

perpetrate, *v.* perpetrar.

perpetual, *a.* perpetuo.

perplex, *v.* confundir.

perplexity, *n.* perplejidad *f.*

persecute, *v.* perseguir.

persecution, *n.* persecución *f.*

perseverance, *n.* perseverancia *f.*

persevere, *v.* perseverar.

persist, *v.* persistir.

persistent, *a.* persistente.

person, *n.* persona *f.*

personage, *n.* personaje *m.*

personal, *a.* personal.

personality, *n.* personalidad *f.*

personnel, *n.* personal *m.*

perspective, *n.* perspectiva *f.*

perspiration, *n.* sudor *m.*

perspire, *v.* sudar.

persuade, *v.* persuadir.

persuasive, *a.* persuasivo.

pertain, *v.* pertenecer.

pertinent, *a.* pertinente.

perturb, *v.* perturbar.

peruse, *v.* leer con cuidado.

pervade, *v.* penetrar; llenar.

perverse, *a.* perverso.

perversion, *n.* perversión *f.*

pessimism, *n.* pesimismo *m.*

pesticide, *n.* pesticida *m.*

pestilence, *n.* pestilencia *f.*

pet, 1. *n.* favorito -ta.; animal doméstico *m.* **2.** *v.* mimar.

petal, *n.* pétalo *m.*

petition, 1. *n.* petición, súplica *f.* **2.** *v.* pedir, suplicar.

petrify, *v.* petrificar.

petroleum, *n.* petróleo *m.*

petticoat, *n.* enagua *f.*

petty, *a.* mezquino, insignificante.

petulant, *a.* quisquilloso.

pew, *n.* banco de iglesia *m.*

pewter, *n.* peltre *m.*

phantom, *n.* espectro, fantasma *m.*

pharmacist, *n.* farmacéutico -ca, boticario -ria.

pharmacy, *n.* farmacia, botica *f.*

phase, *n.* fase *f.*

pheasant, *n.* faisán *m.*

phenomenal, *a.* fenomenal.

phenomenon, *n.* fenómeno *f.*

philanthropy, *n.* filantropía *f.*

philately, *n.* filatelia *f.*

philosopher, *n.* filósofo -fa.

philosophical, *a.* filosófico.

philosophy, *n.* filosofía *f.*

phlegm, *n.* flema *f.*

phlegmatic, *a.* flemático.

phobia, *n.* fobia *f.*

phonetic, *a.* fonético.

phonograph, *n.* fonógrafo *m.*

phosphorus, *n.* fósforo *m.*

photocopier, *n.* fotocopiadora *f.*

photocopy, 1. *n.* fotocopia *f.* **2.** *v.* fotocopiar.

photoelectric, *a.* fotoeléctrico.

photogenic, *a.* fotogénico.

photograph, 1. *n.* fotografía *f.* **2.** *v.* fotografiar; retratar.

photography, *n.* fotografía *f.*

Photostat, *n.* fotocopia *f.*

phrase, 1. *n.* frase *f.* **2.** *v.* expresar.

physical, *a.* físico.

physician, *n.* médico *m.* & *f.*

physics, *n.* física *f.*

physiology, *n.* fisiología *f.*

physiotherapy, *n.* fisioterapia *f.*

physique, *n.* físico *m.*

pianist, *n.* pianista *m.* & *f.*

piano, *n.* piano *m.*

picayune, *a.* insignificante.

piccolo, *n.* flautín *m.*

pick, 1. *n.* pico *m.* **2.** *v.* escoger. **p. up,** recoger.

picket, *n.* piquete *m.*

pickle, 1. *n.* salmuera *f.;* encurtido *m.* **2.** *v.* escabechar.

pickpocket, *n.* cortabolsas *m.* & *f.*

picnic, *n.* picnic *m.*

picture, 1. *n.* cuadro; retrato *m.;* fotografía *f.;* (movie) película *f.* **2.** *v.* imaginarse.

picturesque, *a.* pintoresco.

pie, *n.* pastel *m.*

piece, *n.* pedazo *m.;* pieza *f.*

pieceworker, *n.* destajero -ra, destajista *m.* & *f.*

pier, *n.* muelle *m.*

pierce, *v.* perforar; pinchar; traspasar.

piety, *n.* piedad *f.*

pig, *n.* puerco, cerdo, lechón *m.*

pigeon, *n.* paloma *f.*

pigeonhole, *n.* casilla *f.*

pigment, *n.* pigmento *m.*

pile, 1. *n.* pila *f.;* montón *m.;* (med.) hemorroides *f.pl.* **2.** *v.* amontonar.

pilfer, *v.* ratear.

pilgrim, *n.* peregrino -na, romero -ra.

pilgrimage, *n.* romería *f.*

pill, *n.* píldora *f.*

pillage, 1. *n.* pillaje *m.* **2.** *v.* pillar.

pillar, *n.* columna *f.*

pillow, *n.* almohada *f.*

pillowcase, *n.* funda de almohada *f.*

pilot, 1. *n.* piloto *m.* & *f.* **2.** *v.* pilotar.

pimple, *n.* grano *m.*

pin, 1. *n.* alfiler; broche *m.;* (mech.) clavija *f.* **2.** *v.* prender. **p. up,** fijar.

pinafore, *n.* delantal (de niña) *m.*

pinch, 1. *n.* pellizco *m.* **2.** *v.* pellizcar.

pine, 1. *n.* pino *m.* **2.** *v.* **p. away,** languidecer. **p. for,** anhelar.

pineapple, *n.* piña *f.,* ananás *m.pl.*

pink, *a.* rosado.

pinky, *n.* meñique *m.*

pinnacle, *n.* pináculo *m.;* cumbre *f.*

pint, *n.* pinta *f.*

pioneer, *n.* pionero -ra.

pious, *a.* piadoso.

pipe, *n.* pipa *f.;* tubo; (of organ) cañón *m.*

pipeline, *n.* oleoducto *m.*

piper, *n.* flautista *m.* & *f.*

piquant, *a.* picante.

pirate, *n.* pirata *m.*

pistol, *n.* pistola *f.*

piston, *n.* émbolo, pistón *m.*

pit, *n.* hoyo *m.;* (fruit) hueso *m.*

pitch, 1. *n.* brea *f.;* grado de inclinación; (music) tono *m.;* **2.** *v.* lanzar; (ship) cabecear.

pitchblende, *n.* pechblenda *f.*

pitcher, *n.* cántaro *m.;* (baseball) lanzador -ra.

pitchfork, *n.* horca *f.;* tridente *m.*

pitfall, *n.* trampa *f.,* hoya cubierta *f.*

pitiful, *a.* lastimoso.

pitiless, *a.* cruel.

pituitary gland, glándula pituitaria *f.*

pity, 1. *n.* compasión, piedad *f.* **to be a p.,** ser lástima. **2.** *v.* compadecer.

pivot, 1. *n.* espiga *f.,* pivote *m.;* punto de partida *m.* **2.** *v.* girar sobre un pivote.

pizza, *n.* pizza *f.*

placard, 1. *n.* cartel *m.* **2.** *v.* fijar carteles.

placate, *v.* aplacar.

place, 1. *n.* lugar, sitio, puesto *m.* **2.** *v.* colocar, poner.

placid, *a.* plácido.

plagiarism, *n.* plagio *m.*

plague, 1. *n.* plaga, peste *f.* **2.** *v.* atormentar.

plain, 1. *a.* sencillo; puro; evidente. **2.** *n.* llano *m.*

plaintiff, *n.* demandante *m.* & *f.*

plan, 1. *n.* plan, propósito *m.* **2.** *v.* planear; pensar; planificar. **p. on,** contar con.

plane, 1. *n.* plano; (tool) cepillo *m.* **2.** *v.* allanar; acepillar.

planet, *n.* planeta *m.*

planetarium, *n.* planetario *m.*

plank, *n.* tablón *m.*

planning, *n.* planificación *f.*

plant, 1. *n.* mata, planta *f.* **2.** *v.* sembrar, plantar.

plantation, *n.* plantación *f.* **coffee p.,** cafetal *m.*

planter, *n.* plantador; hacendado *m.*

plasma, *n.* plasma *m.*

plaster, 1. *n.* yeso; emplasto *m.* **2.** *v.* enyesar; emplastar.

plastic, *a.* plástico.

plate, 1. *n.* plato *m.;* plancha de metal. **2.** *v.* planchear.

plateau, *n.* meseta *f.*

platform, *n.* plataforma *f.*

platinum, *n.* platino *m.*

platitude, *n.* perogrullada *f.*

platter, *n.* fuente *f.,* platel *m.*

plaudit, *n.* aplauso *m.*

plausible, *a.* plausible.

play, 1. *n.* juego *m.;* (theat.) pieza *f.* **2.** *v.* jugar; (music) tocar; (theat.) representar. **p. a part,** hacer un papel.

player, *n.* jugador -ra; (music) músico -ca.; (theat.) actor *m.,* actriz *f.*

playful, *a.* juguetón.

playground, *n.* campo de deportes; patio de recreo.

playmate, *n.* compañero -ra de juego.

playwright, *n.* dramaturgo -ga.

plea, *n.* ruego *m.;* súplica *f.;* (legal) declaración *f.*

plead, *v.* suplicar; declararse. **p. a case,** defender un pleito.

pleasant, *a.* agradable.

please, 1. *v.* gustar, agradar. **Pleased to meet you,** Mucho gusto en conocer a Vd. **2.** *adv.* por favor. **Please . . .** Haga el favor de . . ., Tenga la bondad de . . ., Sírvase . . .

pleasure *n.* gusto, placer *m.*

pleat, 1. *n.* pliegue *m.* **2.** *v.* plegar.

plebiscite, *n.* plebiscito *m.*

pledge, 1. *n.* empeño *m.* **2.** *v.* empeñar.

plentiful, *a.* abundante.

plenty, *n.* abundancia *f.* **p. of,** bastante. **p. more,** mucho más.

pleurisy, *n.* pleuritis *f.*

pliable, pliant, *a.* flexible.

pliers, *n.pl.* alicates *m.pl.*

plight, *n.* apuro, aprieto *m.*

plot, 1. *n.* conspiración; (of a story) trama; (of land) parcela *f.* **2.** *v.* conspirar; tramar.

plow, 1. *n.* arado *m.* **2.** *v.* arar.

pluck, 1. *n.* valor *m.* **2.** *v.* arrancar; desplumar.

plug, 1. *n.* tapón; (elec.) enchufe *m.* **spark p.,** bujía *f.* **2.** *v.* tapar.

plum, *n.* ciruela *f.*

plumage, *n.* plumaje *m.*

plumber, *n.* fontanero -era, plomero -era.

plume, *n.* pluma *f.*

plump, *a.* regordete.

plunder, 1. *n.* botín *m.;* despojos *m.pl.* **2.** *v.* saquear.

plunge, *v.* zambullir; precipitar.

plural, *a.* & *n.* plural *m.*

plus, *prep.* más.

plutocrat, *n.* plutócrata *m.* & *f.*

pneumatic, *a.* neumático.

pneumonia *n.* pulmonía *f.*

poach, *v.* (eggs) escalfar; invadir; cazar en vedado.

pocket, 1. *n.* bolsillo *m.* **2.** *v.* embolsar.

pocketbook, *n.* cartera *f.*

podiatry, *n.* podiatría *f.*

poem, *n.* poema *m.*

poet, *n.* poeta *m.* & *f.*

poetic, *a.* poético.

poetry, *n.* poesía *f.*

poignant, *a.* conmovedor.

point, 1. *n.* punta *f.;* punto *m.* **2.** *v.* apuntar. **p. out,** señalar.

pointed, *a.* puntiagudo; directo.

pointless, *a.* inútil.

poise, 1. *n.* equilibrio *m.;* serenidad *f.* **2.** *v.* equilibrar; estar suspendido.

poison, 1. *n.* veneno *m.* **2.** *v.* envenenar.

poisonous, *a.* venenoso.

poke, 1. *n.* empuje *m.,* hurgonada *f.* **2.** *v.* picar; haronear.

Poland, *n.* Polonia *f.*

polar, *a.* polar.

pole, *n.* palo; (geog.) polo *m.*

police, *n.* policía *f.*

policeman, *n.* policía *m.*

policy, *n.* política *f.* **insurance p.,** póliza de seguro.

Polish, *a.* & *n.* polaco -ca.

polish, 1. *n.* lustre *m.* **2.** *v.* pulir, lustrar.

polite, *a.* cortés.

politic, political, *a.* político.

politician, *n.* político -ca.

politics, *n.* política *f.*

poll, *n.* encuesta *f.;* (pl.) urnas *f.pl.*

pollen, *n.* polen *m.*

pollute, *v.* contaminar.

pollution, *n.* contaminación *f.*

polo, *n.* polo *m.*

polyester, *n.* poliéster *m.*

polygamy, *n.* poligamia *f.*

polygon, *n.* polígono *f.*

pomp, *n.* pompa *f.*

pompous, *a.* pomposo.

poncho, *n.* poncho *m.*

pond, *n.* charca *f.*

ponder, *v.* ponderar, meditar.

ponderous, *a.* ponderoso, pesado.

pontiff, *n.* pontífice *m.*

pontoon, *n.* pontón *m.*

pony, *n.* caballito *m.*

ponytail, *n.* cola de caballo *f.*

poodle, *n.* caniche *m.*

pool, *n.* charco *m.* **swimming p.,** piscina *f.*

poor, *a.* pobre; (not good) malo.

pop, *n.* chasquido *m.*

popcorn, *n.* rosetas de maíz, palomitas de maíz *f.pl.*

pope, *n.* papa *m.*

poppy, *n.* amapola *f.*

popsicle, *n.* polo *m.*

popular, *a.* popular.

popularity, *n.* popularidad *f.*

population, *n.* población *f.*

porcelain, *n.* porcelana *f.*

porch, *n.* pórtico *m.;* galería *f.*

pore, *n.* poro *m.*

pork, *n.* carne de puerco.

pornography, *n.* pornografía *f.*

porous, *a.* poroso, esponjoso.

port, *n.* puerto; (naut.) babor *m.* **p. wine,** oporto *m.*

portable, *a.* portátil.

portal, *n.* portal *m.*

portend, *v.* pronosticar.

portent, *n.* presagio *m.,* portento *m.*

porter, *n.* portero *m.*

portfolio, *n.* cartera *f.*

porthole, *n.* porta *f.*

portion, *n.* porción *f.*

portly, *a.* corpulento.

portrait, *n.* retrato *m.*

portray, *v.* pintar.

Portugal, *n.* Portugal *m.*

Portuguese, *a.* & *n.* portugués -esa.

pose, 1. *n.* postura; actitud *f.* **2.** *v.* posar. **p. as,** pretender ser.

position, *n.* posición *f.*

positive, *a.* positivo.

possess, *v.* poseer.

possession, *n.* posesión *f.*

possessive, *a.* posesivo.

possibility, *n.* posibilidad *f.*

possible, *a.* posible.

post, 1. *n.* poste; puesto *m.* **2.** *v.* fijar; situar; echar al correo.

postage, *n.* porte de correo. **p. stamp,** sello *m.*

postal, *a.* postal.

post card, tarjeta postal.

poster, *n.* cartel, letrero *m.*

posterior, *a.* posterior.

posterity, *n.* posteridad *f.*

postgraduate, *a.* & *n.* postgraduado -da.

postmark, *n.* matasellos *m.*

post office, correos *m.pl.*

postpone, *v.* posponer, aplazar.

postscript, n. posdata f.

posture, n. postura f.

pot, n. olla, marmita; (marijuana) marijuana, hierba f. **flower p.,** tiesto m.

potassium, n. potasio m.

potato, n. patata, papa f. **sweet p.,** batata f.

potent, a. potente, poderoso.

potential, a. & n. potencial f.

potion, n. poción, pócima f.

pottery, n. alfarería f.

pouch, n. saco m.; bolsa f.

poultry, n. aves de corral.

pound, 1. n. libra f. **2.** v. golpear.

pour, v. echar; verter; llover a cántaros.

poverty, n. pobreza f.

powder, 1. n. polvo m.; (gun) pólvora f. **2.** v. empolvar; pulverizar.

power, n. poder m.; potencia f.

powerful, a. poderoso, fuerte.

powerless, a. impotente.

practical, a. práctico.

practical joke, inocentada f.

practically, adv. casi; prácticamente.

practice, 1. n. práctica; costumbre; clientela f. **2.** v. practicar; ejercer.

practiced, a. experto.

practitioner, n. practicante m. & f.

pragmatic, a. pragmático.

prairie, n. llanura; (S.A.) pampa f.

praise, 1. n. alabanza f. **2.** v. alabar.

prank, n. travesura f.

prawn, n. gamba f.

pray, v. rezar; (beg) rogar.

prayer, n. oración; súplica f., ruego m.

preach, v. predicar; sermonear.

preacher, n. predicador m.

preamble, n. preámbulo m.

precarious, a. precario.

precaution, n. precaución f.

precede, v. preceder, anteceder.

precedent, a. & n. precedente m.

precept, n. precepto m.

precinct, n. recinto m.

precious, a. precioso.

precipice, n. precipicio m.

precipitate, v. precipitar.

precise, a. preciso, exacto.

precision, n. precisión f.

preclude, v. evitar.

precocious, a. precoz.

precooked, a. precocinado.

predatory, a. de rapiña, rapaz.

predecessor, n. predecesor -ra, antecesor -ra.

predicament, n. dificultad f.; apuro m.

predict, v. pronosticar, predecir.

predictable, a. previsible.

predilection, n. predilección f.

predispose, v. predisponer.

predominant, a. predominante.

prefabricate, v. fabricar de antemano.

preface, n. prefacio m.

prefer, v. preferir.

preferable, a. preferible.

preference, n. preferencia f.

prefix, 1. n. prefijo m. **2.** v. prefijar.

pregnant, a. preñada.

prehistoric, a. prehistórico.

prejudice, n. prejuicio m.

prejudiced, a. (S.A.) prejuiciado.

preliminary, a. preliminar.

prelude, n. preludio m.

premature, a. prematuro.

premeditate, v. premeditar.

premier, n. primer ministro.

première, n. estreno m.

premise, n. premisa f.

premium, n. premio m.

premonition, n. presentimiento m.

prenatal, a. prenatal.

preparation, n. preparativo m.; preparación f.

preparatory, a. preparatorio. **p. to,** antes de.

prepare, v. preparar.

preponderant, a. preponderante.

preposition, n. preposición f.

preposterous, a. prepóstero, absurdo.

prerequisite, n. requisito previo.

prerogative, n. prerrogativa f.

prescribe, v. prescribir; (med.) recetar.

prescription, n. prescripción; (med.) receta f.

presence, n. presencia f.; porte m.

present, 1. a. presente. **to be present at,** asistir a. **2.** n. presente; (gift) regalo m. **at p.,** ahora, actualmente. **for the p.,** por ahora. **3.** v. presentar.

presentable, a. presentable.

presentation, n. presentación; introducción f.; (theat.) representación f.

presently, adv. luego; dentro de poco.

preservative, a. & n. preservativo m.

preserve, 1. n. conserva f.; (hunting) vedado m. **2.** v. preservar.

preside, v. presidir.

presidency, n. presidencia f.

president, n. presidente -ta.

press, 1. n. prensa f. **2.** v. apretar; urgir; (clothes) planchar.

pressing, a. urgente.

pressure, n. presión f.

pressure cooker, cocina de presión f.

prestige, n. prestigio m.

presume, v. presumir, suponer.

presumptuous, a. presuntuoso.

presuppose, v. presuponer.

pretend, v. fingir. **p. to the throne,** aspirar al trono.

pretense, n. pretensión f.; fingimiento m.

pretension, n. pretensión f.

pretentious, a. presumido.

pretext, n. pretexto m.

pretty, 1. a. bonito, lindo. **2.** adv. bastante.

prevail, v. prevalecer.

prevailing, prevalent, a. predominante.

prevent, v. impedir; evitar.

prevention, n. prevención f.

preventive, a. preventivo.

preview, n. vista anticipada f.

previous, a. anterior, previo.

prey, *n.* presa *f.*

price, *n.* precio *m.*

priceless, *a.* sin precio.

prick, 1. *n.* punzada *f.* **2.** *v.* punzar.

pride, *n.* orgullo *m.*

priest, *n.* sacerdote, cura *m.*

prim, *a.* estirado, remilgado.

primary, *a.* primario, principal.

prime, 1. *a.* primero. **2.** *n.* flor *f.* **3.** *v.* alistar.

prime minister, primer ministro *m.* & *f.*

primitive, *a.* primitivo.

prince, *n.* príncipe *m.*

Prince Charming, Príncipe Azul *m.*

princess, *n.* princesa *f.*

principal, 1. *a.* principal. **2.** *n.* principal *m.* & *f.*; director -ra.

principle, *n.* principio *m.*

print, 1. *n.* letra de molde *f.*; (art) grabado *m.* **2.** *v.* imprimir, estampar.

printing, *n.* impresión *f.* **p. office,** imprenta *f.*

printing press, prensa *f.*

printout, *n.* impreso producido por una computadora, impresión *f.*

priority, *n.* prioridad, precedencia *f.*

prism, *n.* prisma *m.*

prison, *n.* prisión, cárcel *f.*

prisoner, *n.* presidiario -ria, prisionero -ra, preso -sa.

privacy, *n.* soledad *f.*

private, 1. *a.* particular. **2.** *n.* soldado raso. **in p.,** en particular.

privation, *n.* privación *f.*

privet, *n.* ligustro *m.*

privilege, *n.* privilegio *m.*

privy, *n.* letrina *f.*

prize, 1. *n.* premio *m.* **2.** *v.* apreciar, estimar.

probability, *n.* probabilidad *f.*

probable, *a.* probable.

probate, *a.* testamentario.

probation, *n.* prueba *f.*; probación *f.*; libertad condicional *f.*

probe, 1. *n.* indagación *f.* **2.** *v.* indagar; tentar.

probity, *n.* probidad *f.*

problem, *n.* problema *m.*

procedure, *n.* procedimiento *m.*

proceed, *v.* proceder; proseguir.

process, *n.* proceso *m.*

procession, *n.* procesión *f.*

proclaim, *v.* proclamar, anunciar.

proclamation, *n.* proclamación *f.*; decreto *m.*

procrastinate, *v.* dilatar.

procure, *v.* obtener, procurar.

prodigal, *n.* & *a.* pródigo - ga.

prodigy, *n.* prodigio *m.*

produce, *v.* producir.

product, *n.* producto *m.*

production, *n.* producción *f.*

productive, *a.* productivo.

profane, 1. *a.* profano. **2.** *v.* profanar.

profanity, *n.* profanidad *f.*

profess, *v.* profesar; declarar.

profession, *n.* profesión *f.*

professional, *a.* & *n.* profesional *m.* & *f.*

professor, *n.* profesor -ra; catedrático -ca.

proficient, *a.* experto, proficiente.

profile, *n.* perfil *m.*

profit, 1. *n.* provecho *m.*; ventaja *f.*; (com.) ganancia *f.* **2.** *v.* aprovechar; beneficiar.

profitable, *a.* provechoso, ventajoso, lucrativo.

profiteer, 1. *n.* explotador - ra. **2.** *v.* explotar.

profound, *a.* profundo, hondo.

profuse, *a.* pródigo; profuso.

prognosis, *n.* pronóstico *m.*

program, *n.* programa *m.*

progress, 1. *n.* progresos *m.pl.* **in p.,** en marcha. **2.** *v.* progresar; marchar.

progressive, *a.* progresivo; progresista.

prohibit, *v.* prohibir.

prohibition, *n.* prohibición *f.*

prohibitive, *a.* prohibitivo.

project, 1. *n.* proyecto *m.* **2.** *v.* proyectar.

projectile, *n.* proyectil *m.*

projection, *n.* proyección *f.*

projector, *n.* proyector *m.*

proliferation, *n.* proliferación *f.*

prolific, *a.* prolífico.

prologue, *n.* prólogo *m.*

prolong, *v.* prolongar.

prominent, *a.* prominente; eminente.

promiscuous, *a.* promiscuo.

promise, 1. *n.* promesa *f.* **2.** *v.* prometer.

promote, *v.* fomentar; estimular; adelantar; promocionar.

promotion, *n.* promoción *f.*; adelanto *m.*

prompt, 1. *a.* puntual. **2.** *v.* impulsar; (theat.) apuntar. **3.** *adv.* pronto.

promulgate, *v.* promulgar.

pronoun, *n.* pronombre *m.*

pronounce, *v.* pronunciar.

pronunciation, *n.* pronunciación *f.*

proof, *n.* prueba *f.*

proof of purchase, certificado de compra *m.*

proofread, *v.* corregir pruebas.

prop, 1. *n.* apoyo, *m.* **2.** *v.* sostener.

propaganda, *n.* propaganda *f.*

propagate, *v.* propagar.

propel, *v.* propulsar.

propeller, *n.* hélice *f.*

propensity, *n.* tendencia *f.*

proper, *a.* propio; correcto.

property, *n.* propiedad *f.*

prophecy, *n.* profecía *f.*

prophesy, *v.* predecir, profetizar.

prophet, *n.* profeta *m.*

prophetic, *a.* profético.

propitious, *a.* propicio.

proponent, *n.* & *a.* proponente *m.*

proportion, *n.* proporción *f.*

proportionate, *a.* proporcionado.

proposal, *n.* propuesta; oferta *f.*; (marriage) declaración *f.*

propose, *v.* proponer; pensar; declararse.

proposition, *n.* proposición *f.*

proprietor, *n.* propietario - ria, dueño -ña.

propriety, n. corrección f., decoro m.

prosaic, a. prosaico.

proscribe, v. proscribir.

prose, n. prosa f.

prosecute, v. acusar, procesar.

prospect, n. perspectiva; esperanza f.

prospective, a. anticipado, presunto.

prosper, v. prosperar.

prosperity, n. prosperidad f.

prosperous, a. próspero.

prostate gland, glándula prostática f.

prostitute, 1. n. prostituta f. **2.** v. prostituir.

prostrate, 1. a. postrado. **2.** v. postrar.

protect, v. proteger; amparar.

protection, n. protección f.; amparo m.

protective, a. protector.

protector, n. protector -ora.

protégé, n. protegido -da.

protein, n. proteína f.

protest, 1. n. protesta f. **2.** v. protestar.

Protestant, a. & n. protestante m. & f.

protocol, n. protocolo m.

proton, n. protón m.

protract, v. alargar, demorar.

protrude, v. salir fuera.

protuberance, n. protuberancia f.

proud, a. orgulloso.

prove, v. comprobar.

proverb, n. proverbio, refrán m.

provide, v. proporcionar; proveer.

provided, conj. con tal que.

providence, n. providencia f.

province, n. provincia f.

provincial, 1. a. provincial. **2.** n. provinciano -na.

provision, 1. n. provisión f.; (pl.) comestibles m.pl. **2.** v. abastecer.

provocation, n. provocación f.

provoke, v. provocar.

prowess, n. proeza f.

prowl, v. rondar.

prowler, n. merodeador -dora m. & f.

proximity, n. proximidad f.

proxy, n. delegado -da. **by p.,** mediante apoderado.

prudence, n. prudencia f.

prudent, a. prudente, cauteloso.

prune, n. ciruela pasa f.

pry, v. atisbar; curiosear; (mech.) alzaprimar.

psalm, n. salmo m.

pseudonym, n. seudónimo m.

psychedelic, a. psiquedélico.

psychiatrist, n. psiquiatra m. & f.

psychiatry, n. psiquiatría f.

psychoanalysis, n. psicoanálisis m.

psychoanalyst, n. psicoanalista m. & f.

psychological, a. psicológico.

psychology, n. psicología f.

psychosis, n. psicosis f.

ptomaine, n. tomaína f.

pub, n. bar m.

public, a. & n. público m.

publication, n. publicación; revista f.

publicity, n. publicidad f.

publicity agent, publicista m. & f.

publish, v. publicar.

publisher, n. editor -ora.

pudding, n. pudín m.

puddle, n. charco, lodazal m.

Puerto Rican, a. & n. puertorriqueño -ña.

Puerto Rico, Puerto Rico m.

puff, 1. n. soplo m.; (of smoke) bocanada f. **powder p.,** polvera f. **2.** v. jadear; echar bocanadas. **p. up,** hinchar; (fig.) engreír.

pugnacious, a. pugnaz.

puh-lease!, ¡Favor!

pull, 1. n. tirón m.; (coll.) influencia f. **2.** v. tirar; halar.

pulley, n. polea f., motón m.

pulmonary, a. pulmonar.

pulp, n. pulpa f.; (of fruit) carne f.

pulpit, n. púlpito m.

pulsar, n. pulsar m.

pulsate, v. pulsar.

pulse, n. pulso m.

pump, 1. n. bomba f. **2.** v. bombear. **p. up,** inflar.

pumpkin, n. calabaza f.

pun, n. juego de palabras.

punch, 1. n. puñetazo; (mech.) punzón; (beverage) ponche m. **2.** v. dar puñetazos; punzar.

punch bowl, ponchera f.

punctual, a. puntual.

punctuate, v. puntuar.

puncture, 1. n. pinchazo m., perforación f. **2.** v. pinchar, perforar.

pungent, a. picante, pungente.

punish, v. castigar.

punishment, n. castigo m.

punitive, a. punitivo.

puny, a. encanijado.

pupil, n. alumno -na; (anat.) pupila f.

puppet, n. muñeco m.

puppy, n. perrito -ta.

purchase, 1. n. compra f. **2.** v. comprar.

purchasing power, poder adquisitivo m.

pure, a. puro.

purée, n. puré m.

purge, v. purgar.

purify, v. purificar.

puritanical, a. puritano.

purity, n. pureza f.

purple, 1. a. purpúreo. **2.** n. púrpura f.

purport, 1. n. significación f. **2.** v. significar.

purpose, n. propósito m. **on p.,** de propósito.

purr, v. ronronear.

purse, n. bolsa f.

pursue, v. perseguir.

pursuit, n. caza; busca; ocupación f. **p. plane,** avión de caza m.

push, 1. n. empuje; impulso m. **2.** v. empujar.

put, v. poner, colocar. **p. away,** guardar. **p. in,** meter. **p. off,** dejar. **p. on,** ponerse. **p. out,** apagar. **p. up with,** aguantar.

putrid, a. podrido.

puzzle, 1. n. enigma; rompecabezas m. **2.** v. dejar perplejo. **p. out,** descifrar.

pyramid, n. pirámide f.

pyromania, n. piromanía f.

Q

quadrangle, *n.* cuadrángulo *m.*

quadraphonic, *a.* cuatrifónico.

quadruped, *a. & n.* cuadrúpedo *m.*

quail, 1. *n.* codorniz *f.* **2.** *v.* descorazonarse.

quaint, *a.* curioso.

quake, 1. *n.* temblor *m.* **2.** *v.* temblar.

qualification, *n.* requisito *m.;* (pl.) preparaciones *f.pl.*

qualified, *a.* calificado, competente; preparado.

qualify, *v.* calificar, modificar; llenar los requisitos.

quality, *n.* calidad *f.*

quandary, *n.* incertidumbre *f.*

quantity, *n.* cantidad *f.*

quarantine, *n.* cuarentena *f.*

quarrel, 1. *n.* riña, disputa *f.* **2.** *v.* reñir, disputar.

quarry, *n.* cantera; (hunting) presa *f.*

quarter, *n.* cuarto *m.;* (pl.) vivienda *f.*

quarterly, 1. *a.* trimestral. **2.** *adv.* por cuartos.

quartet, *n.* cuarteto *m.*

quartz, *n.* cuarzo *m.*

quasar, *n.* cuasar *m.*

quaver, *v.* temblar.

queen, *n.* reina *f.;* (chess) dama *f.*

queer, *a.* extraño, raro.

quell, *v.* reprimir.

quench, *v.* apagar.

query, 1. *n.* pregunta *f.* **2.** *v.* preguntar.

quest, *n.* busca *f.*

question, 1. *n.* pregunta; cuestión *f.* **q. mark,** signo de interrogación. **2.** *v.* preguntar; interrogar; dudar.

questionable, *a.* dudoso.

questionnaire, *n.* cuestionario *m.*

quiche, *n.* quiche *f.*

quick, *a.* rápido.

quicken, *v.* acelerar.

quicksand, *n.* arena movediza.

quiet, 1. *a.* quieto, tranquilo; callado. **be q., keep q.,** callarse. **2.** *n.* calma; quietud *f.* **3.** *v.* tranquilizar. **q. down,** callarse; calmarse.

quilt, *n.* colcha *f.*

quinine, *n.* quinina *f.*

quintet, *n.* (mus.) quinteto *m.*

quip, 1. *n.* pulla *f.* **2.** *v.* echar pullas.

quit, *v.* dejar; renunciar a. **q. doing** (etc.) dejar de hacer (etc.).

quite, *adv.* bastante; completamente. **not q.,** no precisamente; no completamente.

quiver, 1. *n.* aljaba *f.;* temblor *m.* **2.** *v.* temblar.

quixotic, *a.* quijotesco.

quorum, *n.* quórum *m.*

quota, *n.* cuota *f.*

quotation, *n.* citación; (com.) cotización *f.* **q. marks,** comillas *f.pl.*

quote, *v.* citar; (com.) cotizar.

R

rabbi, *n.* rabí, rabino *m.*

rabbit, *n.* conejo *m.*

rabble, *n.* canalla *f.*

rabid, *a.* rabioso.

rabies, *n.* hidrofobia *f.*

race, 1. *n.* raza; carrera *f.* **2.** *v.* echar una carrera; correr de prisa.

race track, hipódromo *m.*

rack, 1. *n.* (cooking) pesebre *m.;* (clothing) colgador *m.* **2.** *v.* atormentar.

racket, *n.* (noise) ruido *m.;* (tennis) raqueta *f.;* (graft) fraude organizado.

radar, *n.* radar *m.*

radiance, *n.* brillo *m.*

radiant, *a.* radiante.

radiate, *v.* irradiar.

radiation, *n.* irradiación *f.*

radiator, *n.* calorífero *m.;* (auto.) radiador *m.*

radical, *a. & n.* radical *m.*

radio, *n.* radio *m. or f.* **r. station,** estación radiodifusora *f.*

radioactive, *a.* radioactivo.

radio cassette, radiocasete *m.*

radish, *n.* rábano *m.*

radium, *n.* radio *m.*

radius, *n.* radio *m.*

raffle, 1. *n.* rifa, lotería *f.* **2.** *v.* rifar.

raft, *n.* balsa *f.*

rafter, *n.* viga *f.*

rag, *n.* trapo *m.*

ragamuffin, *n.* galopín *m.*

rage, 1. *n.* rabia *f.* **2.** *v.* rabiar.

ragged, *a.* andrajoso; desigual.

raid, *n.* (mil.) correría *f.*

rail, *n.* baranda *f.;* carril *m.* **by r.,** por ferrocarril.

railroad, *n.* ferrocarril *m.*

rain, 1. *n.* lluvia *f.* **2.** *v.* llover.

rainbow, *n.* arco iris *m.*

raincoat, *n.* impermeable *m.;* gabardina *f.*

rainfall, *n.* precipitación *f.*

rainy, *a.* lluvioso.

raise, 1. *n.* aumento *m.* **2.** *v.* levantar, alzar; criar.

raisin, *n.* pasa *f.*

rake, 1. *n.* rastro *m.* **2.** *v.* rastrillar.

rally, 1. *n.* reunión *f.* **2.** *v.* reunirse.

ram, *n.* carnero *m.*

ramble, *v.* vagar.

ramp, *n.* rampa *f.*

rampart, *n.* terraplén *m.*

ranch, *n.* rancho *m.*

rancid, *a.* rancio.

rancor, *n.* rencor *m.*

random, *a.* fortuito. **at r.,** a la ventura.

range, 1. *n.* extensión *f.*; alcance *m.*; estufa; sierra *f.*; terreno de pasto. **2.** *v.* recorrer; extenderse.

rank, 1. *a.* espeso; rancio. **2.** *n.* fila *f.*; grado *m.* **3.** *v.* clasificar.

ransack, *v.* saquear.

ransom, 1. *n.* rescate *m.* **2.** *v.* rescatar.

rap, 1. *n.* golpecito *m.* **2.** *v.* golpear.

rapid, *a.* rápido.

rapist, *n.* violador -dora *m.* & *f.*

rapport, *n.* armonía *f.*

rapture, *n.* éxtasis *m.*

rare, *a.* raro; (of food) a medio cocer.

rascal, *n.* pícaro, bribón *m.*

rash, 1. *a.* temerario. **2.** *n.* erupción *f.*

raspberry, *n.* frambuesa *f.*

rat, *n.* rata *f.*

rate, 1. *n.* velocidad; tasa *f.*; precio *m.*; (of exchange; of interest) tipo *m.* **at any r.,** de todos modos. **2.** *v.* valuar.

rather, *adv.* bastante; más bien, mejor dicho.

ratify, *v.* ratificar.

ratio, *n.* razón; proporción *f.*

ration, 1. *n.* ración *f.* **2.** *v.* racionar.

rational, *a.* racional.

rattle, 1. *n.* ruido *m.*; matraca *f.* **r. snake,** culebra de cascabel, serpiente de cascabel *f.* **2.** *v.* matraquear; rechinar.

raucous, *a.* ronco.

ravage, *v.* pillar; destruir; asolar.

rave, *v.* delirar; entusiasmarse.

ravel, *v.* deshilar.

raven, *n.* cuervo *m.*

ravenous, *a.* voraz.

raw, *a.* crudo; verde.

ray, *n.* rayo *m.*

rayon, *n.* rayón *m.*

razor, *n.* navaja de afeitar. **r. blade,** hoja de afeitar.

reach, 1. *n.* alcance *m.* **2.** *v.* alcanzar.

react, *v.* reaccionar.

reaction, *n.* reacción *f.*

reactionary, 1. *a.* reaccionario. **2.** *n.* (pol.) retrógrado *m.*

read, *v.* leer.

reader, *n.* lector -ra; libro de lectura *m.*

readily, *adv.* fácilmente.

reading, *n.* lectura *f.*

ready, *a.* listo, preparado; dispuesto.

ready-cooked, *a.* precocinado.

real, *a.* verdadero; real.

real estate, bienes inmuebles, *m.pl.*

real-estate agent, agente inmobiliario *m.*, agente inmobiliaria *f.*

realist, *n.* realista *m.* & *f.*

realistic, *a.* realista.

reality, *n.* realidad *f.*

realization, *n.* comprensión; realización *f.*

realize, *v.* darse cuenta de; realizar.

really, *adv.* de veras; en realidad.

realm, *n.* reino; dominio *m.*

reap, *v.* segar, cosechar.

rear, 1. *a.* posterior. **2.** *n.* parte posterior. **3.** *v.* criar; levantar.

reason, 1. *n.* razón; causa *f.*; motivo *m.* **2.** *v.* razonar.

reasonable, *a.* razonable.

reassure, *v.* calmar, tranquilizar.

rebate, *n.* rebaja *f.*

rebel, 1. *n.* rebelde *m.* & *f.* **2.** *v.* rebelarse.

rebellion, *n.* rebelión *f.*

rebellious, *a.* rebelde.

rebirth, *n.* renacimiento *m.*

rebound, *v.* repercutir; resaltar.

rebuff, 1. *n.* repulsa *f.* **2.** *v.* rechazar.

rebuke, 1. *n.* reprensión *f.* **2.** *v.* reprender.

rebuttal, *n.* refutación *f.*

recalcitrant, *a.* recalcitrante.

recall, *v.* recordar; acordarse de; hacer volver.

recapitulate, *v.* recapitular.

recede, *v.* retroceder.

receipt, *n.* recibo *m.*; (com., pl.) ingresos *m.pl.*

receive, *v.* recibir.

receiver, *n.* receptor *m.*

recent, *a.* reciente.

recently, *adv.* recién.

receptacle, *n.* receptáculo *m.*

reception, *n.* acogida; recepción *f.*

receptionist, *n.* recepcionista *m.* & *f.*

receptive, *a.* receptivo.

recess, *n.* nicho; retiro; recreo *m.*

recipe, *n.* receta *f.*

recipient, *n.* recibidor -ra, recipiente *m.* & *f.*

reciprocate, *v.* corresponder; reciprocar.

recite, *v.* recitar.

reckless, *a.* descuidado; imprudente.

reckon, *v.* contar; calcular.

reclaim, *v.* reformar; (leg.) reclamar.

recline, *v.* reclinar; recostar.

recognition, *n.* reconocimiento *m.*

recognize, *v.* reconocer.

recoil, 1. *n.* culatada *f.* **2.** *v.* recular.

recollect, *v.* recordar, acordarse de.

recommend, *v.* recomendar.

recommendation, *n.* recomendación *f.*

recompense, 1. *n.* recompensa *f.* **2.** *v.* recompensar.

reconcile, *v.* reconciliar.

recondition, *v.* reacondicionar.

reconsider, *v.* considerar de nuevo.

reconstruct, *v.* reconstruir.

record, 1. *n.* registro; (sports) record *m.* **phonograph r.,** disco *m.* **2.** *v.* registrar.

record player, tocadiscos *m.*

recount, *v.* relatar; contar.

recover, *v.* recobrar; restablecerse.

recovery, *n.* recobro *m.*; recuperación *f.*

recruit, 1. *n.* recluta *m.* **2.** *v.* reclutar.

rectangle, *n.* rectángulo *m.*

rectify, *v.* rectificar.

recuperate, *v.* recuperar.

recur, *v.* recurrir.

recycle, *v.* reciclar.

red, *a.* rojo, colorado.
redeem, *v.* redimir, rescatar.
redemption, *n.* redención *f.*
redhead, *n.* pelirrojo -ja.
red mullet, salmonete *m.*
reduce, *v.* reducir.
reduction, *n.* reducción *f.*
reed, *n.* caña *f.*, (S.A.) bejuco *m.*
reef, *n.* arrecife, escollo *m.*
reel, 1. *n.* aspa *f.*, carrete *m.* **2.** *v.* aspar.
refer, *v.* referir.
referee, *n.* árbitro *m. & f.*
reference, *n.* referencia *f.*
refill, 1. *n.* relleno *m.* **2.** *v.* rellenar.
refine, *v.* refinar.
refinement, *n.* refinamiento *m.; cultura f.*
reflect, *v.* reflejar; reflexionar.
reflection, *n.* reflejo *m.;* reflexión *f.*
reflex, *a.* reflejo.
reform, 1. *n.* reforma *f.* **2.** *v.* reformar.
reformation, *n.* reformación *f.*
refractory, *a.* refractario.
refrain, 1. *n.* estribillo *m.* **2.** *v.* abstenerse.
refresh, *v.* refrescar.
refreshment, *n.* refresco *m.*
refrigerator, *n.* refrigerador *m.*
refuge, *n.* refugio *m.*
refugee, *n.* refugiado -da.
refund, 1. *n.* reembolso *m.* **2.** *v.* reembolsar.
refusal, *n.* negativa *f.*
refuse, 1. *n.* basura *f.* **2.** *v.* negarse, rehusar.
refute, *v.* refutar.
regain, *v.* recobrar. **r. consciousness,** recobrar el conocimiento.
regal, *a.* real.
regard, 1. *n.* aprecio; respeto *m.* **with r. to,** con respecto a. **2.** *v.* considerar; estimar.
regarding, *prep.* en cuanto a, acerca de.
regardless (of), a pesar de.
regent, *n.* regente *m. & f.*
regime, *n.* régimen *m.*

regiment, 1. *n.* regimiento *m.* **2.** *v.* regimentar.
region, *n.* región *f.*
register, 1. *n.* registro *m.* **cash r.,** caja registradora *f.* **2.** *v.* registrar; matricularse; (a letter) certificar.
registration, *n.* registro *m.;* matrícula *f.*
regret, 1. *n.* pena *f.* **2.** *v.* sentir, lamentar.
regular, *a.* regular; ordinario.
regularity, *n.* regularidad *f.*
regulate, *v.* regular.
regulation, *n.* regulación *f.*
regulator, *n.* regulador *m.*
rehabilitate, *v.* rehabilitar.
rehearse, *v.* repasar; (theat.) ensayar.
reheat, *v.* recalentar.
reign, 1. *n.* reino, reinado *m.* **2.** *v.* reinar.
reimburse, *v.* reembolsar.
rein, 1. *n.* rienda *f.* **2.** *v.* refrenar.
reincarnation, *n.* reencarnación *f.*
reindeer, *n.* reno *m.*
reinforce, *v.* reforzar.
reinforcement, *n.* refuerzo *m.;* armadura *f.*
reiterate, *v.* reiterar.
reject, *v.* rechazar.
rejoice, *v.* regocijarse.
rejoin, *v.* reunirse con; replicar.
rejuvenate, *v.* rejuvenecer.
relapse, 1. *n.* recaída *f.* **2.** *v.* recaer.
relate, *v.* relatar, contar; relacionar. **r. to,** llevarse bien con.
relation, *n.* relación *f.;* pariente *m. & f.*
relative, 1. *a.* relativo. **2.** *n.* pariente *m. & f.*
relativity, *n.* relatividad *f.*
relax, *v.* descansar; relajar.
relay, 1. *n.* relevo *m.* **2.** *v.* retransmitir.
release, 1. *n.* liberación *f.* **2.** *v.* soltar.
relent, *v.* ceder.
relevant, *a.* pertinente.
reliability, *n.* veracidad *f.*
reliable, *a.* responsable; digno de confianza.
relic, *n.* reliquia *f.*

relief, *n.* alivio; (sculpture) relieve *m.*
relieve, *v.* aliviar.
religion, *n.* religión *f.*
religious, *a.* religioso.
relinquish, *v.* abandonar.
relish, 1. *n.* sabor; condimento *m.* **2.** *v.* saborear.
reluctant, *a.* renuente.
rely, *v.* **r. on,** confiar en; contar con; depender de.
remain, 1. *n.* (pl.) restos *m.pl.* **2.** *v.* quedar, permanecer.
remainder, *n.* resto *m.*
remark, 1. *n.* observación *f.* **2.** *v.* observar.
remarkable, *a.* notable.
remedial, *a.* reparador.
remedy, 1. *n.* remedio *m.* **2.** *v.* remediar.
remember, *v.* acordarse de, recordar.
remembrance, *n.* recuerdo *m.*
remind, *v.* **r. of,** recordar.
reminisce, *v.* pensar en o hablar de cosas pasadas.
remiss, *a.* remiso; flojo.
remit, *v.* remitir.
remorse, *n.* remordimiento *m.*
remote, *a.* remoto.
remote control, mando a distancia *m.*
removal, *n.* alejamiento *m.;* eliminación *f.*
remove, *v.* quitar; remover.
renaissance, *n.* renacimiento *m.*
rend, *v.* hacer pedazos; separar.
render, *v.* dar; rendir; (theat.) interpretar.
rendezvous, *n.* cita *f.*
rendition, *n.* interpretación, rendición *f.*
renege, *v.* renunciar; faltar a su palabra, no cumplir una promesa.
renew, *v.* renovar.
renewal, *n.* renovación; (com.) prórroga *f.*
renounce, *v.* renunciar a.
renovate, *v.* renovar.
renown, *n.* renombre *m.*, fama *f.*

rent, 1. *n.* alquiler *m.* **2.** *v.* arrendar, alquilar.

repair, 1. *n.* reparo *m.* **2.** *v.* reparar.

repairman, *n.* técnico *m.*

repatriate, *v.* repatriar.

repay, *v.* pagar; devolver.

repeat, *v.* repetir.

repel, *v.* repeler, repulsar.

repent, *v.* arrepentirse.

repentance, *n.* arrepentimiento *m.*

repercussion, *n.* repercusión *f.*

repertoire, *n.* repertorio *m.*

repetition, *n.* repetición *f.*

replace, *v.* reemplazar.

replenish, *v.* rellenar; surtir de nuevo.

reply, 1. *n.* respuesta *f.* **2.** *v.* replicar; contestar.

report, 1. *n.* informe *m.* **2.** *v.* informar, contar; denunciar; presentarse.

reporter, *n.* repórter *m.* & *f.*, reportero -ra.

repose, 1. *n.* reposo *m.* **2.** *v.* reposar; reclinar.

reprehensible, *a.* reprensible.

represent, *v.* representar.

representation, *n.* representación *f.*

representative, 1. *a.* representativo. **2.** *n.* representante *m.* & *f.*

repress, *v.* reprimir.

reprimand, 1. *n.* regaño *m.* **2.** *v.* regañar.

reprisal, *n.* represalia *f.*

reproach, 1. *n.* reprôche *m.* **2.** *v.* reprochar.

reproduce, *v.* reproducir.

reproduction, *n.* reproducción *f.*

reproof, *n.* censura *f.*

reprove, *v.* censurar, regañar.

reptile, *n.* reptil *m.*

republic, *n.* república *f.*

republican, *a.* & *n.* republicano -na.

repudiate, *v.* repudiar.

repulsive, *a.* repulsivo, repugnante.

reputation, *n.* reputación; fama *f.*

repute, 1. *n.* reputación *f.* **2.** *v.* reputar.

request, 1. *n.* súplica *f.*, ruego *m.* **2.** *v.* pedir; rogar, suplicar.

require, *v.* requerir; exigir.

requirement, *n.* requisito *m.*

requisite, 1. *a.* necesario. **2.** *n.* requisito *m.*

requisition, *n.* requisición *f.*

rescind, *v.* rescindir, anular.

rescue, 1. *n.* rescate *m.* **2.** *v.* rescatar.

research, *n.* investigación *f.*

researcher, *n.* investigador - dora.

resemble, *v.* parecerse a, asemejarse a.

resent, *v.* resentirse de.

reservation, *n.* reservación *f.*

reserve, 1. *n.* reserva *f.* **2.** *v.* reservar.

reservoir, *n* depósito; tanque *m.*

reside, *v.* residir, morar.

residence, *n.* residencia, morada *f.*

resident, *n.* residente *m.* & *f.*

residue, *n.* residuo *m.*

resign, *v.* dimitir; resignar.

resignation, *n.* dimisión; resignación *f.*

resist, *v.* resistir.

resistance, *n.* resistencia *f.*

resolute, *a.* resuelto.

resolution, *n.* resolución *f.*

resolve, *v.* resolver.

resonant, *a.* resonante.

resort, 1. *n.* recurso; expediente *m.* **summer r.,** lugar de veraneo. **2.** *v.* acudir, recurrir.

resound, *v.* resonar.

resource, *n.* recurso *m.*

respect, 1. *n.* respeto *m.* **with r. to,** con respecto a. **2.** *v.* respetar.

respectable, *a.* respetable.

respectful, *a.* respetuoso.

respective, *a.* respectivo.

respiration, *n.* respiración *f.*

respite, *n.* pausa, tregua *f.*

respond, *v.* responder.

response, *n.* respuesta *f.*

responsibility, *n.* responsabilidad *f.*

responsible, *a.* responsable.

responsive, *a.* sensible a.

rest, 1. *n.* descanso; reposo *m.;* (music) pausa *f.* **the**

r., el resto, lo demás; los demás. **2.** *v.* descansar; recostar.

restaurant, *n.* restaurante *m.*

restful, *a.* tranquilo.

restitution, *n.* restitución *f.*

restless, *a.* inquieto.

restoration, *n.* restauración *f.*

restore, *v.* restaurar.

restrain, *v.* refrenar.

restraint, *n.* limitación, restricción *f.*

restrict, *v.* restringir, limitar.

rest room, aseos *m.pl.*

result, 1. *n.* resultado *m.* **2.** *v.* resultar.

resume, *v.* reasumir; empezar de nuevo.

résumé, *n.* resumen *m.*

resurgent, *a.* resurgente.

resurrect, *v.* resucitar.

resuscitate, *v.* resucitar.

retail, *n.* **at r.,** al por menor.

retain, *v.* retener.

retaliate, *v.* vengarse.

retard, *v.* retardar.

retention, *n.* retención *f.*

reticent, *a.* reticente.

retire, *v.* retirar.

retirement, *n.* jubilación *f.*

retort, 1. *n.* réplica; (chem.) retorta *f.* **2.** *v.* replicar.

retreat, 1. *n.* retiro *m.;* (mil.) retirada, retreta *f.* **2.** *v.* retirarse.

retribution, *n.* retribución *f.*

retrieve, *v.* recobrar.

return, 1. *n* vuelta *f.*, regreso; retorno *m.* **by r. mail,** a vuelta de correo. **2.** *v.* volver, regresar; devolver.

reunion, *n.* reunión *f.*

reveal, *v.* revelar.

revelation, *n.* revelación *f.*

revenge, *n.* venganza *f.* **to get r.,** vengarse.

revenue, *n.* renta *f.*

revere, *v.* reverenciar, venerar.

reverence, 1. *n.* reverencia *f.* **2.** *v.* reverenciar.

reverend, 1. *a.* reverendo. **2.** *n.* pastor *m.*

reverent, *a.* reverente.

reverse, 1. *a.* inverso. **2.** *n.* revés, inverso *m.* **3.** *v.* invertir; revocar.

revert, *v.* revertir.

review, 1. *n.* repaso *m.;* revista *f.* **2.** *v.* repasar; (mil.) revistar.

revise, *v.* revisar.

revision, *n.* revisión *f.*

revival, *n.* reavivamiento *m.*

revive, *v.* avivar; revivir, resucitar.

revoke, *v.* revocar.

revolt, 1. *n.* rebelión *f.* **2.** *v.* rebelarse.

revolting, *a.* repugnante.

revolution, *n.* revolución *f.*

revolutionary, *a. & n.* revolucionario -ria.

revolve, *v.* girar; dar vueltas.

revolver, *n.* revólver *m.*

revolving door, puerta giratoria *f.*

reward, 1. *n.* pago *m.;* recompensa *f.* **2.** *v.* recompensar.

rhetoric, *n.* retórica *f.*

rheumatism, *n.* reumatismo *m.*

rhinoceros, *n.* rinoceronte *m.*

rhubarb, *n.* ruibarbo *m.*

rhyme, 1. *n.* rima *f.* **2.** *v.* rimar.

rhythm, *n.* ritmo *m.*

rhythmical, *a.* rítmico.

rib, *n.* costilla *f.*

ribbon, *n.* cinta *f.*

rib cage, caja torácica *f.*

rice, *n.* arroz *m.*

rich, *a.* rico.

rid, *v.* librar. **get r. of,** deshacerse de, quitarse.

riddle, *n.* enigma; rompecabezas *m.*

ride, 1. *n.* paseo (a caballo, en coche, etc.) *m.* **2.** *v.* cabalgar; ir en coche.

ridge, *n.* cerro *m.;* arruga *f.;* (of a roof) caballete *m.*

ridicule, 1. *n.* ridículo *m.* **2.** *v.* ridiculizar.

ridiculous, *a.* ridículo.

riding, *n.* equitación *f.*

riding school, picadero *m.*

rifle, 1. *n.* fusil *m.* **2.** *v.* robar.

rig, 1. *n.* aparejo *m.* **2.** *v.* aparejar.

right, 1. *a.* derecho; correcto. **to be r.,** tener razón. **2.** *adv.* bien, correctamente. **r. here,** etc., aquí mismo, etc. **all r.,** está bien, muy bien. **3.** *n.* derecho *m.;* justicia *f.* **to the r.,** a la derecha. **4.** *v.* corregir; enderezar.

righteous, *a.* justo.

rigid, *a.* rígido.

rigor, *n.* rigor *m.*

rigorous, *a.* riguroso.

rim, *n.* margen *m. or f.;* borde *m.*

ring, 1. *n.* anillo *m.;* sortija *f.;* círculo; campaneo *m.* **2.** *v.* cercar; sonar; tocar.

ring finger, dedo anular *m.*

rinse, *v.* enjuagar, lavar.

riot, *n.* motín; alboroto *m.*

rip, 1. *n.* rasgadura *f.* **2.** *v.* rasgar; descoser.

ripe, *a.* maduro.

ripen, *v.* madurar.

ripoff, *n.* robo, atraco *m.*

ripple, 1. *n.* onda *f.* **2.** *v.* ondear.

rise, 1. *n.* subida *f.* **2.** *v.* ascender; levantarse; (moon) salir.

risk, 1. *n.* riesgo *m.* **2.** *v.* arriesgar.

rite, *n.* rito *m.*

ritual, *a. & n.* ritual *m.*

rival, *n.* rival *m. & f.*

rivalry, *n.* rivalidad *f.*

river, *n.* río *m.*

rivet, 1. *n.* remache, roblón *m.* **2.** *v.* remachar, roblar.

road, *n.* camino *m.;* carretera *f.*

roadside, *n.* borde de la carretera *m.*

roam, *v.* vagar.

roar, 1. *n.* rugido, bramido *m.* **2.** *v.* rugir, bramar.

roast, 1. *n.* asado *m.* **2.** *v.* asar.

rob, *v.* robar.

robber, *n.* ladrón -na.

robbery, *n.* robo *m.*

robe, *n.* manto *m.*

robin, *n.* petirrojo *m.*

robust, *a.* robusto.

rock, 1. *n.* roca, peña *f.;* (music) rock *m.,* música

(de) rock *f.* **2.** *v.* mecer; oscilar.

rocker, *n.* mecedora *f.*

rocket, *n.* cohete *m.*

rocking chair, mecedora *f.*

Rock of Gibraltar, Peñón de Gibraltar *m.*

rocky, *a.* pedregoso.

rod, *n.* varilla *f.*

rodent, *n.* roedor *m.*

rogue, *n.* bribón, pícaro *m.*

roguish, *a.* pícaro.

role, *n.* papel *m.*

roll, 1. *n.* rollo *m.;* lista *f.;* panecillo *m.* **to call the r.,** pasar lista. **2.** *v.* rodar. **r. up,** enrollar. **r. up one's sleeves,** arremangarse.

roller, *n.* rodillo, cilindro *m.*

roller skate, patín de ruedas *m.*

Roman, *a. & n.* romano -na.

romance, 1. *a.* románico. **2.** *n.* romance *m.;* amorío *m.*

romantic, *a.* romántico.

romp, *v.* retozar; jugar.

roof, 1. *n.* techo *m.;* **2.** *v.* techar.

room, 1. *n.* cuarto *m.,* habitación *f.;* lugar *m.* **2.** *v.* alojarse.

roommate, *n.* compañero -ra de cuarto.

rooster, *n.* gallo *m.*

root, 1. *n.* raíz *f.* **to take r.,** arraigar.

rootless, *a.* desarraigado.

rope, *n.* cuerda, soga *f.*

rose, *n.* rosa *f.*

rosy, *a.* róseo, rosado.

rot, 1. *n.* putrefacción *f.* **2.** *v.* pudrirse.

rotary, *a.* giratorio; rotativo.

rotate, *v.* girar; alternar.

rotation, *n.* rotación *f.*

rotten, *a.* podrido.

rouge, *n.* colorete *m.*

rough, *a.* áspero; rudo; grosero; aproximado.

round, 1. *a.* redondo. **r. trip,** viaje de ida y vuelta. **2.** *n.* ronda *f.;* (boxing) asalto *m.*

rouse, *v.* despertar.

rout, 1. *n.* derrota *f.* **2.** *v.* derrotar.

route, *n.* ruta, vía *f.*
routine, 1. *a.* rutinario. **2.** *n.* rutina *f.*
rove, *v.* vagar.
rover, *n.* vagabundo -da.
row, 1. *n.* fila; pelea *f.* **2.** *v.* (naut.) remar.
rowboat, *n.* bote de remos.
rowdy, *a.* alborotado.
royal, *a.* real.
royalty, *n.* realeza *f.;* (pl.) regalías *f.pl.*
rub, *v.* frotar. **r. against,** rozar. **r. out,** borrar.
rubber, *n.* goma *f.;* caucho *m.;* (pl.) chanclos *m.pl.,* zapatos de goma.
rubbish, *n.* basura *f.;* (nonsense) tonterías *f.pl.*
ruby, *n.* rubí *m.*
rudder, *n.* timón *m.*
ruddy, *a.* colorado.
rude, *a.* rudo; grosero; descortés.

rudiment, *n.* rudimento *m.*
rudimentary, *a.* rudimentario.
rue, *v.* deplorar; lamentar.
ruffian, *n.* rufián, bandolero *m.*
ruffle, 1. *n.* volante fruncido. **2.** *v.* fruncir; irritar.
rug, *n.* alfombra *f.*
rugged, *a.* áspero; robusto.
ruin, 1. *n.* ruina *f.* **2.** *v.* arruinar.
ruinous, *a.* ruinoso.
rule, 1. *n.* regla *f.* **as a r.,** por regla general. **2.** *v.* gobernar; mandar; rayar.
ruler, *n.* gobernante *m.* & *f.;* soberano -na; regla *f.*
rum, *n.* ron *m.*
rumble, *v.* retumbar.
rumor, *n.* rumor *m.*
run, *v.* correr; hacer correr. **r. away,** escaparse. **r. into,** chocar con.

runner, *n.* corredor -ra; mensajero -ra.
runner-up, *n.* subcampeón -ona.
runproof, *a.* indesmallable.
rupture, 1. *n.* rotura; hernia *f.* **2.** *v.* reventar.
rural, *a.* rural, campestre.
rush, 1. *n.* prisa *f.;* (bot.) junco *m.* **2.** *v.* ir de prisa.
rush hour, hora punta *f.*
Russia, *n.* Rusia *f.*
Russian, *a.* & *n.* ruso -sa.
rust, 1. *n.* herrumbre *f.* **2.** *v.* aherrumbrarse.
rustic, *a.* rústico.
rustle, 1. *n.* susurro *m.* **2.** *v.* susurrar.
rusty, *a.* mohoso.
rut, *n.* surco *m.*
ruthless, *a.* cruel, inhumano.
rye, *n.* centeno *m.*
rye bread, pan de centeno *m.*

S

saber, *n.* sable *m.*
sable, *n.* cebellina *f.*
sabotage, *n.* sabotaje *m.*
sachet, *n.* perfumador *m.*
sack, 1. *n.* saco *m.* **2.** *v.* (mil.) saquear.
sacred, *a.* sagrado, santo.
sacrifice, 1. *n.* sacrificio *m.* **2.** *v.* sacrificar.
sacrilege, *n.* sacrilegio *m.*
sad, *a.* triste.
saddle, 1. *n.* silla de montar. **2.** *v.* ensillar.
sadness, *n.* tristeza *f.*
safe, 1. *a.* seguro; salvo. **2.** *n.* caja de caudales.
safeguard, 1. *n.* salvaguardia *m.* **2.** *v.* proteger, poner a salvo.
safety, *n.* seguridad, protección *f.*
safety belt, cinturón de seguridad *m.*
safety pin, imperdible *m.*
safety valve, válvula de seguridad *f.*
sage, 1. *a.* sabio, sagaz. **2.** *n.* sabio *m.;* (bot.) salvia *f.*

sail, 1. *n.* vela *f.;* paseo por mar. **2.** *v.* navegar; embarcarse.
sailboat, *n.* barco de vela.
sailor, *n.* marinero *m.*
saint, *n.* santo -ta.
sake, *n.* **for the s. of,** por; por el bien de.
salad, *n.* ensalada *f.* **s. bowl,** ensaladera *f.*
salad dressing, aliño *m.*
salary, *n.* sueldo, salario *m.*
sale, *n.* venta *f.*
salesman, *n.* vendedor *m.;* viajante de comercio.
sales tax, impuesto sobre la venta.
saliva, *n.* saliva *f.*
salmon, *n.* salmón *m.*
salt, 1. *a.* salado. **2.** *n.* sal *f.* **3.** *v.* salar.
salute, 1. *n.* saludo *m.* **2.** *v.* saludar.
salvage, *v.* salvar; recobrar.
salvation, *n.* salvación *f.*
salve, *n.* emplasto, ungüento *m.*
same, *a.* & *pron.* mismo. **it's all the s.,** lo mismo da.

sample, 1. *n.* muestra *f.* **2.** *v.* probar.
sanatorium, *n.* sanatorio *m.*
sanctify, *v.* santificar.
sanction, 1. *n.* sanción *f.* **2.** *v.* sancionar.
sanctity, *n.* santidad *f.*
sanctuary, *n.* santuario, asilo *m.*
sand, *n.* arena *f.*
sandal, *n.* sandalia *f.*
sandpaper, *n.* papel de lija *m.*
sandwich, *n.* emparedado, sándwich *m.*
sandy, *a.* arenoso; (color) rufo.
sane, *a.* cuerdo; sano.
sanitary, *a.* higiénico, sanitario. **s. napkin,** toalla sanitaria.
sanitation, *n.* saneamiento *m.*
sanity, *n.* cordura *f.*
Santa Claus, Papá Noel *m.*
sap, 1. *n.* savia *f.;* (coll.) estúpido, bobo *m.* **2.** *v.* agotar.
sapphire, *n.* zafiro *m.*
sarcasm, *n.* sarcasmo *m.*

sardine, *n.* sardina *f.*
sash, *n.* cinta *f.*
satellite, *n.* satélite *m.*
satellite dish, antena parabólica *f.*
satin, *n.* raso *m.*
satire, *n.* sátira *f.*
satisfaction, *n.* satisfacción; recompensa *f.*
satisfactory, *a.* satisfactorio.
satisfy, *v.* satisfacer. **be satisfied that . . .,** estar convencido de que.
saturate, *v.* saturar.
Saturday, *n.* sábado *m.*
sauce, *n.* salsa; compota *f.*
saucer, *n.* platillo *m.*
saucy, *a.* descarado, insolente.
sauna, *n.* sauna *f.*
sausage, *n.* salchicha *f.*
savage, *a. & n.* salvaje *m. & f.*
save, 1. *v.* salvar; guardar; ahorrar, economizar. **2.** *prep.* salvo, excepto.
savings, *n.* ahorros *m.pl.*
savings account, cuenta de ahorros *m.*
savings bank, caja de ahorros *f.*
savior, *n.* salvador -ora.
savor, 1. *n.* sabor *m.* **2.** *v.* saborear.
savory, *a.* sabroso.
saw, 1. *n.* sierra *f.* **2.** *v.* aserrar.
saxophone, *n.* saxofón, saxófono, *m.*
say, *v.* decir; recitar.
saying, *n.* dicho, refrán *m.*
scaffold, *n.* andamio; (gallows) patíbulo *m.*
scald, *v.* escaldar.
scale, 1. *n.* escala; (of fish) escama *f.*; (pl.) balanza *f.* **2.** *v.* escalar; escamar.
scalp, 1. *n.* pericráneo *m.* **2.** *v.* escalpar.
scan, *v.* hojear, repasar; (poetry) escandir.
scandal, *n.* escándalo *m.*
scanner, *n.* escáner *m.*
scant, *a.* escaso.
scar, *n.* cicatriz *f.*
scarce, *a.* escaso; raro.
scarcely, *adv. & conj.* apenas.

scare, 1. *n.* susto *m.* **2.** *v.* asustar. **s. away,** espantar.
scarf, *n.* pañueleta, bufanda *f.*
scarlet, *n.* escarlata *f.*
scarlet fever, escarlatina *f.*
scatter, *v.* esparcir; dispersar.
scavenger, *n.* basurero *m.*
scenario, *n.* escenario *m.*
scene, *n.* vista *f.*, paisaje *m.*; (theat.) escena *f.* **behind the scenes,** entre bastidores.
scenery, *n.* paisaje *m.*; (theat.) decorado *m.*
scent, 1. *n.* olor, perfume; (sense) olfato *m.* **2.** *v.* perfumar; (fig.) sospechar.
schedule, 1. *n.* programa, horario *m.* **2.** *v.* fijar la hora para.
scheme, 1. *n.* proyecto; esquema *m.* **2.** *v.* intrigar.
scholar, *n.* erudito -ta; becado -da.
scholarship, *n.* beca; erudición *f.*
school, 1. *n.* escuela *f.*; colegio *m.*; (of fish) banco *m.* **2.** *v.* enseñar.
sciatica, *n.* ciática *f.*
science, *n.* ciencia *f.*
science fiction, ciencia ficción.
scientific, *a.* científico.
scientist, *n.* científico -ca.
scissors, *n.* tijeras *f.pl.*
scoff, *v.* mofarse, burlarse.
scold, *v.* regañar.
scoop, 1. *n.* cucharón *m.*; cucharada *f.* **2.** *v.* **s. out,** recoger, sacar.
scope, *n.* alcance; campo *m.*
score, 1. *n.* tantos *m.pl.*; (music) partitura *f.* **2.** *v.* marcar, hacer tantos.
scorn, 1. *n.* desprecio *m.* **2.** *v.* despreciar.
scornful, *a.* desdeñoso.
Scotland, *n.* Escocia *f.*
Scottish, *a.* escocés.
scour, *v.* fregar, estregar.
scourge, *n.* azote *m.*; plaga *f.*
scout, 1. *n.* explorador -ra. **2.** *v.* explorar, reconocer.
scramble, 1. *n.* rebatiña *f.* **2.** *v.* bregar. **scrambled eggs,** huevos revueltos.

scrap, 1. *n.* migaja *f.*; pedacito *m.*; (coll.) riña *f.* **s. metal,** hierro viejo *m.* **s. paper,** papel borrador. **2.** *v.* desechar; (coll.) reñir.
scrapbook, *n.* álbum de recortes *m.*
scrape, 1. *n.* lío, apuro *m.* **2.** *v.* raspar; (feet) restregar.
scratch, 1. *n.* rasguño *m.* **2.** *v.* rasguñar; rayar.
scream, 1. *n.* grito, chillido *m.* **2.** *v.* gritar, chillar.
screen, *n.* biombo *m.*; (for window) tela metálica; (movie) pantalla *f.*
screw, 1. *n.* tornillo *m.* **2.** *v.* atornillar.
screwdriver, *n.* destornillador *m.*
scribble, *v.* hacer garabatos.
scroll, *n.* rúbrica *f.*; rollo de papel.
scrub, *v.* fregar, estregar.
scruple, *n.* escrúpulo *m.*
scrupulous, *a.* escrupuloso.
scuba diving, submarinismo *m.*
sculptor, *n.* escultor -ra.
sculpture, 1. *n.* escultura *f.* **2.** *v.* esculpir.
scythe, *n.* guadaña *f.*
sea, *n.* mar *m. or f.*
seabed, *n.* lecho marino *m.*
sea breeze, brisa marina *f.*
seafood, *n.* mariscos *m.pl.*
seal, 1. *n.* sello *m.*; (animal) foca *f.* **2.** *v.* sellar.
seam, *n.* costura *f.*
seaplane, *n.* hidroavión *m.*
seaport, *n.* puerto de mar.
search, 1. *n.* registro *m.* **in s. of,** en busca de. **2.** *v.* registrar. **s. for,** buscar.
seasick, *a.* mareado. **to get s.,** marearse.
season, 1. *n.* estación; sazón; temporada *f.* **2.** *v.* sazonar.
seasoning, *n.* condimento *m.*
season ticket, abono *m.*
seat, 1. *n.* asiento *m.*; residencia, sede *f.*; (theat.) localidad *f.* **s. belt,** cinturón de seguridad. **2.** *v.* sentar. **be seated,** sentarse.
seaweed, *n.* alga, alga marina *f.*

second, 1. *a.* & *n.* segundo *m.* **2.** *v.* apoyar, segundar.

secondary, *a.* secundario.

secret, *a.* & *n.* secreto *m.*

secretary, *n.* secretario -ria; (govt.) ministro -tra; (furniture) papelera *f.*

sect, *n.* secta *f.;* partido *m.*

section, *n.* sección, parte *f.*

sectional, *a.* regional, local.

secular, *a.* secular.

secure, 1. *a.* seguro. **2.** *v.* asegurar; obtener; (fin.) garantizar.

security, *n.* seguridad; garantía *f.*

sedative, *a.* & *n.* sedativo *m.*

seduce, *v.* seducir.

see, *v.* ver; comprender. **s. off,** despedirse de. **s. to,** encargarse de.

seed, 1. *n.* semilla *f.* **2.** *v.* sembrar.

seek, *v.* buscar. **s. to,** tratar de.

seem, *v.* parecer.

seep, *v.* colarse.

segment, *n.* segmento *m.*

segregate, *v.* segregar.

seize, *v.* agarrar; apoderarse de.

seldom, *adv.* rara vez.

select, 1. *a.* escogido, selecto. **2.** *v.* elegir, seleccionar.

selection, *n.* selección *f.*

selective, *a.* selectivo.

selfish, *a.* egoísta.

selfishness, *n.* egoísmo *m.*

sell, *v.* vender.

semester, *n.* semestre *m.*

semicircle, *n.* semicírculo *m.*

semolina, *n.* sémola *f.*

senate, *n.* senado *m.*

senator, *n.* senador -ra.

send, *v.* mandar, enviar; (a wire) poner. **s. away,** despedir. **s. back,** devolver. **s. for,** mandar buscar. **s. off,** expedir. **s. word,** mandar recado.

senile, *a.* senil.

senior, *a.* mayor; más viejo. **Sr.,** padre.

senior citizen, persona de edad avanzada.

sensation, *n.* sensación *f.*

sensational, *a.* sensacional.

sense, 1. *n.* sentido; juicio *m.* **2.** *v.* percibir; sospechar.

sensible, *a.* sensato, razonable.

sensitive, *a.* sensible; sensitivo.

sensual, *a.* sensual.

sentence, 1. *n.* frase; (gram.) oración; (leg.) sentencia *f.* **2.** *v.* condenar.

sentiment, *n.* sentimiento *m.*

sentimental, *a.* sentimental.

separate, 1. *a.* separado; suelto. **2.** *v.* separar, dividir.

separation, *n.* separación *f.*

September, *n.* septiembre *m.*

sequence, *n.* serie *f.* **in s.,** seguidos.

serenade, 1. *n.* serenata *f.* **2.** *v.* dar serenata a.

serene, *a.* sereno; tranquilo.

sergeant, *n.* sargento *m.*

serial, *a.* en serie, de serie.

series, *n.* serie *f.*

serious, *a.* serio; grave.

sermon, *n.* sermón *m.*

serpent, *n.* serpiente *f.*

servant, *n.* criado -da; servidor -ra.

serve, *v.* servir.

service, 1. *n.* servicio *m.* **at the s. of,** a las órdenes de. **be of s.,** servir; ser útil. **2.** *v.* (auto.) reparar.

service station, estación de servicio *f.*

session, *n.* sesión *f.*

set, 1. *a.* fijo. **2.** *n.* colección *f.;* (of a game) juego; (mech.) aparato; (theat.) decorado *m.* **3.** *v.* poner, colocar; fijar; (sun) ponerse. **s. forth,** exponer. **s. off, s. out,** salir. **s. up,** instalar; establecer.

settle, *v.* solucionar; arreglar; establecerse.

settlement, *n.* caserío; arreglo; acuerdo *m.*

settler, *n.* poblador -ra.

seven, *a.* & *pron.* siete.

seventeen, *a.* & *pron.* diecisiete.

seventh, *a.* séptimo.

seventy, *a.* & *pron.* setenta.

sever, *v.* desunir; romper.

several, *a.* & *pron.* varios.

severance pay, indemnización de despido.

severe, *a.* severo; grave.

severity, *n.* severidad *f.*

sew, *v.* coser.

sewer, *n.* cloaca *f.*

sewing, *n.* costura *f.*

sewing basket, costurero *m.*

sewing machine, máquina de coser *f.*

sex, *n.* sexo *m.*

sexism, *n.* sexismo *m.*

sexist, *a.* & *n.* sexista *m.* & *f.*

sexton, *n.* sacristán *m.*

sexual, *a.* sexual.

shabby, *a.* haraposo, desaliñado.

shade, 1. *n.* sombra *f.;* tinte *m.;* (window) transparente *m.* **2.** *v.* sombrear.

shadow, *n.* sombra *f.*

shady, *a.* sombroso; sospechoso.

shaft, *n.* (columna) fuste; (mech.) asta *f.*

shake, *v.* sacudir; agitar; temblar. **s. hands with,** dar la mano a.

shallow, *a.* poco hondo; superficial.

shame, 1. *n.* vergüenza *f.* **be a s.,** ser una lástima. **2.** *v.* avergonzar.

shameful, *a.* vergonzoso.

shampoo, *n.* champú *m.*

shape, 1. *n.* forma *f.;* estado *m.* **2.** *v.* formar.

share, 1. *n.* parte; (stock) acción *f.* **2** *v.* compartir.

shareholder, *n.* accionista *m.* & *f.*

shark, *n.* tiburón *m.*

sharp, *a.* agudo; (blade) afilado.

sharpen, *v.* aguzar; afilar.

shatter, *v.* estrellar; hacer pedazos.

shave, 1. *n.* afeitada *f.* **2.** *v.* afeitarse.

shawl, *n.* rebozo, chal *m.*

she, *pron.* ella *f.*

sheaf, *n.* gavilla *f.*

shear, *v.* cizallar.

shears, *n.* cizallas *f.pl.*

sheath, *n.* vaina *f.*

shed, 1. *n.* cobertizo *m.* **2.** *v.* arrojar, quitarse.

sheep, *n.* oveja *f.*

sheet, *n.* sábana; (of paper) hoja *f.*

shelf, *n.* estante, *m.*, repisa *f.*

shell, 1. *n.* cáscara; (sea) concha *f.*; (mil.) proyectil *m.* **2.** *v.* desgranar; bombardear.

shellac, *n.* laca *f.*

shelter, 1. *n.* albergue; refugio *m.* **2.** *v.* albergar; amparar.

shepherd, *n.* pastor *m.*

sherry, *n.* jerez *m.*

shield, 1. *n.* escudo *m.* **2.** *v.* amparar.

shift, 1. *n.* cambio; (work) turno *m.* **2.** *v.* cambiar, mudar. **s. for oneself,** arreglárselas.

shine, 1. *n.* brillo, lustre *m.* **2.** *v.* brillar; (shoes) lustrar.

shiny, *a.* brillante, lustroso.

ship, 1. *n.* barco *m.*, nave *f.* **2.** *v.* embarcar; (com.) enviar.

shipment, *n.* envío; embarque *m.*

shirk, *v.* faltar al deber.

shirt, *n.* camisa *f.*

shiver, 1. *n.* temblor *m.* **2.** *v.* temblar.

shock, 1. *n.* choque *m.* **2.** *v.* chocar.

shoe, *n.* zapato *m.*

shoelace, *n.* lazo *m.*; cordón de zapato.

shoemaker, *n.* zapatero *m.*

shoot, *v.* tirar; (gun) disparar. **s. away, s. off,** salir disparado.

shop, *n.* tienda *f.*

shopping, *n.* **to go s.,** hacer compras, ir de compras.

shop window, escaparate *m.*

shore, *n.* orilla; playa *f.*

short, *a.* corto; breve; (in stature) pequeño, bajo. **a s. time,** poco tiempo. **in s.,** en suma.

shortage, *n.* escasez; falta *f.*

shorten, *v.* acortar, abreviar.

shortly, *adv.* en breve, dentro de poco.

shorts, *n.* calzoncillos *m.pl.*

shot, *n.* tiro, disparo *m.*

shoulder, 1. *n.* hombro *m.* **2.** *v.* asumir; cargar con.

shoulder blade, *n.* omóplato *m.*, paletilla *f.*

shout, 1. *n.* grito *m.* **2.** *v.* gritar.

shove, 1. *n.* empujón *m.* **2.** *v.* empujar.

shovel, 1. *n.* pala *f.* **2.** *v.* traspalar.

show, 1. *n.* ostentación *f.*; (theat.) función *f.*; espectáculo *m.* **2.** *v.* enseñar, mostrar; verse. **s. up,** destacarse; (coll.) asomar.

shower, 1. *n.* chubasco *m.*; (bath) ducha *f.* **2.** *v.* ducharse.

shrapnel, *n.* metralla *f.*

shrewd, *a.* astuto.

shriek, 1. *n.* chillido *m.* **2.** *v.* chillar.

shrill, *a.* chillón, agudo.

shrimp, *n.* camarón *m.*

shrine, *n.* santuario *m.*

shrink, *v.* encogerse, contraerse. **s. from,** huir de.

shroud, 1. *n.* mortaja *f.* **2.** *v.* (fig.) ocultar.

shrub, *n.* arbusto *m.*

shudder, 1. *n.* estremecimiento *m.* **2.** *v.* estremecerse.

shun, *v.* evitar, huir de.

shut, *v.* cerrar. **s. in,** encerrar. **s. up,** (coll.) callarse.

shutter, *n.* persiana *f.*

shy, *a.* tímido, vergonzoso.

sick, *a.* enfermo. **s. of,** aburrido de, cansado de.

sickness, *n.* enfermedad *f.*

side, 1. *n.* lado; partido *m.*; parte *f.*; (anat.) costado *m.* **2.** *v.* **s. with,** ponerse del lado de.

sidewalk, *n.* acera, vereda *f.*

siege, *n.* asedio *m.*

sieve, *n.* cedazo *m.*

sift, *v.* cerner.

sigh, 1. *n.* suspiro *m.* **2.** *v.* suspirar.

sight, 1. *n.* vista *f.*; punto de interés *m.* **lose s. of,** perder de vista. **2.** *v.* divisar.

sign, 1. *n.* letrero; señal, seña *f.* **2.** *v.* firmar. **s. up,** inscribirse.

signal, 1. *n.* señal *f.* **2.** *v.* hacer señales.

signature, *n.* firma *f.*

significance, *n.* significación *f.*

significant, *a.* significativo.

signify, *v.* significar.

silence, 1. *n.* silencio *m.* **2.** *v.* hacer callar.

silent, *a.* silencioso; callado.

silk, *n.* seda *f.*

silken, silky, *a.* sedoso.

sill, *n.* umbral de puerta *m.*, solera *f.*

silly, *a.* necio, tonto.

silo, *n.* silo *m.*

silver, *n.* plata *f.*

silver-plated, *a.* chapado en plata.

silverware, *n.* vajilla de plata *f.*

similar, *a.* semejante, parecido.

similarity, *n.* semejanza *f.*

simple, *a.* sencillo, simple.

simplicity, *n.* sencillez *f.*

simplify, *v.* simplificar.

simulate, *v.* simular.

simultaneous, *a.* simultáneo.

sin, 1. *n.* pecado *m.* **2.** *v.* pecar.

since, 1. *adv.* desde entonces. **2.** *prep.* desde. **3.** *conj.* desde que; puesto que.

sincere, *a.* sincero.

sincerely, *adv.* sinceramente.

sincerity, *n.* sinceridad *f.*

sinew, *n.* tendón *m.*

sinful, *a.* pecador.

sing, *v.* cantar.

singe, *v.* chamuscar.

singer, *n.* cantante *m.* & *f.*

single, *a.* solo; (room) sencillo; (unmarried) soltero. **s. room,** habitación individual.

singular, *a.* & *n.* singular *m.*

sinister, *a.* siniestro.

sink, 1. *n.* fregadero *m.* **2.** *v.* hundir; (fig.) abatir.

sinner, *n.* pecador -ra.

sinuous, *a.* sinuoso.

sinus, *n.* seno *m.*

sip, 1. *n.* sorbo *m.* **2.** *v.* sorber.

siphon, *n.* sifón *m.*

sir, *title.* señor.

siren, *n.* sirena *f.*

sirloin, *n.* solomillo *m.*

sisal, *n.* henequén *m.*

sister, *n.* hermana *f.*

sister-in-law, *n.* cuñada *f.*

sit, *v.* sentarse; posar. **be sitting,** estar sentado. **s. down,** sentarse. **s. up,** incorporarse; quedar levantado.

site, *n.* sitio, local *m.*

sitting, **1.** *n.* sesión *f.* **2.** *a.* sentado.

situate, *v.* situar.

situation, *n.* situación *f.*

sit-up, *n.* abdominal *m.*

six, *a. & pron.* seis.

sixteen, *a. & pron.* dieciseis.

sixth, *a.* sexto.

sixty, *a. & pron.* sesenta.

size, *n.* tamaño; (of shoe, etc.) número *m.;* talla *f.*

sizing, *n.* upreso *m.;* sisa, cola de retazo *f.*

skate, **1.** *n.* patín *m.* **2.** *v.* patinar.

skateboard, *n.* monopatín *m.*

skein, *n.* madeja *f.*

skeleton, *n.* esqueleto *m.*

skeptic, *n.* escéptico -ca.

skeptical, *a.* escéptico.

sketch, **1.** *n.* esbozo *m.* **2.** *v.* esbozar.

ski, **1.** *n.* esquí *m.* **2.** *v.* esquiar.

skid, **1.** *v.* resbalar. **2.** *n.* varadera *f.*

skill, *n.* destreza, habilidad *f.*

skillful, *a.* diestro, hábil.

skim, *v.* rasar; (milk) desnatar. **s. over, s. through,** hojear.

skin, **1.** *n.* piel; (of fruit) corteza *f.* **2.** *v.* desollar.

skin doctor, dermatólogo -ga *m. & f.*

skip, **1.** *n.* brinco *m.* **2.** *v.* brincar. **s. over,** pasar por alto.

skirmish, *n.* escaramuza *f.*

skirt, *n.* falda *f.*

skull, *n.* cráneo *m.*

skunk, *n.* zorrillo *m.*

sky, *n.* cielo *m.*

skylight, *n.* tragaluz *m.*

skyscraper, *n.* rascacielos *m.*

slab, *n.* tabla *f.*

slack, *a.* flojo; descuidado.

slacken, *v.* relajar.

slacks, *n.* pantalones flojos.

slam, **1.** *n.* portazo *m.* **2.** *v.* cerrar de golpe. **slamming on the brakes,** frenazo *m.*

slander, **1.** *n.* calumnia *f.* **2.** *v.* calumniar.

slang, *n.* jerga *f.*

slant, **1.** *n.* sesgo *m.* **2.** *v.* sesgar.

slap, **1.** *n.* bofetada, palmada *f.* **2.** *v.* dar una bofetada.

slash, **1.** *n.* cuchillada *f.* **2.** *v.* acuchillar.

slat, **1.** *n.* tablilla *f.* **2.** *v.* lanzar.

slate, **1.** *n.* pizarra *f.;* lista de candidatos. **2.** *n.* destinar.

slaughter, **1.** *n.* matanza *f.* **2.** *v.* matar.

slave, *n.* esclavo -va.

slavery, *n.* esclavitud *f.*

Slavic, *a.* eslavo.

slay, *v.* matar, asesinar.

sled, *n.* trineo *m.*

sleek, *a.* liso y brillante.

sleep, **1.** *n.* sueño *m.* **to get much s.,** dormir mucho. **2.** *v.* dormir.

sleeping car, coche cama.

sleeping pill, pastilla para dormir, somnífero *m.*

sleepy, *a.* soñoliento. **to be s.,** tener sueño.

sleet, **1.** *n.* cellisca *f.* **2.** *v.* cellisquear.

sleeve, *n.* manga *f.*

slender, *a.* delgado.

slice, **1.** *n.* rebanada; (of meat) tajada *f.* **2.** *v.* rebanar; tajar.

slide, *v.* resbalar, deslizarse.

slide rule, regla de cálculo *f.*

slight, **1.** *n.* desaire *m.* **2.** *a.* pequeño; leve. **3.** *v.* desairar.

slim, *a.* delgado.

slime, *n.* lama *f.*

sling, **1.** *n.* honda *f.;* (med.) cabestrillo *m.* **2.** *v.* tirar.

slink, *v.* escabullirse.

slip, **1.** *n.* imprudencia; (garment) combinación *f.;* (of paper) trozo *m.;* ficha *f.* **2.** *v.* resbalar; deslizar. **s. up,** equivocarse.

slipper, *n.* chinela *f.*

slippery, *a.* resbaloso.

slit, **1.** *n.* abertura *f.* **2.** *v.* cortar.

slogan, *n.* lema *m.*

slope, **1.** *n.* declive *m.* **2.** *v.* inclinarse.

sloppy, *a.* desaliñado, chapucero.

slot, *n.* ranura *f.*

slot machine, tragaperras *f.*

slouch, **1.** *n.* patán *m.* **2.** *v.* estar gacho.

slovenly, *a.* desaliñado.

slow, **1.** *a.* lento; (watch) atrasado. (v.) **s. down, s. up,** retardar; ir más despacio.

slowly, *adv.* despacio.

slowness, *n.* lentitud *f.*

sluggish, *a.* perezoso, inactivo.

slum, *n.* barrio bajo *m.*

slumber, *v.* dormitar.

slur, **1.** *n.* estigma *m.* **2.** *v.* menospreciar.

slush, *n.* fango *m.*

sly, *a.* taimado. **on the s.** a hurtadillas.

smack, **1.** *n.* manotada *f.* **2.** *v.* manotear.

small, *a.* pequeño.

small letter, minúscula *f.*

smallpox, *n.* viruela *f.*

smart, **1.** *a.* listo; elegante. **2.** *v.* escocer.

smash, *v.* aplastar; hacer pedazos.

smear, **1.** *n.* mancha; difamación *f.* **2.** *v.* manchar; difamar.

smell, **1.** *n.* olor; (sense) olfato *m.* **2.** *v.* oler.

smelt, **1.** *n.* eperlano *m.* **2.** *v.* fundir.

smile, **1.** *n.* sonrisa *f.* **2.** *v.* sonreír.

smite, *v.* afligir; apenar.

smock, *n.* camisa de mujer *f.*

smoke, **1.** *n.* humo *m.* **2.** *v.* fumar; (food) ahumar.

smokestack, *n.* chimenea *f.*

smolder, *v.* arder sin llama.

smooth, **1.** *a.* liso; suave; tranquilo. **2.** *v.* alisar.

smother, *v.* sofocar.

smug, *a.* presumido.

smuggle, *v.* pasar de contrabando.

snack, *n.* bocadillo *m.*

snag, *n.* nudo; obstáculo *m.*

snail, *n.* caracol *m.*

snake, *n.* culebra, serpiente *f.*

snap, 1. *n.* trueno *m.* **2.** *v.* tronar; romper.

snapshot, *n.* instantánea *f.*

snare, *n.* trampa *f.*

snarl, 1. *n.* gruñido *m.* **2.** *v.* gruñir; (hair) enredar.

snatch, *v.* arrebatar.

sneak, *v.* ir, entrar, salir (etc.) a hurtadillas.

sneaker, 1. *n.* sujeto ruín *m.* **2.** zapatilla de tenis.

sneer, 1. *n.* mofa *f.* **2.** *v.* mofarse.

sneeze, 1. *n.* estornudo *m.* **2.** *v.* estornudar.

snicker, *n.* risita *m.*

snob, *n.* esnob *m.*

snore, 1. *n.* ronquido *m.* **2.** *v.* roncar.

snow, 1. *n.* nieve *f.* **2.** *v.* nevar.

snowball, *n.* bola de nieve *f.*

snowdrift, *n.* ventisquero *m.*

snowplow, *n.* quitanieves *m.*

snowstorm, *n.* nevasca *f.*

snub, *v.* desairar.

snug, *a.* abrigado y cómodo.

so, 1. *adv.* así; (also) también. **so as to,** para. **so that,** para que. **so . . . as,** tan . . . como. **so . . . that,** tan . . . que. **2.** *conj.* así es que.

soak, *v.* empapar.

soap, 1. *n.* jabón *m.* **2.** *v.* enjabonar.

soap powder, jabón en polvo *m.*

soar, *v.* remontarse.

sob, 1. *n.* sollozo *m.* **2.** *v.* sollozar.

sober, *a.* sobrio; pensativo.

sociable, *a.* sociable.

social, 1. *a.* social. **2.** *n.* tertulia *f.*

socialism, *n.* socialismo *m.*

socialist, *a. & n.* socialista *m. & f.*

society, *n.* sociedad; compañía *f.*

sociological, *a.* sociológico.

sociologist, *n.* sociólogo -ga *m. & f.*

sociology, *n.* sociología *f.*

sock, 1. *n.* calcetín; puñetazo *m.* **2.** *v.* dar un puñetazo a.

socket, *n.* cuenca *f.; (*elec.) enchufe *m.*

sod, *n.* césped *m.*

soda, *n.* soda; (chem.) sosa *f.*

sodium, *n.* sodio *m.*

sofa, *n.* sofá *m.*

soft, *a.* blando; fino; suave.

soft drink, bebida no alcohólica.

soften, *v.* ablandar; suavizar.

soil, 1. *n.* suelo *m.* **2.** *v.* ensuciar.

sojourn, *n.* morada *f.,* estancia *f.*

solace, 1. *n.* solaz *m.* **2.** *v.* solazar.

solar, *a.* solar.

solar system, sistema solar *m.*

solder, 1. *v.* soldar. **2.** *n.* soldadura *f.*

soldier, *n.* soldado *m. & f.*

sole, 1. *n.* suela; (of foot) planta *f.; (*fish) lenguado *m.* **2.** *a.* único.

solemn, *a.* solemne.

solemnity, *n.* solemnidad *f.*

solicit, *v.* solicitar.

solicitous, *a.* solícito.

solid, *a. & n.* sólido *m.*

solidify, *v.* solidificar.

solidity, *n.* solidez *f.*

solitary, *a.* solitario.

solitude, *n.* soledad *f.*

solo, *n.* solo *m.*

soloist, *n.* solista *m. & f.*

soluble, *a.* soluble.

solution, *n.* solución *f.*

solve, *v.* solucionar; resolver.

solvent, *a.* solvente.

somber, *a.* sombrío.

some, *a. & pron.* algo (de), un poco (de); alguno; (pl.) algunos, unos.

somebody, someone, *pron.* alguien.

somehow, *adv.* de algún modo.

someone, *n.* alguien o alguno.

somersault, *n.* salto mortal *m.*

something, *pron.* algo, alguna cosa.

sometime, *adv.* alguna vez.

sometimes, *adv.* a veces, algunas veces.

somewhat, *adv.* algo, un poco.

somewhere, *adv.* en (*or* a) alguna parte.

son, *n.* hijo *m.*

song, *n.* canción *f.*

son-in-law, *n.* yerno *m.*

soon, *adv.* pronto. **as s. as possible,** cuanto antes. **sooner or later,** tarde o temprano. **no sooner . . . than,** apenas . . . cuando.

soot, *n.* hollín *m.*

soothe, *v.* calmar.

soothingly, *adv.* tiernamente.

sophisticated, *a.* sofisticado.

sophomore, *n.* estudiante de segundo año *m.*

soprano, *n.* soprano *m. & f.*

sorcery, *n.* encantamiento *m.*

sordid, *a.* sórdido.

sore, 1. *n.* llaga *f.* **2.** *a.* lastimado; (coll.) enojado. **to be s.,** doler.

sorority, *n.* hermandad de mujeres *f.*

sorrow, *n.* pesar, dolor *m.,* aflicción *f.*

sorrowful, *a.* doloroso; afligido.

sorry, *a.* **to be s.,** sentir, lamentar. **to be s. for,** compadecer.

sort, 1. *n.* tipo *m.;* clase, especie *f.* **s. of,** algo, un poco. **2.** *v.* clasificar.

soul, *n.* alma *f.*

sound, 1. *a.* sano; razonable; firme. **2.** *n.* sonido *m.* **3.** *v.* sonar; parecer.

soundproof, 1. *a.* insonorizado. **2.** *v.* insonorizar.

soundtrack, *n.* banda sonora *f.*

soup, *n.* sopa *f.*

sour, *a.* agrio; ácido; rancio.

source, *n.* fuente; causa *f.*

south, *n.* sur *m.*

South Africa, Sudáfrica *f.*

South African, *a. & n.* sudafricano.

South America, Sud América, América del Sur.

South American, *a. & n.* sudamericano -na.
southeast, *n.* sudeste *m.*
southern, *a.* meridional.
South Pole, *n.* Polo Sur *m.*
southwest, *n.* sudoeste *m.*
souvenir, *n.* recuerdo *m.*
sovereign, *n.* soberano -na.
sovereignty, *n.* soberanía *f.*
Soviet Russia, Rusia So-
viética *f.*
sow, 1. *n.* puerca *f.* 2. *v.*
sembrar.
space, 1. *n.* espacio *m.* 2. *v.*
espaciar.
space out, *v.* escalonar.
spaceship, *n.* nave espacial,
astronave *f.*
space shuttle, transbordador
espacial *m.*
spacious, *a.* espacioso.
spade, 1. *n.* laya; (cards) espada *f.* 2. *v.* layar.
spaghetti, *n.* espaguetis *m.pl.*
Spain, *n.* España *f.*
span, 1. *n.* tramo *m.* 2. *v.*
extenderse sobre.
Spaniard, *n.* español -ola.
Spanish, *a. & n.* español -
ola.
spank, *v.* pegar.
spanking, *n.* tunda, zumba *f.*
spar, *v.* altercar.
spare, 1. *a.* de repuesto. 2.
v. perdonar; ahorrar;
prestar. **have ... to s.,**
tener ... de sobra.
spare tire, neumático de recambio *m.*
spark, *n.* chispa *f.*
sparkle, 1. *n.* destello *m.* 2.
v. chispear. **sparkling
wine,** vino espumoso.
spark plug, *n.* bujía *f.*
sparrow, *n.* gorrión *m.*
sparse, *a.* esparcido.
spasm, *n.* espasmo *m.*
spasmodic, *a.* espasmódico.
spatter, *v.* salpicar; manchar.
speak, *v.* hablar.
speaker, *n.* conferencista *m.*
& f.
spear, *n.* lanza *f.*
spearmint, *n.* menta romana *f.*
special, *a.* especial. **s. delivery,** entrega inmedi-
ata, entrega urgente.

specialist, *n.* especialista *m.*
& f.
specialty, *n.* especialidad *f.*
species, *n.* especie *f.*
specific, *a.* específico.
specify, *v.* especificar.
specimen, *n.* espécimen *m.;*
muestra *f.*
spectacle, *n.* espectáculo *m.;*
(pl.) lentes, anteojos *m.pl.*
spectacular, *a.* espectacular,
aparatoso.
spectator, *n.* espectador -ra.
spectrum, *n.* espectro *m.*
speculate, *v.* especular.
speculation, *n.* especulación
f.
speech, *n.* habla *f.;* lenguaje;
discurso *m.* **part of s.,**
parte de la oración.
speechless, *n.* mudo.
speed, 1. *n.* velocidad; rapidez *f.* 2. *v.* **s. up,** acelerar, apresurar.
speed limit, velocidad máxima *f.*
speedometer, *n.* ve-
locímetro *m.*
speedy, *a.* veloz, rápido.
spell, 1. *n.* hechizo; rato;
(med.) ataque *m.* 2. *v.* escribir; relevar.
spelling, *n.* ortografía *f.*
spend, *v.* gastar; (time) pasar.
spendthrift, *a. & n.*
pródigo; manirroto *m.*
sphere, *n.* esfera *f.*
spice, 1. *n.* especia *f.* 2. *v.*
especiar.
spider, *n.* araña *f.*
spider web, *n.* telaraña *f.*
spike, *n.* alcayata *f.;* punta
f., clavo *m.*
spill, 1. *v.* derramar. 2. *n.*
caída *f.,* vuelco *m.*
spillway, *n.* vertedero *m.*
spin, *v.* hilar; girar.
spinach, *n.* espinaca *f.*
spine, *n.* espina dorsal *f.*
spinet, *n.* espineta *m.*
spinster, *n.* solterona *f.*
spiral, *a. & n.* espiral *f.*
spire, *n.* caracol *m.,* espiral
f.
spirit, *n.* espíritu; ánimo *m.*
spiritual, *a.* espiritual.
spiritualism, *n.* espiritismo
m.

spirituality, *n.* espiritualidad *f.*
spit, *v.* escupir.
spite, *n.* despecho *m.* **in s.
of,** a pesar de.
splash, 1. *n.* salpicadura *f.*
2. *v.* salpicar.
splendid, *a.* espléndido.
splendor, *n.* esplendor *m.*
splice, 1. *v.* empalmar. 2. *n.*
empalme *m.*
splint, *n.* tablilla *f.*
splinter, 1. *n.* astilla *f.* 2. *v.*
astillar.
split, 1. *n.* división *f.* 2. *v.*
dividir, romper en dos.
splurge, 1. *v.* fachendear. 2.
n. fachenda *f.*
spoil, 1. *n.* (pl.) botín *m.* 2.
v. echar a perder; (a
child) mimar.
spoke, *n.* rayo (de rueda) *m.*
spokesman, *n.* portavoz *m.*
& f.
spokesperson, *n.* portavoz
m. & f.
sponge, *n.* esponja *f.*
sponsor, 1. *n.* patrocinador
m. 2. *v.* patrocinar;
costear.
spontaneity, *n.* espontaneidad *f.*
spontaneous, *a.* espontáneo.
spool, *n.* carrete *m.*
spoon, *n.* cuchara *f.*
spoonful, *n.* cucharada *f.*
sporadic, *a.* esporádico.
sport, *n.* deporte *m.*
sport jacket, chaqueta deportiva *f.*
sports center, pabellón de
deportes, polideportivo *m.*
sportsman, 1. *a.* deportivo.
2. *n.* deportista *m. & f.*
spot, 1. *n.* mancha *f.;* lugar,
punto *m.* 2. *v.* distinguir.
spouse, *n.* esposo -sa.
spout, 1. *n.* chorro *m.;* (of
teapot) pico *m.* 2. *v.* correr a chorro.
sprain, 1. *n.* torcedura *f.,*
esguince *m.* 2. *v.*
torcerse.
sprawl, *v.* tenderse.
spray, 1. *n.* rociada *f.* 2. *v.*
rociar.
spread, 1. *n.* propagación;
extensión; (for bed)

colcha *f.* **2.** *v.* propagar; extender.

spreadsheet, *n.* hoja de cálculo *f.*

spree, *n.* parranda *f.*

sprig, *n.* ramita *f.*

sprightly, *a.* garboso.

spring, *n.* resorte, muelle *m.;* (season) primavera *f.;* (of water) manantial *m.*

springboard, *n.* trampolín *m.*

spring onion, cebolleta *f.*

sprinkle, *v.* rociar; (rain) lloviznar.

sprint, *n.* carrera *f.*

sprout, *n.* retoño *m.*

spry, *a.* ágil.

spun, *a.* hilado.

spur, 1. *n.* espuela *f.* **on the s. of the moment,** sin pensarlo. **2.** *v.* espolear.

spurious, *a.* espurio.

spurn, *v.* rechazar, despreciar.

spurt, 1. *n.* chorro *m.;* esfuerzo supremo. **2.** *v.* salir en chorro.

spy, 1. espía *m.* & *f.* **2.** *v.* espiar.

squabble, 1. *n.* riña *f.* **2.** *v.* reñir.

squad, *n.* escuadra *f.*

squadron, *n.* escuadrón *m.*

squalid, *a.* escuálido.

squall, *n.* borrasca *f.*

squalor, *n.* escualidez *f.*

squander, *v.* malgastar.

square, 1. *a.* cuadrado. **2.** *n.* cuadrado *m.;* plaza *f.*

square dance, *n.* contradanza *f.*

squat, *v.* agacharse.

squeak, 1. *n.* chirrido *m.* **2.** *v.* chirriar.

squeamish, *a.* escrupuloso.

squeeze, 1. *n.* apretón *m.* **2.** *v.* apretar; (fruit) exprimir.

squirrel, *n.* ardilla *f.*

squirt, 1. *n.* chisguete *m.* **2.** *v.* jeringar.

stab, 1. *n.* puñalada *f.* **2.** *v.* apuñalar.

stability, *n.* estabilidad *f.*

stabilize, *v.* estabilizar.

stable, 1. *a.* estable, equilibrado. **2.** *n.* caballeriza *f.*

stack, 1. *n.* pila *f.* **2.** *v.* apilar.

stadium, *n.* estadio *m.*

staff, *n.* personal *m.* **editorial s.,** cuerpo de redacción. **general s.,** estado mayor.

stag, *n.* ciervo *m.*

stage, 1. *n.* etapa; (theat.) escena *f.* **2.** *v.* representar.

stagflation, *n.* estagflación.

stagger, *v.* (teeter) tambalear; (space out) escalonar.

stagnant, *a.* estancado.

stagnate, *v.* estancarse.

stain, 1. *n.* mancha *f.* **2.** *v.* manchar.

stainless steel, acero inoxidable *m.*

staircase, stairs, *n.* escalera *f.*

stake, *n.* estaca; (bet) apuesta *f.* **at s.,** en juego; en peligro.

stale, *a.* rancio.

stalemate, *n.* estancación *f.;* tablas *f.pl.*

stalk, 1. *n.* caña *f.;* (of flower) tallo *m.* **2.** *v.* acechar.

stall, 1. *n.* tenderete; (for horse) pesebre *m.* **2.** *v.* demorar; (motor) atascar.

stallion, *n.* (S.A.) garañón *m.*

stalwart, *a.* fornido.

stamina, *n.* vigor *m.*

stammer, *v.* tartamudear.

stamp, 1. *n.* sello *m.,* estampilla *f.* **2.** *v.* sellar.

stamp collecting, filatelia *f.*

stampede, *n.* estampida *f.*

stand, 1. *n.* puesto *m.;* posición; (speaker's) tribuna *f.;* (furniture) mesita *f.* **2.** *v.* estar; estar de pie; aguantar. **s. up,** pararse, levantarse.

standard, 1. *a.* normal, corriente. **2.** *n.* norma *f.* **s. of living,** nivel de vida.

standardize, *v.* uniformar.

standing, *a.* fijo; establecido.

standpoint, *n.* punto de vista *m.*

staple, *n.* materia prima *f.;* grapa *f.*

stapler, *n.* grapadora *f.*

star, *n.* estrella *f.*

starboard, *n.* estribor *m.*

starch, 1. *n.* almidón *m.;* (in diet) fécula *f.* **2.** *v.* almidonar.

stare, *v.* mirar fijamente.

stark, 1. *a.* severo. **2.** *adv.* completamente.

start, 1. *n.* susto; principio *m.* **2.** *v.* comenzar, empezar; salir; poner en marcha; causar.

startle, *v.* asustar.

starvation, *n.* hambre *f.*

starve, *v.* morir de hambre.

state, 1. *n.* estado *m.* **2.** *v.* declarar, decir.

statement, *n.* declaración *f.*

stateroom, *n.* camarote *m.*

statesman, *n.* estadista *m.*

static, 1. *a.* estático. **2.** *n.* estática *f.*

station, *n.* estación *f.*

stationary, *a.* estacionario, fijo.

stationery, *n.* papel de escribir.

statistics, *n.* estadística *f.*

statue, *n.* estatua *f.*

stature, *n.* estatura *f.*

status, *n.* condición, estado *m.*

statute, *n.* ley *f.*

staunch, *a.* fiel; constante.

stay, 1. *n.* estancia; visita *f.* **2.** *v.* quedar, permanecer; parar, alojarse. **s. away,** ausentarse. **s. up,** velar.

steadfast, *a.* inmutable.

steady, 1. *a.* firme; permanente; regular. **2.** *v.* sostener.

steak, *n.* biftec, bistec *m.*

steal, *v.* robar. **s. away,** escabullirse.

stealth, *n.* cautela *f.*

steam, *n.* vapor *m.*

steamboat, steamer, steamship, *n.* vapor *m.*

steel, 1. *n.* acero *m.* **2.** *v.* **s. oneself,** fortalecerse.

steep, *a.* escarpado, empinado.

steeple, *n.* campanario *m.*

steer, 1. *n.* buey *m.* **2.** *v.* guiar, manejar.

stellar, *a.* astral.

stem, 1. *n.* tallo *m.* **2.** *v.* parar. **s. from,** emanar de.

stencil, 1. *n.* estarcido. **2.** *v.* estarcir.

stenographer, *n.* estenógrafo -fa.

stenography, *n.* taquigrafía *f.*

step, 1. *n.* paso *m.*; medida *f.*; (stairs) escalón *m.* **2.** *v.* pisar. **s. back,** retirarse.

stepladder, *n.* escalera de mano *f.*

stereophonic, *a.* estereofónico.

stereotype, 1. *n.* estereotipo *m.* **2.** *v.* estereotipar.

sterile, *a.* estéril.

sterilize, *v.* esterilizar.

sterling, *a.* esterlina, genuino.

stern, 1. *n.* popa *f.* **2.** *a.* duro, severo.

stethoscope, *n.* estetoscopio *m.*

stevedore, *n.* estibador *m.*

stew, 1. *n.* guisado *m.* **2.** *v.* estofar.

steward, *n.* camarero.

stewardess, *n.* azafata *f.*, aeromoza *f.*

stick, 1. *n.* palo, bastón *m.* **2.** *v.* pegar; (put) poner, meter.

sticky, *a.* pegajoso.

stiff, *a.* tieso; duro.

stiffness, *n.* tiesura *f.*

stifle, *v.* sofocar; (fig.) suprimir.

stigma, *n.* estigma *m.*

still, 1. *a.* quieto; silencioso. **to keep s.,** quedarse quieto. **2.** *adv.* todavía, aún; no obstante. **3.** *n.* alambique *m.*

stillborn, *n.* & *a.* nacido -da muerto -ta.

still life, *n.* naturaleza muerta *f.*

stillness, *n.* silencio *m.*

stilted, *a.* afectado, artificial.

stimulant, *a.* & *n.* estimulante *m.*

stimulate, *v.* estimular.

stimulus, *n.* estímulo *m.*

sting, 1. *n.* picadura *f.* **2.** *v.* picar.

stingy, *a.* tacaño.

stipulate, *v.* estipular.

stir, 1. *n.* conmoción *f.* **2.** *v.* mover. **s. up,** conmover; suscitar.

stitch, 1. *n.* puntada *f.* **2.** *v.* coser.

stock, *n.* surtido *f.*; raza *f.*; (finance) acciones. *f.pl.* **in s.,** en existencia. **to take s. in,** tener fe en.

stock exchange, bolsa *f.*

stockholder, *n.* accionista *m.* & *f.*

stocking, *n.* media *f.*

stockyard, *n.* corral de ganado *m.*

stodgy, *a.* pesado.

stoical, *a.* estoico.

stole, *n.* estola *f.*

stolid, *a.* impasible.

stomach, *n.* estómago *m.*

stomachache, *n.* dolor de estómago *m.*

stone, *n.* piedra *f.*

stool, *n.* banquillo *m.*

stoop, 1. *v.* encorvarse; (fig.) rebajarse. **2.** espaldas encorvadas *f.pl.*

stop, 1. *n.* parada *f.* **to put a s. to,** poner fin a. **2.** *v.* parar; suspender; detener; impedir. **s. doing** (etc.), dejar de hacer (etc.).

stopgap, *n.* recurso provisional *m.*

stopover, *n.* parada *f.*

stopwatch, *n.* cronómetro *m.*

storage, *n.* almacenaje *m.*

store, 1. *n.* tienda; provisión *f.* **department s.,** almacén *m.* **2.** *v.* guardar; almacenar.

store window, escaparate *m.*

stork, *n.* cigüeña *f.*

storm, *n.* tempestad, tormenta *f.*

stormy, *a.* tempestuoso.

story, *n.* cuento; relato *m.*; historia *f.* **short s.,** cuento.

stout, *a.* corpulento.

stove, *n.* hornilla; estufa *f.*

straight, 1. *a.* recto; derecho. **2.** *adv.* directamente.

straighten, *v.* enderezar. **s. out,** poner en orden.

straightforward, *a.* recto, sincero.

strain, 1. *n.* tensión *f.* **2.** *v.* colar.

strainer, *n.* colador *m.*

strait, *n.* estrecho *m.*

strand, 1. *n.* hilo *m.* **2.** *v.* **be stranded,** encallarse.

strange, *a.* extraño; raro.

stranger, *n.* extranjero -ra; forastero -ra; desconocido -da.

strangle, *v.* estrangular.

strap, *n.* correa *f.*

stratagem, *n.* estratagema *f.*

strategic, *a.* estratégico.

strategy, *n.* estrategia *f.*

stratosphere, *n.* estratosfera *f.*

straw, *n.* paja *f.*

strawberry, *n.* fresa *f.*

stray, 1. *a.* vagabundo. **2.** *v.* extraviarse.

streak, 1. *n.* racha; raya *f.*; lado *m.* **2.** *v.* rayar.

stream, *n.* corriente *f.*; arroyo *m.*

street, *n.* calle *f.*

streetcar, *n.* tranvía *m.*

street lamp, *n.* farol *m.*

strength, *n.* fuerza *m.*

strengthen, *v.* reforzar.

strenuous, *a.* estrenuo.

streptococcus, *n.* estreptococo *m.*

stress, 1. *n.* tensión *f.*; énfasis *m.* **2.** *v.* recalcar; acentuar.

stretch, 1. *n.* trecho *m.* **at one s.,** de un tirón. **2.** *v.* tender; extender; estirarse.

stretcher, *n.* camilla *f.*

strew, *v.* esparcir.

stricken, *a.* agobiado.

strict, *a.* estricto; severo.

stride, 1. *n.* tranco *m.*; (fig., pl.) progresos. **2.** *v.* andar a trancos.

strife, *n.* contienda *f.*

strike, 1. *n.* huelga *f.* **2.** *v.* pegar; chocar con; (clock) dar.

striker, *n.* huelguista *m.* & *f.*

string, *n.* cuerda *f.*; cordel *m.*

string bean, *n.* habichuela *f.*

stringent, *a.* estricto.

strip, 1. *n.* tira *f.* **2.** *v.* despojar; desnudarse.

stripe, *n.* raya *f.*; (mil.) galón *m.*

strive, *v.* esforzarse.

stroke, *n.* golpe *m.;* (swimming) brazada *f.;* (med.) ataque *m.* **s. of luck,** suerte *f.*

stroll, 1. *n.* paseo *m.* **2.** *v.* pasearse.

stroller, *n.* vagabundo *m.;* cochecito (de niño).

strong, *a.* fuerte.

stronghold, *n.* fortificación *f.*

structure, *n.* estructura *f.*

struggle, 1. *n.* lucha *f.* **2.** *v.* luchar.

strut, 1. *n.* pavonada *f.* **2.** *v.* pavonear.

stub, 1. *n.* cabo; (ticket) talón *m.* **2.** *v.* **s. on one's toes,** tropezar con.

stubborn, *a.* testarudo.

stucco, 1. *n.* estuco *m.* **2.** *v.* estucar.

student, *n.* alumno -na, estudiante -ta.

studio, *n.* estudio *m.*

studious, *a.* aplicado; estudioso.

study, 1. *n.* estudio *m.* **2.** *v.* estudiar.

stuff, 1. *n.* cosas *f.pl.* **2.** *v.* llenar; rellenar.

stuffing, *n.* relleno *m.*

stumble, *v.* tropezar.

stump, *n.* cabo; tocón *m.*; muñón *m.*

stun, *v.* aturdir.

stunt, 1. *n.* maniobra sensacional *f.* **2.** *v.* impedir crecimiento.

stupendous, *a.* estupendo.

stupid, *a.* estúpido.

stupidity, *n.* estupidez *f.*

stupor, *n.* estupor *m.*

sturdy, *a.* robusto.

stutter, 1. *v.* tartamudear. **2.** *n.* tartamudeo *m.*

sty, *n.* pocilga *f.;* (med.) orzuelo.

style, *n.* estilo *m.;* moda *f.*

stylish, *a.* elegante; a la moda.

suave, *a.* afable, suave.

subconscious, *a.* subconsciente.

subdue, *v.* dominar.

subject, 1. *a.* sujeto. **2.** *n.* tema *m.;* (of study) materia *f.;* (pol.) súbdito -ta;

(gram.) sujeto *m.* **3.** *v.* someter.

subjugate, *v.* sojuzgar, subyugar.

subjunctive, *a. & n.* subjuntivo *m.*

sublimate, *v.* sublimar.

sublime, *a.* sublime.

submarine, *a. & n.* submarino *m.*

submerge, *v.* sumergir.

submission, *n.* sumisión *f.*

submit, *v.* someter.

subnormal, *a.* subnormal.

subordinate, 1. *a. & n.* subordinado -da. **2.** *v.* subordinar.

subscribe, *v.* aprobar; abonarse.

subscriber, *n.* abonado -da *m. & f.*

subscription, *n.* abono *m.*

subsequent, *a.* subsiguiente.

subservient, *a.* servicial.

subside, *v.* apaciguarse, menguar.

subsidy, *n.* subvención *f.*

subsoil, *n.* subsuelo *m.*

substance, *n.* substancia *f.*

substantial, *a.* substancial; considerable.

substitute, 1. *a.* substitutivo. **2.** *n.* substituto -ta. **3.** *v.* substituir.

substitution, *n.* substitución *f.*

subterfuge, *n.* subterfugio *m.*

subtitle, *n.* subtítulo *m.*

subtle, *a.* sutil.

subtract, *v.* substraer.

suburb, *n.* suburbio *m.;* (pl.) afueras *f.pl.*

subversive, *a.* subversivo.

subway, *n.* metro *m.*

succeed, *v.* lograr, tener éxito; (in office) suceder a.

success, *n.* éxito *m.*

successful, *a.* próspero; afortunado.

succession, *n.* sucesión *f.*

successive, *a.* sucesivo.

successor, *n.* sucesor -ra; heredero -ra.

succor, 1. *n.* socorro *m.* **2.** *v.* socorrer.

succumb, *v.* sucumbir.

such, *a.* tal.

suck, *v.* chupar.

suction, *n.* succión *f.*

sudden, *a.* repentino, súbito. **all of a s.,** de repente.

suds, *n.* jabonaduras *f.pl.*

sue, *v.* demandar.

suffer, *v.* sufrir; padecer.

suffice, *v.* bastar.

sufficient, *a.* suficiente.

suffocate, *v.* sofocar.

sugar, *n.* azúcar *m.*

sugar bowl, azucarero *m.*

suggest, *v.* sugerir.

suggestion, *n.* sugerencia *f.*

suicide, *n.* suicidio *m.;* (person) suicida *m. & f.* **to commit s.,** suicidarse.

suit, 1. *n.* traje; (cards) palo; (law) pleito *m.* **2.** *v.* convenir a.

suitable, *a.* apropiado; que conviene.

suitcase, *n.* maleta *f.*

suite, *n.* serie *f.*, séquito *m.*

suitor, *n.* pretendiente *m.*

sullen, *a.* hosco.

sum, 1. *n.* suma *f.* **2.** *v.* **s. up,** resumir.

summarize, *v.* resumir.

summary, *n.* resumen *m.*

summer, *n.* verano *m.*

summon, *v.* llamar; (law) citar.

summons, *n.* citación *f.*

sumptuous, *a.* suntuoso.

sun, 1. *n.* sol *m.* **2.** *v.* tomar el sol.

sunbathe, *v.* tomar el sol.

sunburn, *n.* quemadura de sol.

sunburned, *a.* quemado por el sol.

Sunday, *n.* domingo *m.*

sunken, *a.* hundido.

sunny, *a.* asoleado. **s. day,** día de sol. **to be s.,** (weather) hacer sol.

sunshine, *n.* luz del sol.

suntan, *n.* bronceado *m.* **s. lotion,** loción bronceadora *f.,* bronceador *m.*

superb, *a.* soberbio.

superficial, *a.* superficial.

superfluous, *a.* superfluo.

superhuman, *a.* sobrehumano.

superintendent, *n.* superintendente *m. & f.;* (of building) conserje *m.;*

(of school) director -ra general.

superior, *a. & n.* superior *m.*

superiority, *n.* superioridad *f.*

superlative, *a.* superlativo.

supernatural, *a.* sobrenatural.

supersede, *v.* reemplazar.

superstar, *n.* superestrella *m. & f.*

superstition, *n.* superstición *f.*

superstitious, *a.* supersticioso.

supervise, *v.* supervisar.

supper, *n.* cena *f.*

supplement, 1. *n.* suplemento *m.* **2.** *v.* suplementar.

supply, 1. *n.* provisión *f.;* (com.) surtido *m.;* (econ.) existencia *f.* **2.** *v.* suplir; proporcionar.

support, 1. *n.* sustento; apoyo *m.* **2.** *v.* mantener; apoyar.

suppose, *v.* suponer. **be supposed to,** deber.

suppository, *n.* supositorio *m.*

suppress, *v.* suprimir.

suppression, *n.* supresión *f.*

supreme, *a.* supremo.

sure, *a.* seguro, cierto. **for s.,** con seguridad. **to make s.,** asegurarse.

surety, *n.* garantía *f.*

surf, *n.* oleaje *m.*

surface, *n.* superficie *f.*

surge, *v.* surgir.

surgeon, *n.* cirujano -na.

surgery, *n.* cirugía *f.*

surmise, *v.* suponer.

surmount, *v.* vencer.

surname, *n.* apellido *m.*

surpass, *v.* superar.

surplus, *a. & n.* sobrante *m.*

surprise, 1. *n.* sorpresa **2.** *v.* sorprender. **I am surprised . . . ,** me extraña . . .

surrender, 1. *n.* rendición *f.* **2.** *v.* rendir.

surround, *v.* rodear, circundar.

surveillance, *n.* vigilancia *f.*

survey, 1. *n.* examen; estudio *m.* **2.** *v.* examinar; (land) medir.

survival, *n.* supervivencia *f.*

survive, *v.* sobrevivir.

susceptible, *a.* susceptible.

suspect, 1. *v.* sospechar. **2.** *n.* sospechoso -sa.

suspend, *v.* suspender.

suspense, *n.* incertidumbre *f.* **in s.,** en suspenso.

suspension, *n.* suspensión *f.*

suspension bridge, *n.* puente colgante *m.*

suspicion, *n.* sospecha *f.*

suspicious, *a.* sospechoso.

sustain, *v.* sustentar; mantener.

swallow, 1. *n.* trago *m.;* (bird) golondrina *f.* **2.** *v.* tragar.

swamp, 1. *n.* pantano *m.* **2.** *v.* (fig.) abrumar.

swan, *n.* cisne *m.*

swap, 1. *n.* trueque *m.* **2.** *v.* cambalachear.

swarm, *n.* enjambre *m.*

sway, 1. *n.* predominio *m.* **2.** *v.* bambolearse; (fig.) influir en.

swear, *v.* jurar. **s. off,** renunciar a.

sweat, 1. *n.* sudor *m.* **2.** *v.* sudar.

sweater, *n.* suéter *m.*

sweatshirt, *n.* sudadera *f.*

Swede, *n.* sueco -ca.

Sweden, *n.* Suecia *f.*

Swedish, *a.* sueco.

sweep, *v.* barrer.

sweet, 1. *a.* dulce; amable, simpático. **2.** *n.* (pl.) dulces *m.pl.*

sweetheart, *n.* novio -via.

sweetness, *n.* dulzura *f.*

sweet-toothed, *a.* goloso.

swell, 1. *a.* (coll.) estupendo, excelente. **2.** *n.* (mar.) oleada *f.* **3.** *v.* hincharse; aumentar.

swelter, *v.* sofocarse de calor.

swift, *a.* rápido, veloz.

swim, 1. *n.* nadada *f.* **2.** *v.* nadar.

swimming, *n.* natación *f.*

swimming pool, alberca, piscina *f.*

swindle, 1. *n.* estafa *f.* **2.** *v.* estafar.

swine, *n.* puercos *m.pl.*

swing, 1. *n.* columpio *m.* **in full s.,** en plena actividad. **2.** *v.* mecer; balancear.

swirl, 1. *n.* remolino *m.* **2.** *v.* arremolinar.

Swiss, *a. & n.* suizo -za.

switch, 1. *n.* varilla *f.;* (elec.) llave *f.*, conmutador *m.;* (railway) cambiavía *m.* **2.** *v.* cambiar; trocar.

switchboard, *n.* cuadro conmutador *m.*, centralita *f.*

Switzerland, *n.* Suiza *f.*

sword, *n.* espada *f.*

syllable, *n.* sílaba *f.*

symbol, *n.* símbolo *m.*

sympathetic, *a.* compasivo. **to be s.,** tener simpatía.

sympathy, *n.* lástima; condolencia *f.*

symphony, *n.* sinfonía *f.*

symptom, *n.* síntoma *m.*

synagogue, *n.* sinagoga *f.*

synchronize, *v.* sincronizar.

syndicate, *n.* sindicato *m.*

syndrome, *n.* síndrome *m.*

synonym, *n.* sinónimo *m.*

synthetic, *a.* sintético.

syringe, *n.* jeringa *f.*

syrup, *n.* almíbar; (med.) jarabe *m.*

system, *n.* sistema *m.*

systematic, *a.* sistemático.

T

tabernacle, *n.* tabernáculo *m.*

table, *n.* mesa; (list) tabla *f.*

tablecloth, *n.* mantel *m.*

table of contents, índice de materias *m.*

tablespoon, *n.* cuchara *f.*

tablespoonful, *n.* cucharada *f.*

tablet, *n.* tableta; (med.) pastilla *f.*

tack, *n.* tachuela *f.*

tact, *n.* tacto *m.*

tag, *n.* etiqueta *f.*, rótulo *m.*

tail, *n.* cola *f.*, rabo *m.*

tailor, *n.* sastre *m.*

take, *v.* tomar; llevar. **t. a bath,** bañarse. **t. a shower,** ducharse. **t. away,** quitar. **t. off,** quitarse. **t. out,** sacar. **t. long,** tardar mucho.

tale, *n.* cuento *m.*

talent, *n.* talento *m.*

talk, 1. *n.* plática, habla *f.*; discurso *m.* 2. *v.* hablar.

talkative, *a.* locuaz.

tall, *a.* alto.

tame, 1. *a.* manso, domesticado. 2. *v.* domesticar.

tamper, *v.* **t. with,** entremeterse en.

tampon, *n.* tampón *m.*

tan, 1. *a.* color de arena. 2. *v.* curtir; tostar. 3. *n.* bronceado.

tangerine, *n.* clementina *f.*

tangible, *a.* tangible.

tangle, 1. *n.* enredo *m.* 2. *v.* enredar.

tank, *n.* tanque *m.*

tap, 1. *n.* golpe ligero. 2. *v.* golpear ligeramente; decentar.

tape, *n.* cinta *f.*

tape recorder, magnetófono *m.*, grabadora *f.*

tapestry, *n.* tapiz *m.*; tapicería *f.*

tar, 1. *n.* brea *f.* 2. *v.* embrear.

target, *n.* blanco *m.*

tarnish, 1. *n.* deslustre *m.* 2. *v.* deslustrar.

tarpaulin, *n.* lona *f.*

task, *n.* tarea *f.*

taste, 1. *n.* gusto; sabor *m.* 2. *v.* gustar; probar. **t. of,** saber a.

tasty, *a.* sabroso.

tattoo, *v.* tatuar.

taut, *a.* tieso.

tavern, *n.* taberna *f.*

tax, 1. *n.* impuesto *m.* 2. *v.* imponer impuestos.

tax collector, *n.* recaudador -ra *m.* & *f.*

taxi, *n.* taxi, taxímetro *m.* **t. driver,** taxista *m.* & *f.*

taxpayer, *n.* contribuyente *m.* & *f.*

tax reform, reforma tributaria *f.*

tax return, declaración de la renta *f.*

tea, *n.* té *m.*

teach, *v.* enseñar.

teacher, *n.* maestro -tra, profesor -ra.

team, *n.* equipo *m.*; pareja *f.*

tear, 1. *n.* rasgón *m.*; lágrima *f.* 2. *v.* rasgar, lacerar. **t. apart,** separar.

tease, *v.* atormentar; embromar.

teaspoon, *n.* cucharita *f.*

technical, *a.* técnico.

technician, *n.* técnico -ca *m.* & *f.*

technique, *n.* técnica *f.*

technology, *n.* tecnología *f.*

teddy bear, oso de felpa *m.*

tedious, *a.* tedioso.

telegram, *n.* telegrama *m.*

telegraph, 1. *n.* telégrafo *m.* 2. *v.* telegrafiar.

telephone, 1. *n.* teléfono *m.* **t. book,** directorio telefónico. 2. *v.* telefonear; llamar por teléfono.

telescope, 1. *n.* telescopio *m.* 2. *v.* enchufar.

television, *n.* televisión *f.*

tell, *v.* decir; contar; distinguir.

temper, 1. *n.* temperamento, genio *m.* 2. *v.* templar.

temperament, *n.* temperamento.

temperamental, *a.* sensitivo, emocional.

temperance, *n.* moderación; sobriedad *f.*

temperate, *a.* templado.

temperature, *n.* temperatura *f.*

tempest, *n.* tempestad *f.*

tempestuous, *a.* tempestuoso.

temple, *n.* templo *m.*

temporary, *a.* temporal, temporario.

tempt, *v.* tentar.

temptation, *n.* tentación *f.*

ten, *a.* & *pron.* diez.

tenant, *n.* inquilino -na.

tend, *v.* tender. **t. to,** atender.

tendency, *n.* tendencia *f.*

tender, 1. *a.* tierno. 2. *v.* ofrecer.

tenderness, *n.* ternura *f.*

tennis, *n.* tenis *m.*

tennis court, cancha de tenis, pista de tenis *f.*

tenor, *n.* tenor *m.*

tense, 1. *a.* tenso. 2. *n.* (gram.) tiempo *m.*

tent, *n.* tienda, carpa *f.*

tenth, *a.* décimo.

term, 1. *n.* término; plazo *m.* 2. *v.* llamar.

terminal, *n.* terminal *f.*

terrace, *n.* terraza *f.*

terrible, *a.* terrible, espantoso; pésimo.

territory, *n.* territorio *m.*

terror, *n.* terror, espanto, pavor *m.*

test, 1. *n.* prueba *f.*; examen *m.* 2. *v.* probar; examinar.

testament, *n.* testamento *m.*

testify, *v.* atestiguar, testificar.

testimony, *n.* testimonio *m.*

test tube, tubo de ensayo *m.*

text, *n.* texto; tema *m.*

textbook, *n.* libro de texto.

textile, 1. *a.* textil. 2. *n.* tejido *m.*

texture, *n.* textura *f.*; tejido *m.*

than, *conj.* que; de.

thank, *v.* agradecer, dar gracias; **thanks, th. you,** gracias.

thankful, *a.* agradecido; grato.

that, 1. *a.* ese, aquel. 2. *dem. pron.* ése, aquél; eso, aquello. 3. *rel. pron.* & *conj.* que.

the, *art.* el, la, los, las; lo.

theater, *n.* teatro *m.*

theft, *n.* robo *m.*

their, *a.* su.

theirs, *pron.* suyo, de ellos.

them, *pron.* ellos, ellas; los, las; les.

theme, *n.* tema; (mus.) motivo *m.*

themselves, *pron.* sí, sí mismos -as. **they th.,** ellos mismos, ellas mismas. **with th.,** consigo.

then, *adv.* entonces, después; pues.

thence, *adv.* de allí.

theology, *n.* teología *f.*

theory, *n.* teoría *f.*

there, *adv.* allí, allá, ahí. **there is, there are,** hay.

therefore, *adv.* por lo tanto, por consiguiente.

thermometer, *n.* termómetro *m.*

thermostat, *n.* termostato *m.*

they, *pron.* ellos, ellas.

thick, *a.* espeso, grueso, denso; torpe.

thicken, *v.* espesar, condensar.

thief, *n.* ladrón -na.

thigh, *n.* muslo *m.*

thimble, *n.* dedal *m.*

thin, 1. *a.* delgado; raro; claro; escaso. 2. *v.* enrarecer; adelgazar.

thing, *n.* cosa *f.*

think, *v.* pensar; creer.

thinker, *n.* pensador -ra.

third, *a.* tercero.

Third World, Tercer Mundo *m.*

thirst, *n.* sed *f.*

thirsty, *a.* sediento. **to be th.,** tener sed.

thirteen, *a. & pron.* trece.

thirty, *a. & pron.* treinta.

this, 1. *a.* este. 2. *pron.* éste; esto.

thoracic cage, *n.* caja torácica *f.*

thorn, *n.* espina *f.*

thorough, *a.* completo; cuidadoso.

though, 1. *adv.* sin embargo. 2. *conj.* aunque. **as th.,** como si.

thought, *n.* pensamiento *m.*

thoughtful, *a.* pensativo; considerado.

thousand, *a. & pron.* mil.

thread, *n.* hilo *m.;* (of screw) rosca *f.*

threat, *n.* amenaza *f.*

threaten, *v.* amenazar.

three, *a. & pron.* tres.

thrift, *n.* economía, frugalidad *f.*

thrill, 1. *n.* emoción *f.* 2. *v.* emocionar.

thrive, *v.* prosperar.

throat, *n.* garganta *f.*

throne, *n.* trono *m.*

through, 1. *prep.* por; a través de; por medio de. 2. *a.* continuo. **th. train,** tren directo. **to be th.,** haber terminado.

throughout, 1. *prep.* por todo, durante todo. 2. *adv.* en todas partes; completamente.

throw, 1. *n.* tiro *m.* 2. *v.* tirar, lanzar. **th. away,** arrojar. **th. out,** echar.

thrust, 1. *n.* lanzada *f.* 2. *v.* empujar.

thumb, *n.* dedo pulgar, pulgar *m.*

thumbtack, *n.* chincheta *f.*

thunder, 1. *n.* trueno *m.* 2. *v.* tronar.

Thursday, *n.* jueves *m.*

thus, *adv.* así, de este modo.

thwart, *v.* frustrar.

ticket, 1. *n.* billete, boleto *m.* **t. window,** taquilla *f.* **round trip t.,** billete de ida y vuelta.

tickle, 1. *n.* cosquilla *f.* 2. *v.* hacer cosquillas a.

ticklish, *a.* cosquilloso.

tide, *n.* marea *f.*

tidy, 1. *a.* limpio, ordenado. 2. *v.* poner en orden.

tie, 1. *n.* corbata *f.;* lazo; (game) empate *m.* 2. *v.* atar; anudar.

tier, *n.* hilera *f.*

tiger, *n.* tigre *m.*

tight, *a.* apretado; tacaño.

tighten, *v.* estrechar, apretar.

tile, *n.* teja *f.;* azulejo *m.*

till, 1. *prep.* hasta. 2. *conj.* hasta que. 3. *n.* cajón *m.* 4. *v.* cultivar, labrar.

tilt, 1. *n.* inclinación; justa *f.* 2. *v.* inclinar; justar.

timber, *n.* madera *f.;* (beam) madero *m.*

time, *n.* tiempo *m.;* vez *f.;* (of day) hora *f.; v.* cronometrar.

timetable, *n.* horario, itinerario *m.*

time zone, huso horario *m.*

timid, *a.* tímido.

timidity, *n.* timidez *f.*

tin, *n.* estaño *m.;* hojalata *f.* **t. can,** lata *f.*

tin foil, papel de estaño *m.*

tint, 1. *n.* tinte *m.* 2. *v.* teñir.

tiny, *a.* chiquito, pequeñito.

tip, 1. *n.* punta; propina *f.* 2. *v.* inclinar; dar propina a.

tire, 1. *n.* llanta, goma *f.,* neumático *m.* 2. *v.* cansar.

tired, *a.* cansado.

tissue, *n.* tejido *m.* **t. paper,** papel de seda.

title, 1. *n.* título *m.* 2. *v.* titular.

to, *prep.* a; para.

toast, 1. *n.* tostada *f.;* (drink) brindis *m.* 2. *v.* tostar; brindar.

toaster, *n.* tostador *m.*

tobacco, *n.* tabaco *m.* **t. shop,** tabaquería *f.*

toboggan, *n.* tobogán *m.*

today, *adv.* hoy.

toe, *n.* dedo del pie.

together, 1. *a.* juntos. 2. *adv.* juntamente.

toil, 1. *n.* trabajo *m.* 2. *v.* afanarse.

toilet, *n.* tocado; excusado, retrete *m.* **t. paper,** papel higiénico.

token, *n.* señal *f.*

tolerance, *n.* tolerancia *f.*

tolerate, *v.* tolerar.

toll-free number, teléfono gratuito *m.*

tomato, *n.* tomate *m.*

tomb, *n.* tumba *f.*

tomorrow, *adv.* mañana. **day after t.,** pasado mañana.

ton, *n.* tonelada *f.*

tone, *n.* tono *m.*

tongue, *n.* lengua *f.*

tonic, *n.* tónico *m.*

tonight, *adv.* esta noche.

tonsil, *n.* amígdala *f.*

too, *adv.* también. **t. much,** demasiado. **t. many,** demasiados.

tool, *n.* herramienta *f.*

tooth, *n.* diente *m.;* (back) muela *f.*

toothache, *n.* dolor de muela.

toothbrush, *n.* cepillo de dientes.

toothpaste, *n.* crema dentífrica, pasta dentífrica.

top, 1. *n.* parte de arriba. **2.** *v.* cubrir; sobrepasar.

topic, *n.* (S.A.) tópico *m.*

topical, *a.* tópico.

torch, *n.* antorcha *f.*

torment, 1. *n.* tormento *m.* **2.** *v.* atormentar.

torrent, *n.* torrente *m.*

torture, 1. *n.* tortura *f.* **2.** *v.* torturar.

toss, *v.* tirar; agitar.

total, 1. *a.* total, entero. **2.** *n.* total *m.*

touch, 1. *n.* tacto *m.* **in t.,** en comunicación. **2.** *v.* tocar; conmover.

tough, *a.* tosco; tieso; fuerte.

tour, 1. *n.* viaje *m.* **2.** *v.* viajar.

tourist, 1. *n.* turista *m.* & *f.* **2.** *a.* turístico.

tournament, *n.* torneo *m.*

tow, 1. *n.* remolque *m.* **2.** *v.* remolcar.

toward, *prep.* hacia.

towel, *n.* toalla *f.*

tower, *n.* torre *f.*

town, *n.* pueblo *m.*

town meeting, cabildo abierto *m.*

tow truck, grúa *f.*

toy, 1. *n.* juguete *m.* **2.** *v.* jugar.

trace, 1. *n.* vestigio; rastro *m.* **2.** *v.* trazar; rastrear; investigar.

track, 1. *n.* huella, pista *f.* **race t.,** hipódromo *m.* **2.** *v.* rastrear.

tract, *n.* trecho; tracto *m.*

tractor, *n.* tractor *m.*

trade, 1. *n.* comercio, negocio; oficio; canje *m.* **2.** *v.* comerciar, negociar; cambiar.

trader, *n.* comerciante *m.*

tradition, *n.* tradición *f.*

traditional, *a.* tradicional.

traffic, 1. *n.* tráfico *m.* **2.** *v.* traficar.

traffic jam, atasco, embotellamiento *m.*

traffic light, semáforo *m.*

tragedy, *n.* tragedia *f.*

tragic, *a.* trágico.

trail, 1. *n.* sendero; rastro *m.* **2.** *v.* rastrear; arrastrar.

train, 1. *n.* tren *m.* **2.** *v.* enseñar; disciplinar; (sport) entrenarse.

traitor, *n.* traidor -ora.

tramp, 1. *n.* caminata *f.;* vagabundo *m.* **2.** *v.* patear.

tranquil, *a.* tranquilo.

tranquilizer, *n.* tranquilizante *m.*

tranquillity, *n.* tranquilidad *f.*

transaction, *n.* transacción *f.*

transfer, 1. *n.* traslado *m.;* boleto de transbordo. **2.** *v.* trasladar, transferir.

transform, *v.* transformar.

transfusion, *n.* transfusión *f.*

transistor, *n.* transistor *m.*

transition, *n.* transición *f.*

translate, *v.* traducir.

translation, *n.* traducción *f.*

transmit, *v.* transmitir.

transparent, *a.* transparente.

transport, 1. *n.* transporte *m.* **2.** *v.* transportar.

transportation, *n.* transporte *m.*

transsexual, *a.* & *n.* transexual *m.* & *f.*

transvestite, *n.* travestí *m.* & *f.*

trap, 1. *n.* trampa *f.* **2.** *v.* atrapar.

trash, *n.* desecho *m.;* basura *f.*

trash can, cubo de la basura *m.*

travel, 1. *n.* tráfico *m.;* (pl.) viajes *m.pl.* **2.** *v.* viajar.

travel agency, agencia de viajes *f.*

traveler, *n.* viajero -ra.

traveler's check, cheque de viaje *m.*

tray, *n.* bandeja *f.*

tread, 1. *n.* pisada *f.;* (of a tire) cubierta *f.* **2.** *v.* pisar.

treason, *n.* traición *f.*

treasure, *n.* tesoro *m.*

treasurer, *n.* tesorero -ra.

treasury, *n.* tesorería *f.*

treat, 1. *v.* tratar; convidar.

treatment, *n.* trato, tratamiento *m.*

treaty, *n.* tratado, pacto *m.*

tree, *n.* árbol *m.*

tremble, *v.* temblar.

tremendous, *a.* tremendo.

trench, *n.* foso *m.;* (mil.) trinchera *f.*

trend, 1. *n.* tendencia *f.* **2.** *v.* tender.

trespass, *v.* traspasar; violar.

triage, *n.* clasificación de los heridos después del combate.

trial, *n.* prueba *f.;* (leg.) proceso, juicio *m.*

triangle, *n.* triángulo *m.*

tribulation, *n.* tribulación *f.*

tributary, *a.* & *n.* tributario *m.*

tribute, *n.* tributo *m.*

trick, 1. *n.* engaño *m.;* maña *f.;* (cards) baza *f.* **2.** *v.* engañar.

trifle, 1. *n.* pequeñez *f.* **2.** *v.* juguetear.

trigger, *n.* gatillo *m.*

trim, 1. *a.* ajustado; acicalado. **2.** *n.* adorno *m.* **3.** *v.* adornar; ajustar; cortar un poco.

trinket, *n.* bagatela, chuchería *f.*

trip, 1. *n.* viaje *m.* **2.** *v.* tropezar.

triple, 1. *a.* triple **2.** *v.* triplicar.

tripod, *n.* trípode *m.*

trite, *a.* banal.

triumph, 1. *n.* triunfo *m.* **2.** *v.* triunfar.

triumphant, *a.* triunfante.

trivial, *a.* trivial.

trolley, *n.* tranvía *m.*

trombone, *n.* trombón *m.*

troop, *n.* tropa *f.*

trophy, *n.* trofeo *m.*

tropical, *a.* trópico.

tropics, *n.* trópico *m.*

trot, 1. *n.* trote *m.* **2.** *v.* trotar.

trouble, 1. *n.* apuro *m.;* congoja; aflicción *f.* **2.** *v.* molestar; afligir.

troublesome, *a.* penoso, molesto.

trough, *n.* artesa *f.*

trousers, *n.* pantalones, calzones *m.pl.*

trout, *n.* trucha *f.*

truce, *n.* tregua *f.*

truck, *n.* camión *m.*

true, *a.* verdadero, cierto, verdad.

visit, 1. *n.* visita *f.* **2.** *v.* visitar.
visitor, *n.* visitante *m. & f.*
visual, *a.* visual.
vital, *a.* vital.
vitality, *n.* vitalidad, energía vital *f.*
vitamin, *n.* vitamina *f.*
vivacious, *a.* vivaz.
vivid, *a.* vivo; gráfico.
vocabulary, *n.* vocabulario *m.*

vocal, *a.* vocal.
vodka, *n.* vodca *m.*
vogue, *n.* boga; moda *f.* **be in vogue** estilarse.
voice, 1. *n.* voz *f.* **2.** *v.* expresar.
void, 1. *a.* vacío. **2.** *n.* vacío *m.* **3.** *v.* invalidar.
voltage, *n.* voltaje *m.*
volume, *n.* volumen; tomo *m.*
voluntary, *a.* voluntario.

volunteer, 1. *n.* voluntario -ria. **2.** *v.* ofrecerse.
vomit, *v.* vomitar.
vote, 1. *n.* voto *m.* **2.** *v.* votar.
voter, *n.* votante *m. & f.*
vouch, *v.* **v. for,** garantizar.
vow, 1. *n.* voto *m.* **2.** *v.* jurar.
vowel, *n.* vocal *f.*
voyage, *n.* viaje *m.*
vulgar, *a.* vulgar; común; soez.
vulnerable, *a.* vulnerable.

W

wade, *v.* vadear.
wag, *v.* menear.
wage, 1. *n.* (pl.) sueldo, salario *m.* **2.** *v.* **w. war,** hacer guerra.
wagon, *n.* carreta *f.*
wail, 1. *n.* lamento, gemido *m.* **2.** *v.* lamentar, gemir.
waist, *n.* cintura *f.*
wait, 1. *n.* espera *f.* **2.** *v.* esperar. **w. for,** esperar. **w. on,** atender.
waiter, waitress, *n.* camarero -ra.
waiting room, sala de espera.
wake, *v.* **w. up,** despertar.
walk, 1. *n.* paseo *m.;* vuelta; caminata *f.;* modo de andar. **2.** *v.* andar; caminar; ir a pie.
wall, *n.* pared; muralla *f.*
wallcovering, *n.* tapizado de pared *m.*
wallet, *n.* cartera *f.*
wallpaper, 1. *n.* empapelado *m.* **2.** *v.* empapelar.
walnut, *n.* nuez *f.*
waltz, *n.* vals *m.*
wander, *v.* vagar.
want, 1. *n.* necesidad *f.* **2.** *v.* querer.
war, *n.* guerra *f.*
ward, 1. *n.* (pol.) barrio *m.;* (hospital) cuadra *f.* **2.** *v.* **w. off,** parar.
warehouse, *n.* almacén *m.*
wares, *n.* mercancías *f.pl.*
warlike, *a.* belicoso.
warm, 1. *a.* caliente; (fig.) caluroso. **to be w.,** tener calor; (weather) hacer calor. **2.** *v.* calentar.

warmth, *n.* calor *m.*
warn, *v.* advertir.
warning, *n.* aviso *m.*
warp, *v.* alabear.
warrant, *v.* justificar.
warrior, *n.* guerrero -ra.
warship, *n.* navío de guerra, buque de guerra *m.*
wash, *v.* lavar.
washing machine, máquina de lavar, lavadora *f.*
wasp, *n.* avispa *f.*
waste, 1. *n.* gasto *m.;* desechos *m.pl.* **2.** *v.* gastar; perder.
watch, 1. *n.* reloj *m.;* (mil.) guardia *f.* **2.** *v.* observar, mirar. **w. for,** esperar. **w. out for,** tener cuidado con. **w. over,** guardar; velar por.
watchful, *a.* desvelado.
watchmaker, *n.* relojero -ra.
watchman, *n.* sereno *m.*
water, 1. *n.* agua *f.* **w. color,** acuarela *f.* **2.** *v.* aguar.
waterbed, *n.* cama de agua *f.*
waterfall, *n.* catarata *f.*
watering can, regadera *f.*
waterproof, *a.* impermeable.
wave, 1. *n.* onda; ola *f.* **2.** *v.* ondear; agitar; hacer señas.
waver, *v.* vacilar.
wax, 1. *n.* cera *f.* **2.** *v.* encerar.
way, *n.* camino; modo *m.,* manera *f.* **in a w.,** hasta cierto punto. **a long w.,** muy lejos. **by the w.,** a propósito. **this w.,** por aquí. **that w.,** por allí. **which w.,** por dónde.
we, *pron.* nosotros -as.

weak, *a.* débil.
weaken, *v.* debilitar.
weakness, *n.* debilidad *f.*
wealth, *n.* riqueza *f.*
wealthy, *a.* adinerado.
wean, *v.* destetar.
weapon, *n.* arma *f.*
wear, 1. *n.* uso; desgaste *m.;* (clothes) ropa *f.* **2.** *v.* usar, llevar. **w. out,** gastar; cansar.
weary, *a.* cansado, rendido.
weather, *n.* tiempo *m.*
weave, *v.* tejer.
weaver, *n.* tejedor -ra.
web, *n.* tela *f.*
wedding, *n.* boda *f.*
wedge, *n.* cuña *f.*
Wednesday, *n.* miércoles *m.*
weed, *n.* maleza *f.*
week, *n.* semana *f.* **w. end,** fin de semana.
weekday, *n.* día de trabajo.
weekly, *a.* semanal.
weep, *v.* llorar.
weigh, *v.* pesar.
weight, *n.* peso *m.*
weightless, *v.* ingrávido.
weightlessness, *n.* ingravidez *f.*
weird, *a.* misterioso, extraño.
welcome, 1. *a.* bienvenido. **you're w.,** de nada, no hay de qué. **2.** *n.* acogida, bienvenida *f.* **3.** *v.* acoger, recibir bien.
welfare, *n.* bienestar *m.*
well, 1. *a.* sano, bueno. **2.** *adv.* bien; pues. **3.** *n.* pozo *m.*
well-done, *a.* (food) bien cocido.

well-known, *a.* bien conocido.

well-mannered, *a.* educado.

west, *n.* oeste, occidente *m.*

western, *a.* occidental.

westward, *adv.* hacia el oeste.

wet, 1. *a.* mojado. **to get w.,** mojarse. **2.** *v.* mojar.

whale, *n.* ballena *f.*

what, 1. *a.* qué; cuál. **2.** *interrog. pron.* qué. **3.** *rel. pron.* lo que.

whatever, 1. *a.* cualquier. **2.** *pron.* lo que; todo lo que.

wheat, *n.* trigo *m.*

wheel, *n.* rueda *f.* **steering w.,** volante *m.*

when, 1. *adv.* cuándo. **2.** *conj.* cuando.

whenever, *conj.* siempre que, cuando quiera que.

where, 1. *adv.* dónde, adónde. **2.** *conj.* donde.

wherever, *conj.* dondequiera que, adondequiera que.

whether, *conj.* si.

which, 1. *a.* qué. **2.** *interrog. pron.* cuál. **3.** *rel. pron.* que; el cual; lo cual.

whichever, *a. & pron.* cualquiera que.

while, 1. *conj.* mientras; mientras que. **2.** *n.* rato *m.* **to be worth w.,** valer la pena.

whip, 1. *n.* látigo *m.* **2.** *v.* azotar.

whipped cream, nata batida *f.*

whirl, *v.* girar.

whirlpool, *n.* vórtice *m.*

whirlwind, *n.* torbellino *m.*

whisk broom, escobilla *f.*

whisker, *n.* bigote *m.*

whiskey, *n.* whisky *m.*

whisper, 1. *n.* cuchicheo *m.* **2.** *v.* cuchichear.

whistle, 1. *n.* pito; silbido *m.* **2.** *v.* silbar.

white, 1. *a.* blanco. **2.** *n.* (of egg) clara *f.*

who, whom, 1. *interrog. pron.* quién. **2.** *rel. pron.* que; quien.

whoever, whomever, *pron.* quienquiera que.

whole, 1. *a.* entero. **the wh.,** todo el. **2.** *n.* totalidad *f.* **on the wh.,** por lo general.

wholesale, *n.* **at wh.,** al por mayor.

wholesaler, *n.* mayorista *m. & f.*

wholesome, *a.* sano, saludable.

wholly, *adv.* enteramente.

whose, 1. *interrog. adj.* de quién. **2.** *rel. adj.* cuyo.

why, *adv.* por qué; para qué.

wicked, *a.* malo, malvado.

wickedness, *n.* maldad *f.*

wide, 1. *a.* ancho; extenso. **2.** *adv.* **w. open,** abierto de par en par.

widen, *v.* ensanchar; extender.

widespread, *a.* extenso.

widow, *n.* viuda *f.*

widower, *n.* viudo *m.*

width, *n.* anchura *f.*

wield, *v.* manejar, empuñar.

wife, *n.* esposa, señora, mujer *f.*

wig, *n.* peluca *f.*

wild, *a.* salvaje; bárbaro.

wilderness, *n.* desierto *m.*

wildlife, *n.* fauna silvestre *f.*

will, 1. *n.* voluntad *f.;* testamento *m.* **2.** *v.* querer; determinar; (leg.) legar.

willful, *a.* voluntarioso; premeditado.

willing, *a.* **to be w.,** estar dispuesto.

willingly, *adv.* de buena gana.

wilt, *v.* marchitar.

win, *v.* ganar.

wind, 1. *n.* viento *m.* **2.** *v.* torcer; dar cuerda a.

windmill, *n.* molino de viento *m.*

window, *n.* ventana; (of car) ventanilla *f.;* (of shop or store) escaparate *m.*

windshield, *n.* parabrisas *m.*

windy, *a.* ventoso. **to be w.,** (weather) hacer viento.

wine, *n.* vino *m.*

wing, *n.* ala *f.;* (theat.) bastidor *m.*

wink, 1. *n.* guiño *m.* **2.** *v.* guiñar.

winner, *n.* ganador -ra.

winter, *n.* invierno *m.*

wipe, *v.* limpiar; (dry) secar. **w. out,** destruir.

wire, 1. *n.* alambre; hilo; telegrama *m.* **2.** *v.* telegrafiar.

wireless, *n.* telégrafo sin hilos.

wisdom, *n.* juicio *m.;* sabiduría *f.*

wise, *a.* sensato, juicioso; sabio.

wish, 1. *n.* deseo; voto *m.* **2.** *v.* desear; querer.

wit, *n.* ingenio *m.,* sal *f.*

witch, *n.* bruja *f.*

with, *prep.* con.

withdraw, *v.* retirar.

wither, *v.* marchitar.

withhold, *v.* retener, suspender.

within, 1. *adv.* dentro, por dentro. **2.** *prep.* dentro de; en.

without, 1. *adv.* fuera, por fuera. **2.** *prep.* sin.

witness, 1. *n.* testigo; testimonio *m. & f.* **2.** *v.* presenciar; atestar.

witty, *a.* ingenioso, gracioso, ocurrente.

wizard, *n.* hechicero *m.*

woe, *n.* dolor *m.;* pena *f.*

wolf, *n.* lobo -ba.

woman, *n.* mujer *f.*

womb, *n.* entrañas *f.pl.,* matriz *f.*

wonder, 1. *n.* maravilla; admiración *f.* **for a w.,** por milagro. **no w.,** no es extraño. **2.** *v.* preguntarse; maravillarse.

wonderful, *a.* maravilloso; estupendo.

woo, *v.* cortejar.

wood, *n.* madera; (for fire) leña *f.*

wooden, *a.* de madera.

wool, *n.* lana *f.*

word, 1. *n.* palabra *f.* **the words** (of a song), la letra. **2.** *v.* expresar.

work, 1. *n.* trabajo *m.;* (of art) obra *f.* **2.** *v.* trabajar; obrar; funcionar.

worker, *n.* trabajador -ra; obrero -ra.

workman, *n.* obrero *m.*

work station, estación de trabajo *f.*

work week, semana laboral *f.*

world, *n.* mundo *m.* **w. war,** guerra mundial.

worldly, *a.* mundano.

worldwide, *a.* mundial.

worm, *n.* gusano *m.*

worn, *a.* usado. **w. out,** gastado; cansado, rendido.

worrisome, *a.* inquietante.

worry, 1. *n.* preocupación *f.* **2.** *v.* preocupar.

worrying, *a.* inquietante.

worse, *a.* peor. **to get w.,** empeorar.

worship, 1. *n.* adoración *f.* **2.** *v.* adorar.

worst, *a.* peor.

worth, 1. *a.* **to be w.,** valer. **2.** *n.* valor *m.*

worthless, *a.* sin valor.

worthy, *a.* digno.

wound, 1. *n.* herida *f.* **2.** *v.* herir.

wrap, 1. *n.* (pl.) abrigos *m.pl.* **2.** *n.* envolver.

wrapping, *n.* cubierta *f.*

wrath, *n.* ira, cólera *f.*

wreath, *n.* guirnalda; corona *f.*

wreck, 1. *n.* ruina *f.;* accidente *m.* **2.** *v.* destrozar, arruinar.

wrench, *n.* llave *f.* **monkey w.,** llave inglesa.

wrestle, *v.* luchar.

wretched, *a.* miserable.

wring, *v.* retorcer.

wrinkle, 1. *n.* arruga *f.* **2.** *v.* arrugar.

wrist, *n.* muñeca *f.* **w. watch,** reloj de pulsera.

write, *v.* escribir. **w. down,** apuntar.

write-protect, *v.* proteger contra escritura.

writer, *n.* escritor -ra.

writhe, *v.* contorcerse.

writing paper, papel de escribir *m.*

wrong, 1. *a.* equivocado; incorrecto. **to be w.,** equivocarse; no tener razón. **2.** *adv.* mal, incorrectamente. **3.** *n.* agravio *m.* **right and w.,** el bien y el mal. **4.** *v.* agraviar, ofender.

X, Y, Z

x-ray, 1. *n.* rayo X *m.,* radiografía; *f.* **2.** *v.* radiografiar.

xylophone, *n.* xilófono *m.*

yacht, *n.* yate *m.*

yard, *n.* patio, corral *m.;* (measure) yarda *f.*

yarn, *n.* hilo.

yawn, 1. *n.* bostezo *m.* **2.** *v.* bostezar.

year, *n.* año *m.*

yearly, *a.* anual.

yearn, *v.* anhelar.

yell, 1. *n.* grito *m.* **2.** *v.* gritar.

yellow, *a.* amarillo.

yes, *adv.* sí.

yesterday, *adv.* ayer.

yet, *adv.* todavía, aún.

Yiddish, *n.* yídish *m.*

yield, *v.* producir; ceder.

yogurt, *n.* yogur *m.*

yoke, *n.* yugo *m.*

yolk, *n.* yema *f.*

you, *pron.* usted, (pl.) ustedes; lo, la, los, las; le, les; (familiar) tú, (pl.) vosotros -as; ti; te, (pl.) os. **with y.,** contigo, con usted.

young, *a.* joven.

youngster, *n.* muchacho -cha *m.* & *f.*

your, *a.* su; (familiar) tu; (pl.) vuestro.

yours, *pron.* suyo; (familiar) tuyo; (pl.) vuestro.

yourself, -selves, *pron.* sí; se; (familiar) ti; te. **with**

y., consigo; contigo. **you y.,** usted mismo, ustedes mismos; tú mismo, vosotros mismos.

youth, *n.* juventud *f.;* (person) joven *m.* & *f.*

youth club, club juvenil *m.*

youthful, *a.* juvenil.

zap, *v.* desintegrar, aniquilar.

zeal, *n.* celo, fervor *m.*

zealous, *a.* celoso, fervoroso.

zero, *n.* cero *m.*

zest, *n.* gusto *m.*

zip code, número de distrito postal.

zipper, *m.* cremallera *f.*

zone, *n.* zona *f.*

zoo, *n.* jardín zoológico.

Useful Phrases/Locuciones Útiles

Good day, Good morning.	Buenos días.
Good afternoon.	Buenas tardes.
Good night, Good evening.	Buenas noches.
Hello.	¡Hola!
Welcome!	¡Bienvenido!
See you later.	Hasta luego.
Goodbye.	¡Adiós!
How are you?	¿Cómo está usted?
I am fine, thank you.	Estoy bien, gracias.
I am pleased to meet you.	Mucho gusto en conocerle.
May I introduce . . .	Quisiera presentar . . .
Thank you very much.	Muchas gracias.
You're welcome.	De nada *or* No hay de qué.
Please.	Por favor.
Excuse me.	Con permiso.
Good luck.	¡Buena suerte!
To your health.	¡Salud!
Please help me.	Ayúdeme, por favor.
I don't know.	No sé.
I don't understand.	No entiendo.
Do you understand?	¿Entiende usted?
I don't speak Spanish.	No hablo español.
Do you speak English?	¿Habla usted inglés?
I need an interpreter.	Necesito intérprete.
How do you say . . . in Spanish?	¿Cómo se dice . . . en español?
What do you call this?	¿Cómo se llama esto?
Speak slowly, please.	Hable despacio, por favor.
Please repeat.	Repita, por favor.
I don't like it.	No me gusta.
I am lost.	Ando perdido *or* Me he extraviado.
What is your name?	¿Cómo se llama usted?
My name is . . .	Me llamo . . .
I am an American.	Soy norteamericano (male) *or* Soy norteamericana (female).
Where are you from?	¿De dónde es usted?
I'm from . . .	Soy de . . .
How is the weather?	¿Qué tiempo hace?
It's cold (hot) today.	Hace frío (calor) hoy.
It's raining.	Está lloviendo.
It's snowing.	Está nevando.
What time is it?	¿Qué hora es?
How much is it?	¿Cuánto es?
It is too much.	Cuesta mucho.
I'm just looking.	Estoy viendo.
What do you wish?	¿Qué desea usted?
I want to buy . . .	Quiero comprar . . .

May I see something better?	¿Tiene algo mejor?
May I see something cheaper?	¿Tiene algo menos caro?
It is not exactly what I want.	No es precisamente lo que quiero.

I am hungry.	Tengo hambre.
I am thirsty.	Tengo sed.
Where is there a restaurant?	¿Dónde hay un restaurante?
I have a reservation.	Tengo una reservación.
I would like ...	Quisiera . . .; Me gustaría . . .
Please give me ...	Me trae . . .
Please bring me ...	Me trae . . .
May I see the menu?	¿Podría ver el menú?
The bill, please.	La cuenta, por favor.
Is service included in the bill?	¿El servicio está incluido en la cuenta?
Where is there a hotel?	¿Dónde hay un hotel?
Where is the post office?	¿Dónde está el correo?
Is there any mail for me?	¿Hay correo para mí?
Where can I mail this letter?	¿Dónde puedo echar esta carta?

Take me to ...	Lléveme a . . .
I believe I am ill.	Creo que estoy enfermo (male) or Creo que estoy enferma (female).
Please call a doctor.	Por favor, llame al médico.
Please call the police.	Por favor, llame a la policía.
I want to send a telegram.	Quiero poner un telegrama.
As soon as possible.	Cuanto antes.

Round trip.	Ida y vuelta.
Please help me with my luggage.	Por favor, ayúdeme con mi equipaje.

Where can I get a taxi?	¿Dónde puedo tomar un taxi?
What is the fare to ...	¿Cuánto es el pasaje hasta . . . ?
Please take me to this address.	Por favor, lléveme a esta dirección.
Where can I change my money?	¿Dónde puedo cambiar dinero?
Where is the nearest bank?	¿Dónde está el banco más cercano?
Can you accept my check?	¿Puede aceptar usted mi cheque?
Do you accept traveler's checks?	¿Aceptan cheques de viaje?
What is the postage?	¿Cuánto es el franqueo?
Where is the nearest drugstore?	¿Dónde está la farmacia más cercana?
Is there an all-night pharmacy?	¿Hay una farmacia de turno?
Where is the men's (women's) room?	¿Dónde está el servicio de caballeros (de señoras)?
Please let me off at ...	Por favor, déjeme bajar en . . .

Right away.	¡Pronto!
Help.	¡Socorro!
Who is it?	¿Quién es?
Just a minute!	¡Un momento no más!
Come in.	¡Pase usted!
Pardon me.	Dispense usted.
Stop.	¡Pare!
Look out.	¡Cuidado!
Hurry.	¡De prisa! or ¡Dése prisa!
Go on.	¡Siga!
To (on, at) the right.	A la derecha.
To (on, at) the left.	A la izquierda.
Straight ahead.	Adelante.

Signs/Señales

Caution	Precaución	**No smoking**	Prohibido fumar
Danger	Peligro	**No admittance**	Entrada prohibida
Dead End	Callejón sin salida	**One way**	Dirección única
Exit	Salida	**No entry**	Dirección prohibida
Entrance	Entrada	**Women**	Señoras, Mujeres, Damas
Stop	Alto	**Men**	Señores, Hombres, Caballeros
Closed	Cerrado	**Ladies' Room**	El cuarto de damas
Open	Abierto	**Men's Room**	El servicio
Slow	Despacio		

Spanish speakers aren't just from Spain.
They're from all over Latin America, and each
country shapes and adds to the language.
Become a *global* speaker of Spanish—look for:

RANDOM HOUSE
LATIN-AMERICAN
SPANISH DICTIONARY
SPANISH-ENGLISH/ENGLISH-SPANISH

Featuring more than 50,000 entries and
100,000 definitions, including vocabulary and
usages unique to Mexico, Cuba, Venezuela,
Chile, and other Latin-American countries.

RANDOM HOUSE
LATIN-AMERICAN
SPANISH DICTIONARY
by David L. Gold

Published by Ballantine Books.
Available in bookstores everywhere.

As the world gets smaller, we need to communicate with more people than ever. Don't miss this valuable tool:

RANDOM HOUSE JAPANESE-ENGLISH ENGLISH-JAPANESE DICTIONARY

Reliable, detailed, and up-to-date.

Featuring more than 50,000 entries, including the most common meanings, romanization and Japanese characters, and hundreds of new words.

Also with explanatory glosses to specify meaning and assure appropriate translation!

RANDOM HOUSE
JAPANESE-ENGLISH
ENGLISH-JAPANESE
DICTIONARY
by Seigo Nakao

Published by Ballantine Books.
Available in bookstores everywhere.